THE LIFE OF
S. T. COLERIDGE

The Early Years

S. T. COLERIDGE IN 1795

"This portrait of Mr Coleridge was taken in oils, by a Mr Vandyke (a descendant of the great Vandyke.) . . . a better likeness was never taken; and it has the additional advantage of exhibiting Mr C. in one of his animated conversations."   JOSEPH COTTLE

" . . . my face, unless when animated by immediate eloquence, expresses great sloth, and great, indeed, almost idiotic good nature. 'Tis a mere carcass of a face; fat, flabby, and expressive chiefly of inexpression. Yet I am told that my eyes, eyebrows, and forehead are physiognomically good; but of this the deponent knoweth not. As to my shape, 'tis a good shape enough if measured, but my gait is awkward, and the walk of the whole man indicates *indolence capable of energies.* . . . I cannot breathe through my nose, so my mouth, with sensual thick lips, is almost always open. In conversation I am impassioned, and oppose what I deem error with an eagerness which is often mistaken for personal asperity; but I am ever so swallowed up in the *thing* that I perfectly forget my *opponent*. Such am I."   COLERIDGE

" . . . a tall, dark, handsome young man, with long, black, flowing hair; eyes not merely dark, but black, and keenly penetrating; a fine forehead, a deep-toned, harmonious voice; a manner . . . full of life, vivacity, and kindness; dignified in person."   THE REV. LEAPIDGE SMITH

Hail to thee, Coldridge, youth of various powers!
I love to hear thy soul pour forth the line,
To hear it sing of love and liberty
As if fresh breathing from the hand divine.

I love to mark that soul-pervaded clay,
To see the passions in thine eyeballs roll—
Their quick succession on thy weighty brow—
Thy trembling lips express their very soul.
                                                     THOMAS POOLE

" . . . a young man of brilliant understanding, great eloquence, desperate fortune, democratick principles, and entirely led away by the feelings of the moment."   CHARLOTTE POOLE

THE LIFE OF
S. T. COLERIDGE

The Early Years

by

LAWRENCE HANSON

New York

RUSSELL & RUSSELL

1962

FIRST PUBLISHED IN 1938
REISSUED, 1962, BY RUSSELL & RUSSELL, INC.
BY ARRANGEMENT WITH THE AUTHOR
L. C. CATALOG CARD NO: 61—13766

PRINTED IN THE UNITED STATES OF AMERICA

TO THE

REV. G. H. B. COLERIDGE

PREFACE

No-ONE CAN ATTEMPT a biography of S. T. Coleridge without first recording his peculiar indebtedness to the labours of two men who first kept alive, then steadily increased interest in the poet when other pens were still. Of the published works of Ernest Hartley Coleridge it is scarcely necessary to speak. His *Anima Poetae* and his editions of the *Poems* and the *Letters* are familiar to all interested in S. T. Coleridge. What can perhaps be appreciated fully only by those following a path similar to the one trodden by E. H. Coleridge is the prodigious labour that took place in preparation for the writing of the ill-fated Life of his grandfather. To see and examine the mass of material gathered patiently and over a long period of years by E. H. Coleridge is to realize and so to attempt to express the very great obligation incurred by those who follow after and enjoy the benefit of another man's industry. I now and very gladly make this acknowledgment.

To James Dykes Campbell, friend of E. H. Coleridge, a debt scarcely less heavy remains to be paid. By his editions of the *Poems* and the *Christabel* and by his many articles and speeches upon Coleridgean subjects, J. Dykes Campbell has placed future biographers under a deep obligation; but perhaps by nothing so much as his *Narrative* of the Life of S. T. Coleridge, which, intended to serve only until the full Life by E. H. Coleridge became available, has remained to this day the standard Life of its subject—a work for which the biographer of Coleridge must have not only gratitude, not only admiration, but upon which he is dependent to a quite unusual degree.

I wish to express my very deep appreciation of the kindness of the Rev. G. H. B. Coleridge, who has given me every facility to examine his Coleridge MSS. and permission to draw upon it in my work.

To Miss Catherine M. Maclean I am indebted for her kindness in reading the book in proof and for making valuable suggestions. I must also thank Mr Edmund Blunden for reading through proofs of the book and for his very helpful annotations. Professor

John H. Muirhead I wish to thank for his kindness in agreeing to read through the philosophical sections of the completed Life, and I would also like to take this opportunity of expressing my indebtedness to his writings upon the philosophy of Coleridge.

My thanks are also due to Professor Alice D. Snyder for her kindness in sending (for the third time) her photostat copy of Coleridge's MS. *On the Divine Ideas* across the Atlantic; to Dr Ernest de Selincourt for so obligingly searching for a Coleridge letter on my behalf; to Miss Gwenda David for her suggestions and encouragement; to Miss Helen Cam for her most valuable suggestions and transcripts of Coleridge material in her possession; and to the Master of Jesus College, Cambridge, for kindly furnishing me with information.

I wish also to thank Mrs George Beamish for the care she has taken in the making of the Index to this book; Miss N. Angell Lane and Miss D. Choules for their patient and careful transcriptions of Coleridge MSS.; Mr G. A. T. Allen, of Christ's Hospital, for his unfailing willingness to supply information; Miss Jenny Haywood for reading and correcting the proofs; Mr Stephen K. Jones of the Dr Williams's Library for his helpfulness; members of the Staff of the Reading and Manuscript Rooms of the British Museum for their assistance; the late Mr T. J. Wise for his kindness in permitting me to inspect Coleridge material in his Ashley Library; and all those Ministers and Secretaries of Unitarian Congregations in towns visited by Coleridge, who have been so generous with their help in seeking for and providing me with information.

I am indebted to the kindness of Mrs W. Holcroft Cam for permission to reproduce the portrait of Coleridge in Germany; Mr Gilbert S. Poole for permission to reproduce the portrait of Thomas Poole; Mr and Mrs Gerald Rhodes for permission to reproduce the photograph of Alfoxden; the National Trust for permission to reproduce the photograph of Coleridge's cottage at Stowey; Messrs William George's Sons Ltd. for permission to reproduce the Shuter portrait of Wordsworth from their reproduction of the original painting; and the Trustees of the National Portrait Gallery for permission to reproduce the remaining portraits of Coleridge, Wordsworth, Southey, and Lamb.

I have to thank the Trustees of the Henry E. Huntingdon

Library, San Marino, California, for their permission to quote from the chapters of Coleridge's *Opus Maximum* and from a letter of Charles Lamb in their possession; Dr E. de Selincourt and the Delegates of the Clarendon Press for permission to quote from *The Early Letters of Dorothy and William Wordsworth* and from Wordsworth's *Prelude*; Professor E. L. Griggs and Messrs Constable & Co., Ltd., for permission to quote from the *Unpublished Letters of Samuel Taylor Coleridge*; also Mr John Murray, Messrs G. Bell & Sons, Ltd., Messrs Macmillan & Co., Ltd., Messrs J. M. Dent & Sons, Ltd., Messrs Methuen & Co., Ltd., Messrs William Heinemann, Ltd., and the Proprietors of the *London Illustrated News* for permission to quote from *Charles Lamb and the Lloyds*, *Biographia Literaria*, *Thomas Poole and his Friends*, *The Journals of Dorothy Wordsworth*, *The Letters of Charles Lamb*, *The Letters of Samuel Taylor Coleridge*, and *Unpublished Letters of S. T. Coleridge* respectively.

Finally I wish to thank my wife, whose sympathy and encouragement have made the writing of this book so much easier and so much more enjoyable.

L. H.

BARLAVINGTON, 1938

CONTENTS

CHAPTER	PAGE
I	11
2	29
3	71
4	90
5	145
6	163
7	182
8	203
9	244
10	287
11	313
12	353
13	378
BIBLIOGRAPHY	417
NOTES	421
INDEX	519

LIST OF ILLUSTRATIONS

S. T. COLERIDGE IN 1795   *Frontispiece*

BETWEEN PAGES

THOMAS POOLE   48–49

S. T. COLERIDGE IN 1796   112–113

ROBERT SOUTHEY IN 1796   128–129

COLERIDGE'S COTTAGE AT NETHER STOWEY   144–145

CHARLES LAMB IN 1798   160–161

ALFOXDEN LOOKING NORTH-EAST   208–209

WILLIAM WORDSWORTH IN 1798   240–241

WILLIAM WORDSWORTH IN APRIL, 1798   256–257

S. T. COLERIDGE IN 1799   336–337

THE EARLY YEARS

I

TURNING SEAWARD off the main London to Exeter road west of Honiton, a lane [1] winds between high Devonshire hedges to the little town of Ottery St. Mary.

Ottery is an old town without commercial importance. Despite a disastrous fire in the middle of last century, it appears to-day much as it must have done when Coleridge mooned about it one hundred and sixty years ago. The narrow streets remain, the jumbled houses, the low-browed shops. The mighty church—his father's benefice—thrusts its transept towers above the huddle of roofs as dominantly as ever, even if its bells ring less often and a nineteenth-century restoration has been let loose upon it. The churchyard—his playground—differs only in the number of its occupants. The vicarage—his home—retains its original character. [2] The Otter still winds its way down to the sea; the waterside is still grey with willows, the sandy bed veined with many colours; and the bank on which Coleridge slept could have been no greener, no damper, than it is of an evening now.

In the Vicar's House at Ottery on Wednesday, October 20, 1772, Samuel Taylor [3] Coleridge was born "about 11 o'clock in the forenoon." His father, John Coleridge, Vicar of the Parish, Master of the King's New Grammar School, and Chaplain Priest of the Collegiate Church, was the son of John Coleridge of Crediton, weaver, woollen draper or possibly both. [4] S. T. Coleridge was the youngest of fourteen children, ten of them the children of his mother, John Coleridge's second wife. Seven of his eight brothers grew to manhood; and as his parents treated their last-born with special fondness he was at times regarded by these brothers with a certain hostility and contempt. To this fact much of his precocity must be attributed.

At the age of three, when he would normally have followed

his brothers into his father's school, the young Coleridge was put in the 'reading' school of old Dame Key [5]—he was considered too small to be left to the tender mercies of his father's scholars. This step did him no service either with his brothers or with the other boys—for the size of the town forbade even the movements of a small boy to pass without notice—and it is not altogether surprising to learn that the boys frequently drove him from play and occasionally tormented him—actions which increased his inclination to tell tales and his revulsion against those of his own age. His popularity with some of the elder townsfolk, who marvelled at the flow of speech, capacious memory and adult understanding in one so young, could not compensate for his lack of natural companions.

At home, Coleridge was by no means free from trouble. Not only was he encompassed by numerous older and, on the whole, unfriendly brothers; he was also, and perhaps even more uncomfortably, the victim of one Molly. This woman was the old nurse of his handsome brother Francis, the ninth child, from whom Coleridge had snatched, unwittingly, the honours of the family baby.

The way of such children as the young Coleridge is pretty clearly marked. His natural inclination towards reading grew into a passion. Whenever possible he liked to pay a visit to his aunt Susannah's 'everything' shop at Crediton, where he read steadily through her stock of little gilt-covered books and uncovered tales. Everything in print came alike to him. By the age of six, he had read books as diverse as *Tom Hickathrift, Jack the Giant-Killer, Robinson Crusoe, Belisarius,* the *Adventures of Philip Quarll,* and the *Arabian Nights*—"one tale of which," he wrote later, "(the tale of a man who was compelled to seek for a pure virgin) made so deep an impression on me (I had read it in the evening while my Mother was mending stockings), that I was haunted by spectres, whenever I was in the dark: and I distinctly recollect the anxious and fearful eagerness with which I used to watch the window in which the books lay, and whenever the sun lay upon them, I would seize it, carry it by the wall, and bask and read." [6]

When he could not be in Crediton, Coleridge's favourite haunt was the churchyard where, huddled close to the wall, he would read and mope and dream; until of a sudden "my spirits used to come upon me suddenly; and in a flood" [7]—he would transmute himself temporarily into the characters of whom he had just been reading; acting solitarily, with gravestones for audience, the scenes that had particularly taken hold of his imagination; "cutting down weeds and nettles, as one of the seven champions of Christendom." [8]

In his sixth year, Coleridge was placed in his father's school,[9] where he rapidly outshone every boy of his own age. Of this period he told a curious and significant anecdote. He and his brother George fell ill of a fever. "Frequently have I (half-awake and half-asleep, my body diseased and fevered by my imagination), seen armies of ugly things bursting in upon me, and . . . . four angels keeping them off." [10] The boys were isolated in separate rooms. Nevertheless, despite orders to the contrary, Francis stole up, not to George's room, but to the place where his younger brother lay. He brought with him Pope's 'Homer' which he proceeded to read to the sick boy. This speaks well for Francis, who disliked books rather more than he despised his brother, but it also suggests the power of the magnetism which, even at that early age, and in those unfavourable circumstances, the young Coleridge must have possessed.

It is often possible to trace in a house, a town, a type of country, or in all three, an influence of profound importance upon the life and work of certain men and women. The Brontës present one of the plainest examples of such an influence. Much of the best work of Wordsworth is identified with the mountains of the Lake District. But Coleridge cannot be associated with any one place in this way. His appreciation of nature was unlocalized; it was equally active at Ottery, at Stowey, at Keswick, wherever he happened to be. If Ottery is visited to-day it is because of the sentimental interest which usually attaches to the birthplace of the great. Not only did Coleridge leave the town at an early age and never return for more than a few weeks at a time, but his years there, few as they were, held more unhappy than happy memories; and he dwelt regretfully upon this period of his childhood only during his first brief and natural homesickness and in the more insincere moments of his later days.

The mark which Ottery did in all probability leave upon Coleridge, however, is no less important for being singularly unromantic. The climate of the sheltered little town—mild and moist—cannot have been good for one who appears to have inherited a rheumatic tendency. And an adventure when Coleridge was eight years old doubtless began, if it was not entirely responsible for, those neuralgic attacks which increased rapidly with the years and which brought so early in their train the too masterful solace of opium.

Francis again takes part in this incident. The trouble began over a piece of cheese. The young Coleridge asked his mother to cut his cheese in one slice so that he might toast it. His mother complied; but Francis, unwisely left alone for a moment with the slice of cheese, not unnaturally minced it to express his disapproval of favouritism. The returning Coleridge flew at his brother in a rage when he saw the state of his cheese. Francis fell and shammed dead. Then, while the terrified boy was bending over him in search of some sign of life, Francis suddenly rose and dealt his young brother a severe blow in the face. Coleridge, beside himself, seized a knife and attacked his tormentor. And at that moment his mother returned.

There is nothing in all this that might not be seen in any large household of brothers; but Coleridge evidently was unused either to baring his temper to such an extent or to being caught in the act by his mother. In fear of a thrashing he rushed from the house until he reached the top of a small hill about a mile away. Here he sat down and, drawing from his pocket a small book in which were printed morning and evening prayers, he spent some time repeating them in a devout voice; thinking at the same time with a certain satisfaction how miserable his mother must be feeling at his prolonged absence.

He determined not to return. But it was October and the Otter, flowing round the bottom of the hill, threw up damp chilly mists. Calves in the fields across the river lowed dismally. A man crossed the bridge some distance away without noticing the boy. Darkness descended. Eventually Coleridge fell asleep. While he slept he rolled down the hill until, awakened finally by the dawn, he found himself no more than a few yards away from the water. He attempted to get up and walk but was too stiff to move. He called out, but his voice was so feeble that shepherds nearby did not hear him.

Meanwhile, in Ottery, there had been an uproar when he was not to be found. He was 'cried' in the town. Search parties turned out. The river near the town was dragged. No one thought of looking so far away until by a fortunate chance a former pupil of his father, Sir Stafford Northcote, straying in his direction, discovered the boy. "I remember and never shall forget my father's face as he looked upon me while I lay in the servant's arms— so calm, and the tears stealing down his face; for I was the child of his old age. My mother, as you may suppose, was outrageous with joy." [11] Coleridge was put to bed, where he lay for a day or two; but the effects of that night were never completely to leave him.

Sir Stafford Northcote [12] was the squire of the district. The Great House, as Coleridge termed the Squire's mansion, was early connected in his mind with the tales of the Arabian Nights— its size elevating the building to the dignity and grandeur of a palace. He doubtless was sent there after his recovery to thank his rescuer. Inside, the feature which most struck his imagination was the great spiral staircase with its three spacious landing places, giving the impression of merely "using" the ground from which it sprang. He did not forget this staircase; and the landing places reappear in *The Friend* of later years.

Between Coleridge and his father there existed the companionship not infrequently found between a parent and his youngest child. The great span of years which divided them—the old man was fifty-three when his Benjamin was born—seems only to have brought them closer in thought. And if his father burned some of the more lurid of the books Coleridge was reading, he made amends in their many walks by introducing his son to the wonders of the sky and the magnitude of its inhabitants—"how Jupiter was a thousand times larger than our world and that the other twinkling stars were suns that had worlds rolling round them; and when I came home he shewed me how they rolled round" [13]— a lesson which, in addition to the wonder and delight with which it was heard, confirmed in Coleridge's mind the impression left by much of his reading. It taught him even at that early age that his belief need be limited only by the extent of his imagination.

Father and son might be expected to have something in common; for, as he has been described, the Reverend John Coleridge bears an unmistakable resemblance to his youngest son. He was good-hearted, absent-minded, unworldly, something of an eccentric, optimistic. In his *Critical Latin Grammar*, among other changes for the benefit of the scholar, some of which have since been adopted, the names of the cases were altered.[14] The ablative case, as his son remarks with affectionate delight, was in future to be known as the 'quippe-quare-quale-quia-quidditive' case; and even when it has been discovered that the proposed name was in fact the 'quale-quare-quidditive' case, the proposal remains worthy the father of Coleridge.

John Coleridge lacked parental ambition: and it seems that Coleridge's brothers would have fared badly but for their mother's insistence that they be given an adequate education. Coleridge himself appears to have been in no such danger. His destiny, from childhood, was the Church, and his father took many pains to forward the project.

Coleridge's mother, formerly Anne Bowden,[15] came of sound Devon stock[16] and was, fortunately, a practical woman who managed her large family with considerable success. But there seems little doubt that, despite her affection for her youngest son, the sudden death of her husband in October 1781, on the eve of Coleridge's ninth birthday, deprived the boy of the companionship he most valued.

The death of his father brought about a change of home for Coleridge. The new vicar took up residence at the vicarage and the Coleridge family moved next door. The new schoolmaster [17] did not commend himself to Mrs Coleridge as a teacher—the boy used to come home and relate his master's deficiencies in grammar —and it was not long before she began looking for a school more suited to her youngest son's abilities. She soon met with success. A presentation to Christ's Hospital was obtained from a Mr John Way, through the interest of Mr Francis Buller,[18] an old pupil of her husband; and in April 1782 Coleridge left Ottery for London.

He did not go straight to school. It had been arranged that he should spend a few weeks with his maternal uncle, John Bowden, who had a tobacconist's shop in Threadneedle Street and was also clerk to an underwriter: and from here the boy was taken occasionally to see Mr Buller.

This short period before Coleridge entered the school is interesting because it reveals in the boy what was to become in the man a power as rare as it is remarkable. His uncle was of a convivial disposition; and in his spare time, which seems to have been extensive, he and his nephew made the round of the coffee houses and taverns. Here, amidst the hubbub of argument, the country boy, instead of succumbing to the shyness which might have been expected of him, plunged into the battle of words. Indeed, he did more than this; for it was not long before his opponents fell silent as he talked. At Ottery, Coleridge had become a 'character' to the old ladies, who listened to him open-mouthed. Now, his tongue stilled the men of the City. But this triumphal progress soon came to an end. On the 18th of July Coleridge was sent to the Christ's Hospital Junior School at Hertford. Six weeks later he was back in London, being placed in the Jeffries Ward in the Under Grammar School; and here began his nine years of serious school life.

Lamb, Wordsworth, and Coleridge himself, seem to have been at some pains to draw a pathetic picture of the "liveried schoolboy," [19] the "poor friendless boy" [20] whose few acquaintances soon tired of his visits and neglected him. Coleridge, at a later date and in his best conventional manner, bewails the fate of his "weeping childhood, torn By early sorrow from my native seat." [21] But it is difficult to believe that this "depressed, moping, friendless, poor orphan, half starved" [22] represents more than a phase through which most of the boys had to pass. The conditions at the school must indeed have seemed grim to a newcomer: the brutality of some monitors, the fearsomeness of the punishments, the inadequacy of the food, were alone sufficient to chill the stoutest heart. [23] But they were not the whole of school life, they did not even form the major part of it; and to set against them, Coleridge had the wonders of a great city, access to unlimited books, and, above all, a capacity which he quickly revealed of drawing to himself, first friends and later disciples also. Coleridge doubtless did lie upon the school roof at times watching the skies, as Wordsworth pictured him in The Prelude; [24] and doubtless at such times his thoughts did go back to the only countryside he had known. He possessed, even at that age, a highly developed capacity for bemoaning the loss of that which he had never enjoyed; and if he mistook a love of nature for a longing for home and shed some tears, it is not surprising.

Coleridge describes himself as leading the life of a "playless day-dreamer" [25] until he was fourteen years old; and his earlier years would naturally be more solitary and less disciplined—if it is possible to use such a word in connection with Coleridge— than those which followed. But that he was unhappy for long, even at this time, is unlikely. He had not only his uncle in London, but a maternal aunt, Mrs Short, who was good to him, as his letters reveal. [26] The number of his friends was increasing. From 1785 his brother George was a schoolmaster at Hackney. And he had soon the incalculable consolation of books.

One day, walking along the Strand, Coleridge was enacting one of his day-dreams—in this instance, he was Leander swimming the Hellespont. But the pavement was crowded and the swimmer's outstretched arms caught the pocket of a passer-by. The alarmed boy, when challenged, denied any intention of picking the stranger's pocket and explained his unusual actions with such charm and ability that he not only escaped censure but was actually presented with a free ticket to the circulating library in King Street, Cheapside. [27] Every day Coleridge would slip out of school and hurry along to Cheapside to get the two books allowed at a time. His plan of selection was simple; he started at the beginning of the catalogue and worked steadily through until he had read every book in the library. The subject of a book was never questioned; his ability to understand what he read was no hindrance; he read because he must. It is a measure of Coleridge's talents rather than of his industry, that in spite of this formidable obstacle to the pursuit of routine studies, his progress from class to class was almost mechanical. The acquirement and expression of knowledge seemed as effortless to him as the flow of his conversation.

Soon after his arrival at Christ's Hospital, Coleridge had been taken under the wing of T. F. Middleton. [28] Charles Lamb, [29] though two years younger, had joined the school a few months before Coleridge; and they quickly struck up a friendship. To these were added Charles Valentine Le Grice, [30] Robert Allen [31] and a continually growing host of admirers. Later still the number of disciples increased, though it is now only necessary to remember four—Samuel Favell; [32] Samuel Le Grice; [33] T. Hartwell Horne, [34] whom Coleridge coached in the summer holidays of

1790 and at whose house the elder boy, then head Grecian, spent some pleasant holidays teaching his host the Greek alphabet; and finally, a boy named Evans.[35]

Coleridge passed from Under to Upper Grammar School with unusual speed and in 1787 was marked down for University training, a step which received impressive confirmation in his sixteenth year when he was admitted into the select band of Grecians [36]—the finest classical scholars of the school, who worked for a University Exhibition (usually with the Church in view) under the upper grammar master, the Reverend James Boyer.[37]

To this man Coleridge owed a great deal. Quite early, Boyer's attention (a distinction not without its disadvantages) was said to have been drawn to Coleridge by Middleton, who had been astonished to discover the boy reading Virgil for pleasure in a corner of the playground at a time when his class had not even reached the subject. But it seems unlikely, in any event, that Boyer, as Coleridge's master, would overlook a boy who topped his classes with such regularity.

Boyer has been described by Lamb and eulogized by Coleridge; [38] and though the aspect with which they regard him differs as their outlook and their position in the school differed, they are at one in their appreciation of his powers with the birch—Lamb, not working regularly under Boyer, with all the pleasure of an onlooker; Coleridge, as a member of his class, with the more painful recollection of a sufferer.

Boyer believed in knocking nonsense out of his pupils' heads and knocking sense into them by the same drastic means; but it does not seem that he did Coleridge anything but good—in some respects his influence, however violently imposed, played a considerable part in Coleridge's future development.

In 1786, if Coleridge's dating is correct (an assumption which in this instance cannot be made with confidence), he wrote the first poem that has been preserved. A tradition at Christ's Hospital said that this poem *Genevieve* was written to the daughter of his dormitory 'Nurse' for whom Coleridge—following a school custom—had developed an early passion. The words of the poem certainly support this tradition; and the susceptibility of Coleridge to good looks and kindness of heart suggests that if his Nurse's daughter possessed such advantages he succumbed to them.

[19]

Coleridge spent much time in the sick-ward. He swam the New River in his clothes, let them dry upon him and was ill for months with rheumatic fever and jaundice (a further reason for later pain); but he confounds tradition by placing this event between his seventeenth and eighteenth birthdays, when his affections were being attracted elsewhere.[39]

In 1787, however, a Coleridge poem is safely dated; for in that year the transcriptions into Boyer's album [40] begin. This album recorded what Boyer considered his pupils' best exercises. They were regarded by Coleridge as little more than exercises. One, at least, *Monody on the Death of Chatterton*, even in its original form, shows a promising and unusual power and imaginativeness. Coleridge describes his interest in poetry at this time as insipid, but there is little doubt that he was not even then wholly without pride in his compositions. He had received compliments (not from Boyer) upon the facility shown by him in the writing of verses. Nevertheless, he had other enthusiasms; and these, though in subject not unlike the passions of any intelligent boy, were carried to far greater lengths by the ardour with which Coleridge pursued them. His sudden infatuation, probably in 1785, for a cobbler's calling—the first effort of Coleridge to devote himself to a life of manual labour, heightened in this instance by his reluctance to face the honour of becoming a Grecian, with its unwelcome implications of his future career—did not end until the unfortunate cobbler had been persuaded by his ardent pupil to apply in person to Boyer for the release of the boy from his studies and had been driven, not without bodily injury, from that impetuous man's presence.[41]

Hard upon this debacle followed the decision to become a doctor. Coleridge was not content to haunt the wards of London Hospital where his brother Luke was training under Sir William Blizard. His zeal demanded nothing less than mastery of the art. He read every book on medicine and surgery that he could find. Much that he read must have been incomprehensible to him, but if he did not acquire medical knowledge in proportion to the bulk of his reading, he became acquainted with a realistic and analytical aspect of life as new to him as it was disturbing. A more unsuitable doctor than Coleridge would be difficult to imagine. His habit of relapsing unexpectedly into a profound and almost impenetrable inward cogitation for an indefinite period would alone have made him suspect, if not positively dangerous, to patients requiring attention; but his aversion to witnessing any form of suffering was perhaps an even greater disadvantage. It is possible that some unusually atrocious sight in one of the wards began to dissipate his enthusiasm. In any event, it was fortunate for Coleridge and others when a more congenial influence took possession of his mind.

Coleridge had begun to dabble in the Neo-Platonists. He attributes his first interest in them to the essays on Liberty and Necessity in Cato's *Letters*.[42] The subject was probably followed up by means of the Latin translations frequently supplied with the original Greek. He may have come across Thomas Taylor's translations, which were just beginning to appear,[43] and which at a later date he described rather unkindly as "difficult Greek transmuted into incomprehensible English."[44] But it seems likely, as well as characteristic, that Coleridge did not wait long before he went to the originals. Lamb's description of the youthful Coleridge in the Christ's Hospital cloisters for sheer pleasure holding forth in Greek to his audience[45] cannot be wholly imaginative. And if Coleridge is to be believed, he translated eight Hymns of Synesius into anacreontics before his fifteenth birthday.[46]

On the school 'leave days' Coleridge would often wander about the city seeking kindred souls. When he had struck up an acquaintance with a likely stranger—an act which never presented any difficulty to him—he would guide the conversation at the earliest possible moment to the mystical regions whose profundities he would probe, question, eulogize and dispute as long as the patience of his companion held out. He preferred clergymen as his victims—doubtless because the inevitable turning of the conversation was less likely to be delayed; before a word was spoken he could expect to be met halfway.[47]

And if theology was a natural step from metaphysics, atheism, hovering invitingly on the outskirts, presented a contrast which no enquiring mind could avoid. Coleridge sampled all three. He named Voltaire's *Philosophical Dictionary* as the originator of his doubts;[48] but Erasmus Darwin's arguments against the existence of God and criticism of the evidence of revealed religion, played their part; and the scientific outlook of the medical books he had read lessened his first natural revulsion.

Boyer, who must have been regarding this era of mysticism and scepticism with considerable impatience, at last fell upon his metaphysical-atheistic pupil and administered a sound flogging. This particular punishment after he had "sported infidel" [49] earned Coleridge's gratitude in after years. He said that it effectually drove all temptation to continue infidel from his mind. But even this drastic treatment did not put an end to his metaphysical investigations. That feat was to be achieved—temporarily—by a gentler agency.

A corrective to the impression of Coleridge as wholly a mystic questioner, or as a solitary perpetually bent over a book, is provided by the two essays of Lamb. The bathing parties in the New River, with Coleridge an active and joyous member, recall a side of his nature that is easily forgotten.[50] And the far more famous picture of Coleridge in the cloisters expounding Iamblicus and Plotinus, reciting Homer and Pindar in his deep, sweet voice; the casual passer-by listening amazed; the quick, brilliant counter-argument of C. V. Le Grice; the laugh of handsome Bob Allen bringing the 'wit-combat' to an unpremeditated end; this, whether accurate in detail or not, does reveal unmistakably the characteristic Coleridge in a characteristic setting. There is also the picture, similar in character, of Coleridge "declaiming [Greek] verses as he went about the school grounds." [51] His 'fag' of Grecian days remarks that "he was not very nice in his person or his dress. He seldom had two garters at one time, in consequence of which his stockings used to drop into a series of not very elegant folds." [52]

In 1788, according to Coleridge, his acquaintance with the Evans family began.[53] One of his young disciples, William Evans, persuaded the mighty Grecian to visit the Evans' home in Villiers Street. Coleridge leaped into intimacy with the family. In a remarkably short time he was 'Brother Coly,' as much an inmate of the home as the school permitted. Mrs Evans and her three daughters were not slow to welcome this youth of "natural gladness" [54] with his remarkable gift of speech, his affectionate disposition and his appealing lack of nearby home or parents. As for Coleridge, he was then, as always, heavy with love for those who would love him; grateful to those who would guide him by example rather than by precept; seeking even then for those who would take from him the paralysing responsibility of decision.

This household of three lively, attractive girls and their mother took hold of Coleridge's metaphysical yearnings and gave them a common sense twist from which they did not recover easily. At Villiers Street, Coleridge discovered something of a home life that had not been his before; and he gave generously in return, for all places were the brighter for his presence, all minds the richer for listening to him. The Evanses helped him to be a boy again, and for a time, at least, he almost ceased to wrestle with abstruse problems, identifying himself instead with the liveliness of an affectionate family.

It was not long before Coleridge was dipping his hand into romance. Very soon he and his friend Allen were meeting the elder girls, Mary and Anne, on a Saturday as the sisters left the milliner's shop in which they worked; presenting them with bouquets of uncertainly acquired flowers wrapped with a sonnet or love poem.[55] Coleridge quickly became interested in Mary. Her vivacity, her attractive appearance and her directness, not to say bluntness of manner at times, would naturally appeal to him. They began lightheartedly enough, and it seems probable that Mary, though she enjoyed them, never took Coleridge's attentions too seriously. There was certainly nothing in the nature of a declaration on his part whilst at Christ's Hospital. The 'Brother Coly' of their letters may be genuine on Mary's side at least. It is not even certain when Coleridge realised his love for her. He, as usual, contradicts himself in his reminiscences of this time.

What is quite certain is that, with this coming of family life and affection, with the awakening of a tenderer emotion, and with the beginning of his first interest in poetry, these years, the last four of his schooldays, were years of real, satisfying happiness for Coleridge.

As a Grecian, though he may have wilted at times before the thoughts of the future, there were consolations. He was becoming something of a great man. He recited the Latin Oration on St. Matthew's Day 1789 before the Lord Mayor, William Gill, and dignitaries [56]—an occasion which gave rise to the irreverent but decidedly clever burlesque *The Nose, An Odaic Rhapsody* [57]— and, the circulation of the poem successfully restricted to his friends, the invitation to the dinner of the Amicable Society of Blues at the Nag's Head the following St. Matthew's Day issued to

[23]

Coleridge, Allen and the elder Le Grice went forward without hindrance and the dinner was duly enjoyed.

It is scarcely surprising that Coleridge's metaphysical investigations paused, discouraged, before these new interests. If not necessarily the fruits of unhappiness, they depend to a considerable extent upon long, companionless meditation; and such time he was increasingly unable to spare.

But if his metaphysics met with a check in 1788, they were quite unmanned the following year and no more is heard of them for a long period. For it was in 1789 that Coleridge first became acquainted with the poems of Bowles.

Middleton, Coleridge's old protector at the school, was the man who set the poet in motion. From Cambridge he sent Coleridge the *Sonnets on Picturesque Spots* by the Reverend W. L. Bowles.[58] The immediate reaction which these sonnets had upon Coleridge was not entirely unexpected. Boyer drilled his boys drastically, purging them, so far as he was able, of the tendency in exercises to imitate their betters of the time by the liberal use of stock similes, metaphors, personified abstractions and the like, which might have been, and usually were, interchangeable without serious harm to the sense of the passage. Boyer was wise enough to see that this pernicious habit in his scholars, though it arose out of laziness, would lead inevitably, if unchecked, to a permanent corruption of taste—the kind of corruption, in fact, which was then widespread. He was sufficiently ahead of his age to recoil from the artificiality of the classical school; and his arm did not rest until the more thoughtful of his pupils saw the contemporary poets and their venerated masters through his eyes.

Coleridge was therefore taught rigorously why he should prefer Demosthenes to Cicero, Homer and Theocritus to Virgil, Virgil to Ovid, and Lucretius, Terence and Catullus to the later Roman poets; he was made to see and explain the logic and inevitability in thought and consequently in expression of the one as against the artificiality, the mere epigrammatic brilliance of the other. He was obliged to study Shakespeare and Milton; to acknowledge and to prove the inevitability of every word they used and of its position. The profound logic of great poetry was dinned into his mind. The application of this logic was pressed home when the time came for submission of his own work. Boyer would allow the exercises [59] to accumulate unexamined until several prepared by each boy were ready for inspection. He would then spread out the exercises together and compare the phrases or sentences used. Whenever some particularly atrocious generality met his eye, he would ask whether it could not have been employed with equal effect in any one of the other exercises. If the culprit was unable to convince him of the inevitability of the words chosen, the exercise was torn up and ordered to be rewritten.[60]

In this way, reluctantly perhaps, but certainly, there grew in Coleridge's mind an appreciation of the principles of true poetry and, as a natural corollary, a criticism unspoken no doubt and possibly unrealised (since his heart was not then set on the subject) of the poetry that ruled during his youth—a criticism which he expressed later as "matter and diction . . . characterized not so much by poetic thoughts, as by thoughts *translated* into the language of poetry." [61]

So armed, it is plain to see that Coleridge needed only example to follow precept for him to break the shackles. The releasing medium happened to be the sonnets of Bowles—and if Bowles moved him to action where Shakespeare and Milton had failed, the fact, as Coleridge has explained, that Bowles was a young man, a contemporary, his work recommended by a revered friend, and not a school 'subject' is reason enough.[62]

What may puzzle the reader to-day is the power of Bowles to exercise any marked effect upon an intelligent person. But in order to read Bowles as Coleridge read him, one hundred and fifty years of poetry would need to be obliterated from the mind; the nineteenth century must become the eighteenth; Pope must become the revered prophet of an all-powerful creed rather than a verbal juggler of unusual dexterity; and Erasmus Darwin, his last disciple for a hundred years or more, must be still at work upon the *Botanical Garden*. Burns must be overlooked; Cowper not yet discovered.

Then and then only would it be possible to estimate fully the power of Bowles over the young Coleridge—and over Wordsworth and Southey, to name two other famous admirers.[63] In fact, it is not possible; but to those who make such an effort there do appear certain mild but unmistakable merits in the work of

Bowles. Astonishing though it may seem, he was an innovator. He was not alone in what he did. He was not the first to transgress although the first known to Coleridge. The Wartons, Akenside, Burns, Cowper, were all before him, and to the first, at least, he owed much, as his poems show. Yet when all is said, the fact remains that this man set himself, however faultily, against the taste of his time. He was a rebel. That the tide was about to turn, he could not possibly have known; that he was to be a momentous agent of its turning would have seemed to him incredible.

It is simple enough to see the failings in the book of sonnets that came down from Cambridge to Coleridge. There is little need to study the work of Bowles; the formal simile, the trite moralizing, the uninspired reflection may all be found in the poems of his new disciple for the next few years; just as may be seen at the same time the expression of natural thoughts in natural diction, a simplicity that owed little to art, together with an unmistakable sincerity of feeling towards nature and a new tenderness in its treatment.

Coleridge could never keep a discovery to himself. All must know. On such a momentous occasion they must be put into possession of the vital work at the earliest possible moment. He had no money to buy copies of the sonnets so he set to work to transcribe them. Within the next eighteen months he had transcribed and presented to deserving friends or likely converts more than forty copies. Every new work of Bowles was treasured. More important, he began for the first time to write poems with zeal and with feeling. The training of Boyer, the emotional awakening at the Evans house, and the poems of Bowles, following closely one upon another, released his poetical power—immature as yet and faulty but the genuine expression of a faculty so far dormant.

Bowles had a further important effect upon Coleridge; for in his dissemination of the newly acquired faith, Coleridge often found himself obliged to defend and explain the tenets which he held. To do this was to attempt nothing less than an analysis of the nature of poetry; and much of the time of his last years at school was spent in establishing to his satisfaction a solid foundation of poetical criticism "on which permanently to ground my opinions, in the component faculties of the human mind itself, and their comparative dignity and importance." [64] So before he had left school he had turned philosopher inasmuch as he was applying philosophical principles to his literary criticism: and the conclusions to which he came at this time were "first, that not the poem which we have *read*, but that to which we *return*, with the greatest pleasure, possesses the genuine power, and claims the name of *essential poetry*. Second, that whatever lines can be translated into other words of the same language, without diminution of their significance, either in sense, or association, or in any worthy feeling, are so far vicious in their diction." [65]

With this proselytizing activity, with the writing of poems, and with an increasing devotion to Mary Evans, Coleridge passed his remaining school terms. The dating of the poem *Life*,[66] if correct, suggests that he visited his home in September 1789 despite the expense, the presence of George [67] in London, the companionship of the Short, Bowden, and the Evans families, to say nothing of his visits to the homes of other school friends. His brother Luke [68] had already left London.

On January 12, 1791, the Committee of Almoners of Christ's Hospital appointed Coleridge to an Exhibition at Jesus College, Cambridge. In addition to the common apparel allowance of £40, the Exhibition was worth £40 a year for four years and £30 a year for a further three years. In addition, Coleridge had hope of a Rustat scholarship—available only to sons of the clergy —for a further £29 a year.

Coleridge was still destined for the Church; the List of Christ's Hospital University Exhibitioners notes the fact that he was sent to Jesus as "the prospect of [his] preferment in the Church would be very favorable if he was to be preferred to Jesus College." [69]

Coleridge was entered on the books of Jesus as a sizar on February 5 following his appointment. On August 17, 1791, just over nine years since he joined Christ's Hospital, he left the school and went down to Ottery to stay until it was time to go into residence at Cambridge.

If his poem *Happiness*, written at this time, is a guide to his feelings, it would seem that all was not well with Coleridge at home. Possibly the memories of his sister and his brother Luke, both of whom had died recently, affected him. The depression

[27]

may have been caused by his first serious absence from Mary Evans. Or it may have been occasioned by a still more personal reason. After all, he was barely nineteen years old, he was in love, and, as the transcriber of the poem notes, "The Author was at this time . . . . remarkable for a plump face." The heart of the tragedy has therefore in all probability been exposed by Coleridge in the following cancelled lines: [70]

> Ah! doubly blest, if Love supply
> Lustre to this now heavy eye,
> And with unwonted Spirit grace
> That fat vacuity of face.
> Or if e'en Love, the mighty Love
> Shall find this change his power above;
> Some lovely maid perchance thou'lt find
> To read thy visage in thy mind.

2

AT CAMBRIDGE, Coleridge began well. He began so well that uneasiness grows into apprehension and apprehension hardens into certainty that his assiduity was too good to last.

He went into residence at Jesus on October 16, 1791. He began reading mathematics for three hours a day; classics from teatime until eleven. He read Pindar and composed Greek verse "like a mad dog." [1] In his spare time he translated Anacreon. He was awarded a Rustat scholarship. On November 5 he became a pensioner. The following March 31 he matriculated. In the summer he gained the Browne Gold Medal with his Greek Ode on the Slave Trade. He competed for the Latin Ode and the Epigrams, for the Greek Ode on Astronomy. He was one of the four selected to compete for the Craven Scholarship of 1793.

For the first few months, while Middleton was still at Cambridge, Coleridge maintained something in the nature of methodical reading. He would work in Middleton's rooms at Pembroke while his old school patron was reading for a Fellowship.

But there were early interruptions to this routine. On his arrival at Cambridge, Coleridge began writing letters in earnest. His correspondents were his brother George and the Evans family—Mrs Evans and Mary in particular. He had been in his rooms no more than a month before dampness and draughts gave him a cold, which developed into a rheumatic attack. These ailments called forth the first of the detailed descriptions of his symptoms which were later to occupy an increasingly prominent place in his letters. They also provide the first existing reference which Coleridge made to opium.[2]

There was nothing remarkable in Coleridge's use of opium. It was quite common at this time for doctors to prescribe and administer opium to their patients. Coleridge had watched them do so at the London Hospital and it is a reasonable assumption that he was himself given an opiate when he lay in the school sick ward suffering from rheumatic fever and jaundice. No stigma was

[29]

then attached to those who took opium in moderation. It was obtainable without difficulty. The freedom with which Coleridge comments, in a letter to George, upon its effect on him is proof enough that he saw no harm in the practice.

The Christmas vacation, which he spent with the Evanses, set Coleridge up in health but on his return to Cambridge he was faced with a trouble that was to recur frequently. His brothers began to complain. His requests for money alarmed them. They questioned him about the drinking parties whose existence he had disclosed to George when remarking in an early letter on his abstention from them. They sought some assurance that he was studying hard. And they were particularly disturbed by what they had heard of his intimacy with the notorious William Frend.[3]

Coleridge pacified them through George as best he could. He was being very economical. He avoided the wine parties. He was working hard. His acquaintance with Frend was of the slightest. He included a sermon—one of a number that he wrote for George to use at school.[4] And when would he receive his pecuniary assistance—quarterly or half-yearly? Quarterly, he hoped.[5]

That he succeeded in communicating his optimism to George and the other brothers is improbable. They had more reliable sources of information—from the Christ's Hospital boys, and from the Evans family.

And indeed the truth was not so palatable as Coleridge would have had them believe. He had fallen into debt quickly. He was no stranger to the wine parties. In many escapades he was the leading spirit. His reluctance to any settled form of study had begun to overcome his unnatural bout of industry. The departure of Middleton in 1792 without a Fellowship [6] accelerated an inevitable return to the vast but orderless reading, discussion, and long intervals of repose characteristic of him. As for William Frend, the truth was that Coleridge was fast becoming a disciple of this disturbing man.

In fact, Coleridge's mind, in common with many others at this time, was turning a somersault. Frend's Unitarian teachings and decidedly liberal views in politics were coloured by events in France; and both the personal appeal of Frend and the larger, intoxicating glimpse of freedom from over the Channel, combined to raise his admirer's interest into fervour. The persecution of

Frend and his defiant attitude in the face of it, enhanced the appeal of his doctrines. Coleridge announced—though not to George—that he was a Socinian.[7]

In February 1793 he told Mary Evans that Fox's letter to the Westminster electors was all the "political *go*" at Cambridge.[8] At the same time he was explaining to her mother how the Craven Scholarship had gone finally to Samuel Butler[9] of St. John's, father of the novelist of the same name.[10]

The loss of this scholarship cut the bottom from under Coleridge's feet. He felt little disappointment; and as he had never worked seriously for the examination, he could not have been greatly surprised at the result. But he did fear the effect upon his brothers, already suspicious of his conduct at Cambridge.

And there was another, more important aspect of his failure. With the loss of the scholarship, Coleridge lost, as it were, the last link which held him to respectability, safety, solidity. He was constitutionally averse to the contemplation of unpleasant circumstances and instinctively provided himself with a saving grace, a stretch of sand into which he could bury his head. It might be someone's example, affection, or guidance. It might be no more than a hope, a prospect, which successfully postponed the day of reckoning.

With the passing of Middleton from Cambridge, Coleridge had been left with the Craven Scholarship as his sole bulwark against reality. His mounting debts, his brothers' displeasure, his unrequited love for Mary, even his distracted beliefs, had been held in check, consideration of them had been postponed, by the possibility of a favourable result to the scholarship. He felt that so long as the result was in doubt the responsibility for none of these things was his; their burden slipped off his shoulders automatically. He possessed without effort, without conscious thought, a background of reality before which his mind could play unchecked, his actions range unnoticed.

When the result was declared, there was no rock left to which he could cling, no shield behind which he could shelter. For a moment his Micawber philosophy failed him; he was obliged to face the situation.

But only for a moment. Coleridge's reaction to the result was as characteristic as his attitude to the scholarship while it hung in the balance. After a few days of irresolution he wrote to George, acquainting him with the result. He did not expect to succeed, he informed his brother; but went on to explain that the Master of Jesus, Doctor Pearce, had been not only sadly disappointed but had hinted plainly at unfairness on the part of the examiners: "You would have beat them hollow, I know you would." [11]

Coleridge then hastened to put forward plans which might rehabilitate him in his brothers' eyes and to which he might attach his responsibilities. He blew the first of his many balloons and no sooner had he set eyes on its iridescent beauty than its frailty was no more remembered; he could think only of the heights to which it would soar. He was to undertake a considerable work—a translation of the best lyrics from the Greek and the modern Latin writers. He informed George that he was actually employed upon this book, which he hoped to publish in about six months' time. He did, in fact, make a translation of Casimir's *Ad Lyram* and a handful of other poems from the Latin. He also conducted a brief but enthusiastic canvass for subscribers among his friends.

Fortified by this vision of work done and money earned, Coleridge in his letter passed to a less pleasant subject. For the first time he refers to his debts, which, he says, had "corroded" his spirits for some time. The money from his book, together with frugality of living, would enable him to pay the debts. Dr Pearce had just appointed him Librarian and Chapel Clerk of the College; and the thirty odd pounds a year from this, with the Rustat and school exhibition, would be sufficient to live upon. Indeed, wrote Coleridge, "As I eat no supper or tea, and keep little company . . . I shall be nearly twenty-five pounds plus." [12] He made no appeal for financial help.

This unpleasant task over, Coleridge abandoned himself to conviviality and to the harbouring of opinions of an increasingly revolutionary character. Old Christ's Hospital friends were with him. Allen had gone to Oxford, but G. L. Tuckett [13] and the elder Le Grice were at Cambridge. C. V. Le Grice, at Trinity, saw a great deal of Coleridge, who, he says, "was ready at any time to unbend his mind in conversation; and, for the sake of this, his room (the ground floor room on the right hand of the staircase facing the great gate,) was a constant rendezvous of conversation-loving friends. . . . What evenings have I spent in those rooms! What little suppers, or *sizings*, as they were called, have I enjoyed; when Aeschylus, and Plato, and Thucydides were pushed aside, with a pile of lexicons, to discuss the pamphlets of the day. Ever and anon, a pamphlet issued from the pen of Burke. There was no need of having the book before us. Coleridge had read it in the morning, and in the evening he would repeat whole pages verbatim." [14]

In May, 1793, Frend was tried in the Vice-Chancellor's Court for sedition and defamation of the Church; and the political and theological passions of the undergraduates rose to fever heat. During the trial, as Le Grice wrote, "pamphlets swarmed from the press. Coleridge had read them all; and in the evening, with our negus, we had them *viva voce* gloriously." [15]

But Coleridge was not content with repeating pamphlets to his friends. He attended the trial; and on one of the rare occasions when a point was made in favour of Frend, Coleridge created a mild sensation by clapping aloud. No amount of enthusiasm availed, however. Frend was banished from the University.[16]

That summer Coleridge paid a round of visits on his way to Ottery. He stayed with his brother Edward,[17] who was assistant master at Dr Skinner's school at Salisbury; and after a few days, spent mainly in argument, he moved down to Tiverton where James,[18] the head of the family, lived. He visited Ottery, but was soon back at Tiverton again. James, however, was not the attraction. In the coach from Exeter, Coleridge had made the acquaintance of a girl by the name of Fanny Nesbitt, and, his Cambridge troubles far away, and Mary Evans even more inaccessible than usual, he endeavoured, not without success, to put them both out of mind. Fanny Nesbitt was probably the chief agent in this attempt but Coleridge had other helpers. He attended a Literary Society in Exeter, where the work of a young poet, William Wordsworth, was read and admired.[19] A poem written at this time—*Songs of the Pixies*—provides a record of one of the youthful parties which gathered so naturally about Coleridge.

He also wrote a number of poems to Fanny Nesbitt—*The Rose*, *Cupid Turn'd Chymist* or *Kisses*—whose interest now rests mainly in the fact that the name of Nesbitt in the verses was later crossed out and Sara substituted—the first examples of many that illustrate the manner in which Coleridge was to adapt himself to circumstances.

There was one echo of the past few months which he was obliged to hear, even down in Devonshire. George was seriously displeased with him; would not answer his letters; had written instead to James complaining of his debts, his drinking, his political and religious views. Before he left for Cambridge, however, Coleridge had managed to justify himself with sufficient plausibility to obtain, not only forgiveness, but a sum of money sufficient to settle his debts at the University.

But Coleridge and money were never long together. He had to reach Cambridge before any bills could be settled. In October he returned to the University but the money was no longer with him. The greater part of it had been frittered away on the journey and in London. The sum that remained was small—so small that he was ashamed to offer it to his tutor, the chief creditor. He tried to dismiss the debts from his mind. Christopher Wordsworth,[20] who had just come up to Trinity, successfully engaged his attention for a while. The poet's youngest brother quickly became a frequenter of Coleridge's set. They discussed William Wordsworth's *Descriptive Sketches* which had recently appeared and had been reviewed in the current *Monthly Review*. Coleridge "talked Greek, Max. Tyrius he told us, and spouted out of Bowles." [21] It was decided to form a literary society at which essays from the members were to be read. Two days later Coleridge repeated his *Lines: On an Autumnal Evening* which was then criticized. The society met in Wordsworth's rooms six days after, on the 13th of November. Before supper the members listened to some more readings of his poetry by Coleridge, "he having neglected to write his essay, which is therefore to be produced next week." [22]

But Coleridge had had other matters to occupy his mind. A few days before, on the 7th, a poem appeared in the *Morning Chronicle* entitled *To Fortune: On buying a Ticket in the Irish Lottery*. This poem recorded Coleridge's attempt to retrieve his position. Bewildered by the demands for money, unable to apply again to his brothers for help and dreading the revelation which seemed inevitable, he had fled to London. He gave his own version of these weeks in a letter written some months later to George:

"When the state of my affairs became known to you and by your exertions and my Brothers' generous Confidence a fair Road seemed open to extrication, Almighty God! what a sequel! I loitered away more money on the road, and in town than it was possible for me to justify to my Conscience; and when I returned to Cambridge a multitude of petty embarrassments buzzed round me, like a nest of Hornets, Embarrassments, which in my wild carelessness I had forgotten, and many of which I had contracted almost without knowing it. So small a sum remained, that I could not mock my Tutor with it. My agitations were delirium—I formed a Party, dashed to London at eleven o'clock at night, and for three days lived in all the tempest of Pleasure—resolved on my return—but I will not shock your religious feelings. I again returned to Cambridge—staid a *week*—such a week! Where Vice has not annihilated sensibility, there is little need of a Hell! On Sunday night I packed up a few things, went off in the mail, staid about a week in a strange way, still looking forward with a kind of recklessness to the *dernier ressort* of misery—an accident of a very singular kind prevented me. . . ." [23]

On his first visit to London, he had bought the lottery ticket. So easily and on so slight a foundation did his mind leap from despair to the highest flight of sanguinity that, as the poem *To Fortune* shows, Coleridge was quite capable of believing that the righteous nature of his requirements would influence the lottery drawing in his favour. It is even possible that, with this vision of virtue rewarded before him, Coleridge left some expectation of a speedy settlement in the minds of his creditors—a step which would increase the difficulty of his return to Cambridge should the inconceivable happen.

During his week in Cambridge, the meeting of the Literary Society took place. But Coleridge's position was now even worse than before; he had practically nothing left but his lottery ticket. His Tutor's bills amounted to £132; in all he probably owed about £150. His one hope was the lottery.

Late in November, he returned to London for the drawing. The lottery was drawn. Coleridge did not win. Without money, incapable of forming plans, afraid to go back to Cambridge, and ashamed to remain in London where a meeting with the Evanses was difficult to avoid, he enlisted in the 15th Light Dragoons (the King's Regiment) whose recruiting poster happened to catch his eye. He gave his name as Silas Tomkyn Comberbacke.[24]

Two days later, on December 4, he was inspected, attested and sworn at the regiment headquarters at Reading—an uncritical acceptance which the exigencies of the war with France alone can explain.

As a soldier of any kind, Coleridge would have been misplaced. As a cavalry man, he was a joke. He did not like horses: he could not ride: he was constantly thrown: he never learned to groom his horse: his accoutrements were never clean: he was constantly unwell.

It says a great deal for his adaptability that, in addition to these troubles, Coleridge's life was not made intolerable by the other troopers. In a short time he was writing their love letters for them, telling them stories and prescribing for them when they were unwell, in return for assistance with his grooming and cleaning.

Even this arrangement could not mitigate materially the wretchedness which he quickly began to feel in his situation; nor could it long conceal from the officers his obvious unsuitability for his duties. He was soon relegated to the work of cleaning out the stables and, more particularly, of attending to the sick. It was when he was engaged upon a particularly unpleasant spell of duty, as hospital orderly, that Coleridge received a letter from Tuckett at Cambridge. At this time, early in February, he was isolated in Henley workhouse hospital, in charge of a comrade with smallpox and suffering himself from painful eruptions.

Tuckett's letter did not come as an overwhelming surprise. Only a few weeks after joining the Dragoons, Coleridge had informed some of the Grecians at Christ's Hospital of his situation. They promptly passed on the information to Tuckett. The letter contained welcome news although Coleridge made an attempt to put a dignified face upon it. Tuckett had written immediately to the Coleridge family and to Coleridge's commanding officer. Coleridge's reproaches for the breach of confidence pale before his relief at the prospect of release.

Tuckett enclosed a letter with his own, the sight of which wrung the following soliloquy from Coleridge:

"A letter from my brother George! I feel a kind of pleasure that it is not directed—it lies unopened—am I not already sufficiently miserable? The anguish of those who love me, of him beneath the shadow of whose protection I grew up—does it not plant the pillow with thorns and make my dreams full of terrors? Yet I dare not burn the letter—it seems as if there were a horror in the action. One pang, however acute, is better than long-continued solicitude. My brother George possessed the cheering consolation of conscience—but I am talking I know not what—yet there is a pleasure, doubtless an exquisite pleasure, mingled up in the most painful of our virtuous emotions. Alas! my poor mother! What an intolerable weight of guilt is suspended over my head by a hair on one hand; and if I endure to live—the look ever downward—insult, pity, hell! God or Chaos, preserve me! What but infinite Wisdom or infinite Confusion can do it?" [25]

But this particular letter was soon opened. A correspondence then took place between the two brothers, which discloses in Coleridge a readiness, not to say a genius, for self-abasement. Coleridge's own words are alone adequate to describe the depths to which he appeared willing, if not positively eager, to sink.

"My more than brother!" he wrote. "What shall I say? What shall I write to you? Shall I profess an abhorrence of my past conduct? Ah me! too well do I know its iniquity! But to abhor! this feeble and exhausted heart supplies not so strong an emotion. O my wayward soul! I have been a fool even to madness. What shall I dare to promise? My mind is illegible to myself. I am lost in the labyrinth, the trackless wilderness of my own bosom. Truly may I say, 'I am weary of being saved.' My frame is chill and torpid. The ebb and flow of my hopes and fears has stagnated into recklessness. One wish only can I read distinctly in my heart, that it were possible for me to be forgotten as though I had never been! The shame and sorrow of those who loved me! The anguish of him who protected me from my childhood upwards, the sore travail of her who bore me! Intolerable images of horror! They haunt my sleep, they enfever my dreams! O that the shadow of Death were on my eyelids, that I were like the loathsome form by which I now sit! O that without guilt I might ask of my Maker annihilation! My brother, my brother! pray for me, comfort me, my brother! I am very wretched, and, though my complaint be bitter, my stroke is heavier than my groaning." [26]

In one of these letters, from which a quotation has already been made, Coleridge, not without a certain melancholy pleasure, made a clean breast of certain irregularities in his Cambridge routine:

"I laugh almost like an insane person when I cast my eye backward on the prospect of my past two years. What a gloomy

Huddle of eccentric actions, and dim-discovered motives! To real happiness I bade adieu from the moment, I received my first 'Tutors' Bill'; since that time, since that period my mind has been irradiated by Bursts only of sunshine, at all other times gloomy with clouds, or turbulent with tempests. Instead of manfully disclosing the disease, I concealed it with a shameful cowardice of sensibility, till it cankered my very Heart. I became a proverb to the University for Idleness. The time, which I should have bestowed on the academic studies, I employed in dreaming out wild schemes of impossible extrication. It had been better for me, if my Imagination had been less vivid. I could not with such facility have shoved aside Reflection! How many and how many hours have I stolen from the bitterness of Truth in these soul-enervating Reveries—in building magnificent edifices of Happiness on some fleeting shadow of Reality! My affairs became more and more involved. I fled to Debauchery; fled pure silent and solitary Anguish to all the uproar of senseless mirth. Having, or imagining that I had, no *stock* of Happiness to which I could look forward, I seized the empty gratifications of the moment, and snatched at the Foam, as the wave passed by me. I feel a painful blush on my cheek, while I write it, but even for the Un. Scholarship, for which I affected to have read so severely, I did not read three days uninterruptedly—for the whole six weeks, that preceded the examination, I was almost constantly intoxicated! My Brother! you shudder as you read." [27]

He also wrote a dutiful confession of wrong-doing to James, which began:

"In a mind which vice has not utterly divested of sensibility, few occurrences can inflict a more acute pang than the receiving proofs of tenderness and love where only resentment and reproach were expected and deserved." [28]

Coleridge was not without his helpers. In addition to Tuckett it appears that Boyer, who had been informed of the escapade, interceded with the Coleridge brothers on his former pupil's behalf. Also, according to Coleridge, a Captain Ogle, who belonged to the regiment, became interested in the unhappy trooper after he had discovered the lament:

Eheu! quam infortunii miserrimum
est fuisse felicem!

scrawled on the stable wall; but he played no formal part in obtaining Coleridge's release.[29]

A Cambridge friend, George Cornish, put in a good word for Coleridge and, after running down an elusive and somewhat reluctant Comberbacke in the streets of Reading, offered some money which, as he wrote to his wife: "he refused, but not in a way but what I saw it would be acceptable to him. I therefore gave him a guinea. . . ." [30]

This incident occurred early in March, a few days after Coleridge had left Henley. The weeks he spent with the sick man in the Workhouse Hospital doubtless affected his health and spirits and to some extent may have contributed to the abject tone of the letters written from there. Nevertheless, even in this unpromising situation he contrived to win and enjoy the sympathetic attentions of a "beautiful girl." [31]

The family decided to obtain a discharge for Coleridge but the negotiations were protracted—they were obliged to provide a substitute in his place—and it was not until April 7, 1794 [32] that the discharge was granted. In the meantime, Coleridge was moved from Henley to High Wycombe, where he was billeted at The Compasses—now The Chequers—and from that place to The White Hart at Reading.

As the time of deliverance grew nearer, his letters change their tone. They contain less self-reproach, they become more practical, they concern themselves increasingly with his monetary requirements—for clothes, books, travel—stated in minute detail and accompanied by sundry professions of the new man.

"I received your enclosed," he wrote George. "I am fearful, that as you advise me to go immediately to Cambridge after my discharge, that the utmost contrivances of economy will not enable [me] to make it adequate to all the expenses of my clothes and travelling. I shall go across the country on many accounts. The expense (I have examined) will be as nearly equal as well can be. The *fare* from Reading to High Wycombe on the outside is four shillings, from High Wycombe to Cambridge (for *there is* a coach that passes through Cambridge from Wycombe) I suppose about twelve shillings, perhaps a trifle more. I shall be two days and a half on the road, *two nights*. Can I calculate the expense at less than half a guinea, including all things? An additional guinea would perhaps be sufficient. Surely, my brother, I am not so utterly abandoned as not to feel the *meaning* and *duty* of *economy*." [33]

Toward the end of this time a revival of literary ambitions becomes apparent. He stayed the last three days at Bray revising a work written by his host and writing a dedication and preface. Charles Clagget [34] had set four of Coleridge's lyrics to music: and, more important, suggested that he should write a serious opera. Coleridge recovers his spirits rapidly. "I think of it," he informs George. He feels his powers "greatly strengthened" by the lack of sustained reading whilst in the army.[35]

Coleridge returned to Cambridge with exemplary promptitude. He was back at Jesus on the 11th of April. On the following day he was convened before the Fellows, reprimanded, confined to the College for a month, and obliged to translate *Demetrius Phalareus* into English.[36] Some reason for this leniency emerges from the correspondence between the college authorities and George. Arrangements were made to pay Coleridge's tutor's bills direct—if found necessary, by instalments.[37] George was assured that his brother was highly regarded at the college; and that Coleridge's bearing on returning to the fold was considered "extremely proper." [38]

Coleridge brimmed over with good resolutions. He informed George that he gets up at five o'clock every morning; that he has dropped "solemnly and forever" all his college acquaintances excepting only those who had always remonstrated against his imprudences; that he is finishing a Greek ode; that he intends to write for all the prizes; that he has no time upon his hands; that he is going to aim "at correctness and perspicuity, not *genius.*" He talked hopefully of taking his degree.[39] And he remarked that "every enjoyment, except of *necessary* comforts I look upon as criminal. To *have* practised a severe economy might perhaps have been a merit in me; to practise it now, is only not to be a monster." [40]

There is no reason to believe that this programme ever materialized outside an unduly optimistic imagination. Coleridge was certainly kept busy for a time with the Greek translation. He may have finished his Greek ode. But apart from this, the only tangible signs of his activities from April to June are the Proposals and lengthy Design "for publishing by subscription, *Imitations from the Modern Latin Poets, with a Critical and Biographical Essay on the Restoration of Literature* by S. T. Coleridge, of Jesus College, Cambridge"; [41] possibly one or two of the few poems which alone represented the completed work; and the poem *The Sigh* which was enclosed with a letter to Mary Evans.[42]

The Sigh is interesting because it shows that Coleridge, in verse at least, had abandoned his pretence of friendship with Mary. His passing fancies seem only to have increased his affection. His behaviour on his two disastrous visits to London, although it shamed him from meeting Mary, served only to add to his passion for one who, aware of his excesses, would still correspond with him.

Coleridge spent less than two months at Jesus. On June 5 he became a Foundation Scholar. On the 9th he left Cambridge with Joseph Hucks [43] for a walking tour in Wales. On their way, they called at Oxford to visit Allen, Coleridge's old school friend who was at University College.

The meeting was momentous. Allen introduced Coleridge to his friends, John Stoddart [44] and Robert Southey. Southey was at this time twenty years old, two years younger than Coleridge.[45] He fell an instant victim to the charms of the elder man. On June 12, he wrote to his friend, Grosvenor Bedford: "He [Coleridge] is of most uncommon merit,—of the strongest genius, the clearest judgment, the best heart. My friend he already is, and must hereafter be yours." [46]

Coleridge was not less impressed with Southey. They had a common interest in poetry and in their political views. Southey, however, had more to offer than the customary transports of republican ardour. He had been expelled from Westminster some two years before for disseminating radical and anti-authoritarian sentiments. He had been studying Plato's *Republic* and had been considering emigration and a life of honest toil under conditions at least reminiscent of the philosopher's design.[47]

Here was a heaven-sent opportunity for Coleridge. The treatment of Frend had convinced him of the hopelessness of expecting religious toleration in England. The French Revolution had inspired in him a natural love of freedom which the later excesses of its partisans had been unable to shake, owing largely to what he considered the unjust war made against them by England. Charles Fox in his speeches and Thomas Paine in his *Rights of Man* had convinced him of man's inalienable right to self-government. The repression of free speech had shown him that England would not admit this right, and the gospel of the romanticists that there was virtue and happiness in manual labour not only attracted him but was practically supported, so he argued, by Adam Smith in his *Wealth of Nations*.

The five young men—Coleridge, Hucks, Allen, Southey and his friend, George Burnett,[48] put their heads together and began to evolve a plan by which republicanism in an ideal form might be enjoyed by a select band of enthusiasts.[49] The walking tour was held up. The visit lengthened to close upon a month. Enthusiasm grew to fever heat. The outlines of the scheme became firmer, they filled out, and Coleridge's eloquence poured life into them. Pantisocracy [50]—the name given to the design, at whose hand it is not difficult to imagine—signified, in the words of Southey, "the equal government of all." [51] The details were not at this time fully decided. The most complete description of it, recorded a few months later, was that of Thomas Poole.

"Twelve gentlemen of good education and liberal principles are to embark with twelve ladies in April next. Previous to their leaving this country they are to have as much intercourse as possible, in order to ascertain each other's dispositions, and firmly to settle every regulation for the government of their future conduct. Their opinion was that they should fix themselves at—I do not recollect the place, but somewhere in a delightful part of the new back settlements; that each man should labour two or three hours in a day, the produce of which labour would, they imagine, be more than sufficient to support the colony. As Adam Smith observes that there is not above one productive man in twenty, they argue that if each laboured the twentieth part of time, it would produce enough to satisfy their wants. The produce of their industry is to be laid up in common for the use of all; and a good library of books is to be collected, and their leisure hours to be spent in study, liberal discussions, and the education of their children. A system for the education of their children is laid down, for which, if this plan at all suits you, I must refer you to the authors of it. The regulations relating to the females strike them as the most difficult; whether the marriage contract shall be dissolved if agreeable to one or both parties, and many other circumstances, are not yet determined. The employments of the women are to be the care of infant children, and other occupations suited to their strength; at the same time the greatest attention is to be paid to the cultivation of their minds. Every one is to enjoy his own religious and political opinions, provided they do not encroach on the rules previously made, which rules, it is unnecessary to add, must in some measure be regulated by the laws of the state which includes the district in which they settle. They calculate that each gentleman providing £125 will be sufficient to carry the scheme into execution. Finally, every individual is at liberty, whenever he please, to withdraw from the society." [52]

But although pantisocracy had not yet reached this state of definition, quite enough had been decided for Coleridge to spread the gospel on his journey. Early in July, Southey and Burnett walked down to Bristol together, elaborating the scheme on their way.[53] Coleridge and Hucks set off for Gloucester. Coleridge and Southey were not to be separated for long, however; it was arranged that, when his tour had ended, Coleridge should visit his new friend at Bristol.

The effect of the discussions which had taken place is apparent almost at once in Coleridge.

> "It is *wrong*, Southey," he writes, "for a little girl with a half-famished sickly baby in her arms to put her head in at the window of an inn—'Pray give me a bit of bread and meat!' from a party dining on lamb, green peas, and salad. Why? Because it is *impertinent* and *obtrusive*! 'I am a gentleman! and wherefore the clamorous voice of woe intrude upon mine ear?' My companion is a man of cultivated, though not vigorous understanding; his feelings are all on the side of humanity; yet such are the unfeeling remarks, which the lingering remains of aristocracy occasionally prompt." [54]

He rapidly invents a verb in support of pantisocracy—to aspheterize [55]—"from ἀ, non, and σφέτερος, proprius (we really *wanted* such a word). . . ." Southey later defined aspheterism as "the generalisation of individual property." [56]

From Gloucester—"The women have almost all of them sharp noses" [57]—they went to Ross, staying at the King's Arms, former home of Kyrle, Man of Ross, in whose honour Coleridge wrote a poem on the window shutter of his bedroom.[58]

From Ross, the two made their way through Hereford, Leominster, Bishop's Castle, Montgomery, Welshpool, to Llanfyllin. Coleridge walked prodigious distances and aspheterized freely whenever he found himself in company. At Llanfyllin he secured

[43]

a couple of converts, of "butcher-like appearance" who, after listening to him for a while, gave the toast, " 'God save the King! And may he be the last.' Southey! Such men may be of use. They would kill the golden calf *secundum artem*." [59]

From Llanfyllin, they passed through Llangynog to Bala where they arrived on July 10; at which place the vision of pantisocracy was dangled temptingly before the frequenters of the local inn: clergyman, exciseman, attorney, apothecary, barber—to the no small agitation of the tory section of Coleridge's audience—an agitation redoubled when the loquacious visitor replied to a toast to church and state with a toast to General Washington.[60] Here, too, Coleridge wrote *On Bala Hill* before leaving for Druid House and Llangollen, meeting two Jesus men, Brookes and Berdmore, on the way. Wrexham was reached on July 14.

At Wrexham, pantisocracy and aspheterism were temporarily eclipsed by a distressing incident. Coleridge had forgotten that this town was the dwelling-place of a grandmother of the Evans girls. With her was living Eliza, the youngest daughter; and in Wrexham church Coleridge both saw and was seen by her. Shortly afterwards, looking from the window of the inn to which he had hastily retired, Coleridge was amazed to see on the pavement outside, not only Eliza but her sister Mary. The girls recognized him before he withdrew in confusion, leaving Hucks to report events. They passed and repassed the window in wonder at the vision of a distraught Coleridge in this place and at his refusal to acknowledge them, but he did not appear again.

In his letter of the next day to Southey (almost identical with one written a week later to Henry Martin [61]) Coleridge explained his position. A pantisocrat, a romantic, and a leader of men, could scarcely be expected to say outright that he felt shame or jealousy; so he put it another way:

> "My fortitude would not have supported me, had I *recognized* her—I mean *appeared* to do it! I neither ate not slept yesterday. But love is a local anguish; I am sixteen miles distant, and am not half so miserable. I must endeavour to forget it amid the terrible graces of the wild wood scenery that surround me. I never durst even in a whisper avow my passion, though I knew she loved me. Where were my fortunes? And why should I make her miserable! Almighty God bless her! Her image is in the sanctuary of my heart, and never can it be torn away but with the strings that

grapple it to life. Southey! there are few men of whose delicacy I think so highly as to have written all this. I am glad I have so deemed of you. We are soothed by communications." [62]

At Wrexham, also, Coleridge found cause for alarm in a letter from Southey. His friend, who was very much a creature of moods in those days, and whose pantisocratic fervour tended to subside when apart from Coleridge, was feeling pessimistic about his chances of earning a living. Apparently he had not even dismissed finally from his mind the idea of entering the Church.[63]

Coleridge, fearing that Southey would go the way that Allen, a backslider from the new faith (concerning whom "I say little, but I feel anguish"),[64] appeared to be heading, writes hastily to drive these thoughts out of mind. "For God's sake, Southey! enter not into the church." He bolstered up the spirit of the would-be renegade, assuring him that the creative power of his genius would supply "whatever the stern simplicity of republican wants could require." Alternatively, he suggests a plain but honest clerkship in a counting-house. "A month's application would qualify you for it." Finally, pointing the moral:

"This earnestness of remonstrance! I will not offend you by asking your pardon for it. The following is a *fact*. A friend of Hucks' after long struggles between principle and *interest*, as it is improperly called, accepted a place under government. He took the oaths, shuddered, went home and threw himself in an agony out of a two-pair of stairs window!" [65]

He probably began the first draft of *Lewti* at Wrexham. The poem suggests that Mary had recently been seen and displays the influence of the country through which Coleridge had just walked.[66] *Lewti* shows that Coleridge was beginning to come into his own as a poet. It has colour, something of a dream world in it, and in its rhythm a hint of a new and magic beauty. A certain interest lies in the vicissitudes of its heroine, who was named successively, Mary, Cora, and the non-committal Lewti.

A few hours after seeing the Evans sisters, Coleridge and Hucks had shaken the dust of the town from their feet and were on their way to Ruthin.

The tour then progressed normally. From Ruthin they went to Denbigh, St. Asaph, Holywell, Rhuddlan and Abergele, where Coleridge, observing men, boys and women bathing together naked, comments on the fact that concealment of sex "canthara-dizes" the desires.[67] At Abergele he lost his walking stick which was 'cried' successfully through the town. A little later, at Con-way, they again met Brookes and Berdmore and the four joined forces. From Aber, on July 16, they climbed Penmaenmawr—an excursion which was to produce a memorable phrase in *The Ancient Mariner*. The heat was overpowering and by the time they arrived at the summit, their throats were so constricted that speech was impossible. They discovered a small puddle under a stone, from which they immediately drank. Afterwards, Berd-more, looking at Coleridge, said "You grinned like an idiot!" [68] And from Aber they crossed by ferry to Beaumaris, but Anglesey —Amlwch, Parys Copper Mines, Gwyndu and Moel-y-Don, where their hostess threatened to put the four of them in a single bed—was not a success. Returning to the mainland, they visited Snow-don from Caernarvon on July 20.

The party then made their way south by way of Tan-y-Bwlch, Harlech, Barmouth, Dolgelly and Aberdovey, reaching Aberyst-wyth on July 29. At Llandovery, two days later, Hucks hurried on, leaving the three to pursue a more leisurely course, by Brecon, Aber-gavenny, Tintern, Chepstow and the Old Passage over the river.

Coleridge arrived at Bristol early in August and was intro-duced by Southey to the chosen company of pantisocrats. The backbone of the society consisted of the Fricker family and its connexions, and their house was its headquarters. Mrs Fricker was a widow with five daughters—Sarah,[69] Mary, Edith, Martha and Eliza, and a young son, George. Mary was married to Robert Lovell,[70] a young Quaker, an indifferent poet but an enthusiastic pantisocrat; Edith was engaged to be married to Southey; the other three were unattached. In addition to these, Coleridge made the acquaintance of Heath, the apothecary, and quickly won over Shadrach Weeks, the manservant of Miss Tyler, the aunt with whom Southey had spent much of his boyhood, and upon whose favour he was mainly dependent.

Coleridge was received into the Fricker circle with open arms. Immense enthusiasm reigned throughout the house. Coleridge, Southey and Lovell ranged the town proclaiming the good news. "We preached Pantisocracy and Aspheterism everywhere," wrote Southey to his midshipman brother. "These, Tom, are two

[46]

new words . . . words well understood in the city of Bristol . . . In March we depart for America, Lovell, his wife, brother and two of his sisters; all the Frickers; my mother, Miss Peggy, and brothers; Heath, apothecary, etc.; G. Burnett, S. T. Coleridge, Robert Allen, and Robert Southey. . . . we shall be on the bank of a navigable river, and appoint you admiral of a cock-boat." [71]

In the middle of the month, Coleridge and Southey set out to the Burnett's Somerset farm at Huntspill to report the progress of pantisocracy. Burnett or Henry Poole, a college acquaintance of Coleridge living nearby, introduced the two evangelists to a likely convert, Thomas Poole of Nether Stowey, a village at the foot of the Quantock Hills, a few miles from Bridgwater.

Thomas Poole was at this time twenty-nine years of age.[72] He was a proud, persistent, tender-hearted man, prosaic and blunt in speech, undistinguished in appearance, yet possessed of a rough dignity, a sincerity and a fundamental goodness of heart that won him respect. Rather surprisingly, he professed democratic opinions of an advanced type, and had already antagonized a neighbourhood typical of the extreme conservatism then obtaining in country districts. He was almost entirely a self-educated man who, denied the opportunity of a university education, had, in the intervals afforded by his business, taught himself French and Latin, and made himself acquainted slowly with the Classics, English literature and social and political economy. He had also started the Stowey Book Society the previous year. To one of Thomas Poole's generous nature, who had struggled to achieve some measure of culture, those who had taken learning in their stride were regarded almost with veneration; and when he met Coleridge and Southey, two young university men of promise, professed poets who were also advanced democrats, his heart went out to them without hesitation.

But his words best describe both himself and his visitors:

"Coldridge, whom I consider the Principal in the undertaking [pantisocracy], and of whom I had heard much [from Henry Poole or Burnett] before I saw him, is about five and twenty, belongs to the University of Cambridge, possesses splendid abilities —he is, I understand, a shining scholar, gained the prize for the Greek verses the first or second year he entered the University, and is now engaged in publishing a selection of the best modern Latin poems with a poetical translation. He speaks with much elegance

[47]

and energy, and with uncommon facility, but he, as it generally happens to men of his class, feels the justice of Providence in the want of those inferiour abilities which are necessary to the rational discharge of the common duties of life. His aberrations from prudence, to use his own expression, have been great; but he now promises to be as sober and rational as his most sober friends could wish. In religion he is a Unitarian, if not a Deist; in politicks a Democrat, to the utmost extent of the word.

"Southey, who was with him, is of the University of Oxford, a younger man, without the splendid abilities of Coldridge, though possessing much information, particularly metaphysical, and is more violent in his principles than even Coldridge himself. In Religion, shocking to say in a mere Boy as he is, I fear he wavers between Deism and Atheism." [73]

Coleridge (misspelt by Poole perhaps because the disyllabic pronunciation of the name was common)[74] and Southey explained pantisocracy to their new friend. It is a measure of Poole's earnestness that from their explanation he was able at a later date to describe the scheme with greater accuracy and detail than is to be found in any other existing account of it.

The three, together with Henry Poole and Poole's brother Richard, then repaired to Marsh Mills, Poole's second home, where his cousins, the John Poole's, lived. Poole's cousin John was there. The opportunity was too good to miss. To the scandalized amazement of John Poole (and doubtless to Thomas Poole's embarrassment) Coleridge and Southey—the latter in particular—revealed themselves, rather ostentatiously and with considerable exaggeration, as rabid supporters of the French terrorists.[75] Robespierre had been guillotined on the 28th of the preceding month and the two young republicans seized the occasion to extol his virtues and bewail his untimely end in a most extravagant fashion (Southey, it is said, went so far as to lay his head on his arms and exclaim "I had rather have heard of the death of my own father") [76] and in terms which certainly did not represent their own opinions.

Having charmed, if slightly shocked, Poole, who was henceforth to be regarded by his townsmen with even greater suspicion, and having effectively destroyed their own reputation in Stowey eyes, Coleridge and Southey departed well pleased. Poole was not to be persuaded to emigrate. Though he was apparently prepared

THOMAS POOLE

"A man whom I have seen now in his harvest-field, or the market; now in a committee-room with the Rickmans and Ricardos of the age; at another time with Davy, Woolaston, and the Wedgwoods; now with Wordsworth, Southey, and other friends not unheard of in the republic of letters; now in the drawing-rooms of the rich and the noble; and now presiding at the annual dinner of a Village Benefit Society; and in each seeming to be in the very place he was intended for, and taking the part to which his tastes, talents, and attainments gave him an admitted right. And yet this is not the most remarkable, nor the most individualising trait of our friend's character. It is almost overlooked in the originality and raciness of his intellect; in the life, freshness, and practical value of his remarks and notices, truths plucked as they are growing, and delivered to you with the dew on them, the fair earnings of an observing eye, armed and kept on the watch by thought and meditation; and above all in the integrity, i.e. *entireness* of his being (*integrum et sine cerâ vas*), the steadiness of his attachments, the activity and persistence of a benevolence, which so graciously presses a warm temper into the service of a yet warmer heart."   COLERIDGE

"I used to see much of him and had frequent occasions to admire the course of his daily life, especially his conduct to his labourers and poor neighbours: their virtues he carefully encouraged, and weighed their faults in the scales of charity. . . . I need scarcely add that he felt for all men as his brothers. He was much beloved by distinguished persons—Mr Coleridge, Mr Southey, Sir H. Davy, and many others; and in his own neighbourhood was highly valued as a magistrate, a man of business, and in every other social relation."
                                                    WILLIAM WORDSWORTH

"I found him a stout, plain-looking farmer, leading a bachelor life, in a rustic, old-fashioned house, the house, however, upon further acquaintance, proving to be amply furnished with modern luxuries, and especially with a good library, superbly mounted in all departments bearing at all upon political philosophy; and the farmer turning out a polished and liberal Englishman, who had travelled extensively, and had so entirely dedicated himself to the service of his humble fellow-countrymen . . . that for many miles round he was the general arbiter of their disputes, the guide and counsellor of their difficulties; besides being appointed executor and guardian to his children by every third man who died in or about the town of Nether Stowey."   THOMAS DE QUINCEY

(By permission of Mr Gilbert S. Poole)

to be a pantisocrat in feeling, his business (he was a partner in his father's tanning-yard) and the claims of his mother, prevented his leaving Stowey. But they had his sympathy and support in full measure, and, in the case of Coleridge at least, his very friendly and practical interest.

The visit took place on August 18. For another fortnight, pantisocratic fervour continued in Bristol. Literature was not entirely forgotten, though it cannot be said that it was treated very seriously. The three—Coleridge, Southey and Lovell—decided to write a play upon Robespierre. The first act of this play, *The Fall of Robespierre*, was to be written by Coleridge, the second by Southey, the third by Lovell. All were to be completed by the following evening. In fact, Lovell's act had to be re-written by Southey and Coleridge did not complete his until later. The play was eventually assembled, however, in a somewhat patchy state, a dedication to Hannah More was written and the whole offered to a Bristol bookseller. It was not accepted.[77]

A more important relaxation was being enacted at the Fricker home. Southey had his pantisocratic helpmeet; Lovell had his; Coleridge alone faced the prospect of the Susquehannah solitary and unpaired. The very nature of the scheme demanded that every male should have his opposite—how else could the pantisocrats multiply?

Coleridge was not one to throw obstacles before a child of his own brain—especially when the remedy was so simple, so close at hand and, it appeared, so pleasant.

Everything pointed to a Miss Fricker. As a good pantisocrat, Coleridge must have his partner. The sight of Mary Evans at Wrexham so recently had thrown him into an emotional flurry from which, illogically perhaps but not surprisingly, he emerged eager for feminine sympathy. He was daily, hourly, in the company of three eligible young ladies, all ardent in the cause. And of all the sisters, Sarah, the eldest, was also the prettiest.

What could be clearer? The thought was no sooner in mind than it had become a fact. Engagements and marriages savoured too much of the world he was leaving to commend themselves to a pantisocrat. His scruples were humoured; it was simply understood among the company that Sarah would accompany Coleridge when all set out for America.

D

Early in September Coleridge left for London on his way to Cambridge, taking with him *The Fall of Robespierre*. His precious *Casimir*,[78] after surviving sale and repurchase at Reading in the brief army days, now disappeared for good. Coleridge lost it on the road—a setback to the much proposed *Imitations from the Modern Latin Poets*. Not that the scheme had been abandoned. Postponed, yes, but only for a while. Coleridge was as optimistic as ever about the money it was to bring him. That, and his share of the proceeds from the Robespierre play, were to form his contribution towards the establishment of the pantisocratic state.

In London, he lodged at the Angel Inn, in Butcher Hall Street and close to Christ's Hospital. Most of his days he spent with the Grecians; his evenings were passed at the Salutation and Cat [79] in Newgate Street, where, with Charles Lamb for company and porter and punch for cheer, he was able to talk unstintedly, before a good fire, of poetry, politics, metaphysics, the school, pantisocracy, to a lively and appreciative listener.

His first action was to complete the long-standing first act of *The Fall of Robespierre*. That done, he was introduced by Franklin, an ex-Grecian who was with him at Cambridge, to George Dyer,[80] author of *Complaints of the Poor People of England*, but known now only by reason of his association with Lamb and his appearance in the Elian essays. Dyer, whose critical ability was not his greatest gift, liked "hugely" the fragment of the first act that Coleridge showed him. He straightway offered to speak to the booksellers about it. The booksellers were wiser than he, however, and the play was unable to find a London publisher.

Coleridge occupied himself by aspheterizing briskly. He started upon Dyer, and soon had that guileless man "enraptured" [81] and foretelling the accession to the emigrants of Joseph Priestley,[82] scientist and theologian, whose advanced views had made him the hero of Coleridge, and who was at that time already in America.

Coleridge's success with the Christ's Hospital boys was just as impressive. In particular, the younger Le Grice, who was about to go up to Cambridge, and Samuel Favell, destined for the same place the following year, begged to be allowed to follow the pantisocrats as soon as their education was finished. Favell was driven to express his enthusiasm with a sonnet in which:

With silent sweet survey of tearful Joy
I gaze the Vale, where bloom in fadeless Youth
Love, Beauty, Friendship, Poesy, and Truth.
My Brethren! O my Brethren! then I cry.
And you, Ye mild-eyed Forms! a Brother's Kiss
Give me! [83]

Coleridge also explained the scheme to Grosvenor Bedford, Southey's Westminster friend; and he wrote to Charles Heath of Monmouth, brother of the Bristol pharmacist, a description of pantisocracy—the only description of his at this time that exists:

"A small but liberalized party have formed a scheme of emigration on the principles of an abolition of individual property. Of their political creed, and the arguments by which they support and elucidate it they are preparing a few copies—not as meaning to publish them, but for private distribution. In this work they will have endeavoured to prove the exclusive justice of the system and its practicability; nor will they have omitted to sketch out the code of contracts necessary for the internal regulation of the Society; all of which will of course be submitted to the improvements and approbation of each component member. As soon as the work is printed, one or more copies shall be transmitted to you. Of the characters of the individuals who compose the party I find it embarrassing to speak; yet, vanity apart, I may assert with truth that they have each a sufficient strength of head to make the virtues of the heart respectable, and that they are all highly charged with that enthusiasm which results from strong perceptions of moral rectitude, called into life and action by ardent feelings. With regard to pecuniary matters it is found necessary, if twelve men with their families emigrate on this system, that £2,000 should be the aggregate of their contributions—but infer not from hence that each man's *quota* is to be settled with the littleness of arithmetical accuracy. No; all will strain every nerve; and then, I trust, the surplus money of some will supply the deficiencies of others. The *minutiae* of topographical information we are daily endeavouring to acquire; at present our plan is, to settle at a distance, but at a convenient distance, from Cooper's Town on the banks of the Susquehanna. This, however, will be the object of future investigation. For the time of emigration we have fixed on next March. In the course of the winter those of us whose bodies, from habits of sedentary study or academic indolence, have not acquired their full tone and strength, intend to learn the theory and practice of agriculture and carpentry, according as situation and circumstances make one or the other convenient." [84]

He signed his letter "fellow Citizen." At the Salutation and Cat for a brief, intoxicating spell, he was receiving instead of giving information. He had read Thomas Cooper's *Some Information Respecting America*.[85] By a singular stroke of fortune he struck upon the very fountain-head of knowledge. A young man, once of Christ's Hospital and recently back from America to sell land, dropped into the habit of haunting the room where Coleridge spent his evenings—as he said, to "benefit by conversation." [86] His advice to the pantisocrat was eagerly passed on to Southey:

> "He says two thousand pounds will do—that he doubts not we can contract for our Passage under £400—that we shall buy this Land a great deal cheaper when we arrive at America, than we could do in England—or why (adds he) am I sent over here? That twelve men can *easily* clear *three hundred* Acres in 4 or 5 months—and that for six hundred Dollars a thousand Acres may be cleared, and houses built upon them. He recommends the Susquehannah from its excessive Beauty, and its security from hostile Indians—Every possible assistance will be given us. We may get credit for the Land for ten years or more as we settle upon it—That literary characters make *money* there, that etc., etc. He never saw a Byson in his life, but has heard of them. They are quite backwards. The Mosquitoes are not so bad as our Gnats—and after you have been there a little while, they don't trouble you much. He says the Women's *teeth* are bad there—but not the men's—at least not nearly so much—attributes it to neglect—to particular foods—is by no means convinced it is the necessary effect of Climate." [87]

At last Coleridge tore himself away from London and journeyed up to Cambridge. He arrived there in the middle of September. As soon as he arrived he wrote to Southey in the highest spirits:

> "Well, my dear Southey! I am at last arrived at Jesus. My God! how tumultuous are the movements of my heart. Since I quitted this room what and how important events have been evolved! America! Southey! Miss Fricker! Yes, Southey, you are right. Even Love is the creature of strong motive. I certainly love her. I *think* of her incessantly and with unspeakable tenderness—with that inward melting away of soul that symptomatizes it.
>
> "Pantisocracy! Oh, I shall have such a scheme of it! My

head, my heart, are all alive. I have drawn up my arguments in battle array; they shall have the *tactician* excellence of the mathematician with the enthusiasm of the poet. The head shall be the mass; the heart the fiery spirit that fills, informs, and agitates the whole. Harwood—pish! I say nothing of him.

"SHAD GOES WITH US. HE IS MY BROTHER! I am longing to be with you. Make Edith my sister. Surely, Southey, we shall be *frendotatoi meta frendous*—most friendly where all are friends. She must, therefore, be more emphatically my sister.

"Brookes and Berdmore, as I suspected, have spread my opinions in mangled forms at Cambridge. Caldwell,[88] the most pantisocratic of aristocrats, has been laughing at me. Up I arose, terrible in reasoning. He fled from me, because 'he could not answer for his own sanity, sitting so near a madman of genius.' He told me that the strength of my imagination had intoxicated my reason, and that the acuteness of my reason had given a directing influence to my imagination. Four months ago the remark would not have been more eloquent than just. Now it is nothing." [89]

He also wrote for the first time to Sarah Fricker; but not quickly enough to escape Southey's remonstrance, which arrived the very next day. Coleridge took up his pen again, in sorrow:

"On Wednesday, September 17, I arrived at Cambridge. Perhaps the very hour you were writing in the severity of offended friendship, was I pouring forth the heart to Sarah Fricker. I did not call on Caldwell: I saw no one. On the moment of my arrival I shut my door, and wrote to her. But why not before?

"In the first place Miss F. did not authorize me to direct immediately to her. It was *settled* that through *you* in our weekly *parcels* were the letters to be conveyed. The moment I arrived at Cambridge, and all yesterday, was I writing letters to you, to your mother, to Lovell, etc., to complete a parcel.

"In London I wrote twice to you, intending daily to go to Cambridge; of course I deferred the parcel till then. I was taken ill, very ill. I exhausted my finances, and ill as I was, I sat down and scrawled a few guineas' worth of nonsense for the booksellers, which Dyer disposed of for me. Languid, sick at heart, in the back room of an inn! Lofty conjunction of circumstances for me to write to Miss F. Besides, I told her I should write the moment I arrived at Cambridge. I have fulfilled the promise." [90]

A little later, Coleridge, realizing that his case was imperfect and that in any event attack is the best means of defence, carried the argument on to a higher and more generalized plane:

"Southey! Precipitance is wrong. There may be too high a state of health, perhaps even *virtue* is liable to a *plethora*. I have been the slave of impulse, the child of imbecility. But my inconsistencies have given me a tarditude and reluctance to think ill of any one. Having been often suspected of wrong when I was altogether right, from *fellow-feeling* I judge not too hastily, and from appearances. Your undeviating simplicity of rectitude has made you rapid in decision. Having never erred, you feel more *indignation* at error than *pity* for it. There is *phlogiston* in your heart." [91]

But Southey had not yet done with the matter. Despairing of moving the silent pantisocrat, he had written to Favell at Christ's Hospital complaining of Coleridge's inexplicable tardiness and failure to observe the ordinary forms of an engagement. Favell sent the letter on to Cambridge and Coleridge once more plunged into explanations—this time, not without some irritation.[92]

There followed a few weeks of peace. Coleridge was busy planning "a quarto volume in defence of Pantisocrasy." [93] At last *The Fall of Robespierre* [94] found a home. Benjamin Flower [95] of Cambridge was persuaded to print it. Coleridge's name alone appeared on the title-page; the reason being, as he told Southey, that the sales in Cambridge would be greater because he alone was known there.[96]

A more enthralling period set in when the Bruntons of Norwich [97] brought their theatrical company to play in the Ipswich Fair time. Coleridge and Caldwell quickly became intimate with the family and, in particular, with one of the daughters. Coleridge wrote a poem—*To a Young Lady*, which he sent her together with a copy of *Robespierre*—and seems to have derived considerable comfort from her society.

He began also about this time to criticize his friends' work; and for a while Southey, whose poems naturally received the most attention, submitted with a good grace to the corrections and advice which arrived in generous measure from Cambridge.[98]

At the beginning of October, Coleridge's pantisocratic resolution was shaken to its very foundations. A letter came from Mary Evans—unexpected, disturbing, heartening:

"Is this handwriting altogether erased from your memory? To whom am I addressing myself? For whom am I now violating the rules of female delicacy? Is it for the same Coleridge, whom I once regarded as a sister her best-beloved Brother? Or for one who will *ridicule* that advice from me, which he has *rejected* as offered by his family? I will hazard the attempt. I have no right, nor do I feel myself inclined to reproach you for the Past. God forbid! You have already suffered too much from self-accusation. But I conjure you, Coleridge, earnestly and solemnly conjure you to consider long and deeply, before you enter into any rash schemes. There is an Eagerness in your Nature which is ever hurrying you in the sad Extreme. I have heard that you mean to leave England, and on a Plan so absurd and extravagant that were I for a moment to imagine it *true*, I should be obliged to listen with a more patient Ear to suggestions, which I have rejected a thousand times with scorn and anger. Yes! whatever Pain I might suffer, I should be forced to exclaim, 'O what a noble mind is here o'erthrown, Blasted with ecstacy.' You have a country, does it demand nothing of you? You have doting Friends! Will you break their Hearts? There is a God—Coleridge! Though I have been told (*indeed* I do not believe it) that you doubt of his existence and disbelieve a hereafter. No! You have too much sensibility to be an Infidel. You know I never was rigid in my opinions concerning Religion—and have always thought *Faith* to be only Reason applied to a particular subject. In short, I am the same Being as when you used to say, 'We thought in all things alike.' I often reflect on the happy hours we spent together and regret the Loss of your Society. I cannot easily forget those whom I once loved nor can I easily form new Friendships. I find women in general vain—all of the same Trifle, and therefore little and envious, and (I am afraid) without sincerity; and of the other sex those who are offered and held up to my esteem are very prudent, and very worldly. If you value my peace of mind, you must *on no account* answer this letter, or take the least notice of it. I *would* not for the world *any part* of my Family should suspect that I have written to you. My mind is sadly tempered by being perpetually obliged to resist the solicitations of those whom I love. I need not explain myself. Farewell, Coleridge! I shall always feel that I have been your *Sister*." 99

For three weeks Coleridge kept silence. He was obliged to face the fact that there was an alternative to Sarah and even to pantisocracy. So far as Sarah was concerned, his sonnet, written at this time, *To my Heart* 100—a title changed significantly later to *On a Discovery made too late*—resolves any doubt there may have been about the direction to which his affections inclined. But Sarah was not the only obstacle; she was not even the most important stumbling-block. If he were to have any hope of Mary, pantisocracy would have to be given up.

He was shocked into the realization that his love for Mary Evans was neither a youthful indiscretion, as in the first flush of pantisocratic enthusiasm he had attempted to persuade himself, nor was it necessarily without hope of being returned. Yet its fulfilment—or even the hope of it—was now doubly barred by pantisocracy and by his pantisocratic partner.

With an heroic gesture of renunciation, he made his choice:

"My head throbs so violently and my Spirits are so low, that I shall just add a Sonnet and conclude," he wrote to Francis Wrangham,[101] "It was occasioned by a letter, which I lately received from a young Lady, whom for five years I loved—almost to madness, dissuasive from my American Scheme—but where Justice leads, I will follow—though the Path be through thorns and roughness—The Scotts desire their Compliments. *Compliments!* Cold aristocratic Inanities! I abjure their Nothingness." [102]

He enclosed the sonnet. Southey was also sent a copy of the sonnet. And to Southey was sent a copy of the letter from Mary Evans with instructions to show it to no one.

"I loved her, Southey, almost to madness," he wrote. "Her image was never absent from me for three years, for *more* than three years. My resolution has not faltered, but I want a comforter." [103]

Then followed an ominous reference to his chosen pantisocratic partner:

"I have done nothing, I have gone into company, I was constantly at the theatre here till they left us, I endeavoured to be perpetually with Miss Brunton, I even hoped that her exquisite beauty and uncommon accomplishments might have cured one passion by another. The latter I could easily have dissipated in her absence, and so have restored my affections to her whom I do not love, but whom by every tie of reason and honour I ought to love. I am resolved, but wretched! But time shall do much. You will easily believe that with such feelings, I should have found it no easy task to write to [Miss Fricker]. I should have detested myself, if after my first letter I had written coldly—how could I write *as warmly*?" [104]

This plain speaking by no means commended itself to Southey who, never truly at ease outside the proprieties, viewed this backsliding as yet another instance of Coleridge's extraordinary reluctance to correspond with Sarah Fricker.

Coleridge was driven to bolster up his resolution with pantisocratic dreams. Southey, however, would not afford him even this gratification. He was emerging fairly rapidly from the Coleridge spell. From Bristol and from Bath, where Southey's mother kept a lodging-house, letters arrived severely practical—in Coleridge's view, heretical.

Pantisocracy was undergoing a careful re-examination in the Southey circle; it was being improved; was being rendered more reasonable; related more closely to existing social conditions. As letters from Southey arrived, the unwilling Coleridge found himself confronted by a string of suggestions—all of them doubly unwelcome; for they not only clashed with his pantisocratic principles but tended to reduce his original heroic conception of the adventure—one on a scale worthy the sacrifice even of love itself—to something homespun, ordinary, devoid of romance.

Coleridge struggled manfully against this de-romanticizing tendency. A great part of the trouble arose over Shadrach. Southey had had second thoughts about Shadrach. Why should not he remain their faithful servant, doing a servant's duties, on the bank of the Susquehannah, as he was doing at present in the house on College Green? [105] Coleridge wrote back, grieved at the very thought:

> " 'Let them dine with us and be treated with as much equality as they would wish, but perform that part of labour for which their education has fitted them.' *Southey* should not have written this sentence. My friend, my noble and high-souled friend should have said to his dependents, 'Be my slaves, and ye shall be my equals'; to his wife and sister, 'Resign the *name* of Ladyship and ye shall retain the *thing*.' Again. Is every family to possess one of these unequal equals, these Helot Egalitiés? Or are the few you have mentioned, 'with more toil than the peasantry of England undergo,' to do for all of us 'that part of labour which their education has fitted them for'? If your remarks on the other side are just, the inference is that the scheme of pantisocracy is impracticable, but I hope and believe that it is not a *necessary* inference." [106]

Southey, however, was in no way disconcerted and pressed his point. A triumphant Coleridge found his letter waiting for him:

"I was challenged on the subject of pantisocracy, which is, indeed, the universal topic at the University. A discussion began and continued for six hours. In conclusion, Lushington and Edwards declared the system impregnable, supposing the assigned quantum of virtue and genius in the first individuals. I came home at one o'clock this morning in the honest consciousness of having exhibited closer argument in more elegant and appropriate language than I had ever conceived myself capable of. Then my heart smote me, for I saw your letter on the propriety of taking servants with us. I had answered that letter, and feel conviction that you will *perceive* the error into which the tenderness of your nature had led you." [107]

But neither argument nor appeal moved his friend. He was adamant. He persisted. Coleridge, with many words, began to withdraw:

"My feeble and exhausted heart regards with a criminal indifference the introduction of servitude into our society; but my judgment is not asleep, nor can I suffer your reason, Southey, to be entangled in the web which your feelings have woven. Oxen and horses possess not intellectual appetites, nor the powers of acquiring them. We are therefore justified in employing their labour to our own benefit; mind hath a divine right of sovereignty over body. But who shall dare to transfer 'from man to brute' to 'from man to man'? To be employed in the toil of the field, while *we* are pursuing philosophical studies—can earldoms or emperorships boast so huge an inequality? Is there a human being of so torpid a nature as that placed in our society he would not feel it? A *willing* slave is the worst of slaves! His *soul* is a slave. Besides, I must own myself incapable of perceiving even the temporary *convenience* of the proposed innovation. The *men* do not want assistance, at least none that *Shad* can particularly give; and to the women, what assistance can little Sally, the *wife* of Shad, give more than any other of our married women? Is she to have no domestic cares of her own? No house? No husband to provide for? No children? *Because* Mr and Mrs Roberts are not likely to have children, I see less objection to their accompanying us. Indeed, indeed, Southey, I am fearful that Lushington's prophecy may not be altogether vain. 'Your system, Coleridge, appears strong to the head and lovely to the heart; but depend upon it, you will never give your *women* sufficient strength of mind, liberality of heart, or vigilance of attention. *They* will spoil it.' " [108]

Indeed, Coleridge was himself weakening under the strain.

He became increasingly concerned about the ability of the women to partake successfully in the scheme. His attitude towards the two mothers in particular grew steadily more unfilial:

"If Mrs S. and Mrs F. go with us, they can at least prepare the food of simplicity for us. Let the married women do only what is absolutely convenient and customary for pregnant women or nurses. Let the husband do all the rest, and what will that all be? Washing with a machine and cleaning the house. One hour's addition to our daily labor, and *pantisocracy* in its most perfect sense is practicable. That the greater part of our female companions should have the task of maternal exertion at the same time is very *improbable*; but, though it were to happen, an infant is almost always sleeping, and during its slumbers the mother may in the same room perform the little offices of ironing clothes or making shirts. But the hearts of the women are not *all* with us. I do believe that Edith and Sarah are exceptions, but do even they know the bill of fare for the day, every duty that will be incumbent upon them?" [109]

A little later he enlarges upon his doubts:

"The more perfect our system is, supposing the necessary premises, the more eager in anxiety am I that the necessary premises exist. O for that Lyncean eye that can discover in the acorn of Error the rooted and widely spreading oak of Misery! Quaere: should not all who mean to become members of our community be incessantly meliorating their temper and elevating their understandings? Qu.: whether a very respectable quantity of *acquired* knowledge (History, Politics, above all, *Metaphysics*, without which no man *can* reason but with women and children) be not a prerequisite to the improvement of the head and heart? Qu.: whether our Women have not been taught by us habitually to contemplate the littleness of individual comforts and a passion for the *novelty* of the scheme rather than a generous enthusiasm of Benevolence? Are they saturated with the Divinity of Truth sufficiently to be always wakeful? In the present state of their minds, whether it is not probable that the *Mothers* will tinge the minds of the infants with prejudication? The questions are meant merely as motives to you, Southey, to the strengthening the minds of the Women, and stimulating them to literary acquirements. But, Southey, there are *Children* going with us. Why did I never dare in my disputations with the unconvinced to hint at this circumstance? Was it not because I knew, even to certainty of conviction, that it is subversive of *rational* hopes of a permanent system? These children—the little Frickers, for instance, and your brothers—are they not already deeply tinged with the prejudices and errors of society? Have they not learned from their schoolfellows *Fear* and *Selfishness*, of which the necessary offsprings are Deceit and desultory Hatred? How are we to prevent them from infecting the minds of *our* children? By reforming their judgments? At so early an age, *can* they have *felt* the ill consequences of their errors in a manner sufficiently vivid to make this reformation practicable? How can we ensure their silence concerning God, etc.? Is it possible *they* should enter into our *motives* for this silence? If not, we must produce their *Obedience* by *Terror. Obedience? Terror?* The repetition is sufficient. I need not inform you that they are as inadequate as inapplicable. I have told you, Southey, that I will accompany you on an *imperfect* system. But must our system be thus necessarily imperfect?" [110]

In his effort to maintain the scheme at its original high-pitched level, Coleridge had begun to do some mental weeding out of the proposed company. Southey, however, was impervious to hints; and his friend was obliged to say exactly what was in his mind:

"I wish, Southey, in the stern severity of judgment, that the two mothers were *not* to go, and that the children stayed with them. Are you wounded by my want of feeling? No! how highly must I think of your rectitude of soul, that I should dare to say this to so affectionate a son! *That* Mrs Fricker! We shall have her teaching the infants *Christianity*—I mean, that mongrel whelp that goes under its name,—teaching them by stealth in some ague fit of superstition." [111]

These differences on the theory of pantisocracy and the personnel of the society left Coleridge exposed the more cruelly to the attacks of his affection for Mary. As his pantisocratic fervour faltered, so did his longing for Mary Evans increase. Despite his knowledge of Southey's disapproval, his misery was at times so great, his need for support, even if it were no more than that of one who read his letters, was so overwhelming that he could not always resist the temptation to write of her:

"She *was very* lovely, Southey! We formed each other's minds; our ideas were blended. Heaven bless her! I cannot forget her. Every day her memory sinks deeper into my heart." [112]

At this time, too, Smerdon, the vicar at Ottery, died of a fever. Coleridge wrote an elegy upon him in the course of which he relapsed into the introspectiveness which the subject awoke and which was never very far from his mind. These lines show plainly that Coleridge was as well able to diagnose his character as he was his bodily complaints and weaknesses:

> To me hath Heaven with liberal hand assign'd
> Energic reason and a shaping mind,
> The daring soul of Truth, the patriot's part,
> And Pity's sigh, that breathes the gentle heart—
> Sloth-jaundiced all! and from my graspless hand
> Drop Friendship's precious pearls, like hour-glass sand.[113]

His brothers provided another, even if familiar, source of discomfort. They had heard of Coleridge's political views, which were by this time most difficult to conceal; George, at least, had read *The Fall of Robespierre*; and although he was able to assure Southey that "There is little danger of my being confined," [114] Coleridge was not a little harried.

> "*Advice* offered with *respect* from a brother; *affected coldness*, an assumed *alienation* mixed with involuntary bursts of *anguish* and disappointed *affection*; questions concerning the mode in which I would have it mentioned to my aged mother—these are the daggers which are plunged into *my* peace." [115]

In a letter which is a mixture of sophistry and self-abasement, he endeavoured once again to reassure the persevering George that he was following the appointed path at Cambridge.[116] But although he succeeded in convincing George that he was not out of his mind, this was the full extent of his success. Awkward questions were asked about his future. The Church was definitely dropped as an aim. Coleridge found himself unwillingly contemplating a life in the service of the Law.[117]

From every direction discouragement and disillusionment raised gloomy heads. Coleridge's need for moral support became imperative. Southey was not the man to meet waverings with anything but righteous admonitions. He had had his one weakness with Coleridge; in future, he intended to go his own way, to lead. But Coleridge, though meeting with an intractable Southey in correspondence, had still hope of renewing the old, complete accord—and with it the resolution he so badly needed —by a friendly discussion. Something had also to be done about

Sarah Fricker. If he would not write to her, he must either see her or abandon the whole scheme. Southey gave him little rest on the subject. And possibly a faint hope lingered in him that Sarah's charms would in some degree overcome the image of Mary that he now found increasingly difficult to forget.

With this in mind, he seized the opportunity of a lift to London which was offered him early in November. He would see George and straighten matters out. He would see Lamb and the Christ's Hospital boys, whose sympathy was always his. He would try to arrange for the publication of some of his poems. Then he would go down to Bristol and the old harmony would be restored. He announced his intentions before leaving Cambridge. He even told Southey the date of his arrival in Bristol.[118]

For some time, however, he got no further than London. What with heart-warming hobnobs with Lamb and his Christ's Hospital cronies and a considerable activity in placing poems and endeavouring to aspheterize some of the big men in journalism and letters, his mind was sufficiently occupied for him to pursue his ways without aid from Bristol. The *Morning Chronicle* accepted several of his poems—sonnets[119] on *Burke*,[120] *Priestley*,[121] *Kosciusko*,[122] *Godwin*,[123] *Southey*,[124] and *Sheridan*,[125] appeared in December and January, and the better known *Address to a Young Jack-Ass and its Tether'd Mother* was printed in a revised form on December 30. This is the poem in which Coleridge writes:

> Innocent foal! Thou poor, despis'd forlorn!
> I hail thee Brother, spite of the fool's scorn!
> And fain I'd take thee with me in the Dell
> Of high-souled Pantisocracy to dwell;
> Where Toil shall call the charmer Health his bride,
> And Laughter tickle Plenty's *ribless* side![126]

Southey could get no more from his friend than an occasional letter. These letters show plainly that for the moment all was well again. Southey's poetry is criticized with gusto. Coleridge informs his friend that he had dined with Perry and Grey, respectively proprietor and editor of the *Morning Chronicle*; that he had met Holcroft,[127] just released after being tried for high treason; that he is to dine with Porson[128] and Godwin.[129] He was making himself known—as a promising young poet, a brilliant talker, with highly inflamed political opinions. Godwin said later: "The four principal

oral instructors to whom I feel my mind indebted for improvement were Joseph Fawcet, Thomas Holcroft, George Dyson, and
Samuel Taylor Coleridge."[130] With Godwin, Coleridge visited
Joseph Gerrald[131] in Newgate. His meeting with Holcroft was
faithfully reported:

> "I had the honour of working H[olcroft] a little, and by my
> great *coolness* and command of impressive language certainly *did
> him over*. 'Sir!' said he, 'I never knew so much real wisdom and so
> much rank error meet in one mind before!' 'Which ' answered I,
> 'means, I suppose, that in some things, sir, I agree with you, and in
> others I do not.' He absolutely infests you with *atheism*; and his
> arguments are such that the nonentities of Nugent consolidate
> into oak or ironwood by comparison! As to his taste in poetry, he
> thinks lightly, or rather contemptuously, of Bowles' sonnets; the
> language flat and prosaic and inharmonious, and the sentiments
> only fit for girls! Come, come, Mr Holcroft, as much unintelligible
> metaphysics and as much bad criticism as you please, but no
> *blasphemy* against the divinity of *a Bowles!*"[132]

Coleridge's poetical idol is thus seen to be as firmly set on his
throne as he was four years before, although the pupil's work had
shown signs already of excelling that of his master. But Coleridge's admiration showed no signs of waning; and on December
26 yet another sonnet appeared in the *Morning Chronicle*, of which
it is only necessary to repeat the first line:

My heart has thank'd thee, Bowles! for those soft strains.[133]

A more significant remark, made at this time in a letter to
Southey, deals with a subject to which Coleridge had given considerable thought. He says: "I am a complete necessitarian, and
understand the subject as well almost as Hartley[134] himself, but I
go farther than Hartley, and believe the corporeality of *thought*,
namely, that it is motion."[135]

It is necessary when considering the life of Coleridge constantly
to be on the alert against the dominance of outward incident.
Particularly is this true of his early and more active years. His
indolence at school, at Cambridge, and for a great part of his life,
was an indolence essentially of body. He lived a life of intense,
almost unimaginable mental activity. His curiosity was inexhaustible and had no limits; but whereas, with men of lesser minds, such
curiosity leaves no trace in their lives, apart from temporary

interruptions as they skip from one experience to another, Coleridge's mind was both acquisitive and creative. He rarely read or heard anything from which he did not abstract some aspect of thought to be considered, set in its place, and eventually transformed by a brain whose range and capacity was astounding, an imagination which penetrated a realm where the mortal writ no longer ran. Such a view of Coleridge conflicts often with his actions, at this time as at others; and this conflict is, indeed, part of his peculiar charm.

For this reason, the 'enthusiasms' of Coleridge, of which the present period of his life provides so many examples, have to be set in their right perspective in relation to the whole activity of his mind. Unquestionably they absorbed much of his thought and most of his bodily activity; in most men, they would have exhausted all capacity for thought; but with Coleridge there was a substratum of thought at work which, though it appeared rarely in his writing at this time, was to have an incalculable effect upon the development of his later life and thought.

Pantisocracy, in particular, tends to obscure all other events during the later period at Cambridge; but this, though it provides a rich theme for comedy treatment, must be given its due as a genuine expression, however wildly utopian and impracticable, of important strands of thought to which Coleridge's vast reading, his friendships, and the conditions of the day were together contributing. With its collapse, the ideals which had animated it were to take their places, duly modified by experience, in the fabric of Coleridge's mind, to appear later transfigured by association and reflection.

The two divergent lines of thought—that of the head and that of the heart, the intellectual and the mystical—which had begun in his schooldays with Voltaire and Darwin on the one hand, Plato and the Neo-platonists on the other, continued their development with an even greater intensity. At Cambridge, as in later life, he was searching for some means of reconciling these irreconcilables.

The problem at Cambridge had become more difficult because his friendships (with Frend in particular), the condition of the church, and the trend of events in the world, pressed him irresistibly towards a materialistic theory of life; whereas, his

inclination, then as always, was mystical, his nature fundamentally religious.

It is possible to see, therefore, in Coleridge's hero-worship,
attempts to find in one man—or rather, in that man's teachings—
a theory of life which would satisfy both his reason and his
emotions; and his progression from one master to another
occurred only when he had realized, however reluctantly, that his
wish had proved father to the thought, that his mind had outstretched his teacher, and that the desired combination had
eluded him once again.

While Coleridge was at Cambridge, Thomas Taylor continued
publication of his translations of Plato [136] and Plotinus; [137] and
through their influence there was brought about a revival of
interest in a kind of Indian summer of the Cambridge Platonists.
Jacob Boehme and his fellow Christian mystics drew Coleridge's
mind along similar paths.

Nevertheless, the heirs of Voltaire were in the ascendant in his
mind—Locke, Hume, Hartley, Berkeley, with offshoots in the
persons of Priestley and Godwin.[138] Of these, Locke's disciple,
David Hartley, found an eager follower in Coleridge—the more
so because Hartley's teaching appeared to achieve the desired
amalgam of reason and emotion, of head and heart. Moreover,
Hartley was an old Jesus man and his writ ran strongly there and
throughout the university.

Hartley's *Observations on Man: His Frame, His Duty, and
His Expectations* [139] is composed of two books. The first contains
a re-statement of the doctrine of the laws of the influence of
associations over the opinions and affections "and its use in explaining those things in an accurate and precise way which are
commonly referred to the power of habit and custom in a general
and indeterminate one." [140] He claimed, rightly, to have attained
in several particulars an accuracy and precision in his presentment
of these laws which justified his revision of the theories of Locke
and Hume. In the same part, he also developed the "Hints concerning the Performance of Sensation and Motion which *Sir
Isaac Newton* has given at the end of the *Principia* and in the
Questions annexed to his *Optics.*" [141] The second part of his
treatise makes an abrupt change. It is an exposition of natural
and revealed religion, written as obviously from the standpoint of

a believer as the first part is written from that of a materialist.[142]

The temptation for Coleridge to accept each part uncritically, to let each part satisfy the questionings of reason and heart respectively, without a closer co-ordination of the two parts than the comfortable realisation that one man was responsible for both, was too great to be resisted. He no more attempted to verify the premises upon which Hartley based his conclusions than did Hartley himself. Not until a greater and more profound thinker rose above Coleridge's horizon, was he to jettison completely this insecurely balanced philosophy. For the time, however, his attitude was that expressed in a letter to Southey: "I would ardently that you were a necessitarian, and (believing in an all-loving Omnipotence) an optimist." [143]

Letters to Southey for some time took the place of the proposed visit. The day fixed for Coleridge's journey to Bristol passed and he made no move. The authorities at Jesus were becoming restive at his absence,[144] but still he remained irresolute in London. There, so close to the Evans, and unable, even if he wished, to avoid hearing of Mary from her brother and other Christ's Hospital boys, he was less than ever inclined to think of Sarah, let alone visit her. On the other hand, his interest in pantisocracy had been stimulated by his discussions in London. He did not know what to do and so he did nothing.

Eventually, early in December, action of some kind became imperative. He had either to return to Cambridge or seek fresh comfort from Bristol. To go back, feeling as he did, was out of the question. He set out for Bristol.

The result of his visit was the reverse of his hopes. Southey continued in person his epistolary attitude of disapproval—of Coleridge's pantisocratic scruples and still more of the neglect of Sarah. Indeed, he had an even crueller blow in store for his friend—nothing less than the abandonment, at least for a time, of the original pantisocratic scheme of emigration. Instead, he proposed to a shocked Coleridge that there should be a trial attempt, made no further away than Wales and with the men of the party only.

This prudent retreat from the original bold and romantic conception of pantisocracy—and possibly from the only form in which its principles, as apart from its practicability, could be adequately tested—drove the dismayed Coleridge to take up his pen once again. He did not speak to Southey, preferring characteristically to wait until his friend had gone to his mother at Bath. He then wrote to him from the Frickers' house in Bristol.

"I will not say that you treat me coolly or mysteriously, yet assuredly you seem to look upon me as a man whom vanity, or some other inexplicable cause, has alienated from the system, or what could build so injurious a suspicion? Wherein, when roused to the recollection of my duty, have I shrunk from the performance of it? . . .

"Southey! I must tell you that you appear to me to write as a man who is aweary of the world because it accords not with his ideas of perfection. Your sentiments look like the sickly offspring of disgusted pride. It flies not away from the couches of imperfection because the patients are fretful and loathsome.

"Why, my dear, very dear Southey, do you wrap yourself in the mantle of self-centring resolve, and refuse to us your bounden quota of intellect? Why do you say, '*I, I, I* will do so and so,' instead of saying, as you were wont to do, 'It is all our duty to do so and so, for such and such reasons'?

"For God's sake, my dear fellow, tell me what we are to gain by taking a Welsh farm. Remember the principles and proposed consequences of pantisocracy, and reflect in what degree they are attainable by Coleridge, Southey, Lovell, Burnett, and Co., some five men *going partners* together? In the next place, supposing that we have proved the preponderating utility of our aspheterizing in Wales, let us by our speedy and united enquiries discover the sum of money necessary, whether such a farm with so very large a house is to be procured without launching our frail and unpiloted bark on a rough sea of anxieties. How much is necessary for the maintenance of so large a family—eighteen people for a year at least?

"I have read my objections to Lovell. If he has not answered them altogether to my fullest conviction, he has however shown me the wretchedness that would fall on the majority of our party from any delay in so forcible a light, that if three hundred pounds be adequate to the commencement of the system (which I very much doubt), I am most willing to give up all my views and embark immediately with you." [145]

Southey, however, was not to be moved. And as the three hundred pounds had no existence outside the literary hopes of Coleridge and his friend, there was in any event no hope of an immediate carrying-out of the original scheme. Pantisocracy seemed destined to make its bow, if at all, in Wales.

[67]

Sarah proved as great a disappointment as Southey. In this instance, Coleridge could not complain of his welcome; it was, indeed, more cordial than he had reason to expect. The trouble was fundamental. The attractions of Sarah for him were so bound up with his early enthusiasm for pantisocracy that the whittling down of the scheme to something perilously akin to the prosaic likewise brought their relations into line with everyday conventions and sensibly diminished his ardour.

He returned to London almost in despair. And it was at this moment, when his pantisocratic prop was in process of being struck from under his feet and his sacrifice of two months before rendered vain, that he heard news which snapped further resistance. A rumour reached him that Mary Evans was betrothed. At last he abandoned pretence. He wrote to Mary instantly:

"Too long has my heart been the torture house of suspense. After infinite struggles of irresolution, I will at last dare to request of you, Mary, that you will communicate to me whether or no you are engaged to Mr Todd.[146] I conjure you not to consider this request as presumptuous indelicacy. Upon mine honour, I have made it with no other design or expectation than that of arming my fortitude by total hopelessness. Read this letter with benevolence —and consign it to oblivion.

"For four years I have *endeavoured* to smother a very ardent attachment; in what degree I have succeeded you must know better than I can. With quick perceptions of moral beauty, it was impossible for me not to admire in you your sensibility regulated by judgment, your gaiety proceeding from a cheerful heart acting on the stores of a strong understanding. At first I voluntarily invited the recollection of these qualities into my mind. I made them the perpetual object of my reveries, yet I entertained no one sentiment beyond that of the immediate pleasure annexed to the thinking of you. At length it became a habit. I awoke from the delusion, and found that I had unwittingly harboured a passion which I felt neither the power nor the courage to subdue. My associations were irrevocably formed, and your image was blended with every idea. I thought of you incessantly; yet that spirit (if spirit there be that condescends to record the lonely beatings of my heart), that spirit knows that I thought of you with the purity of a brother. Happy were I, had it been with no more than a brother's ardour!

"The man of dependent fortunes, while he fosters an attachment, commits an act of suicide on his happiness. I possessed

[68]

no establishment. My views were very distant; I saw that you regarded me merely with the kindness of a sister. What expectations could I form? I formed no expectations. I was ever resolving to subdue the disquieting passion; still some inexplicable suggestion palsied my efforts, and I clung with desperate fondness to this phantom of love, its mysterious attractions and hopeless prospects. It was a faint and rayless hope! Yet it soothed my solitude with many a delightful day-dream. It was a faint and rayless hope! Yet I nursed it in my bosom with an agony of affection, even as a mother her sickly infant. But these are the poisoned luxuries of a diseased fancy. Indulge, Mary, this my first, my last request, and restore me to *reality*, however gloomy. Sad and full of heaviness will the intelligence be; my heart will die within me. I shall, however, receive it with steadier resignation from yourself, than were it announced to me (haply on your marriage day!) by a stranger. Indulge my request; I will not disturb your peace by even a *look* of discontent, still less will I offend your ear by the whine of selfish sensibility. In a few months I shall enter at the Temple and there seek forgetful calmness, where only it can be found, in incessant and useful activity.

"Were you not possessed of a mind and of a heart above the usual lot of women, I should not have written you sentiments that would be unintelligible to three fourths of your sex. But our feelings are congenial, though our attachment is doomed not to be reciprocal. You will not deem so meanly of me as to believe that I shall regard Mr Todd with the jaundiced eye of disappointed passion. God forbid! He whom you honour with your affections becomes sacred to me. I shall love him for *your* sake; the time may perhaps come when I shall be philosopher enough not to envy him for *his own*."[147]

He returned to Cambridge and waited. The answer came and his suspense was over. He wrote back to Mary at once:

"I have this moment received your letter, Mary Evans. Its firmness does honour to your understanding, its gentleness to your humanity. You condescend to accuse yourself—most unjustly! You have been altogether blameless. In my wildest day-dream of vanity, I never supposed that you entertained for me any other than a common friendship.

"To love you, habit has made unalterable. This passion, however, divested as it now is of all shadow of hope, will lose its disquieting power. Far distant from you I shall journey through the vale of men in calmness. He cannot long be wretched, who dares be actively virtuous.

[69]

"I have burnt your letters—forget mine; and that I have pained you, forgive me!

"May God infinitely love you!" [148]

He left Cambridge for the last time and buried himself in London. All thought of a degree was abandoned. To the remonstrances of Dr Pearce, who, reluctant to lose a scholar of such brilliant promise, had, it seems, been more than lenient, Coleridge would say only that the Master misunderstood him as "he was neither Jacobin, nor Democrat, but a Pantisocrat." [149] But during this time of bitterness, pantisocracy itself had lost its hold upon him. He could think of nothing but Mary.

He wrote once to Southey, who was enquiring why he did not come down to Bristol. Although he well knew his friend's dislike of the subject, he could not resist writing of Mary:

"Southey! my ideal standard of female excellence rises not above that woman. But all things work together for good. Had I been united to her, the excess of my affection would have effeminated my intellect. I should have fed on her looks as she entered the room, I should have gazed on her footsteps when she went out from me." [150]

There followed an ominous reference to Sarah.

"To lose her! I can rise above that selfish pang. But to marry another. O Southey! bear with my weakness. Love makes all things pure and heavenly like itself—but to marry a woman whom I do *not* love, to degrade her whom I call my wife by making her the instrument of low desire, and on the removal of a desultory appetite to be perhaps not displeased with her absence!" [151]

Then, with belated and scarcely convincing heroics—with underlinings replacing the absent will:

"Enough! These refinements are the wildering fires that lead me into vice. Mark you, Southey! *I will do my duty.*" [152]

He endeavoured to reassure Southey and himself:

"Think you I wish to stay in town? I am all eagerness to leave it; and am resolved, whatever be the consequence, to be at Bath by Saturday." [153]

But his resolve was unequal to the strain. He made no attempt to leave London. The watchers at Bristol watched in vain. No more was heard from him.

3

COLERIDGE RETREATED to the seclusion of the Salutation and Cat. He did not grieve alone, however. Charles Lamb, who had himself just suffered a disappointment in love,[1] joined his friend at every available moment ". . . in that nice little smoky room . . . with all its associated train of pipes, tobacco, Egghot, welch Rabbits, metaphysics and Poetry."[2]

This period of intimacy not only comforted the two young men; it confirmed a friendship which, except for one break, was to endure unruffled to the end of their lives. Lamb, in his letters to Coleridge at a later date, refers again and again to this blissful grimace in the very face of misery. He thinks of Coleridge: ". . . repeating one of Bowles's sweetest sonnets in your sweet manner, while we two were indulging sympathy, a solitary luxury, by the fireside. . . ."[3] He felt that he had even deeper cause for gratitude: "To you I owe much under God. In my brief acquaintance with you in London, your conversations won me to the better cause, and rescued me from the polluting spirit of the world. I might have been a worthless character without you; as it is, I do possess a certain improvable portion of devotional feelings. . . ."[4] As for Coleridge, he had that inestimable boon, a willing and sympathetic listener.

Days passed. Weeks went by. Neither Sarah Fricker nor Southey heard a word from Coleridge. Southey wrote to Favell at Christ's Hospital and was told that Coleridge was staying at the Salutation and Cat. He wrote to that address urging the absentee to do his duty. Coleridge at last replied, naming a day when he would come down to Bristol. On the appointed day Southey and Lovell walked to Marlborough to meet the coach but Coleridge was not in it. He had not come. The two pantisocrats were obliged to return without him.[5]

Meanwhile, the scarcity of money was obliging Coleridge to look about for work. He had now no means. All communication with his family had ceased. He could not pay his bill at the tavern and was forced to leave his clothes behind him as security. He migrated to the Angel, where it is said that the landlord offered to keep him free if only he would talk and so attract admiring crowds.[6] He wrote further sonnets for the *Morning Chronicle* but the money received was insufficient to maintain him. With Dyer's help he eventually made provisional arrangements to go to Scotland as tutor to the sons of the Earl of Buchan.[7]

Before any decision could be taken, however, Southey acted. Spurred on by the Frickers he arrived unexpectedly in London at the end of January. He explained later: "Coleridge did not come back to Bristol till January 1795, *nor would he, I believe, have come back at all,* if I had not gone to London to look for him. For having got there at the beginning of winter, there he remained without writing to Miss F. or to me, until we actually apprehended that his friends had placed him somewhere in confinement."[8]

Southey traced his friend to the Angel. A reconciliation took place, and he brought Coleridge back in triumph to Bristol. There the pantisocratic fire was once again fanned into flame. The reproaches, if such were made, were gentle. And if the charms of Sarah still failed to banish entirely the memory of Mary Evans, the former young lady had her own method of bringing the prodigal to the point. In a letter to Dyer written soon after his arrival, Coleridge explains the position:

> "Intending to return from day to day I postponed writing to you—I will however delay it no longer. I am anxious and perturbed beyond measure concerning my proposed expedition to Scotland—I will pour out my heart before you as water. In the Autumn of last year, you know, we formed our American Plan and with precipitance that did credit to our hearts rather than heads, fixed on the coming April as the time of our embarkation. *This* following circumstances have rendered impracticable—but there are other engagements not so dissoluble. In expectation of embarking on the Pantisocratic Plan I payed my addresses to a young Lady, whom 'οὔτ' αἰνεῖν ἐστι κακοῖσι θέμις'! Independently of the Love and Esteem which her Person, and polished understanding may be supposed to have inspired into a young Man, I consider myself as under particular Ties of Gratitude to her—since in confidence of my Affection she has rejected the Addresses of two Men, one of them of large Fortune—and by her perseverant Attachment to me disobliged her Relations in a very uncomfortable Degree. Perpetually obliged to resist the entreaties

and to endure the reproachful admonitions of her Uncle etc., she vainly endeavors to conceal from me how heavy her heart is with anxiety, how disquieted by Suspense—To leave her for two or three years would, I fear, be sacrificing her health and happiness—In short, why should I write circuitously to you? So commanding are the requests of her Relations, that a short Time must decide whether she marries me whom she loves with an affection to the ardor of which my Deserts bear no proportion—or a man whom she strongly dislikes, in spite of his fortune and solicitous attentions to her. These peculiar circumstances she had with her usual Delicacy concealed from me till my arrival at Bristol." 9

In order to deal with this situation it was found necessary to translate the pantisocratic partnership into the more substantial betrothal of everyday life. And, since it was obviously unwise to let Coleridge once again cast loose from Bristol, the scheme of the Scottish tutorship was allowed to fall through. Coleridge did not return to London again after a few days, as he had intended. His visit to Bristol closed into a settlement.

But a living had still to be sought. Although pantisocracy flourished as a congenial subject for the exercise of Coleridge's rhetorical powers, its execution appeared further away than ever. Not only was the American project postponed indefinitely but the prospects of the Welsh farm settlement grew remote. The energies of the two leading members of the society were absorbed by the effort—prosaic but essential—of maintaining life in themselves. Neither Coleridge nor Southey had means of any kind. Southey had been summarily dismissed his aunt's house when his pantisocratic activities, long disguised, had come to light.10 Since that time he had lived with his mother. He had not returned to Oxford since his first meeting with Coleridge; and the financial assistance from his uncle Hill had therefore ceased.

Both Coleridge and Southey tried to secure positions as reporters on the *Telegraph* 11 until they were able to earn sufficient money in other directions. This, however, came to nothing. They were driven back upon less certain means of earning a living.

They joined Burnett in lodgings at 48 College Street 12 (Lovell and his wife lived in the Old Market) and settled down to earn a living by their pens. Southey and Lovell had been able to persuade Cruttwell of Bath, printer of Bowles' sonnets, to publish their poems in the autumn of the previous year; 13 and, encouraged by this, and doubtless with the success of Bowles in mind, Coleridge and Southey planned greater works. Both had advertised proposals for publishing these works by subscription; Southey, for his *Joan of Arc*; Coleridge, for his *Imitations from the Modern Latin Poets*.

Coleridge's enthusiasm for his *Imitations* blossomed again. He informed Dyer that he would be able to bring it out by the end of the year. He expected to clear one hundred pounds by it.[14] And when Dyer, hopeful soul though he was, cautioned his friend against setting too much store by this work, Coleridge supplied him with figures of promised subscribers. He had 450—half as many again as the minimum required. He assured Dyer, however, that he did not speculate upon the book.[15] It was just as well, for the complete *Imitations* never existed outside a particularly vivid imagination.

Coleridge and Southey had other plans. They were to collaborate in the production of a two-volume book of poems. They were jointly to edit a magazine—*The Provincial Magazine*—containing their work. They were to lecture in Bristol.

But matters would have gone hard with them despite all their planning, had not a benefactor in the person of Joseph Cottle [16] entered their lives at this moment. Cottle was a young Bristol bookseller. He was a vain but generous man who cherished an earnest desire to move in select literary circles; and despite the errors of taste which he displayed in many directions,[17] his enthusiasm for poetry in general did not blind him to the particular promise of Southey and Coleridge. He had first met Lovell in the autumn of 1794 when the latter was endeavouring to procure converts to pantisocracy.[18] Cottle's appreciation of the poetic gifts of the principals of the scheme did not extend to their project; he could not be tempted to join the pantisocrats. He contented himself with encouraging the budding poets to write, spreading their fame throughout the city, and for a time practically supporting them. He met Southey soon after his acquaintance with Lovell began; he did not meet Coleridge until the latter was brought down to Bristol at the beginning of 1795.

Coleridge, Southey, and Cottle quickly became close companions. Cottle showed a faith in his new friends' abilities which played no small part in their development. He not only made it possible for them to live but realized their hopes of publication in a manner which must almost have exceeded their hopes. Southey, in particular, availed himself of the opportunity. Coleridge was too occupied by pantisocratic, political, and religious lectures and conversation to write more than spasmodically.

They told Cottle of their plans. Their immediate object was to secure an income of £100 to £150 between them by writing and lecturing. That stage reached, they proposed to marry, live in and partly on the country, and begin to apply the tenets of pantisocracy until such time as they could collect sufficient funds to attempt the American settlement.[19]

The only part of this plan which showed any sign of materializing was the lecturing. Soon after he arrived in Bristol, Coleridge began a series of political lectures at the Plume of Feathers in Wine Street. These lectures were directed against the repressions of Pitt which at that time were particularly severe. The names of the first three lectures give some impression of their contents. They were respectively: *A Moral and Political Lecture*: *On the Present War*: *The Plot Discovered; or, An Address to the People, against Ministerial Treason*.

Coleridge was obliged to publish the opening lecture in order to rebut the accusation of treason which rapidly followed its delivery. Later,[20] all three were published: the first two as *Conciones ad Populum. Or Addresses to the People*; the third, under its original title.[21]

Many other lectures followed. There was a second series of six political lectures at the Assembly Coffee House. Coleridge's subject was *A Comparative View of the English Rebellion and the French Revolution*. He also delivered a series of six theological lectures *On Revealed Religion, its Corruptions, and its Political Views*,[22] the lectures, according to the prospectus, being "intended for two classes of men, Christians and Infidels; to the Former, that they may be able to give a Reason for the hope that is in them: to the latter, that they may not determine against Christianity, from arguments applicable to its corruptions only," [23] in which Unitarian doctrines were aired with an eloquence which brought the lecturer the admiration, and later the friendship and substantial help of John Prior Estlin,[24] the well-known Unitarian minister and schoolmaster, and his wife—also of Mr Hort (an assistant master), and

Mr Jardine,[25] minister of the chapel at Bath in which Coleridge was first to preach. Coleridge also gave a number of lectures on miscellaneous subjects of topical interest such as the Slave Trade, the Corn Laws, and the Hair Powder Tax, some at the Corn Market in Wine Street, one at a room in Castle Green, some in the Assembly Coffee House on the Quay.

In most of his lectures, Coleridge "preached the gospel to the poor" [26]—the gospel which he urged upon his audiences being a blend of Hartley, Berkeley, pantisocracy, and aspheterism calculated to provide a practicable and more attractive alternative to the existing forms of government and belief.

The attendances at these lectures were good—a fact due at first to Cottle's industrious lionizing of the lecturer. Soon, however, Coleridge began to draw his own crowds. But those who came to hear him were by no means all his followers; there were also those who disapproved of him and his doctrines in an emphatic manner. As Coleridge told Dyer in a somewhat highly coloured account:

> " . . . the opposition of the Aristocrats is so furious and determined, that I begin to fear, that the Good I do is not proportionate to the Evil I occasion—Mobs and Mayors, Blockheads and Brickbats, Plackards and Press gangs have leagued in horrible Conspiracy against me—The Democrats are as sturdy in the support of me—but their number is comparatively small. Two or three uncouth and untrained Automata have threatened my Life— and in the last Lecture the Genus infimum were scarcely restrained from attacking the house in which the 'damn'd Jacobin was jawing away.' " [27]

However, despite the opposition Coleridge encountered, the lectures went on. Southey was lecturing also. His lectures—on history—were neither so successful nor so much resented by a section of his audience. He had not the personal charm and the attractive delivery of Coleridge. He possessed neither the comprehensive grasp of his subject nor the brilliance in the exposition of it that distinguished his friend.

For the first few weeks after the arrival of Coleridge, Cottle was on tenterhooks lest pantisocracy in its full glory—or at least in the form of the proposed settlement in Wales—should suddenly spirit away his precious acquisitions to the cultural society of Bristol.[28] But he had no need to worry. The money from the lectures did not suffice even to pay the rent of the College Street lodgings. Less than two months after he and Southey had settled there, Coleridge was obliged to ask Cottle for the loan of five pounds to settle the bill.[29]

Cottle lent the money readily. Moreover, perceiving that pantisocracy was far from realization, he came forward with some generous offers to the two needy poets. He proposed to each that he should publish a volume of their poems, for which he offered thirty guineas, the money to be paid in advance as it was required. Furthermore, he offered Southey fifty guineas for his *Joan of Arc* and the promise of an unusually lavish production.[30] His offers were accepted.

At first, except for the chronic shortage of money, all went well at College Street. It seemed that the old relationship had returned between Coleridge and Southey, the old enthusiasms had been born again. Southey wrote to Grosvenor Bedford of his friend: "Coleridge is writing at the same table; our names are written in the book of destiny, on the same page."[31]

Coleridge was no less emphatic in a letter to Dyer:

"Southey speaks of you with high esteem and nascent *friendship*. You will esteem and love him. His Genius and acquirements are uncommonly great yet they bear no proportion to his Moral Excellence—He is truly a Man *of perpendicular Virtue a downright upright Republican!* He is *Christianizing* apace—I doubt not, that I shall present him to you right orthodox in the heterodoxy of Unitarianism."[32]

But in fact the reconciliation, the renewal of intimacy, lacked the necessary basis of unity. The flame of pantisocracy which had once held them together, too dazzled to see more than the enhaloed outline of an ideal companion, now burnt low in the one and flickered uncertainly in the other. They were left with characters bared.

For a month or two the novelty of their association under one roof, and the encouragement of Cottle, preserved an amity and an enthusiasm which might have been mistaken for a return of their earlier accord. But the fundamental difference in their characters and aims could not long remain obscured.

The trouble began, as is customary, with small things— mannerisms, habits—but these, though sufficiently disturbing,

[77]

were symptomatic of a profound, unspoken, and, for a time, perhaps, unrealized divergence of thought.

At first Lovell entered the picture. He had once supported with enthusiasm the union of Coleridge and Sarah. Then he changed his attitude. He accused Coleridge of habitual indolence; and considering him, not without justice, as incapable of supporting a wife, began to discourage the idea of a marriage.[33] There were high words. Matters were smoothed out, but the fact that between pantisocrats such division was possible cast grievous doubts in many minds upon the stability of the society.

The establishment at College Street was professedly an aspheteric one. Southey was provided quickly and embarrassingly with a practical demonstration of the principle. His earnings during this period he put later at four times those of Coleridge—a figure which can be accepted as roughly correct.[34] Southey was at heart a careful young man and, aspheterism or no, the disparity annoyed him—the more so, because it seemed unnecessary. In his view, the meagreness of Coleridge's contributions to the common fund was due entirely to an indolence as disgusting to him, and as alien, as it had been to Lovell. While Southey worked, Coleridge talked and planned endlessly. Nor was that all; for the Coleridge monologues not only prevented the speaker from working, but interfered seriously with Southey's own production.

Coleridge's own method of working neither met with Southey's approval nor indeed did it come within the bounds of his comprehension. He complained that Coleridge "goes to work like a hound, nosing his way, turning, and twisting, and winding, and doubling, till you get weary with following the mazy movements. My way is, when I see my object, to dart at it like a greyhound."[35]

In addition, Coleridge's habit of repetition—he would repeat a favourite phrase, argument, or poem almost without end in his conversation and in his correspondence—galled his companion immeasurably.[36] Southey was essentially a man of action. Profound or even prolonged thought was beyond his abilities and outside his sympathies. As he sat in his lodgings day after day steadily turning out poems for Cottle, it was natural that he should regard his erratic companion with some bitterness—it was natural, but by no means conclusive.

Coleridge hit the nail on the head in his reply to Southey's accusations of idleness: "The truth is, you sat down and wrote; I used to saunter about and think what I should write. And we ought to appreciate our comparative industry by the quantum of mental exertion, not the particular mode of it—by the number of thoughts collected, not by the number of lines through which these thoughts are diffused." [37]

Indeed, it is by no means certain that Coleridge was as idle, even relatively, as Southey persuaded himself. He certainly played a considerable part in the revision of *Joan of Arc*; he spent much time criticizing and altering Southey's shorter poems (whether his help was always welcome or not is beside the point); he assisted in the preparation of many of Southey's lectures; he prepared his own lectures, wrote a few short poems and worked upon his *Religious Musings*.

For his part, Coleridge was beginning to feel the strain of the "Moral Excellence" [38] he had been lauding such a short time before. That old enemy, the "phlogiston" [39] in Southey's heart, made an unwelcome appearance at College Street. Coleridge found himself taken to task, first by Lovell, then by Southey, for his short-comings in a manner reminiscent more of the schoolroom than of a pantisocratic association. Southey's insistence upon the letter rather than the spirit of conduct, his lack of consideration, his essential conventionalism, began to show through the pantiso-cratic mask and cast a shadow over their relationship.

But this attitude of increasing disapproval obscured the full truth. Southey's emergence into the man he was to remain was hastened and distorted by the dilemma in which he found himself. He was driven to magnify and harp upon the faults in Coleridge because of his growing consciousness that all was not well in him-self. His rectitude grew more rigid, his remonstrances sharpened, the further he himself slipped from pantisocratic grace.

Coleridge with all his frailties would have been difficult for a man of Southey's disposition, freed from illusion, to stomach for long at close quarters. But in Southey's present state of mind, Coleridge the endlessly planning, fantastically optimistic pan-tisocrat, fast became anathema.

The fact was that Southey had begun seriously to regret his adherence to the scheme. The character of his chief associate as it revealed itself, the fear that, in the name of aspheterism, he might be called upon to support indefinitely an eternally loquacious Coleridge, for ever impeding his work—these aspects of the matter, though sufficiently disturbing, were not the main cause of Southey's loss of faith. This was due to the uprising within him of the demon respectability. He wanted money. He wanted an assured future. He began to hunger for security; for the ordered stability of some profession upon the proceeds and the certainty of which he might found a home for Edith Fricker and at the same time assist his mother.

His present mode of living would do none of these things. On the contrary, he was obliged to face the fact that he had committed himself to a scheme that was worse than impracticable. Not only had his adoption of pantisocracy deprived him of his aunt's goodwill and financial assistance and his uncle's aid in securing a career—it was actually forcing him to share, under most inequitable circumstances, the little money that he was able to earn by his pen.

So he reasoned: and his pantisocratic principles (more especially those inspired by aspheterism) melted like snow under the fire of his indignation; his contempt for his companion grew almost beyond concealment.

Yet he, Southey, had actually set this visionary scheme afoot. He had set the pantisocratic ball rolling. There was the rub. He had bound himself in the most emphatic, not to say lurid terms, to remain faithful to its principles.[40] Honour demanded that he accept his obligations and act a lie. But he flirted with the idea of escape. Hints of his true feelings began to appear in his very manner of speech when referring to the scheme, in the suggestions which escaped from his lips from time to time. He tried to dilute the system. He sought for compromises, for some method of obtaining the substance of a livelihood whilst retaining the shadow of the principles he still professed. Blasphemous perversions of pantisocracy, hideous to Coleridge and bewildering even the faithful Burnett, took shape in his mind and disclosed themselves, willy-nilly. He proposed that the Welsh farm should be run on communal lines but that private resources should remain in the possession of their owners.[41] He proposed earning money for a period of fourteen years and then rejoining pantisocracy.[42]

Coleridge soon began to suspect the truth. In fact, Southey's realistic attitude towards the details of pantisocracy—cause of the vigorous correspondence between Cambridge and Bath the previous autumn—set doubts in Coleridge's mind that the later Bristol reconciliation had no more than lulled.

For a time, however, Southey kept his convictions, if not completely to himself, at least within bounds that made continued co-operation possible. There was no open breach. But some lamentable disagreements took place which, whatever their apparent or initial cause, aroused so considerable a friction and bitterness only because of the steadily growing conviction in Coleridge and the certainty in Southey, that pantisocracy was losing one of its stalwarts.

Such an occasion was the memorable visit to Tintern Abbey planned by the well-meaning Cottle. The party consisted of Cottle, the two young men and their ladies. Only the previous evening, however, a regrettable incident had taken place. Southey was due to lecture on the French Revolution but Coleridge, claiming the subject as one of his special studies, persuaded his friend to let him take the lecture. Unfortunately, at the time appointed for the lecture, no lecturer was to be found, and after waiting a considerable time the audience had been dismissed. The appointment had slipped from Coleridge's mind.[43]

Under these unhappy auspices, the party left Bristol the following morning. At Chepstow they dined at the Beaufort Arms, then visited Piercefield Walks on the way to the Abbey. Southey, however, who regarded the entire jaunt with disapproval, could not contain his anger. He reproached Coleridge for his failure to lecture the previous evening. Coleridge retaliated with an attack on Southey's weakening aspheteric principles. The ladies joined in and Cottle had hard work to restore peace.[44]

For some months the partnership continued this uneasy see-saw between suspicion and reconciliation.[45] But both poets were fighting a losing battle. In August, Southey received two proposals: one, from his old school friend, C. W. W. Wynn, was the confirmation of a previous offer to give Southey an annuity of £160 a year from his twenty-first birthday, in January of the following year, providing that he studied Law; the other was a suggestion from his uncle Hill, just arrived on a visit from Lisbon,

that Southey should return to Oxford and take Orders as determined originally.[46]

The temptation was too great for Southey. He dallied with the
offers, hesitated. The outraged Coleridge, waiting in vain for an
account of the prompt refusal sent to Wynn and Hill, finally
challenged his friend outright. What answer had he given?

> " . . . to think with almost superstitious veneration of you had
> been such a deep-rooted habit of my soul that even then I did not
> dream you could hesitate concerning so infamous a proposal.
> 'None,' you replied, 'nor do I know what answer I shall return.'
> You went to bed. George [Burnett] sat half-petrified, gaping at
> the pigmy virtue of his supposed giant. I performed the office
> of still-struggling friendship by writing you my free sentiments
> concerning the enormous guilt of that which your uncle's doughty
> sophistry recommended." [47]

The argument continued the next morning, but Southey met all
Coleridge's arguments with a devastating frankness, not to say
cynicism, which dumbfounded his questioner. He was almost
given up for lost.[48]

The ménage at 48 College Street dissolved.[49] Southey and
Coleridge maintained a veneer of cordiality but the descent from
pantisocracy was not to be denied. Southey once more joined
his mother at Bath. Burnett returned home. Coleridge moved
alone to No. 25 in the same street. Cottle, with considerable
adroitness, managed to hold, and even to increase, the confidence
of both his shining lights.

On August 20, Coleridge took the decisive step of renting
a cottage at Clevedon, on the Bristol Channel, in preparation for
his marriage.[50]

Coleridge was not to be without a close friend. As he lost
Southey he gained Poole; and the exchange from every point of
view must be reckoned an advantageous one. Soon after Coleridge returned to Bristol the acquaintance, begun the previous
autumn, was resumed. The two men quickly became fast friends.
They were well matched. On the one hand there was the boundless, at times somewhat uncritical, but always entirely selfless admiration of Poole for the brilliant qualities of his friend, coupled
with a childlike faith in his great future. On the other hand, Poole
could discuss Coleridge's work with him as intelligently as

Southey and with the greater generosity of one whose good sense prevented similar ambitions. He would listen to the poet's monologues for hours at a time, without impatience and with an attention and comprehension which alone would have tempted Coleridge to frequent his society. But the influence which he exercised upon the younger man, and the devotion he inspired in him, must be attributed above all to his steadfast yet kindly nature—a comfortable bulwark which bore no resemblance to the "Moral Excellence" [51] of Southey that was proving so chilling and inhospitable a refuge from the storms of the world.

Poole attended some of Coleridge's lectures; made some criticisms; suggested some subjects; even prepared some material for Coleridge's use—as in the lecture on the Hair Powder Tax (one of Poole's pet aversions—he always wore his hair unpowdered). Coleridge, on his part, paid many visits to Stowey. In September he stayed with Poole several days—a visit memorable for the fact that it occasioned the production of two impressions of Coleridge. These were as different from each other as could well be imagined, yet each retained for posterity a record of the poet that is true in its own way, and the two together form a fair picture of the young man.

The first came from Poole himself. On September 12 he wrote a poem to Coleridge; and neither the inferior verses, nor the conventionality which overhangs them, can obscure wholly the truth of the portrait they draw:

> Hail to thee, Coldridge, youth of various powers!
> I love to hear thy soul pour forth the line,
> To hear it sing of love and liberty
> As if fresh breathing from the hand divine.
>
> As if on earth it never yet had dwelt,
> As if from heaven it now had wing'd its way;
> And brought us tidings how, in argent fields,
> In love and liberty blest spirits stray.
>
> I love to mark that soul-pervaded clay,
> To see the passions in thine eyeballs roll—
> Their quick succession on thy weighty brow—
> Thy trembling lips express their very soul.

I love to view the abstracted gaze which speaks
Thy soul to heavenwards towering—then I say,
He's gone—for us to cull celestial sweets
Amid the flowerets of the milky way.

And now at home, within its mortal cage,
I see thy spirit pent—ah me!—and mourn
The sorrow sad, that weighs it down to earth,
As if the Cherub Hope would ne'er return.

And then I mark the starting tear that steals
Adown thy cheek, when of a friend thou speak'st,
Who erst, as thou dost say, was wondrous kind,
But now, unkind, forgets—I feel and weep.

I hear thee speak indignant of the world,
Th' unfeeling world crowded with folly's train;
I hear thy fervent eloquence dispel
The murky mists of error's mazy reign.

And thou, Religion, white-robed Maid of Peace,
Who smil'st to hear him raise his voice on high
To fix thy image on the Patriot's breast—
Remove the bitter tear, the fearful sigh.[52]

So Tom Poole. The second record of Coleridge was made
exactly one week later. Poole had taken his friend to Marsh Mills,
the home of his paternal cousins. He displayed his gifted young
man proudly. But the Pooles at Marsh Mills, who suffered Tom
Poole's political views and eccentricities because of his essential
goodness and gentleness, were by no means inclined to be so for-
bearing with his protégé. Charlotte, the eldest sister, made a note
of the visit:

> "Tom Poole has a friend with him of the name of Coldridge:
> a young man of brilliant understanding, great eloquence, desperate
> fortune, democratick principles, and entirely led away by the feel-
> ings of the moment."[53]

About this time Coleridge and William Wordsworth first met.
In a letter to his friend W. Mathews, Wordsworth said he was
going to Bristol "to see those two extraordinary young men,
Southey and Coleridge," [54] but the date of the meeting is not
known. Wordsworth met Cottle in September and discussed the

possible publication of *Guilt and Sorrow*.[55] In later years he said he recollected meeting Coleridge, Southey, and Edith Fricker in a Bristol lodging-house "about the year 1795."[56] On September 2, and for some days after, he was certainly staying at the Pinneys' house at Bristol[57] (Mr Pinney, a Bristol merchant, owned the house at Racedown which Wordsworth had arranged to rent[58] from his son). Neither Coleridge nor Southey nor Cottle make any mention of a meeting. Coleridge, referring to a note to *Lines written at Shurton Bars* acknowledging the borrowing of a phrase from Wordsworth, says that the note was written before he had met the poet.[59] Nevertheless, some kind of intercourse must have taken place between September and November; for on the 20th of the latter month Wordsworth, sending some lines of a satire in imitation of Juvenal to his friend Wrangham, says that "the two best verses of this extract were given me by Southey, a friend of Coleridge."[60] They began to correspond, Wordsworth sending Coleridge the revised *Guilt and Sorrow* by way of Azariah Pinney and Cottle. Writing to Cottle a few months later, Wordsworth ended his letter: "Best compts. to Coleridge and say I wish much to hear from him."[61]

Meanwhile, the pantisocrats sank deeper into discord. Southey was still undecided what he should do, but his defection from the society was now beyond doubt. The affianced of the two pantisocratic leaders championed the respective causes of their husbands to be and the dispute began to take a less dignified direction. A section of Bristol society became conscious that the protagonists of pantisocracy were falling asunder. Rumour spread. Scandal reared an ugly head. Southey was told that his character was being openly defamed by Coleridge. Coleridge denied the charge and demanded that Southey should honour his pantisocratic vows. There was great bitterness between them.

The position in the Fricker home on Redcliffe Hill became difficult. Possibly it hastened the marriage of Coleridge and Sarah. On October 4, they were married and settled in the Clevedon cottage.[62]

Despite any reluctance Coleridge may have felt to a renewal of his pantisocratic relations with Sarah earlier in the year, and still more their transference into a hard and fast engagement, there is no reason to suppose that he suffered serious qualms when carrying out the almost irrevocable design of matrimony. On the contrary, he threw himself into the pleasures of married life with his customary ardour for new experiences. He announces the news to Poole:

"God bless you; or rather, God be praised for that he *has* blessed you!

"On Sunday morning I was *married* at St. Mary's Redcliffe, poor Chatterton's church! The thought gave a tinge of melancholy to the solemn joy which I felt, united to the woman whom I love best of all created beings. We are settled, nay, quite domesticated, at Clevedon, our comfortable cot!

"*Mrs Coleridge!* I like to write the name. Well, as I was saying, Mrs Coleridge desires her affectionate regards to you. I talked of you on my wedding night. God bless you! I hope that some ten years hence you will believe and know of my affection towards you what I will not now profess.

"The prospect around is perhaps more *various* than any in the kingdom. Mine eyes gluttonizes the sea, the distant islands, the opposite coast! I shall assuredly write rhymes, let the nine Muses prevent it if they can." [63]

In this letter, he also announced the abandonment of one plan —that of *The Provincial Magazine*—for a number of reasons, one of which was "I must be connected with R. Southey in it, which I could not be with comfort to my feelings." [64] But where one plan failed to stay the course, two sprang up anew. An old friend reared its head again. The *Imitations* which had languished as sadly at Bristol as they had done at Cambridge, were to be revived in the latter place, but under more favourable conditions. He proposed to return to Cambridge in six months with his wife; and there, free from University control, he would "finish my great work of 'Imitations' in two volumes. My former works may, I hope, prove somewhat of genius and of erudition. This will be better; it will show great industry and manly consistency." [65] Nor was this all; for when the work was concluded it was his intention to publish proposals for a school. [66]

In this letter the mystery of the Coleridge financial situation is also revealed. Sarah had no money; Coleridge had none. The thirty guineas from Cottle had long since disappeared and the poems on behalf of which it was advanced were not yet finished. Nevertheless, it was Cottle alone who made the marriage possible. Coleridge explains his offer to Poole:

"Cottle has entered into an engagement to give me a guinea and a half for every hundred lines of poetry I write, which will be perfectly sufficient for my maintainance, I only amusing myself on mornings; and all my prose works he is eager to purchase." [67]

In smaller matters, too, Cottle proved most obliging. Though the cottage had been taken some weeks before the marriage a number of articles more or less indispensable were forgotten. Coleridge wrote to Cottle—he had for some months grown into the habit of referring his smaller wants to this seemingly tireless provider—and asked for "A riddle slice; a candle box; two ventilators; two glasses for the wash-hand stand; one tin dust pan; one small tin tea kettle; one pair of candlesticks; one carpet brush; one flower dredge; three tin extinguishers; two mats; a pair of slippers; a cheese toaster; two large tin spoons; a bible; a keg of porter; coffee; raisins; currants; catsup; nutmeg; allspice; cinnamon; rice; ginger; and mace." [68] Cottle obliged; and came down himself the day after the arrival of the goods to see how his young poet had settled in. [69]

In the cottage all went well. Martha Fricker and Burnett, who had transferred his allegiance to Coleridge, joined the married couple. A mild form of pantisocracy was established—all members of the household sharing the work. Burnett endeavoured— probably at this time—to become engaged to Martha, but without success. [70]

The recalcitrant Southey was not forgotten, however. One of Coleridge's first letters was to his old associate urging him not to perjure himself by accepting his uncle's proposal to return to Oxford and take Orders—a letter chiefly remarkable for its admission that the realization of pantisocracy was "distant— perhaps a miraculous millennium." [71] Southey, whose scruples in this matter were not as active as those of Coleridge, did not, in fact, elect either to go to Oxford or to take Orders; but his objection to Coleridge's advice was not the less strong. Further letters passed between them. The situation became too tense even for civility. There came a day when the two pantisocrats passed one another "unsaluted and unsaluting" [72] in the streets of Bristol.

To Coleridge's charges of desertion of the cause, Southey could retort only with accusations of calumny and the plea of common sense—the latter at least being among the last words in the language likely to meet with appreciation from Coleridge.

[87]

Southey chose finally to enter the Law and so secure the Wynn legacy. He openly renounced pantisocracy. He also informed his uncle of his decision; and that patient man, too relieved at the latter news to grieve overmuch about the former, suggested that his nephew should return with him to Lisbon for a few months until the annuity was payable.[73] Possibly he had hopes that the proposed marriage with Edith Fricker would thus go the way of pantisocracy. Southey accepted.

When the news reached Coleridge, he sat down and wrote to Southey a letter of condemnation which occupies fourteen printed pages.[74] He traced the history of their friendship and the fortunes of pantisocracy since its inception. His case was a strong one and he made the most of it. Only when he attempted to deal with the origins of the various rumours that had embittered their differences do his protestations of complete innocence sound somewhat unconvincing.

He repeats his charge against Southey—made previously only to Burnett—that the chief reason for Southey's desire to leave the pantisocratic society was a reluctance to share the annuity.[75] But despite this charge and his spirited defence of pantisocracy, the true grievance was Southey's call to a duty which he had now himself revoked.[76] Coleridge had already lost hope in pantisocracy; he was married, for the moment happily; but he could not forget his feelings at the loss of Mary Evans:

> "Previously to my departure from Jesus College, and during my melancholy detention in London, what convulsive struggles of feeling I underwent, and what sacrifices I made, you know. The liberal proposal from my family affected me no further than as it pained me to wound a revered brother by the positive and immediate refusal which duty compelled me to return. But there was a——I need not be particular; you remember what a fetter I burst, and that it snapt as if it had been a sinew of my heart. However, I returned to Bristol. . . ."[77]

Still less was he able to forget Southey's visit to London and call to duty:

> "My hand trembles when I think what a series of falsehood and duplicity I am about to bring before the conscience of a man who has dared to write me that 'his conduct has been uniformly open.' I must revert to your first letter, and here you say:—

" 'The plan you are going upon is not of sufficient importance to justify me to myself in abandoning a family, who have none to support them but me.' The plan *you* are going upon! What plan was I meditating, save to retire into the country with George Burnett and yourself, and taking by degrees a small farm, there be *learning* to get my own bread by my bodily labour—and then to have all things in common—thus disciplining my body and mind for the successful practice of the same thing in America with more numerous associates? And even if this should never be the case, ourselves and our children would form a society sufficiently large. And was not this your own plan—the plan for the realising of which you invited me to Bristol; the plan for which I abandoned my friends, and every prospect, and every certainty, and the woman whom I loved to an excess which you in your warmest dream of fancy could never shadow out?" [78]

Nevertheless, the letter, despite the occasion that produced it, was in the main the letter of a happy man. The pleasure of being afforded the opportunity of chastising the righteous is not difficult to understand, especially when, as with Coleridge, such an opportunity came so rarely. And when, as on occasions, Coleridge breaks into a purple passage of denunciation, he was obviously enjoying himself exceedingly.

"Is not George Burnett accurate when he undoubtedly ascribes your conduct to an unparticipating propensity—to a total want of the boasted *flocci-nauci-nihili-pilificating* [79] sense? O selfish, money-loving man! What principle have you not given up? Though death had been the consequence, I would have spat in that man's face and called him liar, who should have spoken that last sentence concerning *you* nine months ago? For blindly did I esteem you. O God! that *such a mind* should fall in love with that low, dirty, gutter-grubbing trull, *Worldly Prudence*! Curse on all *pride*! 'Tis a harlot that buckrams herself up in virtue only that she may fetch a higher price." [80]

But his rhetoric was in vain, beyond the satisfaction—not to be despised—which it afforded him in the writing. The letter was sent by hand to Southey on November 13. The day following, Southey and Edith Fricker were married secretly at St. Mary's, Redcliffe.[81] Husband and wife parted at the church. Edith went to Cottle's house, where she was to live with Cottle and his sisters until Southey's return. Southey boarded the Falmouth coach *en route* for Lisbon. Pantisocracy was dead.

[89]

4

THE COTTAGE at Clevedon was occupied for a few weeks only. Neither the company of Sarah nor the beautiful surroundings in which Coleridge found himself could compensate him for the inaccessibility of the library at Bristol, from which he had been a prolific borrower ever since his arrival in the West, and for the distance which separated him from his friends in that city.[1]

Late in November the Coleridges moved to Redcliffe Hill. The poet had his own way of explaining the return to Bristol:

> Ah! quiet Dell! dear Cot, and Mount sublime!
> I was constrain'd to quit you. Was it right,
> While my unnumbered brethren toil'd and bled,
> That I should dream away the entrusted hours
> On rose-leaf beds, pampering the coward heart
> With feelings all too delicate for use?[2]

The new home was not without its disadvantages. Coleridge gained the amenities of Bristol at the expense of an uncomfortably close association with a mother-in-law whom he held in slight esteem and with a large and now often uncongenial household.

From this predicament he was rescued, temporarily, by Poole, who invited the Coleridges to Stowey.[3] The visit was most successful. Sarah liked the Pooles and they liked her. Coleridge was in his element. The petty though inescapable demands of money for housekeeping ceased. He renewed acquaintance with the Stowey 'literaries.' He made numerous enquiries upon the customary methods of tilling the soil, and himself lent a hand in Poole's garden. He even managed to revise the few pages of poems that the long-suffering Cottle had been able to secure for the printer. He was in the throes of his *Religious Musings*—altering, rewriting, adding, without apparent end. So situated and so employed, it was becoming clear to him that in no other place but Stowey could he hope to find the peace and inspiration of that combination of husbandry, poetry, and fellowship—last impulse of pantisocracy that still stirred in him—which was now beginning to take shape as the ultimate aim of his life.

In the meantime, a living had to be earned and Coleridge rescued, if possible, from the disagreeable necessity of producing his hundreds of lines of poetry to order—or at least, from the consideration of such a necessity. That Cottle ever received his due, in sheer bulk of verses, is most unlikely; yet he contributed from time to time to the maintenance of the Coleridges. The fiction adhered to hopefully by Coleridge—"I will repay you in a few weeks" [4]—deceived no one but himself. Moreover, Estlin certainly, Poole probably, and other Bristol familiars possibly, also helped Coleridge with money.[5]

Coleridge, however, had his plans. In December, after his visit to Stowey, he convened a meeting of his friends [6] with great secrecy at the Rummer Tavern in Bristol. The idea which he propounded was none other than the commencement of a magazine. It was little more than two months since Coleridge had dismissed the idea of *The Provincial Magazine* because, apart from the embarrassment of having Southey as a partner, it would be "a thing of *monthly* anxiety and quotidian bustle." [7] But the new magazine was to be very different. The toil to come was forgotten in the heat of enthusiasm. Difficulties were swept aside.

Bills were produced. A prospectus was printed and distributed throughout the city, which announced the coming of a miscellany called *The Watchman* on Friday, February 5, 1796, and every succeeding eighth day. The motto was:

> That All may know the TRUTH;
> And that the TRUTH may make us FREE!![8]

Coleridge went on to explain that:

> IN AN ENSLAVED STATE THE RULERS FORM AND SUPPLY THE OPINIONS OF THE PEOPLE.

that:

> A PEOPLE ARE FREE IN PROPORTION AS THEY FORM THEIR OWN OPINIONS.
> In the strictest sense of the word KNOWLEDGE IS POWER.

and that:

> We actually transfer the Sovereignty to the People, when we make them susceptible of it. In the present perilous state of our

Constitution the Friends of Freedom, of Reason, and of Human Nature, must feel it their duty by every mean in their power to supply or circulate political information.

The public were then informed how *The Watchman* proposed to circulate this information. The contents were to be as follows:

(1) An History of the domestic and foreign Occurrences of the preceding days.

(2) The Speeches in both Houses of Parliament; and during the Recess, select Parliamentary Speeches, from the commencement of the reign of Charles the First to the present aera, with Notes historical and biographical.

(3) Original Essays and Poetry, chiefly or altogether political.

Its chief objects were:

to co-operate (1) with the WHIG CLUB in procuring a repeal of Lord Grenville's and Mr Pitt's bills, now passed into laws, and (2) with the PATRIOTIC SOCIETIES for obtaining a Right of Suffrage general and frequent.

Coleridge ended his manifesto by offering himself to the Public:

as a faithful

WATCHMAN

to proclaim the State of the Political Atmosphere, and preserve Freedom and her Friends from the attacks of Robbers and Assassins!! 9

But Bristol alone, though Cottle and other friends of the editor and founder did their best, could not muster sufficient subscribers to justify the commencement of the magazine. Subscribers had to be sought elsewhere. It was decided that Coleridge should make a tour of the leading cities for this purpose. Financed it is believed by Josiah Wade, a fellow enthusiast to whom he wrote many of his letters at this time, Coleridge set out early in January.

Through Birmingham, Nottingham, Sheffield, Manchester, Liverpool, Lichfield, Coleridge talked his way with growing success. The effect of his coming upon the citizens of these places was electrical. It was as if an angel had appeared in their midst, speaking their own tongue—a somewhat thick-lipped, weak-chinned angel, certainly, but possessing a voice, an eye, a forehead that seemed not to be of this world. And if this visitant from

[92]

the south had an eye to the main chance, such an attitude, in these northern eyes, was nothing but a further merit.

They listened on Sundays to words of more than mortal wisdom and eloquence; and during the week that same voice addressed them, that same glowing persuasiveness enwrapped them, in their homes and at their places of business. These sturdy manufacturers and their friends, these earnest Unitarians, began to realize that their life was incomplete, it was one-sided and not to be endured without the help—at once uplifting and instructive —of *The Watchman* every eighth day.

The evangelist's plan of campaign was simplicity itself. He preached one or more sermons on the Sunday at the local Unitarian chapel:

> " . . . preaching by the way in most of the great towns, as an hireless volunteer, in a blue coat and white waistcoat, that not a rag of the woman of Babylon might be seen on me. For I was at that time and long after, though a Trinitarian (i.e. ad normam Platonis) in philosophy, yet a zealous Unitarian in Religion; more accurately, I was a *psilanthropist*, one of those who believe our Lord to have been the real son of Joseph, and who lay the main stress on the resurrection rather than on the crucifixion." [10]

Following this, mingling with and indeed often overshadowing his proselytizing activities during the succeeding days, were social events, dinners, drives, balls, concerts. And arising out of these, friendships, offers—tempting offers.

Worcester, the first stopping-place, on January 9, was a failure: "The Aristocrats are so numerous and the influence of the Clergy so extensive, that Mr Barr thinks that no bookseller will venture to publish *the* work." [11]

Birmingham, where he arrived two days later, with an introduction from Estlin to the Reverend John Edwards,[12] the Unitarian minister, proved much more satisfactory. Coleridge preached twice: "and, indeed, performed the whole service, morning and afternoon. There were about 1,400 persons present, and my sermons, (great part extempore) were preciously peppered with politics." [13] Despite his distaste for the forms of ritual, however, he allowed himself to be divested of his blue jacket and white waistcoat and arrayed in sombre robes—a slip from conviction which worried his conscience as one of his letters to Wade makes clear:

[93]

"With regard to the gown at Birmingham (of which you enquire), I suffered myself to be over-persuaded. First of all, my sermon being of so political a tendency, had I worn my blue coat, it would have impugned Edwards. They would have said, he had stuck a political lecturer in his pulpit. Secondly, the society is of all sorts,—Socinians, Arians, Trinitarians, etc., and I must have shocked a multitude of prejudices. And thirdly, there is a difference between an inn and a place of residence. In the first, your example is of little consequence; in a single instance only, it ceases to operate as example; and my refusal would have been imputed to affectation, or an unaccommodating spirit. Assuredly I would not do it in a place where I intended to preach often. And even in the vestry at Birmingham, when they at last persuaded me, I told them I was acting against my better knowledge, and should possibly feel uneasy afterwards. So these accounts of the matter you must consider as reasons and palliations, concluding, 'I plead guilty, my Lord!' Indeed I want firmness; I perceive I do. I have that within me which makes it difficult to say, No, repeatedly to a number of persons who seem uneasy and anxious." [14]

At Birmingham occurred the amusing incident of Coleridge's first canvass:

" . . . my first attack was on a rigid Calvinist, a tallow-chandler by trade. He was a tall dingy man, in whom length was so predominant over breadth, that he might almost have been borrowed for a foundery poker. O that face! a face κατ᾽ ἔμφασιν! I have it before me at this moment. The lank, black, twine-like hair—*pingui-nitescent*, cut in a straight line along the black stubble of his thin gunpowder eye-brows, that looked like a scorched *aftermath* from a last week's shaving. His coat collar behind in perfect unison, both of colour and lustre, with the coarse yet glib cordage, that I suppose he called his hair, and which with a *bend* inward at the nape of the neck, (the only approach to flexture in his whole figure,) slunk in behind his waistcoat; while the countenance lank, dark, very *hard*, and with strong perpendicular furrows, gave me a dim notion of someone looking at me through a *used* gridiron, all soot, grease, and iron! But he was one of the *thorough-bred*, a true lover of liberty, and, (I was informed,) had proved to the satisfaction of many, that Mr Pitt was one of the horns of the second beast in the Revelations, that *spoke like a dragon*. A person, to whom one of my letters of recommendation had been addressed, was my introducer. It was a new event in my life, my first *stroke* in the new business I had undertaken of an author, yea, and of an author trading on his own account.

"My companion after some imperfect sentences and a multitude of hums and haas abandoned the cause to his client; and I commenced an harangue of half an hour to Phileleutheros, the tallow-chandler, varying my notes, through the whole gamut of eloquence, from the ratiocinative to the declamatory, and in the latter from the pathetic to the indignant. I argued, I described, I promised, I prophesied; and beginning with the captivity of nations I ended with the near approach of the millennium, finishing the whole with some of my own verses describing that glorious state out of *the Religious Musings*.

"My taper man of lights listened with perseverant and praise-worthy patience, though, (as I was afterwards told, on complaining of certain gales there were not altogether ambrosial,) it was a *melting* day with him. And what, Sir, (he said, after a short pause,) might the cost be? *Only* FOUR-PENCE, (O! how I felt the anti-climax, the abysmal bathos of that *four-pence!*) *only four-pence, Sir, each number, to be published on every eighth day.* That comes to a deal of money at the end of a year. And how much, did you say, there was to be for the money? *Thirty-two pages, Sir! large octavo, closely printed.* Thirty and two pages? Bless me! why except what I does in a family way on the Sabbath, that's more than I ever reads, Sir! all the year round. I am as great a one, as any man in Brummagem, Sir! for liberty and truth and all them sort of things, but as to this, (no offence, I hope, Sir!) I must beg to be excused." [15]

This, the first and almost the last personal canvass that Coleridge made, was followed the same evening by a dinner, which also had its humorous side:

"On returning baffled from the first [attempt], in which I had vainly essayed to repeat the miracle of Orpheus with the Brummagem patriot, I dined with the tradesman who had introduced me to him. After dinner he importuned me to smoke a pipe with him, and two or three other illuminati of the same rank. I objected, both because I was engaged to spend the evening with a minister and his friends, and because I had never smoked except once or twice in my lifetime, and then it was herb tobacco mixed with Oronooko. On the assurance, however, that the tobacco was equally mild, and seeing too that it was of a yellow colour; (not forgetting the lamentable difficulty, I have always experienced, in saying, 'No,' and in abstaining from what the people about me were doing,) I took half a pipe, filling the lower half of the bole with salt. I was soon however compelled to resign it, in consequence of a giddi-ness and distressful feeling in my eyes, which, as I had drunk but a single glass of ale, must, I knew, have been the effect of the tobacco. Soon after, deeming myself recovered, I sallied forth to my engagement; but the walk and the fresh air brought on all the symptoms again, and, I had scarcely entered the minister's drawing-room, and opened a small pacquet of letters, which he had received from Bristol for me; ere I sank back on the sofa in a sort of swoon rather than sleep. Fortunately I had found just time enough to inform him of the confused state of my feelings, and of the occasion. For here and thus I lay, my face like a wall that is white-washing, *deathy* pale and with the cold drops of perspiration running down it from my forehead, while one after another there dropt in the different gentlemen, who had been invited to meet, and spend the evening with me, to the number of from fifteen to twenty. As the poison of tobacco acts but for a short time, I at length awoke from insensibility, and looked round on the party, my eyes dazzled by the candles which had been lighted in the interim. By way of relieving my embarrassment one of the gentlemen began the conversation, with '*Have you seen a paper to-day, Mr Coleridge?*' 'Sir!' (I replied, rubbing my eyes,) 'I am far from convinced, that a christian is permitted to read either newspapers or any other works of merely political and temporary interest.' This remark so ludicrously inapposite to, or rather, incongruous with, the purpose, for which I was known to have visited Birmingham, and to assist me in which they were all then met, produced an involuntary and general burst of laughter; and seldom indeed have I passed so many delightful hours, as I enjoyed in that room from the moment of that laugh to an early hour the next morning.

" . . . Both then and afterwards they all joined in dissuading me from proceeding with my scheme; assured me in the most friendly and yet most flattering expressions, that the employment was neither fit for me, nor I fit for the employment. Yet if I had determined on persevering in it, they promised to exert themselves to the utmost to procure subscribers, and insisted that I should make no more applications in person. . . ." [16]

Coleridge accepted the latter part of their advice and so great was the impression he had made upon the company, with such a will did they set to work, that he was able to report to Wade a few days later that, although he had been feeling "extremely unwell" [17] he had secured about one hundred subscribers. Almost all the subscribers were eventually obtained in this way, by proxy.

At Birmingham, also, Coleridge was heard and admired almost

to the point of idolatry by a young man, Charles Lloyd,[18] son of a wealthy Quaker banker.

From Birmingham, Coleridge travelled at four in the morning of January 22 to Derby.[19] There he met, among others, Joseph Wright[20] the painter; Erasmus Darwin,[21] who twitted him upon his Unitarianism and whose refusal to examine the credentials of revealed religion provoked some strictures from his visitor; and Jedediah Strutt,[22] cotton-spinner and successor to Sir Richard Arkwright, who gave him an introduction to John Fellowes of Nottingham. Coleridge also made the acquaintance of a widow, Mrs Elizabeth Evans of Darley Hall, daughter of Jedediah and sister of William and Joseph Strutt. Dr Crompton, a connexion of Mrs Evans, to whom he had an introduction from Edwards, was not in the town at the time.[23]

At Nottingham, which he visited three days later, his reception was even more cordial. On the evening of his arrival he was invited to a dinner by Mr Fellowes where "On the right hand of the president whom should I see but an old College acquaintance? He hallooed out: *'Coleridge, by God!'* Mr Wright, the president of the day, was his relation—a man of immense fortune. I dined at his house yesterday, and underwent the intolerable slavery of a dinner of three courses. We sat down at four o'clock, and it was six before the cloth was removed."[24]

Coleridge preached a charity sermon at Nottingham[25]—this time in "coloured clothes"[26]—which he hoped would be useful: "as the *Sacred* may eventually help off the *profane*—and my *Sermons* spread a sort of sanctity over my *Sedition*."[27] In this instance, at least, it was ". . . to very good purpose, as far as the plate went. Indeed (altogether) my sermon was the best composition I have ever been guilty of."[28]

He made a most favourable impression on the townsfolk: "I have got among all the first families in Nottingham, and am marvellously caressed, but to tell you the truth I am quite home sick—owing to this long long absence from Bristol. I was at the *Ball*, last night. . . ."[29]

Sheffield was the next town to be visited. Coleridge arrived on February 1. Here, business did not prosper. He called on a Mr Kirby;[30] he was out. Then on a Mr Naylor;[31] he, too, was out. He walked four miles to catch the latter man, who was on a visit to a Mr Meanley [32]—"that tobacco-toothed Parson with a majestic periphery of guts."[33] But he might have spared himself the trouble. Mr Naylor he discovered to be part owner of the *Sheffield Iris*—the paper run by the unfortunate James Montgomery,[34] the poet, who spent much of 1795 and the following year in prison for libel "on a bloody-minded magistrate."[35] As the sale of *The Watchman* might have interfered with that of the *Iris*, Coleridge did not pursue his campaign in that town. He passed to Manchester on the 5th of February,[36] then to Liverpool, where the Cromptons of Eton House feted him. From this town Coleridge was called home by the illness of his wife. He abandoned a visit to London, returning to Bristol by way of Lichfield,[37] where, although he had done unexpectedly well, his spirits began to desert him. He wrote to Wade:

> "I verily believe no poor fellow's idea-pot ever bubbled up so vehemently with fears, doubts, and difficulties, as mine does at present. Heaven grant it may not boil over, and put out the fire! I am almost heartless. My past life seems to me like a dream, a feverish dream—all one gloomy huddle of strange actions and dim-discovered motives;—friendships lost by indolence, and happiness murdered by mismanaged sensibility. The present hour I seem in a quick-set hedge of embarrassments."[38]

In February he arrived back in Bristol. He had with him the names of nearly one thousand subscribers. He had made numerous friends. He appeared to have good reason for elation. But the joys of "projecting,"[39] as Cottle called it, were over. Now, faced with the task of carrying out the projected scheme, his ardour dwindled and died. *The Watchman* began to assume the lineaments of an inescapable and unpleasant eight-day fate. The magazine, so ecstatically conceived, became a drag, a hindrance—its writing and assembly received the epithet of "Watch drudgery."[40] The London booksellers were showing a strange and alarming reluctance to take up *The Watchman*.[41] Pains, aches, domestic strife, illness in the home, together with the editor's chronic inability to achieve anything in the nature of settled work, combined to hinder the production of the magazine. The very fact that *The Watchman* had been promised to appear, that it was no longer a delight but a duty, paralysed the faculties of the unhappy Coleridge. February 5 came and *The Watchman* did not appear.

The days passed and subscribers waited in vain. But on the first day of March the opening number was circulated.

The prospects of *The Watchman* failing were always considerable—the inconvenience to the subscriber of eight-day intervals between publication dates far outweighed the advantage to the publishers of escaping the newspaper tax; the political news was obtainable in greater detail and more frequently in papers devoted especially to that purpose; and the schoolmasterly tone adopted by the editor must have proved almost intolerable to readers who wished to form their own opinions. But Coleridge made assurance doubly sure. The more of a burden *The Watchman* became, the less heart had he for the production of original matter. He fulfilled the prophecy of G. L. Tuckett almost to the letter. Writing to Coleridge, Robert Allen repeats Tuckett's words on hearing of the venture: "You know how subject Coleridge is to fits of idleness. Now, I'll lay any wager, Allen, that after three or four numbers the sheets will contain nothing but parliamentary debates, and Coleridge will add a note at the bottom of the page: 'I should think myself deficient in my duty to the Public if I did not give these interesting debates at *full* length.' " [42]

The chief difference between this and the reality was that Coleridge did not wait three or four numbers. Nor was this all: for, not content with the instruction of his readers by pages of almost unmitigated dullness, Coleridge discomfited radical and conservative reader alike with devastating impartiality—launching attacks on both Godwin and his fellow "Philosophers and Friends of Freedom" [43] for their atheism and immoral teaching, and on Pitt for his reactionary repression.

In the second number he lost, as he calculated some years later, "near five hundred of my subscribers at one blow" [44] by printing an essay *On National Fasts* [45] with the motto from Isaiah, "Wherefore My Bowels shall sound like an Harp." [46] He carried off the indiscretion as best he could, writing to Edwards: "My Essay on Fasting has given *great* offence to the *Slang-men* of *Calvin's Superstition-Shops*, and even Mr Estlin does not altogether relish it, and as to *Hort*,[47] he sighs more than he *says*." [48] But the enormity of his offence began to dawn upon him and very soon he was writing Poole: "The 'Essay on Fasting' I am ashamed of; but it is one of my misfortunes that I am obliged to publish *extempore* as well as compose." [49]

Very soon, his "Jacobin and Democratic Patrons" [50] patronized him no longer. They abandoned *The Watchman* in disgust. There were left only a few faithful Unitarian supporters and the brothers Poole. Richard Poole wrote to congratulate him upon the general excellence of the paper, offering at the same time certain suggestions for its improvement. [51] A letter from Tom Poole on the Slave Trade appeared in the fifth number. For the rest, the editor's correspondence consisted either of abuse or of appeals for more poetry in place of "democratic scurrility." [52] "I detest your principles; your prose I think very so-so; but your poetry is so *exquisitely* beautiful, so *gorgeously* sublime, that I take in your 'Watchman' solely on account of it" [53] wrote one reader, typical of many. Meanwhile the subscribers fell off with ominous regularity.

The poems were slowly being completed amidst pitiful outcries from their author whenever the printer so much as hinted that overdue copy should be supplied. Coleridge's excuses for the nonappearance of promised verses continued to the end as did his lamentations at the demands of the printer. On one occasion, on February 22, his sensitiveness had reached such a pitch that the mere report that a messenger from Cottle had called (actually upon quite another matter) while he was out, brought upon the unoffending head of Cottle the following typical outburst:

"MY DEAR SIR,

"It is my duty and business to thank God for all his dispensations, and to believe them the best possible; but, indeed, I think I should have been more thankful, if he had made me a journeyman shoemaker, instead of an author by trade. I have left my friends; I have left plenty; I have left that ease which would have secured a literary immortality, and have enabled me to give the public works conceived in moments of inspiration, and polished with leisurely solicitude; and, alas! for what have I left them? For [Southey] who deserted me in the hour of distress, and for a scheme of virtue impracticable and romantic! So I am forced to write for bread; write the flights of poetic enthusiasm, when every minute I am hearing a groan from my wife. Groans, and complaints, and sickness! The present hour I am in a quick-set hedge of embarrassment, and whichever way I turn, a thorn runs into me! The future is cloud and thick darkness! Poverty, perhaps, and the thin faces of them that want bread, looking up to me! Nor is this all. My happiest moments for composition are broken in upon by the reflection that I must make haste. I am too late! I am already months behind! I have received my pay beforehand! O, wayward and desultory spirit of Genius. Ill canst thou brook a taskmaster! The tenderest touch from the hand of obligation wounds thee like a scourge of scorpions.

"I have been composing in the fields this morning, and came home to write down the first rude sheet of my preface, when I heard that your man had brought a note from you. I have not seen it, but I guess its contents. I am writing as fast as I can. Depend on it you shall not be out of pocket for me! I feel what I owe you, and independently of this I love you as a friend; indeed, so much, that I regret, seriously regret, that you have been my copyholder.

"If I have written petulantly, forgive me. God knows I am sore all over. God bless you, and believe me that, setting gratitude aside, I love and esteem you, and have your interest at heart full as much as my own." 54

At home, Coleridge faced a situation not perhaps as formidable as his imagination painted it, but bad enough. The romantic bloom of his marriage was being worn off by the constant presence of Mrs Fricker, by Sarah's illness, by chronic financial uncertainty, and by the strain of preparing for the press at regular intervals a magazine in which he had lost interest, and poems for which he had long since been paid.

He had two consolations: opium; and the not inconsiderable pleasure of describing his misery to others. Edwards was his chief confidant at this time.

"Since I last wrote you," he says on March 12, "I have been tottering on the edge of madness—my mind overbalanced on the contra side of Happiness—the repeated blunders of the printer, the forgetfulness and blunders of my associate [the faithful Burnett], etc. etc., abroad, and at home Mrs Coleridge dangerously ill, and expected hourly to miscarry. Such has been my situation for this last fortnight—I have been obliged to take Laudanum almost every night." 55

In the same letter, however, he reports an improvement in the situation, ending, "Mrs Coleridge in languid but not unaffectionate terms desires me to give her love to you." 56

Eight days later he is explaining the comments of some dissatisfied readers of *The Watchman* with a certain amusement:

" . . . But I am perfectly callous except where Disapprobation tends to diminish Profit—there indeed I am all one tremble of Sensibility, marriage having taught me the wonderful uses of the vulgar article of life *Bread*. My wife, my wife's Mother and little Brother, and George Burnett—five mouths opening and shutting as I pull the string! Dear Edwards I know you do not altogether approve of direct Petitions to Deity—but in case there *should* be any efficacy in them, out of pity to the Guts of others pray for the Brains of your friend." [57]

His wife's illness came to a head:

"Yesterday Mrs Coleridge miscarried—but without danger and with little pain. From the first fortnight of pregnancy she has been so very ill with the Fever, that she could afford no nourishment to the Thing which might have been a Newton or an Hartley —it has wasted and melted away. I think the subject of Pregnancy the most obscure of all God's dispensations—it seems coercive against Immaterialism—it starts uneasy doubts respecting Immortality and the pangs which the Woman suffers seem inexplicable in the system of [Nature]. Other pains are only friendly admonitions that we are not acting as Nature requires—but here are pains most horrible in consequence of having obeyed Nature-Queen." [58]

Then his mind stepped a little further:

"How is it," he asks, "that Dr Priestly is not an atheist? He asserts in three different places that God not only *does*, but *is* everything—But if God be everything, everything is God: which is all the Atheists assert. An eating, drinking, lustful God with no unity of *consciousness*—these appear to me the unavoidable Inferences from his philosophy—Has not Dr Priestly forgotten that Incomprehensibility is as necessary an attribute of the First Cause as Love, or Poems, or Intelligence?" [59]

Estlin's sermons did not meet with his entire approval. "Mr Estlin hath not the Catenulating faculty," he tells Edwards. "We want the silk-thread that ought to run through the Pearl Chain of Ratiocination." [60]

Just before the end of the month, the Coleridges moved into a house in Oxford Street, "beautifully situated" [61]—and in which

Coleridge suggested Poole might have a room for seven shillings a week and so attend the lectures of Dr Beddoes.[62] This scheme failing, he was driven to seek comfort in letters; and although his troubles appeared to be on the mend, he could not resist the use of his latest metaphors:

> "Since last you saw me," he wrote Poole, "I have been well nigh distracted. The repeated and most injurious blunders of my printer out of doors, and Mrs Coleridge's increasing danger at home, added to the gloomy prospect of so many mouths to open and shut like puppets, as I move the string in the eating and drinking way— but why complain to you? Misery is an article with which every market is so glutted, that it can answer no one's purpose to export it. *Alas! oh! ah! oh! oh!*" [63]

At last the poems were completed, even *Religious Musings* revised to his satisfaction—"I torture the poem and myself with corrections" [64]—and dispatched finally to Cottle in proof, together with four sonnets by Charles Lamb. On April 16th the poems were published.[65] They were, on the whole, well reviewed. Coleridge, writing to Estlin, drew a picture of triumph: "The Reviews have been wonderful," he says. "The Monthly [66] has *cataracted* panegyric on my poems, the Critical [67] has *cascaded* it; and the Analytical [68] has *dribbled* it with very tolerable civility. The Monthly has at least done justice to my Religious Musings; they place it 'on the very top of the scale of sublimity' ! ! !" [69]

The *Religious Musings* overshadowed all else in bulk; and Coleridge, though he rated it somewhat lower than the *Monthly* reviewer, nevertheless wrote to Benjamin Flower, "I rest all my poetical credit on the *Religious Musings.*" [70]

In fact, Coleridge was mistaken. The poems in the volume which best foreshadow the poet in his maturity are the shorter, lighter pieces. *The Eolian Harp, Songs of the Pixies, Lines written at Shurton Bars,* for instance, are poems which come to mind. Unlike the major poem of the book, these are saved by their spontaneity and lightness from the confusion of overmuch thought. They contain hints of the sensuous mysticism, the delicate precision of imagery, in which Coleridge was to excel.

Religious Musings, on the other hand, suffers from a multiplicity of ideas. As a work of art, it cannot be regarded seriously. It contains occasional passages of beauty, such as:

                        Such delights
As float to earth, permitted visitants!
When in some hour of solemn jubilee
The massy gates of Paradise are thrown
Wide open, and forth come in fragments wild
Sweet echoes of unearthly melodies,
And odours snatched from beds of Amaranth,
And they, that from the crystal river of life
Spring up on freshened wing, ambrosial gales!
The favoured good man in his lonely walk
Perceives them, and his silent spirit drinks
Strange bliss which he shall recognise in heaven.
And such delights, such strange beatitudes
Seize on my young anticipating heart
When that blest future rushes on my view! [71]

In the poem as a whole, however, the influence of Schiller is
too obvious, the endeavour to outstride the existing literary
fashion too crude, the flaming rhetoric and extravagant hyperbole
altogether too blatant.

As a record of Coleridge's thought and beliefs and the influences which had shaped them, however, the poem is important.
It was first conceived at Cambridge late in 1794 and so was close
on two years in the writing. Coleridge's mind had run the gamut
of many emotions during that time. His three great passions of
this period—politics, metaphysics, and theology—all find their
place in the poem. The Revolution in France, translated into
idealistic terms, is heralded (despite the fact that the author was
actually on the point of turning from it in disgust when the poem
was published) as:

                stung to rage by Pity, eloquent men
Have roused with pealing voice the unnumbered tribes
That toil and groan and bleed, hungry and blind. [72]

Though the more menacing aspect of the Revolution was not,
indeed could not, be hidden from him:

                            lo! the Giant Frenzy
Uprooting empires with his whirlwind arm
Mocketh high Heaven; burst hideous from the cell
Where the old Hag, unconquerable, huge,
Creation's eyeless drudge, black Ruin, sits
Nursing the impatient earthquake. [73]

Pantisocracy is here:

> each heart
> Self-governed, the vast family of Love
> Raised from the common earth by common toil
> Enjoy the equal produce.[74]

Priestley, one of the fathers of Unitarianism, receives a tribute:

> patriot, and saint, and sage,
> Him, full of years, from his loved native land
> Statesmen blood stained and priests idolatrous
> By dark lies maddening the blind multitude
> Drove with vain hate.[75]

But more important are signs of Coleridge's emergence, through the philosophy of Hartley and Berkeley, into an intuitive belief rather than a faith wholly explicable by the reason. There is the "sublime system"[76] of Berkeley:

> Believe thou, O my soul,
> Life is a vision shadowy of Truth;
> And vice, and anguish, and the wormy grave,
> Shapes of a dream! The veiling clouds retire,
> And lo! the Throne of the redeeming God
> Forth flashing unimaginable day
> Wraps in one blaze earth, heaven, and deepest hell.
> Contemplant Spirits! ye that hover o'er
> With untired gaze the immeasurable fount
> Ebullient with creative Deity![77]

Hartley is hailed as:

> he of mortal kind
> Wisest, he first who marked the ideal tribes
> Up the fine fibres through the sentient brain.[78]

And his monads

> ye of plastic power, that interfused
> Roll through the grosser and material mass
> In organizing surge! Holies of God!
> (And what if Monads of the infinite mind?)[79]

The idea of reason alone as a basis for a philosophy of life had never flourished in Coleridge's mind—it was indeed fundamentally alien to his nature. A few months before, talking with Darwin at Derby, he had remarked: ". . . it was infinitely consoling to me, to find that the arguments of so great a man, adduced against the existence of a God, and the evidences of revealed religion, were such as had startled me at fifteen, but had become the objects of my smile at twenty." [80]

At the same time as his poems were published, *The Watchman* carried an article of its editor in which he attacked the teachings of the very apostle of reason, Godwin himself.[81] Godwin, it is true, had always been the hero of Southey rather than of his friend [82]— the *Morning Chronicle* sonnet of December two years before was written partly by Southey. Nevertheless, the appearance of *Religious Musings* and the public break with Godwinian doctrines marked a definite change or, more correctly, a righting, of heart on the part of the poet. The *Religious Musings* expresses but the beginnings of a long, unfinished spiritual pilgrimage; yet the faith that is set out there is more settled, more certain than it had ever been before or than it was to be again for many years.

Coleridge had never been truly at ease in the presence of the materialist philosophy. Circumstances had driven his mind in that direction but his heart, his instinct, had shied at the inevitable implications of such a philosophy. For some time, he found in Hartley the consolation of a materialist who was also a believer— or perhaps he would be better described, with his admirer, as a believer who professed himself a materialist.

Hartley, however, was not his only support. He had never entirely lost touch with the Christian mystics; and in a later passage referring to this period, Coleridge expresses his debt to them and sets the stage for a brief consideration of the philosophy shining through the somewhat turgid stanzas of the *Religious Musings*: [83]

> " . . . there exist folios on the human understanding, and the nature of man, which would have a far juster claim to their high rank and celebrity, if in the whole huge volume there could be found as much fulness of heart and intellect, as burst forth in many a simple page of GEORGE FOX, JACOB BEHMEN [Boehme,] and even of Behmen's commentator, the pious and fervid WILLIAM LAW.
>
> "The feeling of gratitude, which I cherish towards these men has caused me to digress further than I had foreseen or proposed; but to have passed them over in an historical sketch of my literary life and opinions, would have seemed to me like the denial of a

debt, the concealment of a boon. For the writings of these mystics acted in no slight degree to prevent my mind from being imprisoned within the outline of any single dogmatic system. They contributed to keep alive the *heart* in the *head*; gave me an indistinct, yet stirring and working presentiment, that all the products of the mere *reflective* faculty partook of DEATH, and were as the rattling twigs and sprays in winter, into which a sap was yet to be propelled from some root to which I had not penetrated, if they were to afford my soul either food or shelter. If they were too often a moving cloud of smoke to me by day, yet they were always a pillar of fire throughout the night, during my wanderings through the wilderness of doubt, and enabled me to skirt, without crossing, the sandy deserts of utter unbelief." [84]

Mainly, however, the mystics had not to convert so much as remind. Coleridge discovered, partly with their aid, but more by instinct, that reason had serious—and for him, unacceptable—limitations. The exercise of reason alone left a vital part of him unsatisfied. It could not, in his experience, attain reality. For that, he came to believe that an act of will, a moral act, was necessary. He must will himself into communion with the Absolute:

> God only to behold, and know, and feel,
> Till by exclusive consciousness of God
> All self-annihilated it shall make
> God its Identity: God all in all!
> We and our Father one! [85]

And this he will do:

> on Meditation's heaven-ward wing
> Soaring aloft I breathe the empyreal air
> Of Love, omnific, omnipresent Love [86]

of which:

> 'Tis the sublime of man,
> Our noontide Majesty, to know ourselves
> Parts and proportions of one wondrous whole! [87]

But this is the ideal, not only unrealized, but by most men unrecognized:

> A sordid solitary thing,
> Mid countless brethren with a lonely heart
> Through courts and cities the smooth savage roams
> Feeling himself, his own low self the whole;

> When he by sacred sympathy might make
> The whole one Self! Self, that no alien knows!
> Self, far diffused as Fancy's wing can travel!
> Self, spreading still! Oblivious of its own,
> Yet all of all possessing! This is Faith! [88]

Indeed, the whole spirit and argument of the poem shows how his faith had steadied and formulated itself by April 1796; but his plainest declaration is made in the lines:

> There is one Mind, one omnipresent Mind,
> Omnific. His most holy name is Love.
> Truth of subliming import! with the which
> Who feeds and saturates his constant soul,
> He from his small particular orbit flies
> With blest outstarting! [89]

Coleridge's satisfaction with the general reception of his poems was soon overshadowed by the precarious position into which *The Watchman* rapidly descended. For a short while—though even this period was longer than the facts warranted—he assumed an optimism, qualified only by the amount of uninteresting work which regular production of the magazine entailed.

On March 30, he informs Poole that *The Watchman* "succeeds so as to yield a *bread-and-cheesish* profit." [90] But in the same letter the ominous hint of new planning appears. "I find," writes Coleridge, "that 'The Watchman' comes more easy to me, so that I shall begin about my Christian Lectures." [91] What he really meant was that he had abandoned his attempts to make the magazine in any serious sense a vehicle for original work. It was his way of announcing the final decease of enthusiasm for the project.

After this, the descent was unimpeded, either by hope or effort, on the part of the editor. As early as April 11, he began to express serious doubts to Poole: "To tell you the truth, I do not think *The Watchman* will succeed. Hitherto I have scarcely sold enough to pay the expenses." [92]

The previous month, foreseeing disaster, he had cast round once more for some fresh means of obtaining money. The activities of Count Rumford, the scientist and economist, had been followed by Coleridge with increasing admiration. He had read in the Count's essays an account of the garden cities which had been established in Bavaria, in which neither beggars nor vagrants had a place and where soldiers might live as small-holders in the intervals of warfare and military training. The Count was a versatile man, his inventiveness extending even to the designing of smokeless chimneys and draughtless fireplaces in the houses of these cities.

These essays awakened all the frustrated horticulturist in Coleridge. He reviewed them with acclamation in *The Watchman* of April 2. He honoured the ingenious nobleman with a sonnet.[93] He became inspired by a plan which would at once benefit England and place a small amount of money in the hands of its author. He proposed nothing less than that he should Rumfordize the cities of Bristol, Birmingham and Manchester by the composition and circulation of one and the same pamphlet, to be entitled *Considerations Addressed to the inhabitants of Bristol, on a subject of importance, (unconnected with Politics) by S.T.C.*—the pamphlet to be suitably altered by the author to fit each city. The pamphlet was to extend to three sheets and to be priced at one shilling. And to spare the civic pride of each centre: "I could so order it, that by writing to a particular friend, at both places, the pamphlet should be thought to have been written *at* each place, as it certainly would be *for* each place."[94] He put it to Cottle. For playing so considerable a part in the replanning of provincial cities, the author asked as recompense, either a division of the profits from the sale of the pamphlet or "(which indeed I should prefer) would you give me three guineas, for the copy-right?"[95] Cottle sent Coleridge the three guineas but "forebore the publication."[96]

On May 5, Coleridge received "a truly fraternal letter" from Poole's brother Richard, "containing good and acceptable advice. He deems my *Religious Musings* 'too metaphysical for common readers.' I answer—the poem was not written for common readers."[97] He had ill news for Poole. "My house," he goes on, "is at present a house of mourning. My wife's mother has lived dying this last six weeks, and she is not yet dead; and the husband of my wife's sister, Robert Lovell, died on Tuesday morning of a putrid fever and has left an infant and widow."[98] He had spent a dreadful night with his sister-in-law while Lovell lay dying.

By this time, the last hope of *The Watchman* had fled. The hours of the magazine were numbered. Coleridge announced the coming demise of the paper. He was resigned, to the point of pleasure:

"With regard to my own affairs they are as bad as the most rampant philo-despot could wish in the moment of cursing. After No. XII [actually X] I shall cease to cry the state of the political atmosphere. . . . *O Watchman, thou hast watched in vain!*—said the Prophet Ezekiel, when, I suppose, he was taking a prophetic glimpse of my sorrow-sallowed cheeks." [99]

In the same breath as he announced defeat from one quarter, however, Coleridge thrust again, twice, at the fates:

"My plans are reduced to two;—the first unpracticable,—the second not likely to succeed.

"Plan 1. I am studying German, and in about six weeks shall be able to read that language with tolerable fluency. Now I have some thoughts of making a proposal to Robinson, the great London bookseller, of translating all the works of Schiller, which would make a portly quarto, on condition that he should pay my journey and my wife's to and from Jena, a cheap German University where Schiller resides, and allow me two guineas each quarto sheet, which would maintain me. If I could realize this scheme, I should there study chemistry and anatomy, and bring over with me all the works of Semler and Michaelis, the German theologians, and of Kant, the great German metaphysician. On my return I would commence a school for eight young men at £105 each, proposing to perfect them in the following studies in this order:—1. Man as an Animal;—including the complete knowledge of anatomy, chemistry, mechanics, and optics:—2. Man as an Intellectual Being;—including the ancient metaphysics, the system of Locke and Hartley—of the Scotch philosophers— and the new Kantean system:—3. Man as a Religious Being;— including an historic summary of all religions, and of the arguments for and against natural and revealed religion. Then proceeding from the individual to the aggregate of individuals, and disregarding all chronology, except that of mind, I should perfect them: 1.—in the history of savage tribes; 2.—of semi-barbarous nations; 3.—of nations emerging from semi-barbarism; 4.—of civilized states; 5.—of luxurious states; 6.—of revolutionary states; 7.—of colonies. During these studies I should intermix the knowledge of languages, and instruct my scholars in *belles lettres* and the principles of composition. . . .

My second plan is to become a Dissenting Minister, and abjure politics and casual literature. Preaching for hire is not right; because it must prove a strong temptation to continue to profess what I may have ceased to believe, *if ever* maturer judgment with wider and deeper reading should lessen or destroy my faith in Christianity. But though not right in itself, it may become right by the greater wrongness of the only alternative—the remaining in neediness and uncertainty. That in the one case I should be exposed to temptation is a mere contingency; that under necessitous circumstances I am exposed to great and frequent temptations is a melancholy certainty." [100]

The Watchman said farewell to its few remaining readers on May 13. The editorial obituary notice came to the point at once. "Henceforward," said the 'Address' to the reader, "I shall cease to cry the state of the Political atmosphere. . . . The reason is short and satisfactory. The work does not pay its expenses." [101] The editor, guide and director of his readers' moral and political education to the bitter end, then took the opportunity of recommending suitable papers for them to read in order that the gap left by the retirement of *The Watchman* might be filled; at the same time doing a good turn to a friend and occasional employer; and perhaps smoothing the path for future contributions of his own:

> " . . . Those who took it [*The Watchman*] in as a mere journal of weekly events, must have been unacquainted with 'FLOWER's CAMBRIDGE INTELLIGENCER'; a Newspaper, the style and composition of which would claim distinguished praise, even among the productions of literary leisure. . . . Those, on the other hand, who expected from it much and varied original composition, have naturally relinquished it in favour of the 'New MONTHLY MAGAZINE'; a work which has almost monopolized the talent of the country. . . ." [102]

Poole had not waited for *The Watchman*'s last moments. Late in March he had been working upon the first draft of the letter which, together with a sum of money amounting to £35 or £40, reached Coleridge on the day the magazine breathed its last. The document read:

> "It has occurred to the undersigned sincere Friends [103] and ardent Admirers of the Author of the 'Monody on the Death of Chatterton,' and of various other pieces in verse and prose of unusual merit,—it has occurred to these to deposit five guineas each in the hands of John Cruikshank, to be by him immediately sent to the person above alluded to. They further propose

[111]

annually, for the six succeeding years, in the week preceding Lady Day, each of them to transmit the like sum to the said John Cruikshank, to be immediately after the receipt thereof applied to the same use as the first deposit now made. And this they pledge themselves to each other to perform, in full confidence that a benevolent Providence will enable them, with unabated cheerfulness, to fulfil their engagement. It is their pride and their pleasure, if it seemeth good to S. T. Coleridge, to offer him this trifling mark of their esteem, gratitude, and admiration: esteem generated from a knowledge of his heart; gratitude for instruction and delight received by his writings and conversation; admiration produced by contemplating the extraordinary marks of sublime genius with which he is endowed.

"They are also irresistibly impelled to make this offer by recollecting the disinterested traits in his character; by recollecting that he has abandoned all, even the most seducing allurements, for a situation which leaves him only the triumphs of an honest heart, which are in truth exquisite, and the power to retain and disseminate those principles which he believes to be true, and to tend to the happiness of man. He also united himself to her he loves, regardless of every other consideration. It is thus that, lifted above the cupidity almost inwoven in the hearts of all who live in such a society as ours, he presents in himself an object which awakens every tender and noble sensation of the soul.

"His friends have now only to exhort him to proceed with a steady and unceasing ardour in the career which he has entered; to exert with kindness his argumentative powers, his forcible eloquence, his keen satire, his learning, in the support and dissemination of what he honestly believes to be the truth; but above all, to invoke that Muse who is the source of his highest delight, who will effectually assist him to that end, and who while she instructs the ignorant, will not cease to charm and elevate the wise.

"They cannot better close this testimony of their mutual regard for him than by the fond wish that all anguish of mind may be removed from his dwelling, and that he may in peace enjoy the most perfect domestic felicity, added to every intellectual delectation, until the awful moment when the curtain shall be withdrawn, and to his soul shall be disclosed that relation existing between man and the great Invisible, which, during his residence here, his ardent eye had often sought in vain." [104]

Coleridge was not deceived by Poole's kindly ruse. He replied instantly:

"Poole! The Spirit, who counts the throbbings of the solitary heart, knows that what my feelings ought to be, such they are. If

S. T. COLERIDGE IN 1796

"This portrait of Mr Coleridge was taken by Mr Robert Hancock, in crayons. The likeness was much admired at the time, and has an additional interest, from having been drawn when Mr C.'s spirits were in a state of depression, on account of the failure of his 'Watchman.' The *dress* is precisely that which Mr Coleridge wore when he preached his first sermon, in Mr Jardine's chapel, at Bath."   JOSEPH COTTLE

" . . . preaching by the way in most of the great towns, as an hireless volunteer, in a blue and white waistcoat, that not a rag of the woman of Babylon might be seen on me."   COLERIDGE

" . . . a round-faced man in a short black coat (like a shooting jacket) which hardly seemed to have been made for him, but who seemed to be talking at a great rate. . . . He did not cease while he staid; nor has he since, that I know of. . . . His forehead was broad and high, light as if built of ivory, with large projecting eyebrows, and his eyes rolling beneath them like a sea with darkened lustre. . . . His mouth was gross, voluptuous, open, eloquent; his chin good-humoured and round; but his nose, the rudder of the face, the index of the will, was small, feeble, nothing. . . . Coleridge in his person was rather above the common size, inclining to the corpulent. . . . His hair was then black and glossy as the raven's, and fell in smooth masses over his forehead."   WILLIAM HAZLITT

"At first I thought him very plain, that is, for about three minutes: he is pale and thin, has a wide mouth, thick lips, and not very good teeth, longish loose-growing half-curling rough black hair. But if you hear him speak for five minutes you think no more of them. His eye is large and full, not dark but grey; such an eye as would receive from a heavy soul the dullest expression; but it speaks every emotion of his animated mind; it has more of the 'poet's eye in a fine frenzy rolling' than I ever witnessed. He has dark eyebrows, and an overhanging forehead."   DOROTHY WORDSWORTH

(By permission of the National Portrait Gallery)

it were in my power to give you anything which I have not already given, I should be oppressed by the letter now before me. But no! I feel myself rich in being poor; and because I have nothing to bestow, I know how much I have bestowed. Perhaps I shall not make myself intelligible; but the strong and unmixed affection which I bear to you seems to exclude all emotions of gratitude, and renders even the principle of esteem latent and inert. Its presence is not perceptible, though its absence could not be endured.

"Concerning the scheme itself, I am undetermined. Not that I am ashamed to receive—God forbid! I will make every possible exertion; my industry shall be at least commensurate with my learning and talents;—if these do not procure for me and mine the necessary comforts of life, I can receive as I would bestow, and, in either case—receiving or bestowing—be equally grateful to my Almighty Benefactor. I am undetermined, therefore—not because I receive with pain and reluctance, but—because I suspect that you attribute to others your own enthusiasm of benevolence; as if the sun should say, 'With how rich a purple those opposite windows are burning!' But with God's permission I shall talk with you on this subject." [105]

He quickly followed his letter with a visit in person to Stowey, Poole meeting his request for a horse "of tolerable meekness" [106] to carry him from Bridgwater.

In consequence of Lovell's death, Coleridge wrote: "We are all become more religious than we were." [107]

At Stowey, he was able to express his thanks in person for the gift, to recover from the shock—whether of relief or of vexation —at *The Watchman*'s ending, and to discuss future plans with his mentor. Coleridge remained with Poole until the 29th of May, meeting the formidable Charlotte again, with even less happy result. This time her remarks on the visitor—whom, strangely enough, she seems to have forgotten—were as brief as, though perhaps less penetrating than, before. In the evening of May 15, her diary says, ". . . who should arrive but the famous Mr Coldridge! I cannot form an opinion of him in so short a time, but could have discovered, if I had not before heard it, that he is clever, and a very short acquaintance will unfold that he is extremely vain of it." [108]

The cessation of his eight-day burden added new vigour to Coleridge's correspondence. He was already writing, spasmodically, to Poole, Estlin, Lamb, Edwards, Wordsworth, and Benjamin Flower. Now he acquired another correspondent in the person of John Thelwall,[109] a notorious revolutionary and sometime poet, who had narrowly escaped transportation for high treason.

Thelwall had taken exception to a description of himself in the *Conciones ad Populum* as an "unsupported Malcontent." No sooner had Coleridge, aided by a gift copy of his poems, smoothed out this misunderstanding—the words, he explained were "caught up from the well-known contemptuous pages of Aristocratic Writers" [110]—than another arose. His *Watchman* article on Godwin distressed Thelwall, a great admirer of *Political Justice*. Coleridge defended his article at some length:

"You have given me the affection of a brother, and I repay you in kind. Your letters demand my friendship and deserve my esteem; the zeal with which you have attacked my supposed *delusions* proves that you are deeply interested for *me*, and interested even to agitation for what you believe to be *truth*. You deem that I have treated 'systems and opinions with the furious prejudices of the conventicle, and the illiberal dogmatism of the cynic'; that I have 'layed about me on this side and on that with the sledge hammer of abuse.' I have, you think, imitated the 'old sect in politics and morals' in their 'outrageous violence,' and have sunk into the 'clownish fierceness of intolerant prejudice.' I have 'branded' the presumptuous children of scepticism 'with vile epithets and hunted them down with abuse.' '*These be hard words, Citizen! and I will be bold to say they are not to be justified*' by the unfortunate page which has occasioned them. The only passage in it which appears *offensive* (I am not now inquiring concerning the truth or falsehood of this or the remaining passages) is the following: 'You have studied Mr. G.'s Essay on Politi[cal] Jus[tice] —but to think filial affection folly, gratitude a crime, marriage injustice, and the promiscuous intercourse of the sexes right and wise, may class you among the despisers of vulgar prejudices, but cannot increase the probability that you are a *patriot*. But you act up to your principles—so much the worse. Your principles are villainous ones. I would not entrust my wife or sister to you; think you I would entrust my country?' My dear Thelwall! how are these opinions connected with the conventicle more than with the Stoa, the Lyceum, or the grove of Academus? I do not perceive that to attack *adultery* is more characteristic of *Christian* prejudices than the prejudices of the disciples of Aristotle, Zeno, or Socrates. In truth, the offensive sentence, 'Your principles are villainous,' was suggested by the Peripatetic Sage who divides bad men into two classes. The first he calls 'wet or intemperate sinners'—men who are hurried into vice by their appetites, but *acknowledge* their actions to be vicious; these are reclaimable. The second class he names *dry* villains—men who are not only vicious but who (the steams from the polluted heart rising up and gathering round the head) have brought themselves and others to believe that *vice* is *virtue*. We mean these men when we say men of bad *principles*—guilt is out of the question. I am a necessarian, and of course deny the possibility of it. However, a letter is not the place for reasoning." [111]

Nevertheless, Coleridge continued to reason for many pages; and the conflict of words, which provoked the customary outburst of epithet but which was conducted on each side with great good humour, quickly established a friendship that was to have an important effect on Coleridge's future. For the time, however, Coleridge contented himself with a prolonged attempt to persuade this aetheistical sheep within the Unitarian fold. Nor, indeed, did he limit himself to the spiritual side of Thelwall's education. The two wrangled solemnly and at great length upon literature. They did not from the very first see eye to eye upon *Religious Musings*; that was scarcely to be expected. Coleridge also sought Thelwall's conversion in certain moral crusades. There was the question of sugar, for instance. The throwing out of the Bill for the Abolition of the Slave Trade had determined its supporters to forgo the use of all commodities produced by slave labour. Sugar was, of course, one of the most important; and Coleridge and Poole, both ardent supporters of the bill, renounced the use of sugar. Thelwall, however, remained impenitent: "On the subject of using sugar, etc.," wrote Coleridge, "I will write you a long and serious letter. This grieves me more than you [imagine]. I hope I shall be able by severe and unadorned reasoning to convince you you are wrong." [112]

In this same letter of May 13, Coleridge refers to "A very dear friend of mine, who is, in my opinion, the best poet of the age. . . ." [113] He spoke of Wordsworth; and although the friendship at this time could have been "very dear" in little more than a literary sense, there is no doubt that the two poets were coming into closer contact with one another. The actual records of their early meetings are obscure and even contradictory.[114] That they met for the first time the previous autumn may be considered certain. Following Wordsworth's letter of January to Cottle in which he sends his compliments to Coleridge,[115] comes Coleridge's reference to the "very dear friend" a few months later; and at the end of the same month Coleridge is sending Lamb the manuscript of Wordsworth's *Guilt and Sorrow* to read and return direct to the author.[116] There was thus already an epistolary friendship between the two, if nothing more. Now another meeting took place, of considerable importance to Coleridge. The exact date of this meeting is not known. It may have occurred in spring, it may have occurred in autumn, but it was certainly in the year 1796. Many years later Coleridge, forgetting the earlier meeting, writes of this second meeting:

"I was in my twenty-fourth year, when I had the happiness of knowing Mr. Wordsworth personally, and while memory lasts, I shall hardly forget the sudden effect produced on my mind, by his recitation of a manuscript poem, which still remains unpublished, but of which the stanza, and tone of style, were the same as those of the 'Female Vagrant,' as originally printed in the first volume of the 'Lyrical Ballads.' There was here no mark of strained thought, or forced diction, no crowd or turbulence of imagery; and, as the poet hath himself well described in his lines 'on revisiting the Wye,' manly reflection, and human associations had given both variety, and an additional interest to natural objects, which in the passion and appetite of the first love they had seemed to him neither to need or permit. The occasional obscurities, which had risen from an imperfect controul over the resources of his native language, had almost wholly disappeared, together with that worse defect of arbitrary and illogical phrases, at once hackneyed, and fantastic, which hold so distinguished a place in the *technique* of ordinary poetry, and will, more or less, alloy the earlier poems of the truest genius, unless the attention has been specifically directed to their worthlessness and incongruity."[117]

The meeting confirmed the interest which each had felt in the other and his work; the recitation went far to formulate in Coleridge's mind the famous distinction, made later, between fancy and imagination; and it encouraged views on poetic theory and practice already held by Coleridge, strengthening both his aversion to the existing poetic order and his determination to supplant it—and so, lending new force to the impulse which was to produce, only two years later, the epoch-making *Lyrical Ballads*.

But these connexions, though the breath of life to Coleridge, were necessarily subservient to the provision of sustenance for himself and his wife. Sarah—unwell, and in the first flush of bewilderment and dismay that a man whom she had understood to possess such brilliant abilities, to be so far above the ordinary run of mankind, should find so much difficulty in making even sufficient money for them to live upon—was not an ideal companion. "Groans, and complaints, and sickness!" [118] writes the harassed Coleridge.

The annuity raised by Poole, together with a smaller gift of fifteen guineas from Estlin, preserved him for a time from complete disaster. His debts on *The Watchman* (some eighty or ninety pounds) were paid by Wade: "a man by no means affluent, a dear friend, who attached himself to me from my first arrival at Bristol." [119] He had received the money for the poems comprising the first volume long before they were completed. He had had neither time nor inclination to write more. He made a little money by reviewing in the *Critical Review* and by occasional contributions to the *Monthly Magazine*, but the sums he received were insufficient to support a family. He had to cast about for some fresh way of earning money.

Coleridge actually went so far as to meditate a revival of *The Watchman*—proof either of desperation or supreme optimism—and Lamb, at the end of May, was advising him to exclude all political matter and confine himself to original literary contributions when he issued the magazine again.[120] But the idea came to nothing. Instead, Coleridge's mind turned naturally enough to the easiest, if not, indeed, the only apparent way out of the dilemma. His preaching on the recent *Watchman* tour had contributed, perhaps more than any other single factor, to the success of the journey. Unlike his first two sermons in Mr Jardine's chapel at Bath in January, which, if Cottle is to be believed, were no more than uninteresting repetitions of lectures at Bristol, on the Corn Laws and the Hair Powder Tax,[121] those in the north and midlands astonished and delighted congregations accustomed to uninspired delivery and threadbare themes. This young man in his blue coat and white waistcoat preached in language as eloquent as his voice was pleasant to hear; expressing thoughts as unconventional as his manner was inspiring. Known and liked before he left Bristol by Estlin, a power among the Unitarians, he quickly made friends and admirers of the ministers and potentates of the chapels wherever he went. Coleridge's conversation flourished most when it assumed the character of a monologue; and although his companions were at almost all times content to remain listeners, possession of a pulpit naturally ensured that his gift was exercised unhindered.

Many who heard him on his tour were reluctant to lose the chance of such a leader for their Congregation, such a power for the cause. That the wish had been expressed is confirmed by the plan which Coleridge had already mentioned to Poole and by his later correspondence with Estlin.[122] Hence his proposal to enliven a decidedly desolate future by entering the ministry—if, indeed, he did not take up the position as tutor which seems to have been mentioned to him at much the same time.[123]

The interest in him as a prospective Unitarian minister culminated in Nottingham. Early in June he was waiting for a definite offer. His scruples, put before Poole, still exercised his mind. He repeated them a little later to Lamb, who urged him to disregard them. "Concerning the unitarian chapel," Lamb wrote, "the salary is the only scruple that the most rigid moralist would admit as valid. Concerning the tutorage—is not the salary low, and absence from your family unavoidable?" [124] For six weeks after his visit to Poole in May, Coleridge did not write to his friend; his reason being: "Suspense has been the real cause of my silence. Day after day I have confidently expected some decisive letter." [125]

Before those in Nottingham had made up their minds, however, before the tutorship could materialize, another, and, on the face of it, more tangible offer had been made. Dr Beddoes,[126] who had been made known to Coleridge by Cottle soon after his arrival in Bristol, stepped into the breach.

Now, on the first day of July, Dr Beddoes passed on to Coleridge a suggestion that Perry of the *Morning Chronicle*, who had just attended, in Bristol, the death of Grey, his co-editor, might engage Coleridge as assistant editor. This would, of course, entail a removal to London. Coleridge had been a fairly regular contributor to this, the best paper of the day. An answer was wanted at once.

Reluctantly, Coleridge agreed. He poured out his doubts and difficulties to Estlin, who was away on a holiday:

"My feet began mechanically to move towards your house—I was most uncomfortably situated. You and Mrs Estlin out of Bristol—and Charles Danvers out of Bristol—and even Mr Wade was absent. So I had nobody to speak to on the subject except Mr Cottle, which I did, and he advised me to write to Perry immediately and accept his proposal. I did so, and expect to-morrow a letter from him with particulars, which I will immediately acquaint you with. My heart is very heavy, for I love Bristol and I do not love London. Besides, local and temporary politics are my aversion—they narrow the understanding, they narrow the heart, they fret the temper. But there are two Giants leagued together, whose most imperious commands I must obey, however reluctant—their names are *BREAD* and *CHEESE*." [127]

He was no more cheerful when he wrote to Poole on the same day: He told his friend of his reluctance to leave Bristol for London, his fears that "local and temporary politics . . . at least acidulate the heart." [128] Nevertheless:

"I have . . . accepted a proposal of Mr Perry's . . . with a heavy and reluctant heart . . . Dr. D. thinks it a good opening on account of Grey's death; but I rather think that the intention is to employ me as a mere hackney without any share of the profits. However, as I am doing nothing, and in the prospect of doing nothing settled, I was afraid to give way to the *omenings* of my heart. . . . I think of hiring a horse for a couple of days, and galloping down to you to have all your advice. . . ." [129]

He also informed Lamb, who had just been refused a week's holiday at Bristol, that he would shortly be coming to live near him in London. [130] From Poole, he received a letter of introduction to a business friend, Purkis of Brentford. [131]

Whether he visited London or not is unknown. In any event, this offer, in common with the tutorship and the Unitarian ministry, came to nothing. It is possible that Coleridge himself rejected all three. For an inhabitant of another town that he had visited on his tour now came to the rescue with a very much more attractive suggestion. From Derby, Coleridge received an invitation from the wealthy Mrs Evans to take up residence with her at Darley Hall as tutor to her two boys. She suggested that he come to Darley with his wife and discuss the matter.

Coleridge accepted the invitation with alacrity. For a week or two he and Sarah basked in the luxury of Darley. The three of them, despite hindrances, became deliciously intimate. After "a very trying week for the Widow"—for "Mr. William Strutt was cold, and his arguments (when he used *any* to Mrs. Evans) dissuasive—and the Grandfather Evans and Mr. Walter Evans decisive in opposition"—Mrs Evans "determined that the sacrifice of her children, which Mammon, gloomy as Moloch, required, should *not* be given." [132] Everything was settled. Coleridge's plan of education was to be adopted. He was to receive £150 a year. Sarah was to come. They were to be of the family.

In the excitement of the moment, Coleridge hastened down to Ottery, leaving his wife "as my hostage" at Darley—moved to this reconciliation by the tender promptings of the women folk no less than by the intoxication of being in a position to announce to his family that respectability and a settled home were at last to be his portion.

At Ottery he was received amiably; with "transports" by his mother; with "joy and tenderness" by George; with "civility" by the others; [133] and on August 7 he returned to Bristol by way of Stowey, well pleased.

A letter—forwarded by Sarah to Wade, "My poor Samuel," she wrote, "I cannot bear to think of his disappointment" [134]—awaited his return. This "impassioned" letter was from Mrs Evans. "She had determined to hazard all consequences rather than lose me," Coleridge told Estlin, [135] but the guardians of her children had vetoed the plan. The boys, they held, needed school training and discipline.

"Farewell, pure and benevolent spirit," wrote Mrs Evans, "Brother in the family of soul. May a happier fate await you." [136] So far and so soon had the spell of Coleridge worked its way with her.

The rejected one bore up well. "After the first moment," he told Poole, "I was perfectly composed, and from that moment to this have continued calm and light-hearted." [137] He enclosed Mrs Evans' letter, then hurried back to Darley. There was an affecting scene. "Mrs. Evans was much agitated when she met me; I hastened to relieve her embarrassment and—I told her to feel nothing on my account. 'I cannot be said to have lost that which I never had, and I have gained what I should not otherwise have possessed, your acquaintance and esteem.' 'Say rather (she exclaimed) my Love and Veneration.' " [138]

Poole, however, denied the charms of Mrs Evans, was by no means so philosophical. He deplored her weakness of will and waxed pessimistic over the status of women: "I am now convinced," he wrote the next day, "of what I doubted before, that woman is inferiour to man. No man who is capable of willing as ardently as she willed, who had the heart and head she possesses, and understood the object to be attained so well, would vacillate. Woman, thou wast destined to be governed. Let us then bow to destiny." [139]

Meanwhile their hostess was trying, not without success, to cheer her disconsolate guests by sending them for excursions. They stayed at Matlock; visited Oakover, Ilam and Dovedale. [140] Coleridge was soon in the highest spirits: "I was the first fiddle;" he wrote to Wade a little later, "—not in the concerts—but everywhere else, and the company would not spare me twenty minutes together. Sunday I dedicated to the drawing up my sketch of education, which I meant to publish, to try to get a school!" [141]

Nothing came of this; but after Coleridge and his wife had spent ten days in and about Darley and were on the point of leaving, Mrs Evans gave more tangible evidence of her appreciation. She presented Coleridge with £95 and Sarah with all her baby clothes, worth £40. [142]

Nor was this all. Before he left, Coleridge was approached by Dr Crompton with a suggestion that he should open a school at Derby. To start the school, Dr Crompton offered to send three of his own children to Coleridge at £100 per year for the three until the suggested total of children—12 in all—was reached, when the regular fee of 20 guineas each was to be paid. The parents were to pay extra for writing- and drawing-masters. Mrs Evans was to use her influence to obtain pupils.

Coleridge agreed immediately. " . . . Now 12 × 20 guineas = 240 guineas = 252£—and my evenings and mornings at my

Disposal—Good things. So I accepted the offer, it being understood, that if anything better offered, I should accept it." [143] A house in course of building was selected and the rent fixed at £12 a year. The house was to be completed by October, the school to commence the following month. After a talk with Coleridge the landlord even agreed to Rumfordize the chimneys, and the future schoolmaster went away quite content.

Sarah went straight home, leaving her husband to spend a week on his way back at Moseley [144] with Mr Thomas Hawkes, [145] a Unitarian minister. He preached twice on the Sunday, August 21. [146] "Words and phrases," he wrote Poole the next day, "which might perhaps have adequately expressed my feelings, the cold-blooded children of this World have anticipated and exhausted in their unmeaning gabber of flattery. I use common expressions —but they do not convey common feelings. My heart has thanked you. In preaching on Faith yesterday I said that Faith was infinitely better than Good Works—as the cause is greater than the effect—as a fruitful tree is better than it's Fruit and as a friendly Heart is of far higher value than the Kindness which it naturally and *necessarily* prompts. It is for that *friendly Heart* that I now have thanked you: and which I so eagerly accept of. . . ." [147]

Of the same Sunday, he told Estlin: "I preached yesterday morning from Hebrews iv. 1, 2. It was my *chef d'œuvre*. I think of writing it down and publishing it with two other sermons. . . . I lament that my political notoriety prevented my relieving you occasionally at Bristol." [148]

Here, yet another hope appeared to present itself: "I have seen a letter from Mr William Roscoe, author of the *Life of Lorenzo the Magnificent*; a work in two 4to volumes (of which the whole first edition sold in a month); it was addressed to Mr Edwards, the minister here, and entirely related to me. Of me and my compositions he writes in terms of high admiration, and concludes by desiring Mr Edwards to let him know my situation and prospects, and saying that if I would come and settle at Liverpool, he thought a comfortable situation might be procured for me. This day Edwards will write to him." [149]

At Moseley, Coleridge again met Charles Lloyd and completed the conquest begun the previous winter. Lloyd, who was the eldest son, showed as great an inaptitude in his father's business as he expressed distaste for the family faith. He wrote poetry of a kind and leaned heavily, though vaguely, towards republicanism. An attempt to place him in the bank had been a failure. A short season at Edinburgh in preparation for the medical profession was no more successful. He had then rusticated with a friend, writing verses of a melancholy nature.

In the circumstances, his devotion to Coleridge appeared heaven-sent. Coleridge was to open a school at Derby. He would have much time on his hands. Why should not Lloyd live with him and drink in daily wisdom? The thought was no sooner uttered then it became Lloyd's life's ambition. Coleridge, too, flattered, and urged by his unconquerable desire to impart knowledge, smiled upon the scheme with a paternal approval that all too soon broke into an enthusiasm indistinguishable from that of his follower.

At the end of the month, while the proposal was being debated in the family circle, Coleridge left for Bristol. He spent a few days at Stowey;[150] every moment in Poole's company increasing, as usual, his longing for a home near this quiet and considerate friend.

Then he received an invitation to stay with the Lloyd family whilst the future of his admirer, Charles Lloyd, was decided. Coleridge, with his wife's permission, accepted[151] and arrived on September 18. He quickly won the confidence of the father. They had a love of the classics and a detestation of the slave trade in common, and Coleridge created an excellent impression—how excellent, in so short a time, can be gathered by the words of the banker when writing to his second son to announce the scheme:

"Charles is gone to Bristol with intention of persuing his studies under the care of S. T. Coleridge, a very sensible, religious man and an extraordinary poet, who was educated for a clergyman, but for conscience sake declined that office. Thou mayst order Coleridge's 'Poems' of the bookseller at S. Walden (a small octavo) and charge them to my account."[152]

The second day following his arrival, Coleridge's emotions were thrown into a tumult by the news that a son had been born to him. "I was quite annihilated with the suddenness of the information," he told Poole, "and retired to my own room to address myself to my Maker, but I could only offer up to Him the silence of stupefied feelings."[153]

He hurried home, taking with him the young Charles Lloyd,

now his inseparable disciple. He found all well at Bristol but his emotion could be satisfied only by the composition of three sonnets to mother and child.[154] "When I first saw the child," he wrote, "I did not feel that thrill and overflowing of affection which I expected. I looked on it with a melancholy gaze; my mind was intensely contemplative and my heart only sad. But when two hours after I saw it at the bosom of its mother, on her arm, and her eye tearful and watching its little features, then I was thrilled and melted, and gave it the Kiss of a *father*." [155]

The child was not baptized—Coleridge having an aversion to sacramental rites [156]—but was named David Hartley. "I hope that ere he be a man, if God destines him for continuance in this life, his head will be convinced of, and his heart saturated with, the truths so ably supported by that great master of *Christian* Philosophy." [157] Even then Coleridge felt restless—so restless, that a visit to Poole became imperative:

> "My dear, very dear Poole," he wrote, "The heart thoroughly penetrated with the flame of virtuous friendship is in a state of glory; but lest it should be exalted above measure there is given it a thorn in the flesh. I mean that when the friendship of any person forms an essential part of a man's happiness, he will at times be pestered by the little jealousies and solicitudes of imbecile humanity. Since we last parted I have been gloomily dreaming that you did not leave me so affectionately as you were wont to do. Pardon this littleness of heart. . . ." [158]

He eulogizes Lloyd:

> "His joy and gratitude to Heaven for the circumstance of his domestication with me I can scarcely describe to you; and I believe that his fixed plans are of being always with me." [159]

They had been together only four days but Coleridge had lost no time. He sends Poole two of Lloyd's sonnets:

> "The latter of them alludes to the conviction of the truth of Christianity, which he had received from me, for he had been, if not a deist, yet quite a sceptic." [160]

He makes his request:

> "My dearest Poole, can you conveniently receive us in the course of a week? We can both sleep in one bed, which we do now. And I have much, very much to say to you and consult with you about. . . ." [161]

The fact was, that the excitement of an heir was not the only, indeed it was no longer the main cause for his craving to be at Stowey. Once again, he informed Poole, his heart was "heavy"— this time, "respecting Derby." [162] Although Lloyd "wins upon me hourly" [163] he was in no sense a substitute for the sturdy moral support of Poole. Quite the contrary; it was he who leaned, or attempted to lean upon the afflicted Coleridge. And Coleridge was in need of support at this time.

The Derby scheme was rapidly losing what attractiveness it had seemed to possess. On reflection, a school, no matter how limited the number of pupils, and how light the duties, compared unfavourably with the occasional tutorship of two boys in luxurious surroundings and with feminine adulation to sweeten what labour was necessary. A school had about it the deadly promise of 'time-table' work so alarming to Coleridge. It was already beginning to assume the dreaded and familiar shape of a duty, a hard and fast agreement, which never failed to sap his resolution and turn his enthusiasm to foreboding.

There was another and more compelling reason which thrust against the Derby plan. The longing to be close to Poole, to live as he lived, was growing in strength. Not until the first day of November did Coleridge express this wish in writing. But the idea behind the wish, the thought itself, was of long standing, it was in Coleridge's mind before he met Poole. As early as 1794 Coleridge and Southey were, at intervals, both fretting; the one, that he had not been brought up to till the ground; the other, that he had not been made a carpenter. The idea of manual labour as the natural, healthy and ideal method of acquiring a livelihood had been one of the basic points of pantisocracy; indeed, the economic edifice of the scheme depended upon communal labour in the fields. Much of this idea survived the collapse of pantisocracy. It dwelt in Coleridge's mind and, when he came to know Poole, it grew in strength. He saw how that admirable man directed farm, quarry, bark mill and tannery, engaged in labour with his own hands during the day, and then, in the evenings, turned to the development of his mind; and he thirsted to do likewise. Hence, too, his continued interest in and admiration for manual labour as a background to mental and spiritual development. In the days of pantisocracy he had no more than an ideal to pursue. Here the

[125]

ideal was translated into the living example of a man who dwelt only a few miles from him.

Behind Coleridge's reluctance to leave the Bristol district for the midlands or north of England at this time, there was always this desire to be near Poole. The continuous struggle for money and position, a struggle for which Coleridge was peculiarly unfitted, enhanced his eagerness to withdraw to Stowey. And there was a further reason. Literature, he decided, could not of itself support a family. It was, he told Thelwall, " . . . but bread and cheese by chance." [164] He decided to retire to Stowey, to live humbly upon the produce of his garden and whatever reviewing he might secure and poems he might write, and in his spare moments to devote himself "to poetry and to the study of ethics and psychology." [165]

Poole sent back an enthusiastic welcome: " . . . Come both directly. I am all alone. And we will *live*. Yes: I hope we will live." [166] Thereupon, Coleridge and Lloyd made their way to Stowey. Lloyd was introduced. The Derby scheme was discussed, Coleridge's fears and objections to it explained and agreement reached that it should be dropped.

On his return to Bristol, Coleridge wrote Dr Crompton "a long letter" [167] abandoning the idea of the school and was able to tell Poole that he had had in return "a very kind letter." [168] From that moment, all his desires were set upon the attainment of a safe harbourage near his friend.

About this time Southey, who had returned to England and taken rooms almost opposite Coleridge in Bristol, made an attempt to renew their friendship. He sent over a conciliatory note in which he quoted in English a sentence from Schiller's *Conspiracy of Fiesco*, "Fiesco! Fiesco! thou leavest a void in my bosom, which the human race, thrice told, will never fill up." [169] Coleridge responded suitably and a reconciliation of sorts took place. Coleridge refers to Southey in a letter to Thelwall, where he says: "Between ourselves the *enthusiasm* of friendship is not with S. and me . . . 'the blasted oak puts not forth its buds anew.' We are *acquaintances*, and feel *kindliness* towards each other, but I do not *esteem* or *love* Southey as I must esteem and love the man whom I dared call by the holy name of *friend*." [170]

Southey, according to his reminiscences of this time, regarded his former associate with no little contempt.[171] The new acquaintanceship, such as it was, may therefore have been made mainly by or on behalf of the respective wives and sisters.

There now came terrible news from London. Coleridge and Lamb had written frequently to one another since the 'rescue' of the former in January of the previous year. Usually these letters were light-hearted affairs—reminiscences of their Christ's Hospital contemporaries and the Salutation and Cat period, playful thrusts by Lamb at Coleridge's enthusiasm for Rumford and his works, together with earnest literary discussions and much mutual criticism of their poetic achievements. Poems were exchanged freely and as freely criticized; though with little apparent effect beyond the enjoyment such criticism afforded them. Lamb's suggested alterations to Coleridge's poems were rarely accepted; and there is no reason to suppose that Coleridge's amendments would have met a happier fate. Coleridge, however, had the advantage of possessing the manuscripts before they were finally handed to the printer. He was quite unable to resist the temptation of making some last-minute alterations to those of Lamb's poems which were being printed with his—much to the mortification of their creator, who first saw his sonnets, printed, in a form which he certainly never intended they should assume. This occurrence it was which occasioned Lamb's reiterated plea, when next he sent poems to Coleridge: "... spare my Ewe Lambs." [172]

Two days before the end of September this correspondence was tragically interrupted. Lamb's sister Mary, in a fit of insanity, stabbed her mother to death and wounded her father. She was confined in an asylum; and Lamb, upon whose shoulders most of the subsequent proceedings fell, wrote on the 27th to Coleridge in deep distress, informing him of the tragedy and begging him to write "—as religious a letter as possible." [173] Coleridge did so:

> "Your letter, my friend," he wrote, "struck me with a mighty horror. It rushed upon me and stupefied my feelings. You bid me write you a religious letter. I am not a man who would attempt to insult the greatness of your anguish by any other consolation. Heaven knows that in the easiest fortunes there is much dissatisfaction and weariness of spirit; much that calls for the exercise of patience and resignation; but in storms like these, that shake

[127]

the dwelling and make the heart tremble, there is no middle way between despair and the yielding up of the whole spirit unto the guidance of faith. And surely it is a matter of joy that your faith in Jesus has been preserved; the Comforter that should relieve you is not far from you. But as you are a Christian, in the name of that Saviour, who was filled with bitterness and made drunken with wormwood, I conjure you to have recourse in frequent prayer to 'his God and your God'; the God of mercies, and father of all comfort. Your poor father is, I hope, almost senseless of the calamity; the unconscious instrument of Divine Providence knows it not, and your mother is in heaven. It is sweet to be roused from a fearful dream by the song of birds and the gladsome rays of the morning. Ah, how infinitely more sweet to be awakened from the blackness and amazement of a sudden horror by the glories of God manifest and the hallelujahs of angels.

"As to what regards yourself, I approve altogether of your abandoning what you justly call vanities. I look upon you as a man called by sorrow and anguish and a strange desolation of hopes into quietness, and a soul set apart and made peculiar to God! We cannot arrive at any portion of heavenly bliss without in some measure imitating Christ; and they arrive at the largest inheritance who imitate the most difficult parts of his character, and, bowed down and crushed underfoot, cry in fulness of faith, 'Father, thy will be done.'

"I wish above measure to have you for a little while here; no visitants shall blow on the nakedness of your feelings; you shall be quiet, and your spirit may be healed. I see no possible objection, unless your father's helplessness prevent you, and unless you are necessary to him. If this be not the case, I charge you write me that you will come.

"I charge you, my dearest friend, not to dare to encourage gloom or despair. You are a temporary sharer in human miseries that you may be an eternal partaker of the Divine nature. I charge you, if by any means it be possible, come to me." [174]

Letters were exchanged between them with greater frequency although the tone of the correspondence became, naturally, more sober. Lamb, in his first agony of mind, forswore literature and forbade Coleridge to mention the subject. He destroyed his poems and his commonplace books of the Elizabethan dramatists. His letters of this time are, indeed, scarcely recognizable as those of the man of a few weeks before. His entire attitude stiffened and became unlovely. Coleridge announced a new change of plan—

ROBERT SOUTHEY IN 1796

"This Portrait of Mr Southey, by Hancock, was a most happy likeness at the period at which it was taken; admitted to be such by all Mr S.'s friends."

JOSEPH COTTLE

"Tall, dignified, possessing great suavity of manners; an eye, piercing, with a countenance full of genius, kindliness, and intelligence."

JOSEPH COTTLE

" . . . a younger man, without the splendid abilities of Coldridge, though possessing much information, particularly metaphysical, and is more violent in his principles than even Coldridge himself. In Religion, shocking to say in a mere Boy as he is, I fear he wavers between Deism and Atheism."

THOMAS POOLE

"He is a young man of the most rigidly virtuous habits and is I believe exemplary in the discharge of all domestic duties, but though his talents are certainly very remarkable for his years (as far as I can judge) I think them much inferior to the talents of Coleridge."   DOROTHY WORDSWORTH

(By permission of the National Portrait Gallery)

his Stowey venture—and must have been astounded to receive the following reply:

> "My dearest friend, I grieve from my very soul to observe you in your plans of life veering about from this hope to the other, and settling no where. Is it an untoward fatality (speaking humanly) that does this for you, a stubborn irresistible concurrence of events? or lies the fault, as I fear it does, in your own mind? You seem to be taking up splendid schemes of fortune only to lay them down again, and your fortunes are an ignis fatuus that has been conducting you, in thought, from Lancaster Court, Strand,[175] to somewhere near Matlock,[176] then jumping across to Dr Somebody's [177] whose son's tutor you were likely to be, and would to God the dancing demon *may* conduct you at last in peace and comfort to the 'life and labors of a cottager.' [178]" [179]

This change in Lamb was apparent in other matters. Coleridge, by request, though doubtless without reluctance, wrote further "religious" letters for the comfort and edification of Lamb and his sister Mary, who had now recovered her reason. But his efforts met with unexpected rebuffs from a Lamb not unnaturally, but certainly unpleasantly, out of character. Even the theology of his original consolatory letter, which Lamb first described as an "inestimable treasure," [180] was later challenged.[181] Fortunately this was only a phase through which Lamb was passing; and before the year was out the discussions in their letters were resumed, together with Lamb's literary activities, with much of the old enthusiasm.

Another person to whom Coleridge announced his change of plans, was Mr Lloyd at Birmingham. He did so with a portentousness befitting the guardian of a man quite two years his junior; almost, indeed, as one father to another:

> "As the father of Charles Lloyd you are of course in some measure interested in any alteration of my schemes of life; and I feel it a kind of Duty to give you my reasons for any such alteration. I have declined my Derby connection, and determined to retire once for all and utterly from cities and towns: and am about to take a cottage and half a dozen acres of land in an enchanting Situation about eight miles from Bridgewater. My reasons are— that I have cause to believe my Health would be materially impaired by residing in a town, and by the close confinement and anxieties incident to the education of children; that as my days would be

[129]   I

dedicated to Dr Crompton's children, and my evenings to a course of study with my admirable young friend, I should have scarcely a snatch of time for literary occupation; and, above all, because I am anxious that my children should be bred up from earliest infancy in the simplicity of peasants, their food, dress, and habits completely rustic. I never shall, and I never will, have any fortune to leave them: I will leave them therefore hearts that desire little, heads that know how little is to be desired, and hands and arms accustomed to earn that little. I am peculiarly delighted with the 21st verse of the 4th chapter of Tobit, 'And fear not, my son! that we are made poor: for thou hast much wealth, if thou fear God, and depart from all sin and do that which is pleasing in His sight.' Indeed, if I live in cities, my children (if it please the All-good to preserve the one I have, and to give me more), my children, I say, will necessarily become acquainted with politicians and politics—a set of men and a kind of study which I deem highly unfavourable to all Christian graces. I have myself erred greatly in this respect; but, I trust, I have now seen my error. I have accordingly snapped my squeaking baby-trumpet of sedition, and have hung up its fragments in the chamber of Penitences. Your son and I are happy in our connection—our opinions and feelings are as nearly alike as we can expect: and I rely upon the goodness of the All-good that we shall proceed to make each other better and wiser. Charles Lloyd is greatly averse from the common run of society—and so am I—but in a city I could scarcely avoid it. And this, too, has aided my decision in favour of my rustic scheme. We shall reside near a very dear friend of mine, a man versed from childhood in the toils of the Garden and the Field, and from whom I shall receive every addition to my comfort which an earthly friend and adviser can give." [182]

The poems had been selling well. By the middle of October, Cottle was considering a second edition of 500 copies. He proposed to pay Coleridge a further twenty guineas for so doing. As he had already purchased the copyright of the poems with the original thirty guineas, this offer was not ungenerous. Nevertheless, Coleridge's assent was given with exceeding dignity:

"I have no mercenary feelings, I verily believe," he wrote; "but I hate bartering at any time, and with any person; with you it is absolutely intolerable. . . . You must see, Cottle, that whatever money I should receive from you, would result from the circumstances that would give me the same, or more—if I published them on my own account. I mean the sale of the poems. I can therefore have no motive to make such conditions with you, except the wish to omit poems unworthy of me, and the circumstance that our separate properties would aid each other by the union; and whatever advantage this might be to me, it would, of course, be equally so to you. The only difference between my publishing the poems on my own account, and yielding them up to you; the only difference, I say, independent of the above stated differences, is, that, in one case, I retain the property for ever, in the other case, I lose it after two editions." [183]

By the end of the month the first edition was exhausted and Coleridge set to work recasting the poems, adding and deleting, in preparation for the next edition. He also wrote at this time the introductory sonnet to Lloyd's privately and sumptuously printed *Poems on the Death of Priscilla Farmer* [184] with which was also included Lamb's *The Grandame*. Two other pamphlets, the first of poems by Coleridge and Lloyd, the second a collection of sonnets by Bowles, Coleridge, Lamb, Southey, Lloyd, and others, were privately printed a little later in the year. All three were sent to Lamb early in December—his "poetical present." [185]

On the first of November, Coleridge wrote to Poole in much agitation about his proposed removal to Stowey: "My heart has been full, yea, crammed with anxieties about my residence near you. I so ardently desire it, that any disappointment would chill all my faculties, like the fingers of death. . . ." [186] In the same letter he tells Poole that Lloyd is "most certainly a young man of great genius." [187]

Four days later he was again writing. He had suggested renting a house at Adscombe near Stowey but nothing had been heard from Cruikshank, agent of Lord Egmont, the owner. ". . .To live in a beautiful country, and to enure myself as much as possible to the labour of the field . . . to see you daily, to tell you all my thoughts in their first birth, and to hear yours, to be mingling identities with you, as it were . . . Disappointment! Disappointment! dash not from my trembling hand the bowl which almost touches my lips." [188]

He suggests that they obtain a temporary home at Stowey until the Adscombe house can be theirs. Will Poole look out a servant for them—"simple of heart, physiognomically handsome, and scientific in vaccimulgence"? "That last word," he tells Poole, "is a new one, but soft in sound and full of expression. Vaccimulgence! I am pleased with the word." [189]

But if this letter is incoherent in places, there was reason for it. Coleridge had suffered a bad attack of neuritis and his spirits were still fluctuating wildly:

"On Wednesday night," he writes, "I was seized with an intolerable pain from my right temple to the tip of my right shoulder, including my right eye, cheek, jaw, and that side of the throat. I was nearly frantic, and ran about the house naked, endeavouring by every means to excite sensations in different parts of my body, and so so to weaken the enemy by creating division. It continued from one in the morning till half past five, and left me pale and fainting. It came on fitfully, but not so violently, several times on Thursday, and began severer threats towards night; but I took between sixty and seventy drops of laudanum, and *sopped* the Cerberus, just as his mouth began to open. On Friday it only *niggled*, as if the chief had departed from a conquered place, and merely left a small garrison behind, or as if he had evacuated the Corsica, and a few straggling pains only remained. But *this morning* he returned in full force, and his name is Legion. Giant-fiends of a hundred hands, with a shower of arrowy death-pangs he transpierced me, and then he became a wolf, and lay a-gnawing at my bones! I am not mad, most noble Festus, but in sober sadness I have suffered this day more bodily pain than I had before a conception of. My right cheek has certainly been placed with admirable exactness under the focus of some invisible burning-glass, which concentrated all the rays of a Tartarean sun. My medical attendant decides it to be altogether nervous, and that it originates either in severe application, or excessive anxiety. My beloved Poole! in excessive anxiety, I believe it might originate. I have a blister under my right ear, and I take twenty-five drops of laudanum every five hours, the ease and *spirits* gained by which have enabled me to write you this flighty but not exaggerated account." [190]

He informs Cottle at the same time of his indisposition, which evidently prevented the fulfilment of an engagement:

"I feel pain in being disappointed—and still greater pain in the idea of disappointing—but I am seriously ill. The complaint, my medical attendant says, is nervous,—and originating in *mental* causes. I have a Blister under my right ear and I take Laudanum every four hours, 25 drops each dose. God be praised for all things! A faith in goodness *makes* all nature good." [191]

[132]

There is no reason to suppose that Coleridge's use of an opiate was now or for some time to come excessive; certainly it had not assumed the proportions of an unbreakable habit. The present attack was doubtless caused in part, as Coleridge and his doctor said, by worry—his anxiety about the acquisition of a house in or near Stowey was fast approaching hysteria—but there is another possible, if not probable, cause of his pain and of his recourse to laudanum both at this and later times. It is now well known that the pain of neuritis can become unbearable: it is a common practice in hospitals to administer hypnotic drugs in such cases to ensure sleep.[192] Coleridge, as has been seen, was particularly susceptible to rheumatic attacks. Moreover, a very common cause of neuritis is septic teeth. Coleridge's teeth were in a bad condition.[193]

The attack passed off and Coleridge recovered sufficiently to take an active interest in the doings of Thelwall. His fatherly concern in his friend's welfare would not have been without irony at any time; at such a moment, it enters the realms of the fantastic:

> " . . . Have you, my dear Thelwall!—no plan for your future Life? What is the state of your body? Are you sickly, or strong? Is your body so weakened by exertion and anxiety, as to make *stimulants* (such as wine and constant *animal* food) necessary to your Health? How many dear little ones have you? I should like to know all things *about* you, for *you*, I am confident, I know already. *My* plan is formed—but of myself hereafter. You mention'd to me that you are not a man of Greek and Roman Literature. Have you read *variously* in your own language? I mean, have you been in university phrase a *Fag*? Or rather have you read little, but reflected much? I ask these perhaps impertinent Questions because I wish to see you engaged in some *great* works—and for these various and profound study is assuredly a thing needful." [194]

A postscript to the letter shows that Coleridge, when writing to Thelwall at least, still retained a style of language to suit his friend:

> "What a foul song Horne Tooke [195] has committed! It has done harm—the aristocrats glory in it, the worthy among *us* shudder, the ignorant whet their *knives*." [196]

But this letter was only an interlude, an oasis, amidst steadily increasing despair over the delay in the Stowey scheme; and within two days, the guide and arbiter of Thelwall's destinies was writing frantically to Poole, from whom he had heard nothing for perhaps ten days: " . . . My anxieties eat me up. I entreat you, write me, if it be only to say, that you have nothing to write." [197]

There had been more trouble in the Coleridge household. This time, their guest was the cause. Lloyd had been taken with a distressing seizure:

> " . . . his distemper (which may with equal propriety be named either Somnambulism, or frightful Reverie, or *Epilepsy from accumulated feelings*) is alarming. He falls all at once into a kind of night-mair: and all the Realities round him mingle with, and form a part of, the strange Dream. All his voluntary powers are suspended; but he perceives every thing and hears every thing, and whatever he perceives and hears he perverts into the substance of his delirious Vision. He has had two principal fits, and the last has left a feebleness behind and occasional flightiness. Dr Beddoes has been called in." [198]

It is scarcely any wonder that Coleridge cries, at the end of his letter: "I want consolation, my friend! my Brother! Write and console me!" [199]

Coleridge had already written to Mr Lloyd informing him of his son's illness and refuting a suggestion that the proposed life at Stowey would be "monastic rather than Christian": [200] ". . . Can he be deemed monastic who is married, and employed in rearing his children?—who *personally* preaches the truth to his friends and neighbours, and who endeavours to instruct tho' Absent by the Press? In what line of Life could I be more *actively* employed? . . . Shall I not be an Agriculturist, an Husband, a Father, and a *Priest* after the order of *Peace*? an *hireless* Priest?" [201] With boundless optimism, he outlined the plan of education which Charles Lloyd would undergo whilst under his supervision at Stowey:

> "While your Son remains with me, he will, of course, be acquiring that knowledge and those powers of Intellect which are necessary as the *foundation* of excellence in all professions, rather than the immediate science of *any*. *Languages* will engross one or two hours in every day: the *elements* of Chemistry, Geometry, Mechanics, and Optics the remaining hours of study. After tolerable proficiency in these, we shall proceed to the study of *Man* and of *Men*—I mean, Metaphysics and History—and finally,

to a thorough examination of the Jewish and Christian Dispensations, their doctrines and evidences; an examination necessary
for all men, but peculiarly so to your son, if he be destined for a
medical man." [202]

Not three weeks had passed, however, before a complete
change came over Coleridge's mind. The reason for this change
was ostensibly Charles Lloyd's unfitness for the profession of a
doctor: "Will you permit me, Sir! to write of Charles Lloyd with
freedom?" asked Coleridge in this new letter. "I do not think he
ever will endure, whatever might be the consequences, to practise
as a physician, or to undertake any commercial employment. . . .
What then remains? I know of nothing but agriculture. . . ." [203]

In his first supposition Coleridge was doubtless right. Nevertheless, his real objection to continuing, or even beginning the
plan he had himself suggested a few days before, was really due
to other considerations. Lloyd's illness had been followed by a fit
of melancholy that brought upon his head the rebuke of a sonnet
from his mentor—*Addressed to a Young Man of Fortune who
abandoned himself to an indolent and causeless melancholy* was the
title of this poem.

Charles Lloyd's delicacy threw much work on to Sarah and her
husband; and his devotion to Coleridge, though flattering, appeared more and more likely, together with the wide gaps in his
knowledge, to put his tutor to greater pains than Coleridge was
prepared to go despite the brave words of the educational plan.
Coleridge therefore decided that their relationship must be rendered more indefinite, the status of Lloyd as pupil altered to the
less compromising one of welcome guest. Hence, on December 4,
Mr Lloyd was informed:

> "I think it my duty to acquaint you with the nature of my con-
> nection with your Son. If he be to stay with me, I can neither be
> his tutor or fellow-student, nor in any way impart a regular system
> of knowledge. My *days* I shall devote to the acquirement of
> *practical* husbandry and horticulture . . . and my evenings will be
> fully employed in fulfilling my engagements with the 'Critical
> Review' and 'New Monthly Magazine.' If, therefore, your Son
> occupy a room in my cottage, he will be there merely as a Lodger
> and Friend; and the only money I shall *receive* from him will be
> the sum which his *board* and *lodging* will cost *me* . . . I shall keep
> no servant." [204]

And so, after Lloyd had paid a visit home, it was arranged. Mr Lloyd agreed to pay the sum of £80 a year on behalf of his son. He had not yet done with his criticisms of the proposed retirement to Stowey, asking what Coleridge would do without companions. He brought upon himself a highly dignified reply —the more so, because Poole also had expressed a fear that Coleridge would feel the loss of his Bristol friends:

> "I shall have six companions," wrote Coleridge: "My Sara, my babe, my own shaping and disquisitive mind, my books, my beloved friend Thomas Poole, and lastly, Nature looking at me with a thousand looks of beauty, and speaking to me in a thousand melodies of love. If I were capable of being tired with all these, I should then detect a vice in my nature, and would fly to habitual solitude to eradicate it." [205]

Still no news was heard from Poole. Coleridge's desire appeared as far from fulfilment as ever. He attempted to console himself by conveying his rural determination to Thelwall. This he did in the midst of an interesting, though unflattering description of himself in response to a request by Thelwall, who had answered his questions of a few days earlier.

> " . . . my face, unless when animated by immediate eloquence, expresses great sloth, and great, indeed, almost idiotic good-nature. 'Tis a mere carcass of a face; fat, flabby, and expressive chiefly of inexpression. Yet I am told that my eyes, eyebrows, and forehead are physiognomically good; but of this the deponent knoweth not. As to my shape, 'tis a good shape enough if measured, but my gait is awkward, and the walk of the whole man indicates *indolence capable of energies*. I am, and ever have been, a great reader, and have read almost everything—a library cormorant. I am *deep* in all out of the way books, whether of monkish times, or of the puritanical era. I have read and digested most of the historical writers; but I do not *like* history. Metaphysics and poetry and 'facts of mind,' that is, accounts of all the strange phantasms that ever possessed 'your philosophy'; dreamers, from Thoth the Egyptian to Taylor the English pagan, are my darling studies. In short, I seldom read except to amuse myself, and I am almost always reading. Of useful knowledge, I am a so-so chemist, and I love chemistry. All else is *blank*; but I *will* be (please God) an horticulturalist and a farmer. I compose very little, and I absolutely hate composition, and such is my dislike that even a sense of duty is sometimes too weak to overpower it.

"I cannot breath through my nose, so my mouth, with sensual thick lips, is almost always open. In conversation I am impassioned, and oppose what I deem error with an eagerness which is often mistaken for personal asperity; but I am ever so swallowed up in the *thing* that I perfectly forget my *opponent*. Such am I." [206]

He asks Thelwall to buy certain books for him—Iamblichus, Proclus, Julian, Porphyry, Plotinus, Sidonius Apollinaris [207]—a list which proves that the Neo-platonists still held his interest.

To Thelwall, also, he replies to certain criticisms of his poems. Thelwall not only accused his friend's poetry of deviating from "nature and simplicity" [208]—he actually attacked the work of Bowles as Della Cruscan; a charge which, as Coleridge says, "cuts the skin and surface of my heart." [209] For himself, Coleridge admits the fault and goes on to explain that:

" . . . I feel strongly and I think strongly, but I seldom feel without thinking or think without feeling. Hence, though my poetry has in general a hue of tenderness or passion over it, yet it seldom exhibits unmixed and simple tenderness or passion. My philosophical opinions are blended with or deduced from my feelings, and this, I think, peculiarises my style of writing, and, like everything else, it is sometimes a beauty and sometimes a fault. But do not let us introduce an Act of Uniformity against Poets. I have room enough in *my* brain to admire, aye, and almost equally, the *head* and fancy of Akenside, and the heart and fancy of Bowles, the solemn lordliness of Milton, and the divine chit-chat of Cowper." [210]

Not all of his correspondence with Thelwall dealt with literature. Many pages of earnest religious argument were poured out before the London free-thinker, partly in defence of Coleridge's own theology as displayed in *Religious Musings* but also, though Coleridge expressly denied any attempt to convert his friend, [211] doubtless not without hope of rescuing Thelwall from the atheistical clutches of Godwin.

Coleridge's contempt for Godwin was steadily increasing—the more so, doubtless, because of Thelwall's championship of him. As Godwin's iniquities appeared to him to increase, Coleridge's indignation rose. He meditated a reply to Godwin's teachings that would once and for all expose their baseness. Indeed, he more than meditated a reply; in his imagination this reply was actually in course of production. It was, in his mind's eye, complete at the booksellers; and it was at no time easy for Coleridge to distinguish between the two stages of reality.

The book was announced in general terms to Thelwall; [212] but to Flower, at Cambridge, Coleridge was more specific:

> "My answer to Godwin," he wrote early in December, "will be a six shilling Octavo; and is designed to shew not only the absurdities and wickedness of *his* system, but to detect what appear to me the defects of all the systems of morality before and since Christ. . . . My last chapter will attack the credulity, superstition, calumnies, and hypocrisy of the present race of Infidels. Many things have fallen out to retard the work; but I hope, that it will appear shortly after Christmas, at the farthest. I have endeavoured to make it a cheap book; and it will contain as much matter as is usually sold for eight shillings." [213]

This work, in common with many another offspring of Coleridge's mind, stopped short as an aspiration in one of Coleridge's notebooks. [214] He had begun keeping these notebooks — his "flycatchers" [215] — a few years before, at Cambridge or Bristol. He continued to keep them until his death. He kept them as he might be expected to do—without order, method, date. They were the repository, scrawled down haphazard, often unfinished, as they occurred to him, of his thoughts, ambitions, and emotions. The notebooks, like their writer, reflect almost every conceivable interest, and, being written without any public in view, they are in many ways the most revealing of all Coleridge's writings.

The most notable single feature shown by the entries is a perception of nature at once exceptionally delicate, truthful, and subtle—the raw material for those exquisite lines to be found scattered throughout Coleridge's greatest poems. But the notebooks serve an even wider purpose in illustrating the range of Coleridge's mind; and above all, something of the charm of a man whose thoughts could leap from the careful recording of a tempting recipe to the note of twenty-seven major works to be written—none of which ever reached a further stage; who could in the same breath express with sublime understanding some particularly complicated and obscure philosophical truth, and bare his heart in an excess of misery and self-pity that the ordinary man can with difficulty begin to comprehend. [216]

At last, towards the end of November, Poole replied. His news was not particularly encouraging. The only cottage he could find to take the place of Adscombe, or to be used until the Adscombe house became available, was a small, ugly building close to the main street in Stowey. Poole did not think this cottage would suit the Coleridges at all. He did not advise his friend to take it. But he quite mistook his man and the intensity of Coleridge's longing to be at Stowey.

Coleridge, in his overwrought condition, would have accepted any accommodation that brought him into the haven of Poole's society. He received the news with enthusiasm. They would be "more than content"[217] to live in the cottage for a time. He asked Poole to take it for a year: "it's vicinity to you shall overbalance its Defects."[218] He hoped they could move in within the next three weeks, for by that time, at Christmas, they would be obliged to leave their present rooms. He ends enthusiastically: "I will *instruct* the maid in *cooking*."[219]

Subsequently, Poole paid a short visit to London. On December 11, Coleridge writes a joyous letter of welcome to the returned friend. He assumes that Poole has taken the necessary steps to rent the cottage, and anticipates the joys of the new home. He is full of new resolutions: "I mean to work *very hard*," he told Poole, "as Cook, Butler, Scullion, Shoe-cleaner, occasional Nurse, Gardener, Hind, Pig-protector, Chaplain, Secretary, Poet, Reviewer, and *omnium-botherum* shilling-Scavenger. In other words, I shall keep no servant, and will cultivate my land-acre and my wise-acres, as well as I can."[220]

But Poole had been thinking matters over. It seemed to him, on reflection, that Coleridge would not benefit by removing to Stowey. The loss of Coleridge's Bristol friends, the expense of moving, the discomfort of the cottage, the probable hostility of neighbours on account of his political views—all decided Poole to advise against the removal. He therefore wrote on his return suggesting gently that Coleridge would be wise to reconsider the idea. He had made enquiries, and told Coleridge of a house that was available at Acton, outside Bristol.

The letters crossed in the post. To Coleridge, Poole's change of front came as a shock, the more severe in that it was totally unexpected. He wrote a heartbroken letter, followed the same night and the next day by one even more frantic:[221]

[139]

" . . . The tumult of my spirits has now subsided, but the Damp struck into my very heart; and there I feel it. O my God! my God! where am I to find rest? Disappointment follows disappointment, and Hope seems given me merely to prevent my becoming callous to Misery. Now I know not where to turn myself. I was on my way to the City Library, and wrote an answer to it there. Since I have returned I have been poring into a book, as a shew for not looking at my wife and the baby. By God, I dare not look at them. Acton! The very name makes me grind my teeth! What am I to do there?

" 'You will have a good garden; you may, I doubt not, have ground.' But am I not ignorant as a child of everything that concerns the garden and the ground? and shall I have one human being there who will instruct me? The House too—what should I do with it? We want but two rooms, or three at the furthest. And the country around is intolerably flat. I would as soon live on the banks of a Dutch canal! And no one human being near me for whom I should, or could, care a rush! No one walk where the beauties of nature might endear solitude to me! There is one Ghost that I *am* afraid of; with that I should be perpetually haunted in this same cursed Acton—the hideous Ghost of departed Hope. O Poole! how could *you* make such a proposal to me? I have compelled myself to reperuse your letter, if by any means I may be able to penetrate into your motives. I find three reasons assigned for my not settling at Stowey. The first, the distance from my friends and the Press. This I answered in the former letter. As to my friends, what can they do for me? And as to the Press, even if Cottle had not promised to correct it for me, yet I might as well be fifty miles from it as twelve, for any purpose of correcting. Secondly, the expense of moving. Well, but I must move to Acton, and what will the difference be? Perhaps three guineas. . . . I would give three guineas that you had not assigned this reason. Thirdly, the wretchedness of that cottage, which alone we can get. But surely, in the house which I saw, *two* rooms may be found, which, by a little green list and a carpet, and a slight alteration in the fireplace, may be made to exclude the cold: and this is all we want. Besides, it will be but for a while. If Cruikshank cannot buy and repair Adscombe, I have no doubt that my friends here and at Birmingham would, some of them, purchase it. So much for the reasons: but these cannot be the real reasons. I was with you for a week, and then we talked over the whole scheme, and you approved of it, and I gave up Derby. More than nine weeks have elapsed since then, and you saw and examined the cottage, and you knew every other of these reasons, if reasons they can be called. Surely, surely, my friend, something has occurred which you have not mentioned to me. Your mother has manifested a strong dislike to our living near you—or something or other; for the reasons you have assigned tell me nothing except that there are reasons which you have not assigned.

"Pardon, if I write vehemently. I meant to have written calmly; but bitterness of soul came upon me. Mrs Coleridge has observed the workings of my face while I have been writing, and is entreating to know what is the matter. I dread to show her your letter. I dread it. My God! my God! What if she should dare to think that my most beloved friend has grown cold towards me!

"Tuesday morning, 11 o'clock.—After an unquiet and almost sleepless night, I resume my pen. As the sentiments over leaf came into my heart, I will not suppress them. I would keep a letter by me which I wrote to a mere acquaintance, lest anything unwise should be found in it; but my friend ought to know not only what my sentiments are, but what my feelings were.

"I am, indeed, perplexed and cast down. My first plan, you know, was this—My family was to have consisted of Charles Lloyd, my wife and wife's mother, my infant, the servant, and myself.

"My means of maintaining them—Eighty pounds a year from Charles Lloyd, and forty from the Review and Magazine. My time was to have been divided into four parts: 1. Three hours after breakfast to studies with C. L. 2. The remaining hours till dinner to our garden. 3. From after dinner till tea, to letter-writing and domestic quietness. 4. From tea till prayer-time to the reviews, magazines, and other literary labours.

"In this plan I calculated nothing on my garden but amusement. In the mean time I heard from Birmingham that Lloyd's father had declared that he should insist on his son's returning to him at the close of a twelvemonth. What am I to do then? I shall be again afloat on the wide sea, unpiloted and unprovisioned. I determined to devote *my whole day* to the acquirement of practical horticulture, to part with Lloyd immediately, and live without a servant. Lloyd intreated me to give up the Review and Magazine, and devote the evenings to him, but this would be to give up a permanent for a temporary situation, and after subtracting £40 from C. Ll.'s £80 in return for the Review business, and then calculating the expense of a servant, a less severe mode of general living, and Lloyd's own board and lodging, the remaining £40 would make but a poor figure. And what was I to do at the end of a twelvemonth? In the mean time Mrs Fricker's son could not be got out as an apprentice—he was too young, and premiumless, and no one would take him; and the old lady herself manifested a great aversion to leaving Bristol. I recurred therefore to my first

[141]

promise of allowing her £20 a year; but all her furniture must of course be returned, and enough only remains to furnish one bedroom and a kitchen-parlour.

"If Charles Lloyd and the servant went with me I must have bought new furniture to the amount of £40 or £50, which, if not Impossibility in person, was Impossibility's first cousin. We determined to live by ourselves. We arranged our time, money, and employments. We found it not only practicable *but easy*; and Mrs Coleridge entered with enthusiasm into the scheme.

"To Mrs Coleridge the nursing and sewing only would have belonged; the rest I took upon myself, and since our resolution have been learning the practice. With only two rooms and two people—their wants severely simple—no great labour can there be in their waiting upon themselves. Our washing we should put out. I should have devoted my whole head, heart, and body to my acre and a half of garden land, and my evenings to literature. Mr and Mrs Estlin approved, admired, and applauded the scheme, and thought it not only highly virtuous, but highly prudent. In the course of a year and a half, I doubt not that I should feel myself independent, for my bodily strength would have increased, and I should have been weaned from animal food, so as never to touch it but once a week; and there can be no shadow of a doubt that an acre and a half of land, divided properly, and managed properly, would maintain a small family in *everything* but clothes and rent. What had I to ask of my friends? Not money; for a temporary relief of my want is nothing, removes no gnawing of anxiety, and debases the dignity of man. Not their interest. What could their interest (supposing they had any) do for me? I can accept no place in state, church, or dissenting meeting. Nothing remains possible but a school, or writer to a newspaper, or my present plan. I could not love the man who advised me to keep a school, or write for a newspaper. He must have a hard heart. What then could I ask of my friends? What of Mr Wade? Nothing. What of Mr Cottle? Nothing.... What of Thomas Poole? O! a great deal. Instruction, daily advice, society—everything necessary to my feelings and the realization of my innocent independence. You know it would be impossible for me to learn *everything* myself. To pass across my garden once or twice a day, for five minutes, to set me right, and cheer me with the sight of a friend's face, would be more to me than hundreds. Your letter was not a kind one. One week only and I must leave my house, and yet in one week you advise me to alter the plan which I had been three months framing, and in which you must have known by the letters I wrote you, during my illness, that I was interested even to an excess and violence of Hope. And to abandon this plan for darkness and a renewal of anxieties which might be fatal to me! Not one word have you mentioned how I am to live, or even exist, supposing I were to go to Acton. Surely, surely, you do not advise me to lean with the whole weight of my necessities on the Press? Ghosts indeed! I should be haunted with ghosts enough—the ghosts of Otway and Chatterton, and the phantasms of a wife broken-hearted, and a hunger-bitten baby! O Thomas Poole! Thomas Poole! if you did but know what a Father and a Husband must feel who toils with his brain for uncertain bread! I dare not think of it. The evil face of Frenzy looks at me. The husbandman puts his seed in the ground, and the goodness, power, and wisdom of God have pledged themselves that he shall have bread, and health, and quietness in return for industry, and simplicity of wants and innocence. The AUTHOR scatters his seed—with aching head, and wasted health, and all the heart-leapings of anxiety; and the follies, the vices, and the fickleness of man promise him printers' bills and the Debtors' Side of Newgate as full and suffi-cient payment.

"Charles Lloyd is at Birmingham. I hear from him daily. In his yesterday's letter he says: 'My dearest friend, everything seems clearing around me. My friends enter fully into my views. They seem altogether to have abandoned any ambitious views on my account. My health has been very good since I left you; and I own I look forward with more pleasure than ever to a permanent con-nection with you. Hitherto I could only look forward to the pleasures of a year. All beyond was dark and uncertain. My father now completely acquiesces in my abandoning the prospect of any profession or trade. If God grant me health, there now remains no obstacle to a completion of my most sanguine wishes.' Charles Lloyd will furnish his own room, and feels it his duty to be in all things his own servant. He will put up a press-bed, so that one room will be his bedchamber and parlour; and I shall settle with him the hours and seasons of our being together, and the hours and seasons of our being apart. But I shall rely on him for nothing except his own maintenance.

"As to the poems, they are Cottle's property, not mine. There is no obstacle from me—no new poems intended to be put in the volume, except the 'Visions of the Maid of Orleans.' . . . But literature, though I shall never abandon it, will always be a secondary object with me. My poetic vanity and my political *furor* have been exhaled; and I would rather be an expert, self-main-taining gardener than a Milton, if I could not unite both.

"My *friend*, wherein I have written impetuously, pardon me! and consider what I have suffered, and still am suffering, in con-sequence of your letter. . . .

"Finally, my Friend! if your opinion of me and your attachment to me remain unaltered, and if you have assigned the true reasons which urged you to dissuade me from a settlement at Stowey, and if indeed (provided such settlement were consistent with my good and happiness), it would give you unmixed pleasure, I adhere to Stowey, and consider the time from last evening as a distempered dream. But if any circumstances have occurred that have lessened your love or esteem or confidence; or if there be objections to my settling in Stowey on your own account, or any other objections than what you have urged, I doubt not you will declare them openly and unreservedly to me, in your answer to this, which I shall expect with a total incapability of doing or thinking of anything, till I have received it. Indeed, indeed, I am very miserable. . . ."* [222]

There was only one answer to such a letter. Poole took the cottage at Stowey. On the last day in the year the Coleridge family—without Lloyd, who had gone home for a few days—were safely installed in their new home.

Shortly before their departure, Coleridge broke into composition again. His heart was full of joy which even a return of neuritis could not subdue—"I am very poorly, not to say ill," he reported to Poole." My face monstrously swollen—my recondite eye sits distent quaintly, behind the flesh-hill, and looks as little as a tomtit's. And I have a sore throat that prevents my eating aught but spoon-meat without great pain. And I have a rheumatic complaint in the back part of my head and shoulders." [223] Nevertheless, he continued, "If we can but contrive to make two rooms *warm* and *wholesome,* we will laugh in the faces of Gloom and Ill-lookingness." [224] He sent Benjamin Flower for publication in the *Cambridge Intelligencer* [225] an *Ode to the Departing Year,* in which, with gloomy relish, he prophesied the extinction of an England that took up arms against the friends of freedom. He also had the poem privately printed in an expanded form as a quarto pamphlet,[226] with a dedication to Poole[227]—fitting end to his triumphant struggle for Stowey.

COLERIDGE'S COTTAGE AT NETHER STOWEY

"Surely, in the house which I saw, *two* rooms may be found, which, by a little green list and a carpet, and a slight alteration in the fireplace, may be made to exclude the cold: and that is all we want."   COLERIDGE in 1796

"Our house is better than we expected—there is a comfortable bedroom and sitting-room for C. Lloyd, and another for us, a room for Nanny, a kitchen, and outhouse. Before our door a clear brook runs of very soft water; and in the back yard is a nice *well* of fine spring water. We have a very pretty garden, and large enough to find us vegetables and employment, and I am already an expert gardener. . . . We have likewise a sweet orchard . . . so that, you see, I ought to be happy, and, thank God, I am so."
COLERIDGE in 1797

"Given from Apollo's temple in the odoriferous Lime-Grove—alias Street."
COLERIDGE in 1799

"the old hovel."   COLERIDGE in 1800

"a miserable cottage."   SARAH COLERIDGE in 1819

5

THE COTTAGE at Stowey is one of a number facing the main road from Bridgwater to Watchet, which runs through the village. The front door is not half a dozen paces from the road.

In January 1797 the accommodation consisted of two small living-rooms, one on each side of the entrance, three bedrooms and a kitchen with a hearth fire. An outhouse and a well (which still exists) were situated just outside the kitchen. The roof was thatched.

The back garden was long and narrow, bounded by Poole's garden and close to the garden of the Cruikshanks. Poole soon had a gate put into the wall of Coleridge's garden, so enabling his friend to visit him without the necessity of walking down two streets. This gate had the further advantage that it led straight to the arbour in Poole's garden (a favourite haunt of Coleridge) beyond the tanning yard.

But this was about the only advantage that the cottage possessed. It was indeed a poor place, as Poole had said. It was cramped, draughty and smoky (the proposed Rumfordizing of the chimney came to nothing [1]), cold and inconvenient—the very joints of meat had to be sent to the baker to be cooked. In January, it was at its least attractive.

But Coleridge, in his relief to be at a distance from Mrs Fricker, his joy to be close to Poole, and in the first flush of his rural enthusiasm, could see nothing amiss with the new home. Even his health took a turn for the better.

"We arrived safe," he told Cottle four days after their descent upon Stowey. "Our house is set to rights. We are all—wife, bratling, and self, remarkably well. Mrs Coleridge likes Stowey, and loves Thomas Poole and his mother, who love her. A communication has been made from our orchard into T. Poole's garden, and from thence to Cruikshank's, a friend of mine, and a young married man, whose wife is very amiable, and she and

Sara are already on the most cordial terms; from all this you will conclude we are happy."[2]

To Estlin he wrote with similar enthusiasm but in greater detail: "Our house is better than we expected—there is a comfortable bedroom and sitting-room for C. Lloyd, and another for us, a room for Nanny, a kitchen, and outhouse. Before our door a clear brook runs of very soft water; and in the back yard is a nice *well* of fine spring water. We have a very pretty garden, and large enough to find us vegetables and employment, and I am already an expert gardener, and both my hands can exhibit a callum as testimonials of their industry. We have likewise a sweet orchard, and at the end of it T. Poole has made a gate, which leads into his garden, and from thence either through the tan yard into his house, or else through his orchard over a fine meadow into the garden of a Mrs Cruikshank, an old acquaintance, who married on the same day as I, and has got a little girl a little younger than David Hartley. Mrs Cruikshank is a sweet little woman, of the same size as my Sara, and they are extremely cordial. T. Poole's mother behaves to *us* as a kind and tender mother. She is very fond indeed of my wife, so that, you see, I ought to be happy, and, thank God, I am so."[3]

"*My farm*," Coleridge had explained to Thelwall, "will be a garden of one acre and a half, in which I mean to raise vegetables and corn for myself and wife, and feed a couple of snouted and grunting cousins from the refuse. My evenings I shall devote to literature; and, by reviews, the magazine [4] and the other shilling-scavenger employments shall probably gain forty pounds a year; which economy and self-denial, gold-beaters, shall hammer till it cover my annual expenses." [5] He disclaimed a longing for present fame, yet was not without a belief in an eventual place in the eye of the public. "I am not *fit* for *public* life; yet the light shall stream to a far distance from my cottage window." [6]

Now, to complete the picture Coleridge had drawn, Thelwall was given a time-table that was nothing if not thorough—so clear-cut, indeed, as to rouse in the mind a doubt whether it ever came to pass: "From seven till half past eight I work in my garden; from breakfast till twelve I read and compose, then read again, feed the pigs, poultry, etc., till two o'clock; after dinner work again till tea; from tea till supper, *review*. . . . I raise potatoes and all manner of vegetables, have an orchard, and shall raise corn with the spade, enough for my family. We have two pigs, and ducks and geese." [7]

Whether this programme was ever more than a good resolve working upon an exuberant fancy is not known. It is certain, however, that the garden, if cultivated at all, was very soon allowed to return to a state of nature.

The news was also passed triumphantly to Lamb who received it with scepticism: ". . . and what does your worship know about farming?" [8] he asked. He did not hide his belief that Coleridge was wasting time. He urged him to write an epic poem—something philosophical, something more worthy of his friend's great powers than the spade. Had not Coleridge once mentioned his intention to write a poem on the origin of evil? he enquired. He suggested section headings, working out the idea, trying to rouse the poet's enthusiasm. [9]

Coleridge considered the suggestion. He went so far as to tell Cottle the preparation he thought an epic poem would require of him:

> "I should not think of devoting less than 20 years to an Epic Poem. Ten to collect materials and warm my mind with universal science . . . the next five to the composition of the poem—and the five last to the correction of it." [10]

But the project, if it may be so called, hung fire. For the first few months of the year Coleridge spent most of his time writing reviews for the magazines and preparing his poems for their second edition. After much talk of drastic changes—he wanted to include this time only his "choicest fish, picked, gutted, and cleaned" [11]—he was persuaded by Cottle, who had an anxious eye on the printing costs, to leave in the new volume most of the original poems.

The place of honour was promised for *The Progress of Liberty* or *The Vision of the Maid of Orleans*—a poem consisting of Coleridge's substantial contribution to Southey's *Joan of Arc* with additions on which he was then at work.

Coleridge asked Cottle to delay the press while he sent this poem uncompleted to Lamb and Wordsworth for their comments; but Lamb's strictures were so severe that Coleridge had not the heart to continue. [12] The poem was left out of the volume and did not appear for many years.

Lamb's criticisms, though withdrawn rather surprisingly in his next letter [13] (too late, however, for the poem to be prepared for the press), seem generally justified. The lines written two years earlier for Southey remain the most interesting part of the *Vision*. There is the denunciation of those:

> who deem themselves most free
> When they within this gross and visible sphere
> Chain down the wingéd thought, scoffing ascent,
> Proud in their meanness: and themselves they cheat
> With noisy emptiness of learnéd phrase. [14]

There is the more specific reference to Hartley:

> Others boldlier think
> That as one body seems the aggregate
> Of atoms numberless, each organized;
> So by a strange and dim similitude
> Infinite myriads of self-conscious minds
> Are one all-conscious Spirit, which informs
> With absolute ubiquity of thought
> (His one eternal self-affirming act!)
> All his involvéd Monads, that yet seem
> With various province and apt agency
> Each to pursue its own self-centering end." [15]

And the description of the various functions of the monads:

> Some nurse the infant diamond in the mine;
> Some roll the genial juices through the oak;
> Some drive the mutinous clouds to clash in air, [16]
>   ... Others, more wild,
> With complex interests weaving human fates,
> Duteous or proud, alike obedient all,
> Evolve the process of eternal good. [17]

The fact that Coleridge contemplated the use of these lines in 1797 to the point of giving them pride of place among his poems, shows that his faith in Hartley was still strong, his inability or reluctance to perceive the fundamental contradiction in Hartley's doctrines still persisted.

Lamb had decided to include more of his poems in this volume than in the first edition; and the bulk of the book was further increased when, at Lloyd's request, Coleridge arranged with Cottle for his pupil's poems to be included also; he expected, he said, in support of the suggestion, that Lloyd's connexions would "take off a great many, more than a hundred" copies. [18]

The projected hours of study with Lloyd did not bear much fruit—but in this instance Coleridge was blameless. When the family moved to the cottage Lloyd was in Birmingham. In the middle of January he visited his brother in London. He made himself acquainted with Lamb, who was then solitary, and the two men discovered an instant liking for one another. Lamb was impressed by his visitor, wrote highly of him to Coleridge and saw much of him for the few days he was in London. [19]

When, late in the month, Lloyd did rejoin the Coleridge family his room was not yet furnished and he stayed with Poole until the last week in February.

Lloyd was a kind and thoughtful companion, though constantly in danger of becoming an alarming one. Sarah liked him. He was considerate to young Hartley (he always appeared at his best with children). But Lloyd's "painfully sensitive" [20] disposition, then, unknown to his host and hostess, much aggravated by his passion for a Birmingham heiress, Sophia Pemberton, though at times accentuating his natural gentleness, was never very far removed from downright melancholia. Sometimes this melancholia would work itself off in verse, but eventually, and as it seems inevitably, it overflowed as a recurrence of the fits he had suffered at Bristol.

Only a short while after he recommenced habitation with the Coleridges these fits began again more frequently and with greater violence than ever before. ". . . poor Charles Lloyd has been ill indeed," wrote a distraught Coleridge to Wade in the middle of March; "—within these ten days he has had five fits, all of them followed by a continued and agonizing Delirium of five or six hours.—So that what with bodily struggles and mental anguish and loss of sleep from sitting up with him, my temples ache, and my frame is feeble." [21]

Shortly after this, Lloyd departed again. He went first to Bath, meeting Southey, with whom he was fast becoming intimate; then to London; and finally to Derby, where he put himself under the care of Dr Darwin and was recommended to a sanitorium at Lichfield.

Lloyd's illness apart, Coleridge was a happier man at this time than he had been since the early days of pantisocracy. His health improved. The scarcity of money, less pressing for the moment than at Bristol, became acute only on occasions. Hartley was growing sturdy; already Coleridge, living again in childhood, had begun to record impressions of the boy which were to take memorable shape in his notebooks and poems.[22] Sarah was well and, closeted with Mrs Poole,[23] Mrs Cruikshank, and other ladies of the village, could talk to her heart's content of the ailments of children, the price of food, the local deeds and misdeeds, which made up her world. Had Coleridge's genius showed any signs of bringing an adequacy of money into the home, his wife would have been quite content. As it was, she basked, not unconsoled, in the glow of confidences given and received.

Socially, Coleridge was as usual proving a great success, but in different circles. "There are a number of very pretty young women in Stowey," he told Thelwall, "all musical, and I am an immense favourite: for I pun, conundrumize, *listen*, and dance."[24]

He preached frequently at the Unitarian chapels at Taunton and Bridgwater.[25] He had also the satisfaction of an industry less intermittent than usual. Even if the cultivation of the cottage garden had ceased—or had never been begun; even though his pupil was usually absent or indisposed; still, Coleridge was by no means idle. In addition to revising old and writing new poems for the second edition, he was reviewing for the magazines. Reviews which appeared in the *Critical Review* dealt with leading examples of the 'Gothic' school of novels which had leaped into full favour. To Coleridge, the tendency of these books was regrettable: "The horrible and the preternatural," he wrote, "have usually seized on the popular taste, at the rise and decline of literature. . . . The same phaenomenon, therefore, which we hail as a fair omen in the belles lettres of Germany, impresses a degree of gloom in the compositions of our countrymen."[26] Nevertheless they and their like, crudely but effectively, were in some sense educating their public in mental acts of faith and exercise of the imaginative faculty—a necessary preliminary to full acceptance of the true romantic poetry which Coleridge was soon to play so distinctive a part in establishing.

There was thus a definite kinship between the mind of Coleridge and the books he was reviewing; and his reviews show, not only a sound critical understanding of the means by which the

'Gothic' writers sought their effects, but an appreciation of them which could come only from one in whom sympathy as well as intelligence had been engaged, and which provided a pointer to his future activities.

Close upon three years before, reviewing Mrs Radcliffe's *Mysteries of Udolpho* in the same magazine, he was writing appreciatively of the "mysterious terrors . . . continually exciting in the mind the idea of a supernatural appearance, keeping us, as it were, upon the very edge and confines of the world of spirits, and yet . . . ingeniously explained by familiar causes." [27]

Now, in a more substantial review of Lewis's *The Monk*, Coleridge showed both a development of his critical powers and a deepening of his sympathies: " . . . we feel no great difficulty in yielding a temporary belief to any, the strangest, situation of *things*. But that situation once conceived, how beings like ourselves would feel and act in it, our own feelings sufficiently instruct us; and we instantly reject the clumsy fiction that does not harmonise with them," [28] he writes, in the course of an analysis of the supernatural element in romantic literature which is as penetrating a piece of criticism as it is significant of the trend of his mind.

Coleridge was not yet fully conscious of the direction in which he would move. Despite more than one reference to " . . . predestinated wreaths, Bright with no fading colours!" [29] his powers of self-analysis at times still appeared undeveloped; just as his critical judgments were apt still to become confused by personal relationships.

In March, while the second edition of the poems was in the press, a request came from Sheridan at Drury Lane. [30] Would Coleridge write a play for him? Coleridge was flattered. "I have no genius that way," he tells Cottle, and goes on to make the astonishing prediction: "Robert Southey has. I think highly of his *Joan of Arc*, and cannot help prophesying that he will be known to posterity, as Shakespeare's great grandson." [31] But notwithstanding his professions of inability he promptly set to work. Soon, *Osorio*, the play, was occupying most of his time and a great deal of his enthusiasm.

So the weeks passed. Lloyd had gone. Last-minute alterations to the poems were still being made. *Osorio* added act to act: "I have written 1500 lines of *my Tragedy*," he informed Cottle in May; "—T. Poole is in extacies with it—he says, it has passion, well-conducted plot, stage-effect, and the Spirit of poetic language without its *technicalities*." [32]

The garden, the library, and the company of Poole were his every day to be enjoyed. The people of Stowey, deciding that a man who preached frequently on Sunday could not be a very harmful radical on the other days of the week, for the most part succumbed to Coleridge's advances. To set the seal upon enjoyment came another meeting with Wordsworth, who stayed at Bristol from March 19 to 29. [33] Poole thought Wordsworth "the greatest man he ever knew." [34] Coleridge, who concurred, arranged to visit the Wordsworths at Racedown at the earliest convenient moment. [35]

But even in the midst of joy the brooding imminence of monetary embarrassment threw a shadow across exhilaration. The Coleridge affairs were once more approaching a crisis. Lloyd's contribution to the household expenses could no longer be depended upon. In Hartley, there was another mouth to feed. Mrs Fricker needed assistance. Cottle's twenty guineas for the second edition of the poems had shared the fate of his payment for the first edition—it had gone long before the poems appeared in print. The payment for the reviews was negligible. The garden, whatever else it might do, could grow neither meat nor bread. A printer's bill from Biggs for the privately printed poems of the previous autumn awaited payment. Coleridge rebounded rapidly into melancholy; ". . . when last in Bristol," he wrote Cottle, "the day I meant to have devoted to you was such a day of sadness, that I could do *nothing*. . . . I felt a depression too dreadful to be described. . . . Wordsworth's conversation, etc., roused me somewhat; but even now I am not the man I have been—and I think never shall. A sort of calm hopelessness diffuses itself over my heart. Indeed every mode of life which has promised me bread and cheese, has been, one after another torn away from me—but God remains. I have no immediate pressing distress, having received ten pounds from Lloyd's father at Birmingham. I employ myself now on a book of Morals in answer to Godwin, and on my Tragedy." [36]

Then, to make matters worse, a difference with Cottle arose

over one of Coleridge's many failures to send 'copy' to the printer at the time promised for the poems then in the press. As Biggs was Cottle's partner, this little trouble, though not of long duration, made the bill of £10 a particular embarrassment. Coleridge applied to Wade. He enclosed the bill with his letter. Would Wade be so good as to settle it? Coleridge promised to repay the sum, together with his other debts to Wade, by instalments.[37]

The position was still serious; early in June, Poole was circularizing the signatories of the original annuity scheme, together with Lloyd, pointing out that another contribution was most necessary.[38] For the moment, however, the uppermost difficulty deferred, Coleridge resumed his way happily enough for a few more weeks.

By May all the poems, revised, were in Cottle's hands with two unimportant exceptions, which arrived after the printer's patience had finally given way.[39] *Osorio* was making good progress. Coleridge had time and spirits enough to relate an experience he had in Huntspill, the village where Burnett lived. He was visiting Burnett, who had yellow jaundice, when a woman of the village stopped him and asked: ". . . if I knew one Coleridge, of Bristol? I answered, I had heard of him. 'Do you know (quoth she) that that vile jacobin villain drew away a young man of our parish, one Burnett,' etc., and in this strain did the woman continue for near an hour; heaping on me every name of abuse that the parish of Billingsgate could supply. I listened very particularly; appeared to approve all she said, exclaiming, 'dear me!' two or three times, and, in fine, so completely won the woman's heart by my civilities, that I had not courage enough to undeceive her."[40]

Burnett recovered from his attack, but he was suffering from another malady which was to prove incurable. He had been anything but a moving spirit in the concoction of pantisocracy; yet, to him, eventually, the fortunes of this scheme became of greater moment than to any other member of the band. He had early put his whole faith in its successful conclusion; like Southey, abandoning the university and all thought of a career that this implied; but unlike that resourceful young man, his interests being restricted, his mind possessing neither the power nor the elasticity to move away from disappointment, Burnett deteriorated slowly but steadily as the scheme drew further and further from hope of realization.

After Southey's defection, Burnett attached himself to Coleridge, the sole remaining bulwark of the pantisocratic faith. He became a kind of handyman on *The Watchman*—a not very handy one, if Coleridge is to be believed—his chief duty, the preparation of the parliamentary reports, frequently needing to be done over again by the editor.[41]

When Coleridge moved to Stowey, Burnett became a constant visitor to the cottage. His attachment to Coleridge had by this time grown instinctive—his real hero had always been Southey. He clung to Coleridge, not because he was encouraged to do so by any professions of pantisocratic intentions from that quarter, but because in the poet's person rested the mortal remains of the scheme and because, in Coleridge's description of his manner of life, if not precisely in his actual manner of living, a sufficient glimmer of the old pantisocratic fire still remained to keep utter despair from his follower's mind.

Nevertheless, to one nourished upon the bright hopes and glorious promises of pantisocracy showered red hot from the mind which had conceived their existence, whose whole hope for the future was bound up with the fortunes of the scheme, and who had insufficient strength of mind to extricate himself from its inevitable end, the thin fare now obtainable at the Stowey cottage must have been poor comfort.[42] The increasing devotion of Coleridge to his poetry was rapidly turning the last vestiges of his enthusiasm and mind from pantisocracy.

The acquaintance with William Wordsworth completed the transition from the airing of a theory of an ideal existence to the active demonstration of a theory of poetry.

On Sunday, June 4, Coleridge preached at Bridgwater—"an excellent sermon . . . on the necessity of religious zeal in these times." [43] The next morning he breakfasted with Dr Toulmin, the minister at Taunton, then set out with the greater part of *Osorio* in his pocket to walk to Racedown.

His arrival was characteristic: "He did not keep to the high road, but leapt over a gate and bounded down the pathless field, by which he cut off an angle." [44] A few minutes later, he had quite won his way into Dorothy Wordsworth's heart. "You had a great loss in not seeing Coleridge," she tells a friend.[45] "He is a wonderful man. His conversation teems with soul, mind, and spirit. Then he is so benevolent, so good tempered and cheerful, and, like William, interests himself so much about every little trifle. At first I thought him very plain, that is, for about three minutes: he is pale and thin, has a wide mouth, thick lips, and not very good teeth, longish loose-growing half-curling rough black hair. But if you hear him speak for five minutes you think no more of them. His eye is large and full, not dark but grey; such an eye as would receive from a heavy soul the dullest expression; but it speaks every emotion of his animated mind, it has more of the 'poet's eye in a fine frenzy rolling' than I ever witnessed. He has fine dark eyebrows, and an overhanging forehead." [46]

As for Coleridge, he leaped into their friendship, into the inmost thoughts of his companions, with the same glowing assurance that he had leaped their gate. The Wordsworths, brother and sister, followed him into intimacy with surprise but no reluctance. It was difficult at any time to remain formal with Coleridge: on this occasion, the speed with which he melted Wordsworth's formidable north-country reserve was little short of miraculous.

For his part, Coleridge was overcome by the joy of finding in Wordsworth one who could not only give him affection but who appeared of comparable intellectual standing, whose views on the development of poetry appeared identical with his own, and who, like himself, considered that he possessed poetic gifts of more than ordinary brilliance. Indeed, Coleridge, in his first enthusiasm as in later years, had no hesitation in hailing his new friend as his superior. "I feel myself *a little man by his side*," he told Cottle, "and yet do not think myself the less man than I formerly thought myself." [47]

They wasted no time. "The first thing that was read after he came," wrote Dorothy, "was William's new poem *The Ruined Cottage* with which he was much delighted; and after tea he repeated to us two acts and a half of his tragedy *Osorio*. The next morning William read his tragedy *The Borderers*." [48]

Coleridge, his critical judgment quite unseated by admiration for the author, claimed for *The Borderers* in a letter to Cottle that it was: "absolutely wonderful. . . . There are in the piece those *profound* touches of the human heart which I find three or four times in 'The Robbers' of Schiller, and often in Shakespeare, but in Wordsworth there are no *inequalities*." [49] Coleridge's own tragedy did not lack praise and was in fact slightly more deserving of it; but fortunately the discussions of the two men rolled far wider than the distinctly limited horizons of the plays which had occupied so much of their time during the past few months.

For some ten days the three of them talked and walked. "We can see the sea 150 or 200 yards from the door," writes Dorothy, "and at a little distance have a very extensive view terminated by the sea seen through different openings of the unequal hills. We have not the warmth and luxuriance of Devonshire though there is no want either of wood or cultivation, but the trees appear to suffer from the sea blasts. We have hills which, seen from a distance almost take the character of mountains, some cultivated nearly to their summits, others in their wild state covered with furze and broom. These delight me the most as they remind me of our native wilds." [50]

The three friends were inseparable; Coleridge breaking away only to write brief but enthusiastic letters to Cottle and necessary ones to Estlin—asking that good friend on June 9 to send five guineas to his wife and to Mrs Fricker, and the following day requesting a five-pound note for his own use. "At present, I am almost shillingless." [51] This money was to come out of the annuity fund held by Estlin which, with customary hopefulness, Coleridge evidently considered elastic.

Coleridge's £5 was intended to enable him to visit his old idol, Bowles, and place *Osorio* before the shrine. But this plan had been made before the Wordsworths had become intimate with him—Racedown was originally to be a mere halt on the way to Bowles in his rectory at Shaftesbury. In fact, the company of the Wordsworths proved far too attractive to be sacrificed even for such a purpose. On the contrary, Coleridge felt he could not have enough of it. On June 16 he returned to Stowey [52] but was back in a day or two—this time with a pressing invitation for his new friends to stay at the cottage. The Wordsworths accepted gladly. There was a further orgy of talk, reading of poems and plays and rambles on the hills for a few more days. On the 28th Coleridge once more went back to Stowey,[53] to reappear four days later with a one-horse chaise in which he conveyed his friends proudly if insecurely to the cottage.

The Wordsworths were delighted with Stowey and its surroundings, which they found more akin to their beloved northern scenery than the Racedown district. They wandered over the long back of the Quantock Hills, which rise almost from the Stowey streets, and explored many of the deep combes by which the hills are scored. "There is everything there," wrote Dorothy; "sea, woods wild as fancy ever painted, brooks clear and pebbly as in Cumberland, villages so romantic; and William and I, in a wander by ourselves, found out a sequestered waterfall in a dell formed by steep hills covered with full-grown timber trees. The woods are as fine as those at Lowther, and the country more romantic; it has the character of the less grand parts of the neighbourhood of the Lakes." [54]

The waterfall and dell actually formed part of the grounds of Alfoxden, "a large mansion, in a large park, with seventy head of deer" [55] some three miles from Stowey. The brother and sister discovered the house on their walk. It was empty; but the mansion was so large, no thought of occupying it occurred to them; instead, their minds were filled with "dreams of happiness in a little cottage, and passing wishes that such a place might be found out." [56]

In this and other walks they were without their host. On the second day after their arrival, Coleridge met with a misadventure: "dear Sara accidentally emptied a skillet of boiling milk on my foot." [57] An effort to go for a walk only made the wound worse and Coleridge was obliged to rest his foot for several days.

At this moment, on July 7, yet another friend arrived. Charles Lamb had at last obtained his much deferred week's leave from the India House. The party was now very lively. If Sarah already had misgivings, she kept them to herself for the time. There was much work to be done in the cottage, and the sight of Dorothy walking like a man and hobnobbing on terms of equality with the poets must have struck Sarah as strange, to say the least of it. [58]

During this period of forced inactivity, Coleridge solaced himself when his friends were absent by reading even more voraciously than usual. He wrote Cottle a letter notable for its description of Dorothy—the first time Coleridge had mentioned her by more than name:

"Wordsworth and his exquisite sister are with me," he wrote. "She is a woman indeed! in mind I mean, and heart; for her person is such, that if you expected to see a pretty woman, you would think her rather ordinary; if you expected to see an ordinary woman, you would think her pretty! but her manners are simple, ardent, impressive. In every motion, her most innocent soul out-beams so brightly, that who saw would say

Guilt was a thing impossible in her.[59]

Her information various. Her eye watchful in minutest observation of nature; and her taste, a perfect electrometer. It bends, protrudes, and draws in, at subtlest beauties, and most recondite faults." [60]

He was able also to examine at leisure the second edition of his poems, which was at last published.[61]

The motto which Coleridge in a rush of friendly ardour affixed to the volume and which he was soon to regret, was a quotation from "Groscoll." [62] His fraternal offering, a lengthy Dedication to George, the credit for which was claimed by Cottle,[63] proved scarcely more successful. George took exception to certain passages in the poem and the compliment found itself in danger of extinction by the chill of moral disapproval which emanated from Ottery.[64]

There were several unimportant poems left out of this edition; and the few new poems which took their place—two sonnets to the child Hartley,[65] the *Ode to the Departing Year*, considerably revised, and the *Reflections on having left a Place of Retirement*, a companion piece to *The Eolian Harp*, were the most notable additions—need little consideration.

Coleridge's Preface is one of the most interesting features of the new edition. The first part of it breathes an unexpected spirit of humility and high endeavour:

"I return my acknowledgments to the different Reviewers for the assistance, which they have afforded me, in detecting my poetic deficiencies," he began. "I have endeavoured to avail myself of their remarks: one-third of the former Volume I have omitted, and the imperfections of the republished part must be considered as errors of taste, not faults of carelessness. My poems have been rightly charged with a profusion of double-epithets, and a general turgidness. I have pruned the double-epithets with no sparing hand; and used my best efforts to tame the swell and glitter both of thought and diction. This latter fault however had insinuated itself into my 'Religious Musings' with such intricacy of union, that sometimes I have omitted to disentangle the weed from the fear of snapping the flower." [66]

The charge of obscurity, Coleridge was not so ready to accept:

"... this is a charge which every poet, whose imagination is warm and rapid, must expect from his *contemporaries*" he went on to say with a decided change of tone. "Milton did not escape it. . . . If any man expect from my poems the same easiness of style which he admires in a drinking song, for him I have not written. *Intelligibilia, non intellectum adfero.*" [67]

The 'pruning,' however, remained more a matter of word than deed; the temptation to deviate "from nature and simplicity" [68] still lingered, unconquered. It would be difficult indeed to tell from the poems in this volume that the time was near when inspiration was to accomplish completely and almost without effort what good resolution had, after struggle, contrived to produce in part alone.

Yet only a few days after the arrival of the Wordsworths and Lamb at Stowey a new note was sounded. Sitting in his "lime-tree bower" [69] at the end of Poole's garden, Coleridge wrote what may be regarded as the first poem to show unmistakable signs of the beauty, the true poetry of nature so soon to come from his pen; signs already of the Wordsworth influence at work; the 'pruning' process really in operation. But above all, an example, a foretaste, of what was to be expected when Coleridge freed himself from the shackles of the Augustan idiom and outlook on nature he had so long despised. Abstractions, at times exquisitely expressed, begin to give place to minute descriptions of nature not less beautifully phrased, which could have come only from one who had discovered the pleasures in detailed observation of the outside world.

Coleridge's notebooks show the beginnings of this new and fascinating passion for the exact recording of nature, particularly in its less obvious manifestations, the re-establishment of contact with the life of the objective world around him. *This Lime-Tree Bower my Prison* begins to put this new passion into poetry.

The poem was written when Coleridge's three guests had left him underneath the lime tree early one evening. They had gone for a walk. In imagination, he follows them—his "Sister" [70] Dorothy, with Wordsworth—"Friends, whom I never more may meet again" [71]—and his "gentle-hearted Charles" [72] (an epithet which Lamb was to repudiate indignantly) [73] winding down

> To that still roaring dell of which I told;
> The roaring dell, o'erwooded, narrow, deep,
> And only speckled by the mid-day sun.[74]

Then viewing again

> The many-steepled tract magnificent
> Of hilly fields and meadows, and the sea,
> With some fair bark, perhaps, whose sails light up
> The slip of smooth clear blue betwixt two Isles
> Of purple shadow! [75]

Whilst he at home for solace

>   watched
> Some broad and sunny leaf, and lov'd to see
> The shadow of the leaf and stem above
> Dappling its sunshine! . . . [76]

>   the ancient ivy, which usurps
> Those fronting elms, and now, with blackest mass
> Makes their dark branches gleam a lighter hue.[77]

And for company:

>   the solitary humble-bee
> Sings in the bean-flower!" [78]
>   the last rook
> Beat its straight path along the dusky air [79]

in the direction of his friends and, perhaps,

>   when all was still,
> Flew creeking o'er thy head.[80]

He imagines Lamb's feelings on the Quantock heights in a passage memorable for its precise and beautiful expression of his own mystical yet minutely perceptive view of nature, showing plainly how already he was passing beyond description, driven by the need not merely to record but to *use* his experience from nature, to give it conscious purpose and direction in the belief that he had discovered "Religious meanings in the forms of Nature": [81]

CHARLES LAMB IN 1798

"This portrait of Charles Lamb, by Hancock, was a masterly likeness. Mr Coleridge often used to look at this image of his old friend and schoolfellow, and express his warmest approbation of its accuracy."

JOSEPH COTTLE

". . . he *blurts* out the finest wit and sense in the world. . . . There is a primitive simplicity and self-denial about his manners, and a Quakerism in his personal appearance, which is, however, relieved by a fine Titian head, full of dumb eloquence."

WILLIAM HAZLITT

" . . . a figure remarkable at a glance, with a fine head, on a small spare body, supported by two almost immaterial legs . . . a striking intellectual face, full of wiry lines, physiognomical quips and cranks. . . . There was much earnestness about the brows, and a deal of speculation in the eyes, which were brown and bright, and 'quick in turning.' "

THOMAS HOOD

" . . . the *leanest* of mankind, tiny black breeches buttoned to the kneecap and no further, surmounting spindle legs also in black, face and head fineish, black, bony, lean, and of a Jew type rather; in the eyes a kind of *smoky* brightness or confused sharpness; spoke with a stutter; in walking tottered and shuffled."

THOMAS CARLYLE

"He always made the best pun and the best remark in the course of the evening. . . . No one ever stammered out such fine, piquant, deep, eloquent things in half-a-dozen half-sentences as he does. His jests scald like tears; and he probes a question with a play upon words. What a keen, laughing, hare-brained vein of home-felt truth! What choice venom!"

WILLIAM HAZLITT

" . . . he has an affectionate heart, a mind *sui generis*; his taste acts so as to appear like the unmechanic simplicity of an instinct . . . Lamb every now and then *irradiates*, and the beam, though single and fine as a hair, is yet rich with colours, and I both see and feel it."

COLERIDGE

(By permission of the National Portrait Gallery)

So my friend

Struck with deep joy may stand, as I have stood,
Silent with swimming sense; yea, gazing round
On the wide landscape, gaze till all doth seem
Less gross than bodily; and of such hues
As veil the Almighty Spirit, when yet he makes
Spirits perceive his presence.[82]

But Coleridge, when physically inactive, was more than usually busy in mind. Already the presence of the Wordsworths near him, not just for this short visit, but permanently, as close neighbours, had assumed the now inevitable form of a necessity. The possibility of their absence forty miles away at Racedown was a calamity he could not face and would not endure. Instead, he agonized himself with plans for their retention. As he could not move to Racedown, they must come to Stowey or near by. And indeed, having once experienced the exhilaration of his companionship, the Wordsworths were scarcely less anxious than Coleridge that they should live within easy reach of the cottage.

They had discovered Alfoxden. It was near Stowey. It was empty. But to them, the renting of such a large house was so ambitious, it appeared to be so far beyond their means, that they had not even considered it.

Not so Coleridge. The conjunction of the two circumstances, the empty house near by and his imperative, not to be denied, wish that these new friends should live near him, was quite sufficient for him to agitate for the consummation of the coincidence.

To Coleridge at this time nothing was impossible, no obstacle too formidable to be overcome when he had set his mind upon the attainment of an object. It was when there was no obstacle, when his course lay plain before him, when the call of an inescapable duty sounded, that he hesitated, faltered, drew back, and was lost. On all other occasions, he persisted in his purpose; differing only from many others similarly situated or determined, in the manner of overcoming the difficulty—for Coleridge, with clock-like regularity, prevailed upon his friends and companions to undertake the removal of the obstacle.

So, now, the faithful Poole was pressed into service. He must secure Alfoxden for the Wordsworths. He made enquiries and difficulties dropped away. The great house and grounds were to be

[161]

let for the remarkably small annual sum of £23 including rates and taxes.

The Wordsworths seized the opportunity with alacrity; on the recommendation of Poole, they were accepted as tenants. On the 14th July, the day Lamb left sadly (and without his greatcoat) for London, the year's lease from Midsummer was signed.[83] The one-horse chaise came into perilous activity again, this time between Stowey, Racedown and Alfoxden ("I . . . am now no inexpert whip," claimed Coleridge).[84] Three days later the Wordsworths were established in their new home.

" . . . I brought him and his sister back with me, and here I have *settled them*," [85] Coleridge announced triumphantly to Southey.

" . . . we heard that this house was to let, applied for it, and took it. Our principal inducement was Coleridge's society," [86] explained Dorothy to her friend Mary Hutchinson.

6

WHEN WORDSWORTH greeted Coleridge at Racedown in June 1797, he was twenty-seven years of age,[1] rather more than two years older than his friend. In almost every respect he was the antithesis of Coleridge. He was born and had spent childhood and boyhood in the Lake District. He was dour by nature, uncommunicative, and stern in outward appearance—tall, spare, grim-faced, eagle-nosed. Even his voice was harsh.[2]

In character, Wordsworth was sincere, self-willed, strong-minded, uncompromising. His outlook was inclined towards rigidity, his mind thereby narrowed. His passionate affections were often concealed by a manner habitually cold and reserved. He possessed, however, an abnormal sensibility to natural phenomena together with a poetic enthusiasm no less ardent, if more controlled, than that of Coleridge, and a capacity for steady application of which Coleridge was entirely innocent.

His less attractive qualities had become enhanced by misfortune by the time Coleridge met him. The younger man, however, already one of the first to be convinced after reading Wordsworth's *Descriptive Sketches* and *Guilt and Sorrow* that their author was the greatest poet of the day, burst in upon the Racedown household equally certain that Wordsworth must be one of the greatest men.

Wordsworth had neither the power nor the desire to withstand this tempestuous good fellowship, this absence of pride and reticence and this unquestioned acceptance of his importance. Had he been a lesser man, Wordsworth might have recoiled from his impetuous visitor; as it was, he responded quickly and surely to Coleridge's artless expectation of mutual confidence; cast off his shell of reserve with unexampled rapidity; and showed an admiring but not surprised Coleridge the sound, deep, sensitive soul which dwelt within.

This very relaxation alone—unknown in the past except when he was with Dorothy—was in the nature of a healing and restorative process to Wordsworth's sorely disturbed mind. Yet it was only a foretaste of the rebirth to come in which Coleridge was to play so large a part.

Outwardly, Wordsworth had been a boy and youth like many another. He had spent the greater part of his spare time in the open—skating on the frozen lakes in winter, riding, rowing, walking, bird-nesting and indulging in horse-play with the best of them.[3] But the mountains and lakes with their accompanying crust of beauty early laid a commanding hand upon the poetic spirit that slept undisturbed beneath the commonplace exterior and scarcely less commonplace actions of the boy. Sometimes, fearless of the dark, the young Wordsworth would spend a night in contemplation of and communion with his sombre and majestic surroundings [4]—presaging an affinity with nature which, though suspected neither by himself nor by those about him, was silently distinguishing him from his companions. Later, he finds words for his early sensations:

> The sounding cataract
> Haunted me like a passion: the tall rock,
> The mountain, and the deep and gloomy wood,
> Their colours and their forms, were then to me
> An appetite: a feeling and a love,
> That had no need of a remoter charm,
> By thought supplied, or any interest
> Unborrowed from the eye.[5]

Not until, at the age of seventeen, he was withdrawn from daily contact with his familiar haunts and set among alien scenes at Cambridge did Wordsworth begin to realize how deeply his happiness depended upon this unconscious communion, how great a force in his life the influence of nature had become.

But an event which thrust a rude hand across so many lives diverted his early passion almost as soon as he had begun to measure its significance. The French Revolution broke out two years after he had gone to St. John's College.

Like most young men of the time, Wordsworth greeted the Revolution with some excitement; but it was not until he spent the summer vacation of 1791 on a walking tour of France and Switzerland and came into intimate contact with the French people that the movement may really be said to have affected his life.

From that time he became, if not an understanding, at least an ardent, republican. He abandoned all thought of entering the Church—chief reason for his going to Cambridge. His poems breathed fervid congratulations to the new republic and expressed an ardent, romantic love of France and her people. No longer could nature content him; love of mankind was now his religion; he had lofty visions of man as a great and free spirit, naturally noble, faced with a prospect of earthly felicity. The up-rush of freedom blazed an ecstatic rhythm through his days:

> Bliss was it in that dawn to be alive,
> But to be young was very heaven; O times,
> In which the meagre, stale, forbidding ways
> Of custom, law, and statute, took at once
> The attraction of a Country in Romance;
> When Reason seem'd the most to assert her rights
> When most intent on making of herself
> A prime Enchanter to assist the work,
> Which then was going forwards in her name.
> Not favour'd spots alone, but the whole earth
> The beauty wore of promise . . .
> . . . earth was then
> To me what an inheritance new-fallen
> Seems, when the first time visited, to one
> Who thither comes to find in it his home
> He walks about and looks upon the place
> With cordial transport, moulds it, and remoulds,
> And is half pleased with things that are amiss,
> 'Twill be such joy to see them disappear.[6]

In January 1791, Wordsworth took his B.A. Degree and left Cambridge—the very year and month that Coleridge was appointed to a scholarship at Jesus. Wordsworth's future was undecided and it cannot be said that he assisted his guardians to come to a decision. On the contrary, his attitude hindered the carrying out of any plan. He possessed money, which, though dwindling rapidly, had not yet been entirely spent. He also had expectations of a further sum[7]—but these were ill-founded. And he was, of course, filled with the independence that the worship of freedom inevitably entails. Many suggestions were made to him as to the way in which he might best occupy his time and talents; he rejected them all out of hand. He would neither enter the Church nor go into the Law. Tutoring, soldiering, journalism, were considered and put aside. As far as he had a definite wish to do any one thing, Wordsworth wished only to retain his freedom. He did not intend to be bound in any way so long as he had money left on which to exist. He could scarcely at this time be described as a poet. The poems he was writing in a desultory manner and which were published two years later were, despite the flashes of impressive imagery which caught the imagination of Coleridge, little more than a hotch-potch—though a clever one—of the most favoured mannerisms of Thomson, Collins, Gray, Pope, Young, Bowles, Erasmus Darwin. They contained in full measure abstractions personified, archaic words, sentimentality, obscurity, strung together by a highly artificial style; their young author in many respects a compendium of the faults, not only of the poetic age creeping to its end, but of the tentative, often exaggerated stirrings of its successor.

Coleridge, many years later, summed up the matter in words that were true, even if not entirely to the liking of Wordsworth:

"During the last year of my residence at Cambridge, I became acquainted with Mr Wordsworth's first publication entitled 'Descriptive Sketches'; and seldom, if ever, was the emergence of an original poetic genius above the literary horizon more evidently announced. In the form, style, and manner of the whole poem, and in the structure of the particular lines and periods, there is an harshness and acerbity connected and combined with words and images all a-glow, which might recall those products of the vegetable world, where gorgeous blossoms rise out of the hard and thorny rind and shell, within which the rich fruit was elaborating. The language was not only peculiar and strong, but at times knotty and contorted, as by its own impatient strength; while the novelty and struggling crowd of images, acting in conjunction with the difficulties of the style, demanded always a greater closeness of attention, than poetry, (at all events, than descriptive poetry) has a right to claim. It not seldom therefore justified the complaint of obscurity." [8]

Wordsworth had yet to realize fully his poetic destiny. His heart was little more in the writing of verses than was Coleridge's a few years later when the thirst for politics, or rather, sociology, possessed him. The ferment of the times had entered into Wordsworth. He was restless, ill at ease, champing at the bit of material circumstances. He was fretting to take some active part in the fight for freedom, to live among those so lately and so gloriously self-enfranchised, to joy—and perhaps work—with them in their newly found freedom.

Eventually, in November, he obtained permission to spend a year in France—primarily, to learn the language thoroughly[9] so that he might later, if he wished, take up the duties of a tutor—but his choice of country and language was not uninfluenced by his political sympathies.[10] He made his way to Orleans that he might the more thoroughly sever himself from the English people and language.

In France, Wordsworth formed two momentous connexions. The first, his friendship with the thirty-seven-year-old Michel Beaupuy,[11] nobly born revolutionary officer, instilled into him a philosophy of revolution. Under the passionate sincerity of the elder man's doctrine, expounded during months of intimacy and strengthened by what he saw around him, Wordsworth's vague and heavily romanticized view of mankind, subordinated still to the "passion," "rapture often, and immediate joy"[12] of nature, rose into a love, a pity, and something of an understanding of the poor, the miserable, and the oppressed, and a faith in the seemingly glorious future then being prepared for them under his very eyes, that seized upon his imagination and caught him by the heart.

> I with him believed
> Devoutly that a spirit was abroad
> Which could not be withstood, that poverty
> At least like this, would in a little time
> Be found no more, that we should see the earth
> Unthwarted in her wish to recompense
> The industrious, and the lowly Child of Toil,
> All institutes for ever blotted out
> That legalised exclusion, empty pomp
> Abolish'd, sensual state and cruel power
> Whether by edict of the one or few,
> And finally, as sum and crown of all,
> Should see the People having a strong hand
> In making their own Laws, whence better days
> To all mankind.[13]

The second, and entirely unexpected connexion, was that which Wordsworth formed at Orleans with Annette Vallon, a girl of royalist sympathies, four years his senior. Her brother Paul lived at Orleans, where she was staying at the time the young poet arrived. He met her in his first days in the town, during his search for suitable lodgings. She began to give him the lessons in French that he could not afford to purchase.[14] Very quickly their friendship ripened into passion. When she was obliged to return to her home, at Blois, he followed. They became lovers. On December 15 of the following year a daughter, Caroline, was born to them.

By this time, however, Wordsworth had already been obliged to leave Annette. His money was coming to an end.[15] He lingered in Paris until news came from Orleans, to which place Annette had fled before her condition became obvious, that the child had been born. Then he went back to England, his mind in a turmoil.

His inability to aid the cause of freedom and justice, or even to obtain a near view of the triumph which he now firmly believed to be in sight, served only to fan the flame of his enthusiasm for "Man and his noble nature."[16]

No less poignant were his feelings for Annette and her child. He had agreed to return to England so that he might explain his position to his uncles. He intended to ask them for financial help in order that he might marry and bring up his daughter. Neither explanation nor solicitation, however, was made by Wordsworth in person. His sole confidante in England at that time, his sister Dorothy, at once began an affectionate correspondence with Annette. It was arranged that Dorothy should approach one of the uncles, in whose house she was then living. She did so without success. Her uncles, their opinion of nephew and ward still further lowered by this latest proof of his worthlessness, refused to give him money or in any way help the marriage to take place.[17]

At this juncture, when it seemed that stalemate had been reached, a second calamity fell upon the poet's bright hopes. An event occurred in February of 1793, not indeed unconsidered by Wordsworth but thrust stubbornly to the back of his mind. The outbreak of war between England and France, contemplated by him, when contemplated at all, as some hideous possibility of the far future, came to him in its reality as a profound and long-lasting shock.

The ardency of the English 'Jacobins' at this time is not easy to recapture, nor is their sense of desolation, of betrayal, when they saw their own countrymen fighting those whom they believed to be upholding the sacred cause of freedom. Nevertheless, their feelings were as sincere as they were impassioned.[18]

Wordsworth was in worse straits than most; for he was robbed at one stroke, not only of a country in which he could feel a natural love and pride, but of his daughter and prospective wife. For a time he was stricken into aimlessness. Practically without money and entirely without purpose, cut off from his most compelling interests, he wandered from friend to friend accepting hospitality without very good grace. Communication with Annette grew difficult. What letters he or Dorothy received were such as to drive him closer to despair. Annette begged him to come and marry her—chiefly, it may be, with the object of re-covering Caroline who had been given into the care of another woman in order that the respectability of the family might be preserved. She was able to catch a glimpse of the baby only when it was brought past her door each day. Her letters revealed great distress [19] and both Wordsworth and his sister were at their wits' end to know how to give her either comfort or reassurance.

Later in the year, it is possible that Wordsworth crossed to France from the Isle of Wight; but if he did so, he returned very quickly, he may not even have seen Annette and he certainly did not marry her.[20]

The inevitable effect of England's entrance into the war was seen when, in October, the Terrorists gained the upper hand in France. On the last day of the month the leaders of the Girondists, whom Wordsworth followed in thought, were guillotined. Paul Vallon was arrested and thrown into prison, his family rendered suspect. The Reign of Terror had begun.

Wordsworth sank deeper into despair:

Most melancholy at that time, O Friend!
Were my day-thoughts, my dreams were miserable;
Through months, through years, long after the last beat
Of those atrocities. . . .
I scarcely had one night of quiet sleep
Such ghastly visions had I of despair
And tyranny, and implements of death.[21]

The war preyed more and more on his mind in all its injustice and misery and hindrance to man's freedom. He had not yet lost faith in the basic goodness of man's nature. For the terrorism he blamed the action of England in fighting France; and amid all the horror he was still able to discern qualities in man—his heroism under persecution, his courage in the face of danger—worthy of love and affording some sort of comfort.[22]

He seemed unable, if not unwilling, to attach himself to any movement in the country or even to organize his own life or work. For the most part he simply drifted unhappily from place to place; his sister, the one person who could give him comfort and a measure of understanding, out of reach at her uncle's house at Forncett, where Wordsworth was forbidden to call.

The only blow Wordsworth struck for his cause in the first part of 1793 was a letter of reproach that he wrote to the Bishop of Llandaff, one-time 'Jacobin' supporter, on the latter's recantation, and in which he set forth his own political faith.[23] Unfortunately, it is by no means certain that the letter was ever sent; and if the writer tried to get it into print he did not succeed.

Later in the year Wordsworth began writing his sombre poem *Guilt and Sorrow*—"to expose the vices of the penal law, and the calamities of war as they affect individuals." This was the first poem he had written since *Descriptive Sketches* which, although only just published in an attempt to get money, had been completed more than a year. Despite the not unexpected morbidity which runs throughout the poem it was a considerable advance, even in its early state, upon anything he had written before. Coleridge, to whom Wordsworth sent the poem and who returned it by way of Lamb,[24] had recognized instantly the vast stride which, partly by sheer necessity of his subject matter but more by the elimination of poetical affectations, the author had made. He spoke enthusiastically of it, to Lamb and to Wordsworth; and many years later, in his *Biographia Literaria*, confirmed the soundness of his youthful judgment.[25]

Apart from this poem, which dragged on in revision for a number of years, Wordsworth did nothing of moment. Like Coleridge and Southey, he proposed to start a monthly magazine, which was to be in character "republican, not revolutionary,"[26] but, lacking support, abandoned it. He tried, unsuccessfully, to get a post on an Opposition newspaper. He also began, a little later, his imitation of Juvenal[27] in which, with the aid of Wrangham, he satirized the leading English figures and habits. This, however, was never completed and he made no attempt to publish what had been written. This record of unfinished activities reflected his state of mind in part only. Fundamentally, Wordsworth was a careful man and his lapses from caution, with their disastrous consequences, accentuated this natural characteristic.

In contrast to the ambiguous attitude of Coleridge and Southey, Wordsworth hated Robespierre without reserve, casting upon the French leader most of the blame for the deterioration which was now becoming unmistakable in the carrying out of the original principles of the Revolution. Indeed, it was slowly growing apparent, even to the well-wishers of the Revolution, that the French people had in many respects exchanged one form of oppression for another. This impression was still far from general, however, and when Robespierre fell Wordsworth was able to rejoice in the belief that the cause of freedom would go forward with renewed vigour.[28]

Before Wordsworth could be finally disillusioned, Pitt began his attack against the English 'Jacobins.' The Habeas Corpus Act was suspended at the end of 1794. The papers of the London Corresponding Society were seized. Hardy,[29] Horne Tooke and Thelwall were arrested and charged with high treason. As the months went by, the drive against English sympathizers with the French was intensified. Transportations on the most flimsy charges were frequent—such a one was that of Gerrald, visited in Newgate by Coleridge at this time. Meetings were forbidden on the slightest provocation. Papers were proceeded against if they dared print anything savouring of sympathy with the French.

Against this manifestation of repression, both Wordsworth and Coleridge fumed and raged, in company with their fellow thinkers in England. But whereas Coleridge was working off his excitement by organizing and addressing tempestuous, often abusive, and always highly provocative meetings, Wordsworth, without this facility for self-expression or for placing himself in situations which invited conflict with the forces of law and order, was hugging to himself his anger, his humiliation and his disgust with his own countrymen and his sorrow at the course of events in France—so driving his feelings ever inward.

In the next two years, events—particularly the instruction of

Napoleon to his soldiers in Italy to pillage, and the attack by France upon Switzerland in peace time—were to bring Wordsworth's faith in France as the home of freedom to a very low ebb. But long before the end of that period, he had sought solace in contemplation of the ideas in which many disillusioned and ardent spirits alike for a time found refuge—William Godwin's doctrine of the perfectibility of man.[30]

On the outbreak of war between England and France, in February 1793, Godwin published his *An Enquiry concerning Political Justice*. In brief, this work was an exaltation of the reason and an exhortation to men to be ruled by it. All else, Godwin taught—the will, prejudices, instincts, innate ideas, the affections, the moral laws—were either chimeras or weaknesses of which education must and, properly conducted, would rid men.

"The true dignity of human reason," he wrote, "is as much as we are able to go beyond them [general laws], to have our faculties in act upon every occasion that occurs, and to conduct ourselves accordingly"[31]—a statement of doctrine which Wordsworth was later to paraphrase poetically when describing his beliefs of that time:

> This was the time when all things tending fast
> To depravation, the Philosophy
> That promised to abstract the hopes of man
> Out of his feelings, to be fix'd thenceforth
> For ever in a purer element
> Found ready welcome. Tempting region that
> For Zeal to enter and refresh herself,
> Where passions had the privilege to work,
> And never hear the sound of their own names;
> But, speaking more in charity, the dream
> Was flattering to the young ingenuous mind
> Pleas'd with extremes, and not the least with that
> Which makes the human Reason's naked self
> The object of its fervour. What delight!
> How glorious! in self-knowledge and self-rule,
> To look through all the frailties of the world,
> And, with a resolute mastery shaking off
> The accidents of nature, time, and place,
> That make up the weak being of the past,
> Build social freedom on its only basis,
> The freedom of the individual mind,

Which, to the blind restraints of general laws
Superior, magisterially adopts
One guide, the light of circumstances, flash'd
Upon an independent intellect.[32]

Godwin himself was sincere in what he taught. He was an upright man, singularly free from the passions that beset humanity.
Thus, when he taught that justice alone should be the sole rule of
conduct, reason the sole arbiter of right and wrong, of what is
expedient, he was able to bear out his teachings by a life which
must in general be considered exemplary by almost any standard
of conduct. He did not see the consequences, the moral chaos that
might easily ensue if men less honest, less sincere, less thoughtful
and less self-controlled than himself were to take his teachings
literally.

Coleridge early perceived the possibilities of such an event. He
was by no means so perturbed by the course of events in France
as Wordsworth, having numerous interests in other directions to
divert his mind. Also, his nature being fundamentally opposed to
Godwin's teachings, he paid but the briefest homage at that court.
As early as 1796 he was trying to rescue Thelwall from Godwin's
clutches and was hard at work upon his lengthy, though imaginary,
Evidences of Natural and Revealed Religion[33]—his answer to what
he regarded as Godwin's attempted corruption of the morals of the
people.

To Wordsworth, on the other hand, lonely, self-repressed,
miserable, his earnest faith in man gradually dimmed under
the successive shocks administered to it both by events in England and in France, Godwin's doctrines, familiar to him from their
first appearance, gathered increasing mastery over his mind.
Moreover, he was not unwilling to hear, as Godwin taught,
that marriage was a definite menace to the calmness of mind
essential to the proper exercise of the reason. He was beginning
to understand that it was not love, but an outbreak of passion, an
opportunity, almost a challenge to put his new ideas of freedom
in the moral sphere into practice, that had united him to Annette.
This humiliating realization and the conviction that he had no longer
any desire to overcome the severance occasioned by war could no
longer be turned aside. Thus, beset on all sides—by his conscience,
his broken faith in man and in his country — Wordsworth

turned gladly to the teaching that invited the disillusioned equally
with the ingenuous. Here was an ideal which the bestiality, the
faultiness of man could not disturb, which it seemed only to
confirm; an ideal which positively enjoined its adherents to avoid
the complications and the commitments of passion. He fell rapidly
under Godwin's spell. Secure as it seemed under the wing of the
necessitarianism implicit in Godwin's teaching, Wordsworth:

> . . . took the knife in hand
> And stopping not at parts less sensitive,
> Endeavoured with my best of skill to probe
> The living body of society
> Even to the heart; I push'd without remorse
> My speculations forward; yea, set foot
> On Nature's holiest places . . .
> Dragging all passions, notions, shapes of faith
> Like culprits to the bar, suspiciously
> Calling the mind to establish in plain day
> Her titles and her honours.[34]

The end of this futile search, this hopeless analysis, left Wordsworth in a far worse state than when he began:

> . . . till, demanding *proof*,
> And seeking it in everything, I lost
> All feeling of conviction, and, in fine,
> Sick, wearied out with contrarieties,
> Yielded up moral questions in despair.[35]

This pilgrimage of despair lasted a considerable period. All the
time, there was a background of movement, of personal relationships in a state of flux. Having antagonized his guardians doubly,
by his refusal to take up settled work and by his liaison, or
rather by his wish to regularize it, Wordsworth had early, in
agreement with Dorothy, decided to live away from the rest of
his family. They planned to live in the utmost simplicity in a
little cottage with Annette and Caroline. The brother and sister
actually experimented by themselves for a few weeks, proving to
their satisfaction that they were able to subsist on the minimum
of food and that they were content in so doing.[36]

For the greater part of the time, however, they were separated.
Wordsworth wandered about, visiting friends, acting as travelling companion, and finally taking care of one, Raisley Calvert,

who was dying of consumption and who, sympathizing with Wordsworth's struggle to remain independent and having faith in his poetic destiny, made arrangements to leave him some money. When Calvert died in January 1795, Wordsworth received a legacy of £900.[37]

This gift at one stroke lifted Wordsworth out of dependence and offered an immediate fulfilment of the plans he and Dorothy had made so eagerly a few years before. For the present, at least, they were not obliged even to restrict themselves to a cottage; true to the fact that good fortune does not come singly, they were offered the use of Racedown. By the late autumn, just before Coleridge and Sarah were married at Bristol, the Wordsworth brother and sister had settled in their first home together.

But the Wordsworth who had planned such an event no longer existed. In place of the once eager crusader against the evils of society was a young man who saw nothing but a world "poisoned at the heart"[38] against which his only defence was the exercise of reason—a defence which in its turn was failing to afford assuagement or satisfaction of both a mental and spiritual ache. The eager lover who had dreamed of Annette making her home with them, a loved and loving wife, now dreaded mention of the subject. The once eager poet dreaming of new worlds to conquer when alone with Dorothy now applied himself to the science of mathematics in an endeavour to satisfy the habit of abstract reasoning into which he had fallen.[39]

Nevertheless, Wordsworth's spiritual degeneration had reached its lowest ebb. The settlement at Racedown was one of the most important events of his life; it was the turning point; and though some time was to elapse before he reached peace of mind, he was never again to know such utter despair and bewilderment as in the period that had just passed.

At first the solitude of Racedown, the peaceful contrast it offered to the mental turmoil inseparable from the life of a town, together with the constant and affectionate presence of his sister, acted merely as a sedative, deadening his conscience and ceaseless self-questioning. Before peace could come to him it was necessary that his mind should be occupied and indeed absorbed by other interests: this, time, his sister, and perhaps above all Coleridge, were to achieve.

[175]

He did not at once begin to write—his mind was far too disturbed, too alienated from the sources of poetry to do so. His whole output at Racedown—in fact, until he knew Coleridge intimately—was insignificant in everything but its slow indication of his change, his rebirth of mind.

Most of his day was spent walking with his sister many miles about the countryside. The rest of the time he was engaged in manual labour—attending to the garden, chopping wood, drawing water—and in reading. It was during these walks that his interest was eventually aroused by Dorothy in the infinite variety, the delicate distinctions to be found in nature by those with a loving, watchful eye and sensitive soul.

But at first not only was his poetic vision clouded and disturbed: an indiscriminate use of the reason had strained and weakened his power to accept even passively the message of nature.

When, after many months at Racedown with none but Dorothy for companion, his eyes began to see the world about him with something of her own simplicity and sensibility, he found himself tempted constantly, almost instinctively, to use nature as no more than an anodyne for his bruised feelings, his loss of faith in man, country, and now even in the power of the reason; struggling the while against a feeling that even this degree of surrender savoured of sentimental backsliding from the unemotional dominion of the reason. Thus he saw nature at first, not with his old, intense, easily satisfied love (that had gone for ever) but as an influence which, without conscious effort on his part, would fulfil the need of a mind:

> Still craving combinations of new forms,
> New pleasures . . .
> To lay the inner faculties asleep.[40]

Thus, too, and for the same reason, he was a victim of the restless, comparative malady; setting himself up instinctively as a critic, a judge of nature, of something far greater than himself:

> . . . giving way
> To a comparison of scene with scene
> . . . to the moral power
> The affections, and the spirit of the place,
> Less sensible.[41]

As far as Annette was concerned, Wordsworth had to fight his battle alone. Indeed it is possible that Dorothy in this matter even proved an unconscious hindrance to his wishes. For some time she certainly visualized the three of them living humbly together in England.[42] But her brother, though determined to acknowledge his obligations to Annette and his child by aiding them as far as possible, no longer wished to marry Annette, nor did he entertain serious thought of so doing. He corresponded with her as regularly as conditions would allow. He sent her money. But already his heart was passing elsewhere. His early love for Mary Hutchinson was stirring in him again. Nevertheless, he could neither easily nor soon throw off his conscience the weight that lingered there. When it became possible for him to visit France he did not at once do so. His only relief was the more cheerful tone which was entering Annette's letters. At last, setting up as a widow at Blois under the assumed name of Madame Williams, she had been able to secure Caroline once more; and her maternal anxiety and affection thus set at rest and satisfied, her interests, especially since the unjust arrest and ill-treatment of her brother Paul, had gradually become engaged in the royalist cause which was to occupy her time and attention increasingly; and her desire for Wordsworth's return and the regularizing of her position grew correspondingly less acute.[43]

To this extent Wordsworth found relief of mind—but although Annette's greater contentment eased his self-reproaches, it could not erase them; he remained oppressed in spirit by the pain of contemplating his lapse from a natural sobriety and the havoc it had wrought to the peace of more than one mind.

In other directions the companionship of Dorothy and the peace of Racedown together began slowly but surely to lift Wordsworth out of despair, inertia and fruitless cynicism. Together they began to instil into him the beginnings of a saner and more optimistic outlook; a new courage; an attempt to look the problems of the world and mankind in the face once again; a readiness to take man for what he is rather than yearn after unrealizable perfection; a desire to slip on the poet's mantle once again, but with a deeper purpose and a surer hand.

Dorothy formed as it were the spearhead of her brother's conscious return to nature. She could and did by loving example break the surface of his indifference. She could not lead him deeper than she herself could penetrate, but a fresh apprehension of nature, a new understanding and love of it, an appreciation of its "charms minute"[44] and a new contentment with them; these things she gave him:

> I too exclusively esteem'd that love,
> And sought that beauty, which, as Milton sings,
> Hath terror in it. Thou didst soften down
> This over-sternness; but for thee, sweet Friend,
> My soul, too reckless of mild grace, had been
> Far longer what by Nature it was framed,
> Longer retain'd its countenance severe,
> A rock with torrents roaring, with the clouds
> Familiar, and a favourite of the Stars:
> But thou didst plant its crevices with flowers,
> Hang it with shrubs that twinkle in the breeze,
> And teach the little birds to build their nests
> And warble in its chambers.[45]

An understanding and appreciation of her quick and delicate perceptions of the world about them quickened his own sensibilities:

> She gave me eyes, she gave me ears;
> And humble cares, and delicate fears.[46]

And as he watched her day by day, happy in the simplicities of life, his assurance grew that

> Our meddling intellect
> Mis-shapes the beauteous forms of things:—
> We murder to dissect.[47]

Nor was this all. By her strong and unwavering belief in Wordsworth's high poetic destiny, she set in motion eventually the even slower process of his return of interest in poetry. His enthusiasm for composition crept back, strengthened by her encouragement and more solidly grounded by reason of his comprehension, through bitter experience, of the verities.

To Dorothy, also, must be attributed indirectly the final crumbling in her brother's mind of the main Godwinian doctrines. Whilst certain teachings of Godwin remained a matter of principle with him—the advocation of transportation in place of the death penalty, for instance, and a staunch fatalism that for long withstood even Coleridge's arguments and example[48]—his faith in humanity crept back, stronger and more soundly based than ever before. Prompted by Dorothy's general friendliness, he began a search for truth about the nature of man amongst those who seemed, in simplicity of thought and of life, to lie nearest the heart of nature. The cottager, the labourer in the field, the pedlar on the road, the poor woman in her tumbledown shack—these he accosted, questioned, began to know on his walks; and in their generosity one to another, their sincerity, uprightness, and touching belief in the sanctity of private property, he discovered a refutation of Godwin's theories more heartening than any attempt of his own to set reason against reason. In the child, Basil, who was living with them at Racedown, natural son of his friend Basil Montague,[49] Wordsworth also discovered an innate source of wisdom and food for thought.[50]

But to enumerate the benefits that Dorothy conferred upon her brother is also to realize the dangers into which, unconsciously, she was leading him. She brought him back to nature, refined his vision of it, giving him a new version of an old happiness for his later inspiration and present peace of mind. She revived in him an enthusiasm for poetry, a sense almost that it was his duty to write. She brought about by example and encouraged the beginnings of his discovery of man's true nature and virtues. All these things she did for him:

> ... At a time
> When Nature, destined to remain so long
> Foremost in my affections, had fallen back
> Into a second place, well pleas'd to be
> A handmaid to a nobler than herself,
> When every day brought some new sense
> Of exquisite regard for common things,
> And all the earth was budding with these gifts
> Of more refined humanity, thy breath,
> Dear Sister, was a kind of gentler spring
> That went before my steps.[51]

But at this point Dorothy's ability to help her brother came to an end. What she could not do was to point the way to the full use of these new powers when acquired. Indeed, it was obvious that she discerned no omission in what Wordsworth did—and therein lay his danger. Partly, her anxiety for the relief of his mental perturbation was responsible—when that seemed on the wane, her watchfulness slackened, her care diminished. Partly, an excessive admiration for him and his work must be held to blame. But mainly the fault lay in the weakness of her critical faculty, which extended little further than reference to downright description or the expression of a simple emotion. She could and did criticise minutely the poems he wrote; but her criticisms were concerned mainly with his interpretation of nature.[52] Beyond that stage, and his fidelity to the reactions of simple people, she was able only to offer a sympathy in which neither the imagination nor the understanding played a large part. She would have been quite content—possibly she would have been more content—had Wordsworth restricted his genius to the writing of short descriptive poems, confined in the main to simple, when not positively insignificant, happenings—often not even suited to poetic expression. She failed to see that this should properly be a stage only in his mental and poetic convalescence. His status as poet, already determined in her heart, did not seem to her to need confirmation by the judgment of the world.

Had this complaisance gone no further than her own feelings, perhaps no harm would have resulted and Wordsworth would slowly and unaided have risen to his rightful position. But the intimacy of brother and sister, her strong influence upon him, his reliance upon her judgment, the lack of outside stimulus or antidote to her fond assurance of his genius, rendered such a restriction out of the question. Moreover, Wordsworth's own limitations at this time and the natural reluctance of the convalescent to venture further, tempted him to accept with a certain relief her present satisfaction with his state.

Thus, though Dorothy had rendered her brother a service of magnitude, she stopped, through no fault of her own, on the edge of his final recovery. She could and did begin Wordsworth's rehabilitation—a task of love that she and she alone could perform; but, to complete her work, another and a greater influence was needed.

So far could Wordsworth go and no further, unless new stimulus came. He could see the merits of those who made up the greater number of mankind—but he had not realized that in them lack of intelligence was amply compensated by a fine, true and almost unfailing instinct. He could see the myriad wonders, the delicate distinctions of nature and could write disconnectedly about them —but he had failed to discover a bond of unity which would enable him fully to utilize his discovery and his new powers. He could at last reject the philosophy of Godwin—but he had no philosophy to put in its place. He was like a man released from a prison, freed from his shackles, yet with no place to lay his head, no purpose for which he could work, no aim to sustain his enthusiasm. He was like that man who swept his house clean only for worse devils to take possession. Dorothy had indeed given him eyes to see and ears to hear; now he needed feet with which to walk and a place towards which he could direct them; he needed a mind to guide him, and a heart to comprehend the way he should go.

And at this, the crucial moment in Wordsworth's career, there leaped over his gate and into his life on that fateful Monday in June 1797, perhaps the one man who could and would give him what, unknowingly, he wanted—Samuel Taylor Coleridge.

7

AFTER THE EXCESSES of thought following upon acquaintance with Beaupuy and *Political Justice* and his subsequent aridity of spirit, Wordsworth regained much of his native caution. He became amenable no longer to outside influence; as his true nature reasserted itself he withdrew increasingly into the ample shelter of his own self-sufficiency. The two exceptions which he acknowledged publicly have therefore the more significance. They were Dorothy and Coleridge.

Although Wordsworth has more to say of his sister's help than that of his friend, there is no reason to suppose that he underestimated Coleridge's value to him and the timeliness of his friend's aid, however reluctant later events and his own vanity might make him of enlarging upon the subject. Looking back, the elder man could not fail to see the momentous, almost miraculous nature of Coleridge's arrival, of the exercise of his influence at this precise moment:

> . . . Ah! then it was
> That Thou, most precious Friend! about this time
> First known to me, didst lend a living help
> To regulate my soul.[1]

Coleridge came to Wordsworth as a profound and salutary surprise, as an exhilarating education. Although at a superficial glance it might seem that the French Revolution would affect them similarly, in the event its effect proved as different as their characters. Whilst Wordsworth's republicanism drove him into scepticism, Coleridge lost none of his religious convictions, turning merely against the hired priest and to the Unitarians, under whose wing he might enjoy both the expression of advanced political sympathies and the aesthetic satisfaction of a nature naturally religious.

Wordsworth burned to join the people who had, as it seemed, shown the practical way to freedom, whilst Coleridge played with great earnestness at the establishment of an ideal home of freedom on the banks of the Susquehannah River.

Even more marked was the contrast later, when England warred—first against the revolutionaries in France, then against the English 'Jacobins.' Whilst Wordsworth was fighting in silence and without much success the disgust and bitter shame he felt for his country, Coleridge was sailing impetuously into the very teeth of treason in his endeavours to stir up the city of Bristol against Pitt the oppressor—and enjoying himself uncommonly well in the process.

The fact was that Coleridge, sustained by his innate religiosity, skated with much noise but little real danger to his peace of mind over the deep waters of the revolution. He was a man of many enthusiasms; and the collapse of one, though causing him some inconvenience and leading to loud outcries, never at this time did more than graze the skin of his feelings. Coleridge found it necessary to confide his troubles, to share his enthusiasms and detestations alike; and in the tumult, the flow of words, the circle of solicitous friends or frenzied audience, indignation, sorrow and despair for the most part trickled peacefully away. Wordsworth, whose manner commonly repelled and whose instinct was for silence, had rarely the opportunity when he had the desire to obtain such relief. Coleridge, with his vast reading behind him, with a mind that ran naturally to the formation of a philosophy and who was impelled to synthesize, had a background of thought upon which he could retire for consolation; Wordsworth, no systematic reader and at this time without a philosophy or the means of making one, sank unconsoled into almost uninterrupted melancholy and cynicism.

The two men were complementary. Coleridge lacked the will to achieve greatness, rarely the desire. Wordsworth lacked the unifying power so essential if he were to lift his recovered but unco-ordinated love of nature, his new interest in man, into a synthesis, a philosophy worthy of his genius.

Therein lay a fundamental distinction between the two friends. The restlessness, the instinctive creativeness, the buoyancy of Coleridge's mind urged him ever forward; its vast capacity drove his thought ever wider and deeper. To experience anything was to Coleridge a challenge to understand; and to know anything was a challenge to use that knowledge. Not only could he never rest satisfied with mere static experience for himself; he could not bear the thought that one whom he loved and admired, as he did Wordsworth, should continue in what he deemed positive error.

To some, this characteristic of Coleridge betokens a generosity beyond the normal, to others the same action expresses nothing but an intolerable inability to let well, and other people, alone. However that may be, the distinction between *meum* and *tuum* was never clear to Coleridge; and later, taking as he would give, he created trouble that has never been and probably never will be settled satisfactorily. To those of rigid mind, borrowing without acknowledgment is close upon a sin. To those who remember that Coleridge gave with an even greater lavishness and disregard for convention than he took, the offence seems less heinous.

To Wordsworth, at least, Coleridge's outpouring, whether of knowledge that stimulated and inspired or, as more commonly at first, of an admiration in itself creative, was nothing but a blessing. He spoke later of his friend's conversation as "like a majestic river, the sound or sight of whose course you caught at intervals; which was sometimes concealed by forests, sometimes lost in sand; then came flashing out broad and distinct; and even when it took a turn which your eye could not follow, yet you always felt and knew that there was a connection in its parts, and that it was the same river."[2] He declared that Coleridge was "most *wonderful*"[3]—a description which, coming from that undemonstrative source and after the passing of many years, gives unusual meaning to an overworked word. Wordsworth was thinking then of "the originality" of Coleridge's mind and "the power he possessed of throwing out in profusion grand central truths from which might be evolved the most comprehensive systems"[4]—a habit of the younger man which came to him so naturally as to constitute a serious hindrance to the possibility of settled work by one always averse to concentration upon a single object—but which to Wordsworth, who lacked a philosophical design to direct his work, proved precisely the unifying force he required. The instinct of his friend to synthesize his thoughts, his breadth of view and his depth of thought served to pull together in Wordsworth's mind the scattered emotions which possessed it, to turn his work from fragmentary descriptions of impressions and emotions into the expression of a comprehensive philosophy.

Wordsworth never acknowledged his debt with adequate fullness; but that he was aware of it a number of passages suggest:

> With such a theme,
> Coleridge! with this my argument, of thee
> Shall I be silent? O most loving Soul!
> Placed on this earth to love and understand,
> And from thy presence shed the light of love,
> Shall I be mute ere thou be spoken of?
> Thy gentle Spirit to my heart of hearts
> Did also find its way; and thus the life
> Of all things and the mighty unity
> In all which we behold, and feel, and are,
> Admittedly more habitually a mild
> Interposition, and closelier gathering thoughts
> Of man and his concerns, such as become
> A human Creature, be he who he may!
> Poet, or destined for a humbler name;
> And so the deep enthusiastic joy,
> The rapture of the Hallelujah sent
> From all that breathes and is, was chasten'd, stemm'd
> And balanced by a Reason which indeed
> Is reason; duty and pathetic truth;
> And God and Man divided, as they ought,
> Between them the great system of the world
> Where Man is sphered, and which God animates.[5]

But this came later. It acknowledges a part only, though an
important part, of the influence upon Wordsworth of the man
who greeted him so ardently when for the first time, at Racedown,
they had an extensive opportunity of knowing one another.

Wordsworth regarded with amazement and admiration this
man who, in speech at least, not less emphatically opposed to
oppression, scarcely less fanatically anxious for the victory of the
French than himself, could in the midst of the campaign against
the English 'Jacobins' sit down and write *Religious Musings* and
The Destiny of Nations (as the *Vision* was later to become) in
which love is hailed as the law of the world and God, "Nature's
essence, mind, and energy,"[6] the soul of the universe—only the
person of the priest too often hiding the true face and nature of
God. He heard with increasing sympathy, if with surprise, Coleridge's interpretation of Hartley's doctrines, that all visible things

—man, creature, vegetation alike—were symbols of reality, "Monads of the infinite mind."[7]

To one for whom the word freedom had come to be synonymous with shame and despair, for whom religion was but another word for hypocrisy, for gross and unbelievable superstition, Coleridge's attitude came as a revelation—a new world of thought. The effect on Wordsworth was far from immediate. The elder man had resumed his natural deliberateness, reverting to the true nature of one slow to absorb new ideas, the more so when they penetrated depths unknown and almost fearful to him. Now, rendered doubly cautious by past events, he hesitated, advancing in thought step by step. Coleridge's influence in this direction was thus not at once apparent. In truth, his influence from the commencement of their acquaintance was profound; not the less so in that, when it fully appeared, it had already taken on the aspect of Wordsworth's own poetical lineaments. Its power was to be demonstrated, signally but unhappily, in years to come, when that influence was withdrawn. But the sincerity and earnestness of Coleridge had the effect almost at once of lifting his friend's attention in part at least to a consideration, not without scepticism, certainly, but with a steady decline of it, of matters reaching beyond the immediate affairs of the world, and so played no small part in Wordsworth's eventual emancipation. Wordsworth's admiration of passages in the *Religious Musings*—for example, the passage describing the joys of those in communion with Heaven —was given doubtless to the poetry; but it is difficult entirely to divorce the verses from their meaning, and in fact, as Wordsworth could not have failed to realize, much of the merit of the poem was blended inextricably with the thought which had inspired the utterance.[8]

Evil, said Coleridge, was not only essential (with Spinoza he saw it as a necessary part of God, since to him at this time all things were integral parts of God) but was actually a positive though unconscious agent of eventual good. Freedom, he saw largely as a matter of the spirit. His approach to pantheism struck a ready chord in the mind of Wordsworth, tending already to credit nature with Godlike attributes.

But Wordsworth's greatest need as a poet was to overcome the temptation, aided and abetted unconsciously by Dorothy, to be satisfied with isolated expressions of emotion arising from contact with nature or with those who lived close to nature and expressed it in their lives. Here he might have stopped, the fullness of his genius undeveloped. The raising and fusing of these emotions into a philosophy—an essential act before he could hope to become a great poet—was scarcely within his power or the range of his mind unaided; certainly the suggestion, by example at least, had to be left to another.

The influence of Coleridge upon Wordsworth was apparent long before their meeting at Racedown. When they had met first in Bristol the younger man was in the full flood of enthusiasm for Hartley. He would rarely suffer the most transient listener to pass without attempting (usually with success) to leave with the visitor something of his own passion for whatever creed at the time possessed him. To a man such as Wordsworth, admired by Coleridge for his work before they met, the younger man would speak of Hartley and his doctrines with uncommon warmth and conviction, his eagerness to share his enthusiasms rising with his opinion of the man he addressed. It is even possible that Coleridge actually introduced his friend to the work of the then revered doctor-philosopher. But whether Coleridge was the first to bring Hartley to Wordsworth's notice, or whether he first gave Wordsworth an interest in Hartley, by so doing he rendered the elder man the beginning of a double service of which it would be difficult to overestimate the benefit. To a Wordsworth familiar or unfamiliar with Hartley in the autumn of 1795, the interpretation put upon the philosopher's doctrines by Coleridge would come as a novelty of surpassing interest and excitement, as a releasing power of which he would not be slow to take advantage.

Hartley, so presented, was to perform a far more vital function in the liberation and enlargement of Wordsworth's thought than ever his philosophy had been able to do for Coleridge himself.

The Coleridgean Hartley substantiated in Wordsworth's mind during the poet's time at Racedown what Dorothy's example and his own observation had led him to suspect but of which, otherwise, he would have lacked proof.

Wordsworth's introduction to Hartley's attempted derivation of the moral emotions through association from elementary sensations, the doctrine that the growth of the moral being was

[187]

due to these sense-impressions acting one upon another, building up a moral character in conformity with the laws of the association—this was timely. It appeared to give the sanction of physiology, cast in philosophic form, to what had hitherto been no more than an instinct of self-preservation in Wordsworth's mind, a grasping at belief in the power and importance of the senses and of the goodness inherent in man.

So Hartley, through Coleridge, confirmed in Wordsworth—however unsoundly—a natural and valuable instinct that helped the poet to recover self-respect and develop a new interest in man, that set him forward with renewed confidence and hope to the prosecution of poetry in which man would take his rightful place by the side and as an integral part of nature.

At first Wordsworth—too relieved, too joyful at this escape from doubt and perplexity to question Hartley's premises too closely—did not discover the fundamental weakness of a doctrine that explained man's mystical yearnings and achievement in terms of elementary sensations and the laws of association. But eventually, of course, the discovery was unavoidable. Wordsworth could neither deny the independent existence of mind apart from sense nor could he reconcile such an existence with the doctrines to which he owed so much.

At this moment, when Wordsworth had reached an impasse, he met Coleridge for the third time, at Racedown. But it was no longer a Coleridge sounding high heaven with praise for Hartley and his works. He had fallen silent on that subject. He occupied himself instead by directing the minds of his hearers to the study of Berkeley, the idealist, whose later doctrines had been possessed and transformed by his own mind.

This new leaven of thought broke upon Wordsworth the sensationalist as a shining light, a resolvent of his difficulties. Here was the missing part of his philosophy. It enabled him to hold the balance between his existing sensationalism and his gropings after idealism. It gave him the knowledge and the power to transcend the senses by an imaginative act, a state of ecstasy, in which he was able to achieve an

> interior life
> —In which all beings live with god, themselves
> Are god . . .[9]

[188]

a statement of faith highly reminiscent of Coleridge's earlier lines in the *Religious Musings*;[10] and indicating plainly, if further indication were needed, the derivation of Wordsworth's new and satisfying philosophy, in the light of which so much of his greatest work was to be written.

Coleridge's praise of superstition and of the instinct in *The Destiny of Nations* came just at the right moment:

> Fancy is the power
> That first unsensualises the dark mind,
> Giving it new delights; and bids it swell
> With wild activity; and peopling air,
> By obscure fears of Beings invisible,
> Emancipates it from the grosser thrall
> Of the present impulse, teaching Self-control,
> Till Superstition, with unconscious hand
> Seat reason on her throne.[11]
>
> For all that meets the bodily sense I deem
> Symbolical, one mighty alphabet
> For infant minds; and we in this low world
> Placed with our backs to bright Reality,
> That we may learn with young unwounded ken
> The substance from its shadow.[12]

When Wordsworth heard these lines recited by Coleridge at Racedown, the message they carried fell into fertile soil. His mind was ready, unconsciously anxious, for such a thought. He was in the midst of investigating the minds of those in whose lives, as in those of animals, instinct plays a prominent part. The suggestion put forward by Coleridge explained what had puzzled him—the lack of intelligence in these people—showing him that nature's compensation—a fine, true instinct and a responsiveness to superstition and the natural feelings—led to greater truth and a deeper because simpler joy. It went far to determine him in his purpose of basing his poetic material upon the minds, the lives, and even the speech of the poor and the young.

But there was another and perhaps more powerful influence which Coleridge exerted upon Wordsworth.

When Coleridge arrived at Racedown with the greater part of *Osorio* in his pocket he found his friend with the tragedy *The Borderers* completed. This work, anything but a great piece of literature, is nevertheless almost as important a key to its author's development as is *Religious Musings* to that of Coleridge. By means of *The Borderers* Wordsworth was purging himself, consciously or not, of his extreme faith in Godwin and his teachings. He was doing so by the simple but effective expedient of following Godwin's teachings to their natural, logical, even if improbable, conclusion. Suppose, he postulated, a murderer was to use his reason to justify his crime. He would then be but throwing off

> . . . the tyranny
> Of the world's masters, with the musty rules
> By which they uphold their craft.

He would obey instead

> . . . the only law that sense
> Submits to recognise; the immediate law,
> From the clear light of circumstances, flashed
> Upon an independent Intellect.[13]

This typical piece of Godwinian reasoning uttered by Oswald, the villain of the tragedy, made plain, aided by the course of the plot, that with the reason as sole guide excellent justification could be presented for any crime, any outrage upon society or the individual. Thus, while Wordsworth was letting off some Godwinian steam, he was at the same time rendering untenable the firm hold of Godwinian theories over his mind the moment he could regard his play objectively.

Coleridge's admiration for *The Borderers* was excessive. His appreciation of *Guilt and Sorrow*, with which he was acquainted already before his Racedown visit, was based upon firmer ground. Wordsworth was not an instinctive artist. He had at the best of times little sense of form. He had to work hard to force his material into the mould of poetry—and his choice of subject was often so slight or so unsuitable as to render his attempt open to ridicule. But in *Guilt and Sorrow* he had begun to master his material and his story, though melodramatic, was suitable for poetic representation.

The advance in style, form and manner of this poem from the *Descriptive Sketches* was profound; and this it was that occasioned the eulogies of his friend. Later, Coleridge was to write with true critical insight of the merits, the more than touch of genius in

Guilt and Sorrow which justified his earlier championship of Wordsworth completely:

> " . . . no mark of strained thought, or forced diction, no crowd or turbulence of imagery . . . manly reflection, and human associations had given both variety, and an additional interest to natural objects, which in the passion and appetite of the first love they had seemed to him neither to need or permit. The occasional obscurities, which had risen from an imperfect controul over the resources of his native language, had almost wholly disappeared, together with that worse defect of arbitrary and illogical phrases." [14]

Now Coleridge was able to express his appreciation in person and at length. He did not fail. When he heard, not only *The Borderers* but *The Ruined Cottage*—"the finest poem in our language, comparing it with any of the same or similar length," [15] he said later—his admiration for the author soared close to worship.

This admiration, constantly affirmed against the opinions of others and defended even at the jeopardy of his own reputation, was one of the most important, certainly one of the most immediately apparent influences which the new friendship brought to Wordsworth. It restored the elder man's self-respect, gave him a new and constructive enthusiasm for poetry.

Coleridge, where he loved, counted not cost, certainly not the cost of his own critical status. Loving, he was generous to a fault —the fault in this instance being an unnecessary exaggeration of Wordsworth's personal and poetical virtues at his own expense. But this humility, this reverence, was accepted in all solemnity by Wordsworth. He did not question its essential rightness; on the contrary, his self-esteem having risen to its ordained height, from whence it was destined never again to fall, he penned some lines which describe the writer far better than they state the exact truth:

> . . . thou, O Friend!
> Pleased with some unpremeditated strains
> That served those wanderings to beguile, hast said
> That then and there my mind had exercised
> Upon the vulgar forms of present things,
> The actual world of our familiar days,
> Yet higher power; had caught from them a tone,
> An image, and a character, by books

Not hitherto reflected. Call we this
A partial judgment—and yet why? for *then*
We were as strangers; and I may not speak
Thus wrongfully of verse, however rude,
Which on thy young imagination, trained
In the great City, broke like light from far.[16]

This reference to Coleridge's glad admission of his debt to
the elder poet was written many years later, when Wordsworth,
whose second thoughts were not always his best, looked back
over the years with diminished sensibility but no lack of the
appreciation shown of his work. It refers in particular to Coleridge's acknowledgment of two particular benefits which this early
acquaintance with Wordsworth and his work had brought him.
Both were due primarily to *Guilt and Sorrow*.

The first was Wordsworth's handling of nature; partly a
reflection of Dorothy's quick vision in his work but due also
to his lifelong familiarity with his subject. It is not necessary
to agree completely with Coleridge's estimate of this influence
to see that a very strong influence was at work upon him.
It is a question of degree; and bearing in mind Coleridge's
enthusiastic gratitude and its tendency to overflow easily into
exaggeration, a mean can be taken. In fact, Coleridge had shown
a sensibility to the influence of nature before coming into contact
with Wordsworth. His nature pictures commonly took the
form of visions, of delicate and curiously sensuous imaginings.
Wordsworth said of him: "Coleridge was not under the
influence of external objects. He had extraordinary powers of
summoning up an image or series of images in his own mind."[17]
He relied less upon intimate knowledge of nature, for which
neither his life hitherto nor perhaps his inclinations wholly fitted
him, than upon his powers of evocation, which he was so soon
to put to even greater use. Nevertheless, possessed as he was of a
perception as fine as that of Dorothy and far more widespread,
his acquaintance with Wordsworth enabled him instantly to
recognize and appreciate in the elder man's work that which he
would have had, if possible, in his own. Thus it was that he had
been one of the first to see and applaud in Wordsworth's earlier
work the signs—rare indeed but unmistakable—of a new, sincere
and at times masterly hand at work in the depiction of nature;

this, too, just when Coleridge was himself coming into contact with nature once again and it was appearing in his own work, climbing steadily out of the formalized style he had railed against for so long without wholly following his own precepts. When Coleridge met Wordsworth and became familiar with the source from which this refreshing naturalism had sprung, his admiration trembled into little less than reverence.

But another and greater characteristic of Wordsworth's poetry touched Coleridge even more closely. This was, in Coleridge's own words:

> "It was not however the freedom from false taste, whether as to common defects, or to those more properly his own, which made so unusual an impression on my feelings immediately, and subsequently on my judgement. It was the union of deep feeling with profound thought; the fine balance of truth in observing, with the imaginative faculty in modifying the objects observed; and above all the original gift of spreading the tone, the *atmosphere*, and with it the depth and height of the ideal world around forms, incidents, and situations, of which, for the common view, custom had bedimmed all the lustre, had dried up the sparkle and the dew drops. 'To find no contradiction in the union of old and new; to contemplate the ANCIENT of days and all his works with feelings as fresh, as if all had then sprang forth at the first creative fiat; characterizes the mind that feels the riddle of the world, and may help to unravel it. To carry on the feelings of childhood into the powers of manhood; to combine the child's sense of wonder and novelty with the appearances, which every day for perhaps forty years had rendered familiar:
>
> > With sun and moon and stars throughout the year,
> > And man and woman;
>
> this is the character and privilege of genius, and one of the marks which distinguish genius from talents.' " [18]

Something of this had been in Coleridge's mind ever since he had first read an early draft of *Guilt and Sorrow*; but it was not until he met Wordsworth at Racedown that the importance of this "original gift" became impressed upon him. Aided perhaps by Wordsworth's conversation and his impassioned recitation of the poem; aided too by contemplation over a period since he had first read it; and still more by his acquaintance with Wordsworth's latest work, *The Ruined Cottage*, which displayed this gift with even greater clarity, freed from encumbering melo-drama, Coleridge realized the more clearly that this demonstration of the creative imagination was new to contemporary English poetry. It had not been seen before. And it bore within it the seeds of greatness.

Perceiving that he was in the presence of a novelty of moment, Coleridge characteristically would not rest until he understood what at first he only felt and what to the author was a matter of instinct rather than deliberate judgment:

> "This excellence, which in all Mr Wordsworth's writings is more or less predominant, and which constitutes the character of his mind, I no sooner felt, than I sought to understand. Repeated meditations led me first to suspect, (and a more intimate analysis of the human faculties, their appropriate marks, functions, and effects matured my conjecture into full conviction,) that fancy and imagination were two distinct and widely different faculties, instead of being, according to the general belief, either two names with one meaning, or, at furthest, the lower and higher degree of one power and the same power . . . Milton had a highly *imaginative*, Cowley a very *fanciful* mind. If therefore I should succeed in establishing the actual existences of two faculties generally different, the nomenclature would be at once determined. To the faculty by which I had characterized Milton, we should confine the term *imagination*; while the other would be contra-distinguished as *fancy*. Now were it once fully ascertained, that this division is no less grounded in nature, than that of delirium from mania, or Otway's

> Lutes, lobsters, seas of milk, and ships of amber,

> from Shakespear's

> What! have his daughters brought him to this pass?

> or from the preceding apostrophe to the elements; the theory of the fine arts, and of poetry in particular, could not, I thought, but derive some additional and important light. It would in its im-mediate effects furnish a torch of guidance to the philosophical critic; and ultimately to the poet himself." [19]

Here was matter for earnest discussion between the two men, discussion which was to extend far beyond the few Racedown days. And in this is seen something of the magnitude of Cole-ridge's contribution to the association of himself and his friend and yet another demonstration of the difference between them.

Coleridge it was who fought out in his own mind what this new "excellence" was, how it arose, how it could be fostered, developed, where it would lead. Hence it was the younger man's instant recognition of and response to a touch of genius in Wordsworth which was to form the nucleus of their joint attempt to change the face of English poetry.

Eventually indeed, it was the pen of the elder poet which set this point down before the public, as it was his work in the first instance that had set the idea in Coleridge's mind. For while, in Coleridge's words, ". . . it was Mr Wordsworth's purpose to consider the influences of fancy and imagination as they are manifested in poetry, and from the different effects to conclude their diversity in kind," [20] Coleridge had already stepped beyond poetry and was busy investigating "the seminal principle, and then from the kind to deduce the degree." [21] But this was later. For the time, the excitement of the discovery and its relation to a new theory of poetry absorbed the attention of both men during many months of happy discussion.

In the first flush of this enthusiasm for Wordsworth's work, Coleridge paid his friend the most practical compliment of immediate imitation. Thereby he gave a misleading impression of their spheres of influence upon each other. Coleridge's facile imitations of *The Borderers* and *Guilt and Sorrow* in parts of *Osorio* and *The Vision of The Maid of Orleans* respectively actually disguise the real and lasting trend of influence, which in this respect moved mainly in the reverse direction. The difficulty of discovering the truth is enhanced by Wordsworth's power of absorbing, ruminating upon, and finally reproducing a thought so typically Wordsworthian in construction as to obscure its origins. Thus, years later, thoughts of Coleridge appeared in Wordsworth's poetry, transformed outwardly, a lasting and not the least important part of his work and mind—joy of existence, love of his country, of man and, eventually, of God. A plain instance of this 'taking over' of Coleridgean ideas and attitudes towards life is the pantheism first suggested tentatively in Coleridge's *Eolian Harp* which reappears in full bloom in his friend's *Lines Written in Early Spring*—an interval of more than two years separating the poems. And, arising out of this, an equally plain instance of a further push by Coleridge at the Wordsworthian conception of life;

always liable to dig itself in deeper on a thought, but rarely indeed to expand a thought unhelped. ". . . surely," wrote Coleridge, recording a discussion he had with Wordsworth and Hazlitt, later in time indeed, but characteristic of the process at work from the beginning of their acquaintance, "always to look at the superficies of objects for the purpose of taking delight in their beauty, and sympathy with their real or imagined life, is as deleterious to the health and manhood of intellect as, always to be peering and unravelling contrivance may be to the simplicity of the affection and the grandeur and unity of the imagination." [22]

Coleridge's personal debt to Wordsworth, on the other hand, was scarcely the less considerable. He was not, as was his friend, in mental turmoil when they met at Racedown. His need of moral support was inveterate, however, and Wordsworth's true nature —cool, steadfast, and rocklike—which Coleridge helped to revive, returned the compliment by stiffening the chronic weakness of will and resolving the indecision which fell so often like a blight upon the younger man's brilliant promise.

In this and in a general agreement upon politics Wordsworth was perhaps no more than another Poole. Coleridge had now two broad backs against which he could lean. But though temporarily less well-balanced than Poole, less versatile, less generally useful, and certainly less generally beloved, Wordsworth nevertheless obtained necessarily and soon the greater influence over Coleridge. Poole possessed sympathy with Coleridge's aspirations and a heartening belief in his ability to achieve them. Wordsworth was in a position to offer more. He was a fellow poet, like-minded in poetic aspiration, and able to give Coleridge the encouragement of a favourable verdict by one of longer poetic experience. He also and more importantly presented Coleridge with the inspiration of one, in the younger man's view, far greater in genius than himself; at once comrade and example, helpmate and shining light, friend and guiding star. To one of Coleridge's hero-worshipping temperament the very promise of association regularly with the man he admired to the point of idolatry, both as man and as poet, and whose thoughts in so many things echoed his own, was sufficient to inspire him to action and to conquer, for a time at least, the procrastination that hung like a skirt about every attempted translation of his activity of mind into permanent performance.

One of Poole's greatest virtues in Coleridge's eyes was the fact that, as Coleridge said: he was ". . . one of those men who have one good quality, namely, that they always *do* one thing at a time."[23] But this virtue possessed its corresponding defect; for Poole, continues Coleridge, "can seldom *think* but of one thing at a time."[24] "My mind," he adds, "is in general of the contrary make."[25] Wordsworth was also a man of like orderliness and perseverance with Poole. But he possessed at this time a mental liveliness closer to that of his friend. He was naturally a cooler man than Poole, even more level-headed, and far less liable to extravagance in word or action. In his reactions to the arts, something of Poole's normal wisdom seemed at times to desert him. Acting perhaps in the nature of an outlet from the sameness of his day of farming and tanning, a certain sentimentalism often got the better of his usual shrewdness—his poetic enthusiasms were apt to grow over-sweet.

Not so Wordsworth; generally cool, dependable, reserved, slow to express enthusiasm, he gave the impression of greater dependability as in poetry he certainly possessed the greater knowledge, and so had the greater appeal for Coleridge who, naturally enough, was apt to admire men in proportion as their strength of character soared above his own. In fact, he not only admired but in their actual or near presence, by an ingenious process of inversion, passed his infirmities of will on to their shoulders, the while he assumed mentally their strength, the qualities which he so conspicuously lacked, so gaining confidence, virtue, and encouragement from their friendship. His own weaknesses seemed, if not excused by their strength, at least overawed and put conveniently out of sight.

To this new admiration Poole, who had little jealousy in his nature, not only assented but at first actually fostered by his encomiums upon Wordsworth. He would have been scarcely human had the possibility of the gradual loss of his position as Coleridge's greatest friend and adviser not pained him; but Coleridge had love enough in his heart for many friends and Poole's unselfishness was such that, seeing in Wordsworth a man who would help Coleridge to give the world what he firmly believed only Coleridge could give, he stepped for the time into second place uncomplaining, content in the knowledge that Coleridge's esteem for him had not lessened—had indeed only been increased by this new and greater friendship which was now to transfigure life in the cottage and at Alfoxden.

And, of course, Wordsworth was the means by which Coleridge met Dorothy.

In a sense the natural sympathies of these two marched closer than those of the brother and sister. Though Coleridge had not the knowledge of nature born of long and close association with it, as had the Wordsworths, he possessed a subtle delicacy of perception and an appreciation of minute distinctions between the moods of the countryside at least as fine as that of Dorothy and finer than that of Wordsworth.

Dorothy broke upon Coleridge with all the delight of unsuspected novelty. In addition to the readiness of sympathy and quick understanding of her sex she brought a double joy; Coleridge found in her a love of nature more knowledgeable than, if not as profound as, his own. He also discovered in her for the first time a woman to whom the pursuit of poetry ranked high—one who applauded and sympathized with his efforts to achieve beauty, even when his final aim was beyond her comprehension.

In most respects Dorothy was unlike any other woman he had known. Her mind moved on a plane to which few had access. She thought little of herself or of the things commonly associated with the likes and desires of her sex. Her heart was with nature and with her brother; and now, with Coleridge also. Appearance, financial success or stability, reputation, social standing—these were details, common enough and natural enough, with which she was little concerned. She was a creature with much that was elemental in her, at moments as akin to the wild things she loved so dearly as to those whose form she bore. Her very manner, her expression, proclaimed Dorothy's true standing. Simple and unassuming she was. But a shy, abrupt wildness—that was her peculiar quality. It is not surprising that after his first meeting with brother and sister together Coleridge had words only for Wordsworth's greatness. Dorothy had to grow upon him. Small, shy, stooping, darting, like a bird, with the dark bright eyes of a bird, wild, restless, and missing nothing, stammering with eagerness to express herself, to pass on to those she loved what she had seen—that was Dorothy. But 'wild' best fits her. Many people were to notice this particular quality that separated her from her fellows. Wordsworth spoke of

the shooting lights
Of thy wild eyes.[26]

This was the keynote to De Quincey's, the fullest description of Dorothy that exists; and which, though it refers to her many years later, is in essentials a true portrait of the younger Dorothy:

"Immediately behind her [Mary Wordsworth] moved a lady, shorter, slighter. . . . 'Her face was of Egyptian brown'; rarely, in a woman of English birth, had I seen a more determinate gypsy tan. Her eyes were not soft, as Mrs Wordsworth's, nor were they fierce or bold; but they were wild and startling, and hurried in their motion. Her manner was warm and even ardent; her sensibility seemed constitutionally deep; and some subtle fire of impassioned intellect apparently burned within her, which, being alternately pushed forward into a conspicuous expression by the irrepressible instincts of her temperament, and then immediately checked, in obedience to the decorum of her sex and age, and her maidenly condition, gave to her whole demeanour, and to her conversation, an air of embarrassment and even of self-conflict, that was almost distressing to witness. Even her very utterance and enunciation often suffered, in point of clearness and steadiness, from the agitation of her excessive organic sensibility. At times, the self-counteraction and self-baffling of her feelings caused her even to stammer. . . . The greatest deductions from Miss Wordsworth's attractions . . . were the glancing quickness of her motions, and other circumstances in her deportment (such as her stooping attitude when walking), which gave an ungraceful, and even an unsexual character to her appearance when out-of-doors. She did not cultivate the graces which preside over the person and its carriage. But, on the other hand, she was a person of very remarkable endowments intellectually; and, in addition to the other great services which she rendered to her brother, this I may mention, as greater than all the rest, and it was one which equally operated to the benefit of every casual companion in a walk—viz. the exceeding sympathy, always ready and always profound, by which she made all that one could tell her, all that one could describe, all that one could quote from a foreign author, reverberate, as it were, à plusieurs reprises, to one's own feelings, by the manifest impression it made upon hers. The pulses of light are not more quick or more inevitable in their flow and undulation, than were the answering and echoing movements of her sympathizing attention. Her knowledge of literature was

[199]

irregular, and thoroughly unsystematic. She was content to be ignorant of many things; but what she knew and had really mastered lay where it could not be disturbed—in the temple of her own most fervid heart." [27]

Dorothy was a creature of abnormal sensibility, finely drawn, highly strung, from whom the faintest breath of nature could draw answering music like the lute in Coleridge's *Eolian Harp*. Not a poet herself, she had the poetic instinct highly developed. Coleridge marvelled at her, loved her. Such sympathy with his work, with his aspirations; such accurate interpretation (like the electrometer of his description) of every mood and phase of the nature he longed to know and understand more fully—this seemed too much to expect from a single source—yet there it was, embodied in, of all people, the sister of the man he most admired. His joy, his thankfulness, passed beyond words.

Yet in the midst of all this almost unbelievable good fortune, Coleridge was able to see that in certain circumstances Dorothy might actually become a menace to the development of her brother's genius. Coleridge was not only devoted to her—he understood her. If her limitations tended to become overshadowed by admiration and gratitude, they were never, fortunately, entirely unperceived. He saw clearly that her deeply affectionate nature might easily mislead a critical sense which tended to lose its keenness after the question of detail had passed. He saw that her absorption in the minutae of nature rendered her too easily contented with poems that were little more than a framework for exquisite imagery produced often in collaboration between her remarkable gift of perception and Wordsworth's equally remarkable gift of committing this perception to paper in verses of rugged and austere beauty. Her affection, in pandering to Wordsworth's vanity—always easily kindled—was setting a snare for his self-criticism—none too strong at the time and in danger of being weakened by her uncritical admiration. Jealous for Wordsworth's great future, Coleridge saw moreover that the lack of variety in Dorothy's interests, her dearth of ambition and complete absence of philosophical insight, often rendered her advice and her influence of questionable value. When Coleridge met them and for some time after, Wordsworth often appeared content, in the warmth of Dorothy's enthusiasm, to attempt the portrayal in poetic form of emotions which had been aroused by incidents fit only for prose, whose message was too slight to justify poetic treatment. This tendency it was in Wordsworth, encouraged by Dorothy (at such times in her element, fully comprehending what her beloved brother was writing and fully sharing his thoughts), of which Coleridge foresaw the danger and which he was able in great measure to overcome. He perceived that Dorothy's sensitiveness to the moods and beauties of nature unfitted her for depth of thought in directions which to him were of the utmost importance—and which he had determined must be so regarded by Wordsworth.[28]

Both Dorothy and Coleridge idolized Wordsworth. But they did not idolize the same part of him. Dorothy loved and admired the Wordsworth that was; Coleridge, though he loved and admired the man he saw, gave his chief devotion, his reverence almost, to the Wordsworth and his work that could be, that, in the phraseology of Coleridge's unquestioning faith, was to come, the Wordsworth he perceived still hidden, still, it may be, undreamed of by the very man in whom greatness sheltered.

In these different manifestations of affection, sister and friend were true to their sex. Dorothy asked no more of her brother than to remain the man she knew and adored. Coleridge burned with anxiety to see the man he felt was contained in his friend; he could neither rest, nor would he let Wordsworth rest, until the genius in Wordsworth was out, was fulfilled, had enforced man's homage. Dorothy's love for Wordsworth was creative inasmuch as her brother accepted something of the quietude of her simple philosophy, looked through her eyes, transformed her prose visions into poetry, at times of exceeding beauty; but at others, such was his and her lack of discrimination, of exceeding pedestrianism and triviality. Coleridge's love was creative on a more grandiose scale; for it is at least questionable whether Wordsworth's greater works would ever have been written but for the constant exhortations, the illimitable belief in his genius, the broadening and synthesizing mind, of his friend. The very praise that Coleridge lavished upon Wordsworth was in the nature of a goad to further achievement; for, though Wordsworth was capable of accepting laudation as no more than the rightful due to his genius, there had to come and, in fact, was soon to come, a time when, parted from Coleridge, he looked further into himself and discovered that his talent did not measure up fully to the praise he had accepted, and that without his friend he was the lesser man. So did the influence of Coleridge take its effect.

Alone with Wordsworth, once his mental recovery had been assured, Dorothy might well have proved an actual deterrent to the full greatness which Coleridge knew was hidden in his friend. Together with her brother and with Coleridge, acting as the sensitive, quivering antennae of the three, her value was inestimable, her place in posterity not only secured but unshadowed.

". . . three people, but only one soul,"[29] said Coleridge of them; and he spoke truly.

8

ON THE FOURTEENTH of July 1797, the Wordsworths took possession of Alfoxden. They were accompanied by Coleridge and Sarah who came to help them settle in their new home. Although too big—the household was to consist only of Dorothy and William, Peggy the maid, and Basil—the house appealed to them, mainly because of its beautiful and extensive surroundings. Dorothy described the house and grounds in a letter:

"The house is a large mansion, with furniture enough for a dozen families like ours. There is a very excellent garden, well stocked with vegetables and fruit. The garden is at the end of the house, and our favourite parlour, as at Racedown, looks that way. In front is a little court, with grass plot, gravel walk, and shrubs; the moss roses were in full beauty a month ago. The front of the house is to the south, but it is screened from the sun by a high hill which rises immediately from it. This hill is beautiful, scattered irregularly and abundantly with trees, and topped with fern, which spreads a considerable way down it. The deer dwell here, and sheep, so that we have a living prospect. From the end of the house we have a view of the sea, over a woody meadow-country; and exactly opposite the window where I now sit is an immense wood, whose round top from this point has exactly the appearance of a mighty dome. In some parts of this wood there is an under grove of hollies which are now very beautiful. In a glen at the bottom of the wood is the waterfall of which I spoke, a quarter of a mile from the house. We are three miles from Stowey, and not two miles from the sea. Wherever we turn we have woods, smooth downs, and valleys with small brooks running down them through green meadows, hardly ever intersected with hedgerows, but scattered over with trees. The hills that cradle these valleys are either covered with fern and bilberries, or oak woods, which are cut for charcoal. . . .

"Walks extend for miles over the hill-tops; the great beauty of which is their wild simplicity; they are perfectly smooth, without rocks. The Tor of Glastonbury is before our eyes during more than half of our walk to Stowey; and in the park wherever we go, keeping about fifteen yards above the house, it makes a part of our prospect." [1]

Some time before, Thelwall had announced his intention of walking down from London; partly to meet Coleridge in person, but also with the object of discovering a cottage nearby in which he and his family might live—for he had now decided to abandon politics altogether and take up the semi-horticultural, semi-literary life, which Coleridge had given him to understand was the procedure at the Stowey cottage.

Lamb had been hoping for a glimpse of Thelwall whilst at Stowey but had been disappointed. "Is the Patriot come yet?" he asks in his first letter to Coleridge on reaching London. "I was looking out for John Thelwall all the way from Bridgewater, and had I met him, I think it would have moved almost me to tears." [2] As it was, he missed him by a matter of three days. Late on the evening of the 17th, Thelwall arrived at Stowey. The cottage was not deserted, because Sarah had that day returned "to superintend the wash-tub." [3]

"I have spoiled the soapsuds, however," he wrote to his wife from Alfoxden the next evening. "I slept at Coleridge's cot, and this morning we rose by times, and came here time enough to call Samuel and his friend Wordsworth up to breakfast. Faith, we are a most philosophical party." [4] They visited the dell and waterfall during the course of the day. "There have we . . . a literary and political triumvirate, passed sentence on the productions and characters of the age, burst forth in poetical flights of enthusiasm, and philosophised our minds into a state of tranquillity, which the leaders of nations might envy, and the residents of cities can never know." [5] Of this time and place, Wordsworth years later could still recollect Coleridge exclaiming, "This is a place to reconcile one to all the jarrings and conflicts of the wide world." "Nay," said Thelwall, "to make one forget them altogether." [6]

The next day the Coleridges took their guest back to Stowey for a few days. The Wordsworths escorted the little party along the way, so commencing the traffic between Stowey and Alfoxden which was to remain constant for the next year.

Thelwall settled down at Stowey for a few days, visiting Poole, indulging in endless discussions with his host on politics, education, religion, and literature and looking in vain for any sign of the horticultural activity he had heard about in the early part of the year. Coleridge's anecdote of later years brings this to mind.

> "Thelwall," he said, "thought it very unfair to influence a child's mind by inculcating any opinions before it should have come to years of discretion, and be able to choose for itself. I showed him my garden, and told him it was my botanical garden. 'How so?' said he; 'it is covered with weeds.' 'Oh,' I replied, *that* is only because it has not yet come to its age of discretion and choice. The weeds, you see, have taken the liberty to grow, and I thought it unfair in me to prejudice the soil towards roses and straw-berries.' " [7]

Coleridge, as his correspondence with Thelwall had already shown, was by no means disturbed by the gulf of contrast in mind and habit which yawned between himself and his guest. On the contrary, the fact added spice to Thelwall's presence; there was always the possibility of conversion, and failing that, he was not at this time averse to considering points of view other than his own.

Hospitality flowed from him. He was not content with Lamb, with Thelwall, with Wordsworth. All must come and share his new-found joy. The Southeys must come. He would fetch them himself. He thought—he felt sure—he could secure a one-horse chaise. Will they come? He will fetch them. They need fear nothing. "I have driven back Miss Wordsworth over forty miles of execrable roads [8] and have been always very cautious, and am now no inexpert whip." [9]

Cottle too must come. He had not been well but soon he would have recovered and then he must certainly come. [10] Wade must come. Writing on the first day of August, Coleridge with his customary impetuosity bursts forth: ". . . my dear fellow! do not let there be such pauses in our correspondence." [11] And then, with that fatal facility for promulgating impossibly good resolutions which gushed irresistibly from him at penitential moments, "I will pledge myself to write you once every *fortnight*." [12]

In this same letter to Wade, Coleridge displayed further characteristics. He describes Thelwall with prescience, yet the accuracy with which he summed up character was of little use to him; with Thelwall, as with others, he failed as usual to profit by his discernment when dealing with the person concerned.

"John Thelwall," he writes, "is a very warm hearted honest man—and disagreeing, as we do, on almost every point of religion, of morals, of politics, and of philosophy, we like each other uncommonly well—He is a great favorite with Sara. *Energetic Activity*, of *mind* and of *heart*, is his Master-feature. He is prompt to *conceive*, and still prompter to *execute*—But I think, that he is deficient in that *patience* of mind, which can look *intensely* and *frequently* at the same subject. He believes and disbelieves with impassioned confidence—I wish to see him *doubting* and *doubting*. However, he is the man for *action*—he is intrepid, eloquent, and— honest. Perhaps the only *acting* Democrat, that *is* honest—for the *Patriots* are ragged cattle—a most execrable herd—arrogant because they are ignorant, and boastful of the strength of reason, because they have never tried it enough to know its *weakness*. O my poor Country! The Clouds cover thee—there is not one spot of clear blue in the whole heaven." [13]

To Southey, he had written from Alfoxden soon after the Wordsworths had settled in. Southey, who was trying to arrange a reprint of Chatterton's poems to help the poet's sister, had asked Coleridge if he would try to obtain subscribers, write an essay on Chatterton, and agree to a reprint of his *Monody on the Death of Chatterton*. To the first two requests, Coleridge agreed—in principle at least. He also offered to attempt a new poem on Chatterton. But he refused to allow his *Monody* to be reprinted; and the reasons he gives for his refusal—a thorough-going denunciation of his past work—show how far he had travelled in self-criticism since that time and point the way his mind was moving:

"... on a life and death so full of heart-going *realities* as poor Chatterton's, to find such shadowy nobodies as cherub-winged *Death*, Trees of *Hope*, bare-bosomed *Affection* and simpering *Peace*, makes one's blood circulate like ipecacuanha. But so it is. A young man by strong feelings is impelled to write on a particular subject, and this is all his feelings do for him. They set him upon the business and then they leave him. He has such a high idea of what poetry ought to be, that he cannot conceive that such things as his natural emotions may be allowed to find a place in it; his learning therefore, his fancy, or rather conceit, and all his powers of buckram are put on the stretch. It appears to me that strong feeling is not so requisite to an author's being profoundly pathetic as taste and good sense." [14]

[206]

In this letter, Coleridge sends Southey the first draft of his poem written a few days earlier, *This Lime-Tree Bower my Prison*. Wordsworth is lauded: he is "a very great man, the only man to whom *at all times* and *in all modes of excellence* I feel myself inferior ";[15] and Dorothy, Coleridge describes as "a most exquisite young woman in her mind and heart." [16] Hot upon these inducements Coleridge on behalf of Wordsworth offered the Southeys a suite of rooms at Alfoxden. But, whether their reason was fear of the one-horse chaise or whether it was due to something less friendly, the Southeys did not come.

No one visited Alfoxden for a long time save Thelwall. The three of them—Coleridge and the Wordsworths—were free to walk the hills and explore the combes, there to meditate upon and to discuss unendingly the poetic theories steadily taking shape in their minds. And, also, to scandalize the neighbourhood. From this point of view, Thelwall had been visitors enough and to spare.

This time, Coleridge was utterly undone. Just as he had begun to wear down opposition, to win some acceptance as a village decoration, an amiable curiosity almost, with a wife who was perfectly normal, one of themselves in fact, and a baby apparently as others; just at this time the Stowey neighbourhood was affronted by the sub-letting of Alfoxden to the Wordsworths, two doubtful characters, brother and sister by name, yet who had with them a mysterious small boy, who lived solitary, unnatural lives, walking at all hours on the hills, murmuring strings of meaningless words, staring at a tree, a piece of bracken, a fall of water, an unconscionable time together; strange, suspicious people, revolutionaries for certain.[17]

This last suspicion was confirmed when the notorious John Thelwall appeared at Alfoxden within a few days of the Wordsworths settling there. That this man—gaol-bird, traitor, acknowledged republican, who denied the existence of God, whose name was known and hated throughout England—that this man should dare to set foot in patriotic Stowey, religious Stowey, staunch Stowey, was more than sufficient to damn those who had dared to ask him there, to give him shelter. Poor, loyal, eminently respectable Poole, together with Coleridge, fell once again into disrepute.

Miss Charlotte Poole appears once more upon the scene. Her diary entry for July 23 reads:

"We are shocked to hear that Mr Thelwall has spent some time at Stowey this week with Mr Coleridge, and consequently with Tom Poole. Alfoxton house is taken by one of the fraternity, and Woodlands by another. To what are we coming?"[18]

To what, indeed! They did not know, except that it boded no good to the community. It seemed best to find out what new treachery was hatching. The Government was informed by a Dr Lysons of Bath (not by Sir Philip Hale of Cannington as Coleridge supposed) that he had received information of a suspicious emigrant family occupying Alfoxden. In due time, down came a government spy whose activities, not of the most secretive, afforded Coleridge some excellent fun.[19]

"The dark guesses of some zealous Quidnunc," wrote Coleridge, "met with so congenial a soil in the grave alarm of a titled Dogberry of our neighbourhood, that a SPY was actually sent down from the government *pour surveillance* of myself and friend. There must have been not only abundance, but *variety* of these 'honorable' men at the disposal of Ministers: for this proved a very honest fellow. After three weeks' truly Indian perseverance in tracking us, (for we were commonly together,) during all which time seldom were we out of doors, but he contrived to be within hearing, (and all the while utterly unsuspected; how indeed *could* such a suspicion enter our fancies?) he not only rejected Sir Dogberry's request that he would try yet a little longer, but declared to him his belief, that both my friend and myself were as good subjects, for aught he could discover to the contrary, as any in His Majesty's dominions. He had repeatedly hid himself, he said, for hours together behind a bank at the sea-side, (our favorite seat), and overheard our conversation. At first he fancied, that we were aware of our danger; for he often heard me talk of one *Spy Nozy*, which he was inclined to interpret of himself, and of a remarkable feature belonging to him; but he was speedily convinced that it was the name of a man who had made a book and lived long ago. Our talk ran most upon books, and we were perpetually desiring each other to look at *this*, and to listen to *that*; but he could not catch a word about politics. Once he had joined me on the road . . . and, passing himself off as a traveller, he had entered into conversation with me, and talked of purpose in a *democrat* way in order to draw me out. The result, it appears, not only convinced him that I was no friend of Jacobin-

ALFOXDEN LOOKING NORTH-EAST

"Here we are in a large mansion, in a large park, with seventy head of deer around us. . . . The garden is at the end of the house, and our favourite parlour, as at Racedown, looks that way. . . . The front of the house is to the south, but it is screened from the sun by a high hill which rises immediately from it. This hill is beautiful, scattered irregularly and abundantly with trees, and topped with fern, which spreads a considerable way down it. . . . From the end of the house we have a view of the sea, over a woody meadow-country; and exactly opposite the window where I now sit is an immense wood, whose round top from this point has exactly the appearance of a mighty dome."   DOROTHY WORDSWORTH

"I slept that night in an old room with blue hangings, and covered with the round-faced family-portraits of the age of George I and II, and from the wooded declivity of the adjoining park that overlooked my window, at the dawn of day, could 'hear the loud stag speak.' "   WILLIAM HAZLITT

"We spent a fortnight at Coleridge's; in the course of that time we heard that this house was to let, applied for it, and took it. Our principal inducement was Coleridge's society."   DOROTHY WORDSWORTH

"I had been on a visit to Wordsworth's at Racedown, near Crewkerne, and I brought him and his sister back with me, and here I have *settled them*. By a combination of curious circumstances a gentleman's seat, with a park and woods, elegantly and completely furnished, with nine lodging rooms, three parlours, and a hall, in the most beautiful and romantic situation by the seaside, four miles from Stowey—this we have got for Wordsworth at the *rent of twenty-three pounds a year, taxes included!* The park and woods are *his* for all purposes *he* wants them, and the large gardens are altogether and entirely his."   COLERIDGE

(W. F. Taylor, London)

ism; but, (he added), I had 'plainly made it out to be such a silly as well as wicked thing, that he felt ashamed though he had only *put it on.*' "[20]

Thus Coleridge on an incident, a little touched up in retrospect perhaps, but essentially true. But the most foolish part of this spy scare, illustrating how easily the country people at that time panicked in the face of anything unusual, was the report, forwarded to the Government, that the strangers were making a plan of the countryside, asking whether a certain brook was navigable to the sea and were later seen examining the brook from its beginnings to its mouth—the brook being that one upon which Coleridge was meditating the writing of a poem in the manner of Cowper's *The Task*, to be entitled *The Brook*; the plans being his notes as he was "*making studies*"[21] for the poem. He continues his account of the spy:

"Had I finished the work, it was my purpose in the heat of the moment to have dedicated it to our then committee of public safety as containing the charts and maps, with which I was to have supplied the French Government in aid of their plans of invasion. And these too for a tract of coast that, from Clevedon to Minehead, scarcely permits the approach of a fishing-boat!"[22]

This affair, though not the immediate result of Thelwall's visit, was carried further only because the spy heard of his presence in the neighbourhood. Less quick but as certain was the dashing of all hopes of Thelwall finding permanent refuge in the district. At the end of July, he went to Wales, leaving Coleridge to try and secure a cottage for him. After a visit to Thelwall at Bristol,[23] Coleridge went so far as to write and approach the necessary people[24] to this end, but he was informed that Thelwall could settle at Stowey only if Poole were to vouch for his behaviour. To this Coleridge would not agree, as he told Thelwall with unwonted firmness.

". . . the hope which I had entertained, that you could have settled without the remotest interference of Poole, *has vanished*. To such interference on his part there are insuperable difficulties: the whole malignity of the aristocrats will converge to him as to the one point; his tranquillity will be perpetually interrupted, his business and his credit hampered and distressed by vexatious calumnies, the ties of relationship weakened, perhaps broken; and,

O

lastly, his poor old mother made miserable—the pain of the stone aggravated by domestic calamity and quarrels betwixt her son and those neighbours with whom and herself there have been peace and love for these fifty years. Very great odium T. Poole incurred by bringing *me* here. My peaceable manners and known attachment to Christianity had almost worn it away when Wordsworth came, and he, likewise by T. Poole's agency, settled here. You cannot conceive the tumult, calumnies, and apparatus of threatened persecutions which this event has occasioned round about us. If *you*, too, should come, I am afraid that even riots, and dangerous riots, might be the consequence. Either of us separately would perhaps be tolerated, but *all three* together, what can it be less than plot and damned conspiracy—a school for the propagation of Demagogy and Atheism? And it deserves examination, whether or no as moralists we should be justified in hazarding the certain evil of calling forth malignant passions for the contingent good, that might result from our living in the same neighbourhood? Add to which, that in point of the *public interest*, we must take into the balance the Stowey Benefit Club. Of the present utility of this T. Poole thinks highly; of its possible utility, very, very highly indeed; but the interests, nay, perhaps the existence of this club, is interwoven with his character as a peaceable and *undesigning* man; certainly, any future and greater excellence which he hopes to realize in and through the society will vanish like a dream of the morning. If, therefore, you can get the land and cottage near Bath of which you spoke to me, I would advise it on many accounts; but if you still see the arguments on the other side in a stronger light than those which I have stated, come, but not yet. Come in two or three months—take lodgings at Bridgwater—familiarise the people to your name and appearance, and, when the *monstrosity* of the thing is gone off, and the people shall have begun to consider you as a man whose mouth won't eat them, and whose pocket is better adapted for a bundle of sonnets than the transportation or ambush place of a French army, then you may take a house; but indeed (I say it with a very sad but a very clear conviction), at *present* I see that much evil and little good would result from your settling here." 25

Coleridge was, in fact, over optimistic in supposing that Thelwall would ever be able to make a home in Stowey—the retired firebrand was destined to get no nearer than Llyswen, in Wales, where he eventually settled.

Thelwall was not the only sufferer of Stowey's political staunchness. His visit hastened, if it did not settle, the departure of the Wordsworths and so, eventually, that of Coleridge also. Although they were not immediately aware of the fact, the Wordsworths' tenancy of Alfoxden was doomed from the moment Thelwall crossed the threshold.

In August, Coleridge had another visitor, a certain Richard Reynell. His comments on the household at Stowey are not profound. He appears to have been struck chiefly by Coleridge's ability—in which Coleridge was matched by the Wordsworths and many of his friends—to walk long distances. When the visitor called, the poet was out: ". . . having set out for Bristol to see Mrs Barbauld[26] a few days before. I think he had never seen her, and that he now had *walked* all the way to gratify his curiosity. He returned on Saturday evening after a walk of 40 miles in one day, apparently not much fatigued."[27]

Lloyd, released from the sanatorium, had turned up again, but not at Stowey. Because of parental opposition to the match with Sophia Pemberton, he was planning to run away with her and make a Scotch marriage at Gretna Green. His fellow conspirator, or possibly moderator, was none other than Southey, with whom he was now on very cordial terms. Lamb, also, coming within the orbit of this friendship, paid a visit to them at Southey's cottage at Burton, near Christchurch. He spent a couple of days there and left much alarmed about the plans that were going forward.[28] The following week Lloyd and Southey were at Bath on their way to Birmingham to try and persuade Sophia to agree to the plan. Although so near to Stowey, however, they did not visit Coleridge, nor did Lloyd seek his help or advice.

Lamb, who wrote in haste to Coleridge as soon as he had returned from Burton, said that Lloyd had excused himself from going to Stowey; "He said if he *had* come to you, he could never have brought himself to leave you."[29] This was cold comfort to Coleridge, as sensitive almost as Lloyd himself to neglect, mindful of his former pupil's professions of attachment to him, ready if not positively eager to bestow advice, and not a little jealous of Southey's increasing influence. Lloyd began to come under his displeasure. After a time Coleridge ceased writing to him. Lamb appealed in vain; worse than in vain: "You use Lloyd very ill, never writing to him. I tell you again that his is not a mind with which you should play tricks. He deserves more tenderness from you."[30]

But only an advance by Lloyd could repair the injury to Coleridge's affections and pride: and of that there was no sign. So Lamb's appeal met with no response; indeed, the very fact that it was made and its assumption that Coleridge was not as familiar with Lloyd's mind as was Lamb, did harm, not good. The coolness began to spread between the would-be mediator and his old friend.

After Thelwall had gone, Coleridge paid his long-deferred visit to Bowles. He left Stowey on September 6,[31] for Shaftesbury, carrying with him *Osorio*, now completed to the middle of the fifth act.[32] From that place he proposed to visit his brother at Salisbury, then Southey at Burton.[33]

The meeting of Bowles and Coleridge was not a success according to Cottle, who remarked that: "I noticed a marked change in his commendation of Mr B. from the time he paid that man of genius a visit . . . an altered feeling . . . not so much expressed by words, as by his subdued tone of applause."[34] Certainly, Cottle would seem to be borne out by the shortness of the visit, for on September 12 Coleridge wrote a sonnet to Linley, Sheridan's secretary and brother-in-law, inscribed at Donhead, Wiltshire.[35] A few days later, he was writing to Cottle from London in great haste. Sarah was to come up to London. They were to live there for the next four months.[36]

Sarah stayed where she was. Soon Coleridge was back again at Stowey, writing to Thelwall with a certain pessimism. Money troubles were weighing upon him again. He had finished his tragedy, but had not much hope that it would be accepted. ". . . I suppose that at last I must become a Unitarian minister, as a less evil than starvation. For I get nothing by literature. . . ."[37]

The recollection of an incident in his childhood of which he had recently been writing to Poole in response to the latter's request for particulars of his early life, came back to him, but without enthusiasm—indeed, with positive misrepresentation:

"... I can *at times* feel strongly the beauties you describe, in themselves and for themselves; but more frequently *all things* appear *little*, all the knowledge that can be acquired child's play; the universe itself! what but an immense heap of *little* things? I can contemplate nothing but *parts*, and parts are all *little*. My mind feels as if it ached to behold and know something *great*, something *one* and *indivisible*. And it is only in the faith of that that rocks or waterfalls, mountains or caverns, give me the sense of sublimity or majesty! But in this faith *all things* counterfeit infinity." [38]

He goes on to quote from *This Lime-Tree Bower my Prison*,[39] showing clearly both the hold which Spinoza was gaining upon him and why—for he was but affirming his inability to rest content with the thought of a universe of little things and with the common conception of nature, no matter how deeply loved or understood. His reaffirmation of his belief in nature as a symbol of God was the more significant at this time, after months of intimacy with the Wordsworths, who loved nature for itself and were content with a knowledge of its outward manifestations and the inward peace that contemplation of it ensured. The strength of Coleridge's instinct to *use* nature, to step upon it, as it were, to treat it as a vantage-point from which he might observe what nature stood for and to what it led, could have had no sterner test than this silent but unmistakable conflict with the less penetrative, less ambitious views of the friends he loved and depended upon so deeply.

What the two men displayed in their poems—Wordsworth a magnificent example of observation, Coleridge of penetration; Wordsworth content to set down what he saw, Coleridge obliged to record what he felt—did but march a step further in their beliefs at this time: the one, satisfied by the vague acceptance of a God in nature, the other, struggling ever to pierce beyond the façade of the external world to the all-embracing unity his intellect suspected, his faith demanded.

The fact was, Coleridge could no more help this God-search than he could help his innately religious mind. It was he and there was no more to be said. But scarcely less necessary was the demand of his intellect to make religion not only a living but a provable thing, a spiritual force in men's lives that could yet be demonstrated to the satisfaction of the reason. What one part of him felt, the other part insisted upon proving. It was this conflict which, at first instinctively, he was beginning to strive to resolve; this, that drove him at times to pessimism; and this, a reaction from which, in his same letter to Thelwall, made him say: "It is but seldom that I raise and spiritualize my intellect to

[213]

this height; and at other times I adopt the Brahmin creed, and say, 'It is better to sit than to stand, it is better to lie than to sit, it is better to sleep than to wake, but Death is the best of all!' I should much wish, like the Indian Vishnu, to float about along an infinite ocean cradled in the flower of the Lotus, and wake once in a million years for a few minutes just to know that I was going to sleep a million years more." [40] This thought he had put into the mouth of a character, Alhadra, in *Osorio*.[41]

It was probably true that these thoughts were rare at the moment. His mind was occupied for the most part with money troubles, with the possibility that he might be obliged to enter the Ministry. Estlin, anxious to secure this brilliant young man for his Church, was keeping his eyes open for suitable vacancies— one of which, at Norwich,[42] Coleridge had already refused to consider on account of the town's distance from his friends and its lack of amenities; indeed he had some hard words to say of Norwich.[43] Now, however, his fate seemed bound up with the fate of *Osorio*, about which he was uncertain, to say the least of it, even when an author's modesty has been discounted. The news of Mrs Evans' marriage to her husband's half-brother, Walter Evans—one of her children's guardians and a steadfast opponent of the tutorship scheme—could bring from Coleridge only a melancholy "I saw it even from the first week I was at Darley." [44]

Affairs at Alfoxden, far from consoling, roused him to in-dignation. The owner of the house, Mrs St. Albyn, had censured the tenant for sub-letting to the Wordsworths. Poole, as a party to the sub-letting (he had witnessed the agreement and drafted it), was involved in this reprimand. His letter defending Words-worth, which he wrote promptly, had no effect.[45] Coleridge was enraged. "The aristocrats seem to persecute *even Wordsworth*," [46] he told Thelwall.

In November he was back in London, waiting to hear the fate of his tragedy. There was no news; but he was successful in arranging an introduction to Harris, of Covent Garden, who said that he would be prepared to consider Wordsworth's tragedy. Coleridge wrote post-haste to his friend with the news, begging him to send the play.[47] Wordsworth did so, also without "the faintest expectation that it will be accepted." [48]

Coleridge had been busy at this time with a less useful activity. He had written and sent to the *Monthly Magazine*, wherein they appeared in the November issue, three sonnets under the name of Nehemiah Higginbottom.[49] These sonnets were parodies. Coleridge explains them in a letter to Cottle. "I sent three mock Sonnets in ridicule of my own & Charles Lloyd's, & Lamb's, &c. &c.—in ridicule of that affectation of unaffectedness, of jumping & misplaced accent on common-place epithets, flat lines forced into poetry by Italics, (signifying how well & *mouthisly* the Author would read them) puny pathos, &c. &c.—the instances are almost all taken from mine & Lloyd's poems."[50] He adds, in the paternal manner which it sometimes pleased him to adopt: "I think they may do good to our young Bards."[51]

But if that was really his intention, he thought wrongly. Later he explained his action more fully but not perhaps with any greater conviction. "The first,"[52] he wrote, "had for its object to excite a good-natured laugh at the spirit of *doleful egotism*, and at the recurrence of favorite phrases, with the double defect of being at once trite and licentious."[53] This was a hit at Lloyd. The second,[54] parodying Lamb, exposed: ". . . low, creeping language and thoughts, under the pretence of *simplicity*. And the third,[55] the phrases of which were borrowed entirely from my own poems, on the indiscriminate use of elaborate and swelling language and imagery."[56]

The result of this blend of humour and fatherly concern, not perhaps entirely devoid of pique at the new intimacy of Lloyd and Lamb, from which Coleridge found himself excluded, was unfortunate. Lamb, whose sense of humour was more than equal to the occasion, could appreciate the double joke—that intended by Coleridge and the picture, perhaps more humorous, of the author in parental mood. But Lloyd, whose sensitiveness was abnormal, who lacked a sense of humour, and in whom malice and an unquiet tongue were never far apart, was no person to expose publicly in this way. He held his work in great seriousness. He is unlikely to have appreciated the necessity for Coleridge's sonnet *Addressed to a Young Man of Fortune who Abandoned Himself to an Indolent and Causeless Melancholy*. This far heavier blow, over-estimated both by his vanity and his excess of sensitiveness, rankled, stayed in his mind, and bore ugly results.

A more useful employment of Coleridge whilst in London was to busy himself about the learning of French and German. He intended to translate Wieland's *Oberon*. He may even have begun it. Nor was this all. He asks Cottle to procure him a German-English Grammar[57] and goes on to say: "I have written a ballad of about 300 lines[58]—& the Sketch of a Plan of General Study."[59] He returned to Stowey in November to wait with Wordsworth until the decision of the two theatres was known. Their walks were resumed. But Coleridge was now set upon the composition of a poem on a subject: ". . . that should give equal room and freedom for description, incident, and impassioned reflections on men, nature, and society, yet supply in itself a natural connection to the parts, and unity to the whole. Such a subject I conceived myself to have found in a stream, traced from its source in the hills among the yellow-red moss and conical glass-shaped tufts of bent, to the first break or fall, where its drops become audible, and it begins to form a channel; thence to the peat and turf barn, itself built of the same dark squares as it sheltered; to the sheep-fold; to the first cultivated plot of ground; to the lonely cottage and its bleak garden won from the heath; to the hamlet, the villages, the market-town, the manufactories, and the seaport. My walks therefore were almost daily on the top of Quantock, and among its sloping combes. With my pencil and memorandum book in my hand, I was *making studies*, as the artists call them, and often moulding my thoughts into verse, with the objects and imagery immediately before my senses."[60]

The poem was to be called *The Brook*. But as Coleridge was not alone in his walks on the hills, neither was he alone in his meditations upon the poem. Wordsworth was consulted. His friend's enthusiasm kindled a like flame in him. Thus, out of the conception of this poem which was never written, arose the beginnings of a greater work to be written later by Wordsworth. Here was the true birthplace of *The Prelude*, during those idyllic days on the Quantocks, while Coleridge's future, as a poet at least, seemed to hang in the balance.

For the time, however, care was pushed aside in the manner which Coleridge was so well able to do, no man better. *The Brook* seemed half written, enthusiasm mounted high as the grandeur of the theme took shape in the poets' minds. But it was not destined to be written by Coleridge. Nevertheless, despite the fact that *The Brook* was to come to nothing and despite the trepidation with which he awaited the fate of his tragedy, Coleridge was actually upon the brink of an era, brief but magical, which, although unable to ensure him a financial competence, was eventually to secure him a place among the major English poets.

The next few months were to see, with true Coleridgean dramatic effect, not only the swift emergence of Coleridge the poet in full stature but—what he was not to know—the appearance of his greatest poetry. For a moment of time—for an all too brief moment—Coleridge was destined to outstrip the wildest hopes, the fondest imaginings of his friends.

This remarkable creative outburst—the more remarkable in that, in metre, treatment of subject, atmosphere, in almost every respect Coleridge was to break new ground—was a tribute to the influence of the Wordsworths; not so much by what they did, by what they were able to teach, neither by precept nor by example, so much as by what they were, what they stood for. To Coleridge they came as a releasing power. They enabled the poetic greatness in him to escape at last from the excessively human foibles and weaknesses which had encompassed and imprisoned it. They spelt release from self-distrust, from paralysing inhibitions, from dragging sloth, from mental loneliness. They brought about the full expression of a poetic fancy whose flowering had waited upon the coming of a kindred soul. Released of his often self-imposed burdens, Coleridge soared into greatness.

Even when, as was often the fact, Wordsworth neither appreciated nor fully understood the subtle beauties of his friend's work, he still stood for Coleridge as the greatest poet of his time, the joint advocate of progress, fellow fighter against poetic reaction and artificiality; and so, as a companion of the heart even when not of the mind. Indeed, in one respect at least, Wordsworth was preparing to step further than Coleridge in the direction of realism; both men were already busy with the beginnings of the theory of poetic diction which Wordsworth was later to develop to questionable lengths.

The tasks of the two men in this endeavour to reinspire poetry were to be allotted mutually so as to fit the directions in which inclinations and abilities alike pointed. Coleridge has explained the position to which their consideration of the function of the creative imagination, together with their determination to uproot artificial language, abstractions, and sentimental bathos led them:

"During the first year that Mr Wordsworth and I were neighbours, our conversations turned frequently on the two cardinal points of poetry, the power of exciting the sympathy of the reader by a faithful adherence to the truth of nature, and the power of giving the interest of novelty by the modifying colors of imagination. The sudden charm, which accidents of light and shade, which moon-light or sun-set, diffused over a known and familiar landscape, appeared to represent the practicability of combining both. These are the poetry of nature. The thought suggested itself (to which of us I do not recollect) that a series of poems might be composed of two sorts. In the one, the incidents and agents were to be, in part at least, supernatural; and the excellence aimed at was to consist in the interesting of the affections by the dramatic truth of such emotions, as would naturally accompany such situations, supposing them real. And real in *this* sense they have been to every human being who, from whatever source of delusion, has at any time believed himself under supernatural agency. For the second class, subjects were to be chosen from ordinary life; the characters and incidents were to be such, as will be found in every village and its vicinity, where there is a meditative and feeling mind to seek after them, or to notice them, when they present themselves.

"In this idea originated the plan of the 'Lyrical Ballads'; in which it was agreed, that my endeavours should be directed to persons and characters supernatural, or at least romantic; yet so as to transfer from our inward nature a human interest and a semblance of truth sufficient to procure for these shadows of imagination that willing suspension of disbelief for the moment, which constitutes poetic faith. Mr Wordsworth, on the other hand, was to propose to himself as his object, to give the charm of novelty to things of every day, and to excite a feeling analogous to the supernatural, by awakening the mind's attention from the lethargy of custom, and directing it to the loveliness and the wonders of the world before us; an inexhaustible treasure, but for which, in consequence of the film of familiarity and selfish solicitude we have eyes, yet see not, ears that hear not, and hearts that neither feel nor understand." [61]

This passage was written some years after the event and consequently states the division of aims with a greater precision than actually existed in November 1797. At this time, although

Wordsworth and Coleridge had clarified their minds as to their eventual aims, their respective functions in the attainment of these aims remained unfixed. But they were soon to have an unmistakable demonstration of the need for division of labour and a fair indication of the direction that this division should take.

For it was with *The Ancient Mariner* that Coleridge's great period began. The poem itself was unpremeditated, coming about through the conjunction of several circumstances.

Early in November, the three of them—Coleridge, Wordsworth, and Dorothy—had made a longer walk than usual, to Porlock, Lynmouth, the Valley of Rocks and home by Dulverton.[62] The excursion was a great success. Nothing would do but that it should be repeated. They decided to try and make the second journey profitable in more senses than one; hoping to sell to the *Monthly Magazine*—the scene of Coleridge's recent satirical feat—a poem to be composed jointly during the walk— ". . . the profits of which were to defray the expenses of a little excursion we were to make together." [63]

But the determining factor, the reason why *The Ancient Mariner* and not perhaps *The Brook* achieved existence, was a dream of John Cruikshank, Coleridge's back-garden neighbour. In this dream, he told Coleridge, he "fancied he saw a skeleton ship, with figures in it." [64] Not on the face of it a great deal to stir the imagination, but to Coleridge this strange vision, together with the suggestion made by Wordsworth after a reading of Shelvocke's *Voyages*, that a man killing an albatross should bring upon his head the vengeance of the tutelary spirits of the regions,[65] linked itself mysteriously with a host of strange facts Coleridge had garnered from his "out-of-the-way books,"[66] moved his imagination to work, gave it the impetus that was all it needed to blossom into strange and wonderful beauty.

At half-past four on the "dark and cloudy" afternoon of Monday, November 13, they set out again.[67] For the first eight miles, Dorothy wrote, the two men were busy "employing themselves in laying the plan of a ballad, to be published with some pieces of William's." [68]

But Coleridge the poet had found himself at last. The subject took an irresistible hold upon him. With every step they took towards Watchet, he saw the scope of the poem expand, its possibilities grow, its attractiveness increase.

His imagination took wing. Wordsworth made one or two suggestions, added a few lines, but collaboration soon grew difficult. It became impossible: ". . . our respective manners," wrote Wordsworth, stately to the last, "proved so widely different that it would have been quite presumptuous in me to do anything but separate from an undertaking upon which I could only have been a clog." [69]

So, after they had left Watchet the next morning, Coleridge took over the entire composition of the poem. As the excursion proceeded, so his absorption intensified and the poem grew until it became obvious that it would be too long to secure acceptance by the magazine for which it had been destined. Also, it was far from completion.

They reached home. Coleridge continued to work on the poem, his creative imagination at full stretch. Everything was to be put aside for *The Ancient Mariner*. But the pressure of poverty (for his state was barely above indigence) would not be denied. He was obliged to revisit London to try and discover news of his play. "I have heard nothing about my Tragedy, except some silly remarks of Kemble's, to whom Linley shewed it," [70] he wrote Cottle. His patience was wearing thin. "Sheridan, most certainly, has not used me with common Justice. The proposal came from himself—and altho' this circumstance did not bind him to accept the Tragedy, it certainly bound him to pay every & that the earliest, attention to it. I suppose, it lies snugly in his green Bag—if it have not emigrated to the Kitchen or the Cloāca." [71]

He had not long to wait. The second day in December he wrote Poole from Bristol. He had had a letter from Linley. *Osorio* had been rejected by Sheridan—". . . his *sole* objection is—the obscurity of the last three acts." [72]

He was not alone in his disappointment; Wordsworth's tragedy was also rejected a few days later, despite a hurried visit to London by brother and sister to make certain alterations which it was hoped might fit the play for performance. [73] But while this was little more than disappointment for the Wordsworths, for Coleridge his play's rejection, despite his apparent lack of optimism as to its reception, meant that he must cease to hope for a living from literature.

The one tangible result of his London visits was an arrangement reached with Daniel Stuart,[74] editor of the *Morning Post*, a paper in which Coleridge's work had already appeared, that he should contribute poems and articles regularly in future, his remuneration being fixed at a guinea a week.[75] Even this sum, welcome though it was, seemed insufficient and too insecure to release Coleridge from his financial plight.

In any event, in the first bitterness of disappointment and "in all the despondency of the new taxes" considering the Plan of General Study as "absolutely romantic,"[76] Coleridge "offered to supply Mr Row's place for a few Sundays at Shrewsbury, to see whether I liked the place and whether the congregation liked me, and would endure my opinions, which, softened and modified as they had been, did still retain a degree of *peculiarity*."[77] His decision was strengthened by an event which occurred while he waited. This was nothing less than a sharp attack by Southey, accusing Coleridge of satirizing his work when printing the 'simplicity' Higginbottom poem the previous November. This suggestion, in which Lloyd's hand may perhaps be seen, Coleridge denied vigorously:

> "... I am sorry, Southey! very sorry, that I wrote or published those sonnets—but 'sorry' would be a tame word to express my feelings, if I had written them with the motives which you have attributed to me. I have not been in the habit of treating our separation with levity—nor ever since the first moment thought of it without deep emotion—and how could you apply to yourself a sonnet written to ridicule infantine simplicity, vulgar colloquialisms and ladylike friendships? I have no conception, neither I believe could a passage in your writings have suggested to me or any man the notion of *your* 'plainting plaintively.' I am sorry that I wrote thus, because I am sorry to perceive a disposition in you to believe evil of me, of which your remark to Charles Lloyd was a painful instance. I say this to you, because I shall say it to no other being. I feel myself wounded and hurt and write as such . . ."[78]

but apparently without carrying conviction, for not only did he fall foul of Lamb, who said plainly that he did not believe his denials;[79] but Southey, succumbing to the very misdemeanour he attributed to Coleridge, copied him—his imitation extending even to the style of pen-name, his choice being the unoriginal Abel Shufflebottom.

On Christmas Day, Coleridge received two letters. One was from Estlin enclosing a letter from John Rowe, Unitarian minister at Shrewsbury who had accepted a similar position in Bristol. Estlin had recommended Coleridge to Rowe as his successor. The idea was received favourably. "Mr Coleridge," wrote Rowe, "is almost the only one I would wish to settle here."[80] He agreed to consult those in authority at Shrewsbury. He promised to write as soon as he was able to forward a definite offer.

The other letter to Coleridge was from Josiah Wedgwood, writing from Penzance. A draft for £100 was enclosed.

> "My brother Thomas and myself," the letter said, "had sepa-
> rately determined that it would be right to enable you to defer
> entering into an engagement, we understand you are about to
> form, from the most urgent of motives. We therefore request you
> will accept the enclosed Draft with the same simplicity with which
> it is offered."[81]

Tom[82] and Josiah[83] Wedgwood were sons of Josiah, the famous potter of Etruria. Although only a year older than Coleridge, Tom Wedgwood had already begun to fail in health. In the hope of a correct diagnosis and a cure of the mysterious ailment from which he suffered, he remained in Bristol in 1797 under Dr Beddoes—one of the many fruitless attempts he was destined to make in search of health. In Bristol he and Josiah met Poole; and through Poole he came to know and quickly to appreciate Coleridge.[84] He stayed at Alfoxden in September.[85] He not only found Coleridge's powers and range of conversation a revelation and an inspiration, but soon discovered that they had in common a number of acquaintances, a love of freedom, and above all, a deep interest in metaphysics. When he and Josiah heard of Coleridge's financial plight and method of remedying it, they decided to come to his aid.

Coleridge at first accepted the money—"to console myself for a disappointment,"[86] he told Estlin, having hoped for a decisive offer from Shrewsbury. He waited a day, then wrote Josiah:

> "I received your letter, with the enclosed order yesterday. You
> have relieved me from a state of hesitation and perplexity; and

have given me the tranquillity and leisure of independence for the next two years. I am not deficient in the ordinary feelings of gratitude to you and Mr T. Wedgwood; but I shall not find them oppressive or painful, if in the course of that time I shall have been acquiring knowledge for myself, or communicating it to others; if either in act or preparation I shall have been contributing my quota to the cause of Truth and Honesty." [87]

For a moment the draft seemed to have succeeded in the intention with which it was sent. Coleridge, in his first rush of joy on the reception of this unexpected gift (despite his deprecatory words to Estlin), was able to see no further than the immediate freedom it offered him. On reflection, the impermanence of the means supporting this freedom became apparent to him. The day after he had accepted the money, the expected letter from Rowe arrived, inviting Coleridge to Shrewsbury to preach preparatory to an offer being made him to fill the vacant pulpit should he create a favourable impression.

Coleridge now found himself in a cruel dilemma. It seemed that he must risk offending either Estlin or the Wedgwoods. He had to choose between immediate but apparently temporary freedom and security without freedom and with restrictions that galled his principles.

After another week he made up his mind. Acting for once against the advice of Poole, he wrote to Josiah Wedgwood, returning the draft and setting forth in detail the reasons for his action:

"By the inclosed you will understand the occasion of this letter. Your Brother and yourself will be pleased with my conduct, if I shall make it appear probable to you, that the purposes, for which you sent and I accepted so large a Bill, will be better answered by my returning than by my retaining it. You wished to remove those urgent motives which might make it necessary for me to act in opposition to my principles: you wished to give me leisure for the improvement of my Talents at the same time that my mind should be preserved free from any professional Bias which might pervert, or at least hamper, the exertion of them. I will state to you with great simplicity all that has passed thro' my mind on these subjects. The affectionate esteem, with which I regard your character, makes this openness pleasant to me: and your kindness seems to have authorised the freedom, which I am about to take in being so diffuse concerning my own affairs.

[223]

"If a Man considered himself as acting in opposition to his principles *then only* when he gave his example or support to actions and institutions, the existence of which produces *unmingled* evil he might perhaps with a safe conscience perpetrate any crime and become a member of any Order. If on the other hand a man should make it *his principle* to abstain from all modes of conduct, the general practice of which was not permanently useful, or at least absolutely harmless, he must live, an isolated Being: his furniture, his servants, his very cloathes are intimately connected with Vice and Misery. To preserve therefore our moral feelings without withdrawing ourselves from active life, we should, I imagine, endeavour to discover those evils in society which are the most pressing, and those of which the immediate Removal appears the most practicable: to the removal of these we should concenter our energies, for the removal of them be prepared to make any sacrifices. In other things we *must* compound with a large quantity of evil—taking care to select from the modes of conduct, which may be within our choice, those in which we can do the most good with the least evil. Now I shall apply this to myself. As far as I am able to decide, the most pressing evils and those of which the speedy removal is the most practicable, are these—the union of Religion with the Government, and those other political Institutions and abuses which I need not name; but which not only produce much evil directly and per se, but likewise perpetuate the causes of most other evils. Do not think me boastful when I assert that rather than in any way support any of these, I would undergo Poverty, Dependence, and even Death. There remain within my choice two Sources of Subsistence: the Press and the Ministry. Now as to the Press, I gain at present a guinea a week by writing to the Morning Post—and as my expenses, living as I do now, will not exceed 100£ a year—or but little more, even including the annual 20£, for which my wife's mother has a necessity—I could by means of your kindness subsist for the next two years, and enjoy leisure and external comfort. But anxiety for the future would remain and increase, as it is probable my children will come fast on me: and the Press, considered as a Trade, is perhaps only not the worst occupation for a man who would wish to preserve any delicacy of moral feeling. The few weeks I have written for the Morning Post, I have felt thus—Something must be written and written immediately—if any important Truth, any striking beauty, occur to my mind, I feel a repugnance at sending it garbled to a newspaper: and if any idea of ludicrous personality, or apt anti-ministerial joke, crosses me, I feel a repugnance at rejecting it, because *something must be written*, and nothing else suitable occurs. The longer I continue a hired paragraph-scribbler, the more powerful these Temptations will become; and indeed nothing scarcely that has not a *tang* of personality or *vindictive* feeling, is pleasing or interesting, I apprehend, to my Employers. Of all I most dislike party-politics—yet this sort of gypsie Jargon I am compelled to fire away. To the *Ministry* I adduced the following objections at the time that I decided against entering into it. It makes one's livelihood hang upon the profession of *particular opinions*: and tends therefore to warp the intellectual faculty; to fasten convictions on the mind by the agency of it's wishes; and if Reason should at length dissever them, it presents strong motives to Falsehood or Simulation. Secondly, as the subscriptions of the Congregation form the revenue, the Minister is under an inducement to adapt his moral exhortations to their wishes rather than to their needs. (Poor Pilkington of Derby was, I believe, obliged to resign on account of his sermons respecting Riches and Rich Men.) Thirdly, the routine of Duty brings on a certain sectarian mannerism, which generally narrows the Intellect itself, and always narrows the sphere of its operation. In answer to these objections it may be observed: first, that I see the contingency of these evils very distinctly, and in proportion to my clear perception of them it is probable that I shall be able to guard against them. Secondly, the Press, considered as a *Trade*, presents still greater temptations—and this is not a controversy concerning absolute, but concerning *comparative* good. Thirdly, the income of that place, which is now offered to me, does not depend on the congregation; but is an estate. This weakens certainly, tho' as certainly does not remove, the second objection. Fourthly—The principal of these objections are weak or strong in proportion to the care and impartiality with which the particular opinions had been formed previously to the assumption of the ministerial office; in as much as the probability of a change in these opinions is therefore proportionally lessened. Now, not only without any desire of becoming an hired Teacher in any sect but with decisive intentions to the contrary I have studied the subject of natural and revealed religion—I have read the works of the celebrated Infidels—I have conversed long, and seriously, and dispassionately with Infidels of great Talents and information— and most assuredly, my faith in Christianity has been confirmed rather than staggered. In teaching it therefore, at present, whether I act *beneficently* or no, I shall certainly act *benevolently*. Fifthly— The *necessary* creed in our sect is but short—it will be necessary for me, in order to my continuance as an Unitarian Minister to believe that Jesus Christ was the Messiah—in all other points I may play off my Intellect *ad libitum*. Sixthly—that altho' we ought not to brave temptations in order to shew our strength,

yet it would be slothful and cowardly to retire from an employment, because tho' there *are* no temptations at present, there
may be some hereafter. In favor of my assuming the ministerial
office it may be truly said, that it will give me a regular income
sufficient to free me from all anxiety respecting my absolute wants,
yet not large enough to exempt me from motives, even of a
pecuniary nature, for literary exertion. I can afford to dedicate
three or twice three years to *some one work*, which *may be* of
benefit to society, and will certainly be uninjurious to my own
moral character: for I shall be positive at least that there is no
falsehood or immorality in it proceeding from haste or necessity—
If I do enter on this office, it will be at Shrewsbury—I shall be surrounded by a fine country, no mean ingredient in the composition
of a poet's happiness—I shall have at least five days in every week
of perfect leisure—120£ a year—a good house, valued at 30£ a
year—and if I should die and without any culpable negligence or
extravagance have left my family in want, the Congregations are
in the habit of becoming the guardians. Add to this, that by Law
I shall be exempted from military service—to which, Heaven only
knows how soon we may be dragged. For I think it not improbable, that in case of an invasion our government will serve
all, whom they choose to suspect of disaffection, in the same way
that good King David served Uriah—"set ye Uriah in the fore-
front of the hottest Battle, and retire ye from him, that he may be
smitten and die." I do not wish to conceal from you that I have
suffered more from fluctuation of mind on this occasion than on
any former occasion: and even now I have scarcely courage to
decide absolutely. It is chilling to go among *strangers*—and I leave
a lovely country, and one friend so eminently near to my affections
that his Society has almost been consolidated with my ideas of
happiness. However—I shall go to Shrewsbury, remain a little
while amongst the congregation: if no new argument arise
against the Ministerial office, and if the old ones assume no new
strength, there I shall certainly pitch my *tents*, and *probably* shall
build up my permanent Dwelling. Whatever is conducive to a
man's real comforts is in the same degree conducive to his
utility—a permanent income not inconsistent with my religious
or political creeds, I find necessary to my quietness—without it I
should be a prey to anxiety, and anxiety with me always induces
Sickliness, and too often Sloth: as an overdose of Stimulus proves
a narcotic.

"You will let me know of the arrival of the Bill: and it would
give me very great pleasure to hear, that I had not forfeited your
esteem by first accepting, and now returning it. I acted, each time,
from the purest motives possible on such an occasion: for my

public usefulness being incompatible with personal vexations, an enlightened Selfishness was in this case the only species of Benevolence left to me." [88]

This day and the next Coleridge spent in explaining his actions to Wade, Estlin, and Cottle by letter. Having returned the £100, his position had become critical. As he explained, so he asked for money—the disagreement with Poole making application in that quarter impossible.

"This last fortnight has been eventful," he told Wade. "I received an hundred pounds from Josiah Wedgewood, in order to prevent the necessity of my going into the Ministry—I have received an invitation from Shrewsbury to be the Minister there— and after the fluctuations of mind which have for nights together robbed me of sleep, and I am afraid of Health, I have at length returned the order to Mr Wedgewood with a long letter explanatory of my conduct, and accepted the Shrewsbury Invitation—so I shall be with you by the Middle of next week—But I am moneyless, and want 20£. For 10£ I have written to Mr Estlin, 5£ I will get, somehow or other from the Editor of the New Monthly Magazine, and 5£ I must borrow of you, if you can lend it me with perfect convenience but, I beseech, do not put yourself out of your way in these hard times—for if it be not perfectly convenient to you, I doubt not, I shall be able to get it somewhere or other—

"My dear friend, T. Poole, is not convinced of the *expediency*, either to the public or myself, of my returning the Draft and accepting the congregation—It would have been a heart saddening thing to have parted from him in any way, but to part from him, he not satisfied that there is any necessity or propriety in my parting from him, is *very* painful." [89]

Estlin, who knew already of the Wedgwood gift, was told merely that it had been returned. Coleridge was deep in the first reaction to what he considered a right decision; but his despondency in this instance was due as much to the difference with Poole as to the prospect of leaving Stowey. Nor, perhaps, was it entirely unpremeditated; for Estlin it was who so earnestly desired to see his protégé in the Ministry.

"The first sunny morning that I walk out, at Shrewsbury, will make my heart die away within me," he wrote, "for I shall be in a *land of Strangers*! For I shall have left a Friend whose sympathies were perfect with my manners, feelings and opinions—and what is yet more painful, I shall have left him unconvinced of the *expediency* of my going, public or personal. I could not *stay* with an easy conscience; but whether I shall be happy so far removed from any who love me, I know not. This I know—I will make myself contented by struggling to do my Duty." [90]

Coleridge in his finest letters discloses not only the best of his own character but that of the person to whom he is writing. This occurs, as might be expected, when Coleridge is most genuine in what he says and least conscious of himself. But there were other Coleridge letters; few enough at this time, but even then not entirely absent. A Coleridge less admirable but not less human is then made plain by his own hand. It is expected of a man, for instance, to choose his words with care, even to an old friend, when asking for money. But such care was not enough for Coleridge. He wanted more than money. With the gift must come approbation, an assurance that he had in no way deteriorated in the estimation of the person addressed; that, indeed, his request had if anything endeared him further. He must lose no shred of affection or sympathy, understanding or esteem, for these things radiating to him from his friends nourished in him the will to live actively, virtuously, creatively. Without such assurance, he was stricken into despondency and inaction. Of moral stamina he had little or none. A rebuff, criticism that sprang from dislike, contempt, or even indifference was not only hurtful to him—it struck vitally at his self-esteem; to him, the very source of energy and hope. It withdrew from him the love on which alone he flourished. Thus it was not enough to feel such esteem in himself; it must be propped from outside, by love and trust from all his friends. And when, as was often to occur, there existed little or no cause for self-esteem in his actions, he continued still to attempt to wrest a belief in the purity, the spotlessness of his motives from an incredulous reader; to win it by words and so create the illusion of it—attempts whose success was almost invariably confined to their effect upon his own mind. No man ever made more determined efforts to dull and deceive himself with words, to build around himself a character of patently fictitious beauty, strength, and determination—an illusion shattered almost by his every act.

This self-deception became more evident—became for a time,

indeed, almost his whole life—later. But the germ of it was often to be seen even in happier days. On such occasions, Coleridge considered it necessary to mould his letters into the kind of shape he fancied the recipient would wish. The resulting contortions were not always pretty. When, for instance, in his letter to Estlin he writes of duty with a capital D and with the sentiments of a martyr, it can be assumed with some certainty that his conscience was uneasy because he had little intention of performing what he promised; that he is about to make a request for assistance of some kind; or, what was more common, that he is writing what he believes (usually upon the slenderest foundation and often mistakenly) is expected of him.

He tells Estlin that he is taking the duty of the minister at Bridgwater, John Howell,[91] the next day and that he goes to Shrewsbury the end of the week following. Then he draws his friend's attention to his need of money; and no sooner does he deal with this real difficulty than his manner grows refreshingly natural:

"I am now, utterly without money; and my account stands thus. I owe Biggs 5£, Parsons, the bookseller, owes me more than this considerably; but he is a rogue, and will not pay me. I have not paid Mrs Fricker her quarterly allowance—in short—

	£	s	d
Biggs	5	0	0
Mrs Fricker	5	5	0
A quarter's rent due Dec. 25th	2	2	0
Maid's Wages	1	1	0
Shoemaker	1	13	0
Coals	2	6	0
Chandler	0	12	0
Sundries	0	12	0
	£18	11	0

This is all I owe in the world: now in order to pay it I must borrow ten pounds of you, 5£ of Mr Wade, and will sell my Ballad to Phillips who I doubt not will give me 5£ for it—I suppose, that my Friends will not withdraw their annual subscription of 5£ this year—so that, you see, I propose to anticipate your's, Mr Hobhouse's, and Mr Wade's subscriptions.

"God love you! I will be with you as soon as Riches, instead of

[229]

making *themselves* wings, shall make a pair for *my* shoulders—at present, I am absolutely unfledged." [92]

Despite the fact that the ballad was not sold for £5, for the very good reason that it was not completed,[93] Coleridge received £15 from Estlin which enabled him to settle his Stowey debts and, with a little money in his pocket, to take coach for Shrewsbury, at which place he arrived on January 13.

At this point the narrative is taken up by one who has written unforgettably of his first meeting with Coleridge. William Hazlitt,[94] twenty years old at the time, has left a brilliant, if at times bitter, description of Coleridge—a description written many years later, when his admiration for the elder man had turned to contempt:

"My father was a Dissenting Minister at W[e]m in Shropshire; and in the year 1798 (the figures that compose that date are to me like the 'dreaded name of Demogorgon') Mr Coleridge came to Shrewsbury, to succeed Mr Rowe in the spiritual charge of a Unitarian Congregation there. He did not come till late on the Saturday afternoon before he was to preach; and Mr Rowe, who himself went down to the coach in a state of anxiety and expectation, to look for the arrival of his successor, could find no one at all answering the description but a round-faced man in a short black coat (like a shooting jacket) which hardly seemed to have been made for him, but who seemed to be talking at a great rate to his fellow-passengers. Mr Rowe had scarce returned to give an account of his disappointment, when the round-faced man in black entered, and dissipated all doubts on the subject, by beginning to talk. He did not cease while he staid; nor has he since, that I know of. He held the good town of Shrewsbury in delightful suspense for three weeks that he remained there, 'fluttering the *proud Salopians* like an eagle in a dove-cote'; and the Welch mountains that skirt the horizon with their tempestuous confusion, agree to have heard no such mystic sounds since the days of

'High-born Hoel's harp or soft Llewellyn's lay!'

As we passed along between W[e]m and Shrewsbury, and I eyed their blue tops seen through the wintry branches, or the red rustling leaves of the sturdy oak-trees by the roadside, a sound was in my ears as of a Siren's song; I was stunned, startled with it, as from deep sleep; but I had no notion then that I should ever be able to express my admiration to others in motley imagery or quaint allusion, till the light of his genius shone into my soul, like

[230]

the sun's rays glittering in the puddles of the road. I was at that time dumb, inarticulate, helpless, like a worm by the way-side, crushed, bleeding, lifeless; but now, bursting from the deadly bands that bound them,

'With Styx nine times round them,'

my ideas float on winged words, and as they expand their plumes, catch the golden light of other years. My soul has indeed remained in its original bondage, dark, obscure, with longings infinite and unsatisfied; my heart, shut up in the prison-house of this rude clay, has never found, nor will it ever find, a heart to speak to; but that my understanding also did not remain dumb and brutish, or at length found a language to express itself, I owe to Coleridge. But this is not to my purpose.

"My father lived ten miles from Shrewsbury, and was in the habit of exchanging visits with Mr Rowe, and with Mr Jenkins of Whitchurch (nine miles farther on) according to the custom of Dissenting Ministers in each other's neighbourhood. A line of communication is thus established, by which the flame of civil and religious liberty is kept alive, and nourishes its smouldering fire unquenchable, like the fires in the Agamemnon of Æschylus, placed at different stations, that waited for ten long years to announce with their blazing pyramids the destruction of Troy. Coleridge had agreed to come over to see my father, according to the courtesy of the country, as Mr Rowe's probable successor; but in the meantime I had gone to hear him preach the Sunday after his arrival. A poet and a philosopher getting up into a Unitarian pulpit to preach the Gospel, was a romance in these degenerate days, a sort of revival of the primitive spirit of Christianity, which was not to be resisted.

"It was in January, 1798, that I rose one morning before daylight, to walk ten miles in the mud, and went to hear this celebrated person preach. Never, the longest day I have to live, shall I have such another walk as this cold, raw, comfortless one, in the winter of the year 1798. *Il y a des impressions que ni le tems ni les circonstances peuvent effacer. Dusse-je vivre des siècles entiers, le doux tems de ma jeunesse ne peut renaître pour moi, ni s'effacer jamais dans ma mémoire.* When I got there, the organ was playing the 100th psalm, and, when it was done, Mr Coleridge rose and gave out his text, 'And he went up into the mountain to pray, HIMSELF, ALONE.' As he gave out his text, his voice 'rose like a steam of rich distilled perfumes,' and when he came to the two last words, which he pronounced loud, deep, and distinct, it seemed to me, who was then young, as if the sounds had echoed from the bottom of the human heart, and as if that prayer might have floated in solemn silence through the universe. The idea of St John came into mind, 'of one crying in the wilderness, who had his loins girt about, and whose food was locusts and wild honey.' The preacher then launched into his subject, like an eagle dallying with the wind. The sermon was upon peace and war; upon church and state—not their alliance, but their separation—on the spirit of the world and the spirit of Christianity, not as the same, but as opposed to one another. He talked of those who had 'inscribed the cross of Christ on banners dripping with human gore.' He made a poetical and pastoral excursion,—and to shew the fatal effects of war, drew a striking contrast between the simple shepherd boy, driving his team afield, or sitting under the hawthorn, piping to his flock, 'as though he should never be old,' and the same poor country-lad, crimped, kidnapped, brought into town, made drunk at an alehouse, turned into a wretched drummer-boy, with his hair sticking on end with powder and pomatum, a long cue at his back, and tricked out in the loathsome finery of the profession of blood.

'Such were the notes our once-lov'd poet sung.'

And for myself, I could not have been more delighted if I had heard the music of the spheres. Poetry and Philosophy had met together. Truth and Genius had embraced, under the eye and with the sanction of Religion. This was even beyond my hopes. I returned home well satisfied. The sun that was still labouring pale and wan through the sky, obscured by thick mists, seemed an emblem of the *good cause*; and the cold dank drops of dew that hung half melted on the beard of the thistle, had something genial and refreshing in them; for there was a spirit of hope and youth in all nature, that turned every thing into good. The face of nature had not then the brand of JUS DIVINUM on it:

'Like to that sanguine flower inscrib'd with woe.'

"On the Tuesday following, the half-inspired speaker came. I was called down into the room where he was, and went half-hoping, half-afraid. He received me very graciously, and I listened for a long time without uttering a word. I did not suffer in his opinion by my silence. 'For those two hours,' he afterwards was pleased to say, 'he was conversing with W. H.'s forehead!' His appearance was different from what I had anticipated from seeing him before. At a distance, and in the dim light of the chapel, there was to me a strange wildness in his aspect, a dusky obscurity, and I thought him pitted with the small-pox. His complexion was at that time clear, and even bright—

'As are the children of yon azure sheen.'

His forehead was broad and high, light as if built of ivory, with large projecting eyebrows, and his eyes rolling beneath them like a sea with darkened lustre. 'A certain tender bloom his face o'er-spread,' a purple tinge as we see it in the pale thoughtful complexions of the Spanish portrait-painters, Murillo and Velasquez. His mouth was gross, voluptuous, open, eloquent; his chin good-humoured and round; but his nose, the rudder of the face, the index of the will, was small, feeble, nothing—like what he has done. It might seem that the genius of his face as from a height surveyed and projected him (with sufficient capacity and huge aspiration) into the world unknown of thought and imagination, with nothing to support or guide his veering purpose, as if Columbus had launched his adventurous course for the New World in a scallop, without oars or compass. So at least I comment on it after the event. Coleridge in his person was rather above the common size, inclining to the corpulent, or like Lord Hamlet, 'somewhat fat and pursy.' His hair (now, alas! grey) was then black and glossy as the raven's, and fell in smooth masses over his forehead. This long pendulous hair is peculiar to enthusiasts, to those whose minds tend heavenward; and is traditionally insepar-able (though of a different colour) from the pictures of Christ. It ought to belong, as a character, to all who preach *Christ crucified*, and Coleridge was at that time one of those! . . .

"No two individuals were ever more unlike than were the host and his guest. A poet was to my father a sort of nondescript: yet whatever added grace to the Unitarian cause was to him welcome. He could hardly have been more surprised or pleased, if our visitor had worn wings. Indeed, his thoughts had wings; and as the silken sounds rustled round our little wainscoted parlour, my father threw back his spectacles over his forehead, his white hairs mixing with its sanguine hue; and a smile of delight beamed across his rugged cordial face, to think that Truth had found a new ally in Fancy! Besides, Coleridge seemed to take considerable notice of me, and that of itself was enough. He talked very familiarly, but agreeably, and glanced over a variety of subjects. At dinner-time he grew more animated, and dilated in a very edifying manner on Mary Wolstonecraft and Mackintosh.[95] The last, he said, he considered (on my father's speaking of his *Vindiciæ Gallicæ* as a capital performance) as a clever scholastic man—a master of the topics,—or as the ready warehouseman of letters, who knew exactly where to lay his hand on what he wanted, though the goods were not his own. He thought him no match for Burke, either in style or matter. Burke was a metaphysician, Mackintosh a mere logician. Burke was an orator (almost a poet) who reasoned in figures, because he had an eye for nature:

Mackintosh, on the other hand, was a rhetorician, who had only an eye to common-places. On this I ventured to say that I had always entertained a great opinion of Burke, and that (as far as I could find) the speaking of him with contempt might be made the test of a vulgar democratical mind. This was the first observation I ever made to Coleridge, and he said it was a very just and striking one. I remember the leg of Welsh mutton and the turnips on the table that day had the finest flavour imaginable. Coleridge added that Mackintosh and Tom Wedgwood (of whom, however, he spoke highly) had expressed a very indifferent opinion of his friend Mr Wordsworth, on which he remarked to them—'He strides on so far before you, that he dwindles in the distance!' Godwin had once boasted to him of having carried on an argument with Mackintosh for three hours with dubious success; Coleridge told him—'If there had been a man of genius in the room, he would have settled the question in five minutes.' He asked me if I had ever seen Mary Wolstonecraft, and I said, I had once for a few moments, and that she seemed to me to turn off Godwin's objections to something she advanced with quite a playful, easy air. He replied, that 'this was only one instance of the ascendancy which people of imagination exercised over those of mere intellect.' He did not rate Godwin very high* (this was caprice or prejudice, real or affected) but he had a great idea of Mrs Wolstonecraft's powers of conversation, none at all of her talent for book-making. We talked a little about Holcroft. He had been asked if he was not much struck *with* him, and he said, he thought himself in more danger of being struck *by* him. I complained that he would not let me get on at all, for he required a definition of every the commonest word, exclaiming, 'What do you mean by a *sensation*, Sir? What do you mean by an *idea*?' This, Coleridge said, was barricadoing the road to truth:—it was setting up a turnpike-gate at every step we took. I forget a great number of things, many more than I remember; but the day passed off pleasantly, and the next morning Mr Coleridge was to return to Shrewsbury. When I came down to breakfast, I found that he had just received a letter from his friend T. Wedgwood, making him an offer of 150£ a-year if he chose to waive his present pursuit, and devote himself entirely to the study of poetry and philosophy. Coleridge seemed to make up his mind to close with this proposal in the act of tying on one of his shoes. It threw an additional damp on his departure. It took the wayward

* He complained in particular of the presumption of attempting to establish the future immortality of man "without" (as he said) "knowing what Death was or what Life was"—and the tone in which he pronounced these two words seemed to convey a complete image of both. [Hazlitt.]

[234]

enthusiast quite from us to cast him into Deva's winding vales, or by the shores of old romance. Instead of living at ten miles distance, of being the pastor of a Dissenting congregation at Shrewsbury, he was henceforth to inhabit the Hill of Parnassus, to be a shepherd on the Delectable Mountains. Alas! I knew not the way thither, and felt very little gratitude for Mr Wedgwood's bounty. I was presently relieved from this dilemma; for Mr Coleridge, asking for a pen and ink, and going to a table to write something on a bit of card, advanced towards me with undulating step, and giving me the precious document, said that that was his address, *Mr Coleridge, Nether-Stowey, Somersetshire*; and that he should be glad to see me there in a few weeks' time, and, if I chose, would come half-way to meet me. I was not less surprised than the shepherd-boy (this simile is to be found in Cassandra) when he sees a thunder-bolt fall close at his feet. I stammered out my acknowledgments and acceptance of this offer (I thought Mr Wedgwood's annuity a trifle to it) as well as I could; and this mighty business being settled, the poet-preacher took leave, and I accompanied him six miles on the road. It was a fine morning in the middle of winter, and he talked the whole way. The scholar in Chaucer is described as going

—'Sounding on his way.'

So Coleridge went on his. In digressing, in dilating, in passing from subject to subject, he appeared to me to float in air, to slide on ice. He told me in confidence (going along) that he should have preached two sermons before he accepted the situation at Shrewsbury, one on Infant Baptism, the other on the Lord's Supper, shewing that he could not administer either, which would have effectually disqualified him for the object in view. I observed that he continually crossed me on the way by shifting from one side of the foot-path to the other. This struck me as an odd movement; but I did not at that time connect it with any instability of purpose or involuntary change of principle, as I have done since. He seemed unable to keep on in a strait line.[96] He spoke slightingly of Hume (whose Essay on Miracles he said was stolen from an objection started in one of South's sermons—*Credat Judæus Apella!*). I was not very much pleased at this account of Hume, for I had just been reading, with infinite relish, that completest of all metaphysical *choke-pears*, his *Treatise on Human Nature*, to which the *Essays*, in point of scholastic subtlety and close reasoning, are mere elegant trifling, light summer-reading. Coleridge even denied the excellence of Hume's general style, which I think betrayed a want of taste or candour. He however made me amends by the manner in which he spoke of Berkeley. He dwelt particularly on his *Essay on Vision* as a masterpiece of analytical reasoning. So it undoubtedly is. He was exceedingly angry with Dr Johnson for striking the stone with his foot, in allusion to this author's Theory of Matter and Spirit, and saying, 'Thus I confute him, Sir.' Coleridge drew a parallel (I don't know how he brought about the connection) between Bishop Berkeley and Tom Paine. He said the one was an instance of a subtle, the other of an acute mind, than which no two things could be more distinct. The one was a shop-boy's quality, the other the characteristic of a philosopher. He considered Bishop Butler as a true philosopher, a profound and conscientious thinker, a genuine reader of nature and of his own mind. He did not speak of his *Analogy*, but of his *Sermons at the Rolls' Chapel*, of which I had never heard. Coleridge somehow always contrived to prefer the *unknown* to the *known*. In this instance he was right. The *Analogy* is a tissue of sophistry, of wire-drawn, theological special-pleading; the *Sermons* (with the Preface to them) are in a fine vein of deep, matured reflection, a candid appeal to our observation of human nature, without pedantry and without bias. I told Coleridge I had written a few remarks, and was sometimes foolish enough to believe that I had made a discovery on the same subject (the *Natural Disinterestedness of the Human Mind*)—and I tried to explain my view of it to Coleridge, who listened with great willingness, but I did not succeed in making myself understood. . . .

"I remember but one other topic of discourse in this walk. He mentioned Paley, praised the naturalness and clearness of his style, but condemned his sentiments, thought him a mere time-serving casuist, and said that 'the fact of his work on Moral and Political Philosophy being made a text-book in our Universities was a disgrace to the national character.' We parted at the six-mile stone; and I returned homeward pensive but much pleased. I had met with unexpected notice from a person, whom I believed to have been prejudiced against me. 'Kind and affable to me had been his condescension, and should be honoured ever with suitable regard.' He was the first poet I had known, and he certainly answered to that inspired name. I had heard a great deal of his powers of conversation, and was not disappointed. In fact, I never met with any thing at all like them, either before or since. I could easily credit the accounts which were circulated of his holding forth to a large party of ladies and gentlemen, an evening or two before, on the Berkeleian Theory, when he made the whole material universe look like a transparency of fine words; and another story (which I believe he has somewhere told himself) of his being asked to a party at Birmingham, of his smoking tobacco and going to sleep after dinner on a sofa, where the company found him to their no small surprise, which was increased to wonder when he started up of a sudden, and rubbing his eyes, looked about him, and launched into a three-hours' description of the third heaven, of which he had had a dream, very different from Mr Southey's Vision of Judgment, and also from that other Vision of Judgment, which Mr Murray, the Secretary of the Bridge-street Junto, has taken into his especial keeping!

"On my way back, I had a sound in my ears, it was the voice of Fancy: I had a light before me, it was the face of Poetry. The one still lingers there, the other has not quitted my side! Coleridge in truth met me half-way on the ground of philosophy, or I should not have been won over to his imaginative creed. I had an uneasy, pleasurable sensation all the time, till I was to visit him. During those months the chill breath of winter gave me a welcoming; the vernal air was balm and inspiration to me. The golden sunsets, the silver star of evening, lighted me on my way to new hopes and prospects. *I was to visit Coleridge in the spring.*" [97]

The offer to which Hazlitt refers was contained in a letter from Josiah Wedgwood from Penzance dated January 10:

"In the absence of my brother, who has an engagement this morning, I take up the pen to reply to your letter received yesterday. I cannot help regretting very sincerely that, at this critical moment, we are separated by so great a length of the worst road in the kingdom. It is not that we have found much difficulty in deciding how to act in the present juncture of your affairs, but we are apprehensive that, deprived of the benefit of conversation, we may fail somewhat in explaining our views and intentions with that clearness and persuasion which should induce you to accede to our proposal without scruple or hesitation—nay, with that glow of pleasure which the accession of merited good fortune, and the observation of virtuous conduct in others, ought powerfully to excite in the breast of healthful sensibility. Writing is painful to me. I must endeavor to be concise, yet to avoid abruptness. My brother and myself are possessed of a considerable superfluity of fortune; squandering and hoarding are equally distant from our inclinations. But we are earnestly desirous to convert this superfluity into a fund of beneficence, and we have now been accustomed for some time, to regard ourselves rather as Trustees than Proprietors. We have canvassed your past life, your present situation and prospects, your character and abilities. As far as certainty is compatible with the delicacy of the estimate, we have no hesitation in declaring that your claim upon the fund appears to come under more of the conditions we have prescribed for its disposal, and to be every way more unobjectionable, than we could possibly have

[237]

expected. This result is so congenial with our heartfelt wishes, that it will be a real mortification to us if any misconception or distrust of our intentions, or any unworthy diffidence of yourself, should interfere to prevent its full operation in your favour.

"After what my brother Thomas has written I have only to state the proposal we wish to make to you. It is that you shall accept an annuity for life of £150, to be regularly paid by us, no condition whatsoever being annexed to it. Thus your liberty will remain entire, you will be under the influence of no professional bias, and will be in possession of a 'permanent income not inconsistent with your religious and political creeds,' so necessary to your health and activity.

"I do not now enter into the particulars of the mode of securing the annuity, &c.—that will be done when we receive your consent to the proposal we are making; and we shall only say that we mean the annuity to be independent of everything but the wreck of our fortune, an event which we hope is not very likely to happen, though it must in these times be regarded as more than a bare possibility.

"Give me leave now to thank you for the openness with which you have written to me, and the kindness you express for me, to neither of which can I be indifferent, and I shall be happy to derive the advantages from them that a friendly intercourse with you cannot fail to afford me." [98]

This letter, addressed to Coleridge at Stowey, had been opened by Poole and forwarded to Shrewsbury—and from that place to Wem—with a letter of his own, earnestly exhorting the recalcitrant Coleridge to see reason:

"My Dearly Beloved—Such is the answer which is sent to your letter. I received it this morning by nine o'clock, and immediately informed Mrs Coleridge of it, scrawled two notes to you, one directed *the Rev. M. Rowe's, Shrewsbury*, the other enclosed in a short letter I wrote to Estlin, desiring him immediately to send or give it to you, and sent off little Tommy to the post-office, where I trust he arrived before the mail went off. In my letter to Estlin, I informed him of the contents of the above; told him that when I considered the ministry, and your peculiar character, that I thought you ought not to hesitate to accept the annuity proposed, and that I trusted he would be of the same opinion, as I was satisfied that his approbation of every part of your conduct formed no small ingredient of your happiness.

"I now repeat that my opinion is that you ought not to hesitate to accept the annuity. When I consider the MANNER in which the proposal is made, the persons from whom it comes, the property they possess, and the uses to which they have destined that property, I really think it would be palsying that benevolence, which, God be praised, does exist in the human breast, to think of refusing it. This benevolence, in the present case, is deduced from reason; the utility of it is clearly seen before the feelings are permitted to colour the deed with all that can give joy to the heart of man. The existence of such benevolence is the pledge, and the only pledge, of our perfectibility; it is, alas! so overgrown by the various wickedness which has been so systematically excited in the world, that it is rarely seen. You have called it forth in this instance; don't drive it back to the honourable breast where it seems peculiarly to keep its court. Excuse my warmth of expression. You can have but two reasons to hesitate: first, that it is more honourable to gain one's own living than to be dependent upon another; second, that you possibly may be of more use in promoting Christianity as a minister than as a private man. The first can only be answered by considering the *true use* which the possessors of wealth ought to make of it, and by your own immutable resolves of falling in with that use—in which case you are not dependent, but you labour as effectually for that which you receive, as if you took a spade, and worked for me a day, and received a shilling. You and your friends are only moving in the small sphere which approaches to perfection, which is, by beginnings like these, I trust, to conquer and to involve the whole. Would you prefer sticking to the great circle of vice which heavily, very heavily, now drags itself on? The second objection is so frivolous that it need not have been mentioned. The nicest notion of honour can only preclude your being an *hired* minister, while you receive this annuity. You don't think Christianity more pure by coming from the mouth or pen of an hired man? You are not shackled. Your independence of mind is *part of the bond.* You are to give to mankind that which you think they most want. Religion, if you please, may be, as it will be, the basis of your moral writings—it may shine in your lighter productions, inspire and purify your poetry. You may, if you please, occasionally preach, and these occasional addresses are heard with the attention which novelty, as the world is, always excites, and, being gratuitous, possess the aid of disinterestedness on your part, and gratitude on the part of the hearers, to impress on the mind the doctrines you teach." 99

The next day Coleridge replied to Josiah Wedgwood:

"Yesterday morning I received the letter which you addressed to me in your own and your brother's name. Your benevolence appeared so strange and it came upon my mind with such suddenness, that for a while I sat and mused on it with scarce a reference to myself, and gave you a moral approbation almost wholly unmingled with those personal feelings which have since filled my eyes with tears—which do so even now while I am writing to you. What can I say? I accept your proposal not unagitated but yet, I trust, in the same worthy spirit in which you made it.—I return to Stowey in a few days. Disembarrassed from all pecuniary anxieties yet unshackled by any regular profession, with powerful motives and no less powerful propensities to honourable effort, it is my duty to indulge the hope that at some future period I shall have given a proof that as your intentions were eminently virtuous, so the action itself was not unbeneficent." 100

There followed an orgy of letters, explanatory of his good fortune. Estlin alone provided a difficult task. He was much in favour of the Shrewsbury scheme, and it was necessary to proceed with care and write at length. Coleridge's arguments in favour of the annuity were numerous. His letter to Estlin, written on the day he accepted the annuity, demolished the necessity for entering the ministry, but its greatest interest is perhaps in the illustration it provides of the prevailing cast of his thought and for his reference to Hartley, made with a reverence that shows Hartley to be still a power in his mind, but a power now shifted for good to the 'religious' side of that philosopher's doctrines:

"Shall I refuse 150£ a year for life, as certain, as any fortune can be, for (I will call it) another 150£ a year, the attainment of which is not yet certain, and the duration of which is precarious? You answer, 'Yes! the cause of Christianity and practical Religion demands your exertions. The powers of intellect, which God has given you, are given for this very purpose, that they may be employed in promoting the best interests of mankind.' Now the answer would be decisive to my understanding, and (I think you know enough of me to believe me when I say that were the annuity 1,500£ a year instead of 150£) it should be decisive on my conduct, if I could see any reason why my exertions for Christianity and practical Religion depend, I will not say, on my being at Shrewsbury, but—on my becoming a stipendiary and regular minister. It makes me blush, I assure you, sitting *alone* as I now am, at the idea of mentioning two such names as I am about to do, with any supposable reference to my own talents, present or to come, but *the kind is not altered by the degree*. Did Dr. HARTLEY employ himself for the promotion of the best interests

WILLIAM WORDSWORTH IN 1798

"This portrait of Mr Wordsworth, was taken by Hancock, and was an undoubted likeness, universally acknowledged to be such, at the time."

JOSEPH COTTLE

" . . . above the middle size, with marked features and an air somewhat stately and quixotic. He reminds me of some of Holbein's heads: grave, saturnine, with a slight indication of sly humour . . . He has a peculiar sweetness in his smile, and great depth and manliness and a rugged harmony in the tones of his voice. His manner of reading his own poetry is particularly imposing; and in his favourite passages his eye beams with preternatural lustre, and the meaning labours slowly up from his swelling breast . . . In company, even in a *tête-à-tête*, Mr Wordsworth is often silent, indolent, and reserved."

WILLIAM HAZLITT

" . . . a dignified manner, with a deep and roughish but not unpleasing voice, and an exalted mode of speaking. He had a habit of keeping his left hand in the bosom of his waistcoat; and in this attitude, except when he turned round to take one of the subjects of his criticism from the shelves, he sat dealing forth his eloquent but hardly catholic judgments. . . . He was as sceptical on the merits of all kinds of poetry but one, as Richardson was on those of the novels of Fielding."

LEIGH HUNT

"Wordsworth is a very great man, the only man to whom *at all times* and *in all modes of excellence* I feel myself inferior."

COLERIDGE

"T. Poole's opinion of Wordsworth is that he is the greatest man he ever knew; I coincide."

COLERIDGE

of mankind? Most certainly. If instead of being a physician he had been an hired Teacher, that he would not have taught Christianity *better*, I can certainly say, and I suspect, from the vulgar prejudices of mankind that his name might have been less efficacious. That, however, is a Trifle. A man who thinks that Lardner defended Christianity because he received 50 or 60£ a year for preaching at Crouched Friars, must be such a booby that it cannot be of much consequence what he thinks; but Lardner! do you really think, my dear Friend! that it would have been of much detriment to the Christian world if the author of the Credibility, etc., had never received or accepted the invitation at Crouched Friars? Surely not. I should be very unwilling to think that my efforts as a Christian minister depended on my preaching regularly in one pulpit. God forbid! To the cause of Religion I solemnly devote all my best faculties; and if I wish to acquire knowledge as a philosopher and fame as a poet, I pray for grace that I may continue to feel what I now feel, that my greatest reason for wishing the one and the other, is that I may be enabled by my knowledge to defend Religion ably, and by my reputation to draw attention to the defence of it. I regard every experiment that Priestley made in Chemistry, as giving *wings* to his more sublime theological works." [101]

For the rest, his letters were pure joy. Cottle,[102] Poole,[103] Wordsworth, Thelwall,[104] Lamb,[105] all heard post-haste of his good fortune. To Wordsworth he speaks of his acceptance of the "magnificent liberality" of the Wedgwood brothers, "on the presumption that I had talents, honesty, and propensities to perseverant effort."[106] He goes on to say that, "of the pleasant ideas which accompanied this unexpected event, it was not the least pleasant, nor did it pass through my mind the last in the procession, that I should at least be able to trace the spring and early summer at Alfoxden with you, and that wherever your after residence may be, it is probable that you will be within the reach of my tether, lengthened as it now is."[107]

His letter to Thelwall, according to the report of that rather indifferent friend, whose understanding of Coleridge showed cleverness without profundity, passing on the news in a letter to Dr. Crompton, "has a dash of the obscure not uncommon to the rapid genius of C. Whether he did or did not accept the cure of Unitarian Souls, it is difficult from the account to make out. I suppose he did not, for I know his aversion to preaching

God's holy word for hire, which is seconded not a little, I expect, by his repugnance to all regular routine and application. I also hope he did not, for I know he cannot preach very often without travelling from the pulpit to the Tower. Mount him but upon his darling hobby-horse, 'the republic of God's own making,' and away he goes like hey-go-mad, spattering and splashing through thick and thin and scattering more *levelling* sedition and constructive treason than poor Gilly or myself ever dreamed of." [108]

In reply to the news the ecstatic Poole could scarcely contain his joy:

"The receipt of your last letter made me so happy that I went to a party here in town, and was never so chearful; never *sung* so well, never so witty, never so agreeable,—so I was told ten times over! They little knew the cause which made joy beam from every feature and action. Make as much haste home as you can, provided it be *good speed*. You will, of course, stay the necessary time at Cote House. God bless you for ever." [109]

But although Coleridge sent in his resignation of candidature almost immediately after returning to Shrewsbury from Wem on the 19th, [110] he did not at once leave the town. Popularity, which at times, perhaps, he mistook for affection, was sweet to him. With love, which he coupled with esteem, it was a moving spirit of his life and action, and he quitted it at all times with manifest reluctance. "The people here absolutely *consume* me," he assured Poole with disarming naïvety a few days later. "The clergymen of the Church are eminently courteous, and some of them come and hear me. If I had stayed, I have reason to think that I should have doubled the congregation almost immediately" [111]—this being a prelude to the less welcome fact that "you will be vexed to hear, that I have written nothing for the Morning Post." [112]

That his popularity at Shrewsbury was not an illusion of vanity is shown by a letter written by a Mr Wood, one of the Unitarian Church officials, when Coleridge had refused payment for his journey to the town and preaching there:

"The motive for your declining to accept a small remuneration for the expence and trouble you have incurred by your journey to Shrewsbury, affords a fresh proof of those elevated sentiments, which must add to our regret for the disappointment we have experienced. Circumstanced however as you now are, we are compelled to allow the justice of those motives, which have induced you to withdraw yourself from an Office we had promised ourselves you would have filled with so much honour to yourself and satisfaction to our Society.

"Permit me however again to request in the name of that Society, that you will accept of the trifle tendered, as a small compensation for your Services during your residence among us. Feeling as we do, for the unexpected interruption of that pleasure and edification we had so much reason to promise ourselves from your future connection with us; yet believe me dear Sir we are not so selfish as not to feel also the most lively satisfaction, at an occurrence which places you in a situation more conformable to your inclinations and Views. When great and extraordinary abilities, are combined with pure and ardent zeal in the glorious, sacred cause of Truth and Liberty; what may not be expected from the leisure and opportunity retirement will afford you; for employing those powers with which the great Author of the human frame has endowed you, in the defence of all that can be dear to rational Beings? When pure Christianity is so violently assailed on all sides; and suffers almost equally from the intemperate zeal and blind enthusiasm of her mistaken friends, as from the avowed hostility of her open enemies; what can be more worthy of Mr Coleridge, than to enter the lists as a zealous Advocate, for *vital*, and *practical* as well as *pure* religion? Have not we Unitarians, too much deserved the reproach, of being lukewarm Christians, *neither cold nor hot?* Disgusted with the folly, and too general hypocrisy, of those who place the whole of religion in a blind faith, a simple exertion of intellect, or in enthusiastic feelings; have we not passed to the opposite extreme, and been too prone to exclude all those warm and generous affections, which the Almighty has implanted in our frame, as powerful auxiliaries to Virtue?

"If these imperfect hints, should direct your attention to a subject, for the discussion of which it appears to me you are supereminently qualified, I shall have much reason to look back with pleasure upon our shortlived correspondence." [113]

Coleridge had also received "a very affectionate letter from Thomas Wedgwood. . . . He desires me to meet him at Cote House.[114] I shall therefore leave this place on Monday morning and shall, God willing, breakfast with him on Tuesday morning." [115] And on Tuesday morning, January 30, Coleridge had actually reached Cottle's shop in Wine Street, Bristol.[116]

A few days later, Coleridge was back at Stowey—no minister, but a poet, his muse at last set free.

[243]

9

NOW BEGAN the second and most prolific period of Coleridge the poet; when his imagination performed wonders and beauty streamed from his pen. This, the period during which most of Coleridge's great poetry was written, was short, lasting only a few months. It was a time of almost unbroken personal happiness, of full intercourse and ever-increasing intimacy with the Wordsworths, of carefree abandonment of mind and heart to his work, his friends, his family and the delights of the Stowey countryside—the time when he and Wordsworth:

> first
> Together wanton'd in wild Poesy.[1]

This is the period immortalized by Wordsworth's lines:

> beloved Friend,
> When, looking back thou seest in clearer view
> Than any sweetest sight of yesterday
> That summer when on Quantock's grassy Hills
> Far ranging, and among her sylvan Combs,
> Thou in delicious words, with happy heart,
> Didst speak the Vision of that Ancient Man,
> The bright-eyed Mariner, and rueful woes
> Didst utter of the Lady Christabel;
> And I, associate with such labour, walk'd
> Murmuring of him who, joyous hap! was found,
> After the perils of his moonlight ride
> Near the loud Waterfall; or her who sate
> In misery near the miserable Thorn;
> When thou dost to that summer turn thy thoughts,
> And hast before thee all which then we were,
> To thee, in memory of that happiness
> It will be known, by thee at least, my Friend,
> Felt, that the history of a Poet's mind
> Is labour not unworthy of regard:[2]

Already it was known that the lease of Alfoxden would not be renewed.[3] The Wordsworths would have to look elsewhere for a home. But July was many months ahead; and the immediate effect of the knowledge upon the three of them was only to intensify their joy in the present close relationship, their desire that every moment possible should be spent together. Some measure of the extent of this intimacy and of Dorothy's intense interest in the phenomena of nature is to be seen in her *Journal* (preserved for the first time from January to March); and her entries sometimes echo, sometimes precede, similar descriptions in the poems of her brother and his friend.[4]

In these few months Coleridge wrote a number of poems, many of them published in the *Morning Post*, whose manifold beauties have been obscured, when they have not been quite overlooked, by the perfection of the great trio—*The Ancient Mariner*, the first part of *Christabel*, and *Kubla Khan*—completed by the summer.

In the *Morning Post* of April 13 appeared for the first time in print *Lewti; or the Circassian's Love Chant*. The poem was much altered since the days of Mary Evans. The heroine's name had been twice changed. The element of delicate and sensuous imagery had been extended. But *Lewti* is memorable chiefly for its hint of a new and melodious metre upon which Coleridge was working.

In February, Coleridge wrote *France: an Ode*, first published in the *Morning Post* of April 16 under the title *The Recantation* and to the accompaniment of the following editorial effusion:

> "The following excellent Ode will be in unison with the feelings of every friend to Liberty and foe to Oppression; of all who, admiring the French Revolution, detest and deplore the conduct of France towards Switzerland. It is very satisfactory to find so zealous and steady an advocate for Freedom as Mr COLERIDGE concur with us in condemning the conduct of France. . . . What we most admire is the *avowal* of his sentiments, and public censure of the unprincipled and atrocious conduct of France."[5]

The poem was a direct result of the recent unprovoked French invasion of Switzerland, an act which, although it had not the full support of those in the French army, shook the faith of most remaining supporters of the French Government in England, including Wordsworth.[6] To Coleridge, at no time so attached to the French as to the principle of freedom which they were supposed to uphold, this act was decisive. In his own words:

> "In part from constitutional indolence, which in the very heyday of hope had kept my enthusiasm in check, but still more from the habits and influences of a classical education and academic persuits, scarcely a year had elapsed from the commencement of my literary and political adventures before my mind sank into a state of thorough disgust and despondency, both with regard to the disputes and the particular disputant." [7]

In this poem he recanted his belief in the French government as the torchbearer of universal freedom in no uncertain terms:

> Forgive me, Freedom! O forgive those dreams!
> I hear thy voice, I hear thy loud lament,
> From bleak Helvetia's icy caverns sent—
> I hear thy groans upon her blood-stained streams!
> Heroes, that for your peaceful country perished,
> And ye that, fleeing, spot your mountain-snows
> With bleeding wounds; forgive me, that I cherished
> One thought that ever blessed your cruel foes!
> To scatter rage, and traitorous guilt,
> Where Peace her jealous home had built;
> A patriot-race to disinherit
> Of all that made their stormy wilds so dear;
> And with inexpiable spirit
> To taint the bloodless freedom of the mountaineer—
> O France, that mockest Heaven, adulterous, blind,
> And patriot only in pernicious toils!
> Are these thy boasts, Champion of human kind?
> To mix with Kings in the low lust of sway,
> Yell in the hunt, and share the murderous prey;
> To insult the shrine of Liberty with spoils
> From freemen torn; to tempt and to betray?
>
> The Sensual and the Dark rebel in vain,
> Slaves by their own compulsion! In mad game
> They burst their manacles and wear the name
> Of Freedom, graven on a heavier chain! [8]

So run some of the concluding lines: but when the dead political wood has been pruned from the poem there remains the opening apostrophe to nature—a piece of pure poetry, living still and demonstrating what is often passed by in these neglected poems, Coleridge's peculiar power of evoking nature by word pictures as beautiful and as strange as they are exact. His was the watchful gaze of the naturalist born, as quick and as eager to perceive distinctions in the humblest region of nature as in its grander and wilder aspects; adding to this gift one not less rare—the ability of the poet to express, to paint in unforgettable words, what the naturalist has seen so that all men may see. His eye could distinguish and his pen set down a shape, a colour, a movement, a sound, as far beyond the range of perception of less fortunate men as the height and depth of the musical scale are hidden from the ordinary ear.[9] Nor was this the end of his magic; rather, if words are to be taken literally, it was the beginning of magic; for he would wrap what would normally be facts, unusual certainly, but facts still, in a veil of faery glamour—losing no whit of the realistic truth of his picture, but softening and beautifying its outline immeasurably: until it seemed scarcely of this world.

> Ye Woods! that listen to the night-birds singing,
> Midway the smooth and perilous slope reclined,
> Save when your own imperious branches swinging,
> Have made a solemn music of the wind!
> Where, like a man beloved of God,
> Through glooms, which never woodman trod,
> How oft, pursuing fancies holy,
> My moonlight way o'er flowering weeds I wound,
> Inspired, beyond the guess of folly,
> By each rude shape and wild unconquerable sound!
> O ye loud Waves! and O ye Forests high!
> And O ye Clouds that far above me soared!
> Thou rising Sun! thou blue rejoicing Sky!
> Yea, every thing that is and will be free!
> Bear witness for me, whereso'er ye be,
> With what deep worship I have still adored
> The spirit of divinest Liberty.[10]

This mastery of delicate detail, this exactitude in the ways of nature, this romanticism of realism, is repeated again and again in poems outside the major three. In *Frost at Midnight*, for instance, also written in February of that wonderful year—this time, when

> The inmates of my cottage, all at rest,
> Have left me to that solitude, which suits

Abstruser musings: save that at my side
My cradled infant slumbers peacefully.
'Tis calm indeed! so calm, that it disturbs
And vexes meditation, with its strange
And extreme silentness. Sea, hill, and wood,
This populous village! Sea, and hill, and wood,
With all the numberless goings-on of life,
Inaudible as dreams! the thin blue flame
Lies on my low-burnt fire, and quivers not;
Only that film, which fluttered on the grate,
Still flutters there, the sole unquiet thing.
Methinks, its motion in this hush of nature
Gives it dim sympathies with me who live,
Making it a companionable form,
Whose puny flaps and freaks the idling Spirit
By its own moods interprets, every where
Echo or mirror seeking of itself,
And makes a toy of Thought.[11]

In this poem is contained the promise to Hartley that was to
become a prophecy:

I was reared
In the great city, pent 'mid cloisters dim,
And saw nought lovely but the sky and stars.
But *thou*, my babe! shalt wander like a breeze
By lakes and sandy shores, beneath the crags
Of ancient mountain, and beneath the clouds
Which image in their bulk both lakes and shores
And mountain crags: so shalt thou see and hear
The lovely shapes and sounds intelligible
Of that eternal language, which thy God
Utters, who from eternity doth teach
Himself in all, and all things in himself.[12]

And the poem ends with the famous description:

Therefore all seasons shall be sweet to thee,
Whether the summer clothe the general earth
With greenness, or the redbreast sit and sing
Betwixt the tufts of snow on the bare branch
Of mossy apple-tree, while the nigh thatch
Smokes in the sun-thaw; whether the eave-drops fall
Heard only in the trances of the blast,
Or if the secret ministry of frost
Shall hang them up in silent icicles,
Quietly shining to the quiet Moon.[13]

Nor is this descriptive beauty and exactitude the only notable part of *Frost at Midnight*. The lilt of a new technique in versification that had shown itself faintly in *Lewti*, here, in the blank verse, begins to strike on the ear with a strange and mystic beauty. Further joy in the external world, accurately rendered in comparison with Coleridge's stilted eighteenth-century formalities of a few years before, with his introspection of a few months back, is seen in *Fears in Solitude*, a poem written on April 20, when a general invasion by the French was feared.[14] Coleridge goes up to the old earthen 'castle' above Stowey:

> A green and silent spot, amid the hills,
> A small and silent dell![15] O'er stiller place
> No singing sky-lark ever poised himself.
> The hills are heathy, save that swelling slope,
> Which hath a gay and gorgeous covering on,
> All golden with the never-bloomless furze,
> Which now blooms most profusely: but the dell
> Bathed by the mist, is fresh and delicate
> As vernal corn-field, or the unripe flax,
> When, through its half-transparent stalks, at eve,
> The level sunshine glimmers with green light.[16]

So for the setting of the poem. But to Coleridge that is only a part, a lesser part, of its purpose. He leads on to the promise of spiritual peace that awaits the humble man, would he in wisdom but

> lie on fern or withered heath,
> While from the singing lark (that sings unseen
> The minstrelsy that solitude loves best),
> And from the sun, and from the breezy air,
> Sweet influences trembled o'er his frame;
> And he, with many feelings, many thoughts,
> Made up a meditative joy, and found
> Religious meanings in the forms of Nature!
> And so, his senses gradually wrapt
> In a half sleep, he dreams of better worlds,
> And dreaming hears thee still, O singing lark,
> That singest like an angel in the clouds![17]

But the beauty, the peace of his surroundings can at the moment only emphasize the horrors of war which threatened to deflower the country; to fall upon those to whom war had become no more than a breakfast-table titillation:

                                    Boys and girls,
And women, that would groan to see a child
Pull off an insect's leg, all read of war,
The best amusement for our morning meal!
The poor wretch, who has learnt his only prayers
From curses, who knows scarcely words enough
To ask a blessing from his Heavenly Father,
Becomes a fluent phraseman, absolute
And technical in victories and defeats,
And all our dainty terms for fratricide;
Terms which we trundle smoothly o'er our tongues
Like mere abstractions, empty sounds to which
We join no feeling and attach no form!
As if the soldier died without a wound;
As if the fibres of this godlike frame
Were gored without a pang; as if the wretch,
Who fell in battle, doing bloody deeds,
Passed off to Heaven, translated and not killed;
As though he had no wife to pine for him,
No God to judge him! Therefore, evil days
Are coming on us, O my countrymen! [18]

Coleridge admits the justice of the punishment which would
fall upon the nation if the invasion took place; but he pleads that
the French are unworthy to be conquerors, to be the instruments
of God's wrath: he begs God to forgive his fellow countrymen;
then defends his own patriotism:

O native Britain! O my Mother Isle!
How shouldst thou prove aught else but dear and holy
To me, who from thy lakes and mountain-hills,
Thy clouds, thy quiet dales, thy rocks and seas,
Have drunk in all my intellectual life,
All sweet sensations, all ennobling thoughts,
All adoration of the God in nature,
All lovely and all honourable things,
Whatever makes this mortal spirit feel
The joy and greatness of its future being?
There lives not form nor feeling in my soul
Unborrowed from my country! O divine
And beauteous island! thou has been my sole
And most magnificent temple, in the which
I walk with awe, and sing my stately songs,
Loving the God that made me! [19]

And he ends, as he began, with a picture of his surroundings; now, with evening advancing—an evening which Coleridge conjures up in words as truthful as they are vivid, as beautiful as they are unforgettable; words which, characteristically, pass beyond description to the meaning of what is seen—seeing nature as a symbol:

> But now the gentle dew-fall sends abroad
> The fruit-like perfume of the golden furze:
> The light has left the summit of the hill,
> Though still a sunny gleam lies beautiful
> Aslant the ivied beacon. Now farewell,
> Farewell, awhile, O soft and silent spot!
> On the green sheep-track, up the heathy hill,
> Homeward I wind my way; and lo! recalled
> From bodings that have well-nigh wearied me,
> I find myself upon the brow, and pause
> Startled! And after lonely sojourning
> In such a quiet and surrounded nook,
> This burst of prospect, here the shadowy main,
> Dim-tinted, there the mighty majesty
> Of that huge amphitheatre of rich
> And elmy fields, seems like society—
> Conversing with the mind, and giving it
> A livelier impulse and a dance of thought![20]

In April also was composed *The Nightingale*, in which Coleridge wrote the lines:

> And hark! the Nightingale begins its song,
> 'Most musical, most melancholy' bird!
> A melancholy bird? Oh! idle thought!
> In Nature there is nothing melancholy.
> But some night-wandering man whose heart was pierced
> With the remembrance of a grievous wrong,
> Or slow distemper, or neglected love,
> (And so, poor wretch! filled all things with himself,
> And made all gentle sounds tell back the tale
> Of his own sorrow) he, and such as he,
> First named these notes a melancholy strain,
> And many a poet echoes the conceit;[21]

A sentiment with which Wordsworth was in full accord. He wrote later: "What false notions have prevailed, from generation to generation, of the true character of the Nightingale. As far as my

Friend's Poem, in the 'Lyrical Ballads', is read, it will contribute greatly to rectify these."[22]

For the picture of the nightingale as it is, Coleridge drew upon his notebook:[23]

'Tis the merry Nightingale
That crowds, and hurries, and precipitates
With fast thick warble his delicious notes,
As he were fearful that an April night
Would be too short for him to utter forth
His love-chant, and disburthen his full soul
Of all its music![24]

He spoke of

A most gentle Maid,
Who dwelleth in her hospitable home
Hard by the castle, and at latest eve
(Even like a Lady vowed and dedicate
To something more than Nature in the grove)
Glides through the pathways; she knows all their notes,
That gentle Maid! and oft, a moment's space,
What time the moon was lost behind a cloud,
Hath heard a pause of silence; till the moon
Emerging, hath awakened earth and sky
With one sensation, and those wakeful birds
Have all burst forth in choral minstrelsy,
As if some sudden gale had swept at once
A hundred airy harps! And she hath watched
Many a nightingale perch giddily
On blossomy twig still swinging from the breeze,
And to that motion tune his wanton song
Like tipsy Joy that reels with tossing head.[25]

And finally, Coleridge drew the famous picture of Hartley, again using his notebook in which he had set down the incident soon after its occurrence:[26]

My dear babe,
Who, capable of no articulate sound,
Mars all things with his imitative lisp,
How he would place his hand beside his ear,
His little hand, the small forefinger up,
And bid us listen! And I deem it wise
To make him Nature's play-mate. He knows well
The evening-star; and once, when he awoke
In most distressful mood (some inward pain
Had made up that strange thing, an infant's dream),

I hurried with him to our orchard-plot,
And he beheld the moon, and, hushed at once,
Suspends his sobs, and laughs most silently,
While his fair eyes, that swam with undropped tears,
Did glitter in the yellow moon-beam! [27]

But these moments of beauty, though they promise and recall his full glory of utterance, are but parts of an imperfect whole. They are overshadowed inevitably by *The Ancient Mariner*, *Christabel*, and *Kubla Khan*.[28] The poems in which they occur are unfortunate to encounter comparison almost from the moment of composition with three poems so close to perfection as to be almost indistinguishable from it.

Of the three, *The Ancient Mariner*, finished on March 23, was destined to remain Coleridge's one complete poem. "The 'Ancient Mariner' cannot be imitated," [29] he said of it later. He did it no more than justice. *The Ancient Mariner* is not merely one of the great English poems. It is the strangest. It approaches closer to the heart of the supernatural than any other poem. It demonstrates with a subtler mastery and completeness than ever before or after his "shaping spirit of Imagination" [30] in action—a blend of the realistic and the romantic so complete, so indivisible, as to silence the most critical reader.

The Ancient Mariner was Coleridge's first attempt to procure a "willing suspension of disbelief" in the reader, using "characters supernatural, or at least romantic." [31] In this poem he succeeds with such thoroughness that the consummate skill which has effected the amalgam is apt to receive less than its due reward. The final inception of the poem has been described earlier. Yet what occurred on that November evening on the way to Watchet was little more than the setting of a match to a fire already laid.

The genesis of *The Ancient Mariner* is open to interpretation to a degree unusual if not unique among examples of masterly lyricism. And more than most great poems, perhaps, it needs this explanation if its full greatness is to be understood and appreciated.

To a point—a point further than most great poems go—the creation of *The Ancient Mariner* was deliberate. It was composed with a purpose which was never let out of mind. To this extent there is about it little of the bright flash of genius, unexpected, inexplicable. But it gains, not loses, in wonder in that it is susceptible, to a point, of explanation since it leads the ordinary mortal into the mind of a poet, following his processes of thought, only to stop on the brink beyond which no man may follow, marvelling the more at the sudden leap into genius, when explanations hitherto prosaic are glorified and pass into mystery.

Coleridge chose the ballad form—a vehicle used customarily for the conveyance of folk song and story, now for the first time lifted into the region of great poetry.

The story he told was more than ordinarily interesting. It is deceptively simple—the simplicity masking prodigious labour and infinite skill. It holds the reader's attention without difficulty, from the departure of the ship to its homecoming.

The poem consists of three analysable elements. There is the material background—the voyage of the ship. There is the spiritual background—what Wordsworth recorded as "the spectral persecution."[32] And permeating the whole there is the moral background—the fatal act of the mariner and its inevitable consequences.

For the voyage, Coleridge drew upon two sources. The first source was the recollection of everything relevant to the subject (which was considerable) that he had read. It is difficult to decide which is the more memorable—the vast quantity and wide range of his reading or the power he possessed of preserving knowledge when so acquired.

The second source was his own careful and exquisite appreciation of the myriad intricacies of nature. His nature study was, in this instance, more deliberately directed than his reading; he went out upon the hills, as has already been seen, with his notebook, "moulding my thoughts into verse, with the objects and imagery immediately before my senses."[33] The result was a creative use of imagery, the use of an imagery not only exact, not only carefully selected and sparingly used, but playing no mean part in forwarding the author's design upon his readers.

So far, the procedure, though beyond the general capability, is not beyond comprehension. Much of Coleridge's reading on subjects touching *The Ancient Mariner* had been necessarily haphazard. The general direction and inclination only were there. As he had told Thelwall many months before: "Metaphysics and poetry and 'facts of mind,' that is, accounts of all the strange phantasms that ever possessed 'your philosophy'; dreamers, from Thoth the Egyptian to Taylor the English pagan, are my darling studies." [34] Yet that accounts only for a part, even if the main part, of the type of reading that went to form the poem. All of it passed into his subconscious memory as disconnected fragments. There, deep down, a process of unconscious selection, purification, merging, took place. The things that had been impressed upon the eye and the mind, by seeing and by reading, were then moulded in dream: "my Dreams become the Substances of my Life," [35] said Coleridge. They played a vital part in the final, the subconscious perfecting of *The Ancient Mariner*.

Omnivorous reading and a capacious memory; acute perception of the phenomena of nature; dreams as weird as they were constructive; these were the strands of which the poem was to be woven. Then, stirred by his "shaping spirit of Imagination," [36] there was drawn from Coleridge's unconscious mind, transfigured, the stuff of the poem; but, not least of the marvels, with the exactitude of his details of nature unimpaired—the strangest and possibly the greatest demonstration of this, in his view and in Wordsworth's, the supreme poetic quality.

Yet when all has been said, the miracle remains a miracle. The marvel of the poem, its fascination and its beauty, is found in its triumphant amalgam—in itself savouring of the supernatural—of realism and phantasy. Despite the presence in it of these hitherto supposed incompatibles, the poem is one, it achieves a unity which seems as impossible as it is certainly inexplicable. With great daring, Coleridge set out deliberately to reconcile the irreconcilable. And he succeeded. He succeeded so thoroughly, so completely, so satisfyingly, that from that day to this readers of the poem have suspended disbelief—not so much willingly or with acclamation as because they must, because a power greater than themselves is at work upon them as they read; because this suspension is at once demanded by the poem's realism and cajoled by its witchery; because they are in the presence of a magic alchemy that turns romance to realism and realism to romance before their very eyes, yet all unseen.

With the writing of *The Ancient Mariner*, Coleridge at one bound achieved greatness. His poetical dross slipped away, leaving pure gold. After years of overmuch protestation that he had stepped for good outside the formality, the stiltedness, of eighteenth century poetry, he really, suddenly, unexpectedly did so—not by degrees, not by stages of development clearly marked, but at this one incredible bound. Indeed, the magnitude of the change from comparative ineffectiveness to the glory of *The Ancient Mariner* is almost as great a wonder as the poem itself.

Gone were the ponderous diction, the double-epithets which months before Coleridge was supposed to have pruned "with no sparing hand"[37] from the second edition of his poems. Gone, turgidity, false heat, bombast. Gone, all echoes of Gray, Collins and Bowles. Gone, that disastrous "deviation from nature and simplicity"[38] which dogged his best work to the last moment—and which, together with a frequent and overwhelming intrusion of philosophical and religious argument, was defacing the beauty of poems actually written while *The Ancient Mariner* was being completed.[39]

The only signs remaining of the old unregenerate Coleridge were two: an attempt to clothe the story with a false and quite unnecessary glamour by the use of archaic forms—an example of this pseudo-romantic diction until that time customary in the ballad, and which appeared only in the first edition of the *Lyrical Ballads*, is seen in the original title, *The Rime of the Ancyent Marinere*; and possibly a slight over-emphasis of the moral of the story—Coleridge himself later admitted as much to Mrs Barbauld, who, inexplicably, had complained that the poem was without a moral.[40]

The first part of *Christabel*, begun after and finished before[41] *The Ancient Mariner*, suffers in comparison with it only because remaining a part of an uncompleted whole. Its language is as clear and as simple, the ease and mastery of construction as marked, as in *The Ancient Mariner*. It effects a similar magical blending of the real and the fantastic. Coleridge's hand in this poem has lost none of its cunning; indeed in one respect *Christabel* may be said to excel *The Ancient Mariner*; for in it Coleridge set himself the harder task—to bewitch the reader in the open light of day.

His theme in this poem was witchcraft and his handling of the subject is necessarily more subtle. He gains his effects by sugges-

WILLIAM WORDSWORTH IN APRIL, 1798

"I think I see him now. He answered in some degree to his friend's description of him, but was more gaunt and Don Quixote-like. He was quaintly dressed (according to the *costume* of that unconstrained period) in a brown fustian jacket and striped pantaloons. There was something of a roll, a lounge in his gait, not unlike his own Peter Bell. There was a severe, worn pressure of thought about his temples, a fire in his eye (as if he saw something in objects more than the outward appearance), an intense high narrow forehead, a Roman nose, cheeks furrowed by strong purpose and feeling, and a convulsive inclination to laughter about the mouth, a great deal at variance with the solemn, stately expression of the rest of his face . . . He sat down and talked very naturally and freely, with a mixture of clear gushing accents in his voice, a deep guttural intonation, and a strong tincture of the northern *burr*, like the crust on wine."   WILLIAM HAZLITT

"Meantime, his face—that was one which would have made amends for greater defects of figure. . . . The forehead . . . is not remarkable for its height; but it *is*, perhaps, remarkable for its breadth and expansive development . . . his eyes are not, under any circumstances, bright, lustrous, or piercing; but, after a long day's toil in walking, I have seen them assume an appearance the most solemn and spiritual that it is possible for the human eye to wear. The light which resides in them is at no time a superficial light; but, under favourable accidents, it is a light which seems to come from unfathomed depths. . . . The nose, a little arched, is large. . . . The mouth, and the whole circumjacencies of the mouth, composed the strongest feature in Wordsworth's face."   THOMAS DE QUINCEY

"I have now known him a year and some months, and my admiration, I might say my awe, of his intellectual powers has increased even to this hour, and (what is of more importance) he is a tried good man."   COLERIDGE

"I feel myself *a little man by his side*."   COLERIDGE

(By permission of Messrs William George's Sons Ltd.)

tion rather than by direct statement—by innumerable touches so delicate, so skilfully woven into the fabric of the poem, that they take their places unchallenged as an inalienable part of it.

Coleridge announced his intention of prefixing to *The Ancient Mariner* an essay "on the uses of the Supernatural in poetry, and the principles which regulate its introduction"; [42] and to *Christabel* an essay on the uses of the Preternatural—a distinction which is its own explanation of his outlook upon the two poems and the methods he adopted in their making. Unfortunately these essays, although referred to by Coleridge with confidence as existing, must, it seems, take their places with the great unwritten.

Christabel seems, more perhaps than any other poem, to represent the fruit of close collaboration between Coleridge and Dorothy. Both the subject and the time were propitious. In any event, the images in the poem are to be found reproduced in Dorothy's *Journal* in more than one instance.[43]

There is, of course, the classic example of Coleridge's:

> There is not wind enough to twirl
> The one red leaf, the last of its clan,
> That dances as often as dance it can,
> Hanging so light, and hanging so high,
> On the topmost twig that looks up at the sky,[44]

which became an entry in the *Journal* for March 7 of

> "One only leaf upon the top of a tree—the sole remaining leaf
> —danced round and round like a rag blown by the wind." [45]

And there were other examples of the two minds close together, less notable but suggestive of mutual influence. Coleridge's

> And the Spring comes slowly up this way [46]

is almost repeated in the *Journal* of March 24:

> "The spring continues to advance very slowly."[47]

And in the reverse direction, Dorothy's note on January 27:

> "The manufacturer's dog makes a strange, uncouth howl,
> which it continues many minutes after there is no noise near it
> but that of the brook," [48]

may very well have connexion with the "toothless mastiff" of
Christabel and his

> Sixteen short howls, not over loud.[49]

More striking are the *Journal* descriptions; on January 25:

> "The sky spread over with one continuous cloud, whitened by
> the light of the moon," [50]

on January 27:

> "the sky flat . . . a white, thin cloud," [51]

and on January 31:

> "When we left home the moon immensely large, the sky
> scattered over with clouds. These soon closed in, contracting the
> dimensions of the moon without concealing her," [52]

which turned into a Coleridge notebook entry:

> Behind the thin
> Grey cloud that cover'd but not hid the sky
> The round full moon look'd small,[53]

emerging finally into its mature and glamorous beauty in *Christabel*:

> The thin gray cloud is spread on high,
> It covers but not hides the sky.
> The moon is behind, and at the full;
> And yet she looks both small and dull.[54]

Comparison of the *Journal* entries and the verses of the poem
suggests that Coleridge was as often the teacher as the taught
in the observation of nature. But the question can become academic and can, in fact, never be solved. He and Dorothy met
so frequently at this time, their interests were so similar, their
delicate perception so alike, that it would seem invidious, even
were it possible, to assign to the one or to the other the credit for
the original observation which led to so many passages of exquisite beauty in the poems. That Dorothy played a considerable
part in Coleridge's poetical development can be seen. That he
played a large part in opening even her eyes to hidden beauties
may be assumed with confidence. The result, in any event, was
beauty in which all shared; a beauty to which, often enough,
Dorothy, Coleridge, and Wordsworth all contributed. To ascer-

tain the exact proportion of their individual contributions is fortunately, perhaps, as far beyond the power of man as it would most certainly be beyond the wish of those concerned. The beauty exists; and that should satisfy.

Christabel was, less notably, the scene of the "toothless mastiff bitch" comedy. In response to the request of an "honoured friend"[55] the word "bitch" was struck out, and until 1834, the year of Coleridge's death, the lifeless "which" appeared in all printed editions of the poem. Coleridge made an effort to improve the variation, but without success. He replaced it, tentatively, with:

> Sir Leoline the Baron bold
> Hath a toothless mastiff old;[56]

Lamb, who must have regarded these evasions with no little amusement, lent a hand. Why not

> Sir Leoline, the baron round
> Had a toothless mastiff hound,[57]

he suggested. But no; the substituted "which" was allowed to stand.

The last of the three great poems, *Kubla Khan*, was written in May 1798.[58] Coleridge has explained the circumstances attending the writing of the poem in a note attached to it:

"In the summer of the year 1797, the Author, then in ill health, had retired to a lonely farm-house between Porlock and Linton, on the Exmoor confines of Somerset and Devonshire. In consequence of a slight indisposition, an anodyne had been prescribed, from the effects of which he fell asleep in his chair at the moment that he was reading the following sentence, or words of the same substance, in 'Purchas's Pilgrimage': 'Here the Khan Kubla commanded a palace to be built, and a stately garden thereunto. And thus ten miles of fertile ground were inclosed with a wall.' The Author continued for about three hours in a profound sleep, at least of the external senses, during which time he has the most vivid confidence, that he could not have composed less than from two to three hundred lines; if that indeed can be called composition in which all the images rose up before him as *things*, with a parallel production of the correspondent expressions, without any sensation or consciousness of effort. On awaking he appeared to himself to have a distinct recollection of the whole, and taking his pen, ink and paper, instantly and eagerly wrote down the lines that are here preserved. At this moment he was unfortunately called out by a person on business from Porlock, and detained by him above one hour, and on his return to his room, found, to his no small surprise and mortification, that though he still retained some vague and dim recollection of the general purport of the vision, yet, with the exception of some eight or ten scattered lines and images, all the rest had passed away like the images on the surface of a stream into which a stone has been cast, but, alas! without the after restoration of the latter!" [59]

That Coleridge had made a mistake of a year in his dating of the poem is known by a later note, of November 3, 1810, [60] in which he says that this retirement to the farm-house and use of opium was an effort to relieve his "nervous disquietude and misery" [61] due to trouble with Lloyd—a trouble which also prevented the completion of *Christabel*, and which did not arise until 1798. He describes his use of opium on this occasion as "the first" [62] —but, assuming that he is referring to its use as a mental opiate, it has already been seen that as far back as the winter of 1796 he had resorted to opium for this purpose. Even without this check from Coleridge himself on the date of the composition of *Kubla Khan*, the perfection of the poem, and particularly of its metrical beauty, would suggest that it was the last and not the first of the three great poems. Wordsworth later spoke of "the extreme care and labour which he [Coleridge] applied in elaborating his metres . . . when he was intent on a new experiment in metre, the time and labour he bestowed were inconceivable." [63] His labour was not wasted; for in this, the great and inimitable dream poem, the metrical beauty that stirred in the earlier poems, shone weirdly and variously in *The Ancient Mariner*, and lent *Christabel* no small part of its magical witchery, breaks into perfection. *Kubla Khan* is pure lyricism—sound, picture, sensation—clothed in the sensuous beauty of imagery that none knew so well as its author how to evoke. It is also the supreme example in English literature of the workings of the creative subconscious, unhelped—or unhindered —by conscious composition. That large and seemingly limitless pool of Coleridge's memory, into which was cast every conscious impression, is here allowed its one matchless expression, and returns its precious contents, refined, glorified, selected by the imagination, working secretly, undreamed of, but with great and abundant power. The taking of the opium, about which much has been said, may have provided the opportunity for this sub-conscious creation to take place, but that is the full extent of its power. Indeed, when all is said, this fragment of poem, together with the unfinished *Christabel* and the completed *The Ancient Mariner*, defy analysis.[64] All three leave the reader, finally, wondering the more at such magic, such unearthly beauty, such miraculous hoverings between worlds, and above all, at the mortal brain that could have conceived such poems. The familiar plaint that Coleridge wrote so little great poetry turns, on reflection, into thankfulness and amazement that any man should have been enabled to break the bounds of mortality for so long.

Wordsworth, too, in this blissful period of uninterrupted intimacy, of happiness and productivity, had been "very rapidly adding to my stock of poetry."[65] But quantity was not all. That much was to be expected of him. Beyond it he was now to pass, thanks in no small measure to Coleridge. He was beginning to spread his wings. Rather stiff wings they were, not a little formal and inclined to hover over trivialities, but wings of tremendous power, rough, untamed, with passion in their beat.

As Wordsworth stimulated his friend by application to work, by careful thought and constant enthusiasm for the new principles of poetry upon which both he and Coleridge were basing their work, so Coleridge repaid the compliment in another but not less important direction. By his habit of systematizing, of expanding an emotion into a thought, of directing his work by philosophical design; by his insistence, at home and abroad, upon Wordsworth's genius—(". . . my admiration, I might say my awe, of his intellectual powers has increased even to this hour,"[66] he tells Estlin, for instance, while Tom Wedgwood and Mackintosh are informed that "He strides on so far before you, that he dwindles in the distance!");[67] and, perhaps above all, by his deprecation of his friend's squandering of this mighty genius upon a multitude of short, slight, and sometimes positively unworthy poems, by his insistence that Wordsworth should write a long poem in which a philosophy of life might alone be adequately expressed:[68] by all these things Coleridge was helping to bring out the greatness in the elder man.

So it was that, on March 6, Wordsworth could tell his friend Tobin:[69] "I have written 1300 lines of a poem in which I contrive to convey most of the knowledge of which I am possessed. My object is to give pictures of Nature, Man, and Society. Indeed, I know not any thing which will not come within the scope of my plan."[70] And Coleridge, with customary enthusiasm, writes two days later to Cottle: "The Giant Wordsworth—God love him! Even when I speak in the terms of admiration due to his intellect, I fear lest those terms should keep out of sight the amiableness of his manners. . . . He has written more than 1,200 lines of a blank verse, superior, I hesitate not to aver, to anything in our language which any way resembles it. Poole (whom I feel so consolidated with myself that I seem to have no occasion to speak of him out of myself) thinks of it as likely to benefit mankind much more than anything Wordsworth has yet written."[71]

While this, the projected *The Recluse*, was being written by Wordsworth, and Coleridge was beginning his inspired spell of composition, Lamb had added to the general contentment by writing to his friend in terms which suggested that the 'tattle'[72] of Lloyd, who was now living in London, was being judged at its true worthlessness. "You have writ me many kind letters," he wrote, "and I have answered none of them. I don't deserve your attentions. An unnatural indifference has been creeping on me since my last misfortunes, or I should have seized the first opening of a correspondence with *you*."[73]

The first cloud in their sky—the refusal of Mrs St. Albyn, owner of Alfoxden, to sanction the renewal of the Wordsworths' lease,[74] was dispelled without trouble. At first it seemed that the Wordsworths would succeed in settling even nearer to Coleridge than Alfoxden. "Tom Poole drank tea with us yesterday afternoon," wrote Dorothy on March 5; "he gives us great hopes that we shall get a very pleasant house a quarter of a mile from this place. . . ."[75] Even when this plan failed, as, with their reputation in the neighbourhood, it must inevitably have failed, they still talked of keeping near Coleridge. "It is most probable that we shall go back again to Racedown," reported Dorothy, "as there is little chance of our getting a place in this neighbourhood. We have no other very strong inducement to stay but Coleridge's society, but that is so important an object that we have it much at heart."[76]

But an even more attractive plan was mooted; a plan that had been germinating in Coleridge's mind for over two years. It was discussed, amplified, and accepted enthusiastically. Wordsworth explains it in a letter of March 11 to his friend, James Losh: [77] "Do contrive to come and see us before we go away," he writes. "Coleridge is now writing by me at the same table. I need not say how ardently he joins with me in this wish, and how deeply interested he is in everything relating to you. We have a delightful scheme in agitation, which is rendered still more delightful by a probability which I cannot exclude from my mind that you may be induced to join in the party. We have come to a resolution, Coleridge, Mrs Coleridge, my Sister, and myself of going into Germany, where we purpose to pass the two ensuing years in order to acquire the German language, and to furnish ourselves with a tolerable stock of information in natural science. Our plan is to settle, if possible, in a village near a University, in a pleasant, and if we can a mountainous, country; it will be desirable that the place should be as near as may be to Hamburg, on account of the expense of travelling." [78]

The carrying-out of this plan called for money. For once, unnatural though it sounds, Coleridge remained comparatively untroubled by the thought (although as late as February 18 he was driven to borrow £5 from Cottle, the first payment of the Wedgwood annuity having still to be made).[79] Wordsworth was not so fortunately placed, as he had lent a great deal of his legacy to Basil Montague. The only hope for him of sufficient money lay in the publishing of his poems.

In this dilemma they both turned to Cottle. Coleridge, knowing Cottle the better, wrote first. The question of a third edition of his poems is raised without a great deal of enthusiasm—a fact which is understandable if Cottle proposed, for the sake of economy, to reprint without alterations. Rather, Coleridge would prefer to "make it a volume worthy of me, and omit utterly near one-half of the present volume—a sacrifice to pitch black oblivion." [80]

More important at the moment, however, was money for Wordsworth.

"I am requested by Wordsworth, to put to you the following questions," continued Coleridge. "What could you, conveniently and prudently, and what would you give for—first, our two

Tragedies, with small prefaces, containing an analysis of our principal characters? Exclusive of the prefaces, the tragedies are, together, five thousand lines; which, in printing, from the dialogue form, and directions respecting actors and scenery, are at least equal to six thousand. To be delivered to you within a week of the date of your answer to this letter; and the money which you offer, to be paid to us at the end of four months from the same date; none to be paid before, all to be paid then. Second.—Wordsworth's *Salisbury Plain*, and *Tale of a Woman*; which two poems, with a few others which he will add, and the notes, will make a volume. This to be delivered to you within three weeks of the date of your answer, and the money to be paid as before, at the end of four months from the present date.

"Do not, my dearest Cottle, harass yourself about the imagined great merit of the compositions, or be reluctant to offer what you can prudently offer, from an idea that the poems are worth more. But calculate what you can do, with reference simply to yourself, and answer as speedily as you can; and believe me your sincere, grateful, and affectionate friend and brother." [81]

Cottle promptly offered thirty guineas for the tragedies and a similar sum for Wordsworth's poems.[82] But the two poets had made the suggestion with reluctance—they cherished a hope, faint but persistent (somewhat justified by Sheridan's offer to stage *Osorio*—an offer reported by Coleridge to George in May with due cynicism as a "promise he will . . . . certainly break"),[83] that the two plays might eventually find a producer. After consideration, they declined Cottle's offer on those grounds. The offer for the poems, on the other hand, was accepted, but details of the contents of the volume were reserved for further discussion. The fact was, that the project of a joint book of poems— the *Lyrical Ballads* to be—was now one of their chief interests. Animated as they were by a similar enthusiasm for the re-orientation of poetry in keeping with the true principles that they considered should govern it, each now with a substantial body of work completed which illustrated their theories, and with a preface to the volume, if not on paper, at least very much alive in their heads, they were anxious to see Cottle, obtain his opinion, and hasten the day when both principles and the proofs of them could be offered to the public.

Coleridge broke the news of the Wordsworths' coming separation from Alfoxden—"Wordsworth has been caballed against *so*

[264]

long and so loudly"[84]—and urges Cottle to come down and see them in their lovely home before it is too late. Wordsworth twice wrote, urging Cottle to come.[85] Soon after his last letter, on May 9, Cottle arrived. He visited Stowey and Alfoxden—and comments with a certain humour but without too great a regard for exactitude on his experiences at these two homes.[86] It was finally arranged that Cottle should publish a selection of the work of each poet, the volume or volumes to be entitled *Lyrical Ballads*. As an earnest of progress he carried back with him *The Ancient Mariner*, which was to head the volume.[87]

He was followed almost at once by the young Hazlitt, whose visit, though postponed, had not been forgotten. Writing to a Mr Wicksteed of Wem on March 9, Coleridge ended his letter: ". . . tell young Mr Hazlitt that I remember him with respect due to his talent, and that the wish which I expressed of seeing him at Stowey still lives within me."[88]

Hazlitt arrived, eager to see and hear the wonderful Coleridge again; doubly enthralled by the thought that he would also meet the great Wordsworth, of whom it is certain Coleridge had told him much. Again, his experiences are best told in his own words:

> "I arrived, and was well received. The country about Nether Stowey is beautiful, green and hilly, and near the sea-shore. . . . In the afternoon, Coleridge took me over to All-Foxden, a romantic old family-mansion of the St Aubins, where Wordsworth lived. . . . Wordsworth himself was from home, but his sister kept house, and set before us a frugal repast; and we had free access to her brother's poems, the *Lyrical Ballads*, which were still in manuscript, or in the form of *Sybilline Leaves*. I dipped into a few of these with great satisfaction, and with the faith of a novice. I slept that night in an old room with blue hangings, and covered with the round-faced family-portraits of the age of George I and II, and from the wooded declivity of the adjoining park that overlooked my window, at the dawn of day, could
>
> '. . . hear the loud stag speak.'
>
> "That morning, as soon as breakfast was over, we strolled out into the park, and seating ourselves on the trunk of an old ash-tree that stretched along the ground, Coleridge read aloud, with a sonorous and musical voice, the ballad of *Betty Foy*. I was not critically or sceptically inclined. I saw touches of truth and nature, and took the rest for granted. But in the *Thorn*, the *Mad Mother*,

and the *Complaint of a Poor Indian Woman*, I felt that deeper power and pathos which have been since acknowledged,

'In spite of pride, in erring reason's spite,'

as the characteristics of this author; and the sense of a new style and a new spirit in poetry came over me. It had to me something of the effect that arises from the turning up of the fresh soil, or of the first welcome breath of Spring,

'While yet the trembling year is unconfirmed.'

Coleridge and myself walked back to Stowey that evening, and his voice sounded high

'Of Providence, foreknowledge, will, and fate,
Fix'd fate, free-will, foreknowledge absolute,'

as we passed through echoing grove, by fairy stream or waterfall, gleaming in the summer moonlight! He lamented that Wordsworth was not prone enough to believe in the traditional superstitions of the place, and that there was a something corporeal, a *matter-of-fact-ness*, a clinging to the palpable, or often to the petty, in his poetry, in consequence. His genius was not a spirit that descended to him through the air; it sprung out of the ground like a flower, or unfolded itself from a green spray, on which the gold-finch sang. He said, however (if I remember right), that this objection must be confined to his descriptive pieces, that his philosophic poetry had a grand and comprehensive spirit in it, so that his soul seemed to inhabit the universe like a palace, and to discover truth by intuition, rather than by deduction. The next day Wordsworth arrived from Bristol at Coleridge's cottage. I think I see him now. He answered in some degree to his friend's description of him, but was more gaunt and Don Quixote-like. He was quaintly dressed (according to the *costume* of that unconstrained period) in a brown fustian jacket and striped pantaloons. There was something of a roll, a lounge in his gait, not unlike his own Peter Bell. There was a severe, worn pressure of thought about his temples, a fire in his eye (as if he saw something in objects more than the outward appearance), an intense high narrow forehead, a Roman nose, cheeks furrowed by strong purpose and feeling, and a convulsive inclination to laughter about the mouth, a good deal at variance with the solemn, stately expression of the rest of his face. . . . He sat down and talked very naturally and freely, with a mixture of clear gushing accents in his voice, a deep guttural intonation, and a strong tincture of the northern *burr*, like the crust on wine. He instantly began to make havoc of the half of a Cheshire cheese on the table, and said triumphantly that 'his marriage with experience had not been so unproductive as Mr Southey's in teaching him a knowledge of the good things of this life.' He had been to see the *Castle Spectre* by Monk Lewis, while at Bristol, and described it very well. He said 'It fitted the taste of the audience like a glove.' This *ad captandum* merit was however by no means a recommendation of it, according to the severe principles of the new school, which reject rather than court popular effect. Wordsworth, looking out of the low, latticed window, said, 'How beautifully the sun sets on that yellow bank!' I thought within myself, 'With what eyes these poets see nature!' and ever after, when I saw the sun-set stream upon the objects facing it, conceived I had made a discovery, or thanked Mr Wordsworth for having made one for me! We went over to All-Foxden again the day following, and Wordsworth read us the story of Peter Bell in the open air; and the comment made upon it by his face and voice was very different from that of some later critics! Whatever might be thought of the poem, 'his face was as a book where men might read strange matters,' and he announced the fate of his hero in prophetic tones. There is a *chaunt* in the recitation both of Coleridge and Wordsworth, which acts as a spell upon the hearer, and disarms the judgment. Perhaps they have deceived themselves by making habitual use of this ambiguous accompaniment. Coleridge's manner is more full, animated, and varied; Wordsworth's more equable, sustained, and internal. The one might be termed more *dramatic*, the other more *lyrical*. Coleridge has told me that he himself liked to compose in walking over uneven ground, or breaking through the straggling branches of a copse-wood; whereas Wordsworth always wrote (if he could) walking up and down a straight gravel-walk, or in some spot where the continuity of his verse met with no collateral interruption. Returning the same evening, I got into a metaphysical argument with Wordsworth, while Coleridge was explaining the different notes of the nightingale to his sister, in which we neither of us succeeded in making ourselves perfectly clear and intelligible. Thus I passed three weeks at Nether Stowey and in the neighbourhood, generally devoting the afternoons to a delightful chat in an arbour made of bark by the poet's friend Tom Poole, sitting under two fine elm-trees, and listening to the bees humming round us, while we quaffed our *flip*. It was agreed, among other things, that we should make a jaunt down the Bristol-Channel, as far as Linton. We set off together on foot, Coleridge, John Chester, and I. This Chester was a native of Nether Stowey, one of those who were attracted to Coleridge's discourse as flies are to honey, or bees in swarming-time to the sound of a brass pan. He 'followed in the chase, like a dog who hunts, not like one that made up the cry.' He had on a brown cloth coat, boots, and corduroy breeches, was low in stature, bow-legged, had a drag in his walk like a drover, which he assisted by a hazel switch, and kept on a sort of trot by the side of Coleridge, like a running footman by a state coach, that he might not lose a syllable or sound that fell from Coleridge's lips. He told me his private opinion, that Coleridge was a wonderful man. He scarcely opened his lips, much less offered an opinion the whole way: yet of the three, had I to chuse during that journey, I would be John Chester. He afterwards followed Coleridge into Germany, where the Kantean philosophers were puzzled how to bring him under any of their categories. When he sat down at table with his idol, John's felicity was complete; Sir Walter Scott's, or Mr Black-wood's, when they sat down at the same table with the King, was not more so. We passed Dunster on our right, a small town between the brow of a hill and the sea. I remember eyeing it wistfully as it lay below us: contrasted with the woody scene around, it looked as clear, as pure, as *embrowned* and ideal as any landscape I have seen since, of Gaspar Poussin's or Domenichino's. We had a long day's march—(our feet kept time to the echoes of Coleridge's tongue)—through Minehead and by the Blue Anchor, and on to Linton, which we did not reach till near midnight, and where we had some difficulty in making a lodgment. We however knocked the people of the house up at last, and we were repaid for our apprehensions and fatigue by some excellent rashers of fried bacon and eggs. The view in coming along had been splendid. We walked for miles and miles on dark brown heaths overlooking the Channel, with the Welsh hills beyond, and at times descended into little sheltered valleys close by the seaside, with a smuggler's face scowling by us, and then had to ascend conical hills with a path winding up through a coppice to a barren top, like a monk's shaven crown, from one of which I pointed out to Coleridge's notice the bare masts of a vessel on the very edge of the horizon and within the red-orbed disk of the setting sun, like his own spectre-ship in the *Ancient Mariner*. At Linton the character of the sea-coast becomes more marked and rugged. There is a place called the *Valley of Rocks* (I suspect this was only the poetical name for it) bedded among precipices overhanging the sea, with rocky caverns beneath, into which the waves dash, and where the sea-gull for ever wheels its screaming flight. On the top of these are huge stones thrown transverse, as if an earth-quake had tossed them there, and behind these is a fretwork of perpendicular rocks, something like the *Giant's Causeway*. A thunder-storm came on while we were at the inn, and Coleridge was running out bare-headed to enjoy the commotion of the elements

[268]

in the *Valley of Rocks*, but as if in spite, the clouds only muttered a few angry sounds, and let fall a few refreshing drops. Coleridge told me that he and Wordsworth were to have made this place the scene of a prose-tale, which was to have been in the manner of, but far superior to, the *Death of Abel*, but they had relinquished the design. In the morning of the second day, we breakfasted luxuriously in an old-fashioned parlour, on tea, toast, eggs, and honey, in the very sight of the bee-hives from which it had been taken, and a garden full of thyme and wild flowers that had produced it. On this occasion Coleridge spoke of Virgil's Georgics, but not well. I do not think he had much feeling for the classical or elegant. It was in this room that we found a little worn-out copy of the *Seasons*, lying in a window-seat, on which Coleridge exclaimed, '*That* is true fame!' He said Thomson was a great poet, rather than a good one; his style was as meretricious as his thoughts were natural. He spoke of Cowper as the best modern poet. He said the *Lyrical Ballads* were an experiment about to be tried by him and Wordsworth, to see how far the public taste would endure poetry written in a more natural and simple style than had hitherto been attempted; totally discarding the artifices of poetical diction, and making use only of such words as had probably been common in the most ordinary language since the days of Henry II. Some comparison was introduced between Shakespear and Milton. He said 'he hardly knew which to prefer. Shakespear appeared to him a mere stripling in the art; he was as tall and as strong, with infinitely more activity than Milton, but he never appeared to have come to man's estate; or if he had, he would not have been a man, but a monster.' He spoke with contempt of Gray, and with intolerance of Pope. He did not like the versification of the latter. He observed that 'the ears of these couplet-writers might be charged with having short memories, that could not retain the harmony of whole passages.' He thought little of Junius as a writer; he had a dislike of Dr Johnson; and a much higher opinion of Burke as an orator and politician, than of Fox or Pitt. He however thought him very inferior in richness of style and imagery to some of our elder prose-writers, particularly Jeremy Taylor. He liked Richardson, but not Fielding; nor could I get him to enter into the merits of *Caleb Williams*.* In short, he was profound and discriminating with respect to those authors whom he liked, and where he gave his judgment fair play; capricious, perverse, and prejudiced in his antipathies and distastes. We loitered on the 'ribbed sea-sands,' [89] in such talk as

* He had no idea of pictures, of Claude or Raphael, and at this time I had as little as he. [Hazlitt.]

this, a whole morning, and I recollect met with a curious sea-weed, of which John Chester told us the country name! A fisher-man gave Coleridge an account of a boy that had been drowned the day before, and that they had tried to save him at the risk of their own lives. He said 'he did not know how it was that they ventured, but, Sir, we have a *nature* towards one another.' This expression, Coleridge remarked to me, was a fine illustration of that theory of disinterestedness which I (in common with Butler) had adopted. I broached to him an argument of mine to prove that *likeness* was not mere association of ideas. I said that the mark in the sand put one in mind of a man's foot, not because it was part of a former impression of a man's foot (for it was quite new) but because it was like the shape of a man's foot. He assented to the justness of this distinction (which I have explained at length elsewhere, for the benefit of the curious) and John Chester listened; not from any interest in the subject, but because he was astonished that I should be able to suggest any thing to Coleridge that he did not already know. We returned on the third morning, and Coleridge remarked the silent cottage-smoke curling up the valleys where, a few evenings before, we had seen the lights gleaming through the dark.

"In a day or two after we arrived at Stowey, we set out, I on my return home, and he for Germany. It was a Sunday morning, and he was to preach that day for Dr Toulmin of Taunton. I asked him if he had prepared any thing for the occasion? He said he had not even thought of the text, but should as soon as we parted. I did not go to hear him,—this was a fault,—but we met in the evening at Bridgewater. The next day we had a long day's walk to Bristol, and sat down, I recollect, by a well-side on the road, to cool ourselves and satisfy our thirst, when Coleridge repeated to me some descriptive lines from his tragedy of Remorse; which I must say became his mouth and that occasion better than they, some years after, did Mr Elliston's and the Drury-lane boards,—

'Oh memory! shield me from the world's poor strife,
And give those scenes thine everlasting life.'

"I saw no more of him for a year or two, during which period he had been wandering in the Hartz Forest in Germany; and his return was cometary, meteorous, unlike his setting out. It was not till some time after that I knew his friends Lamb and Southey. The last always appears to me (as I first saw him) with a common-place book under his arm, and the first with a *bon-mot* in his mouth. It was at Godwin's that I met him with Holcroft and Coleridge, where they were disputing fiercely which was the best—*Man as he was, or man as he is to be.* 'Give me,' says Lamb, 'man as he is *not* to be.' This saying was the beginning of a friendship between us, which I believe still continues." [90]

The prose tale mentioned by Hazlitt, of which the Valley of Rocks was to have been the scene, was *The Wanderings of Cain*. The proposed collaboration between Coleridge and Wordsworth came to a speedy end, as related by Coleridge:

"The work was to have been written in concert with another, whose name is too venerable within the precincts of genius to be unnecessarily brought into connection with such a trifle, and who was then residing at a small distance from Nether Stowey. The title and subject were suggested by myself, who likewise drew out the scheme and the contents for each of the three books or cantos, of which the work was to consist, and which, the reader is to be informed, was to have been finished in one night! My partner undertook the first canto; I the second: and which ever had *done first*, was to set about the third. Almost thirty years have passed by; yet at this moment I cannot without something more than a smile moot the question which of the two things was the more impracticable, for a mind so eminently original to compose another man's thoughts and fancies, or for a taste so austerely pure and simple to imitate the Death of Abel? Methinks I see his grand and noble countenance as at the moment when having despatched my own portion of the task at full finger-speed, I hastened to him with my manuscript—that look of humourous despondency fixed on his almost blank sheet of paper, and then its silent mock-piteous admission of failure struggling with the sense of the exceeding ridiculousness of the whole scheme—which broke up in a laugh: and the Ancient Mariner was written instead." [91]

The effort at collaboration over *The Ancient Mariner*, as has been seen, met with no greater success. Of *The Wanderings of Cain* only fragments exist.

Hazlitt was mistaken in thinking that the end of his visit coincided with Coleridge's departure for Germany. At that time the Wordsworths were still at Alfoxden. The German plan was still some months from fruition.

Coleridge referred to the Lynton walk—there in one day and back in one day—in a letter to Cottle. Wordsworth and he had decided definitely, he said, that the *Lyrical Ballads* should occupy one volume only: "We deem that the volumes offered to you, are, to a certain degree, one work in kind, though not in degree, as an ode is one work; and that our different poems are, as stanzas, good, relatively rather than absolutely: mark you, I say in kind, though not in degree."[92] They also insisted that the poems must be published anonymously: "Wordsworth's name is nothing to a large number of persons; mine stinks."[93]

He ends this letter with a few words on typography. The printer was a bugbear to him, then and always—the proof sheets of his works are littered with exclamations of despair at the typographical errors and signs of slovenliness that abound there. "Cottle, my dear Cottle," he says, "I meant to have written you an Essay on the Metaphysics of Typography, but I have not time. Take a few hints, without the abstruse reasons for them, with which I mean to favour you. 18 lines in a page, the line closely printed, certainly more closely printed than those of the *Joan* ('Oh, by all means, closer, *W. Wordsworth*'); equal ink, and large margins; that is beauty; it may even, under your immediate care, mingle the sublime! And now, my dear Cottle, may God love you and me, who am, with most unauthorish feelings, Your true friend."[94]

Early in April Coleridge had occasion to write to his brother George—a letter which, in common with most of his letters to his family, is instructive but not always edifying. Coleridge writes to defend himself, not for the first time, against the charge of harbouring republican sentiments. In some respects his letter is an uneasy mixture of sophistry and affectation, an essay in apologetics. Anxious, as usual, to represent himself to George as he conceives George wishes him to be, he contrives to draw the picture of one so eminently reasonable, so saintly in thought and behaviour, that the true, faulty, yet vastly more attractive Coleridge is swallowed up in words. Nevertheless, the letter, in which great good sense and clap-trap, penetrating thought and hypocritical ranting jostle one another, has much value. For in it is seen the movement of Coleridge's mind from the politics of the city to the poetry and philosophy of the country, from men to man—a movement in part anticipated, in part followed by Wordsworth. But first:

"An illness, which confined me to my bed, prevented me from returning an immediate answer to your kind and interesting letter. My indisposition originated in the stump of a tooth over which some matter had formed; this affected my eye, my eye my stomach, my stomach my head, and the consequence was a general fever, and the sum of pain was considerably increased by the vain attempts of our surgeon to extract the offending member. Laudanum gave me repose, not sleep; but you, I believe, know how divine that repose is, what a spot of enchantment, a green spot of fountains and flowers and trees in the very heart of a waste of sands!" [95]

He then proceeded to the point at issue:

"I collect from your letter that our opinions and feelings on political subjects are more nearly alike than you imagine them to be. Equally with you (and perhaps with a deeper conviction, for my belief is founded on actual experience), equally with you I deprecate the moral and intellectual habits of those men, both in England and France, who have modestly assumed to themselves the exclusive title of Philosophers and Friends of Freedom. I think them at least *as* distant from greatness as from goodness. If I know my own opinions, they are utterly untainted with French metaphysics, French politics, French ethics, and French theology. As to *the Rulers* of France, I see in their views, speeches, and actions nothing that distinguishes them to their advantage from other animals of the same species. History has taught me that rulers are much the same in all ages, and under all forms of government; they are as bad as they dare to be. The vanity of ruin and the curse of blindness have clung to them like an hereditary leprosy. Of the French Revolution I can give my thoughts most adequately in the words of Scripture: 'A great and strong wind rent the mountains, and brake in pieces the rocks before the Lord; but the Lord was not in the wind; and after the wind an earthquake; and after the earthquake a fire; and the Lord was not in the fire'; and now (believing that no calamities are permitted but as the means of good) I wrap my face in my mantle and wait, with a subdued and patient thought, expecting to hear 'the still small voice' which is of God. In America (I have received my information from unquestionable authority) the morals and domestic habits of the people are daily deteriorating; and one good consequence which I expect from revolution is that individuals will see the necessity of individual effort; that they will act as good Christians, rather than as citizens and electors; and so by degrees will purge off that error, which to me appears as wild and more pernicious than the πάγχρυσον and panacea of the alchemists, the error of attributing to governments a talismanic influence over our virtues and our happiness, as if governments were not rather effects than causes. It is true that all effects react and become causes, and so it must be in some degree with governments; but there are other agents which act more powerfully because by a nigher and more continuous agency, and it remains true that governments are more the *effect* than the cause of that which we are. Do not therefore, my brother, consider me as an enemy to government and its rulers, or as one who says they are evil. I do not say so. In my opinion it were a species of blasphemy! Shall a nation of drunkards presume to babble against sickness and the headache? I regard governments as I regard the abcesses produced by certain fevers —they are necessary consequences of the disease, and by their pain they increase the disease; but yet they are in the wisdom and goodness of Nature, and not only are they physically necessary as effects, but also as causes they are morally necessary in order to prevent the utter dissolution of the patient. But what should we think of a man who expected an absolute cure from an ulcer that only prevented his dying. Of guilt I say nothing, but I believe most steadfastly in original sin; that from our mothers' wombs our understandings are darkened; and even where our understandings are in the light, that our organization is depraved and our volitions imperfect; and we sometimes see the good without wishing to attain it, and oftener *wish* it without the energy that wills and performs. And for this inherent depravity I believe that the *spirit* of the Gospel is the sole cure; but permit me to add, that I look for the spirit of the Gospel 'neither in the mountain, nor at Jerusalem.'

"You think, my brother, that there can be but two *parties* at present, for the Government and against the Government. It may be so. I am of no party. It is true I think the present Ministry weak and unprincipled men; but I would not with a safe conscience vote for their removal; I could point out no substitutes. I think very seldom on the subject; but as far as I have thought, I am inclined to consider the aristocrats as the most respectable of our three factions, because they are more decorous. The Opposition and the Democrats are not only vicious, they wear the *filthy garments* of vice.

> He that takes
> Deep in his soft credulity the stamp
> Design'd by loud disclaimers on the part
> Of liberty, themselves the slaves of lust,
> Incurs derision for his easy faith
> And lack of knowledge, and with cause enough:
> For when was public virtue to be found
> Where private was not? Can he love the whole
> Who loves no part? He be a *nation's* friend,
> Who is, in truth, the friend of *no* man there?

[274]

Can he be strenuous in his country's cause
Who slights the charities, for whose dear sake
That country, if at all, must be belov'd?

Cowper

"I am prepared to suffer without discontent the consequences
of my follies and mistakes; and unable to conceive how that which
I am of Good could have been without that which I have been of
evil, it is withheld from me to regret anything. I therefore consent
to be deemed a Democrat and a Seditionist. A man's character
follows him long after he has ceased to deserve it; but I have
snapped my squeaking baby-trumpet of sedition, and the fragments lie scattered in the lumber-room of penitence. I wish to be
a good man and a Christian, but I am no Whig, no Reformist, no
Republican, and because of the multitude of fiery and undisciplined
spirits that lie in wait against the public quiet under these titles,
because of them I chiefly accuse the present ministers, to whose
folly I attribute, in a great measure, their increased and increasing
numbers. You think differently, and if I were called upon by you
to prove my assertions, although I imagine I could make them
appear plausible, yet I should feel the insufficiency of my data.
The Ministers may have had in their possession facts which alter
the whole state of the argument, and make my syllogisms fall as
flat as a baby's card-house. And feeling this, my brother! I have
for some time past withdrawn myself totally from the consideration of *immediate causes*, which are infinitely complex and un
certain, to muse on fundamental and general causes, the 'causae
causarum.' I devote myself to such works as encroach not on the
anti-social passions—in poetry, to elevate the imagination and set
the affections in right tune by the beauty of the inanimate im-
pregnated as with a living soul by the presence of life—in prose
to the seeking with patience and a slow, very slow mind, 'Quid
sumus, et quidnam victuri gignimus,'—what our faculties are and
what they are capable of becoming. I love fields and woods and
mountains with almost a visionary fondness. And because I have
found benevolence and quietness growing within me as that
fondness has increased, therefore I should wish to be the means
of implanting it in others, and to destroy the bad passions not
by combating them but by keeping them in inaction."[96]

At this point, he quotes Wordsworth—a bold yet subtle reference, as it was doubtless the reputation of his friend, with that
of Thelwall, which had brought upon Coleridge the brotherly
rebuke.

[275]

                    Not useless do I deem
These shadowy sympathies with things that hold
An inarticulate Language; for the Man—
Once taught to love such objects as excite
No morbid passions, no disquietude,
No vengeance, and no hatred—needs must feel
The joy of that pure principle of love
So deeply, that, unsatisfied with aught
Less pure and exquisite, he cannot choose
But seek for objects of a kindred love
In fellow-nature and a kindred joy.
Accordingly he by degrees perceives
His feelings of aversion softened down;
A holy tenderness pervade his frame!
His sanity of reason not impair'd,
Say, rather, that his thoughts now flowing clear
From a clear fountain flowing, he looks round,
He seeks for good; and finds the good he seeks. [97]

"I have laid down for myself two maxims, and, what is more I am in the habit of regulating myself by them. With regard to others, I never controvert opinions except after some intimacy, and when alone with the person, and at the happy time when we both seem awake to our own fallibility, and then I rather state my reasons than argue against his. In general conversation to find out the opinions common to us, or at least the subjects on which difference of opinion creates no uneasiness, such as novels, poetry, natural scenery, local anecdotes, and (in a serious mood and with serious men) the general evidences of our religion. With regard to myself, it is my habit, on whatever subject I think, to endeavour to discover all the good that has resulted from it, that does result, or that can result. To this I bind down my mind, and after long meditation in this tract slowly and gradually make up my opinions on the quantity and nature of the evil. I consider this as the most important rule for the regulation of the intellect and the affections, as the only means of preventing the passions from turning reason into a hired advocate." [98]

Shortly after writing this letter, he followed it up with a visit to Ottery, where George, who had taken Orders, was now Chaplain Priest and Master of the King's School. He returned to Stowey on April 18.[99]

His next letter to George, on May 14,[100] announced the birth that day of a second son, to be known as Berkeley, after the philosopher Bishop of that name.[101] Almost in the same breath as he announces the good news to Estlin and to Poole and comments upon his new son's appearance with paternal pride: "... already almost as large as Hartley .... strong and shapely, and has the paternal beauty in his upper lip ...."[102] he has to refer to less pleasant matters; to the daughter of Dr Toulmin, who "... in a melancholy derangement suffered herself to be swallowed up by the tide on the coast between Sidmouth and Bere ...",[103] the lamentable though quaintly expressed cause of Coleridge taking the minister's duty at Taunton the day before the birth of Berkeley; and, above all, he has to refer to Lloyd.

For, at this very moment, when all seemed well, when, as he told Cottle, "... new and tender health is all over me like a voluptuous feeling"[104]—at this moment Lloyd, unknowingly, struck.

The apologetic letter from Lamb of a few months before turned out to be but a flash in the pan. Indeed, if, as the wording of the letter suggests, Lamb's conscience was stirred, it may have been as much by thoughts of events in the making as by those past. In that letter he told Coleridge that he was collaborating with Lloyd in putting out a volume of poems entitled *Blank Verse*. Soon after, in March, Lloyd, hearing that there was a possibility of a third edition of Coleridge's poems being published, informed Cottle that he did not wish his poems to be printed again with those of Coleridge, requesting that they should be omitted from any future edition.

Coleridge, when told of this by Cottle, replied ruefully: "... it is curious that *I* should be applied to to be 'persuaded to resign, and in hope that I might' *consent* to *give up* (unknown by whom) a number of poems which were published at the earnest request of the author, who assured me that the circumstance was 'of no trivial import to his happiness.' Times change and people change; but let us keep our souls in quietness! I have no objection to any disposal of C. Lloyd's poems, except that of their being republished with mine. The motto which I had prefixed, 'Duplex,' etc. from Groscollius, has placed me in a ridiculous situation; but it was a foolish and presumptuous start of affectionateness, and I am not unwilling to incur punishments due to my folly. By past experiences we build up our moral being." [105]

He continues with an example of the exaggerated terms in which he at times indulged—thereby giving the impression of an insincerity which did not always exist: "How comes it," he asks, "that I have never heard from dear Mr Estlin, my fatherly and brotherly friend? The idea haunted me through my sleepless nights, till my sides were sore in turning from one to the other, as if I were hoping to turn from the idea." [106]

Lloyd's action, though Coleridge made light of it, hurt him deeply. But worse was to come. In the spring [107] Lloyd published his novel *Edmund Oliver*. The novel was published by Cottle and dedicated to Lamb. It contained obvious and malicious references to Coleridge. His love affairs, his indiscretions leading up to the period with the Hussars, his sloth, his recourse to opium— all were referred to in an exaggerated form as adventures and characteristics of the leading figure in the book. In the Preface, Lloyd wrote: "The incidents relative to the army were given me by an intimate friend who was himself eyewitness of one of them." [108] The intimate friend—intimate no longer—had, however, no notion that his reminiscences were to be used thus, to blacken his character in public.

Coleridge was dumbfounded. Lloyd had wounded him in his weakest part. His pride was hurt, inevitably; but more grievous was the rebuff to his affections. That Lloyd should so write of him, that Cottle should publish, that Lamb should permit the dedication to himself of such a book—these indications of the apparent indifference, if not actual dislike, with which he was regarded where once, so short a time before, love and admiration reigned, preyed upon the affectionate Coleridge like a fever.

But Lloyd had not yet done with his former idol. Certain injudicious references to Southey and Lamb which Coleridge had made in confidence at the Stowey fireside—for instance: "Charles Lloyd in one of his fits had shown to Lamb a letter, in which Coleridge had illustrated the cases of vast genius in proportion to talent and predominance of talent in conjunction with genius, in the persons of Lamb and himself" [109]—were repeated by Lloyd, not necessarily with deliberate intent to injure Coleridge, but rather because he seemed at times in incomplete control of his

[278]

tongue and his imagination. That he restricted himself to the bare truth, unpalatable hearing though that may have proved at times, appears unlikely in view of the result of his scandal-mongering; for Southey, already displeased by the supposed attack on him by way of the 'simplicity' sonnet, now retreated in high dudgeon into a cold and almost impenetrable hauteur, whilst Lamb—the grateful, apologetic Lamb of a few months back—actually intimated through Dorothy that he wished the correspondence between himself and Coleridge to cease.

At this final blow, Coleridge was quite unmanned. That his old friend should thus, unlovingly, lacking even the courage to write to him direct, go over to the enemy, struck at his heart. In the face of the contempt of those to whom he had given his affection, his new-found joy in life and his confidence and enthusiasm in his work alike deserted him. There was no strength, no virtue left in him.

Coleridge once wrote:

> To be beloved is all I need,
> And whom I love, I love indeed.[110]

He was right; so right, that when love was withdrawn from him, denied him, his need of it repulsed, his spirits sank like those of a sick man. His health failed.

He wrote to Lamb, a letter not without dignity:

"Lloyd has informed me through Miss Wordsworth that you intend no longer to correspond with me. This has given me little pain; not that I do not love and esteem you, but on the contrary because I am confident that your intentions are pure. You are performing what you deem a duty, and humanly speaking have that merit which can be derived from the performance of a painful duty. Painful, for you would not without struggles abandon me in behalf of a man who, wholly ignorant of all but your name, became attached to you in consequence of my attachment, caught *his* from *my* enthusiasm, and learned to love you at my fireside, when often while I have been sitting and talking of your sorrows and afflictions I have stopped my conversations and lifted up wet eyes and prayed for you. No! I am confident that although you do not think as a wise man, you feel as a good man.

"From you I have received little pain, because for you I suffer little alarm. I cannot say this for your friend; it appears to me evident that his feelings are vitiated, and that his ideas are in their combination merely the creatures of those feelings. I have received letters from him, and the best and kindest wish which, as a Christian, I can offer in return is that he may feel remorse.

"Some brief resentments rose in my mind, but they did not remain there; for I began to think almost immediately, and my resentments vanished. There has resulted only a sort of fantastic scepticism concerning my own consciousness of my own rectitude. As dreams have impressed on him the sense of reality, my sense of reality may be but a dream. From his letters it is plain that he has mistaken the heat and bustle and swell of self-justification for the approbation of his own conscience. I am certain that *this* is not the case with me, but the human heart is so wily and inventive that possibly it may be cheating me, who am an older warrior, with some newer stratagem. When I wrote to you that my Sonnet to Simplicity was not composed with reference to Southey, you answered me (I believe these were the words): 'It was a lie too gross for the grossest ignorance to believe'; and I was not angry with you, because the assertion which the grossest ignorance would believe a lie the Omniscient knew to be truth. This, however, makes me cautious not too hastily to affirm the falsehood of an assertion of Lloyd's that in Edmund Oliver's love-fit, leaving college and going into the army he had no sort of allusion to or recollection of my love-fit, leaving college, and going into the army, and that he never thought of my person in the description of Oliver's person in the first letter of the second volume. This cannot appear stranger to me than my assertion did to you, and therefore I will suspend my absolute faith.

"I wrote to you not that I wish to hear from you, but that I wish you to write to Lloyd and press upon him the propriety, nay the necessity, of his giving me a meeting either *tête-à-tête* or in the presence of all whose esteem I value. This I owe to my own character; I owe it to him if by any means he may even yet be extricated. He assigned as reasons for his rupture my vices; and he is either right or wrong. If right, it is fit that others should know it and follow his example; if wrong, he has acted very wrong. At present, I may expect everything from his heated mind rather than continence of language, and his assertions will be the more readily believed on account of his former enthusiastic attachment, though with wise men this would cast a hue of suspicion over the whole affair; but the number of wise men in the kingdom would not puzzle a savage's arithmetic—you may tell them in every [community] on your fingers. I have been unfortunate in my connections. Both you and Lloyd became acquainted with me when your minds were far from being in a composed or natural state, and you clothed my image with a suit of notions and feelings which could

[280]

belong to nothing human. You are restored to comparative sane-
ness, and are merely wondering what is become of the Coleridge
with whom you were so passionately in love; *Charles Lloyd's*
mind has only changed his disease, and his is now arraying his
ci-devant Angel in a flaming San Benito—the whole ground of the
garment a dark brimstone and plenty of little devils flourished out
in black. Oh, me! Lamb, 'even in laughter the heart is sad!' My
kindness, my affectionateness, he deems wheedling; but, if after
reading all my letters to yourself and to him, you can suppose him
wise in his treatment and correct in his accusations of me, you
think worse of human nature than poor human nature, bad as it is,
deserves to be thought of. God bless you." [111]

But his resistance to unlovingness quickly crumbled despite the
philosophical front he showed to Lamb. In a letter written the day
Berkeley was born, he complained bitterly to Estlin: "I ought to
have written to you before; and have done very wrong in not
writing. But I have had many sorrows and some that bite deep;
calumny and ingratitude from men who have been fostered in the
bosom of my confidence!" [112] And a few days later in a letter to
Poole, who had just lost his brother Richard, Coleridge was unable
wholly to restrain his personal misery:

> "My dearest Poole," he wrote, "I was all day yesterday in a
> distressing perplexity whether or no it would be wise or con-
> solatory for me to call at your house, or whether I should write
> to your mother, as a Christian friend, or whether it would not be
> better to wait for the exhaustion of that grief which must have its
> way. So many unpleasant and shocking circumstances have hap-
> pened to me in my immediate knowledge within the last fortnight,
> that I am in a nervous state, and the most trifling thing makes me
> weep. Poor Richard! May Providence heal the wounds which it
> hath seen good to inflict! Do you wish me to see you to-day? Shall
> I call on you? Shall I stay with you? or had I better leave you
> uninterrupted? In all your sorrows as in your joys, I am, indeed,
> my dearest Poole, a true and faithful sharer!" [113]

Even in his relations with Wordsworth he can see for the
moment a darker side.

> "On one subject," he tells Estlin, "we are habitually silent; we
> found our data dissimilar, and never renewed the subject. It is his
> practice and almost his nature to convey all the truth he knows
> without any attack on what he supposes falsehood, if that false-

hood be interwoven with virtues or happiness. He loves and venerates Christ and Christianity. I wish he did more, but it were wrong indeed if an incoincidence with one of our wishes altered our respect and affection to a man of whom we are, as it were, instructed by one great Master to say that not being against us he is for us." [114]

Unable to endure the torment of his reflections upon this breach of friendship, he sought the obscurity of the lonely farmhouse between Porlock and Lynton, [115] at which place, taking opium to escape for a while from his unhappiness, he composed in his dreams the magical *Kubla Khan*.

Hearing that Lloyd was in the neighbourhood, Coleridge and Wordsworth tried to lay him by the heels—"to bring back poor Lloyd" [116] as Coleridge explains to Estlin, writing from the village of Cross, whence Wordsworth had just left to continue the search in Bristol. He describes Lloyd's infirmities with solemn mystery as "made the instruments of another man's darker passions." [117] But the elusive Lloyd had already gone back to Birmingham, where Lamb was due shortly for a fortnight's holiday.

Cottle attempted to patch up the quarrel. He wrote to Lloyd, who replied: "I love Coleridge, and can forget all that has happened." [118] But by this time Coleridge, apparently unprepared to forget with such facility, had already widened the rift. After emerging from his temporary retirement he made an effort to carry off the situation with a high hand. In an attempt to convince himself and those around him that he remained indifferent to the loss of Lamb's friendship, and still more, perhaps, of his esteem, he spoke of him with assumed loftiness. What exactly he said is not known. But it is unlikely to have differed materially from the words repeated by Lamb to Southey. "Samuel Taylor Coleridge, to the eternal regret of his native Devonshire, emigrates to Westphalia—'Poor Lamb (these were his last words), if he wants any *knowledge*, he may apply to me,'—in ordinary cases, I thanked him, I have an 'Encyclopaedia' at hand, but on such an occasion as going over to a German university, I could not refrain from sending him the following propositions, to be by him defended or oppugned (or both) at Leipsic or Gottingen." [119]

This was the actual letter Lamb had sent Coleridge:

"THESES QUÆDAM THEOLOGICÆ

1. Whether God loves a lying Angel better than a true Man?
2. Whether the Archangel Uriel *could* affirm an untruth? and if he *could* whether he *would*?
3. Whether Honesty be an angelic virtue? or not rather to be reckoned among those qualities which the Schoolmen term '*Virtutes minus splendidæ et terræ et hominis participes*'?
4. Whether the higher order of Seraphim Illuminati ever sneer?
5. Whether pure intelligences can love?
6. Whether the Seraphim Ardentes do not manifest their virtues by way of vision and theory? and whether practice be not a sub-celestial and merely human virtue?
7. Whether the Vision Beatific be anything more or less than a perpetual representment to each individual Angel of his own present attainments and future capabilities, somehow in the manner of mortal looking-glasses, reflecting a perpetual complacency and self-satisfaction?
8. and last. Whether an immortal and amenable soul may not come to be damned at last, and the man never suspect it beforehand?

Learned Sir, my Friend,

Presuming on our long habits of friendship and emboldened further by your late liberal permission to avail myself of your correspondence, in case I want any knowledge, (which I intend to do when I have no Encyclopædia or Lady's Magazine at hand to refer to in any matter of science,) I now submit to your enquiries the above Theological Propositions, to be by you defended, or oppugned, or both, in the Schools of Germany, whither I am told you are departing, to the utter dissatisfaction of your native Devonshire and regret of universal England; but to my own individual consolation if thro' the channel of your wished return, Learned Sir, my Friend, may be transmitted to this our Island, from those famous Theological Wits of Leipsic and Gottingen, any rays of illumination, in vain to be derived from the home growth of our English Halls and Colleges. Finally wishing, Learned Sir, that you may see Schiller and swing in a wood (*vide* Poems) and sit upon a Tun, and eat fat hams of Westphalia,
I remain,
Your friend and docile Pupil to instruct." [120]

Coleridge did not answer the letter. "Mr Coleridge," said Cottle, "gave me this letter, saying, 'These young visionaries will do each other no good.' " [121] But the assumption of this paternal air, which would be ludicrous were it not pathetic, could not save Coleridge from unenviable reflections or prevent Lamb's vicious stabs from casting a shadow over the remainder of his days in England.

In June, Coleridge visited the Wedgwoods at Stoke d'Abernon, where the German expedition was discussed and where he learned that Godwin wished to be introduced to him again.[122] Coleridge wrote Poole while he was away, his journey also taking in Bristol, and Brentford where Poole's business friend, Purkis, lived:

> "I arrived in Bristol on Monday evening, spent the next day at Estlin's, who opposed my German expedition *furore per-religioso, amicissimo furore*. At Brentford I arrived Wednesday evening, and was driven by Mr Purkis great part of the way to Stoke on Thursday evening. . . . The Wedgwoods received me with joy and affection. I have been metaphysicizing so long and so closely with T. Wedgwood, that I am a *caput mortuum* mere lees and residuum. . . . This place is a noble, large house in a rich, pleasant country; but the little Toe of Quantock is better than the head and shoulders of Surrey and Middlesex." [123]

The Wordsworths left Alfoxden on June 25, spent a week at Stowey with the Coleridges, came to Bristol on July 2 and stayed a few days with Cottle until they could get into lodgings they had taken at Shirehampton, in order that Wordsworth should be able to "superintend the printing" [124] of his poems by Cottle's printer, Biggs. "I have not often felt more regret than when we quitted Allfoxden," Dorothy wrote to her aunt, Mrs Rawson, from Cottle's shop; "I should however have felt much more if we were not likely in so short a time to have again the pleasure of Coleridge's society, an advantage which I prize the more, the more I know him." [125]

In the same letter, Dorothy speaks of Southey. "You ask me if I am acquainted with Southey. I know a little of him personally, that is I dined three times at his house when I was in town and called there once or twice; and I know a good deal of his character from our common friends. He is a young man of the most rigidly virtuous habits and is I believe exemplary in the discharge of all domestic duties, but though his talents are certainly very remarkable for his years (as far as I can judge) I think them much inferior to the talents of Coleridge." [126]

The Wordsworths, after leaving Cottle, went for a short walking tour along the banks of the Wye to Tintern Abbey, which Wordsworth was eager that Dorothy should see. This walk produced the famous *Lines written a few miles above Tintern Abbey*.

A few days later Coleridge visited the Wordsworths at Bristol to make final arrangements about the journey to Germany. He had misgivings about the wisdom of his family coming with them. He writes to Poole on August 3, one of his eminently 'reasonable' letters—a high moral tone in evidence as usual when a difficult point had to be won:

> "I still think the realization of the scheme of high importance to my intellectual utility; and of course to my moral happiness. But if I go with Mrs C. and little ones, I must *borrow*—an imprudent, perhaps an immoral thing—and the uncertainties attendant on all human schemes; the uncertainty of our happiness, comfort, cheap living etc., when in Germany; and the unsettled state of Germany itself; force on me the truth that I ought not to hazard any considerable sum. I propose therefore, if, as I guess, Mrs Coleridge's wishes tend the same way, to go myself (comparatively a trifling expense) stay 3 or 4 months, in which time I shall at least have learnt the language; then, if all is well, all comfortable, and I can rationally propose to myself a scheme of weighty advantages—to fetch over my family—if not to return, with my German for my pains, and the wisdom that 3 or 4 months sojourn among a new people must give to a watchful and thinking man. Make up your mind on my scheme—I shall return in a week. All, whom I have seen, are well. Wordsworth and his Sister, Wade and Cottle, desire their best love to you—I shall dart into Wales, and return per viam Swansea usque ad Bridgewater sive Cummage." [127]

Together with Dorothy and Wordsworth, Coleridge 'darted' into Wales, to see Thelwall at his farm of Llyswen near Swansea and to visit the scenes which had inspired *Tintern Abbey*.[128] On his return, it was of course decided that Sarah and the children should remain at Stowey under the care of Poole. It is difficult to understand any reason, except that of politeness, why the original suggestion should ever have been made.

The Wordsworths reached London on their way to Yarmouth on August 27. Coleridge, with the faithful John Chester, who was to accompany him to Germany, met them there on or about

September 10. He occupied himself with the arrangements for the publication of a little quarto of 23 pages by Johnson of St. Paul's Churchyard, to be sold at one shilling and sixpence. It contained *Fears in Solitude, France: an Ode,* and *Frost at Midnight.*[129] In the excitement and pleasure of these last few days he omitted to pay a call of considerable importance—his expected visit to Daniel Stuart to arrange about future contributions to the *Morning Post.*

On the 13th, Dorothy writes that the poems ". . . are printed, but not published . . . in one small volume, without the name of the author; their title is 'Lyrical Ballads, with other Poems.' Cottle has given thirty guineas for William's share of the volume."[130]

The following day they left for Yarmouth. On the 15th Coleridge wrote Poole, prompted by affection, of course, yet not unaccompanied, perhaps, by a twinge of conscience: "I am on the point of leaving my native country for the first time, a country which, God Almighty knows, is dear to me above all things for the love I bear to you. Of many friends whom I love and esteem, my head and heart have ever chosen you as the friend —as the one being in whom is involved the full and whole meaning of that sacred title."[131]

The next day they sailed for Germany.

10

As THE LITTLE party receded into the obscurity of a foreign country the *Lyrical Ballads* were published.[1] The event aroused no enthusiasm. No one foresaw in this little volume of poems the precursor of a new poetical age. No one hailed the coming of a fresh power into poetry. The *Lines written a few miles above Tintern Abbey*, Wordsworth's masterly contribution which ended the book, was referred to once only. *The Ancient Mariner* aroused only the contempt when it did not stir the wrath of those who mentioned it. Yet *Tintern Abbey* was Wordsworth's finest composition; *The Ancient Mariner* the greatest poem in the volume; and the *Lyrical Ballads* themselves were destined to form the spearhead of a poetry at once romantic and truthful, naturalistic and beautiful; that gave common things the lustre of novelty and uncommon things the assurance of nature; that spelt the end of eighteenth-century poetry and ushered in a period, brief in time but memorable in effect—a period which, though its main impulse was not destined to span even the remainder of Coleridge's life, was to crowd within its few years a wealth of unaffected beauty, of romance, of a quiet, moving, and sincere naturalism, of a sheer lyrical sweetness in poetry the like of which has been known only once before in the whole life of English literature.

By means of this small volume, Coleridge and Wordsworth blazed a trail along which Shelley,[2] Keats, Scott, Byron, with a host of minor poets were to follow, shedding a new, tender, and truthful beauty behind them; a trail which in later years was to reach as far as Tennyson in his greater lyrics.

The poems were preceded by an Advertisement:

> It is the honourable characteristic of Poetry that its materials are to be found in every subject which can interest the human mind. The evidence of this fact is to be sought, not in the writings of Critics, but in those of Poets themselves.
>
> The majority of the following poems are to be considered as

experiments. They were written chiefly with a view to ascertain how far the language of conversation in the middle and lower classes of society is adapted to the purposes of poetic pleasure. Readers accustomed to the gaudiness and inane phraseology of many modern writers, if they persist in reading this book to its conclusion, will perhaps frequently have to struggle with feelings of strangeness and aukwardness: they will look round for poetry, and will be induced to enquire by what species of courtesy these attempts can be permitted to assume that title. It is desirable that such readers, for their own sakes, should not suffer the solitary word Poetry, a word of very disputed meaning, to stand in the way of their gratification; but that, while they are perusing this book, they should ask themselves if it contains a natural delineation of human passions, human characters, and human incidents; and if the answer be favourable to the author's wishes, that they should consent to be pleased in spite of that most dreadful enemy to our pleasures, our own pre-established codes of decision.

Readers of superior judgment may disapprove of the style in which many of these pieces are executed; it must be expected that many lines and phrases will not exactly suit their taste. It will perhaps appear to them, that wishing to avoid the prevalent fault of the day, the author has sometimes descended too low, and that many of his expressions are too familiar, and not of sufficient dignity. It is apprehended, that the more conversant the reader is with our elder writers, and with those in modern times who have been the most successful in painting manners and passions, the fewer complaints of this kind will he have to make.

An accurate taste in poetry, and in all the other arts, Sir Joshua Reynolds has observed, is an acquired talent, which can only be produced by severe thought, and a long continued intercourse with the best models of composition. This is mentioned not with so ridiculous a purpose as to prevent the most inexperienced reader from judging for himself; but merely to temper the rashness of decision, and to suggest that if poetry be a subject on which much time has not been bestowed, the judgment may be erroneous, and that in many cases it necessarily will be so.

The tale of Goody Blake and Harry Gill is founded on a well-authenticated fact which happened in Warwickshire. Of the other poems in the collection, it may be proper to say that they are either absolute inventions of the author, or facts which took place within his personal observation or that of his friends. The poem of the Thorn, as the reader will soon discover, is not supposed to be spoken in the author's own person: the character of the loquacious narrator will sufficiently shew itself in the course of the story. The Rime of the Ancyent Marinere was professedly written in imitation of the *style*, as well as of the spirit of the elder poets; but with a few exceptions, the Author believes that the language adopted in it has been equally intelligible for these three last centuries. The lines entitled Expostulation and Reply, and those which follow, arose out of conversation with a friend who was somewhat unreasonably attached to modern books of moral philosophy.[3]

But this Advertisement barely attempts to explain the real significance of the venture. That was to be the duty of the famous Preface to the second edition of the *Lyrical Ballads* which, though written by Wordsworth, must be considered a joint production. As Coleridge said, it "is half a child of my own brain, and arose out of conversations so frequent that, with few exceptions, we could scarcely either of us, perhaps, positively say which first started any particular thought."[4] At this stage, Coleridge associated himself with the theory of Poetic Diction [5] which his friend was later to elaborate by himself.

Coleridge's theory of the creative imagination is not specifically mentioned in this Advertisement or in the Preface to the second edition, though to some extent implicit in both. Nor is any definition attempted of the two sorts of poems which the *Lyrical Ballads* were planned to exhibit. That was to be done some years later by Coleridge in words which have taken high place in the history of literary criticism.[6]

In fact, the division resolved itself into *The Ancient Mariner* on the one hand, and certain of Wordsworth's poems (by no means the best) on the other. Of the twenty-three poems in the volume, four only had been written by Coleridge, although these four, owing to the length of *The Ancient Mariner*, occupied nearly a third of the pages in the book; two of them, *The Foster-Mother's Tale* and *The Dungeon*, were fragments from *Osorio*, of little poetical value; the third, *The Nightingale*, was substituted at the last moment for *Lewti* [7]—substituted so hurriedly that the pagination was thereby thrown out of accuracy. None of these three poems conformed to the conditions which had been laid down for Coleridge—namely, the use of the supernatural or romantic incidents or agents; "yet so as to transfer from our inward nature a human interest and a semblance of truth sufficient to procure for these shadows of imagination that willing suspension of

[289]

disbelief for the moment, which constitutes poetic faith" [8]—so that *The Ancient Mariner* alone was left to bear the burden of proving that this particular "excellence" [9] of the creative imagination was practicable.

> "With this view," explained Coleridge, "I wrote 'The Ancient Mariner' and was preparing among other poems, 'The Dark Ladie,' and the 'Christabel,' in which I should have more nearly realized my ideal, than I had done in my first attempt. But Mr. Wordsworth's industry had proved so much more successful, and the number of his poems so much greater, that my compositions, instead of forming a balance, appeared rather an interpolation of heterogeneous matter. Mr. Wordsworth added two or three poems written in his own character, in the impassioned, lofty, and sustained diction, which is characteristic of his genius. In this form the 'Lyrical Ballads' were published; and were presented by him, as an *experiment*, whether subjects, which from their nature rejected the usual ornaments and extra-colloquial style of poems in general, might not be so managed in the language of ordinary life as to produce the pleasureable interest, which it is the peculiar business of poetry to impart." [10]

Nevertheless, despite the greater number of poems attempting the exposition of Wordsworth's allotted function, namely, "to give the charm of novelty to things of every day, and to excite a feeling analogous to the supernatural, by awakening the mind's attention from the lethargy of custom, and directing it to the loveliness and the wonders of the world before us" [11]—the solitary *Ancient Mariner* achieved its purpose with an ease, a mastery, a certainty, and a mystery altogether beyond the capabilities of its companions in the *Lyrical Ballads*.

To say this is rather to emphasize Coleridge's unique achievement than to depreciate the part which Wordsworth played in this demonstration of the newly discovered "synthetic and magical power, to which we have exclusively appropriated the name of imagination." [12] It is only by comparison with a poem close to perfection that the best of Wordsworth's contributions suffer. Moreover, the elder man had what would be generally admitted the more difficult task.

Metrically, Coleridge and Wordsworth created a minor revolution in established practice. They substituted 'equivalent feet' for the even, syllabic metre of eighteenth-century poetry. By varying freely the number of syllables and the accent they banished the monotony of the regular beat of the line—so giving to the sound of their verses the elasticity, the freedom, the impression of spontaneity, the closeness to life, that informed their imagery and meaning.[13]

In *Tintern Abbey*, that exquisite reflective and pantheistic lyric, Wordsworth sounded depths of natural beauty and a calm and philosophic faith in nature as the "hiding-places of man's power," [14] that was new to English poetry. This poem alone, with *The Ancient Mariner*, might well have gained for the *Lyrical Ballads* their reputation for heralding a new era in English poetry.

Indeed, Wordsworth's *Tintern Abbey* and the kindred poems—the "poems written in his own character" [15]—expressed the true direction his genius was to take far more surely than that of the ballads wherein an attempt is made to carry out the principles agreed with Coleridge. Of the latter group of poems, a few, like *We are Seven*, *The Thorn*, *Goody Blake*, and *Simon Lee*, despite their weaknesses, display an advance on what had gone before, an actuality, a rough sincerity, a power of narrative, a certain psychological insight, a sufficient novelty of treatment, to justify their places as worthy agents in the rebirth of the romantic and naturalistic impulse in English poetry that the *Lyrical Ballads* set in firm and resistless motion.

But no hint that they recognized the revolutionary character of the volume escaped the contemporary reviewers. They not only failed to notice that new ground was being broken; for the most part they overlooked the finest poems in the *Lyrical Ballads*. Southey alone had good words to say of *Tintern Abbey* and *Lines on a Yew Tree*. "The experiment, we think, has failed" he wrote of the experimental poems in general, "not because the language of conversation is little adapted to 'the purposes of poetic pleasure,' but because it has been tried upon uninteresting subjects." [16] *The Forsaken Indian Woman* was passed by. *The Ancient Mariner* was unanimously condemned. One reviewer alone praised *The Nightingale*.[17] Only *The Idiot Boy*, *The Thorn*, *The Mad Mother* (later called simply by its first line, *Her Eyes are Wild*), and *Goody Blake* were with some unanimity (though not including Southey) held to contain real merit. For the rest, the book might scarcely have been published. Not one of the early reviews of the volume showed either sympathy with or understanding of the experiment.

The authors, who knew nothing of the reception of their poems, went their way in Germany unconcerned.

The declared aim of the visit to Germany was that the two poets, after learning the language, should "furnish ourselves with a tolerable stock of information in natural science."[18] But these are the words of Wordsworth. And it is Dorothy who adds a further reason: "that translation is the most profitable of all works."[19]

That these sentiments were shared by Coleridge is certain: he had been talking not long before of translating *Oberon*: and he had long been convinced of the desirability, to rate it no higher, of 'warming' his mind "with universal science."[20] But these desiderata did not account for the whole, they did not form even the greater part of the enthusiasm that induced him to carry the plan successfully against the lukewarmness, in the first instance, if it were nothing more, of Poole, Sarah, and Estlin.

To discover his main motive in forwarding the German scheme it is necessary to recall two pronouncements by him; one, in a letter to Poole of May 6, 1796; the other in a letter to Cottle in May of the following year. In the first, he had mooted the idea of a trip to Germany financed by a bookseller, for whom in return he would translate "all the works of Schiller." "If I could realize this scheme," he wrote, "I should there study chemistry and anatomy, and bring over with me all the works of Semler and Michaelis, the German theologians, and of Kant, the great German metaphysician."[21]

In the second letter he had listed the requirements of a poet's education in order to fit himself for the production of an epic poem. Ten years of preparation would be necessary. "I would be a tolerable Mathematician. I would thoroughly understand Mechanics; Hydrostatics; Optics and Astronomy; Botany; Metallurgy; Fossilism; Chemistry; Geology; Anatomy; Medicine; then the mind of man; then the minds of men, in all Travels, Voyages, and Histories."[22]

Here can be seen both the magnitude of the basic idea behind Coleridge's visit to Germany and the reasoning which prompted it; an idea which circumstance rather than change of mind had hitherto frustrated.

[292]

Now, it is true, he possessed the promise of company not dreamed of earlier, and lacking which perhaps he might never have bestirred himself or have discovered the opportunity to go. Yet still he remained essentially alone in what he sought. Thus, though he and Wordsworth set out together, the divergence in the scale and direction of their aims was too considerable to be turned aside by the pull of affection. The break-up of the party may have been due ostensibly to the realization by Coleridge and Wordsworth that the temptation to talk to each other in their native tongue would greatly hinder their conquest of German. The Wordsworths' need for strict economy certainly influenced their decision. But the conclusion remains that separation sooner or later, for a more fundamental reason, was inevitable.

Wordsworth, indeed, made no particular professions of an aim in travelling to Germany beyond his reference to the study of social science in connexion with his projected work on Man, Nature, and Society and to the advantages of mastering another language. He had been long enough in the company of Coleridge to imbibe some, at least, of his friend's views on the necessary studies of a prospective epic poet. Possibly his convictions as to the need of this knowledge were not held with sufficient strength to survive the absence of Coleridge. Possibly his nature was such that, once absorbed finally by affection for his own country, he was destined to remain an onlooker, a stranger, in all others—an observer always, an inmate never. In the event, whatever his intentions, Wordsworth's German tour resolved itself into little more than an intelligent but essentially 'foreign' ramble about the countryside—an amble punctuated or dictated by efforts to find accommodation less expensive than that which he and Dorothy were occupying; an amble growing increasingly tedious the longer he and his sister were separated from Coleridge and from England; and during which even the least of his objectives—the learning of the language—was not achieved. His German tour is memorable only for the poetry he wrote during the course of it.

Coleridge, on the other hand, though his love and his longing for his own land was little, if any, less than that of Wordsworth, set himself to penetrate and make his own the thought of the nation amidst which he found himself; a process which he began, characteristically and correctly, by making himself, as far as was possible, and for the time being, one of that nation. It is significant that, once this opportunity was within his grasp, he seized it, threw off sloth, cast for a time the ties that bound him to his friends, and set himself without delay to achieve his object. A new resolution appeared to animate him. For the next few months he could have compared (had such a thought ever entered his head) the respective activities of Wordsworth and himself to his own advantage; he could have contemplated (had he wished) the rare spectacle of a Coleridge more industrious than the friend he venerated—a veneration which owed not a little of its strength to Wordsworth's diligence.

Wordsworth, it is true, had no desire to emulate Coleridge. In fact, he was later to give as his opinion, what he probably thought and perhaps said at the time, that his friend's desertion of the muse for philosophy was ill-advised. Eventually, he was to see in Coleridge's German trip the seeds of the decay of Coleridge the poet; but he certainly neither foresaw nor suspected such a disaster.[23] His attitude at the time could have been no more than mild disapproval—coupled possibly with surprise—at Coleridge's earnest determination to pursue a plan rather than scrape the surface of the country with himself and Dorothy—a disapproval coupled with, and of course emphasized by, his own inability to comprehend either the force of intellect or the urge of faith that together pushed his friend forward into abstruse studies.

In the beginning, two conflicting forces struggled for possession of Coleridge's mind. One, headed by Voltaire, would thrust God out of court by the exercise of the reason. The other, represented by Plato and the Neo-platonists, taught him, as one of their central doctrines, to regard beauty as the revelation of spirit through matter.

Coleridge, after an initial falling away, quickly regained a belief in Deity—a belief which, an integral part of his nature, satisfying in one form or another a need of his inmost being, he could not for long ignore.

But though he might resume, instinctively, the questionings of faith, his intelligence once exercised would not permit him to discard the reason with a like facility. It remained to dog him with a constant demand for proof of the validity of every emotion. This unceasing surveillance by the reason was responsible for Coleridge's passion to understand what he felt.

Thus he was driven, early, to seek a synthesis of reason and emotion, of philosophy and religion, in an endeavour to quell the strife within him.

His pilgrimage in search of this ideal led through strange territory. Southey wrote in 1808 of Coleridge's philosophical movements: "Hartley was ousted by Berkeley, Berkeley by Spinoza, and Spinoza by Plato; when last I saw him [four years before] Jacob Behmen had some chance of coming in. The truth is that he plays with systems, and any nonsense will serve him for a text from which he can deduce something new and surprising." [24] Southey's order, so far as the first three names were concerned, was probably correct. He may have been correct in all if a certain domination of mind, and not priority of acquaintance, is considered. Nevertheless, correct or not, such a neat and tidy, clear-cut description of Coleridge's philosophical and metaphysical loyalties, however necessary, can be misleading, as Southey's final remark demonstrates excellently. For, although the saying emphasizes the limitations of the man who made it rather than him of whom it is made, the danger of trying to compress years of thought into a simple formula remains very real. The suggestion of certain streams of thought being turned off and on like a series of taps—a suggestion palpably false of any thoughtful being and particularly of one such as Coleridge, who relinquished nothing that his mind had once made his own—can be harmful, can leave an impression the reverse of true in the mind.

Coleridge did not so much discard a thought as transform it, fit it into place in the jig-saw of his mind. How this process would work he demonstrated in his great poems, by the subconscious transformation of facts assimilated in the course of many years of reading—a process equally true, if less unconsciously performed, of his philosophical ruminations, though the result in this instance was to have neither the complete triumph nor the magic of his poetry.

Even at the height of his devotion to Hartley's theories, for example, only a part of Coleridge's mind accepted what he was so fervently praising. There were in his mind, as in most, reservations—but reservations more pronounced in him than in most, as his mind was the more richly stored and as he was the more beset by religious questionings and by hopes of discovering the perfect system that would marry religion and art, philosophy and religion, reason and understanding, without protest from mind, heart, or sense, and in a way that he could not only believe but demonstrate to others.

Coleridge was, in truth, always rather more than the doctrine he adopted. Thus, even at his most Hartleian, his most Berkeleian, he overlaps his own enthusiasm. The creed of the moment cannot contain his whole mind.

His enthusiasms are thus somewhat misleading. As usual, Coleridge contributes generously to his own confusion in other minds. His conversation, his letters, his attempts to procure converts, give the impression of one absorbed, overcome, quite led away by the passion for the doctrine that happens to be uppermost in his mind at the time.

But in fact he was, even when the most ardent and persuasive advocate of a particular system, busy mating, comparing, selecting his freshly gathered and his more matured conceptions; a function for the most part as instinctive as his acquisition and retention of knowledge.

Coleridge had a positive genius for creating the wrong impression. He cringed when he would be firm, flattered when he would be truly helpful, fawned when his gratitude was genuine: and now he left an impression of unbalanced enthusiasms, quickly discarded—aided inevitably by such after-attempts at summaries of his philosophical progress as have been instanced, but which, fortunately, the greatness of his comprehension, its infinite capacity, could not bear out—that certainly does not do justice to the 'universality' of his mind.

Coleridge's belief in Hartley's doctrines lasted a number of years. In 1794 he first fell under Hartley's influence. In 1796, he named his first child after the philosopher. In 1798, when he left for Germany, Hartley still held a place in his mind and estimation.

But not only did Hartley's theories fail at any time to dominate Coleridge's whole mind; they occupied different parts of it at different periods. In the beginning, the necessitarian Hartley was in the ascendant. For a time, Coleridge even outstripped his master. "I am a complete necessitarian," he announced to Southey towards the end of 1794, "and understand the subject as well almost as Hartley himself, and believe the corporeality of *thought*, namely, that it is motion." [25] He invited his friend to join him in his demonstration of the reconciliation of irreconcilables: "I would ardently that you were a necessitarian, and (believing in an all-loving Omnipotence) an optimist." [26]

This extreme position, however, neither Coleridge's common sense nor his religious instinct would suffer him to maintain. He drifted steadily from contemplation of Hartley's doctrine of association to the more comforting exposition of natural and revealed religion by the same versatile philosopher. But he by no means abandoned or wholly repudiated the materialistic Hartley. By a process of mental gymnastics—or possibly self-hypnotism would be a better description of the workings of his mind at this time—aided in no small degree by the example of his master, Coleridge not only did not challenge the incompatibility of Hartley's doctrines, but managed for a remarkably long time to palm off upon his reason shoddy material which his heart could not accept, but which his mind was unable to reject entirely. Until he could refute the necessitarian Hartley as clearly and unmistakably with his head as he did with his heart, he was not able completely to release himself from the implications of the full philosophy. If his faith was unable to rest content with the teachings of "the Great and Excellent Dr Hartley," [27] his reason was equally unable to let them go.

Thus, if the poems (often the surest and most reliable vehicles of Coleridge's philosophy) are examined, in *Religious Musings*, published in 1796 but commenced in the Christmas of 1794, he was able in one breath to hail Hartley as

> he of mortal kind
> Wisest, he first who marked the ideal tribes
> Up the fine fibres through the sentient brain.[28]

And in another breath, in *The Destiny of Nations*—the relevant part of which was written by Coleridge in 1795 for use in Southey's *Joan of Arc*—whilst railing, for the moment impotently, against the demands and limitations of the intellect, he condemned Hartley implicitly, with the materialists, as one of those who

> Chain down the wingéd thought, scoffing ascent,
> Proud in their meanness: and themselves they cheat
> With noisy emptiness of learnéd phrase,
> Their subtle fluids, impacts, essences.[29]

This anomalous state of affairs continued for some years. Coleridge did not openly reject the doctrine of association until much later; at best he felt it to be mistaken, but could not prove it. In a note to his contribution to *Joan of Arc*, later incorporated in *The Destiny of Nations*, Coleridge agrees in general that Sir Isaac Newton's philosophy expressed in his *Optics*—with which he associates Hartley to some degree—leads to atheism.[30] Meanwhile, he solved the problem by turning an eye of increasing dimness to that side of Hartley's teachings. Thus, in 1796, his first son was named after "that great master of *Christian* Philosophy." [31] And later, in his letter to Estlin of January 1798, announcing his decision to accept the Wedgwood annuity, Coleridge concentrated upon the less controversial aspect of Hartley: "Did Dr HARTLEY employ himself for the promotion of the best interests of mankind?" he asks.[32] And answers his own question, "Most certainly. If instead of being a physician he had been an hired Teacher, that he would not have taught Christianity *better*, I can certainly say. . . ." [33]

But long before this, Coleridge had called in outside aid.

First in the field was Berkeley. In 1796 Coleridge tells Cottle: "Bishop Taylor, old Baxter, David Hartley, and the Bishop of Cloyne are my men." [34] The *Religious Musings* include the Berkeleian statement of faith:

> Life is a vision shadowy of Truth;
> And vice, and anguish, and the wormy grave,
> Shapes of a dream! The veiling clouds retire,
> And lo! The Throne of the redeeming God
> Forth flashing unimaginable day
> Wraps in one blaze earth, heaven, and deepest hell.[35]

Thelwall is informed in December of that year: "Now that the thinking part of man, that is, the soul, existed previously to its appearance in its present body may be very wild philosophy, but it is very intelligible poetry; inasmuch as 'soul' is an orthodox word in all our poets, they meaning by 'soul' a being inhabiting our body, and playing upon it, like a musician enclosed in an

[298]

organ whose keys were placed inwards. Now this opinion I do not hold; not that I am a materialist, but because I am a Berkeleyan." [36] Coleridge lists in a notebook at this time twenty-six works which he intends to complete. One of these was to be: "Hymns to the Sun, the Moon, and the Elements—six hymns. In one of them to introduce a dissection of Atheism, particularly the Godwinian System of Pride. Proud of what? An outcast of blind Nature ruled by a fatal Necessity—Slave of an Ideot Nature. In the last Hymn a sublime enumeration of all the charms or tremendities of Nature—then a bold avowal of Berkeley's system!!!!" [37]

In January 1797, Lamb, then following Coleridge's philosophical pilgrimage with an ardent interest and a certain imitativeness, wrote: "Are you yet a Berkeleyan? Make me one. I rejoice in being, speculatively, a necessarian. Would to God, I were habitually a practical one. Confirm me in the faith of that great and glorious doctrine, and keep me steady in the contemplation of it." [38]

In July of the same year, a note to *This Lime-Tree Bower my Prison* transcribed in a letter to Southey says: "You remember I am a *Berkeleian*." [39] In January 1798, when with Hazlitt, Coleridge deprecated Dr Johnson's cavalier dismissal of Berkeley's theory of the impossibility of anything existing independently of perception.[40] And in May 1798, the final honour was bestowed upon the philosopher Bishop — Coleridge's second son was given his name.

Berkeley was able first to support the unsteady edifice of Hartley's doctrines in Coleridge's mind and finally to supplant them, because, whereas Hartley's doctrines remained not only incompatible but static, Berkeley's thought progressed—and progressed in line with Coleridge's own mind.

That Berkeley and Hartley could be mentioned in one breath by Coleridge in 1796 is explicable in one way only: that Coleridge had not at that time made himself familiar with or had not mastered the later Berkeley. He was thinking, when he spoke to Cottle, of the Berkeley who called for a surrender of the mind to the disconnected impressions of the senses—the Berkeley who maintained that "what we call matter has no actual existence, and that the impressions which we believe ourselves to receive from it are not, in fact, derived from anything external to ourselves, but are produced within us by a certain disposition of the mind, the immediate operation of God" [41]—the Berkeley of the *New Theory of Vision*, promulgating the very doctrine which had incurred the wrath of Dr Johnson.

But although the greater part of Berkeley's work was devoted to strengthening and clarifying the new empiricism of Locke, whose direct successor he was, this was not the whole, nor perhaps the most significant part of it. In two directions he stepped tentatively out of his chosen course: first, in his doctrine of notions, partly developed only, in his *Principles of Human Knowledge*, which led directly towards the Kantean analysis of the elements of experience, and, if carried forward sufficiently, must have rendered untenable the very empiricism he spent the greater part of his life explaining and defending; and secondly, in the echoes of Plato to be found in his last considerable work, *Siris*.

These later doctrines of Berkeley began to take charge of Coleridge's enthusiasm; and by means of them Berkeley had, by May 1798, advanced sufficiently in the poet's estimation to receive the supreme compliment of a son's name.

Thus the first part of Southey's 'placing' of Coleridge's philosophies can be enlarged simply, subject to the qualifications already made with regard to such simplifications, as: 1794, Hartley—Necessitarian and Believer; then a gradual diminution of the influence of the materialist element in Hartley's doctrines until in 1796, Hartley, Believer and Berkeley, Empiricist; the influence of the Platonic school steadily reasserting itself until, in 1798, Berkeley—Platonist and Kantean.

But Berkeley had no sooner attained supremacy in Coleridge's mind than he began to lose it. The beginnings of this new change are, of course, to be traced long before the change actually took place. They had existed in Coleridge's mind since orderly thought began: and though thrust down temporarily by the Cambridge passion for Frend and the reason, the balance between intellect and heart soon began to right itself. Coleridge became sickened by the apparent consequences of a complete or even major reliance upon the reason, though unable wholly to refute what an acknowledgment of the reason appeared to imply.

In what, though closer now, was still the other side of his mind,

or, as Coleridge would have said, in his heart, he was continuing
and enlarging the "early study of Plato and Plotinus, with the
commentaries and the THEOLOGIA PLATONICA of the illustrious
Florentine; of Proclus, and the Gemistius Pletho," [42] which was
to lead him through Bruno, Descartes, Boehme again, and in the
direction of the mysticism of Jacobi.

By the end of 1796, Coleridge was writing Benjamin Flower:
"I . . . found no comfort, till it pleased the Unimaginable High
and Lofty One to make my Heart more tender in regard of
religious feelings. My philosophical refinements, and metaphysical Theories lay by me in the hour of anguish, as toys by the
bedside of a child deadly sick." [43] When he settled at Stowey, it
was with the intention of devoting his "thoughts and studies to
the foundations of religion and morals" [44]—a decision brought
about, partly by a wish to convert Thelwall, partly to expose the
teachings of Godwin, but chiefly by the necessity which Coleridge felt in himself, not only of replacing a certain lack of confidence in the necessitarian Hartley, but of resolving the conflict,
never long stilled, between the reason and the emotions which
this re-emergence of the religious impulse in him had once more
aroused.

To this time must be attributed his reversion to the pages of
George Fox, Boehme, and William Law, the mystics who "contributed to keep alive the *heart* in the *head*; gave me an indistinct,
yet stirring and working presentiment, that all the products of
the mere *reflective* faculty partook of DEATH." [45]

An echo of Boehme is seen already, just before the move to
Stowey, in Coleridge's letter to Thelwall of December 1796, in
which, after referring to Plato's interpretation of life as harmony
—"but I love Plato, his dear, *gorgeous* nonsense" [46]—he says:
"On the whole, I have rather made up my mind that I am a mere
apparition, a naked spirit, and that life is, I myself I." [47]

In the *Religious Musings*, completed soon after his arrival at
Stowey, lip-service is still paid to the principle of necessity; but
the major emphasis is placed upon the desirability of unity—that
long-sought unity which it was becoming apparent, however reluctant Coleridge might be finally to admit the fact, Hartley was
unable to effect.

Much of *Religious Musings* was a manifestation of the influence of Plotinus upon the mind of its author. When, for instance, Coleridge writes :

> Lovely was the death
> Of Him whose life was Love! Holy with power
> He on the thought-benighted Sceptic beamed
> Manifest Godhead. . . .
> And first by Fear uncharmed the drowséd Soul.
> Till of its nobler nature it 'gan feel
> Dim recollections; and thence soared to Hope,
> Strong to believe whate'er of mystic good
> The Eternal dooms for His immortal sons.
> From Hope and firmer Faith to perfect Love
> Attracted and absorbed: and centered there
> God only to behold, and know, and feel,
> Till by exclusive consciousness of God
> All self-annihilated it shall make
> God its Identity: God all in all!
> We and our Father one! [48]

his development of the idea becomes unmistakably Plotinian.

At much the same time Coleridge first met Wordsworth. From this unexpected source and from a new angle he received confirmation of a truth the revelation of which he had just begun to believe waited upon faith and a definite exercise of the will. So, he felt, by piercing the bounds of the senses and the reason, he might discover a transcendent reality, a truth which was not realizable in experience, which possibly defied expression, but which, if grasped, might bring him what he sought. He became aware that there was a vital distinction between the truths of abstract science, attained by the reason alone, and the evidence of the doctrines of religion which could not be separated entirely from the exercise of the individual will.

And then came the meeting with Wordsworth. Coleridge, as has been seen, by his realization of the existence and power of the imagination, beginning as an emotion after hearing Wordsworth's reading of *Guilt and Sorrow* in 1796 and ending as a contribution of magnitude to literary criticism, together with Wordsworth quickly applied this new "excellence" to the composition of poetry of which the *Lyrical Ballads* was the direct and immediate result.

But this was only the first and most obvious application of

the "esemplastic power" [49] as Coleridge was to call this ability to bring diversity into unity. So far, Coleridge and Wordsworth moved hand in hand, in sympathy if not in understanding: for it is by no means certain—his few explanatory words do nothing to prove it[50]—that Wordsworth was at this time able to explain critically the great poetic merit of which he was conscious.

It was not long before Coleridge by himself was investigating "the seminal principle" [51] of the creative imagination. As he did so, he came to realize that there was a vital connexion between the function of this imagination and what he had gathered so many years before from Plato and the Neo-Platonists; between the function of this imagination and his tentative expressions of the belief that

> all that meets the bodily sense I deem
> Symbolical, one mighty alphabet
> For infant minds.[52]

This symbolic interpretation of the world round him, the vision of the infinite through the finite, began to assume in his mind its true value and authority. It was, he discovered, by a creative act of the imagination as compared with that of the will in the moral sense that he found religious meanings in the forms of nature; and with eyes open to the manner in which he was able to do so.

Hence his thankfulness, when writing to Poole of his childhood, that by reason of "my early reading of fairy tales and genii, etc., etc., my mind had been habituated *to the Vast*, and I never regarded *my senses* in any way as the criteria of my belief," [53] since it was only thus that he came instinctively to regulate his creeds by his conceptions, not by his sight.

Hence, too, his realization that the majority of people have not this sense : "I know no other way of giving the mind a love of the Great and the Whole. Those who have been led to the same truths step by step, through the constant testimony of their senses, seem to me to want a sense which I possess. They contemplate nothing but *parts*, and all *parts* are necessarily little. And the universe to them is but a mass of *little things*." [54] That it was in fact a gift upon which not great poetry alone, but constructive thought, and perhaps even a satisfactory theology, necessarily depend; nothing less, perhaps, than a means of revealing the eternal verities.

Hence the growing appeal of Spinoza, whose teachings assumed an imaginative interpretation of nature. But Spinoza, great though his influence upon Coleridge was becoming, greater still though it was to become, could offer him unity only at the expense of personality—as Coleridge saw it, at a total sacrifice of his own soul-identity. "For a very long time, indeed," he says, "I could not reconcile personality with infinity; and my head was with Spinoza, though my whole heart remained with Paul and John." [55] To such a man as Coleridge, philosophy could never be accepted as a satisfactory substitute for religion. "We may feel *from* and about a thing, an event, a quality, we can feel *toward* a Person only." [56] That was how he saw it. "The personal in me is the ground and condition of Religion, and the Personal alone is the Object." [57]

The ideal doctrine was yet to be found. But the position had improved. Coleridge was no longer searching vaguely for an explicable union of philosophy, religion, and art, of faith and reason. He had come across a clue that might lead him to an end of the problem. For that sovereign faculty, the shaping power of the imagination, which had started into life as a poetic power— might not the use of it be extended, Coleridge began to ask himself, to perform another and a greater function—none other than that of overleaping the hiatus that, in his mind, still yawned between art and religion, between head and heart.[58]

Moreover, by his realization of the powers of the creative imagination, Coleridge was at once able to make a primary condition, a test, of any system of thought before embracing it; that it should be capable of containing this essential faculty. He held in his mind a measuring rod by which the worth of claimants to his allegiance could in future be meted.

He might perhaps fob off Hartley with the fancy, assuming it to be no more than a non-creative, plastic, sense-and-impression-recording machine in the mind. But the imagination, seen as he now saw it, as an active creative force, the law of association could neither explain nor allow. Nor, indeed, was such a doctrine capable of accommodating the conception, in itself a product of the creative imagination, of the universe as a unity. When, as was inevitable, Coleridge acquired greater familiarity with the function of this vital force, not only could he find no warrant for its existence in Hartley's teachings—belief in these teachings positively forbade belief in the existence of such a power.

Berkeley was in little better case. His theocentric metaphysic offered neither comfort nor certainty to the Coleridge faced with his important discovery. It could not satisfy a mind which believed in the existence of a reality behind every experience to be found by a creative and imaginative effort of will; a mind which could regard every experience with the detachment born of its own peculiar individuality, yet illumined by the wisdom of all experience.

Even Spinoza seemed a broken reed. That his system led to pantheism, Coleridge was convinced : " . . . the inevitable result of all *consequent* Reasoning," he wrote, "in which the speculative intellect refuses to acknowledge a higher or deeper ground than it can itself supply, is—and from Zeno the Eleatic to Spinoza ever has been—Pantheism, under one or other of its modes: the least repulsive of which differs from the rest, *not* by its consequences which are the same in all and in all alike amount to practical Atheism; but only as it may express the striving of the reasoner to hide these consequences from his own consciousness. All speculative Disquisition must begin with Postulates, that derive their legitimacy, substance, and Sanction from the Conscience; and from whichever of the two points the Reason may start, from the things that are seen to the One Invisible, or from the idea of the absolute One to the things that are seen, it will find a chasm, which the *Moral* Being only, which the Spirit and Religion of Man alone can fill up or over-bridge." [59]

So Coleridge was to express what at this time he no more than felt; but the feeling was sufficient to tell him that Spinoza's teachings could not contain this rich and vital significance which cried imperiously for a philosophy which would encompass it.

Coleridge did not, of course, perceive immediately the full significance of this incongruity of thought between his old loyalties and these new visions of a vital poetic and philosophic faculty; but he suspected it where it was not plain, and the German scheme offered him an opportunity, long desired, of trying to effect a reconciliation between reason and imagination, or, as the problem was to become known to him, between reason and understanding.

Nor had Coleridge been content to remain idle until such an opportunity came his way. That he was in revolt against the philosophy of the Age of Reason—whose chief advocates denied the possibility of the existence of God, derided beauty except as a form of utility, admitted no control over the passions, no place for the heart in the government of man or the formation of the laws by which he was to live—that Coleridge could not for a moment subscribe to such a doctrine might be assumed with confidence, bearing in mind his nature, even had he made no statement on the subject. But of course he had done so: "the arguments . . ." (of Dr Darwin), he writes in 1796, "against the existence of a God and the evidences of revealed religion were such as had startled me at fifteen, but had become the objects of my smile at twenty." [60]

He felt already, even if he did not clearly perceive, the bondage into which the minds of men had been led and the consequent barrenness of their philosophy. Later he wrote of it: "Whoever is acquainted with the history of philosophy, during the last two or three centuries, cannot but admit, that there appears to have existed a sort of secret and tacit compact among the learned, not to pass beyond a certain limit in speculative science. The privilege of free thought, so highly extolled, has at no time been held valid in actual practice, except within this limit; and not a single stride beyond it has ever been ventured without bringing obloquy on the transgressor." [61]

But this did not mean that Coleridge would have rejected the use of the reason even had he been able to do so. What he repudiated instinctively was the domination of the reason. He felt the use of the reason alone to be as inadequate to meet the requirements of a new and wholly satisfying philosophy as would the unsupported statement of faith. Both were necessary. To him it seemed as foolish, as unsatisfactory, to use the one or the other, reason or faith, exclusively, as that man would be who persisted in going through life using one arm only, although in full possession of both. The co-operation of the reason in defining and defending such a philosophy as he dreamed of, he not only recognized but welcomed. He was aware, long before he left for

Germany, of the desirability—indeed, the necessity—of a philosophy that would combat the present worship of the reason partly at least on its own ground, by a more intelligent use of the reason. Thus he had already in some sort determined, however vaguely, to bend the weight of his thought, the whole direction of his mind, towards the evolution of a synthesis of reason and understanding which it seemed could alone prove adequate to overcome the existing gap between, on the one hand, the prevalent abuse of the intellect, and on the other, an uncritical reliance upon the individual act of faith.

All this was stirring in Coleridge's head and heart. But it was felt rather than understood. It was by no means clear cut. It was far from full definition. It was nebulous. It was out of focus. But the conception of a synthesis existed; the need for a synthesis moved steadily forward in his mind. Indeed, it might be said that in embryo it had always been there.

At the end of a MS. copy of *The Destiny of Nations* (*The Vision of the Maid of Arc*) Coleridge has written: "N.B.—Within twelve months after the writing of this Poem, my bold Optimism, and Necessitarianism, together with the Infra, seu plusquam-Socinianism, down to which, step by step, I had *un*believed, gave way to the day-break of a more genial and less shallow system. But I contemplate with pleasure these Phases of my Transition." [62]

This note would date his emancipation from late in 1797. But the direction to which he must look for assistance in formulating a philosophy to replace what he might lose by the abandonment of the materialist position had been in and out of his mind since the previous year at least. The answer to the problem of formulating a comprehensive philosophy was half made as early as 1796. In a MS. note to his letter to Thelwell on December 17 of that year he says: "Mendelssohn . . . has written some of the most acute books possible in favour of natural immortality, and Germany deems him her profoundest metaphysician, with the exception of the most unintelligible Immanuel Kant" [63]—a label which Kant would probably have resented less than the description of himself as a metaphysician.

But, unintelligible or not, Kant was one of Coleridge's chief objectives. This "great German metaphysician" it is whose work Coleridge tells Poole he must know if he is to perfect his proposed "school for eight young men" in "the new Kantean system." [64]

Coleridge spent some spare time when in London the following year waiting for news of *Osorio*, by continuing the study of German he had begun at Bristol in 1796. He was, he claimed—too optimistic to be mindful of the labour involved—about to translate Wieland's *Oberon*. This was one of the few German works he had read. Leibnitz; the *Luise* of Voss; some dramas of Schiller; and the *Emilia Galotti* of Lessing, whom Coleridge, happily unable to foresee the future, described to Benjamin Flower in April 1796 as "the most formidable Infidel," [65]—these, with the *Oberon*, were the only German works of moment with which he was acquainted before he went to Germany.

Coleridge stated, years later, that: "I can not only honestly assert, but I can satisfactorily prove by reference to writings (Letters, Marginal Notes, and those in books that have never been in my possession since I first left England for Hamburgh, etc.) that all the elements, the *differentials*, as the algebraists say, of my present opinions existed for me before I had even seen a book of German Metaphysics later than Wolf and Leibnitz, or could have read it, if I had." [66]

In confirmation of this claim, it is certain that he had, to a considerable even if vague extent, anticipated what he sought to find in Kant; and in one from whom he did not anticipate the help he later experienced—Schelling. At least five instances can be adduced to show that his mind was already moving in many ways parallel to those of the German philosophers he was soon to discover.

There was his conviction that Richard Baxter, whose life he had read, in some sense anticipated Kant: " . . . from the following sentence in his life (that invaluable Work published from Baxter's own Manuscript by Matthew Silvester) I cannot doubt, but that the merit of substituting Trichotomy for the then, and alas! the still, prevailing method of Dichotomy, which forms the prominent excellence in Kant's Critique of the pure reason, belongs to R. Baxter, a century before the publication of Kant's Work. Nay, it appears that the claim of our own Countryman rests on a stronger as well as elder plea. For Baxter grounds the necessity of Trichotomy, as the Principle of Real Logic, on an absolute

Idea presupposed in all intelligental Acts: whereas Kant adopts it merely as a fact of Reflection, tho' doubtless as a singularly curious Fact in which he suspects some yet deeper Truth latent and hereafter to be discovered. 'Having long been purposing to draw up a Method of Theology I now began it. I never yet saw a Scheme, or Method either of Physics or of Theology that gave any satisfaction to my Reason. Tho' many have attempted to exercise more accurateness in distribution than all others that went before them, yet I could never see any whose Confusion or great Defects I could not easily discover; but not so easily amend. *I had been twenty-six years convinced that Dichotomyzing will not do it*; but that the Divine Trinity in Unity hath exprest itself in the whole frame of Nature and Morality.' " [67]

Coleridge himself anticipates the critical attitude he was to find in Kant; first in his conviction that a "moral act" was necessary to pierce the limitations of the intellect and attain the ultimate truth: "I became convinced, that religion, as both the cornerstone and the key-stone of morality, must have a *moral* origin; so far at least, that the evidence of its doctrines could not, like the truths of abstract science, be wholly independent of the will. It were therefore to be expected, that its *fundamental* truth would be such as MIGHT be denied; though only by the fool, and even by the fool from the madness of the *heart* alone! The question then concerning our faith in the existence of a God, not only as the *ground* of the universe by his essence, but as its maker and judge by his wisdom and holy will, appeared to stand thus. The sciential *reason*, whose objects are purely theoretical, remains neutral, as long as its name and semblance are not usurped by the opponents of the doctrine. But it *then* becomes an effective ally by exposing the false show of demonstration, or by evincing the equal demonstrability of the contrary from premises equally logical. The *understanding* mean time suggests, the analogy of *experience* facilitates, the belief. Nature excites and recalls it, as by a perpetual revelation. Our feelings almost necessitate it; and the law of conscience peremptorily commands it. The arguments, that at all apply to it, are in its favor; and there is nothing against it, but its own sublimity. It could not be intellectually more evident without becoming morally less effective; without counteracting its own end by sacrificing the *life* of faith to the cold mechanism of a worthless because compulsory assent. The belief of a God and a future state, (if a passive acquiescence may be flattered with the name of *belief*), does not indeed always beget a good heart; but a good heart so naturally begets the belief, that the very few exceptions must be regarded as strange anomalies from strange and unfortunate circumstances. From these premises I proceeded to draw the following conclusions. First, that having once fully admitted the existence of an infinite yet self-conscious Creator, we are not allowed to ground the irrationality of any other article of faith on arguments which would equally prove that to be irrational, which we had allowed to be *real*. Secondly, that whatever is deducible from the admission of a *self-comprehending* and *creative* spirit may be legitimately used in proof of the *possibility* of any further mystery concerning the divine nature. '*Possibilitatem* mysteriorum (Trinitatis, etc.) contra insultus Infidelium et Hæreticorum a contradictionibus vindico; haud quidem *veritatem*, quae revelatione solâ stabiliri possit'; says LEIBNITZ, in a letter to his Duke. He then adds the following just and important remark. 'In vain will tradition or texts of scripture be adduced in support of a doctrine, donec clava impossibilitatis et contradictionis e manibus horum Herculum extorta fuerit. For the heretic will still reply, that texts, the literal sense of which is not so much *above* as directly *against* all reason, must be understood *figuratively*, as Herod is a fox, etc.'

"These principles I held, *philosophically*, while in respect of revealed religion I remained a zealous Unitarian. I considered the *idea* of the Trinity a fair scholastic inference from the being of God, as a creative intelligence; and that it was therefore entitled to the rank of an *esoteric* doctrine of natural religion. But seeing in the same no practical or moral bearing, I confined it to the schools of philosophy. The admission of the Logos, as *hypostasized* (i.e. neither a mere attribute, or a personification) in no respect removed my doubts concerning the incarnation and the redemption by the cross; which I could neither reconcile *in reason* with the impassiveness of the Divine Being, nor in my moral feelings with the sacred distinction between things and persons, the vicarious payment of a debt and the vicarious expiation of guilt." [68]

Secondly, in his anticipation of Kant's mental homeopathy

by an ingenious use of the reason to set a limit to its own capabilities of unveiling the final truths: "there had dawned upon me," he writes, "even before I had met with the Critique of the Pure Reason, a certain guiding light. If the mere intellect could make no certain discovery of a holy and intelligent first cause, it might yet supply a demonstration, that no legitimate argument could be drawn from the intellect *against* its truth. And what is this more than St. Paul's assertion, that by wisdom, (more properly translated by the powers of reasoning) no man ever arrived at the knowledge of God?" [69]

There was his statement, later, that " . . . all Schelling had said he [Coleridge] had thought out for himself, or found in Jacob Boehme" [70]—a bold avowal indeed, yet borne out by two instances at least; one, the remark to Thelwall already quoted when he considers that he is, on the whole, "a mere *apparition*, a naked spirit, and that life is, I myself I"; [71] and again in his ability to see things whole,—that gift which others "seem to me to want" [72]— his faith that "*all things* counterfeit infinity," [73] and his recognition of the importance of this imaginative attitude, which was a further anticipation of Schelling.

And finally, there is the general truth of the fact that the philosophy which he adumbrated many years later, in 1818, could, as he claimed, be derived from a study of the Greek philosophers and "the great men of Europe from the middle of the fifteenth till towards the close of the seventeenth century" some of whose principles "both of taste and philosophy" he upheld. [74]

What he lacked, what he felt increasingly as an imperative need to the successful accomplishment of his attempt at a synthesis, was confirmation of his own progress in philosophy and religion—a broad back of authoritative opinion and thought against which he could lean his mental and spiritual queries, even as he rested his moral problems against the steadfastness of Poole and Wordsworth. The distinction he had begun to draw in his own mind between fancy and imagination needed the confirmation he no more than suspected might exist when restated in terms of reason and understanding.

"A more thorough revolution in my philosophic principles, and a deeper insight into my own heart, were yet wanting" [75]— so he spoke of his condition before leaving for Germany. This clarity, this essential ability to perceive, to uncover the truth, he believed, rightly, he might acquire by study of the work of the German philosophers and theologians—a body of thought still in the main hidden from him by the mists of an unfamiliar language. And here is to be found the primary motive which set Coleridge upon the Hamburg packet that sailed from Yarmouth on August 16, 1798.

I I

AT ELEVEN O'CLOCK on Sunday morning, the packet left Yarmouth. Very soon, half of the eighteen passengers had disappeared. Dorothy was the first to go. Wordsworth, though he afterwards described the trip as "a very pleasant voyage" [1] soon followed his sister. Chester also went below.

Coleridge, unwilling to risk the effect of the odours below deck, curled himself up in a boat on deck. From this retreat he was roused later by one of two Danes on board. Addressing him as "Doctor Teology" on account of his black clothes, large shoes and black worsted stockings, the Dane asked Coleridge to come and drink with his party. Coleridge acquiesced. They drank, talked, sang, and eventually took to dancing reels on deck. At first all went well. The Dane could not speak too highly of Coleridge. "Vat imagination!" he exclaimed, "vat language! vat vast science! and vat eyes! vat a milk-vite forehead! O my heafen! vy, you're a Got!" [2]

But eventually he "commenced an harangue on religion, and mistaking me for 'un philosophe' in the continental sense of the word, he talked of Deity in a declamatory style, very much resembling the devotional rants of that rude blunderer, Mr Thomas Paine, in his Age of Reason, and whispered in my ear, what damned *hypocrism* all Jesus Christ's business was. I dare aver, that few men have less reason to charge themselves with indulging in *persiflage* than myself. I should hate it, if it were only that it is a Frenchman's vice, and feel a pride in avoiding it, because our own language is too honest to have a word to express it by. But in this instance the temptation had been too powerful, and I have placed it on the list of my offences. Pericles answered one of his dearest friends, who had solicited him on a case of life and death, to take an equivocal oath, for his preservation: *Debeo amicis opitulari, sed usque ad Deos.* Friendship herself must place her last and boldest step on this side the altar. What Pericles would not do to save a friend's life, you may be assured, I would not hazard merely to

[313]

mill the chocolate-pot of a drunken fool's vanity till it frothed over. Assuming a serious look, I professed myself a believer, and sunk at once an hundred fathoms in his good graces. He retired to his cabin, and I wrapped myself up in my great coat, and looked at the water. A beautiful white cloud of foam at momently intervals coursed by the side of the vessel with a roar, and little stars of flame danced and sparkled and went out in it: and every now and then light detachments of this white cloud-like foam darted off from the vessel's side, each with its own small constellation, over the sea, and scoured out of sight like a Tartar troop over a wilderness." [3]

From that moment, the rest of the journey passed quietly and without more incident than the sight of "a wild duck swimming on the waves, a single solitary wild duck. It is not easy to conceive, how interesting a thing it looked in that round objectless desert of waters. I had associated such a feeling of immensity with the ocean, that I felt exceedingly disappointed, when I was out of sight of all land, at the narrowness and *nearness*, as it were, of the circle of the horizon. So little are images capable of satisfying the obscure feelings connected with words." [4]

At eleven o'clock on Tuesday morning the boat reached Cuxhaven. By making a small extra payment to the Master, the four of them arranged to continue up the river to Hamburg. The packet proceeded on its way and at nightfall cast anchor thirty-five miles up the river. Coleridge, Wordsworth, Dorothy and Chester had tea on deck by moonlight, all together again, happy and excited by the strangeness of foreign scenes and sounds around them. [5]

But their first sight of Hamburg next morning was disappointing. Coleridge, in particular, was quite disgusted with the town and its people: "huddle and ugliness, stench and stagnation" [6] was his description of Hamburg. While Wordsworth took rooms at Der Wilde Mann, Coleridge visited the English bookseller, who, the following day, gave him an introduction to a Herr Klopstock, brother of the poet. Another introduction followed, to a Professor Ebeling, who was hard of hearing: "so deaf, indeed," said Coleridge, "that it was a painful effort to talk with him, as we were obliged to drop all our pearls into a huge ear-trumpet." [7] From the Professor's house, Coleridge and Wordsworth went back to the home of Herr Klopstock, where was "a very fine portrait of Lessing, whose works are at present the chief object of my admiration. His eyes were uncommonly like mine; if anything, rather larger, and more prominent. But the lower part of his face, and his nose—O what an exquisite expression of elegance and sensibility!—There appeared no depth, weight, or comprehensiveness in the forehead.—The whole face seemed to say, that Lessing was a man of quick and voluptuous feelings; of an active but light fancy; yet acute not in the observation of actual life, but in the arrangements and management of the ideal world, i.e. in taste and in metaphysics. I assure you that I wrote these very words in my memorandum-book with the portrait before my eyes, and when I knew nothing of Lessing but his name, and that he was a German writer of eminence." [8]

Coleridge quickly determined that Hamburg was no place for him. "My spirits certainly, and my health I fancied, were beginning to sink under the noise, dirt, and unwholesome air of our Hamburg hotel." [9] He secured an introduction from the poet Klopstock to the Amtmann of Ratzeburg, a small lakeside town between Hamburg and Lübeck. There he went alone on Sunday, the 23rd. The Amtmann, whom he afterwards described to Poole as "a sort of perpetual Lord Mayor, uniting in himself Judge and Justice of Peace over the bauers of a certain district," [10] was in this instance "almost an Englishman and an idolizer of our nation." [11] He and Coleridge agreed very well. The visitor was introduced to the pastor, who lived on the hillside looking down upon the lake. It was soon decided that Coleridge and Chester would live as paying guests with the pastor and Coleridge returned to Hamburg on the 27th, well pleased.

The next three days were spent at Hamburg. During this time, Coleridge and Wordsworth paid a visit to Klopstock, the poet. The interview, with its difficulties, was described later by De Quincey:

"An anonymous writer," he says, "has made the mistake of supposing Coleridge to have been the chief speaker, who did not speak at all. The case was this: Klopstock could not speak English. . . . Neither Coleridge nor Wordsworth, on the other hand, was able to *speak* German with any fluency. French, therefore, was the only medium of free communication; that being pretty equally familiar to Wordsworth and to Klopstock. But Coleridge found so much difficulty even in *reading* French that, wherever (as in the case of Leibnitz's 'Theodicée') there was a choice between an original written in French and a translation, though it might be a very faulty one, in German, he always preferred the latter. Hence it happened that Wordsworth, on behalf of the English party, was the sole supporter of the dialogue. The anonymous critic says another thing, which certainly has an air of truth—viz. that Klopstock plays a very secondary *role* in the interview (or words to that effect). But how was this to be avoided in reporting the case, supposing the fact to have been such? Now, the plain truth is that Wordsworth, upon his own ground, was an incomparable talker; whereas 'Klubstick' (as Coleridge used to call him) was always a feeble and slovenly one, because a loose and incoherent thinker. Besides, he was now old and decaying. Nor at any time, nor in any accomplishment, could Klopstock have shone, unless in the respectable art of skating. *There* he had a real advantage. The author of 'The Messiah', I have authority for saying, skated with the ease and grace of a regular artist; whereas the poet of the 'Excursion' sprawled upon the ice like a cow dancing a cotillion.

"Wordsworth did the very opposite of that with which he was taxed; for, happening to look down at Klopstock's swollen legs, and recollecting his age, he felt touched by a sort of filial pity for his helplessness. And he came to the conclusion that it would not seem becoming in a young and as yet obscure author to report too consciously the real superiority which he found it easy to maintain in such a colloquy.

"But neither had Klopstock the pretensions as a poet which the Blackwood writer seems to take for granted. Germany, the truth is, wanted a great epic poet. Not having produced one in that early and plastic stage of her literary soil when such a growth is natural and spontaneous, the next thing was to bespeak a substitute. The force of Coleridge's well-known repartee, when, in reply to a foreigner asserting for Klopstock the rank of German Milton, he said: 'True, sir; a very *German* Milton,' cannot be fully appreciated but by one who is familiar with the German poetry, and the small proportion in which it is a natural, racy, and domestic growth." [12]

Coleridge did, in fact, exchange a few sentences with the venerable poet—in English—but the burden of the conversation fell necessarily upon Wordsworth.[13] The interview could scarcely be considered a success. When Klopstock informed his visitors that he considered Glover's blank verse superior to that of Milton; and further, that he knew very little about the history of German poetry or the older German poets; then there seemed little else the younger man could do but summon up pity.

> "I looked at him with much emotion," wrote Coleridge. "I considered him as the venerable father of German poetry; as a good man; as a Christian; seventy-four years old; with legs enormously swoln; yet active, lively, chearful, and kind, and communicative. My eyes felt as if a tear were swelling into them." [14]

But there was one man to whom the news of the meeting brought nothing but pleasure. When Coleridge passed the news to Poole: "You have seen Klopstock!" wrote back that enthusiastic if somewhat indiscriminate admirer of greatness in the Arts, seeking ever the droppings of wisdom, both for himself and his friend. "Be particular in describing the physiognomy and stature of all such men, as well as noting their habits and sayings." [15]

Coleridge and Wordsworth had decided that they must part. Coleridge was anxious, not so much to see the country as to master first its language, then its learning; the position of the place where his study took place was immaterial—the less he had to travel the better he would be pleased. The Wordsworths were more anxious to see the country. They had also to be more careful with their money than Coleridge, who, having obtained permission to anticipate his annuity if necessary, had for a time thrown financial cares to the winds. And already they had begun to realize that so long as the four of them kept together there was little chance of their learning the German language.

So Coleridge informed Poole that the party was to break up. He and Chester were leaving for Ratzeburg on the last day of September. The Wordsworths, who liked Hamburg little better than did their friend, would leave later, probably for a town near the Brocken, Goslar. Lamb, hearing the news, scented a disagreement which did not exist. He wrote Southey:

> "I hear that the Two Noble Englishmen have parted no sooner than they set foot on German earth, but I have not heard the reason—possibly, to give novelists an handle to exclaim, 'Ah me! what things are perfect?' " [16]

Poole was pleased:

> "The Wordsworths have left you—so there is an end of our fears about amalgamation, etc. I think you both did perfectly right. It was right for them to find a cheaper situation; and it was right for you to avoid the expense of travelling, provided you are where *pure German* is spoken. You will, of course, frequently hear from Wordsworth. . . ." [17]

He proceeded to give Coleridge some advice:

> "You are now, dear Col., fixed in Germany, and what you have to do is to attend *wholly* to those things which are better attained in Germany than elsewhere. Let nothing divert you from them. And, on this consideration, I should spend no time to send anything to Stewart [Stuart] but what was involved in the progress of those pursuits. If any matter to *narrate* occurred, which, *for certain*, could be despatched without exertion of mind, or any great *consumption* of time, send it to him. But *begin* no poetry—no original composition—unless translation from German may be so called. One thing which you must determine to acquire while you are in Germany is as perfect a knowledge of the language as possible. You will thus have to show one distinct and almost tangible addition to your stock of knowledge, for the trouble and expence to yourself, for the anxieties and fears of your family and friends, incurred by this journey. . . . Beware of being too much with Chester. I could wish you had not both been in one house. Speak nothing but German. Live with Germans. Read in German. Think in German. Don't mind a few pounds while you are out for any assistance in learning German; nor, while you are out, must you regard a few weeks or months of time. You must *stay long enough to do the business you are gone to do*; but do it as quick as you *can do it* well. . . ." [18]

He then puts his finger, kindly, but not without insight, on the probable (but in this instance unfounded) hindrance to Coleridge's studies:

> "Make a strict arrangement of your time and chain yourself down to it. This may not be advisable for the generality, but I am persuaded it would counteract a *disease* of your mind—which is an active subtilty of imagination ever suggesting reasons to push off whatever excites a moment of languor or *ennui*. This many of your friends falsely call irresolution. No one has more resolution and decision than you; no one sooner sees the side of a question on which the balance of argument turns. But then

[318]

that same habit of giving free scope to the activity of your imagination, makes it death to you to chain the mind long to any particular object. This habit to *acquire a language must be conquered*, and I am sure is conquerable. To acquire a language—nay, to acquire excellence in any point . . ."[19]

Coleridge had asked for some details of English agriculture to be sent on behalf of Chester, who was to spend some of his time studying German agriculture:

"I should think it would be a good object for Chester to take a very accurate account of the agriculture, horticulture, implements relating to those objects, and, in short, of every species of rural and domestic management which he has the opportunity of observing, or collecting information on."[20]

Coleridge took literally Poole's advice about contributions to the *Morning Post*. He sent nothing whatever to Stuart; not even what he had already promised to write. Poole, in his letter of November 22 says:

"Stuart has written a very kind letter to Mrs Coleridge. He is afraid that he offended you, as you did not call before you left London. He says he hopes you consider his engagement as existing with you. He has been anxiously expecting the communication you promised him respecting German literature. . . . Why have you not sent it? Though I repeat that I advise you not to suffer your thoughts to stray from the main objects, to send communications to Stewart, if in pursuing those objects suitable matter occur, transmit it."[21]

Stuart's long-suffering—not for the first or the last time—was the more remarkable when his standing and that of Coleridge were compared. It was a tribute to his good nature, certainly; but far more to the personal charm of Coleridge—a charm that lingered even when the source of radiation was both absent and unaccountably silent; and not least, to the foresight, the penetration of Stuart, who was able to see, not only the fine poet in this obscure young man, but—of more moment to him—the possibilities of a first-rate journalist.

On October 3, Wordsworth wrote to Poole from Hamburg:

"Coleridge has most likely informed you that he and Chester have settled at Ratzeburg. Dorothy and I are going to speculate further up in the country."[22]

Coleridge set off for Ratzeburg on September 30; and a few weeks later gave Sarah a description of his host:

"My room is large and healthy; the house commands an enchanting prospect. The pastor is worthy and a learned man—a widower with eight children, five of whom are at home. The German language is spoken here in the utmost purity. The children often stand round my sofa and chatter away; and the little one of all corrects my pronunciation with a pretty pert lisp and self-sufficient tone, while the others laugh with no little joyance."

He adds: "The Gentry and Nobility here pay me an almost adulatory attention." [23]

Later, he enlarged upon his method of becoming familiar with the language:

"It was a regular part of my morning studies for the first six weeks of my residence at Ratzeburg, to accompany the good and kind old pastor, with whom I lived, from the cellar to the roof, through gardens, farmyard, etc., and to call every, the minutest, thing by its German name. Advertisements, farces, jest books, and the conversation of children while I was at play with them, contributed their share to a more home-like acquaintance with the language, than I could have acquired from works of polite literature alone, or even from polite society." [24]

Sarah remained unmoved at the thought of her husband's grand—and attractive—friends. "There is a very beautiful little woman—less, I think, than you—a Countess Kilmansig," [25] Coleridge wrote to her; and she replied: "I know my dear Samuel in her affliction will not forget entirely his most affectionate wife." [26]

Her confidence, at this time, was not misplaced. Coleridge managed to enjoy himself—the rôle of distinguished Englishman alone (for all practical purposes) in an admiring foreign town was one for which no better man could have been cast—yet was also, at times, genuinely unhappy and homesick. His letters home are almost piteous. When he has not heard from Sarah for some weeks:

"Another and another and yet another post day; and still Chester greets me with, 'No letters from England!' A knell, that strikes out regularly four times a week. How is this, my Love? Why do you not write to me? Do you think to shorten my absence by making it insupportable to me? Or perhaps you anticipate that if I received a letter I should idly turn away from my German to *dream* of you—of you and my beloved babies! Oh, yes! I should indeed dream of you for hours and hours; of you, and of beloved Poole, and of the infant that sucks at your breast, and of my dear, dear Hartley. You would be *present*, you would be with me in the air that I breathe; and I should cease to see you only when the tears rolled out of my eyes, and this naked, undomestic room became again visible." [27]

And when he does hear, a few days later, that Berkeley—of whose illness his father was ignorant—has recovered from smallpox:

"God, the Infinite, be praised that my babes are alive. His mercy will forgive me that late and all too slowly I raised up my heart in thanksgiving. At first and for a time I wept as passionately as if they had been dead; and for the whole day the weight was heavy upon me, relieved only by fits of weeping. I had long expected, I had passionately expected, a letter; I received it, and my frame trembled. I saw your hand, and all feelings of mind and body crowded together. Had the news been cheerful and only 'We are as you left us,' I must have wept to have delivered myself of the stress and tumult of my animal sensibility. But when I read the danger and the agony—My dear Sara! my love! my wife!— God bless you and preserve us. . . . My life, believe and know that I pant to be home and with you." [28]

That Coleridge did so wish, when writing, cannot be doubted. That his chief thought at home was his children, was also becoming apparent. Almost every letter is punctuated by cries of "O my dear Babies! my Babies!" [29] But that this pressure of feeling, of unhappiness, of longing for home, could have been maintained by anyone, let alone the mercurial Coleridge, is out of the question.

There were others, besides his wife and children, for whom Coleridge pined at times. The Wordsworths, who had been at Goslar, deeper in the country, since October 6, received some hexameters from Coleridge.[30] The last two lines were:

William my head and my heart! dear William and dear Dorothea!
You have all in each other; but I am lonely, and want you![31]

Dorothy sends him some poems and fragments of poems that Wordsworth had composed—among these, the famous description, in *The Prelude* to be, of his youthful days in the Lake District:

> All shod with steel,
> We hiss'd along the polish'd ice, in games
> Confederate, imitative of the chace
> And woodland pleasures, the resounding horn,
> The pack loud bellowing, and the hunted hare.
> So through the darkness and the cold we flew,
> And not a voice was idle; with the din
> Meanwhile the precipices rang aloud,
> The leafless trees, and every icy crag
> Tinkled like iron.[32]

The word 'tinkled' caught Coleridge's imagination, and he soon appropriated it when writing to Sarah. The whole piece was transcribed by Dorothy because she thought Coleridge, then enjoying skating for the first time on the lake on which Ratzeburg stood, would appreciate it the more. In her letter, she makes the first mention of the possibility that Coleridge might eventually go north with them on their return:

> "You speak in raptures of the pleasure of skaiting," she writes—"it must be a delightful exercise, and in the North of England amongst the mountains whither we wish to decoy you, you might enjoy it with every possible advantage. A race with William upon his native lakes would leave to the heart and the imagination something more dear and valuable than the gay sight of ladies and countesses whirling along the lake of Ratzeburg."[33]

Coleridge had had some trouble with his eyes—"a stye, or something of that kind, has come upon and enormously swelled my eyelids"[34]—and Dorothy says: "I am afraid they will suffer from this long ill-written letter, and I begin to be *half* afraid that you will be tired before you get through it . . . but no! you will not."[35] She and Wordsworth are thinking of leaving Goslar —their stay has not been a success—and ask Coleridge's advice as to what they should buy in the way of books on their journey.

Dorothy ends her letter: "Farewell! God love you! God bless you! dear Coleridge, our very dear friend."[36]

Another loss that saddened Coleridge, when he thought about it, was, of course, the company of Poole. He poured out vast letters to him:

"My friend, my dear friend!" he wrote on January 4. "Two hours have past since I received your letter. It was so frightfully long since I received one!! My body is weak and faint with the beating of my heart."[37]

He reports his progress and tells Poole of his intentions:

"I am quite well, calm and industrious. I now read German as English—that is, without any *mental* translation as I read. I likewise understand all that is said to me, and a good deal of what they say to each other. On very trivial and on metaphysical subjects I can talk *tolerably*—so, so!—but in that conversation, which is between both, I bungle most ridiculously. I owe it to my industry that I can read old German, and even the old low German, better than most of even the educated natives. It has greatly enlarged my knowledge of the English language."[38]

He pours out his troubles, which are, not uncommonly, monetary:

"Including *all* expenses, I have not lived at less than two pounds a week. Wordsworth (from whom I receive long and affectionate letters) has enjoyed scarcely one advantage, but his expenses have been considerably less than they were in England. . . . For these last two months I have drunk nothing but water, and I eat but little animal food. . . . My dear Poole! I am afraid that, supposing I return in the first week of May, my whole expenses . . . will not have been less than 90 *pounds!*"[39]

This means that he has had to anticipate his Wedgwood annuity. But he has a plan to repay what he has borrowed:

"I despair not but with intense application and regular use of time, to which I have now almost accustomed myself, that by three months' residence at Göttingen I shall have *on paper* at least *all* the materials if not the whole structure of a work that will repay me. The work I have planned, and I have imperiously excluded all waverings about other works. That is the disease of my mind— it is comprehensive in its conceptions, and wastes itself in the contemplations of the many things which it might do. I am aware of the disease, and for the next three months (if I cannot cure it) I will at least suspend its operation. This book is a life of Lessing, and interweaved with it a true state of German literature in its rise and present state. I have already written a little life from three different biographies, divided it into years, and at Göttingen I will read his works regularly according to the years in which they were

[323]

written, and the controversies, religious and literary, which they occasioned. But of this say nothing to anyone. The journey to Germany has certainly *done me good*. My habits are less irregular and my *mind* more in my own power. But I have much still to do!" [40]

He passes on to the questions of Wordsworth, and their future dwelling-places:

"Wordsworth is divided in his mind—unquietly divided between the neighbourhood of Stowey and the North of England. He cannot think of settling at a distance from me, and I have told him that I cannot leave the vicinity of Stowey. His chief objection to Stowey is the want of books. The Bristol Library is a hum, and will do us little service; and he thinks that he can procure a house near Sir Gilford Lawson's by the Lakes, and have free access to his immense library. I think it better once in a year to walk to Cambridge, in the summer vacation—perhaps I may be able to get rooms for nothing, and there for a couple of months read like a Turk on a given plan, and return home with a mass of materials which, with dear, *independent* Poetry, will fully employ the remaining year. But this is idle prating about a future. But indeed, it is time to be looking out for a house for me—it is not possible I can be either comfortable or useful in so small a house as that in Lime Street. If Woodlands can be gotten at a reasonable price, I would have it." [41]

Poole replied:

"When the letters from Hamburg were announced Ward [42] jumped up and twirled round like a whirlygig, in spite of the barricade of chairs and tables that were near him, to the great derangement of the bread and cheese, and two or three full glasses of beer which were splashed over. I sat *grinning* and broke the seal. Why will you make yourself unhappy at not hearing from us? . . . Be assured, unless we are all taken off in a whirlwind, that, if you do not hear from us, it will always arise from the miscarriage or delay of a letter." [43]

Poole tells him that Sarah has gone to Bristol. Berkeley, who, after overcoming the smallpox, had developed a cough, was reported to be getting better.

"I am delighted to hear of your progress in German; delighted to hear of your progress in mastering the untired and unbidden excursions of your mind. Perfect yourself, oh perfect yourself, I pray you, in this latter discipline, for who knows how to do well like you, if you could acquire *power* to do it. . . . I am highly pleased with your intended removal to Göttingen. Being a university it must possess advantages which your present situation does not —to say nothing of the economy of the plan. . . . But once more, my dearly beloved, let me entreat you not to over-interest yourself about your family and friends here; not to incapacitate yourself by idle apprehensions and tender reveries of imagination concerning us. Those things are wrong. They can do no good, and you are not fit to see many people, and many nations, if you indulge in them. Mrs Coleridge has sent me from Bristol the letter you wrote her. Was it well to indulge in, much less to express, such feeling concerning *any* circumstance which could relate to two infants? I do not mean to check tenderness, for in the *folly* of tenderness I can sympathise—but be *rational*, I implore you—in your present situation, your happiness depends upon it. I was grieved to hear of your eyes. Take care of your health, remember that. Water and vegetable food will not do for you. . . . As to the house—I have long felt that in Lime Street is unsuitable for you. The old house at Woodlands, Wilmott intends living in himself; the new house is too large. What think you of the house in which Hancock lived at Stowey? . . . you *may be certain* I shall keep an eye on every house to be had here and in the neighbourhood. *I will not part from you, if you will not part from me*; be assured of that. I can truly say that your society is a principal ingredient of my happiness, a principal source of my improvement. The time will, I trust, come, when it will contribute still more than it has done both to the one and to the other." 44

Before he could receive this letter, Coleridge had written again to Sarah. He began with a further display of excessive sensibility:

"Since the wind changed, and it became possible for me to have letters, I lost all my tranquillity. . . . This morning I awoke long before light, feverish and unquiet. I was certain in my mind that I should have a letter from you, but before it arrived my restlessness and the irregular pulsation of my heart had quite wearied me down, and I held the letter in my hand like as if I was stupid, without attempting to open it. 'Why don't you read the letter?' said Chester, and I read it. Ah, little Berkeley—I have misgivings, but my duty is rather to comfort you, my dear, dear Sara! I am so exhausted that I could sleep. I am well, but my spirits have left me. I am completely homesick." 45

He gave news of the Wordsworths:

"I hear as often from Wordsworth as letters can go backward and forward in a country where fifty miles in a day and night is expeditious travelling! He seems to have employed more time in writing English than in studying German. No wonder! for he might as well have been in England as at Goslar, in the situation which he chose and with his unseeking manners. He has now left it, and is on his journey to Nordhausen. His taking his sister with him was a wrong step; it is next but impossible for any but married women, or in the suit of married women, to be introduced to any company in Germany. Sister here is considered as only a name for mistress. Still, however, male acquaintance he might have had, and had I been at Goslar I would have had them; but W., God love him! seems to have lost his spirits and almost his inclination for it." [46]

The greater part of the lake on which Ratzeburg was situated was still ice-bound. Coleridge described it to Sarah, borrowing on the way from Wordsworth's "tinkled":

"O my God! what sublime scenery I have beheld. Of a morning I have seen the little lake covered with mist; when the sun peeped over the hills the mist broke in the middle, and at last stood as the waters of the Red Sea are said to have done when the Israelites passed; and between these two walls of mist the sunlight burst upon the ice in a straight road of golden fire . . . intolerably bright . . . the walls of mist partaking of the light in a *multitude* of colours. About a month ago the vehemence of the wind had shattered the ice; part . . . was driven to shore and had frozen anew; this was of a deep blue, and represented an agitated sea—the water that ran up between the great islands of ice shone of a yellow-green (it was at sunset), and all the scattered islands of *smooth* ice were *blood*, intensely bright *blood*; on some of the largest islands the fishermen were pulling out their immense nets through the holes made in the ice for this purpose, and the fishermen, the net-poles, and the huge nets made a part of the glory! O my God! how I wished you to be with me! In skating there are three pleasing circumstances—firstly, the infinitely subtle particles of ice which the skate cuts up, and which creep and run before the skater like a low mist, and in sunrise or sunset become coloured; second, the shadow of the skater in the water seen through the transparent ice; and thirdly, the melancholy undulating sound from the skate, not without variety; and, when very many are skating together, the sounds give an impulse to the icy trees, and the woods all round the lake *tinkle*." [47]

He ends with an account of his smoking habits, which had been greatly encouraged since leaving Wordsworth, a non-smoker, and living with the Germans:

". . . a pipe at breakfast is a great addition to the comfort of life. I shall [smoke at] no other time in England. Here I smoke four times a day—1 at breakfast, 1 half an hour before dinner, 1 in the afternoon at tea, and 1 just before bed-time—but I shall give it all up, unless, as before observed, you should happen to like the smoke of a pipe at breakfast. Once when I first came here I smoked a pipe immediately after dinner; the pastor expressed his surprise: I expressed mine that he could smoke before breakfast. 'O Herr Gott!' (that is, Lord God) quoth he, 'it is delightful; it invigorates the frame and *it clears out the mouth so.*' A common amusement at the German Universities is for a number of young men to smoke out a candle! that is, to fill a room with tobacco smoke till the candle goes out." [48]

A few weeks later, on February 3, Dorothy, writing to her brother Christopher, explained that the cold had been too severe for them to leave Goslar earlier. Certainly no love of the place itself had kept them there.

"We have gone on advancing in the language, the main object of our journey, in tolerably regular progress," she wrote, "but if we had had the advantage of good society we should have done much more—this however is a benefit which we have now given up all expectation of attaining, as we find that when a *man and woman* are received into society, they are expected, being considered as a sort of family, to give entertainments in return for what they receive. Now this, in conjunction with the expense of travelling, is absolutely out of our power, though I believe that we could do it, being stationary, for as little expense as we could live for, entirely without company, in England. We have then bounded our desires to seeing a little more of the country, and getting into a family pretty much resembling this, in which we now are, with whom, as now, we may talk upon common subjects. Perhaps if the weather is fine, and we do not find travelling very expensive, we may not fix more than a fortnight in one place; but make a little circuit from town to town. At present however the weather is not very favourable for such a plan. . . ." [49]

Coleridge, it is evident, had not failed to spread—and not improbably overstate—his prowess in Ratzeburg society; and

Dorothy was not sufficiently in touch with the Germans to realize the abundance of titles in that country:

"Coleridge," Dorothy tells her brother, "is in a very different world from what we stir in; he is all in high life, among barons, counts and countesses. He could not be better placed than he is at Ratzeberg for attaining the object of his journey; but his expenses are much more than ours conjointly. I think however he has done perfectly right in consenting to pay so much, as he will not stay longer in Germany than till March or April." [50]

On the 23rd of the month the Wordsworths at last left Goslar; and four days later, on their arrival at Nordhausen, wrote a joint letter to Coleridge. The greater part of Dorothy's contribution to the letter consisted of a detailed description of their journey from Goslar to Nordhausen. She ends:

"I now come to something of more importance, the subject of your letters—but let me first speak of the joy we felt at seeing your handwriting again; I burst open the seals and could almost have kissed them in the presence of the postmaster, but we did not read a word till we got to the inn when we devoured them separately, for at least two hours. With the experience we have had of the possibility of travelling for a very trifling expense, we cannot but think that you have done wisely in quitting Ratzeberg, both on your account and that of Chester. Gottingen seems to be the best possible place for your purpose. William now takes the pen—God bless you dear dear Coleridge." [51]

Wordsworth wrote:

"We do not wish to read much but should both be highly delighted to be chattering and chattered to, through the whole day. As this blessing seems to be destined for some more favoured sojourners, we must content ourselves with pshaw for the ears,—eyes for ever! We are resolved if the weather be tolerable to saunter about for a fortnight or three weeks at the end of which time you may be prepared to see us in Gottingen. I will not say to tarry long there for I do not think it would suit our plan, but to have the pleasure of seeing and conversing with you." [52]

Wordsworth was pessimistic but resigned over his failure to acquite a useful knowledge of the language:

"My progress in German," he says, "considered with reference to literary emolument is not even as dust in the balance. If I had

had opportunities of conversing I should not have cared much if I had not read a line. My hope was that I should be able to learn German as I learn'd French, in this I have been woefully deceived. I acquired more french in two months, than I should acquire German in five years living as we have lived. In short sorry I am to say it I do not consider myself as knowing *any* thing of the German language. Consider this not as spoken in modesty either false or true but in simple verity.—I cannot sufficiently thank you for your two valuable letters particularly that upon the German Poets. Of the excellence of Lessing I can form no distinct idea. My internal prejudgment concerning Wieland and Goethe (of Voss I knew nothing) were, as your letter has convinced me, the result of no *negligent* perusal of the different fragments which I had seen in England." [53]

At the end of his letter, Wordsworth announces a project reminiscent less of the writer than of his sanguine friend of many interests. He says:

"We intend to import into England a new invention for washing. Among other advantages which our patent will set forth we shall not fail to insist upon the immense saving which must result from our discovery which will render only one washing basin necessary for the largest family in the kingdom. We dare not trust this communication to a letter, but you shall be a partner, Chester likewise. Adieu God bless you, Dorothy's best and kindest love. We shall soon be with you." [54]

Then, after an apology for the bad writing, comes: "God love you, my dear very dear friend D.W." [55]

This letter was addressed to Coleridge at Göttingen. On the 6th of February he had left Ratzeburg and, after the coldest journey he had ever experienced, reached Hanover for the week-end, and finally, on the fifth day, the university town of Göttingen, a few miles from Goslar. From there, he next wrote to Sarah, on March 12, describing his journey and his life at Göttingen. But first came a description of his feelings when lonely—feelings which would naturally be renewed more often after moving to a strange town:

"I have thought and thought of you, and pictured you and the little ones so often and so often that my imagination is tired down, flat and powerless, and I languish after home for hours together in vacancy, my feelings almost wholly unqualified by *thoughts*. I

[329]

have at times experienced such an extinction of *light* in my mind—
I have been so forsaken by all the *forms* and *colourings* of existence,
as if Being remained, blind and stagnant. After I have recovered
from this strange state and reflected upon it, I have thought of a
man who should lose his companion in a desart of sand, where his
weary Halloos drop down in the air without an echo. I am deeply
convinced that if I were to remain a few years among objects for
whom I had no affection I should wholly lose the powers of intellect. Love is the vital air of my genius,[56] and I have not seen one
human being in Germany whom I can conceive it *possible* for me
to *love*, no, not *one*; in my mind they are an unlovely race, these
Germans." [57]

Coleridge had been given letters of recommendation—"not
ordinary letters" [58]—by a Herr von Doring, "a nobleman" [59] of
Ratzeburg, to his brother-in-law at Hanover. On arrival at
Hanover, he was introduced "to all the great people," [60] and, what
was of more importance, was presented " 'as an English gentleman of first-rate character and talents' to Baron Steinburg,
the Minister of State, and to Von Brandes, the Secretary of State
and Governor of Göttingen University. The first was amazingly
perpendicular, but civil and polite, and gave me letters to Heyne,
the head Librarian, and, in truth, the real *Governor* of Göttingen.
Brandes likewise gave me letters to Heyne and Blumenbach, who
are his brothers-in-law." [61]

Coleridge remarks that there are only two things worth seeing
in Hanover, one of which was a bust of Leibnitz—the adaptor,
or inventor as Coleridge might have said, of monadism. This,
wrote Coleridge, "impressed on my soul a sensation which has
ennobled it. It is the face of a god! and Leibnitz was almost more
than a man in the wonderful capaciousness of his judgment and
imagination!" [62]

On arrival at Göttingen, Coleridge

" . . . called with my letters on the Professor Heyne, a little,
hopping, over-civil sort of a thing, who talks very fast and with
fragments of coughing between every ten words. However, he
behaved very courteously to me. The next day I took out my
matricula, and commenced student of the University of Göttingen.
Heyne has honoured me so far that he has given me the right,
which properly only professors have, of sending to the Library
for an indefinite number of books in my own name.

"On Saturday evening I went to the concert. Here the other

Englishmen introduced themselves. After the concert Hamilton, a Cambridge man, took me as his guest to the Saturday Club, *where what is called* the first class of students meet and sup once a week. Here were all the nobility and three Englishmen. Such an evening I never passed before—roaring, kissing, embracing, fighting, smashing bottles and glasses against the wall, singing—in short, such a scene of uproar I never witnessed before, no, not even at Cambridge. I drank nothing, but all except two of the Englishmen were drunk, and the party broke up a little after one o'clock in the morning. I thought of what I had been at Cambridge and of what I was, of the wild bacchanalian sympathy with which I had formerly joined similar parties; and of my total inability now to do aught but meditate, and the feeling of the deep alteration in my moral being gave the scene a melancholy interest to me." [63]

However, although it is difficult to believe that Coleridge remained as detached from conviviality as he would have Sarah believe, he did in fact apply himself with a quite uncharacteristic regularity to the conquest of German thought. But he was not without his moments of relaxation—the presence of other Englishmen studying at Göttingen ensured as much. In addition to Hamilton, Coleridge met Charles and Frederick Parry,[64] the elder Parry holding forth at Göttingen upon the moral forces of the ancient religions.[65] Clement Carlyon [66] joined the university on March 22 with a travelling scholarship from Pembroke, Cambridge; with him came G. B. Greenough [67] and others. Carlyon in his reminiscences devotes the greater part of a volume to his impressions and recollections of Coleridge at this time—impressions not in themselves noteworthy or in any way inspired, but indicating, beyond Coleridge's fascination for others, the amount of time that the men must have spent together—a time largely devoted to walks and talks—the latter, as might be expected, mostly monologues by Coleridge upon almost every subject, great and trivial, that the mind can conceive. "Coleridge is much liked," wrote the elder Parry, "notwithstanding many peculiarities. He is very liberal towards all doctrines and opinions and cannot be put out of temper. . . . The great fault which his friends lament is the variety of subjects which he adopts, and the too abstruse nature of his ordinary speculations, *extra homines positas.*" [68]

Yet, despite this good fellowship, and the time it occupied,

Coleridge at times worked diligently in the lecture rooms and in his own lodgings. In addition to his Lessing studies: "I regularly attended the lectures on physiology in the morning, and on natural history in the evening, under BLUMENBACH. . . . Eichorn's lectures on the New Testament were repeated to me from notes by a student from Ratzeburg." [69] Charles Parry explains the reason for Coleridge's non-attendance at Eichorn's lectures. "Coleridge," he writes, "an able vindicator of these important truths [Christian Evidences], is well acquainted with Eichorn, but the latter is a coward, who dreads his arguments and his presence." [70]

> "But my chief efforts," continued Coleridge, "were directed towards a grounded knowledge of the German language and literature. From Professor TYCHSEN I received as many lessons in the Gothic of Ulphilas as sufficed to make me acquainted with its grammar, and the radical words of most frequent occurrence; and with the occasional assistance of the same philosophical linguist, I read through OTTFRIED's metrical paraphrase of the gospel, and the most important remains of the THEOTISCAN, or the transitional state of the Teutonic language from the Gothic to the old German of the Swabian period. . . . I read with sedulous accuracy the MINNESINGER (or singers of love, the provençal poets of the Swabian court) and the metrical romances; and then laboured through sufficent specimens of the *master singers*, their degenerate successors; not however without occasional pleasure from the rude, yet interesting strains of Hans Sachs, the cobler of Nuremberg. . . . In the opinion of LESSING, the most acute of critics, and of ADELUNG, the first of Lexicographers, Opitz, and the Silesian poets, his followers, not only restored the language, but still remain the models of pure diction. A stranger has no vote on such a question; but after repeated perusal of the work my feelings justified the verdict, and I seemed to have acquired from them a sort of *tact* for what is *genuine* in the style of later writers. Of the splendid era, which commenced with Gellert, Klopstock, Ramler, Lessing, and their compeers, I need not speak. With the opportunities which I enjoyed, it would have been disgraceful not to have been familiar with their writings." [71]

After such an indication of the extent of his reading, it would seem ungenerous to wonder at Coleridge's lack of reference to Goethe, to Bürger, and, particularly, to Kant. Of the latter he must have heard much. Three series of lectures—on the *Critiques* of

Reason and *Judgment* respectively and upon Kantean logic and aesthetics—were being held at the university while Coleridge was there.[72] Apparently he attended none of these lectures; but he heard enough on the subject to confirm his determination to study Kant at the earliest available opportunity.[73]

Christian Heyne was at this time lecturing on the Greeks—their learning, constitution, religion, and the domestic condition under which they lived—a course preparatory to one on Greek Literature; [74] but there is no sign that Coleridge attended these lectures. In fact, it is difficult to see how he could have found the time to do so. With the work of Heyne, who had numbered Tieck and the Schlegels among his pupils, Coleridge was familiar before he came to Germany. He had, at Stowey, Heyne's edition of Virgil.[75]

Unknown to Coleridge, sorrow had fallen in earnest upon the little Coleridge family. On February 11, Sarah sent a distracted note to Poole:

> "Oh, my dear Mr Poole, I have lost my dear, dear child! at one o'clock on Sunday Morning a violent convulsive fit put an end to his painful existence, myself and two of his aunts were watching by his cradle. I wish I had not seen it, for I am sure it will never leave my memory; sweet babe! what will thy Father feel when he shall hear of thy sufferings and death!" [76]

Poole had warned Sarah not to excite her husband's emotions over herself or the children as he felt that this might have an adverse effect upon Coleridge's work.[77]

> "I am perfectly aware of every thing you have said on the subject in your letter," Sarah continued; "I shall not yet write to Coleridge, and when I do—I will pass over all disagreeable subjects with the greatest care, for I well know their violent effect on him —but I account myself most unfortunate in being at a distance from him at this time, wanting his consolation as I do, and feeling my griefs almost too much to support with fortitude. . . . I am very miserable!!!" [78]

For over a month, no attempt was made to break the news to Coleridge. Eventually, with reluctance, Poole wrote on March 15:

> "My ever dear Col.—The Hamburg mail at length arrived, but it brought no great weight of pleasure for me. One letter came. . . . I sent it to Mrs C. at Bristol, and desired her not to write to you till

[333]

I had written, and that I would forward her my letter to read. I have this morning heard from her. . . . She is very well, and I shall send her this letter that she may read it and forward it to you. Perhaps even by reading so far, you *feel the reason* for my wishing to write to you before Mrs Coleridge. I suspect you feel it by the anticipations in your last letter. You say there that you have serious misgivings concerning Berkeley—well—you now, my dear Col., know the worst. I thus give you to understand the catastrophe of the drama, without heightening it by first narrating the circumstances which led to it; but, as you will hear by and by, those circumstances were purely natural, and such as probably no human conduct or foresight could have averted. The child was got perfectly well out of the smallpox, and enjoyed a clear interval of health before he was seized with a cough. . . . As he did not get better, the medical men, and indeed all of us, advised Mrs C. to go to Bristol and try change of air, or rather to carry into execution the visit she intended. For some time the child appeared better, but the cough returned, and he lost flesh and grew weaker daily— in short, from the accounts Mrs Coleridge wrote me, I was quite prepared for the event. . . . On examination it was found that he died of a consumption. Mrs Coleridge was much fatigued during the child's illness, but her health was very good, and she very wisely kept up her spirits. . . .

"I have thus, my dear Col., informed you of the whole truth. It was long contrary to my opinion to let you know of the child's death before your arrival in England. And I thought, and still think myself justified in that notion, by the OVER-anxiety you expressed in your former letters concerning the children. Doubtless the affection found to exist between parents and *infant* children is a wise law of nature, a mere instinct to preserve Man in his infant state. . . . But the moment you make this affection the creature of reason, you degrade reason. When the infant becomes a reasonable being, then let the affection be a thing of reason, not before. Brutes can only have an instinctive affection. Hence, when that ceases to be necessary, all affection ceases. This seems to me to be a great line of demarcation between Men and Beasts, between Reason and Instinct. If then the love of infants be a mere instinct, it is extraordinary that sensible men should be much disturbed at the counteraction of it, particularly when the end of that action, if I may so speak, becomes a nullity. Certainly, if I had an only child, and no hopes of another, who alone was to be the solace of my age, who was to take my property, to bear my name, to represent myself; in short, to be another self—certainly, if this child were to die, I should feel my *earthly* being as it were suddenly stopped, and something like a feeling of annihilation would occur, which of all others is the most disconsolate. But this is not your case. Hartley is brave and well, and like to give you grandchildren and great-grandchildren, *ad libitum*; and, I need not add, very likely to have a plenty of brothers and sisters. The truth is, my dear Col., it is idle to reason about a thing of this nature. Therefore I talk quaintly—your mind must suggest everything I can suggest and more. Only let your *mind* act, and not your *feelings*. Don't conjure up any scenes of distress which never happened. Mrs Coleridge felt as a mother . . . and, in an exemplary manner, did all a mother could do. *But she never forgot herself.* She is now perfectly well, and does not make herself miserable by recalling the engaging, though, remember, mere instinctive attractions of an infant a few months old."[79]

This well-meant, though scarcely convincing explanation and appeal to the bereaved father, appeared to meet with unexpected success. Coleridge had so exhausted his emotions in anticipation of calamity that when calamity came he remained comparatively calm:

"Your two letters, dated January 24 and March 15, followed close on each other. I was still enjoying 'the livelier impulse and the dance of thought' which the first had given me when I received the second. At the time, in which I read Sara's lively account of the miseries which herself and the infant had undergone, all was over and well—there was nothing to *think* of—only a mass of pain was brought suddenly and closely within the sphere of my perception, and I was made to suffer it over again. For this bodily frame is an imitative thing, and touched by the imagination gives the hour which is past as faithfully as a repeating watch. But Death—the death of an infant—of one's own infant! I read your letter in calmness, and walked out into the open fields, oppressed, not by my feelings, but by the riddles which the thought so easily proposes, and solves—never! A parent—in the strict and exclusive sense a parent!—to me it is a *fable* wholly without meaning except in the *moral* which it suggests—a fable of which the moral is God. Be it so—my dear, dear friend! Oh let it be so! La Nature (says Pascal) 'La Nature confond les Pyrrhoniens, et la Raison confond les Dogmatistes. Nous avons une impuissance à prouver invincible à tout le Dogmatisme. Nous avons une idée de la vérité invincible à tout le Pyrrhonisme.' I find it wise and human to believe, even on slight evidence, opinions, the contrary of which cannot be proved, and which promote our happiness without hampering our intellect. My baby has not lived in vain—this life has been to him what it is to all of us—education and development! Fling yourself forward into your immortality only a few thousand years, and how small will not the difference between one year old and sixty years appear! Consciousness!—it is no otherwise necessary to our conceptions of future continuance than as connecting the present link of our being with the one immediately preceding it; and *that* degree of consciousness, *that* small portion of *memory*, it would not only be arrogant, but in the highest degree absurd, to deny even to a much smaller infant. 'Tis a strange assertion that the essence of identity lies in *recollective* consciousness. 'Twere scarcely less ridiculous to affirm that the eight miles from Stowey to Bridgwater consist in the eight milestones. Death in a doting old age falls upon my feelings ever as a more hopeless phenomenon than death in infancy; but *nothing* is hopeless. What if the vital force which I sent from my arm in the stone as I flung it in the air and skimmed it upon the water—what if even that did not perish! It was *life!*—it was a particle of *being!*—it was power! and how could it perish? *Life, Power, Being!* Organization may be and probably is their *effect*—their *cause* it *cannot* be! I have indulged very curious fancies concerning that force, that swarm of motive powers which I sent out of my body into that stone, and which, one by one, left the untractable or already possessed mass, and—but the German Ocean lies between us. It is all too far to send you such fancies as these! Grief, indeed,—

> Doth love to dally with fantastic thoughts,
> And smiling like a sickly Moralist,
> Finds some resemblance to her own concern
> In the straws of chance, and things inanimate.

But I cannot truly say that I grieve—I am perplexed—I am sad—and a little thing—a very trifle—would make me weep—but for the death of the baby I have *not* wept! Oh this strange, strange, strange scene-shifter Death!—that giddies one with insecurity and so unsubstantiates the living things that one has grasped and handled! Some months ago Wordsworth transmitted me a most sublime epitaph. Whether it had any reality I cannot say. Most probably, in some gloomier moment he had fancied the moment in which his sister might die.

EPITAPH.

> A slumber did my spirit seal,
> I had no human fears;
> She seemed a thing that could not feel
> The touch of earthly years.

S. T. COLERIDGE IN 1799

"I have at last received your *German picture*. It is a good picture—certainly like you—but it *wants character* . . . it gives one pleasure to look at; but it is *Mr Coleridge* and not *Coleridge*. You are in the drawing-room, and not in the vales of Quantock, or on the top of Skiddaw."   THOMAS POOLE

"I have heard him say, fixing his prominent eyes upon himself (as he was wont to do whenever there was a mirror in the room), with a singularly coxcombical expression of countenance, that his dress was sure to be lost sight of the moment he began to talk, an assertion which, whatever may be thought of its modesty, was not without truth."   CLEMENT CARLYON

"I saw there, likewise, a very fine portrait of Lessing, whose works are at present the chief object of my admiration. His eyes were uncommonly like mine; if any thing, rather larger and more prominent."   COLERIDGE

"The rapt one with the godlike forehead."   WILLIAM WORDSWORTH

> No motion has she now, no force,
> She neither hears nor sees;
> Mov'd round in Earth's diurnal course
> With rocks, and stones, and trees! [80]

He finished the letter two days later, on April 8, with comments on the proposed house at Stowey:

"I must not disguise from you that to live *in* Stowey, and in that house which you mention, is to me an exceedingly unpleasant thought. Rather than go anywhere else I assuredly would do it, and be glad, but the thought is unpleasant to me. I do not like to live *in* a town, still less in Stowey, where, excepting yourself and mother, there is no human being attached to us, and few who do not dislike us. Besides, it is a sad tyranny that all who live in towns are subject to, that of innoculating all at once, etc. And then the impossibility of keeping one's children free from vice and profaneness, etc." [81]

To his wife he wrote, on the same day:

"It is one of the discomforts of my absence, my dearest Love! that we feel the same calamities at different times—I would fain write words of consolation to you; yet I know that I shall only fan into new activity the pang which was growing dead and dull in your heart. Dear little Being! he had existed to me for so many months only in dreams and reveries, but in them existed and still exists so livelily, so like a real thing, that although I know of his death, yet when I am alone and have been long silent, it seems to me as if I did not understand it. Methinks there is something awful in the thought, what an unknown being one's own infant is to one —a fit of sound—a flash of light—a summer gust that is as it were *created* in the bosom of the calm air, that rises up we know not how, and goes we know not whither! But we say well; it goes! it is gone! and only in states of society in which the revealing voice of our most inward and abiding nature is no longer listened to (when we sport and juggle with abstract phrases, instead of representing our feelings and ideas), only then we say it *ceases*! I will not believe that it ceases—in this moving, stirring, and harmonious universe—I *cannot* believe it! Can cold and darkness come from the sun? where the sun is not, there is cold and darkness! But the living God is everywhere, and works everywhere— and where is there room for death? To look back on the life of my baby, how short it seems! but consider it, referently to nonexistence, and what a manifold and majestic *Thing* does it not become? What a multitude of admirable actions, what a multitude of *habits* of actions it learnt even before it saw the light! and who shall count or conceive the infinity of its thoughts and feelings, its hopes, and fears, and joys, and pains, and desires, and presentiments, from the moment of its birth to the moment when the glass, through which we saw him darkly, was broken—and he became suddenly invisible to us?" [82]

He begins, as was ever his habit, to follow the bent of his mind, less to comfort his wife than to convince himself, to test his theories against this keen edge of actual sorrow.

"Out of the Mount that might not be touched, and that burnt with fire, out of darkness, and blackness, and tempest, and with his own Voice, which they who heard entreated that they might not hear it again, the most high God forbade us to use his *name vainly*; And shall we who are Christians, shall we believe that he himself uses his own power vainly? That like a child he builds palaces of mud and clay in the common road, and then he destroys them, as weary of his *pastime*, or leaves them to be trod under by the hoof of Accident? That God works by *general* laws are to me words without meaning or worse than meaningless—ignorance, and imbecility, and limitation must wish in generals. What and who are these horrible shadows necessity and general law, to which God himself must offer *sacrifices*—hecatombs of sacrifices? I feel a deep conviction that these shadows exist not—they are only the dreams of reasoning pride, that would fain find solutions for all difficulties without faith—that would make the discoveries which lie thick sown in the path of the eternal Future unnecessary; and so conceiting that there is sufficiency and completeness in the narrow present, weakens the presentiment of our wide and ever widening immortality. God works in each for all—most true— but more comprehensively true is it, that he works in all for each. I confess that the more I think, the more I am discontented with the doctrines of Priestley. He builds the whole and sole hope of future existence on the words and miracles of Jesus—yet doubts or denies the future existence of infants—only because according to his own system of materialism he has not discovered how they can be made *conscious*. But Jesus has declared that *all* who are in the grave shall arise—and that those who should arise to perceptible progression must be ever as the infant which He held in his arms and blessed. And although the *Man* Jesus had never appeared in the world, yet I am Quaker enough to believe, that in the heart of every man the Christ would have revealed himself, the Power of the Word, that was even in the wilderness. To me who am absent this faith is a real consolation,—and the few, the

[338]

slow, the quiet tears which I shed, are the accompaniments of high and solemn thought, not the workings of pain or sorrow. When I return indeed, and see the vacancy that has been made—when nowhere anything corresponds to the form which will perhaps for ever dwell on my mind, then it is possible that a keener pang will come upon me." [83]

He continues with a thought, natural enough in the circumstances, yet suggesting by the very fact that he considers its mention necessary that the love between Sarah and himself already needed confirmation, needed restatement to strengthen it. His words are open to interpretation merely as an attempt to comfort. That they were so intended, there can be no doubt; but it was not Sarah alone whom Coleridge was endeavouring to reassure; already there are signs that his affections were centring upon his children.

"Yet I trust, my love! I trust, my dear Sara! that this event which has forced us to think of the death of what is most dear to us, as at all times probable, will in many and various ways be good for us. To have shared—nay, I should say—to have divided with any human being any one deep sensation of joy or of sorrow, sinks deep the foundations of a lasting love. When in moments of fretfulness and imbecility I am disposed to anger or reproach, it will, I trust, be always a restoring thought—'We have wept over the same little one,'—and with whom am I angry? With her who so patiently and unweariedly sustained my poor and sickly infant through his long pains—with her, who, if I too should be called away, would stay in the deep anguish over my death-pillow! who would never forget me! Ah, my poor Berkeley!" [84]

This letter had been written and dispatched nearly a fortnight before Coleridge received the first letter, dated March 25, written to him by Sarah since the death of Berkeley.

"My dearest Love," she writes, "I hope you will not attribute my long silence to want of affection. If you have received Mr Poole's letter you will know the reason and acquit me. My darling infant left his wretched mother on the 10th of February, and though the leisure that followed was intolerable to me, yet I could not employ myself in reading or writing, or in any way that prevented my thoughts from resting on him. This parting was the severest trial that I have ever yet undergone, and I pray to God that I may never live to behold the death of another child. For, O my dear Samuel, it is a suffering beyond your conception!

[339]

You will feel and lament the death of your child, but you will only recollect him a baby of fourteen weeks, but I am his mother and have carried him in my arms and have fed him at my bosom, and have watched over him by day and by night for nine months. I have seen him twice at the brink of the grave, but he has returned and recovered and smiled upon me like an angel,—and now I am lamenting that he is gone!"[85]

Coleridge replied at once, on April 23:

"Surely it is unnecessary for me to say how infinitely I languish to be in my native country, and with how many struggles I have remained even so long in Germany! I received your affecting letter, dated Easter Sunday; and, had I followed my impulses, I should have packed up and gone with Wordsworth and his sister, who passed through (and only passed through) this place two or three days ago. If they burn with such impatience to return to their native country, *they* who are all to each other, what must I feel with everything pleasant and everything valuable and everything dear to me at a distance—here, where I may truly say my only amusement is—to labour! But it is, in the strictest sense of the word, impossible to collect what I have to collect in less than six weeks from this day; yet I read and transcribe from eight to ten hours every day. Nothing could support me but the knowledge that if I return now we shall be embarrassed and in debt; and the moral certainty that having done what I am doing we shall be more than *cleared*—not to add that so large a work with so great a quantity and variety of information from sources so scattered and so little known, even in Germany, will of course establish my character for industry and erudition certainly; and, I would fain hope, for reflection and genius. This day in June I hope and trust that I shall be in England. Oh that the vessel could but land at Shurton Bars! Not that I should wish to see you and Poole immediately on my landing. No!—the sight, the touch of my native country, were sufficient for one *whole* feeling, the most deep unmingled emotion—but then and after a lonely walk of three miles—then, first of *all*, whom I knew, to see you and my *Friend*! It lessens the delight of the thought of my return that I must get at you through a tribe of *acquaintances*, damping the freshness of one's joy! My poor little baby! At this time I see the corner of the room where his cradle stood—and his cradle too—and I cannot help seeing him in the cradle. Little lamb! and the snow would not melt on his limbs! I have some faint recollections that he had that difficulty of breathing once before I left England —or was it Hartley?"[86]

Coleridge goes on to describe a Christmas custom in Germany.[87] This letter suggests that for the moment Coleridge has exhausted his emotions but not his reluctance to meet unpleasantness. Although he worked hard at Göttingen, his day was not all labour. Although at times—possibly for the greater part of the time—he longed to be in England and at home, there were periods, frequent periods, when his occupation and his pleasures alike filled his mind to the exclusion of all regrets or longings. And although it need not be doubted that his reason for not returning immediately was sufficiently genuine at the time he wrote his letter, his melancholy was not so long-lasting, his labours were neither so arduous nor so engrossing that they did not permit of excursions. He wrote, on May 6:

"My dear Poole, my dear Poole!—I am homesick. Society is a burden to me; and I find relief only in labour. So I read and transcribe from morning till night, and never in my life have I worked so hard as this last month, for indeed I must sail over an ocean of matter with almost spiritual speed, to do what I have to do in the time in which I *will* do it or leave it undone! O my God, how I long to be at home! My *whole Being* so yearns after you, that when I think of the moment of our meeting, I catch the fashion of German joy, rush into your arms, and embrace you. Methinks my hand would swell if the whole force of my feeling were crowded there. Now the Spring comes, the vital sap of my affections rises as in a tree! . . . But these leafless Spring Woods! Oh, how I long to hear you whistle to the Rippers![88] There are a multitude of nightingales here (poor things! they sang in the snow). I thought of my own verses on the nightingale, only because I thought of Hartley, my *only* Child. Dear lamb! I hope he won't be dead before I get home. There are moments in which I have such a power of life within me, such a *conceit* of it, I mean, that I lay the blame of my child's death to my absence. *Not intellectually*; but I have a strange sort of sensation, as if, while I was present, none could die whom I entirely loved, and doubtless it was no absurd idea of yours that there may be unions and connections out of the visible world."[89]

Five days after writing these words, Coleridge had set out, with a son of Blumenbach, Carlyon, Greenough, the two Parrys and Chester, on a Whitsun tour of the Hartz mountains. The younger Parry, Frederick, being subject to asthma was accommodated with a white pony, on which the party's spare clothes were fastened. There had been some talk of Wordsworth joining the party, but as he had insisted upon Dorothy accompanying him and some of the men considered the journey unsuitable for a woman, the plan fell through.[90] This excursion, says Carlyon, found Coleridge at his most cheerful. He talked most of the time —on Shakespeare, the Miracle plays, peasant customs, Sachs, and the English Divines, particularly Jeremy Taylor, whose prose as well as his theology Coleridge so much admired, to mention but a few of the subjects he touched upon. He defined sublimity as a "suspension of the powers of comparison," [91] pointing out that "no animal but man can be struck with wonder." [92] He adduced as an additional reason for believing in the immortality of the soul that the works of man, though intended, as far as could be seen, for his pleasure, outlast him on earth.[93] As usual, when Coleridge was in high spirits, puns abounded.[94] The expedition went by way of Poelen and St. Andreasberg to the Brocken, coming back in a half-circle, through Elbingerode, where Coleridge wrote in an album his lines, *I stood on Brocken's sovran height*; Blankenburg, where, looking over the Duke of Brunswick's castle, the party was highly diverted by a great rent which had appeared in Coleridge's coat; [95] Wernigerode; Hartzburg; Goslar and Clausthal. In the Brocken Stammbuch, Coleridge wrote his 'homesick' lines—'*Tis sweet to him who all the week*.

The day before they returned to Göttingen, the 17th, Coleridge wrote to Sarah, from Clausthal. He described the journey to the Brocken and down again, partly in verse; but the only notable words were those which confirmed once more Coleridge's preoccupation with the unity of the world, his readiness to discover symbolism in nature:

> "Now again is nothing but firs and pines above, below, around us! How awful is the deep unison of their undividable murmur; what a one thing it is—it is a sound that impresses the dim notion of the Omnipresent!" [96]

Yet Coleridge did work hard; almost as hard, if by no means as interruptedly, as he gives Poole to understand. In the letter of May 6, he tells Poole something of the Wordsworths, who had visited him for the second time,[97] and with whom, it seemed, all was not well—although the tendency of Coleridge to read his own feelings into those of others cannot be disregarded. He announces in firm not to say virtuous tones his resistance to their blandishments. But like so many of Coleridge's utterances, the firmness was less a statement or sign of determination than the expression of a pious hope that, having laid down in black and white a course of conduct, he would thereby be strengthened sufficiently to pursue it:

"Wordsworth and his sister passed through here, as I have informed you. I walked with them five English miles, and spent a day with them. They were melancholy and hypped. W. was affected to tears at the thought of not being near me—wished me of course to live in the North of England near Sir Frederick Vane's great library. I told him that, independent of the expense of removing, and the impropriety of taking Mrs Coleridge to a place where she would have no acquaintance, two insurmountable objections, the library was no inducement to me—for I wanted old books chiefly, such as could be procured anywhere better than in a gentleman's new fashionable collection. Finally I told him plainly that *you* had been the man in whom *first* and in whom alone I had felt an *anchor*! With all my other connections I felt a dim sense of insecurity and uncertainty, terribly incompatible. W. was affected *to tears*, very much affected; but he deemed the vicinity of a library absolutely *necessary* to his health, nay to his existence. It is painful to me, too, to think of not living near him; for he is a *good* and *kind* man, and the only one whom in *all* things I feel my superior—and you will believe me when I say that I have few feelings more pleasurable than to find myself, in intellectual faculties, an inferior.

"But my resolve is fixed, *not to leave you till you leave me*! I still think that Wordsworth will be disappointed in his expectation of relief from reading without society; and I think it highly probable that where I live, there he will live; unless he should find in the North any person or persons, who can feel and understand him, and reciprocate and react on him. My many weaknesses are of some advantage to me; they unite me more with the great mass of my fellow-beings—but dear Wordsworth appears to me to have hurtfully segregated and isolated his being. Doubtless his delights are more deep and sublime; but he has likewise more hours that prey upon the flesh and blood. With regard to *Hancock's* house, if I can get no place within a mile or two of Stowey I must try to get that; but I confess I like it not—not to say that it is not altogether pleasant to live directly opposite to a person who had behaved so rudely to Mrs Coleridge. But these are in the eye of reason trifles, and if no other house can be got—in my eye, too, they shall be trifles." [98]

Coleridge goes on to give some very general details of his work:

"The Professors here," he says, "are exceedingly kind to all the Englishmen, but to me they pay the most flattering attentions, especially Blumenbach and Eichhorn. Nothing can be conceived more delightful than Blumenbach's lectures, and, in conversation, he is, indeed, a most interesting man. The learned Orientalist Tychsen has given me instruction in the Gothic and Theotuscan languages, which I can now read pretty well; and hope in the course of a year to be thoroughly acquainted with all the languages of the North, both German and Celtic. I find being learned is a mighty easy thing, compared with any study else. My God! a miserable poet must he be, and a despicable metaphysician, whose acquirements have not cost him more trouble and reflection than all the learning of Tooke, Porson, and Parr united. With the advantage of a great library, learning is nothing—methinks, merely a sad excuse for being idle. Yet a man gets reputation by it, and reputation gets money; and for reputation I don't care a damn, but money—yes—money I must get by all honest ways. Therefore at the end of two or three years, if God grant me life, expect to see me come out with some horribly learned book, full of manuscript quotations from Laplandish and Patagonian authors, possibly, on the striking resemblance of the Sweogothian and Sanscrit languages, and so on!" [99]

Then follows a typical Coleridge note:

"N.B. Whether a sort of parchment might not be made of old shoes; and whether apples should not be grafted on oak saplings, as the fruit would be the same as now, but the wood far more valuable? *Two ideas of mine*—To extract *aqua fortis* from cucumbers is a discovery not yet made, but sugar from *bete*, oh! all Germany is mad about it. I have seen the sugar sent to Blumenbach from Achard the great chemist, and it is good enough. They say that an hundred pounds weight of *bete* will make twelve pounds of sugar, and that there is no expense in the preparation. It is the *Beta altissima*, belongs to the *Beta vulgaris*, and in Germany is called *Runkelrübe*. Its leaves resemble those of the common red *bete*. It is in shape like a clumsy nine pin and about the size of a middling turnip. The flesh is white but has rings of a reddish cast. I will bring over a quantity of the seed." [100]

He tells Poole that he hopes to be home in the last week of June, and ends, "My dear Poole! don't let little Hartley die before I come home. That's silly—true—and burst into tears as I wrote it." [101]

The description of the Brocken trip was carried on by Coleridge in a letter to Poole written from Göttingen the day after the party returned, on May 19. This very detailed letter takes the journey to within seven miles of Göttingen, Coleridge promising the remainder in a further letter. He is, however, dissatisfied with his efforts at description: "What can be the cause that I am so miserable a describer?" he asks. "Is it that I understand neither the practice nor the principles of Painting? or is it not true, that others have really succeeded? I could half suspect that what are deemed fine descriptions, produce their effects almost purely by a charm of words, with which and with whose combinations, we associate *feelings* indeed, but no distinct *Images*." [102]

He expects to leave Göttingen in about two weeks; but asks Poole to warn Sarah that he may be a week late—a warning of which it is difficult to believe Sarah stood in great need, since Coleridge had already overstepped the date by which she had entreated and he had promised he would return. [103]

On May 21 Coleridge wrote from Göttingen to Josiah Wedgwood. He had written him "six huge letters," [104] he says, all of which had been awaiting the departure to England of Hamilton who had promised to take them with him but who had been delayed. Finally, Coleridge determined to take them home himself, posting the explanatory letter only.

In one of these letters, which certainly merits the description of "huge," covering seven printed pages, Coleridge sets out to give "a definite idea of the word Bauer." [105] It is difficult to do so, he says "without running thro' the origin and history of this Class." [106] This he proceeds to do; with such thoroughness that at the end of the letter he has only reached the Middle Ages. "In the next," he says, "I will give the distinct History of the Hanoverian Bauers to the present day—and in a third the account of them, as they are, in agriculture, size of property, education, etc." [107]

But while this historical essay does credit to Coleridge's researches, the most interesting part of the letter, as is so often the case, is to be found in what Coleridge calls "something like a digression."

" . . . the Roman Empire was too large, and too incongruous in it's parts, for that *national* Religion, which built on national Events and working on the imagination thro' definite forms and on the feelings thro' incessant association of the mythology with the Laws and Scenes, which were *exclusively* theirs, had effected wonders on the Greeks and early Romans! for this, it was grown too large. It gradually therefore suffered the National Religion to sink into contempt, and took up a World-Religion—such as had always existed in Asia, from the largeness of the Asiatic Empires. To this cause I am inclined to attribute the easy Propagation of Christianity—which was in truth the World-Religion common to the great Empires in Asia, divested of Asiatic forms and ceremonies. The consequence of Christianity or a World-Religion as opposed to a *National* Religion appears to me universally this— Personal and Domestic Duties are far better attended to, but Patriotism and all Enthusiasm for the aggrandisement of a country as a country, are weakened or extinguished. In Greece and Rome . . . under the influence of a *national* Religion, we find sorry Fathers, bad Husbands, and cruel Masters: but glowing and generous Patriots. In Christian Countries an excellent Private Character totally devoid of all Public Spirit. . . . But on this subject a man might write a volume and bring out some curious observations on the March of Things in France; and how far a Passion for Statues etc., will be able to smuggle a sort of Idolatry into the Feelings altho' it *may be* too late in the World to introduce it into the understanding. The more I think, the more I am convinced that the greatest of differences is produced when in the one case the feelings are worked upon thro' the Imagination and the Imagination thro' definite Forms (i.e. the Religion of Greece and Rome); and in the other cases where the Feelings are worked upon by Hopes and Fears purely individual, and the Imagination is kept barren in definite Forms and only in cooperation with the Understanding labours after an obscure and indefinite Vastness— this is Christianity, My dear Friend! I have made something like a digression—but it is the first, and shall be the last." [108]

Meanwhile Sarah was spending weeks of unhappiness and perplexity with the Southeys at Westbury. Her baby was dead, and despite what Poole had written to Coleridge, or others might think, she had not forgotten, nor was she ever to forget the little Berkeley while she lived. [109] Then Samuel (a form of address which Coleridge particularly detested but which Sarah used invariably to him and of him to others) had failed to make adequate provision for her. She had no money left and her expenses had, of course, been unusually heavy. Twice, at least, unwilling to borrow from those at Bristol, she was obliged to ask Poole for money.[110] "With regard to money, my Love!" writes her husband light-heartedly, "Poole can write to Mr Wedgwood, if it is not convenient for him to let you have it." [111] But Sarah did not wish it to be convenient. She detested this haphazard, this careless attitude towards money. She dreaded the uncertainty of not knowing where the next penny was to come from. She disliked dependence upon others; unable to conceive a mind to which the asking of a favour presented no difficulties, no obstacle of pride, because conscious of its own readiness, its eagerness to give in other directions. In a well-ordered household—such as the one, for instance, in which she was then staying—there was no hand-to-mouth improvidence, but a steady supply of money, carefully laid out. Sarah regarded her sister's husband with a wistful and increasing admiration.

This admiration was intensified when it was seen by Sarah that the *Lyrical Ballads* were not a great, an immediate success. She writes Poole, her dismay not unmingled with triumph, "The Lyrical Ballads are laughed at and disliked by all with very few excepted." [112] Again she tells him the news from Bristol, "The Lyrical Ballads are not liked at all by any." [113] There was no doubt about it. Why, Southey himself, that model of propriety, of good sense and literary success, had actually pronounced the final word upon these unfortunate poems. He wished to be kind, but he must be just; they had failed. That was his considered opinion. [114]

Sarah regarded the situation with mixed feelings. Was Samuel not a great poet after all? Had his intimacy with the Wordsworths led him only to this—a book of poems reckoned a failure, his own special contribution specially damned? Sarah's doubts about Coleridge's claims to greatness, and more especially about the benefits of the Wordsworths' influence upon him, now seemed confirmed. No fame for him! And as a natural corollary, no greatness. How could there be merit in his work if it did not call forth general esteem? How, indeed! Southey had spoken.

From that moment, her husband's literary endeavours, never very acceptable in Sarah's sight save as possible providers of a substantial or at least regular income, were as dust in her eyes. She did not cease to love Coleridge, but her respect for his work died. Understanding of it, she had never possessed.

But there was a further embarrassment and source of worry to be met by Sarah at this time. People in Bristol, mindful of the wooing Coleridge, ardent pantisocrat, fanatical anti-Government man, of recent years, his tumultuous lectures not yet forgotten, hastened to ask his wife if the rumours they had heard of Coleridge's conversion to the Government cause were true. Sarah did not know. How could she tell which party Coleridge favoured at any given moment? She applied to Poole: "It is very unpleasant to me to be often asked if Coleridge has changed his political sentiments—for I know not properly how to reply—pray furnish me."[115]

"Pray furnish me." How often can the inevitable end of a marriage be summed up so concisely, in three words? "Pray furnish me," Sarah asked. Unfortunately it was beyond the power of Poole, or of anyone else, to furnish her. So far as knowledge of her husband's mind was concerned, she was destined to pass uncomprehending to her grave.

There were further grievances forming. The results of Coleridge's visit to Germany were not, in Sarah's eyes, to seem commensurate with the sacrifices she had endured to make the visit possible and pleasant. Not only had her husband raised up a mighty debt—he had anticipated most of his Wedgwood annuity for 1800, had overdrawn more than his due for 1799, and in addition had borrowed from Carlyon [116]—but the tangible, the immediate effects of that year abroad appeared negligible and profitless. The work which was to establish his character "for industry and erudition " [117] and which detained him in Germany, was not destined to appear. His Life of Lessing never reached a stage further than the collecting of materials and perusal of the great German's works.

When finally Coleridge returned to England, he had little indeed to show Sarah for his stay in Germany; he had accomplished, it appeared, only a fraction of the purpose he set out to achieve. Kant and Schelling remained unread. Hartley remained unconfuted. Coleridge's personal philosophy remained nebulous, undecided, unproven. Yet the difference between achievement and aim was, on this occasion at least, due less to indolence than to a combination of under-estimation of the task he wished to accomplish, and of discoveries made when once familiar with the German language that necessitated changes of plan. For instance, his decision to write a Life of Lessing to recover money spent in Germany; and his conclusion, quite early, that: "Instead of troubling others with my crude notions . . . I was thenceforward better employed in attempting to store my own head with the wisdom of others." [118]

Yet he accomplished much; more than his most ardent friend could have hoped. "What have I done in Germany?" [119] he writes in the Wedgwood letter of May 21, anticipating what must have been the natural desire of his financial supporters for information:

"I have learned the language, both high and low German, I can read both, and speak the former so fluently, that it must be a fortune for a German to be in my company, that is, I have words enough and phrases enough, and I arrange them tolerably; but my pronunciation is hideous. 2ndly, I can read the oldest German, the Frankish, and the Swabian. 3rdly, I have attended the lectures on Physiology, Anatomy, and Natural History, with regularity, and have endeavoured to understand these subjects. 4thly, I have read and made collections for a history of the 'Belles Lettres,' in Germany, before the time of Lessing: and 5thly, very large collections for a *Life of Lessing*; to which I was led by the miserably bad and unsatisfactory biographies that have been hitherto given, and by my personal acquaintance with two of Lessing's friends. Soon after I came into Germany, I made up my mind fully not to publish anything concerning my Travels, as people call them; yet I soon perceived that with all possible economy, my expenses would be greater than I could justify, unless I did something that would to a moral certainty repay them. . . . Accordingly, my main business at Göttingen has been to read all the numerous controversies in which Lessing was engaged, and the works of all those German poets before the time of Lessing, which I could not afford to buy. For these last four months, with the exception of last week, in which I visited the Hartz, I have worked harder than I trust in God Almighty I shall ever have occasion to work again: this endless transcription is such a body-and-soul-wearying purgatory." [120]

Yet perhaps the greatest benefit which his eleven months in Germany had conferred upon him, was the clarification and strengthening of the resolve, now mentioned specifically for the first time, to attempt in one great work, his *Opus Maximum*, to set forth a philosophy which would embrace both philosophy and religion, reason and understanding, would satisfy both head and heart:

> "I shall have bought thirty pounds' worth of books," he says, "chiefly metaphysics, and with a view to the one work, to which I hope to dedicate in silence, the prime of my life." [121]

A little earlier in the same letter a sentence shows clearly how aware Coleridge was of the inadequacy of mere statement, from whichever side it came: "Seiffmilts,[122] in his great work concerning the divine order and regularity in the destiny of the human race, has a chapter entitled a confutation of this idea; I read it with great eagerness, and found therein that this idea militated against the glory and goodness of God, and must therefore be false,—but further confutation found I none!" [123]

A considerable change of mind had taken place since April 1, 1796, when in a letter to Benjamin Flower, long forgotten by Coleridge, he had written, after talking about Bishop Watson's refutation of Paine: "The most formidable Infidel is Lessing, the author of *Emilia Galotti*; I ought to have written, *was*, for he is dead. His book is not yet translated, and is entitled, in German, *Fragments of an Anonymous Author*. It unites the wit of Voltaire with the subtlety of Hume and the profound erudition of *our* Lardner. I had some thoughts of translating it with an Answer, but gave it up, lest men, whose tempers and hearts incline them to disbelief, should get hold of it; and, though the answers are satisfactory to my mind, they may not be equally so to the minds of others." [124]

Now, far from writing a refutation of Lessing's work, he was studying it assiduously with a view to a comprehensive Life of the author; having discovered in the course of his residence in Germany that Lessing, the literary critic, was more worthy of praise than Lessing, the theologian, of reproach, "I chose the *Life of Lessing*," he told Josiah Wedgwood, "because it would give me an opportunity of conveying under a better name than my own ever will be, opinions which I deem of the highest importance." [125]

Not the least difficult of Sarah's problems was to get Coleridge home. She had besought him to return by May.[126] He would do so, he assured her. He would not stay a moment longer than he was obliged.[127] Unfortunately, he alone was the judge of the moment when his work in Germany could be considered as completed. He yearned to be with his family and friends again; yet there was work still to be done—and the talks and rambles with the Göttingen Englishmen were undeniably pleasant. Perhaps, too, he still hoped, as Parry said, "to make metaphysicians of them."[128] For a few more weeks, therefore, he compromised. He worked hard; but he did not omit to play; and so justified in his own mind his procrastination and stifled for the time his longing for England.

One of their excursions—to the castle of the Count Birdlipsch—displayed Coleridge in a typical attitude. The party, having lost their way, struggled after dark into Cassel. At the inn there they were first met by a woman who refused them anything but an unclean floor to lie upon. A man, entering the room afterwards, appeared more amenable and there seemed a good chance that they might after all have fresh straw to lie upon, if not food to eat. Unhappily, Coleridge conceived it his duty to point out to the woman how far she had strayed from the principles of Christianity. His remarks were, not unnaturally, interpreted as a reflection upon the religious convictions of the Hessians. The whole party were driven from the inn, chased by an irate crowd, and had to count themselves fortunate that they escaped bodily injury.[129]

Another excursion, on June 12th, to Wilhemsthal, was memorable chiefly for a rent in Coleridge's breeches which obliged him to wait until the tailor at Göttingen had recovered sufficient sobriety to mend them.[130] Coleridge slept the night at Minden and found the party the next day, not without difficulty, at Cassel.

But these outings were as nothing to the next flight of Coleridge's enthusiasm for walking tours. He suddenly conceived the idea of forming a party to tour Denmark, Sweden, and Norway. Greenough would go. Carlyon would go. Charles Parry wrote off to his father to try and obtain permission to join the party. Enthusiasm mounted high. Then, perhaps fortunately, word did not come from the Parry family before Coleridge had left Göttingen for home. A day or two later, the answer arrived. Parry

[351]

could go. The brothers hurriedly took coach for Brunswick and caught up the travellers. But by that time, actually on his way to England, Coleridge's enthusiasm for Scandinavia had cooled. A map was bought and studied. After lengthy discussion, Coleridge announced that he could not then undertake the expedition. But he would gladly go with them the following spring.[131]

When, at midsummer, his longing for home finally overcame him, Coleridge abruptly set straight off. After a farewell dinner at the Blumenbach house,[132] he left Göttingen in such a hurry that the boxes were not ready and he and Chester were obliged to leave all their books and spare clothes to be forwarded.[133]

It was agreed that Coleridge and Chester must see the sun rise and set from the Brocken before they left Germany.[134] They took a coach. Carlyon and Greenough accompanied them. Then, since Coleridge was in the district, he felt he must visit Woolfenbüttel and examine the Lessing relics. The party walked on to Blankenburg, then by coach to Helmstadt, Woolfenbüttel, which they reached on June 28 and left two days later, arriving at Brunswick on the last day of the month. At Brunswick they visited Richmond, the Duchess of Brunswick's palace. Here, too, Coleridge met a Professor von Zimmerman, who wanted to know what Kant meant "by saying first that the existence of God cannot possibly be proved, and then that this impossibility is the best proof of His existence." [135] Coleridge for once held his peace. He had yet to fathom Kant.

On July 3 Coleridge and Chester parted from the others and made their way to Hamburg and Cuxhaven whilst Greenough, Carlyon, and the Parrys returned to Göttingen. The boxes had not yet arrived. Coleridge's distress was comical.[136] At Cuxhaven he and Chester still awaited the precious boxes of clothes and, for Coleridge, the even more precious box containing his £30 of "metaphysical" books,[137] for the most part unread—books which were destined finally to unseat Hartley from his long resting-place in Coleridge's mind and to present to Coleridge, in Kant particularly, the man who, more than any other, was to take possession of his mind and heart "as with a giant's hand." [138]

12

BUT THESE BOOKS of German philosophy were not yet destined to influence their new owner. When Coleridge finally arrived in England with Chester towards the end of July 1799, he hurried back to Stowey, with no more than a brief stop on the way to greet his friends.[1]

One of his first actions, after the rapture of homecoming had worn down, was to approach Southey and try to effect some sort of reconciliation. Doubtless he did so partly at Sarah's entreaty; but his gratitude to Southey would alone have persuaded him to the attempt. Southey had arranged for the funeral of little Berkeley, Southey had kept the distraught mother at his home for weeks. And if the sight of Southey's steadiness, his regular supply of money, his increasing success and his utter freedom from any suspicion of acting incomprehensibly, had driven Sarah inexorably from hope of comprehension of her husband, and perhaps from the wish to comprehend—even so Southey, though not blameless, was not without excuse. There is reason to believe that already this upright man was finding some difficulty in keeping his virtue to himself. Indeed, the temptation to compare himself to Coleridge, even at this early stage, must have been considerable.

But of this Coleridge knew nothing. If he suspected it, he let the thought remain unanalysed.

> "I am doubtful, Southey," he wrote, "whether the circumstances which impel me to write to you ought not to keep me silent, and, if it were only a feeling of delicacy, I should remain silent, for it is good to do all things in faith. But I have been absent, Southey! ten months, and if *you* knew that domestic affection was hard upon me, and that my own health was declining, would you not have shootings within you of an affection which ('though fallen, though changed') has played too important a part in the event of our lives and the formation of our character, ever to be *forgotten*? I am perplexed what to write, or how to state the object of my writing. Any participation in each other's moral being I do not wish, simply because I know enough of the mind

[353]

of man to know that [it] is impossible. But, Southey, we have similar talents, sentiments nearly similar, and kindred pursuits; we have likewise, in more than one instance, common objects of our esteem and love. I pray and intreat you, if we should meet at any time, let us not withhold from each other the outward expressions of daily kindliness; and if it be no longer in your power to soften your opinions, make your feelings at least more tolerant towards me—(a debt of humility which assuredly we all of us owe to our most feeble, imperfect, and self-deceiving nature). We are few of us good enough to know our own hearts, and as to the hearts of others, let us struggle to hope that they are better than we think them, and resign the rest to our common Maker."[2]

Southey's response to this appeal was a complaint that Coleridge had slandered him;[3] a statement which brought from Coleridge an impassioned denial, hinting strongly that Lamb and Lloyd were the real authors of the misunderstanding, and referring Southey to the testimony of Poole and Wordsworth:

"Suffice it to avow calmly and on my honor as a man and gentleman, that I never charged you with aught but your deep and implacable enmity towards me, and that I founded this on the same authorisation on which you founded your belief of my supposed hatred to you—Southey! for nearly three years Poole has been the repository of my very thoughts. I have not written or received any letter of importance which he has not seen. For more than one whole year I was with Wordsworth almost daily, and frequently for weeks together. Our conversations concerning you have been numberless, and during the affair with Lloyd under suppositions of a highly irritating kind. If Wordsworth and Poole will not affirm to you solemnly that I have ever thought and spoken of you with affection and respect, never charging you with aught else than your restless enmity to me and attributing even that to *Delusion*, I abandon myself for ever to the disesteem of every man whose esteem is worth having. You have received evidence to the contrary and I could shew you written testimonies contradictory to some sentences of your last letter. Yet on my soul I believe you. I do not require you to do at present the same with regard to me. But I pray you, let us be at least in the possibility of understanding each others moral being; and with regard to what you have heard, to think a little on the state of mind in which those were *from* whom you heard it."[4]

His appeal was borne out by Poole in a letter of August 8, sent by special messenger to Minehead, where Southey was staying:

"in the many conversations I have had with Coleridge concerning yourself," wrote Poole, "he has never discovered the least personal enmity against, but, on the contrary, the strongest affection for you stifled only by the untoward events of your separation. . . . As for C. Lloyd, it would be cruel to attribute *his* conduct to aught but a diseased mind." [5]

Southey, who was by this time becoming aware of Lloyd's shortcomings as a friend—"I never knew a man so delighted with the exteriors of friendship," he wrote. "I love him, but I cannot esteem him, and so I told him" [6]—accepted this assurance and the two families met once again in amity. At Stowey, something of the old companionship crept back. "Here I am, and have been some days wholly immersed in conversation," wrote Southey on the 20th of the month. "The hours slip away, and the ink dries upon the pen in my hand." [7] They engaged, probably on Southey's suggestion, upon a joint poem—the squib *The Devil's Thoughts*, later *The Devil's Walk*. The idea behind the poem was "A meeting of devils might make fine confessions of whom they had been visiting." [8] The method of composition was exceedingly free and easy:

> There, while the one was shaving,
>   Would he the song begin;
> And the other, when he heard it at breakfast,
>   In ready accord join in.[9]

They sent the poem to the *Morning Post*, where it appeared as an anonymous contribution on September 6. It was an instant success and caused a minor sensation. Speculation was busy naming the author; the true names not being disclosed publicly until many years later.[10]

Southey discussed with Coleridge the possibility of obtaining from him some contributions to the second number of the *Annual Anthology*, a miscellany of poems by Southey and his friends; it was also agreed that Coleridge and his visitor should collaborate in an epic poem with Mohammed as the subject—a start being made on the spot.[11]

Nor was this the end of Coleridge's good intentions. He returned from Germany, it would seem, loving not only his country but the people in it, the more; determined, for a time, and while no one reminded him of it, to do his duty. Thus, after a week or two, they all left together; the Southeys to try and find lodgings somewhere on the coast; the Coleridges to visit Ottery. Southey, who called at Ottery from Sidmouth, told his friend, John May, that: "We were all a good deal amused by the old lady. She could not hear what was going on, but seeing Samuel arguing with his brothers, took it for granted that he must have been wrong, and cried out, 'Ah, if your poor father had been alive, he'd soon have convinced you.' " [12] Coleridge, however, soon discovered the danger of parading his opinions too blatantly before the family circle if peace was to be maintained and his visit accounted a success.

"George and the colonel," he told Poole, "good men as times go—very good men—but alas! we have neither tastes nor feelings in common. This I wisely learnt from their conversation, and did not suffer them to learn it from mine. What occasion for it? Hunger and thirst—roast fowls, mealy potatoes, pies, and clouted cream! bless the inventors of them! An honest philosopher may find therewith preoccupation for his mouth, keeping his heart and brain, the latter in his scull, the former in the pericardium some five or six inches from the roots of his tongue! Church and King! Why I drink Church and King, mere cutaneous scabs of loyalty which only ape the king's evil, but affect not the interior of one's health. Mendicant sores! it requires some little caution to keep them open, but they heal of their own accord. Who (such a friend as I am to the system of fraternity) could refuse such a toast at the table of a clergyman and a colonel, his brother? So, my dear Poole! I live in peace." [13]

He was able, from time to time, to obtain consolation for this forbearance in the shape of visits to Exeter and "the other party." [14] Of this, he "dined with a Mr Northmore, a pupil of Wakefield, who possesses a fine house half a mile from Exeter. In his boyhood he was at my father's school. . . . But Southey and self called upon him as authors—he having edited a Tryphiodorus and part of Plutarch, and being a notorious anti-ministerialist and free-thinker. He welcomed us as he ought, and we met at dinner Hucks (at whose house I dine Wednesday), the man who toured with me in Wales and afterwards published his 'Tour,' Kendall, a poet, who really looks like a man of genius, pale and gnostic, has the merit of being a Jacobin or so, but is a shallowist—and finally a Mr Banfill, a man of sense, information, and various literature, and most perfectly a gentleman—in short a pleasant man. At his house we dine tomorrow. Northmore himself is an honest, vehement sort of a fellow who splutters out all his opinions like a fiz-gig, made of gunpowder not thoroughly dry, sudden and explosive, yet ever with a certain adhesive blubberliness of elocution. Shallow! shallow! A man who can read Greek well, but shallow! Yet honest, too, and who ardently wishes the well-being of his fellow-men, and believes that without more liberty and more equality this well-being is not possible. He possesses a most noble library." [15]

About the beginning of September, the Coleridges left Ottery and joined the Southeys, who, trying to find suitable lodgings until their cottage at Burton was enlarged, had settled for the time in Exeter.[16] After a few days, on the 11th, Coleridge set off with Southey for a short walking tour. They visited Paignton, Dartmouth, Totnes, and part of Dartmoor, and were back in Exeter in five days. Neither of them was particularly impressed with the country through which they passed: ". . . in general," Coleridge told Poole, "what of Devonshire I have lately seen is tame to Quantock, Porlock, Culbone, and Linton "; [17] though he comments later on "the interesting Bovey waterfall [Becky Fall] through that wild dell of ashes which leads to Ashburton, most like the approach to upper Matterdale." [18]

On the 24th, Coleridge, Sarah, and Hartley returned to Stowey. The little party was not quite at ease, mentally or physically. Young Hartley was believed to have caught the itch, apparently from Fanny, the maid, who left them the morning after they reached Stowey.

"As neither Sara or I have yet any symptoms of infection, I hope and trust, that you and Edith and Eliza are safe," Coleridge wrote Southey the same day. "Believe me tho' obliged to bear up against the *Fresh* [outburst] of my wife's hypersuperlative Grief on the occasion I have nevertheless suffered much anxiety lest poor Eliza or Mrs S. should have been colonized by those damn'd invisible skin-moles. Moses [Hartley] received the Catholic sacrament of unction for the first time last night. He was very merry during the performance, singing or chanting, I be a funny Fellow and my name is Brimstonello. I doubt not that all will be well—well by tomorrow, or at farthest next day—for he slept quiet and has never once scratched himself since his embrimstonement." [19]

Coleridge commissions Southey to ask Dyer the bookseller, "whom my Brother names a dark-hearted Jacobin, is really an honest man and I like him," [20] respecting copies of Bacon's works (for Poole), Milton's prose works, and the sermons of Jeremy Taylor. "The money shall be payed him," he goes on, "by some of my relations in Exeter." [21]

Coleridge assures Southey that he will "go on with the Mohammed" [22]—but he adds the warning "tho' something I must do for pecuniary emoluments." [23] He has had a new idea for raising money: "I think of writing a schoolbook." [24]

He spent a great deal of his time, however, reading Spinoza, whose work, since the visit to Germany, he had rediscovered with much enthusiasm; breaking off only for brief intervals to weave fresh plans for the making of money to repay his debts and overdrawn annuity—plans as ephemeral as the moments he devoted to them.

"Our little Hovel is almost afloat," he tells Southey a few days later; "poor Sara tired off her legs with servantry—the young one fretful and noisy from confinement exerts his activities on all forbidden things—the house stinks of sulphur. I however sunk in Spinoza, remain as undisturbed as a Toad in a Rock; that is to say, when my rheumatic pains are asleep, for you must know that our apothecary persuaded me and Sara to wear Mercurial Girdles, as Preventives, accordingly Sara arrayed herself with this Cest of the Caledonian Venus and Seke [Psyche]. On the first day I walked myself into a perspiration, and O Christus Jesus! how I stunk! Convinced as I was before of the necessity of all parts of the human body, I now received double-damning nose-conviction, that all my pores were necessary *Holes* with a vengeance. I walked one Magnum Mercuri Excrementum, cursed with the faculty of self-sentiency—but the Nose is the most placable of all the senses, and to one's own evil odours one can reconcile oneself almost as easily as to one's own Vices. But whether I caught cold or no, I cannot tell; but the next day a fit of the Rheumatism laid hold of me from the small of my back down to the calves of my Legs, shooting thro' me like hot arrows headed with adder's Teeth: since my Rheumatic Fever at school I have suffered nothing like it! Of course, I threw off my girdle—for such damned Twitches! I would rather have old Scratch himself, whom all the Brimstone in Hell can't cure, than endure them! I am still however not free from them—tho' the latter attacks have decreased in violence —you'd laugh to see how pale and haggard I look—and by way

[358]

of a Clincher, I am almost certain that Hartley has not had the Itch." [25]

He then expatiates on his plans for money-making. Southey had suggested that Coleridge 'write up' [26] the letters descriptive of Germany; but Coleridge rejected the idea, as he did that of attempting to make money by writing poetry. "As to a volume of Poems," he writes, "I am not in a poetical mood, and moreover am resolved to publish nothing with my name till my Great Work. But the School Book which I am planning will I think be a lucrative speculation." [27]

Coleridge asks Southey to approach Taylor of Norwich for the loan of two books necessary to the compilation of his school book—"Herder's Ideas for the History of the Human Race, I do not accurately remember the German Title, the second, Zimmerman's Geographie der Menschen." [28]

He was toying with the idea of another and even more familiar plan. "I have very serious Thoughts of trying to get a couple of Pupils, very serious ones." [29]

The letter ends with an anecdote of Hartley. "Young Brimstonello is fast asleep—he is a quaint boy. When I told him you had sent your love to him in a Letter, he sat and thought and thought, and at last burst into a fit of Laughter." [30]

Despite his aches and pains, Coleridge managed, as usual, to spread a precious leaven of humour through the Poole household. "My dear fellow," he once told Thelwall, "I laugh more and talk more nonsense in a week than [most] other people do in a year." [31]

It was and it remained the truth, if not the whole truth, about him for some years to come. Indeed, his humour, though it was to pass through lean times, never entirely deserted him. For this— his mirth, his intense liveliness, even when it had origin in vanity, and for his interest in others, he was beloved, more readily— indeed, almost spontaneously—by many who cared not at all for his learning and poetical genius.

At this time he wrote his two-word letter, "Thank you!" [32] to Thomas Ward, Poole's little apprentice, whose admiration of his master's friend came close to worship, and who, by taking careful copies of Coleridge's letters to Poole, rendered a service of no mean value to posterity. In this instance Coleridge had thanked Ward in a *"pen*tagonal" [33] punning letter for cutting him some pens which had, in fact, been cut by Govatt, the clerk. Ward then sent over a bundle of pens, the product of his own labour. Coleridge's reply illustrates a not unimportant facet of his nature and indicates unmistakably the happy relationship existing between him and the Poole circle.

> "Ward! I recant, I recant! Solemnly recant and disannul all praise, puff, and panegyric on your damned pens. I have this moment read the note wrapped round your last present, and last night therefore wrote my Elegy on the assured Belief that the first Batch were your's, and before I had tried the second. The second! I'm sick on't. Such execrable Blurrers of innocent white paper, Villains with uneven legs, Hexameter and Pentameter Pens— —Elegy—No—no—no—Elegies written with elegiac Pens (whose L E Gees I wish in your Guts) elegies on my poor Thoughts doing *pen*ance in white sheets, filthily illegible—My rage prevents me from writing sense—but o Govatt, dear Govatt! Kick that spectacle-mongering son of a Pen-hatchet out of creation, and remain alone, from the date herof, invested with the rank and office of Penmaker to my immortal Bardship, with all the dignities and emoluments thereunto annexed.
>
> "Given from Apollo's temple in the odoriferous Lime-Grove—alias Street—in what Olympiad our Inspiration knows not, but of the usurping Christian Æra 1799, Oct. 8.
>
> S. T. COLERIDGE.
>
> "Govatt is expected to express his Gratitude by an immediate Present of half a dozen pens—amended if indeed the reprobates be not incorrigible." [34]

About this time Coleridge first met Humphry Davy.[35] The establishment of Dr Beddoes' Pneumatic Institute, in which experiments with "medicated airs"[36] for the cure or relief of disease, particularly consumption, might take place, had been delayed by popular prejudice. Its existence was made possible, finally, by the generosity of Tom Wedgwood, already a patient of Beddoes, who gave £1000 for that purpose.[37] The money would be well spent, he told his brother Josiah, even if it did no more than discover

[360]

"that 'airs' are *not* efficacious in medicine."[38] A house was taken in Dowry Square, Hot Wells. The next step was to find a suitable man to work under Beddoes as Superintendent of the Institute. Such a man was discovered in the brilliant and enthusiastic young Cornishman, Humphry Davy, "the carver's son"[39] of Tredrea.

In October 1798, Davy had come up to Bristol to begin work. Although no more than nineteen years of age, he was not only a chemist of exceptional promise but had dabbled to some purpose in philosophy and poetry (he had contributed to Southey's *Annual Anthology*). Poole, Southey, and Cottle became friendly with him. Poole and Southey allowed him to experiment upon them. Poole "inhaled his nitrous oxide with the usual extraordinary and transitory sensations."[40] Southey was more enthusiastic: "Oh, Tom!" he wrote to his brother, "such a gas has Davy discovered, the gaseous oxyde! Oh, Tom! I have had some; it made me laugh and tingle in every toe and finger tip. Davy has actually invented a new pleasure, for which language has no name. Oh, Tom! I am going for more this evening; it makes one strong, and so happy! so gloriously happy!"[41]

All three were not only interested in Davy's work, but charmed with the man. Coleridge, who had attended Beddoes' lectures before leaving for Germany, and whose interest in his experiments was perhaps greater than that of the other two, was naturally eager to meet the man of whom he heard so much; and Davy was scarcely less eager.

It is possible that they met for the first time at Upcott, where Coleridge spent a few days with the Wedgwoods early in October.[42] Cottle, however, claims the honour of bringing the two men together.[43] In any event, they discovered an instant affection for one another; and a friendship began that was to exercise a considerable effect upon Coleridge's future. He had "never met with so extraordinary a *young man*,"[44] Coleridge told Tom Wedgwood. Coleridge, of course, must have his fill of nitrous oxide; and began at once to try his hand at innumerable experiments in Davy's laboratory—his interest in physical science, which had flickered uncertainly in the company of Dr Beddoes, now flaming out strongly.

On the 14th of October, he was back at Stowey, again in the toils of rheumatism. "I am harassed with the rheumatism in my head and shoulders, not without arm-and-thigh-twitches," he told Southey the next day, "—but when the pain intermits it leaves my sensitive frame *so* sensitive! My enjoyments are so deep, of the fire, of the candle, of the thought I am thinking, of the old folio I am reading, and the silence of the silent house is so *most and very* delightful, that upon my soul! the rheumatism is no such bad thing as *people make for.*"[45]

News of his acquaintance with Northmore at Exeter had been "creating very serious uneasinesses at Ottery."[46] "Northmore," he explained, "is so pre-eminently an offensive character to the aristocrats. He sent Paine's books as a present to a clergyman of my brother's acquaintance, a Mr Markes."[47]

The completion of *Christabel*, which Coleridge in a moment of enthusiasm had promised Southey as the opening poem for the next *Annual Anthology*, was not progressing. It had not in fact been attempted. There seemed little likelihood that it would be completed. But Coleridge did not tell Southey he felt unequal to the task. On the contrary. "I will set about 'Christabel' with all speed," he wrote; adding "but I do not think it a fit opening poem, and what I would humbly lay before you as the best plan of the next Anthologia, I will communicate shortly in another letter entirely on this subject. Mohammed I will not forsake; but my money-book I must write first."[48] But the money-book, like the completion of *Christabel*, remained a pleasant vision.

Lloyd was slipping fast from Southey's good graces, and Coleridge refers to the backslider with the genial tolerance of the man of conscious rectitude who, much maligned, is at last moving into sight of restitution.[49] He also mentions Lamb, not without humour: "I have great affection for Lamb," he tells Southey, "but I have likewise a perfect Lloyd-and-Lambophobia! Independent of the irritation attending an epistolary controversy with them, their *prose* comes so damn'd dear! Lloyd especially writes with a woman's fluency in a large rambling hand, most dull though profuse of feeling. I received from them in last quarter letters so many, that with the postage I might have bought Birch's Milton."[50]

A few days later, he and Sarah went to Bristol. The money-making scheme was at a standstill. No poetry moved in him. He could not read long for thought of the uncongenial work that faced him before he could concentrate upon his precious German books and the plan which already was forming in his mind and in which they were to play so great a part. The *Life of Lessing*, his offering to the Wedgwoods, was assuming the ominous lineaments of a duty, an obligation, and so was drawing away imperceptibly but surely from realization.

But all his troubles, all plans faded and were as nothing when disturbing news reached him of Wordsworth's illness. "I have heard from W. Wordsworth," he had written Poole a few weeks earlier. "He is ill, and seems not happy. Montague has played the fool, I expect, with him in pecuniary affairs."[51] He adds, "He renounces Alfoxden altogether."[52] Now it seemed that his friend's condition had taken a turn for the worse.

Wordsworth's continued indisposition drew Coleridge north. He left Bristol for Sockburn as soon as possible.[53] On October 22[54] he and Cottle set off for "my most important journey to the North."[55] Four days later, after an uneventful journey during which they passed through Tadcaster and Easingwold, the travellers arrived at Sockburn.[56]

This was the first time Coleridge and the Wordsworths had met since their day together at Göttingen in April. On reaching England in May, Wordsworth and Dorothy had gone straight to the Hutchinsons' farm at Sockburn-on-Tees, between Northallerton and Darlington. There they stayed, happy enough, Dorothy with her friend, William with the woman he loved, in the person of Mary Hutchinson.[57] They could not make up their minds where to settle. As late as July 4, Dorothy was writing Poole: "We are yet quite undetermined where we shall reside—we have no house in view at present. It is William's wish to be near a good library, and if possible in a pleasant country. If you hear of any place in your neighbourhood that will be likely to suit us, we shall be much obliged to you if you will take the trouble of writing to us."[58]

The truth, of course, was that Wordsworth was anxious to see Coleridge before committing himself. The firmness of Coleridge's refusal to leave Stowey and live in the north had not improbably deceived Wordsworth as much as it deceived his friend. It sounded eminently reasonable. How was he to know that it was thrown up as a screen from temptation, as a chain of uttered words that might bind the speaker to his duty? Wordsworth's nature had no need of such subterfuges; it felt itself sufficiently strong to take what it wanted, to put aside that which it must not have. But for all that, Wordsworth found himself more and more reluctant to face a future devoid of the constant companionship of Coleridge. He might be incomparably the stronger and more self-sufficient man. He might concur with some complaisance in his friend's estimate of the superiority of his poetic genius. But these advantages availed him little when the personality of Coleridge was withdrawn. For months the two men had been parted; and Wordsworth was not the less conscious of his loss than Coleridge. Indeed, at this time it is even possible that Wordsworth's strength and stability of character, his fellow-feeling as a poet, were not missed so painfully by Coleridge as was the admiring, the inspiring, the creative enthusiasm of Coleridge by his friend.

There was, after all, but one Coleridge. In Poole, Coleridge was able to enjoy to a certain extent the advantages of Wordsworth. Moreover, given even moderately congenial company, Coleridge could in most circumstances be depended upon to pass the time not unhappily. A solitary listener, even, would suffice for him to spend some hours profitably. Books would hold him absorbed for days at a time.

Wordsworth had no such consolations. During this past year, though he had written some poems and verses of rare beauty and power, Wordsworth had not advanced in his purpose of creating his great, his epic poem on Man, Nature, and Society, to be called *The Recluse*. He was conscious that his predilection for the composition of short poems had returned; and that for this backsliding his absence from the encouragement, the faith of the synthesizing Coleridge must be held mainly responsible.

For some time after reaching England, Wordsworth occupied himself by trying to establish the true position of affairs with regard to the *Lyrical Ballads*. The task was not easy. A few days after his return he tells his brother Richard that he fears there has been "some sad mismanagement."[59] Subsequent correspondence with Cottle did little to change his opinion. Cottle, who told Wordsworth he was leaving the bookselling business, spoke optimistically of the sale of the book—too optimistically for Wordsworth, who fears the account has gained more by "your wish to give pleasure, and your proneness to self-deception"[60] than the actual sales figures warranted.

Two facts alone seemed quite clear. "From what I can gather," he wrote Cottle, "it seems that The Ancyent Marinere has upon the whole been an injury to the volume, I mean that the old words and the strangeness of it have deterred readers from going on."[61] For this, Wordsworth has his remedy, "If the volume should come to a second edition I would put in its place some little things which would be more likely to suit the public taste."[62]

The other certainty was Southey's unfavourable review of the poems in the *Critical Review* the previous October. Wordsworth was much displeased. "He knew that I published those poems for money and money alone. He knew that money was of importance to me. If he could not conscientiously have spoken differently of the volume, he ought to have declined the task of reviewing it."[63]

Altogether, glad though he was to be in England and with Mary, Wordsworth did not feel at ease. He told Cottle that "nothing but pecuniary necessity, will, I think, ever prevail upon me to commit myself to the press again."[64] He receives the rest of his thirty guineas for the volume and invites Cottle, when the retirement from bookselling was effected, to make a tour of Cumberland and Westmorland. If he does so, Wordsworth promises to meet him, with Dorothy, at Greta Bridge, about twenty miles from Sockburn, and later, to accompany him through the Lake District.[65]

But Wordsworth's restlessness could be stilled in one way only. He needed Coleridge. Not only had he not set eyes upon his friend since the day in April at Göttingen—he had heard no word from him. As late as July letters written by Wordsworth and Dorothy to Cottle and Poole and even in one instance to Richard Wordsworth, ask that letters shall be forwarded, express anxiety that no letters have been received despite the fact that Coleridge had promised to write from Göttingen, hope that he is coming home soon—in short, display a lively wish for some sign of the friend who meant so much to them.[66]

At last, on his return from Germany, Coleridge wrote. As usual, his letter flamed with a creative enthusiasm. He urged Wordsworth to continue work on *The Recluse*. And he had a new suggestion to make—for a work peculiarly well fitted to Wordsworth's genius and his personal experience alike.

"I do entreat you to go on with 'The Recluse,'" he wrote; "and I wish you would write a poem, in blank verse, addressed to those, who, in consequence of the complete failure of the French Revolution, have thrown up all hopes of the amelioration of mankind, and are sinking into an almost epicurean selfishness, disguising the same under the soft titles of domestic attachment and contempt for visionary *philosophes*. It would do great good, and might form a part of 'The Recluse,' for in my present mood I am wholly against the publication of any small poems." [67]

Wordsworth seized upon the idea with avidity. He had known, perhaps to a greater degree than most, the despair of one who had seen in the Revolution the coming of a new age. His own story—how he had sunk to the depths of disillusionment, how he had climbed back to sanity and a fresh interest in life—should hold a message of hope for many. Already he had written verses dealing with incidents of his childhood which might well take their place at the commencement of the poem—for if it were treated as such a theme deserved to be treated the poem must present the reader with the whole picture of the man whose thought it was to unfold. Given to introspection, with an ability to portray "emotion recollected in tranquillity," [68] and possessed, as he was to show, of a superb command of blank verse, Wordsworth was suited ideally to record this epic story of "the discipline And consummation of the Poet's mind." [69]

Moreover, he not only responded enthusiastically to Coleridge's first suggestion; he also linked up this new poem with the plan of *The Recluse*. It should be a tailpiece, an appendix: "the two Works have the same kind of relation to each other . . . as the ante-chapel has to the body of a gothic church." [70]

Wordsworth determined to address the poem to Coleridge; and although it was not destined to receive a name until after both poets had died, it came to be known to William and Dorothy from its inception as *The Poem to Coleridge*.[71]

Coleridge was overjoyed by Wordsworth's reception of his suggestions: "I long to see what you have been doing," he wrote in the middle of October in a letter that illustrates excellently the influence he exerted upon his friend and his constant drive after a synthesis; "O let it be the tail-piece of 'The Recluse!' for of nothing but 'The Recluse' can I hear patiently. That it is to be addressed to me makes me more desirous that it should not be a poem of itself. To be addressed, as a beloved man, by a thinker, at the close of such a poem as 'The Recluse,' a poem *non unius populi*, is the only event, I believe, capable of inciting in me an hour's vanity—vanity, nay, it is too good a feeling to be so called; it would indeed be a self-elevation produced *ab extra*." [72]

But Coleridge was to see Wordsworth sooner than he expected. Within a few days of writing this letter, he and Cottle, who had decided to accept the invitation made some months before, had set out together for Sockburn in consequence of Wordsworth's illness.

The visitors were received rapturously by the Wordsworths. William had recovered his health and was already talking about a tour of the Lake District. In a few hours Coleridge had made himself a favourite with the whole household; [73] and in one instance, perhaps, rather more. Here, at Sockburn, Coleridge first met Sarah, Mary Hutchinson's sister.

Sarah Hutchinson was at this time twenty-four, more than two years younger than Coleridge. In person, she was in no way remarkable. Small, inclined to plumpness, her most attractive physical features were her hair, fine, long and light brown, her complexion, fair and delicate, and her expression, which was habitually sweet. But her nature was more than ordinarily serene and kindly, her mind more than ordinarily acute and receptive. Despite her quiet and unassuming manner, she was a thoughtful girl at a time when, and in a part of the country where intellectuality, if not actually used as a term of reproach, was at least commonly considered incompatible with the full discharge of feminine duties. Sarah had been fortunate enough to be brought up by her cousin-in-law, David Patrick, the 'intellectual pedlar,' a man of uncommon power of mind. [74] By him and his wife, the girl's natural sense of humour had been allowed full play, her receptive and capable mind had been given sound material to feed upon. Sarah lacked Dorothy's fine perception of and affection for the moods and minutia of Nature; she did not possess the latter's extreme sensibility. She was altogether less impulsive, less excitable than Dorothy; with a ready sympathy for others and a quick comprehension of their minds that was in great part denied the elder girl. She was naturally more lively, as well as more intelligent, than Mary. "If sense, sensibility, sweetness of temper, perfect simplicity and an unpretending nature joined to shrewdness and entertainingness, make a valuable woman, Sarah H. is so," Coleridge said of her: "for the combination of natural shrewdness and disposition to innocent humour joined with her perfect simplicity and tenderness is what distinguishes her from her sister, whose character is of a more solemn cast." [75]

But Wordsworth wanted to take Coleridge to the Lake District. He wanted his friend to see the scenes of his boyhood, the scenes about which he had written so recently in fragments of his proposed pendant poem to *The Recluse*. And he wanted to find, if possible, by his beloved lakes and mountains a home in which he and Dorothy and later, perhaps, Mary too might live.

So the very next afternoon, on Sunday October 27,[76] the three men set off; Coleridge, at least, more than a little reluctant to leave Sockburn so soon; Cottle, "his legs hugely muffled up, mounted on Tom Hutchinson's mare Lily," [77] not so sorry. They passed Neasham Bank overlooking the "*Peninsulating* Tees" [78] through Hurworth to Croft by footpath, discussing on this last part of the journey "the question of Polytheism and Monotheism, and the contrasted associations of tombs by the roadside and tombs in the churchyard." [79] Here, too, Coleridge had the thought "of translating Schiller's 'Gotten des Griechenland,' and of writing an antiphony to it." [80] On the whole he concluded he had "Better write both myself in the manner of Penseroso and Allegro." [81]

That night they slept at the George Inn [82] at Piercebridge. The next day they passed through Gainford, reading the epitaphs in the churchyard, reaching Castle Barnard late in the afternoon.

On the following day, October 29, they came to Greta Bridge, at which place "near where the Greta falls into the Tees I watched the shooting of water-threads down the slope of the huge green stone. The white rose of eddy-foam, where the stream ran into a scooped or scalloped hollow of the rock in its channel—this shape an exact white rose, was for ever overpowered by the stream rushing down upon it, and still, obstinate in resurrection, it spread up into the scallop, by fits and starts blossoming into a full flower." [83]

[368]

Here, Coleridge "Hung over the Bridge, and wondered to myself how much of this scene of endless variety in identity was Nature's, how much the living organ's! What would it be if I had the eyes of a fly! What if the blunt eye of a Brobdingnag!"[84]

Here, too, they parted company. Cottle, whose journey had not proved a complete success—he had managed to elicit from Wordsworth only a single reference to the *Lyrical Ballads*,[85] and that may be assumed with some confidence to have lacked enthusiasm, so convinced was Wordsworth of Cottle's mismanagement—had abandoned the projected tour and went south to Bristol. Coleridge and Wordsworth took the coach over Stainmore on their way to the Lakes.

The two friends were not alone for long. At Temple Sowerby, where they slept the night, Wordsworth heard that his sailor brother John, in England on leave, was at Newbiggin a mile or two away. They joined forces; and the next morning all three walked on westward.[86]

From Temple Sowerby they walked to Bampton, visiting an uncle of Wordsworth by marriage, the Rev. Thomas Myers, at Barton. At Mayburgh, before Bampton, Coleridge noted "a stone fence and between the stone fence which is circular an upright stone 10 feet high with an ash close by its side umbrellaing it—a scene of religion and seclusion."[87]

The following day they "went over by Long Sleddale to Kentmere, Troutbeck, and thence by Rayrigg, and Bowness; a raw and rainy day."[88] The next day they "went on to the ferry, a cold passage, were much disgusted with the new erections and objects about Windermere,"[89] proceeding to Hawkshead, where Wordsworth had spent his schooldays.

On November 3, they set out to "Leave Esthwaite. On the road survey the whole of the lake on my right—straight before me a peep of Wynandermere, and over a gate on my left five rugged huge mountains rising one above the other in wild relations of posture. Our road turns: we pass by Blelham Tarn, and now the five mountains face us."[90] They proceeded by Rydal to Grasmere where they put up at the cottage of Robert Newton, an old soldier. Here they stopped for a few days.

John was obliged to leave on Tuesday, November the fifth. His brother and Coleridge walked with him as far as Grisedale

Tarn on his way back.[91] They all went "over the fork of Helvellyn, on a day when light and darkness co-existed in contiguous masses, and the earth and sky were but one." [92]

The poets stayed at Grasmere for another two days. They visited Easedale. "Churnmilk Force," [93] wrote Coleridge, "appears over a copse, the steam from the water-fall rising above the trees. As we come nearer, a rock stands up and intercepts all but the marge and rims of the lower half of the fall, but the trees, sometimes yielding and parting in the wind make the lowest fall beneath the rock visible. A little way below the waterfall is a one-arched bridge,[94] with ferns growing on it—its parapet or ledge of single stones not unmortared, yet cemented more by moss and mould." [95]

Both men were much struck by the beauty of the little village and its surroundings. Coleridge called the lakes "divine sisters." [96] "It was to me the vision of a fair country," he wrote on the back of Wordsworth's letter to Dorothy from Grasmere: "why were you not with us?" [97] He scarcely knew what to praise most. His admiration set the seal on the determination of his friend who had known and loved Grasmere years before. Wordsworth decided on the spot that this was the place he had been seeking for a home. He made enquiries. There was a plot of land for sale by the lake side. John had promised to give him the money to buy the land. He thought of building a house upon the site. It would cost about £250, he reckoned. There was also a small cottage empty, only a few yards from the road. It had been an inn, The Dove and Olive Branch. This might suit them. He thought at first that he would not make a decision until he had talked the matter over with Dorothy.[98]

On Friday, the 8th, they walked to Wastdale. They slept the night in the house of Thomas Tyson, below Yewbarrow. The following day they were at Cockermouth, Wordsworth's birthplace. The next day, Sunday, they turned back to the lakes by Bassenthwaite to Keswick. Coleridge was moved especially by the beauty of Derwentwater—which, of all the lakes, he was to love best.[99]

"From the window of the Inn at Ouse Bridge," Coleridge wrote, "we overlook the whole length of Bassenthwaite, a simple majesty of water and mountain, and in the distance the Bank rising like a wedge, and in the second distance, the crags of Derwentwater. What an effect of shades in the water! On the left the conical shadow—on the right a square of splendid black, all the intermediate area a mirror reflecting dark and sunny cloud, but in the distance a black promontory with a circle of melted silver, and a path of silver running from it like a flat cape in the lake. The snowy Borrowdale is seen in the far distance, and a ridge of nearer mountains sloping down, as it were to the bank of Bassenthwaite." [100]

From Keswick, Coleridge wrote Southey, explaining how he came to be in the north. "From hence I go to London, having had (by accident here) a sort of offer made to me of a pleasant kind, which, if it turn out well, will enable me and Sara to reside in London for the next four or five months—a thing I wish extremely on many and important accounts." [101]

He went on to defend his opinion "for thinking 'Christabel' *were* it finished, and finished as spiritedly as it commences, yet still an improper opening poem" [102] for Southey's *Annual Anthology*. He urged Southey, as he had urged Wordsworth, to devote himself to greater work—with customary incaution making an offer as a kind of bait. "Do, do, my dear Southey! publish the 'Madoc' *quam citissime*, not hastily, but yet speedily. I will instantly publish an Essay on Epic Poetry in reference to it. I have been reading the Æneid, and there you will be all victorious, excepting the importance of Æneas and his connection with events existing in Virgil's time." [103]

For a few more days, the two poets continued their tour of the lakes. They went round by Embleton, through Low Lorton, where Coleridge noted the Yew—"prodigious in size and complexity of numberless branches, flings itself on one side entirely over the river" [104]—of which Wordsworth was later to write.[105] They passed Red How, Grasmoor, "a most sublime crag, of a violet colour, patched here and there with islands of the heath-plant, and most picturesquely wrinkled and guttered," [106] the Scalehill Inn, Loweswater, seeing before them "a sweet country . . . Somersetshire Hills, and scattered here and there, many a neat house, with its little group of trees, the homesteads of the Estatesmen." [107] Opposite Grasmoor towered Mellbreak and between the two hills lay Crummock Water. As they approached the upper end of the lake, "'Tis an archipelago of tinest islands, seven fair Pleiades, and two of them hug the opposite shore." [108]

The next day, the 12th of November, they climbed up to Scale Force, then crossed over by Floutern Tarn to Ennerdale, along the lake to Gillerthwaite, and over Black Sail to Wastdale Head.

They slept at T. Tyson's on the Wednesday night, setting out for Borrowdale the next morning—"the brooks in their anger. All the gullies full and white, and the chasms now black, now half-hid by the mist, but ever and anon the waterfall within the chasm flashing through the mist. On one hill I counted seven huge gullies, to say nothing of numberless Tapes, tiny white streams, to which in conjunction with the frost shattered chasms of stone—stone cataracts—the largest stone still at the bottom of the solid stream, the mountains owe much of their form and colouring." [109]

The two men crossed Sty Head Pass and slept the night at Rosthwaite. On Friday, the 15th, they were back at Keswick, passing by Grange and admiring Lodore. "1 mile and $\frac{1}{2}$ from Keswick we come to a Druidical circle," wrote Coleridge. "On the right is the road and Saddleback—on the left a fine but un-watered vale, walled by grassy hills and a fine black crag standing single at the terminus as sentry. Before me, that is, towards Keswick, the mountains stand, one behind the other, in orderly array, as if evoked by and attentive to the assembly of white-vested Wizards." [110]

On the Friday night they slept at Threlkeld, proceeding the following morning over a barren peat moss to Matterdale. At Matterdale, Coleridge is "struck, as by a flash, with its similarity to the Devonshire Cleaves. . . . [111] One cottage we noticed more particularly. It stood two or three hundred yards above a cascade, in a small but sweet curve of the brook, the front to the path—one gable with its two widely-placed windows facing the cascade, and the other gable over-arched by stately trees, and the whole roof greener than the green field in which we stood." [112]

From Matterdale they walked on to Ullswater by way of Aira Force. "The chasm is very fine," wrote Coleridge, "violet coloured beeches and hawthorns as big as forest trees, and apprickle with berries as red as red flowers, grow close at hand. The higher part of the fall, where the two streams run athwart each other, is a thing to itself, but where the wheel-part is broken, it spreads into a muslin apron, and the whole waterfall looks like a long waisted giantess slipping down on her back. But on the bridge, where you see only the wheel, it is very fine. The waters circumvolve with a complete half-wheel." [113]

That night they slept at Patterdale. The next morning, Sunday, November 17, they left their "bad Inn and went down the Lake by the opposite shore. The ground was white with hoar-frost. The Lake lay calm and would have been mirror-like but that it had been breathed on by the mist." [114] Coleridge stood on the apex of the triangular bay past the first great promontory, taking in the whole of the water view. The mist closed down—"now it is all one deep wall of white vapour, save that black streak shaped like strange creatures seem to move in and down it, in the opposite direction to the motions of the greater body of mist. And seen from behind, over the fork of the precipitous ridge, the sun has sent within the wall of mist, ten thousand silky hairs of amber and green light. [115] I step two paces and have lost the glory, but the edge has exactly the soft richness of the silvered-edge of a cloud behind which the sun is travelling. The fog has now closed over the Lake, and we wander in obscurity, save that here and there the vapour is prettily coloured by withered fern over which it hovers." [116]

They could just see Lyulph's Tower, gleaming "like a ghost dim and shadowy in the water—and the bright shadow thereof, how beautiful it is, cut across by that tongue of breezy water! And now the shadow is suddenly gone, and the Tower itself rises emerging from the mist. Two thirds are still hidden, but the pinnacles are clear—and in a moment all is snatched away—A mazy dance, a fleeting pageantry of realities and shadows!" [117]

Finally they come to the house of Wordsworth's friend, Mr Clarkson, at Euscmere. There, sitting on a tree-stump by the brink of the lake, Coleridge saw a scene, "of perfect serenity. That fat round buttock of a hill together with its reflection in the water make together one absolutely undistinguishable form, a kite or a paddle or keel turned towards you. The seamlike road winds up the hill and downwards into the Lake. I never saw so sweet an image!" [118]

Here, on Monday, November 18, the friends separated. Words-

[373]

worth returned to Grasmere, to consider once more the choice before him, and to wander again about the district in which he had decided to make his home. Coleridge went back to the farm at Sockburn.

The offer that Coleridge had received was from Stuart of the *Morning Post*. Stuart invited Coleridge to become a regular contributor to his paper. He offered to find and pay for suitable accommodation in London and to give Coleridge a weekly salary which compared favourably with the rates of pay common in journalism at that time. This offer, which promised to free Coleridge from his financial difficulties if he would apply himself to the work for a few months, was at once accepted.[119] Coleridge did not go back to Stowey. He took the coach direct from Sockburn to London.

But he did not leave the farm immediately. At Sockburn he probably drafted, certainly conceived, the poem *Love* which first appeared in the *Morning Post* on December 21 of the same year as an "Introduction to the Tale of the Dark Ladie." This was the first poem of moment Coleridge had written, had been able or wishful to write, since the summer of the previous year. He had waited in vain for inspiration, for a return of the muse. Now, for a brief space, it returned; if not in full glory, at least in a manner that was memorable, both for the occasion and for future events which it in some sense foreshadowed. Like *The Ancient Mariner*, Coleridge later pronounced *Love* to be inimitable.[120] Possibly he was thinking more of the feelings which had inspired it; for the poem itself, unlike *The Ancient Mariner*, invited not only imitations but improvements; and was, in fact, to have a far greater successor in Keats' *La Belle Dame sans merci*. Nevertheless *Love* is an interesting poem and one which, despite the occasional 'precious' touches, contains much beauty and a pleasing simplicity. This ballad expresses excellently the more 'romantic' side of the Romantic Revival; to which, in this instance, Coleridge's chief contribution may be described as a process of intellectualizing the glorification of the passions.

Coleridge sent the poem to the editor of the *Morning Post* with a foreword:

"The following poem is the introduction to a somewhat longer one, for which I shall solicit insertion on your next open day. The use of the old ballad word *Ladie* for Lady, is the only piece of obsoleteness in it; and as it is professedly a tale of ancient times, I trust that 'the affectionate lovers of venerable antiquity' (as Cambden says) will grant me their pardon, and perhaps may be induced to admit a force and propriety in it. A heavier objection may be adduced against the Author, that in these times of fear and expectation, when novelties *explode* around us in all directions, he should presume to offer to the public a silly tale of old-fashioned love; and five years ago, I own, I should have allowed and felt the force of this objection. But, alas! explosion has succeeded explosion so rapidly that novelty itself ceases to appear new; and it is possible that now, even a simple story wholly unspiced with politics or personality, may find some attention amid the hubbub of Revolutions, as to those who have remained a long time by the falls of Niagara, the lowest whispering becomes distinctly audible." [121]

The influences upon it of Coleridge's visit to Sockburn are plain enough in the poem. There are the physical characteristics—the recumbent figure of the "arméd knight"—Sir Ralph Conyers in the old church at Sockburn; the "Grey Stone" in an adjoining field which is said to commemorate the Knight's victory over a monstrous worme or wiverne; the peninsula, washed by the Tees, in which the parish of Sockburn is situated; and the "ruined tower" below the castle "mount" at Richmond, a few miles away. [122]

But of greater importance is the influence of her whom the poem exalts and but for whom the poem would never have come into existence. When Coleridge writes:

> All thoughts, all passions, all delights,
> Whatever stirs this mortal frame,
> All are but ministers of Love,
> And feed his sacred flame, [123]

he expresses a conviction born of his own recent experience. When he continues:

> Oft in my waking dreams do I
> Live o'er again that happy hour
> When midway on the mount I lay,
> Beside the ruined tower.
>
> The moonshine, stealing o'er the scene
> Had blended with the lights of eve;
> And she was there, my hope, my joy,
> My own dear Genevieve!

[375]

She leant against the arméd man,
The statue of the arméd knight;
She stood and listened to my lay,
Amid the lingering light.

Few sorrows hath she of her own,
My hope! my joy! my Genevieve!
She loves me best, whene'er I sing
The songs that make her grieve,[124]

he is recording, with truth in essentials, happenings at Sockburn.
And when he speaks of Genevieve and his relations with her:

She listened with a flitting blush,
With downcast eyes and modest grace;
For well she knew, I could not choose
But gaze upon her face.

She wept with pity and delight,
She blushed with love, and virgin-shame;
And like the murmur of a dream,
I heard her breathe my name.[125]

I saw her bosom heave and swell,
Heave and swell with inward sighs—
I could not choose but love to see
Her gentle bosom rise.[126]

Her wet cheek glow'd: she stept aside—
As conscious of my look she stepped—
Then suddenly, with timorous eye
She fled to me and wept.[127]

She half enclosed me with her arms,
She pressed me with a meek embrace;
And bending back her head, looked up,
And gazed upon my face.

'Twas partly love, and partly fear,
And partly 'twas a bashful art,
That I might rather feel, than see,
The swelling of her heart,[128]

he is recording something of his own wishes, at the least, if not
those of Sarah Hutchinson.

If doubt still remains concerning the extent to which the affections of the heroine of the poem for Coleridge had in fact been formulated or declared at this early stage, there is little question of Coleridge's feelings.

That some drawing together had already occurred may be more than surmised; for, apart from the poem, there is the evidence of the notebooks—in this instance, by no means decisive, certainly: yet, in view of what was to follow, significant of more than a light-hearted flirtation.

On November 24, Coleridge made the following entry in his notebook: "Conundrums and puns, and stories and laughter with Jack Hutchinson. Stood up round the fire, et Sara manum a tergo longum in tempus prensatam and . . . tunc temporis, tunc primum amor me levi spiculo, venenato eheu et insanabili——" [129]

Three days later he was in London.

13

STUART HAD TAKEN rooms for Coleridge at 21 Bucking-
ham Street, Strand. From these "quiet and healthful"[1] lodgings
Coleridge wrote to Poole, asking for Sarah and Hartley to join
him and inviting his friend up to see him in London.[2] Within
a few days, before December 9, the Coleridge family was under
one roof again.[3] Coleridge wasted no time before resuming his
acquaintance with a number of Londoners. "Godwin is no great
things in intellect," he tells Southey early in December, referring
to a meeting between Godwin, Davy, and himself; "but in heart
and manner he is all the better for having been the husband of
Mary Wollstonecraft."[4] He also refers to Mary Hays,[5] authoress,
feminist, and friend of Mary Wollstonecraft, about whom a small
storm was shortly to agitate the circle of friends just reuniting.

Southey's health was causing some anxiety. "I would to God
your health permitted you to come to London," Coleridge wrote.
"You might have lodgings in the same house with us. And this I
am certain of, that not even Kingsdown is a more healthy or airy
place."[6] But Southey thought of going abroad with his wife to
recuperate.[7] The possibility began to arouse in Coleridge an
emotion reminiscent of the old pantisocratic enthusiasm: "As to
my future residence," he writes, "I can say nothing—only this,
that to be near you would be a strong motive with me for my
wife's sake as well as myself. I think it not impossible that a
number might be found to go with you and settle in a warmer
climate."[8]

Another and more notable resumption of friendship was the
coming together of Coleridge and Lamb. It would be difficult, in
any event, to imagine the two men, strongly attached to each other
despite their disagreement, living in the same city without a
meeting. But there were other more definite reasons for their
renewal of intimacy.

Lamb had reproached Southey for his adverse review of *The
Ancient Mariner* and in so doing had shown his appreciation of

the poem. "If you wrote that review in 'Crit. Rev.,' " he told Southey, "I am sorry you are so sparing of praise to the 'Ancient Marinere';—so far from calling it, as you do, with some wit, but more severity, 'A Dutch Attempt,' etc., I call it a right English attempt, and a successful one, to dethrone German sublimity. You have selected a passage fertile in unmeaning miracles, but have passed by fifty passages as miraculous as the miracles they celebrate. I never so deeply felt the pathetic as in that part,

> A spring of love gush'd from my heart,
> And I bless'd them unaware—

It stung me into high pleasure through sufferings. Lloyd does not like it; his head is too metaphysical, and your taste too correct; at least I must allege something against you both, to excuse my own dotage—

> So lonely 'twas, that God himself
> Scarce seemed there to be!—etc. etc.

But you allow some elaborate beauties—you should have extracted 'em. 'The Ancient Marinere' plays more tricks with the mind than that last poem,[9] which is yet one of the finest written." [10]

That Coleridge, in his new friendliness with Southey, had heard of Lamb's admiration for his poem may be assumed with some confidence.

At much the same time Lamb, like Southey before him, partly perhaps by reason of Southey's changing attitude towards Lloyd, partly through Lloyd's own indiscretions, had begun to realize that Lloyd's actions were at times unpredictable, his words not always to be depended upon; and from this, it was but a step to the conclusion that Lloyd's reminiscences of Coleridge, which had played so large a part in effecting the breach between Lamb and Coleridge, owed something at least to imagination, if not to spite.[11] Moreover, the admiration—in their eyes excessive—of Coleridge for Wordsworth—another factor in the drawing away of Lamb, Lloyd, and Southey from their associate—appeared for the moment, with Wordsworth far away, to have spent itself.

In a very short time the old friends were reunited. During the second week in December Lamb told Lloyd, "I have just learned that Coleridge has taken lodgings with his family in the Adelphi—

but I have seen nothing of him."[12] Two weeks later he had met
Coleridge, dined with him and breakfasted with him and Priscilla,
Lloyd's sister, whom Lamb was hoping to match with Christopher
Wordsworth.[13] From this time, the renewed friendship gathered
warmth and was soon proceeding with much of its former
intimacy.

The correspondence with Southey continued with fair regularity. On Christmas Eve, or rather, on the stroke of Christmas
Day,[14] Coleridge began a letter:

> "My Spinosism (if Spinosism it be, and i' faith 'tis very like it)
> disposed me to consider this big city as that part of the supreme
> One which the prophet Moses was allowed to see—I should be
> more disposed to pull off my shoes, beholding Him in a *Bush*,
> than while I am forcing my reason to believe that even in the
> theatres *He* is, yea! even in the Opera House."[15]

This reflection, induced by recent visits to the theatre, was followed by a description of Coleridge's daily work.

> "I am employed from I-rise to I-set (that is, from nine in the
> morning to twelve at night), a pure scribbler. My mornings to
> booksellers' compilations, after dinner to Stuart, who pays *all* my
> expenses here, let them be what they will; the earnings of the
> morning go to make up an hundred and fifty pounds for my
> year's expenditure; for, supposing *all clear* my year's (1800)
> allowance is anticipated. But this I can do by the first of April (at
> which time I leave London). For Stuart I write often his lead-
> ing paragraphs on Secession, Peace, Essay on the new French
> Constitution,[16] Advice to Friends of Freedom, Critiques on Sir
> W. Anderson's Nose, Odes to Georgiana D. of D. (horribly
> misprinted), Christmas Carols, etc. etc.,—anything not bad in
> the paper that is not yours, is mine. So if any verses there strike
> you as worthy the 'Anthology', 'do me the honour, Sir!' How-
> ever, in the course of a week I *do mean* to conduct a series of essays
> in that paper which may be of public utility. So much for myself,
> except that I long to be out of London; and that my Xstmas
> Carol is a quaint performance, and, in as strict a sense as is *possible*,
> an Impromptu, and, had I done all I had planned, that 'Ode to
> the Duchess' [17] would have been a better thing than it is." [18]

Several times within the past two years Coleridge and his
friends had been attacked by poem and cartoon in the *Anti-
Jacobin* and its successor as wild radicals and indifferent poets.

[380]

One of these poems, *The New Morality*, the relevant verse of which ran:

> And ye five other wandering Bards that move
> In sweet accord of harmony and love,
> C———dge and S—th—y, L—d and L—be & Co.
> Tune all your mystic harps to praise Lepaux! [19]

was reprinted in *The Beauties of the 'Anti-Jacobin'* in 1799. To the poem a footnote on Coleridge was appended. It ended:

> "He has since married, had children, and has now quitted the country, become a citizen of the world, left his little ones father-less, and his wife destitute. *Ex uno disce* his associates Southey and Lambe." [20]

The poem had left Coleridge undisturbed; and indeed, the accusations against him in it were steadily growing more unreal as he moved away from youthful enthusiasms. The libellous foot-note was another matter. It cut Coleridge very deep; the more so, of course, in that, shorn of exaggeration, it did put a finger, not only on an act of Coleridge about which he felt sensitive to criticism, but on a state of mind, a disloyalty of thought, which was fast becoming habitual in his relations with his wife.

He told Southey that he had been advised to sue for libel,[21] but nothing came of it; and the words remained in his mind for years to come; to rankle the more bitterly, the nearer Coleridge drifted towards the act which would go far to justify the gibe.

But at the moment he had a more immediate worry. The tentacles of duty were binding him tightly, pinioning his mind. His effort to force himself to the carrying out of a purpose by announcing his intentions in decisive and even enthusiastic terms had returned upon him like a boomerang—contemplation of the hopes and expectations he had aroused benumbing his energies, stultifying his capabilities and leaving his projected work even further from fulfilment. All he could do was to place a further barrier of months before the time when he might be expected to carry out his promises.

> "My dear Southey!" he continued, "I have said nothing con-cerning that which most oppresses me. Immediately on my leaving London I fall to the 'Life of Lessing'; till that is done, till I have given the Wedgwoods some proof that I am *endeavouring* to do well for my fellow-creatures, I cannot stir." [22]

Southey had asked if Coleridge would really consider leaving England with him. "That being done," continued the optimist, having successfully pushed the task away from immediate consideration, having accomplished it in words, "I would accompany you, and see no impossibility of forming a pleasant little colony for a few years in Italy or the South of France. Peace will soon come. God love you, my dear Southey!" [23]

He ended, as often, with Hartley:

"Hartley is quite well, and my talkativeness is his, without diminution on my side. 'Tis strange, but certainly many things go in the blood, beside gout and scrophula. Yesterday I dined at Longman's and met Pratt, and that honest piece of prolix dullity and nullity, young Towers, who desired to be remembered to you. To-morrow Sara and I dine at Mister Gobwin's, as Hartley calls him, who gave the philosopher such a rap on the shins with a ninepin that Gobwin in huge pain *lectured* Sara on his boisterousness. I was not at home. *Est modus in rebus.* Moshes is somewhat too rough and noisy, but the cadaverous silence of Godwin's children is to me quite catacombish, and, thinking of Mary Wollstonecraft, I was oppressed by it the day Davy and I dined there." [24]

The idea of the party abroad was pursued when Coleridge wrote Davy on New Year's Day:

"Davy! Davy! if the public Good did not iron and adamant you to England and Bristol, what a little colony might we ... not make. Tobin, I am sure, would go, and Wordsworth, and I—and Southey. Precious stuff for Dreams—and God knows, I have no time for them!" [25]

So he passed from dreams to physical sensations, displaying the lively curiosity in their causes that characterized his approach to most aspects of life:

"Questions—
On dipping my foot and leg into very hot water, the first sensation was identical with that of having dipped it into very cold. This identity recurred as often as I took my leg out in order to pour in the hot water from the kettle, and put it in again. How is this explained in philosophical Language divested of corpuscular Theories? Define Disgust in philosophical Language. Is it not, speaking as a materialist, always a stomach-sensation conjoined with an idea? What is the cause of that sense of cold, which accompanies inhalation, after having eat peppermint Drops?"

[382]

"I wish," he went on, "in your Researches that you and Beddoes would give a compact compressed History of the Human Mind for the last century, considered simply as to the acquisition of Ideas or new arrangement of them. Or if you won't do it there, do it for me—and I will print it with an Essay I am now writing on the principles of Population and Progressiveness." [26]

Coleridge's intimacy with Godwin was growing—though it carried with it always something of amused toleration in the attitude of the younger man.

"Godwin talks evermore of you with lively affection 'What a pity that such a man should degrade his vast Talents to Chemistry,' cried he to me—Why, quoth I, how, Godwin! can you thus talk of a science, of which neither you nor I understand an iota etc. etc.; and I defended Chemistry as knowingly at least as Godwin attacked it—affirmed that it united the opposite advantages of immaterializing the mind without destroying the definiteness of the Ideas—nay even while it gave clearness to them . . . we both agreed (for G., as well as I, thinks himself a Poet) that *the Poet* is the greatest possible character etc. etc. Modest Creatures! Hurra, my dear Southey!—you [and I] and Godwin, and Shakespeare, and Milton, with what an athanasiophagous grin we shall march together—*we poets*: Down with all the rest of the World!— By the word athanasiophagous I mean devouring Immortality by anticipation! Tis a sweet word!—

"God bless you, my dear Davy! Take my nonsense like a pinch of snuff—sneeze it off, it clears the head. . . ." [27]

The previous day, New Year's Eve, Coleridge had written a short note to Poole. He repeats his "I-rise to I-set," hopes that Poole receives the papers regularly (copies of the *Morning Post* so that Poole can read his friend's contributions), and ends:

"Being so hurried for time I should have delayed writing till tomorrow; but to-day is the last day of the year, and a sort of superstitious feeling oppressed me that the year should not end without my writing, if it were only to subscribe myself with the old words of an old affection. . . . God bless you, and him who is ever, ever yours—who, among all his friends, has ever called and ever felt you the Friend." [28]

Despite this demonstration of affection, the genuineness of which need not be doubted, all was not well between the two friends. Poole was disturbed. He was hurt. Coleridge's sudden

[383]

decision to accept Stuart's offer; his omission to seek his friend's advice; his precipitate rush to London direct from Sockburn, an avoidance of Stowey dictated in part at least by cowardice, by a dislike of facing disapproval—these things had given Poole much pain.

Nor was that all: Coleridge's attitude towards the choice of a home after he had finished in London was far from satisfactory. He was becoming increasingly particular. Gone were the days when the meanest cottage would suffice if it brought him close to his friend. Now, the house must be roomy, it must contain a study, and its situation must please everybody. He wavered between situations he liked and situations which would suit Sarah. Thus, early, a house is discovered at Aisholt in a somewhat remote Quantock combe.

"The situation is delicious; all I could wish,"[29] he wrote; but upon second thoughts his determination, if not enthusiasm, to take it, faltered.

"Sara being Sara " he continued "and I being I, we must live in a town or else close to one, so that she may have neighbours and acquaintances. For my friends form not that society which is of itself sufficient to a woman. I know nowhere else but Stowey (for to Bristol my objections are insurmountable), but our old house in Stowey, and that situation will not do for us. God knows where we can go; for that situation which suits my wife does not suit me, and what suits me does not suit my wife. However, that which is, is—a truth which always remains equally clear, but not always equally pleasant."[30]

There was no doubt about his dilemma, which was very real; but its restatement more than once was small comfort to Poole, whichever way he regarded it—as a confession that his friend's marriage was not completely happy or as an excuse for postponing the issue of choosing the situation for a future home.

And the fact that Poole, in this instance too, was aware of the real cause of the struggle in his friend's mind did nothing to ease his hurt. Though less selfish than most men, Poole was not utterly immune from jealousy; and though he admired and respected Wordsworth, he was unable to believe him the great genius that Coleridge declared; he considered the adulation poured upon the elder poet by Coleridge excessive, undeserved, and harmful to ` is friend's best interests. He was by no means convinced that

Coleridge would be the gainer if choosing to live near Wordsworth rather than at Stowey, though he remained open to conviction. And of course he longed for the exhilaration of Coleridge's society once more—even for a renewal of the occasions, not infrequent, when he could remove or lighten his friend's fits of heavy depression.

At the moment, these feelings expressed themselves mainly through Poole's disapproval of Coleridge's journalistic work, his fear that his friend's true genius might become overlaid, buried by ephemeral but more immediately profitable work—a fear which, unjustified though it was to prove, was none the less powerful in Poole's mind. He feared, too, for the soiling of Coleridge's mind in London, not by inclination but by a too easygoing toleration of bad company.

Topping all this came the suspicion—equally unjustified—that Coleridge was tiring of his Stowey friend; that his letters were dictated more by duty than by affection. So that it was a sad and a stiff letter written by Poole to Coleridge on January 21.

"Whether by the employment you have chosen," he says, "you have exactly performed the *duty* you owe *yourself*, is what you can determine much better than I. However that may be, *I* in truth long for the period when you shall have gained that sum of money which is necessary to replace what you last year expended beyond your income, as it will give me solid satisfaction to see you resume, or rather begin, employments more consonant to your former intentions, more worthy of your abilities, more permanently useful to society, to yourself now, and to your family *hereafter, for ever*. Where you begin those employments it is for you to choose. I need not say, if it be here, or in this neighbourhood, it will contribute greatly to my happiness and wellbeing, as it would be supposing affectation in you not to be aware that your society here is that sort of acquisition which nothing can replace. Yes, Coleridge, I am much indebted to you, and though you've found in my mind perhaps an unfruitful, you shall never in my heart, an ungrateful soil.

"I write to you with restraint, because I think you treated me with unmerited silence, and when you wrote you seemed to perform a duty, not a pleasure. I remarked to Mrs Coleridge that I was afraid my disposition was altered, and that I was acquiring the *heart-withering* faculty of losing men's *hearts* though I retained their *heads*. If this be true I must and will endeavour to rectify it, and when I can see errors and inconsistencies in those

2 B

whom I love, where I can't sympathise I will at any rate be silent. Thus much, my dear Col., I have written, and let it not give you pain, or draw from you a long reply. The former would distress me beyond measure, and the latter would take up more of your time than I would wish you to expend in letter-writing. . . . When I anxiously wish you to reside here, it is on this sole condition, *that you can do as well here what you propose doing, as elsewhere.* If this be not the case, it would be weakness and imprudence, at any rate for the present, to think of residing here." [31]

Despite his feeling that Coleridge was debasing his genius, Poole was constrained to admit that the journalism was well done.

"I cannot but approve of what you have written in the papers. It is done in a masterly manner. Your observations . . . are, without doubt, just, though I think you have borne hard on Buonaparte and the French Constitution. . . . Your ode to the Duchess was a delightful thing—the letter from Talleyrand [32] excellent." [33]

He ends with a warning:

"Purkis tells me he dined with you, and was gratified at meeting those I would not have given a louse to meet. He speaks that in conversation men talk boldly of Atheism, etc. I implore you, my dear Col., not by any *levity* for a moment to countenance such principles and sentiments; not to share the withering curse which God now scatters upon men—a curse which causes men of *no* feeling to give up all to *feeling*, contrary to the conviction which intellect must award if allowed to act. You often, from good nature, or from a certain perverseness of disposition, or from vanity, give countenance to men and principles at which in the moments of *true* self-possession, you would spurn. . . ." [34]

Coleridge, replying some weeks later, reproached Poole for his doubts.

"How could you take such an absurd idea into your head, that my affections have weakened towards you?" he wrote. "Sometimes I have thought you rash in your judgments of my conduct, but I perceived rather than felt it. But, enough of this. My affections are what they are, and, in all human probability, ever will be. I write merely to desire you to be on the look-out for a house. I shall, beyond all doubt, settle at Stowey, if I can get . . . a house with a garden, and large enough for me to have a study out of the noise of women and children. This is absolutely necessary for me." [35]

This statement of his intentions, as of his affections, sounded, at first hearing, definite enough. Yet the former only too probably masked, and was intended partly to bolster up, a sagging purpose. That Coleridge was genuine in his wish, so often expressed, to be at Stowey, need not be doubted. But he had other wishes, at least of equal strength; and these it was he set himself, half-heartedly, to fight; employing a favourite weapon of the weak, the announcement of intentions—but promptly nullifying its effect in the next breath, by attaching to it qualifications providing easy and endless avenues of escape from the implications of his own words.

The company he kept was truly varied—in addition to the 'regulars,' Godwin, Lamb, and Stuart, he met or renewed acquaintance with, at this time, Longman,[36] John Pinney, Basil Montague, father of little Basil of Alfoxden, Horne Tooke, Sir James Mackintosh, Sir Francis Burdett,[37] George Dyer, Mrs Barbauld, Sir Richard Phillips,[38] Mary Hays, Miss Wesley,[39] Miss Benger,[40] Mrs 'Perdita' Robinson,[41] and Charlotte Smith.[42] At times, no doubt, the company would not have earned Poole's approval—Coleridge, indeed, though much later, declared that on one occasion, when dining with Horne Tooke and Burdett, he took exception to the grossness of the conversation and withdrew, whereupon Burdett, as compensation, invited the distressed Coleridge to his house at Wimbledon.[43] However this may be—and Coleridge's propriety of later years was not above exaggerating the effect of undue coarseness upon himself when younger—although Poole's estimate of his friend's character was, up to a point, correct, his fears for him in this connexion were unfounded, not because Coleridge declined to associate with those against whom Poole warned him—he did not—but because there was in him something too fine, too deep, to be sullied. Like many another, he needed the froth blown off him occasionally before the rich, true man beneath could be tasted.

Further details of his work were given by Coleridge to Tom Wedgwood in a letter written in January, when his activities were at their height. "I am sitting by a fire in a rug great coat," he began; and then went on; "It is most barbarously cold."[44] He told Wedgwood of Southey's loss of health and determination to leave the country as soon as the poem he was working on was completed.[45]

Coleridge continued with a significant passage—a pointer to the state of mind which was eventually to influence, in part at least, the momentous decision as to his future dwelling-place.

"Thank God," he wrote "*I have my health perfectly*, and I am working hard; yet the present state of human affairs presses on me for days together, so as to deprive me of all my cheerfulness. It is probable that a man's private and personal connexions and interests ought to be uppermost in his daily and hourly thoughts, and that the dedication of much hope and fear to subjects which are perhaps disproportionate to our faculties and powers, is a disease. But I have had this disease so long, and my early education was so undomestic, that I know not how to get rid of it; or even to wish to get rid of it. Life were so flat a thing without enthusiasm, that if for a moment it leaves me, I have a sort of stomach sensation attached to all my thoughts, *like those which succeed to the pleasurable operations of a dose of opium.*

"Now I make up my mind to a sort of heroism in believing the progressiveness of all nature, during the present melancholy state of humanity, and on this subject *I am now writing*; and no work on which I ever employed myself makes me so happy while I am writing." [46]

Here there was, in effect, a cry for the companionship of Wordsworth and Dorothy, the two who alone had manifested the power of arousing and maintaining enthusiasm in Coleridge. He then described his financial position and the steps he was taking to set it right.

"I shall remain in London till April," he wrote. "The expenses of my last year made it necessary for me to exert my industry, and many other good ends are answered at the same time. Where I next settle I shall continue, and that must be in a state of retirement and rustication. It is therefore good for me to have a run of society, and that various and consisting of marked characters. Likewise, by being obliged to write without much elaboration, I shall greatly improve myself in naturalness and facility of style, and the particular subjects on which I write for money are nearly connected with my future schemes. My mornings I give to compilations which I am sure cannot be wholly useless, and for which, by the beginning of April I shall have earned nearly £150. My evenings to the *Theatres*, as I am to conduct a sort of Dramaturgy or series of Essays on the Drama, both its general principles, and likewise in reference to the present state of the English Theatres. This I shall publish in the *Morning Post*. My attendance on the theatres costs me nothing, and Stuart, the Editor, covers my expenses in London. Two mornings, and one whole day, I dedicate to these Essays on the possible progressiveness of man, and on the principles of population. In April I retire to my greater works, —*The Life of Lessing*. My German chests are arrived, but I have them not yet, but expect them from Stowey daily; when they come I shall send a letter.

"I have seen a good deal of Godwin, who has just published a Novel. I like him for thinking so well of Davy. He talks of him everywhere as the most extraordinary of human beings he has ever met with. I cannot say that, for I know *one* whom I feel to be the superior." [47]

There is no question that although Coleridge did not in fact "give up his whole time and services" to the *Morning Post*, [48] he was undeniably busy. In the first five weeks of the new year he wrote more than twenty articles for the paper. Before the end of the year Longman had asked him to undertake the translation of Schiller's unpublished drama *Wallenstein*, [49] the English copyright of which had been taken over from a publisher by the name of Bell. [50] He contributed fourteen poems and several epigrams to Southey's second *Annual Anthology*. [51] And there is reason to believe that he may have begun one or more of the 'pot-boilers' suggested intermittently to Southey as money-makers at this time. To these labours must be added theatre-going, social visits, letter-writing, and, surely not the least, his flow of conversation, which it is not possible to believe the most exhausting programme of work could entirely subdue.

As a journalist, Coleridge was instantly successful. The degree of his success was later to be the subject of controversy but the fact itself has not been questioned. The great poets have commonly shown themselves possessors of a notable prose style. Coleridge at his best displays a close affinity with Hooker and Jeremy Taylor whose sonorous prose he admired but which could scarcely be considered an ideal medium for the leading article of a newspaper. Coleridge, however, was more often long winded and obscure; two faults that, of all weaknesses, can least be suffered in journalism. Yet in the event Coleridge responded to the requirements of his new profession with an ease that was masterly, a speed that was admirable, and a regularity that was astonishing. His early articles read well. They are clear. They have dignity.

They are well knit, are admirably phrased and possess considerable power. They can be read with pleasure although the subjects with which they deal have long since ceased to possess more than an academic interest at best. Yet this adaptation of his prose to the occasion, though surprising, was not the most remarkable feature of Coleridge's achievement in journalism. His ability to master, at short notice, the intricacies of a situation, to sum it up vividly, at times crisply and succinctly, and usually with a sound selective as well as prophetic sense is, in these articles, most pronounced—a necessary concomitant of successful journalism, certainly, but not one with which Coleridge would have been credited readily. That he possessed many of the requirements of a first-class journalist—simplicity, wit, humour, practicality, eloquence, ability to see or make the point (if not to keep to it) was, with the possible exception of practicality, never in question—the trouble commonly being not lack of these abilities but an excess of them, the possession of a depth of thought altogether unsuited to the journalistic outlook. But that he could exercise these powers regularly, rapidly, and to a degree precisely suited to the requirements of the profession—this was, indeed, an unsuspected demonstration, if a short-lived one, of a new talent and self-control.[52]

In his contributions to the *Morning Post* at this time, Coleridge makes his first considerable move towards the conservative attitude. In his *France: an Ode* more than a year before, Coleridge had abandoned youthful hopes with his denunciation of the militarists who appeared to be taking control of the country. This undoubted lapse from the cause of freedom seemed to him, in 1800, to have hardened into something approaching permanent aggression. He declaimed against Napoleon and in this connexion it is as difficult to see wherein lay the inconsistency with which he was to be charged by Hazlitt and others as it is to see in Napoleon the high-priest of freedom.[53]

Coleridge still opposed the Government, and Pitt in particular. His poem *Fire, Famine, and Slaughter*, a denunciation of Pitt for letting loose the horrors of war, was followed by a string of leading articles in which the Prime Minister was more often than not the villain of the piece. The *Morning Post* was, of course, a supporter of Fox. But, like Wordsworth, Coleridge had discovered whilst in Germany the depth of his love for England.

Realization of his affection, coupled now with a practical vision of what a country could be, torn by strife, fearful of the future, disunited, with no common love of land or ruler to impose order and give hope—this necessarily imposed upon his political opinions a cautiousness formerly foreign to him—a certain tendency at times to remoteness which his philosophical activities of the past years would necessarily forward. After he had seen how much worse justice, public opinion, honesty, happiness, and freedom could fare in another country than in his own, his animosity against the policy of the Government could not but moderate as his republican fervour died. As might be supposed, following upon his close association with a newspaper, Coleridge for the time and on paper, at least, became more of a party man. Instead of demanding freedom, he called for the elevation of the Liberals to power, with appropriate abuse of those already in office. He called for the ending of the war, denounced Pitt for refusing to treat for peace, and took the line that the French, as a nation, were not to be blamed, even for the proposed Constitution of Sieyes.

> "The eighteenth Century is now at its close," he wrote on the last day of the year, "a century venerable for its discoveries, terrific in its events! This impudent offer of these mountebank liberticides—was it to mortify pride, that *this* is doomed to be the *last* incident of such a century? Is it to deaden the extravagance of human hope, that the general acceptance of it will probably be the *first* incident of the new age? Alas, poor human nature! or rather, indeed, alas, poor Gallic nature! For Γραῖοι ἀεὶ παῖδες: the French are always children, and it is the infirmity of benevolence to wish, or dread aught concerning them." [54]

Coleridge stated later that when "solicited to undertake the literary and political department in the *Morning Post*" he accepted "on the condition that the paper should thenceforwards be conducted on certain fixed and announced principles, and that I should neither be obliged nor requested to deviate from them in favour of any party or any event." [55] But while it will scarcely be disputed that he gave a new vigour and popularity to the columns of the *Morning Post*, it is not easy to see that the policy of the paper changed in any marked degree from its original Liberal, anti-Pitt attitude. Rather would it be more correct to say that, of the two, it was Coleridge who conformed to the policy he found in occupation. He did, however, play a considerable part in raising the standard of contributions to the paper, and so eventually of journalism itself—a consummation for which the deliberate plan of Stuart must also claim much credit.

Proof of Coleridge's success in journalism is best found neither in his somewhat extravagant assertions of later days [56] nor in the equally extravagant denials of a hurt and angry Stuart,[57] but in the offer Stuart made when Coleridge withdrew from regular work for the *Morning Post*. Also in Stuart's willingness, if not positive anxiety, to retain Coleridge's services at a later date, despite his knowledge of his brilliant contributor's utter unreliability in the matter of producing work to time. Kindness (of which, with forbearance, Stuart was to display much) could not alone account satisfactorily for the editor's actions.

Coleridge's journalistic excellence was in no sense a question of merit acquired after long practice. His work was as spontaneous as such work could be; and the merit in it was, almost necessarily, present from the first; for by February 14, barely ten weeks after he had come to London, Coleridge, tired and harassed by his unwonted exertions and the many demands upon his time, anxious to get on with *Wallenstein*, informed Poole that "I have given up the *Morning Post*, but the editor is importunate against it." [58] He explains his position to Stuart who, not unnaturally, had protested against this abrupt withdrawal from the service of his paper. The usual "Dear Stuart" had frozen temporarily to "Dear Sir."

"I feel more uncomfortably respecting my conduct to *you* for these last ten days, than I have had occasion to feel on any occasion for these last twenty months. Your last note has just reached me. The former is here, but I have not read it, having been out of London to avoid interruptions. Whether we continue connected or no, I consider myself as two full weeks' work in your debt for that which I have already received. These cursed Plays play the devil with me. I have been writing from morning till night, and almost half the night too, and yet get on too slowly for the printer; and Mr Longman is kept in constant [dread] that some rival translation may pop out before mine. And besides this, my wife and child leave London tomorrow; and I was particularly desirous to have done enough to give me some *claim* to draw on him for the few pounds which I must draw on him for their journey. These things I mention, not as justifications of my breach of promise, but as palliations. So much for the past. For the future, thus much. In about four or five days I shall have finished the first Play; and that being finished, I may go on more leisurely with the others. I shall then be able to give you some assistance, probably as much as you may want. A certain number of Essays I consider myself bound to send you AS SOON AS POSSIBLE, in common honesty. AFTER these, if it be worth your while, I will do what I can, only not for any regular *stipend*. That harasses me. I know that hitherto I have received from you much more than I have earned, and this must not be. I have no objection to be paid for what I *do*, but a great objection to be paid for what I OUGHT to do. This translation-Fag has almost knocked me up, and I am so confused that I scarcely know whether I have expressed myself intelligibly. My wife goes tomorrow evening, and I shall be at No. 36 Chapel St., Pentonville."

He adds: "I will certainly fill you out a good paper on Sunday." [59]

Whether or not the "good paper" was filled out that Sunday is unknown, but as Coleridge's estimate of the time needed for the completion of even the first part of *Wallenstein* was woefully inaccurate the promise is unlikely to have been fulfilled. However, Coleridge's connexion with Stuart was not severed completely although his contributions to the *Morning Post* for the time being dwindled rapidly and soon ceased altogether.

Stuart made an effort to revive his contributor's flagging interest. He asked Coleridge to report a debate in Parliament. Thus, in the next breath after telling Poole that he had finished with the *Morning Post*, Coleridge adds, "Tonight I must go with him [Stuart] to the House of Commons." [60] And goes on to explain that "on the great debate I was in the terrible crowd from 8 Monday Morning to 3 Tuesday morning and continued after this writing and correcting till 9." [61]

A few days later, in a letter to Josiah Wedgwood, who had just told him of Tom's intention to try a journey to the West Indies in the hope of recovering health, Coleridge described his experiences in Parliament, enclosing a copy of the *Morning Post* containing his report:

"I have been three times to the House of Commons," he wrote; "each time earlier than the former; and each time hideously crowded. The two first days the debate was put off. Yesterday I went at a quarter before eight, and remained till three this morning,

[393]

and then sat writing and correcting other men's writing till eight —a good twenty-four hours of unpleasant activity! I have not felt myself sleepy yet. Pitt and Fox completely answered my pre-formed ideas of them. The elegance and high finish of Pitt's periods, even in the most sudden replies, is *curious*, but that is all. He argues but so so, and does not reason at all. Nothing is rememberable of what he says. Fox possesses all the full and over-flowing eloquence of a man of clear head, clear heart, and im-petuous feelings. He is to my mind a great orator; all the rest that spoke were mere creatures. I could make a better speech myself than any that I heard, except Pitt and Fox. I reported that part of Pitt's which I have enclosed in brackets, not that I report ex-officio, but my curiosity having led me there, I did Stuart a service by taking a few notes." [62]

He goes on to tell Wedgwood of his approaching release from work in London, together with some animadversions upon the craft he had for all practical purposes forsaken; though he showed himself not without pride in his own achievements:

"I work from morning to night," he wrote, "but in a few weeks I shall have completed my purpose, and then adieu to London for ever. We newspaper scribes are true galley-slaves. When the high winds of events blow loud and frequent then the sails are hoisted, or the ship drives on of itself. When all is calm and sunshine then to our oars. Yet it is not unflattering to a man's vanity to reflect that what he writes at twelve at night, will before twelve hours are over, have perhaps, five or six thousand readers! To trace a happy phrase, good image, or new argument, running through the town and sliding into all the papers. Few wine merchants can boast of creating more sensa-tion. Then to hear a favourite and often-urged argument, repeated almost in your own particular phrases, in the House of Commons; and, quietly in the silent self-complacence of your own heart, chuckle over the plagiarism, as if you were monopolist of all good reasons. But seriously, considering that I have newspapered it merely as means of subsistence, while I was doing other things, I have been very lucky. *The New Constitution*; *The Proposal for Peace*; *The Irish Union*; etc. etc.; they are important in themselves, and excellent vehicles for general truths. I am not ashamed of what I have written." [63]

He ends by telling Wedgwood that he has attended Mackintosh's lectures regularly.[64]

In a letter to Southey just after his visit to Parliament, Coleridge speaks of his reporting activities. "I shall give up this Newspaper business," he writes; "it is too, too fatiguing. I have attended the Debates twice, and the first time I was twenty-five hours in activity, and that of a very unpleasant kind; and the second time, from ten in the morning till four o'clock the next morning." [65] A few days later he advises Southey to "Read Pitt's speech in the 'Morning Post' of today. I reported the whole with notes so scanty, that—Mr Pitt is much obliged to me. For, by Heaven, he never talked half as eloquently in his life-time. He is a *stupid, insipid* charlatan, that *Pitt*." [66]

The Pitt report,[67] also destined to be the seat of controversy in later years, possibly did not cause the sensation that Coleridge was later to claim for it, but certainly was not as unremarkable as Stuart made out.[68]

As the first effort of a man to whom such work, and the conditions under which the work was carried out, was unfamiliar, this report of Pitt on the necessity of continuing the war, written up from exceedingly brief notes, shows a brilliant grasp of the requirements of political reporting. What it lacked in accuracy it more than made up for in interest, in conviction and in dramatic appeal. The report does credit to Pitt, if indeed it does not openly flatter him. The gist of the matter was his if the eloquence was not. That it further advanced the reputation of the *Morning Post* is by no means unlikely.[69]

Poole, though worried by Coleridge's abrupt throwing up of his engagement with Stuart, was pleased with the Pitt report:

"I was highly pleased with the last of your Pitt's speeches," he wrote. "It was an eminent instance of the magick of language upon truth and reason—the finest manufacture from the worst materials. But wherefore deck out the minister in this way? Why had you not reported Sheridan and his side?" [70]

But he is anxious that Coleridge shall not rashly jeopardize his future:

"You have closed, you say, with the *Morning Post,*" Poole says in the same letter. "I never liked your being a newspaper writer, but I trust as you entered into an engagement, that you have fulfilled it, and that you have not closed without answering your *own* and Stuart's purpose. To do this would make the last errour greater than the first. When I say I do not wish you to be a newspaper writer, I do not simply speak impartially, but contrary to my own pleasure and interest; for the regular receipt of the *Morning Post*, and what you have written in it, have given me great delight." He asks anxiously: "If you have given up the paper, what are you doing? Let me know."[71]

One fact was quite certain to Coleridge: he was not going to continue working for the *Morning Post*. The Pitt report, though the result of it had afforded him some gratification, had, at the same time, by its revelation of the rigours and waste of energy involved in Parliamentary reporting, finally set the seal on Coleridge's determination to be done with journalism, for the time being at least.

"I can without any straining gain 500 guineas a year, if I give up poetry—i.e. original poetry," he told Poole a few days later. "If I had the least love of money I could make almost sure of £2,000 a year, for Stuart has offered me half shares in the two papers, the *Morning Post* and the *Courier*, if I would devote myself with him to them—but I told him that I would not give up the country, and the lazy reading of old folios for two thousand times two thousand pound—in short, that beyond £250 a year I considered money as a real evil—at which he stared. I think there are but two good ways of writing—one for immediate and wide impression, though transitory—the other for permanence. Newspapers are the first—the best one can do is the second. That middle class of translating books is neither the one nor the other. When I have settled myself *clear*, I shall write nothing for money but for the newspaper."[72]

Like most of Coleridge's dealings with Stuart at this time, the authenticity of this offer has been doubted. The possibility that Coleridge was exaggerating is certainly far from unlikely. The likelihood that Stuart, a good business man, would be prepared to make so definite an offer, or risk so unpractical a man as Coleridge as partner, seems remote. Nevertheless, the substance of Coleridge's statement is undoubtedly true. Stuart did not want to lose this valuable contributor. To keep him, he would be prepared to pay handsomely—more than usual, more than the generous terms he had paid hitherto. He would doubtless be prepared at the least to hint of the possible financial advantages of a permanent association with the paper.[73]

In any event, Coleridge would do no more than give a promise of further contributions. He would not be tied. For the present he had determined, goaded by the worried Longman, to devote most of his time to making an end of the translation.

So, Sarah and Hartley gone in the first days of March to visit Mrs Roskilly—wife of the former curate at Stowey, now Rector of Kempsford[74]—for five weeks at least, with a further two contemplated with Mrs Fricker at Bristol,[75] Coleridge moved, not as he had told Southey previously, to the house of Purkis, with whom he had become intimate—"one of your lovers,"[76] Poole had described him, laughingly—but to Lamb's lodgings at Pentonville.

The friendship with Lamb had revived quickly. By January Coleridge was recommending Lamb's "My Great Aunt's Manuscript" to Stuart for use in the *Morning Post*;[77] and Lamb was acting as courier between Southampton Street and Stuart's offices when Coleridge felt indisposed.[78]

On the 23rd of the month, Lamb wrote to Coleridge, thanking him for "the very novel and exquisite manner in which you combined political with grammatical science, in your yesterday's dissertation on Mr Wyndham's unhappy composition. It must have been the death-blow to that ministry. I expect Pitt and Grenville to resign."[79]

He went on: "I expect Manning[80] of Cambridge in town tonight —will you fulfil your promise of meeting him at my house? He is a man of a thousand. Give me a line to say what day, whether Saturday, Sunday, Monday, etc., and if Sara and the Philosopher can come. I am afraid that if I did not at intervals call upon you, I should *never see you*. But I forget, the affairs of the nation engross your time and your mind."[81]

The dinner with Manning duly took place and the Cambridge man fell under the spell of Coleridge's personality and conversation[82]—a fact the more remarkable in that Manning must have been far from favourably predisposed towards Coleridge, for he had as a pupil and friend none other than Charles Lloyd, now a student of Caius and married to his Sophia.[83]

Coleridge advanced further in Lamb's favour as Lloyd slipped from it. An incident at this time hastened the process. Lloyd, it seems, had at one time encouraged the affections of Mary Hays, whom Coleridge met in London. Coleridge was far from impressed by this early feminist and materialist, of whose intellect he tells Southey: "I think not *contemptuously* but certainly *despectively* . . . for to hear a thing, ugly and petticoated, ex-syllogize a God with cold-blooded precision, and attempt to run religion through the body with an icicle, an icicle from a Scotch Hog-trough! *I* do not endure it." [84] Nevertheless, he could not but regard with indignation—mingled with which, the culprit being who he was, a certain satisfaction, perhaps even pleasure, is to be discerned—the attitude of Lloyd towards her. "Charles Lloyd's conduct," he writes Southey in the same letter, "has been atrocious beyond what you stated. Lamb himself confessed to me that during the time in which he kept up his ranting, sentimental correspondence with Miss Hayes, he frequently read her letters in company, as a subject for *laughter*, and then sate down and answered them quite *à la Rousseau!*" [85]

His disquisition ends more in sorrow than in anger, and not unmingled with righteous triumph: "Poor Lloyd! Every hour new-creates him; he is his own posterity in a perpetually flowing series, and his body unfortunately retaining an external identity, *their* mutual contradictions and disagreeings are united under one name, and of course are called lies, treachery, and rascality! I would not give him up, but that the same circumstances which have wrenched his morals prevent in him any salutary exercise of genius. And therefore he is not worth to the world that I should embroil and embrangle myself in his interests." [86]

All this was faithfully repeated by Southey to Lloyd and Manning; and by the latter, with protests, back to Lamb, together with an accusation against Coleridge in quite another connexion, of telling lies.[87] But this time, helped no doubt by Coleridge's presence in London, Lamb stood by his old friend.

"Lloyd's letter to Miss Hays I look upon to be a most curious specimen of the apologetic style," he wrote Manning in reply. "How a man could write such a letter to a woman, and dream that there was in it any tendency to soothe or conciliate, from no analogous operations in my own wrong Brain can I explain. . . . Now, Manning, seriously what do you think of this letter? does it appear that Coleridge has added one jot to what Miss Hays might fairly represent from Lloyd's own confession?—You doubt, whether Southey ever exprest himself so strongly on this subject. I suppose you refer to Coleridge's account of him. I can tell you, that Southey did express himself in very harsh terms of Lloyd's conduct, when he was last in town. He came fresh from Miss Hays, who had given him all the story, as I find she tells everybody! and told Southey she despised Lloyd. I am not sure, that Southey was not in a humour, after this representation, to say all that Coleridge declared he did say. Particularly, if he saw this Letter, which I believe he did. Now, do not imagine, that Col. has prejudiced my mind in this *at all*,—the truth is, I write from my own single judgment, and when I showed the Letter to Coleridge, he read it in silence, or only once muttered the word 'indelicate.' But I should not have been easy in concealing my true sentiment from you. My whole moral sense is up in arms against the Letter. . . . I will sum up the controversy in the words of Coleridge, all he has since said to me, 'Miss Hayes has acted like a fool, & Charles Lloyd not very wisely.' " [88]

The further accusation against Coleridge met with no greater success:

"I cannot but smile," Lamb continued, "at Lloyd's beginning to find out, that Col. can tell lyes. He brings a serious charge against him—that he told Caldwell he had no engagements with the Newspapers! As long as Lloyd or I have known Col. so long have we known him in the daily & hourly habit of quizzing the world by lyes, most unaccountable & most disinterested fictions. With a correct knowledge of these inaccuracies on both sides, I am still desirous of keeping on kind terms with Lloyd, and I am to sup with Coleridge tonight—Godwin will be there, whom I am rather curious to see—& Col. to partake with me of Mannings Bounty [89] tomorrow." [90]

In the following month, this second charge was discovered by Manning to have no foundation in fact. "You recollect, I suppose," he told Lamb, "the story about Coleridge's humming Caldwell of Jesus College concerning his newspaper engagements—well it is turned out to be all a mistake—Caldwell has never imputed any such declaration to Coleridge." [91]

Thus Coleridge emerged from this not very edifying welter of gossip, back-chat, and accusations more or less scatheless and— what is much more to the point—refixed with greater firmness in the good graces of Lamb. Indeed, good graces is scarcely the right expression; for although the old Coleridge worship had disappeared as Lamb discovered a mind of his own and realized the extreme fallibility of his old idol, there took its place a more settled, a better balanced admiration and affection.

Their new intimacy came on apace. "Coleridge has conceived a most high (Quaere if just) opinion of you, most illustrious Archimedes," [92] Lamb wrote Manning on February 9. "Philosopher Godwin dines with me on your Turkey this day—I expect the roof to fall in & crush the Atheist. I have been drunk two nights running at Coleridge's." [93]

Coleridge's move to Lamb's lodgings at Pentonville when Sarah and Hartley had left London was therefore only to be expected. The two settled down to much of their former conviviality. That some work was done on *Wallenstein* there need be no doubt; but Coleridge's assurance to Poole at this time, that he was "very quiet" [94] and wished to be at Stowey requires some qualification. That he was sometimes quiet, that he often felt a longing for the peace of Stowey and Poole's steadying influence, is unquestionable; but that he had other interests, other means of occupying his mind, some far from quiet, is equally certain.

By March 3 he had made himself at home at No. 36 Chapel Street, and was writing Godwin, now fast becoming an intimate:

> "The punch, after the wine, made me tipsy last night. This I mention, not that my head aches, or that I felt, after I quitted you, any unpleasantness or titubancy; but because tipsiness has, and has always, one unpleasant effect—that of making me talk very extravagantly; and as, when sober, I talk extravagantly enough for any common tipsiness, it becomes a matter of nicety in discrimination to know when I am or am not affected. An idea starts up in my head,—away I follow through thick and thin, wood and marsh, brake and briar, with all the apparent interest of a man who was defending one of his old and long-established principles. Exactly of this kind was the conversation with which I quitted you. I do not believe it possible for a human being to have a greater horror of the feelings that usually accompany such principles as I then supposed [supported], or a deeper conviction of their irrationality, than myself; but the whole thinking of my life will not bear me up against the accidental crowd and press of my mind, when it is elevated beyond its natural pitch. We shall talk wiselier with the ladies on Tuesday. God bless you, and give your dear little ones a kiss a-piece from me." [95]

As soon as he had joined forces with Lamb, Coleridge's energizing influence began to take effect. This gift of pouring into the minds and hearts of his friends an almost illimitable inspirational force, of lifting them above the trammels of their own personality, of discerning and freeing the true man, was the more remarkable for its inability to benefit the source from which it sprang. Thus it is often in his friends that the truest expression of the inner Coleridge is to be seen. They are all, in fact, in one way or another, little Coleridges, faint, minor, and somewhat melancholy symbols of the Coleridge that might have been.

In a letter of Lamb to Manning on March 17, the effect of Coleridge's presence is shown clearly, and is none the less striking for all Lamb's half-humorous, half deprecatory method of announcing his new activity, and for the fact Coleridge did not stay to complete what he had begun. When Lamb's situation is considered; his seclusion; his constant dread of further outbreaks on the part of his sister, Mary; his lack of concentration; his aimlessness, if not positive lack of ambition; then something of the true effect upon him of less than three weeks' close contact with Coleridge becomes apparent.

> "I am living in a continuous feast," he writes. "Coleridge has been with me now for nigh three weeks, and the more I see of him in the quotidian undress and relaxation of his mind, the more cause I see to love him, and believe him a *very good man*, and all those foolish impressions to the contrary fly off like morning slumbers. He is engaged in translations, which I hope will keep him this month to come. He is uncommonly kind and friendly to me. He ferrets me day and night to *do something*. He tends me, amidst all his own worrying and heart-oppressing occupations, as a gardener tends his young *tulip*. . . . He has lugged me to the brink of engaging to a newspaper, and has suggested to me for a first plan the forgery of a supposed manuscript of Burton, the anatomist of melancholy." [96]

Southey, his nerves frayed and his digestion impaired, finally, early in April, set out for Lisbon with Edith, on his uncle Hill's invitation; [97] but not before, in the course of a considerable correspondence with Coleridge, the project of a common dwelling-place, until abandoned by Coleridge on account of the 'Life of Lessing', had in imagination peopled a home in many parts of the world. The islands of Greece, Turkey, Poland, Hungary, Trieste, Italy, Constantinople—these were some of the suggested places wherein the little colony was to have discovered peace and quiet.[98] But the South of France—barred to them by the war—was, they felt, the most desirable centre.[99]

Southey's need for money to go abroad produced a crop of suggestions, some fantastic, others closer to reality. For most of them Coleridge was responsible. Why should not Southey and he "*toss up*" a novel, he asks.[100] Godwin, he tells his friend, has made £400 from his *St. Neon*. "As sure as ink flows in my pen," he wrote, "by help of an amanuensis I could write a volume a week."[101] If Southey does not care for the suggestion, Coleridge is ready with another—and another. "You'll write another quarter for Mr Stuart? You will torture yourself for twelve or thirteen guineas?" he asks. "I pray you do not do so!"[102] He presents Southey with some more profitable alternatives. "You might easily make twice the money you receive from Stuart by the use of the scissors; for your name is prodigiously high among the London publishers."[103] Longman, he says, paid Cottle £370 for the copyright of Southey's *Joan of Arc* and 1797 *Poems*. Cottle had himself made a profit of £250 on them. "You are a strong swimmer, and have borne up poor Joey with all his leaden weights about him,"[104] Coleridge assured Southey. "Nothing has answered to him but your works. By me he has lost somewhat—by Fox, Amos, and himself *very much*."[105] Moreover, Coleridge knows Longman to be "most and very eager to have the property of your works at almost any price."[106] This should show Southey that his name was beginning to become known, that it was worth money.

"Thus, for instance," Coleridge suggests, "bring together on your table, or skim over successively Brücker, Lardner's 'History of Heretics,' Russell's 'Modern Europe,' and Andrew's 'History of England,' and write a history of levellers and the levelling principle under some goodly title. . . . I will gladly write a philosophical introduction that shall enlighten without offending."[107] But the idea fell through because Southey would not consent to set his name to such a book and the booksellers would not publish anonymously.[108]

Coleridge, undismayed, continued to pour out suggestions. He urges Southey to finish *Thalaba* quickly. It will, he assures his friend, "beyond all doubt bring you two hundred pounds, if you will sell it at once; but *do* not print at a venture, under the notion of selling the edition. . . . I can sell your 'Thalaba' quite as well in your absence as in your presence."[109] Again, however, the plan fell through; Southey did not feel able, or inclined, to rush the completion of the poem.[110] The indefatigable Coleridge then sounded the booksellers afresh, and with some success: "Phillips," he told Southey, "would be very glad to engage you to write a school book for him, the History of Poetry in all nations, about 400 pages: but this, too, *must* have your name. He would give sixty pounds."[111] Southey again demurred: he complained that Phillips was not all he might be.[112]

"Phillips is a good-for-nothing fellow," agreed Coleridge, "but what of that? He will give you sixty pounds, and advance half the money now for a book you can do in a fortnight, or three weeks at farthest."[113] But Southey still held out. He did not know sufficient French, German or Italian, he said; and he was chary of setting his name haphazard to a book of which he might not approve.[114]

Coleridge brushed these objections aside: "I do not see that a book said by you in the preface to have been written merely as a book for young persons could injure your reputation more than Milton's 'Accidence' injured *his*. I *would do it*, because you can do it so easily. It is not necessary that you should say much about French or German literature. Do it so. Poetry of savage nations— Poetry of rudely civilized—Homer and the Hebrew Poetry, etc. —Poetry of civilized nations under Republics and Polytheism, State of Poetry under the Roman and Greek Empires—Revival of it in Italy, in Spain, and England—then go steadily on with England to the end, except one chapter about German Poetry to conclude with, which I can write for you."[115]

Southey, unconvinced, made some suggestions himself. Let them write a drama.[116] But Coleridge was emphatic. "The theatre! the theatre! my dear Southey! it will never, never, never do! . . . for present money, novels or translations."[117]

And of Southey's other suggestion, that they might run jointly a magazine with signed articles,[118] Coleridge fought equally shy: "Your review-plan *cannot* answer for this reason," he explained. "It could exist only as long as the ononymous anti-anonymists remained in life, health, and the humour, and no publisher would undertake a periodical publication on so gossamery a tie. Besides, it really would not be right for any man to make so many people have strange and uncomfortable feelings towards him; which must be the case, however kind the reviews might be—and what but nonsense is published?"[119]

In the event, none of the money-making plans materialized; and Southey, who received £100 unexpectedly from a friend, was able to make his way to Portugal without the aid of this hack work.[120]

The correspondence between the two men at this time also produced some isolated but interesting glimpses of Coleridge. There was, for instance, the question of George, the youngest Fricker child. Southey approached Coleridge to see whether the latter would help to improve the boy's prospects. With superb optimism, Coleridge at once expressed his willingness "to become his bondsman for five hundred pounds."[121] For, said he, kind-hearted as usual, if unpractical, "To remain all his life an under clerk, as many have done, and earn fifty pounds a year in his old age with a trembling hand—alas! that were a dreary prospect. No creature under the sun is so helpless, so unfitted, I should think, for any other mode of life as a clerk, a mere clerk."[122]

He is on surer ground when he goes on to suggest, "We might between us keep him neat in clothes from our own wardrobes, I should think, and I am ready to allow five guineas this year."[123]

More is heard of Hartley, of whom Coleridge was never tired of quoting; "he sported of his own accord a theologico-astronomical hypothesis," he told Southey. "Having so perpetually heard of good boys being put up into the sky when they are dead, and being now beyond measure enamoured of the lamps in the streets, he said one night coming through the streets, 'Stars are dead lamps, they be'nt naughty, they are put up in the sky.'"[124]

Still further of the boy's goings-on. "Hartley is rampant," his proud father writes, "and emperorizes with your pictures. Harry is a fine boy. Hartley told a gentleman, 'Metinks you are *like Southey*,' and he *was* not wholly unlike you—but the chick calling you simple 'Southey,' so pompously!"[125]

Southey had accused Coleridge of 'illuminizing';[126] and he starts Coleridge off on a brief excursion into sociology and political economy. "I think that property will some time or other be modified by the predominance of intellect, even as rank and superstition are now modified by and subordinated to property, that much is to be hoped of the future; but first those particular modes of property which more particularly stop the diffusion must be done away, as injurious to property itself; these are priesthood and the too great patronage of Government. Therefore, if to act on the belief that all things are the process, and that inapplicable truths are moral falsehoods, be to illuminize, why then I illuminize!"[127]

On February 18 he tells Southey, "I shall do no more for Stuart."[128] Certainly he had ceased regular work for the paper. Yet what was possibly the most successful of all his contributions —his *Character of Pitt*—did not appear in the *Morning Post* until March 19, when he had been domesticated with Lamb for more than a fortnight. This article, which increased the sales and reputation of the paper considerably, is a brilliant piece of writing, though its estimate of the Prime Minister is not uncoloured by party politics.[129]

In a letter to Estlin a little earlier, Coleridge makes some scathing remarks about education of the wrong type at Oxford and Cambridge and expresses a horror of festivities on the Sabbath— remarks wholly explicable only by the known views of his correspondent.[130] Dr Disney, the man who indirectly provoked the censure was Unitarian minister in Essex Street. The minister himself, Coleridge told Estlin, "I *respect*, highly respect: in the Pulpit he is an *Apostle*, but *there—there it stops*."[131]

As for the Sunday party: 'My dear Friend! in the crowded, heartless Party at Dr Disney's, O! how I did think of your Sunday Suppers, their light uncumbrous simplicity, the heartiness of manner, the literary Christianness of Conversation."[132]

Coleridge's strictures on the universities were excited by Dr Disney's sons. "The younger," wrote Coleridge, "with his shirt collar halfway up his cheek, gave me no high idea of the propriety of Unitarian Dissenters sending their Sons to Established and Idolatrous Universities."[133]

In a postscript—so often the most complete revelation of Coleridge's mind—he enlarges on the subject with what may be estimated variously as a blithe, not to say hypocritical, disregard of his own quite recent experiences or as a determination to profit by them:

> "Nothing is more common than for conscious Infidels to go into the *Church*. Conscious Arians or Socinians swarm in it—so much for the *Morals* of Oxford and Cambridge. With their too early reasonings, and logic-cuttings, and reading Hume and such like

Trash, the young Dissenters are prone to Infidelity, but do you know any Instance of such an Infidel accepting an office that implied the belief of Christianity? It cannot be said, that it is owing to *our* Preferments being so much smaller: for the majority are but Curates in the Established Church, or on small Livings and not so well off as George Burnett was, or Sam Reed would have been, but this is it, my dear Friend! The Education, which Dissenters receive among Dissenters, generates Conscientiousness and a scrupulous Turn: will this be gained at the Wine Parties at Cambridge?" [134]

A second postscript, ostensibly dealing in praise of Mrs Barbauld, gains its greatest interest from Coleridge's diagnosis of his own character.

"The more I see of Mrs Barbauld the more I admire her—that wonderful *Propriety* of Mind! She has great *acuteness*, very great—yet how steadily she keeps it within the bounds of practical Reason. This I almost envy as well as admire—my own Subtleties too often lead me into strange (though God be praised) transient out-of-the-way-nesses. Oft like a winged spider, I am entangled in a new-spun web, but never fear for me, 'tis but the flutter of my wings—and off I am again!" [135]

But while Southey, for the time at least, had made his plans, Coleridge remained no nearer the choice of a home that should reconcile his conflicting desires. The only certainty was that Sarah must be settled in a house by the late summer.[136] Where that house should be, was still undecided. Coleridge's mind can be seen veering hither and thither. Or, it may be, endeavouring only, and with much unwillingness, to escape the pull towards Wordsworth. On December 24, it was the "pleasant little colony . . . in Italy or the South of France." [137] In January: "I must stay in England." [138] A fortnight later: "we are under the absolute necessity of fixing somewhere, and that somewhere will, I suppose, be Stowey." [139]

"In May," he tells Southey, "I am under a kind of engagement to go with Sara to Ottery. My family wish me to fix there, but *that* I must decline in the names of public liberty and individual free-agency. Elder brothers, not senior in intellect, and not sympathising in main opinions, are subjects of occasional visits, not temptations to a co-township." [140]

He adds: "if you go to Burton, Sara and I will waive the Ottery plan, if possible. . . ." [141] Then: "Alfoxden would make two houses

[406]

sufficiently divided for unimpinging independence." [142] At the same time he was writing Poole: "I shall, beyond all doubt, settle at Stowey, if I can get . . . a house." [143] Failing that: "we shall take lodgings at Minehead or Porlock." [144]

But never a word about going north to live. The possibility, it would seem, had not occurred to Coleridge. As far as Poole was to know, Coleridge remained as adamant to Wordsworth's suggestion as he had appeared to be when in Germany. Yet Coleridge had known for months and was not without reminders, that the Wordsworths still earnestly wished, still hoped for his settlement near them. He knew the direction in which his most powerful indication pointed. Finally, writing to Poole from Lamb's, Coleridge, facing facts at last, burst out in despair: "I would to God I could get Wordsworth to retake Allfoxden. The society of so great a being is of priceless value." [145] Not only would he be sundering himself from the strong and vitalizing influence of Wordsworth if he decided upon a house in the south; he was also being made increasingly conscious that he would be amidst men who either could not or would not appreciate Wordsworth's greatness—whose attitude was, in fact, that he, Coleridge, would be well advised to think less of his friend's powers and more of profiting by his own: Lamb, the Wedgwoods, Godwin, Southey, even Poole, sinned in this respect: "No one," he told Poole, "neither you or the Wedgwoods, although you far more than any one else, ever entered into the feeling due to a man like Wordsworth, of whom I do not hesitate in saying that, since Milton, no one has *manifested* himself equal to him." [146]

Poole, who could scarcely have avoided putting his finger upon the main cause of his friend's vacillations and sudden, mysterious fussiness about the amenities of a Stowey dwelling-place, was at this last straw unable to restrain his impatience. He replied sharply, a letter not without its tinge of jealousy, reproaching Coleridge for prostrating himself before Wordsworth.

On the last day of the month Coleridge replied:

> "You charge me with prostration in regard to Wordsworth. Have I affirmed anything miraculous of W? Is it impossible that a greater poet than any since Milton may appear in our days? Have there any *great* poets appeared since him? . . . Future greatness! Is it not an awful thing, my dearest Poole? What if you had

known Milton at the age of thirty, and believed all you now know of him?—What if you should meet in the letters of any then living man, expressions concerning the young Milton *totidem verbis* the same as mine of Wordsworth, would it not convey to you a most delicious sensation? Would it not be an assurance to you that your admiration of the *Paradise Lost* was no superstition, no shadow of flesh and bloodless abstraction, but that the *Man* was even so, that the greatness was incarnate and personal? Wherein blame I you, my best friend? Only in being borne down by other men's rash opinions concerning W." [147]

He goes on to reject yet another suggestion by Poole for a Stowey house—this time, a proposal that the Coleridges should occupy part of a farmhouse, sharing the kitchen with the occupants of the other half. Coleridge could see the seeds of much trouble in such an arrangement which, he said, would "be worse than the old hovel fifty times over." [148]

After this unusual bluntness of speech, he felt that Poole needed some reassurances:

"Do not, my dearest Poole, deem me cold, or finical, or indifferent to Stowey, full and fretful in objection; but on so important an affair to a man who has, and is likely to have, a family, and who *must* have silence and a *retired study*, as a house is, it were folly not to consult one's own feelings, folly not to let them speak audibly, and having heard them, hypocrisy not to utter them. . . . My dearest friend, when I have written to you lately, I have written with a mind and heart completely worn out . . . I trust in God you have not misinterpreted this into a change of character. I was a little jealous at an expression in your last letter— 'I am happy you begin to feel your power.' . . . my dear Tom, I feel not an atom more power than I have ever done, except the power of gaining a few more paltry guineas than I had supposed. On the contrary, my faculties appear to myself dwindling, and I do believe if I were to live in London another half year, I should be dried up wholly." [149]

But although the tone of his letter was in general mild and conciliatory, the effect of the charge of prostration seems to have been to drive him into Wordsworth's arms. Indeed, the very lack of recrimination in his letter, the assurances of his affection and the suggestion of his determination to settle in Stowey, while they speak of Coleridge's kindliness and love of Poole, mask also a further and less acceptable meaning; one that, in his anxiety not to hint to his friend, Coleridge, treading again the familiar path of weakness, would be at some pains to deny. From this moment it is probable that Coleridge's decision was made, even if, as would almost certainly be the case, he took care not to admit the fact even to himself. At the least, Poole's outbreak doubtless hastened his departure from London. Five days later Lamb was writing somewhat disconsolately to Manning:

"Coleridge has left us, to go into the north, on a visit to his god Wordsworth. With him have flown all my splendid prospects of engagement with the 'Morning Post,' all my visionary guineas." [150]

Wallenstein was not yet finished; Coleridge took it with him. He told Stuart he would be away for ten days and, having borrowed a few pounds for his journey, left London with all possible speed. [151]

If only Wordsworth would retake Alfoxden! So Coleridge had besought the fates in his letter to Poole. But this wish for time to be set back—one of the most earnest, most genuine wishes ever uttered by Coleridge—was vain. The last chance of persuading the Wordsworths to take a house in the south had gone after the summer of the previous year—a time when Coleridge had left his friends, waiting anxiously to hear of his plans so that they might suit their own to his convenience, without a letter for months. Now the Wordsworths had acted on their own. They were settled at last. And not at Alfoxden. If Coleridge wished to be near them, he had no alternative but to go north.

Coleridge knew this well enough: "he will never quit the North of England," [152] he had prophesied to Poole of Wordsworth, sadly. The day after Coleridge had left Sockburn the previous November, Wordsworth had returned in triumph. He had taken the little cottage, once an inn, that stood by the roadside at Grasmere. Into this place, Dove Cottage, he and Dorothy moved on December 20, having walked most of the way from Sockburn. [153]

On Christmas Eve, Wordsworth had written at length to Coleridge, describing their journey: "We talk of you perpetually," he said, "and for me I see you everywhere." [154] He enquired anxiously after his friend's health and told him not to trouble to contradict the story that the *Lyrical Ballads* were entirely the work of Coleridge. [155] "Such a rumour is the best thing that can befall them," he

[409]

ended, after Dorothy had scribbled, "Write soon I pray you. God bless you. My love to Mrs Coleridge and a kiss for Hartley."[156]

Neither Wordsworth nor Dorothy concealed their earnest hope that Coleridge would join them. On April 11 Dorothy reported to her brother Richard that Dove Cottage was quite full, for, in addition to Coleridge, John was there and their friend Cooke.[157]

Coleridge was hard at work on *Wallenstein*. "Tomorrow morning I send off the last sheet of my irksome, soul-wearying labour," he wrote Josiah Wedgwood ten days later. "Of its success I have no hope,"[158] he added, "but with all this I have learnt that I have Industry and Perseverance—and before the end of the year, if God grant me health, I shall have my wings wholly un-bird-limed."[159]

Wordsworth, who watched his friend's progress with admiration, said later that "there was nothing more astonishing than the ease and rapidity with which it was done."[160]

Coleridge himself felt far from satisfied with the work, which he called "a dull heavy play, but I entertain hopes that you will think the language for the greater part, natural, and good common-sense English."[161] But his judgment was clouded by recent memories of a dreaded 'task.' Later, he was to take a not unmerited pride in his work.[162]

Schiller had attested the copy from which the translation was to be made, on September 30 the previous year; but he had not been informed by Bell of the transfer of the English copyright to Longmans. Hence, when the play appeared in print—*The Piccolomini* in April and *The Death of Wallenstein* in June—*The Camp*, the first, introductory part of the trilogy had not been attempted —Schiller wrote to Coleridge, asking how he had come into possession of the German MS. The transaction had to be explained to him.[163]

Coleridge's prognostication was only too well founded. The work was a complete failure; a fact due neither to its demerits as literature nor its unsuitability for representation on the stage so much as to the political conditions of the time. German drama, so popular a few years before, had declined rapidly in favour as the cause of Republicanism fell into disrepute.[164] Schiller had gone out of fashion. And the man about whom the play revolved appeared to possess far too many of the characteristics of the

dreaded Napoleon to stand a chance of acceptance as the hero
Schiller made him. His character rendered the whole work suspect.

The *Anti-Jacobin Review*, the *Monthly Review*, the *British
Critic* were unanimous in condemning play, hero, and translator
alike. They found the play tedious, extravagant, and often absurd;
Wallenstein's actions disgusting and profligate; the translation
lame and without harmony or elegance. The true merits of both
drama and translation were obscured by this onslaught; and even
its translator considered that an explanation which was not far
removed from an apology was due from him for undertaking the
work: The *Monthly Review* described Coleridge as "by far the
most rational partisan of the German theatre," [165] and he hastened
to protest.

> "As I am confident there is no passage in my preface or notes
> from which such an opinion can be legitimately formed," he
> wrote, "and as the truth would not have been exceeded if the
> direct contrary had been affirmed, I claim it of your justice that in
> your Answers to Correspondents you would remove this misrepre-
> sentation. The mere circumstance of translating a manuscript play
> is not even evidence that I admired that one play, much less that I
> am a general admirer of plays in that language." [166]

Not only was the representation of *Wallenstein* on the stage
rendered out of the question; even the sales of the published play
fell flat. The work was quickly remaindered by the publishers
against Coleridge's advice,[167] and in a few years when the translation began to acquire a good name, copies were practically un-
obtainable. Yet the play has many merits; and Coleridge's free
translation of it, though not without errors, is a noble piece of
work—one which, when taste had disassociated itself from political
principles, was hailed, not without justice, as greater than the
original. Whilst perpetuating Schiller's grandiose treatment of the
subject, Coleridge's version is often simpler, his lines having greater
beauty, his words greater power than the German. His interpola-
tions possess both poetic merit and personal interest.[168]

A letter from Lamb at this time, signed C Lamb, *Umbra*, from
Land of shadows, and dated Shadow-month the 16th or 17th,
reproaches Coleridge for dwelling overmuch on metaphysical
subjects in his last letter—a letter in which Coleridge had asked
his friend if he would look after the proof sheets of *Wallenstein*.

"You read us a dismal homily upon 'Realities,' " wrote Lamb. "We know, quite as well as you do, what are shadows and what are realities. You, for instance, when you are over your fourth or fifth jorum, chirping about old school occurrences, are the best of realities." [169]

After *Wallenstein* was off his hands, Coleridge fell again into the full effortless intimacy of day-long rambles and talks with Wordsworth and Dorothy; the only difference being that now, instead of wandering down the combes and over the heathery smoothness of the Quantocks, their feet took them up the rocky sides of Lakeland fells and in the mornings their eyes looked over Grasmere in place of Alfoxden's park and rounded hill.

Moreover, these walks, unlike most of those in Somerset, had an object beyond the mere pleasure the three of them felt in walking and talking together.

Coleridge was looking for a suitable home—just in case the Stowey district should still yield nothing satisfactory, he told himself. He found a house. Greta Hall stood on a little hill in a loop of the River Greta, facing Derwent Water, with Skiddaw rising up behind, with mountains in front and upon each side. Bassenthwaite Lake and the waterfall of Lodore were both visible from the house. Keswick was only a few minutes' walk away. The house was roomy; the rent low; and the distance from Grasmere, although some four times the distance between Alfoxden and Stowey,[170] was no kind of obstacle to such doughty walkers as Coleridge and his friends.

Coleridge was enraptured by the situation of Greta Hall.

"I left Wordsworth on the 4th of this month," he wrote Godwin from Poole's house on May 21. "If I cannot procure a suitable house at Stowey I return to Cumberland and settle at Keswick, in a house of such a prospect, that if according to you and Hume, impressions and ideas *constitute* our being, I shall have a tendency to become a god, so sublime and beautiful will be the series of my visual existence." [171]

He continues: "But whether I continue here or migrate thither, I shall be in a beautiful country, and have house-room and heart-room for you, and you must come and write your next work at my house." [172]

But despite his words, it is difficult, indeed it is well-nigh impossible, to believe that he had any longer, or wished to have, a choice. His mind was made up; and although his visit to Stowey was in part undertaken ostensibly for the purpose of seeking a convenient house, there seems little doubt that he spent most of his time preparing himself to break the news to Poole and to Sarah.[173]

Godwin had missed Coleridge. "He seems, above all men, mortified at your going away," reported Lamb. "Suppose you were to write to that good-natured heathen—'or is he a *shadow?*'"[174]—a suggestion with which Coleridge, though always intending to comply, had never quite succeeded in doing. Now Godwin, waiting no longer, had written warmly, attributing to the influence of Coleridge his own advance in appreciation of poetry and philosophy during the past few months.[175]

"I received your letter this morning," Coleridge replied, adding with unblushing faith both in his own good intentions and in his friend's continued belief in their existence "and had I not, still I am almost confident that I should have written to you before the end of the week . . . I remember you with so much pleasure and our conversations so distinctly, that I doubt not we have been mutually benefitted; but as to your poetic and physiopathic feelings, I more than suspect that dear little Fanny and Mary have had more to do in that business than I. Hartley sends his love to Mary. 'What? and not to Fanny?' 'Yes, and to Fanny, but I'll *have* Mary.' He often talks about them."[176]

There had fallen upon Lamb another blow. Hetty, the Lambs' old servant, had died. The shock had unseated his sister's reason—her first serious attack since the death of their father—and she had to be removed and placed in confinement.

Lamb, in despair, wrote to Coleridge:

"I am left alone in a house with nothing but Hetty's dead body to keep me company. To-morrow I bury her, and then I shall be quite alone, with nothing but a cat to remind me that the house has been full of living beings like myself. My heart is quite sunk, and I don't know where to look for relief. Mary will get better again; but her constantly being liable to such relapses is dreadful; nor is it the least of our evils that her case and all our story is so well known around us. We are in a manner *marked*. . . . I am completely shipwrecked. My head is quite bad. I almost wish that Mary were dead."[177]

Godwin, in his letter, commented upon Lamb's misfortunes:

"My poor Lamb! How cruelly afflictions crowd upon him!" agreed Coleridge. "I am glad that you think of him as I think; he

[413]

has an affectionate heart, a mind *sui generis*; his taste acts so as to appear like the unmechanic simplicity of an instinct—in brief he is worth an hundred men of *mere* talents. Conversation with the latter tribe is like the use of leaden bells—one warms by exercise —Lamb every now and then *irradiates*, and the beam, though single and fine as a hair, is yet rich with colours, and I both see and feel it." [178]

He passed to Davy:

"In Bristol I was much with Davy, almost all day; he always talks of you with great affection. . . . If I settle at Keswick, he will be with me in the fall of the year, and so meet you—And let me tell you, Godwin, four such men as you, I, Davy, and Wordsworth, do not meet together in one house every day of the year. I mean, four men so distinct with so many sympathies." [179]

Coleridge had heard from Southey the previous day.

"He arrived at Lisbon, after a prosperous voyage, on the last day of April. His letter to me is dated May-Day. He girds up his loins for a great history of Portugal, which will be translated into the Portuguese in the first year of the Lusitanian Republic." [180]

'Perdita,' Mrs Robinson, was ill.

"I wish I knew the particulars of her complaint. For Davy has discovered a perfectly new acid, by which he has restored the use of limbs to persons who had lost them for years. . . ." [181]

Early in the following month, Coleridge wrote to Davy asking for "a little tiny bottle of the acid." [182]

Another project looms up on the horizon.

"I think of translating Blumenbach's Manual of Natural History," he told Davy; "—it is very well written, and would, I think, be useful to students as an admirable direction to their studies, and to others it would supply a *general* knowledge of the subject. . . . Now I wish to know from you whether there is in English already any work of one volume (this would make 800 pages) that renders this useless. In short, should I be right in advising Longman to undertake it? Answer me as soon as you conveniently can. Blumenbach has been no very great discoverer, tho' he has done some respectable things in that way; but he is a man of enormous knowledge, and has an *arranging* head." [183]

[414]

A further request shows Coleridge upon the point of opening the books acquired in Germany and of returning to the problems neither heart nor head would suffer him to lay aside for long.

"When you have leisure," he wrote, "you would do me a great service, if you would briefly state your metaphysical system of Impressions, Ideas, Pleasures, and Pains, the laws that govern them, and the reasons which induce you to consider them as essentially distinct from each other. My motive for this request is the following. As soon as I settle, I shall read Spinoza and Leibnitz, and I particularly wish to know wherein they agree with and wherein they differ from you. If you will do this, I promise you to send you the result—and with it my own creed." [184]

At this time—the end of May and the first days of June— there was a general hush among his friends. The Coleridge circle seems for the moment immobilized, withdrawn from the central figure, as though awaiting his decision. Southey in Portugal; Tom Wedgwood at sea nearing Falmouth; Davy at Bristol, Godwin about to visit Ireland, both engaged to stay with Coleridge if he went north; Lamb swallowed up in desolation of heart; Stuart, with whom Coleridge's position was still unsettled, waiting for the elapse of "the ten days of my absence" [185] which were to lengthen into months—"Since I quitted you I have never been within 150 miles of London. I left Grasmere with that intention indeed, but at Kendal received letters which forced me Stowey-ward," Coleridge explained [186]—and who was beginning to feel that Coleridge wished to shun him; [187] and of course, nearer home, Poole and Sarah, waiting for him to speak—all stood apart in these crucial moments—moments of suspense and of significance. Upon Coleridge's choice there depended not only his own happiness and destiny, not only the happiness and destiny of those about him, but, it might be, the very future of English poetry.

And yet there was no decision. No decision remained to be made. It had been taken without words, without conscious thought, months before.

When Coleridge told Davy in those early June days "I have now finally determined on the North," [188] he was but announcing the inevitable. Even Poole, hurt and sad as he was, even Sarah, close to the birth of her third child, faced with the companionship of those she had little cause to love, the loss of her friends, knew well enough that Coleridge and the Wordsworths could not be separated for long.

Realization of the inevitability of the decision did not necessarily imply resignation to it. That there were protests, tears, even recrimination, seems certain. But they were without avail because they had to face, not so much Coleridge himself, as the Wordsworths in Coleridge; and—a fact which Sarah and Poole did not, could not know—because of that other influence, destined to challenge even the domination of the Wordsworths, and which unconsciously perhaps was helping even then to impel Coleridge irresistibly northward.

"I parted from Poole with pain and dejection, for him, and for myself in him," [189] Coleridge wrote. Nevertheless, they parted. And on Thursday, June 12, 1800, Sarah, Hartley and Coleridge left Stowey and set their faces towards the north.

LIST OF WORKS
TO WHICH FREQUENT REFERENCE IS MADE
IN THE NOTES FOLLOWING

L.   Letters of Samuel Taylor Coleridge. Edited by Ernest Hartley Coleridge. 2 vols., 1895.

U.L.   Unpublished Letters of Samuel Taylor Coleridge. Edited by Earl Leslie Griggs. 2 vols., 1932.

B.E.   Biographia Epistolaris. Being the Biographical Supplement of Coleridge's Biographia Literaria. With Additional Letters, etc. Edited by A. Turnbull. 2 vols., 1911.

A.   Letters, Conversations and Recollections of S. T. Coleridge. [Collected and edited by Thomas Allsop.] 2 vols., 1836.

E.   Unpublished Letters from Samuel Taylor Coleridge to the Rev. John Prior Estlin. Communicated by Henry A. Bright to the Miscellanies of the Philobiblon Society. Vol. XV, 1884.

L.P.   Letters from the Lake Poets, Samuel Taylor Coleridge, William Wordsworth, Robert Southey, to Daniel Stuart. 1889.

M.C.   Memorials of Coleorton. Being Letters from Coleridge, Wordsworth and his Sister, Southey, and Sir Walter Scott to Sir George and Lady Beaumont of Coleorton, Leicestershire, 1803 to 1834. Edited, with Introduction and Notes, by William Knight. 2 vols., 1887.

J.G.   The Life of Samuel Taylor Coleridge. By James Gillman. Vol. I, 1838.

E.R.   Early Recollections, Chiefly Relating to the late Samuel Taylor Coleridge, During his long residence in Bristol. By Joseph Cottle. 2 vols., 1837.

R.   Reminiscences of Samuel Taylor Coleridge and Robert Southey. By Joseph Cottle. 1847

M.   Samuel Taylor Coleridge. A Narrative of the Events of his Life. By James Dykes Campbell. 1894.

J.D.C. The Poetical Works of Samuel Taylor Coleridge. Edited with a Biographical Introduction. By James Dykes Campbell. Globe edition. 1924.

P.   The Complete Poetical Works of Samuel Taylor Coleridge, including Poems and Versions of Poems now published for the first time. Edited with textual and bibliographical notes by Ernest Hartley Coleridge. 2 vols., 1912.

C.W. The Complete Works of Samuel Taylor Coleridge. With an Introductory Essay. Edited by Professor W. G. T. Shedd. 7 vols., 1853–54.

P.D.W. The Poetical and Dramatic Works of Samuel Taylor Coleridge, founded on the Author's latest Edition of 1834, with many additional pieces now first included, and with a collection of various readings. Re-issued, with additions. 4 vols., 1880.

L.R. The Literary Remains of Samuel Taylor Coleridge. Collected and edited by Henry Nelson Coleridge. 4 vols., 1836–39.

F.A. The Friend: A Series of Essays, in Three Volumes. By S. T. Coleridge. A new edition. 1818.

F.B. The Friend. Third edition. 3 vols., 1837.

B.Lit.A. Biographia Literaria: or, Biographical Sketches of my Literary Life and Opinions. By S. T. Coleridge, Esq. 2 vols., 1817.

B.Lit.B. Biographia Literaria. Second Edition. Prepared for publication in part by the late Henry Nelson Coleridge. Completed and published by his widow. 2 vols., 1847.

B.Lit.C. Biographia Literaria by S. T. Coleridge. Edited with his Aesthetical Essays, by J. Shawcross. 2 vols., 1907.

T.T. The Table Talk and Omniana of Samuel Taylor Coleridge. With additional Table Talk from Allsop's 'Recollections,' and manuscript matter not before printed. Arranged and edited by T. Ashe. 1884.

O.T. Essays on his own Times; forming a second series of "The Friend." By Samuel Taylor Coleridge. Edited by his daughter. 3 vols., 1850.

C.M.C. Coleridge's Miscellaneous Criticism. Edited by Thomas Middleton Raysor. 1936.

A.P. Anima Poetæ. From the Unpublished Note-Books of Samuel Taylor Coleridge. Edited by Ernest Hartley Coleridge. 1895.

G.M.B. The Gutch Memorandum Book. B.M. Add. MSS. 27901.

MS.C. Chapters of Coleridge's Opus Maximum in Three Volumes. MS. in the possession of the Rev. G. H. B. Coleridge.

MS.H. On the Divine Ideas—a chapter of Coleridge's Opus Maximum. MS. in the possession of the Henry E. Huntingdon Library.

X. The Road to Xanadu. A Study in the Ways of the Imagination. By John Livingston Lowes. 1931.

C.P. Coleridge as Philosopher. By John H. Muirhead. 1930.

C.M.V. Coleridge: Studies by Several Hands on the Hundredth Anniversary of his Death. Edited by Edmund Blunden and Earl Leslie Griggs. 1934.

S.C. Minnow among Tritons. Mrs S. T. Coleridge's letters to Thomas Poole, 1799–1834. Edited by Stephen Potter. 1934.

C.L.	The Letters of Charles Lamb: to which are added those of his sister Mary Lamb. Edited by E V. Lucas. 3 vols., 1935.
L.L.	The Life of Charles Lamb. By E. V. Lucas. Revised edition. 2 vols., 1921.
C.LL.	Charles Lamb and the Lloyds. Edited by E. V. Lucas. 1898.
R.S.	The Life and Correspondence of Robert Southey. Edited by his son, the Rev. Charles Cuthbert Southey. Second edition. 6 vols., 1849–1850.
R.S.L.	Selections from the Letters of Robert Southey. Edited by his son-in-law, John Wood Warter. 4 vols., 1856.
R.S.W.	The Complete Poetical Works of Robert Southey. Collected by himself. 10 vols., 1837–38.
H.S.	The Early Life of Robert Southey, 1774–1803. By William Haller. 1917.
T.P.	Thomas Poole and his Friends. By Mrs Henry Sandford. 2 vols., 1888.
W.L.	The Letters of William and Dorothy Wordsworth. Arranged and Edited by Ernest de Selincourt: I. The Early Letters, 1787–1805. 1935. II. The Middle Years—Vol. 1. 1806–June 1811. 1937. III. do. Vol. 2. August 1811–1820. 1937.
W.P.	The Prelude or Growth of a Poet's Mind. By William Wordsworth. Edited from the Manuscripts with Introduction, Textual and Critical Notes, by Ernest de Selincourt. 1926.
W.W.	The Prose Works of William Wordsworth. Edited by the Rev. Alexander B. Grosart. 3 vols., 1876.
C.P.W.	The Complete Poetical Works of William Wordsworth. Edited by John Morley. 1888.
M.W.	Memoirs of William Wordsworth. By Christopher Wordsworth, D.D., Canon of Westminster. 2 vols., 1851.
K.W.	The Life of William Wordsworth. By William Knight. 3 vols., 1889.
L.W.	The Early Life of William Wordsworth, 1770–1798. By Émile Legouis. Translated by J. W. Matthews. With additional Appendix. 1921.
A.V.	William Wordsworth and Annette Vallon. By Émile Legouis. 1922.
H.	William Wordsworth. His Life, Works, and Influence. By George McLean Harper. Revised edition. 1929.
D.W.M.	Dorothy Wordsworth. The Early Years. By Catherine Macdonald Maclean. 1932.
D.W.S.	Dorothy Wordsworth. A Biography. By Ernest de Selincourt. 1933.

D.W.J.   Journals of Dorothy Wordsworth. Edited by William Knight. One-volume edition. 1924.

T.W.   Tom Wedgwood, the First Photographer. An Account of his Life, his Discovery and his Friendship with Samuel Taylor Coleridge, including the letters of Coleridge to the Wedgwoods. By R. B. Litchfield. 1903.

W.H.   The Complete Works of William Hazlitt. Centenary Edition. Edited by P. P. Howe. 21 vols., 1930–34.

H.D.M.   Memoirs of the Life of Sir Humphry Davy, Bart. By his Brother, John Davy. 2 vols., 1836.

H.D.F.   Fragmentary Remains, Literary and Scientific, of Sir Humphry Davy, Bart. With a Sketch of His Life and Selections from His Correspondence. Edited by his Brother, John Davy. 1858.

W.G.   William Godwin: His Friends and Contemporaries. By C. Kegan Paul. 2 vols., 1876

Q.   The Collected Writings of Thomas de Quincey. Edited by David Masson. 14 vols., 1896.

C.R.D.   Henry Crabb Robinson on Books and their Writers. Edited by Edith J. Morley. 3 vols., 1938.

E.S.   Essays and Studies. By Members of the English Association.

P.M.L.A.   Publications of the Modern Language Association of America.

D.N.B.   The Dictionary of National Biography.

O.E.D.   The Oxford English Dictionary.

N.&Q.   Notes and Queries.

BIBLIOGRAPHIES

Bibliography by John P. Anderson in *Life of Samuel Taylor Coleridge*, by Hall Caine, 1887.

The Bibliography of Coleridge by the late Richard Herne Shepherd. Revised, corrected and enlarged by Colonel W. F. Prideaux, 1900.

A Bibliography of Samuel Taylor Coleridge. By John Louis Haney. 1903.

Short Bibliography of Coleridge by A. A. Jack and A. C. Bradley, No 23, English Association Pamphlets, 1912.

A Bibliography of the writings in prose and verse of Samuel Taylor Coleridge. By T. J. Wise. 1913–19.

The Marginalia of S. T. C. By John Louis Haney. 1923.

Two Lake Poets. A Catalogue of printed books by William Wordsworth and Samuel Taylor Coleridge. Collected by T. J. Wise. 1927.

Samuel Taylor Coleridge. A selected bibliography compiled by V. W. Kennedy. 1935.

NOTES

CHAPTER 1

11   1   But the 'lane' even now may have taken on the more formal aspect
         of a road, better suited to the motorist no doubt, but in no sense
         peculiar to Devonshire.

     2   Several additions have been made to the Vicar's House at
         Ottery since Coleridge's time but it remains in part a fourteenth-
         century building.

     3   One of his godfathers was named Samuel Taylor.   Letter to
         Thomas Poole, March 1797.   L. I, p. 9.   Later one of the
         Housekeepers who signed Coleridge's Presentation to Christ's
         Hospital.   Coleridge was baptized on December 30, 1772.

     4   See *The Story of a Devonshire House*, by Lord Coleridge, K.C.,
         1905.   E. H. Coleridge has summarized what is known about
         the Coleridge family in C.M.V. p. 5 et seq.   See also L. I, p. 4
         et seq.; note 2, p. 4; and notes 1 and 2, p. 5.

12   5   "My schoolmistress, the very image of Shenstone's . . . was
         nearly related to Sir Joshua Reynolds."   Letter to Thomas
         Poole, March 1797, L. I, pp. 9–10.

     6   To Thomas Poole, October 9, 1797.   L. I, p. 12.

13   7   Ibid.

     8   J.G. p. 10.   Autobiographical note by Coleridge.   It continues
         "Alas! I had all the simplicity, all the docility of the little child,
         but none of the child's habits.   I never thought as a child, never
         had the language of a child."

     9   Adjoining the Vicar's House.   Pulled down in or about 1873.
         The King's School is now a Secondary School under the Devon
         County Education Committee.   The present buildings date
         from 1910.

    10   To Thomas Poole, October 9, 1797.   L. I, p. 13.

15 11   To Thomas Poole, October 16, 1797.   L. I, p. 15.   This
         reminiscence, with others, is retold in F.A. I, p. 251 et seq.
         Also in J.G. p. 11; A.P. p. 29; E.R. I, pp. 240–243.

    12   The Seventh Baronet.   Grandfather of the first Lord Iddesleigh.
         He had been a pupil of Coleridge's father.   Coleridge's "Great
         House" was Escot, near Ottery.   See C.W. II, pp. 137–138;
         also A.P. p. 157.

    13   To Thomas Poole, October 16, 1797.   L. I, p. 16.

16 14   Possessive for Genitive, for example.

    15   Or Bowdon.

    16   See *The Story of a Devonshire House*, also C.M.V. p. 7, for further
         particulars.

    17   Warren by name.

16 18 Later Judge Sir Francis Buller. The Presentation was No. 67, dated March 28, 1782.

17 19 W.P. 1805, VI, l. 276.

20 Charles Lamb, *Christ's Hospital Five-and-Thirty Years Ago*. *Essays of Elia*, 1820–23.

21 *Sonnet: On Quitting School for College*, 1791. J.D.C. p. 15; P. I, p. 29

22 *Christ's Hospital Five-and-Thirty Years Ago*.

23 Ibid. Cf. J.G. p. 20; Leigh Hunt's *Autobiography*, revised edn., 1860.

24 1805, VI, ll. 274–284. Cf. *Sonnet: To the River Otter*, J.D.C. p. 23; P. I, p. 48; *Lines: To a Beautiful Spring in a Village*, J.D.C. p. 24; P. I, p. 58; *Frost at Midnight*, J.D.C. p. 126; P. I, p. 240; *Lines composed in a Concert-room*, J.D.C. p. 148; P. I, p. 324; *A Letter to——* E.S. XXII, pp. 17–18.

18 25 J.G. p. 17.

26 See, for instance, Coleridge's letter to his mother, February 4, 1785. *Unpublished Letters of S. T. Coleridge*. Edited by E. H. Coleridge, *Illustrated London News*, April 1, 1893, and foll.

27 J.G. pp. 17, 20.

28 Thomas Fanshaw Middleton, 1769–1822. Elected to Pembroke College, Cambridge, September 26, 1788. Curate at Gainsborough. Published essays *Country Spectator*, 1793. First Bishop of Calcutta. Sonnet (1793) mentioning Coleridge, see E.S. XXII, p. 52.

29 Born February 10, 1775.

30 1773–1858. Left Cambridge 1796 to become tutor to W. J. G. Nicholls of Trereife, near Penzance. Ordained 1798. Married Mrs Nicholls (the mother) a year later. Perpetual curate of Madron, Penzance, 1806–31. See Lamb's *Christ's Hospital Five-and-Thirty Years Ago* and *Grace Before Meat*. See Wordsworth's letter to Wrangham, July 12, 1807, W.L. II, p. 134; also Le Grice's reminiscences of Coleridge in the *Gentleman's Magazine*, December 1834; also his *Sonnet in Reminiscence of the Poet Coleridge*, E.S. XXII, p. 57. Also see C.R.D. II, pp. 512, 513, 833; L. I, pp. 111, 325; T.T. August 16, 1832, p. 180.

31 1772–1805. Went to Balliol College, Oxford, 1792. Then Westminster Hospital; M.B., M.D. Appointed deputy-surgeon to the 2nd Royals, on service in Portugal. Married a widow. Later became a journalist. See Leigh Hunt's *Autobiography*, Lamb's *Newspapers Five-and-Thirty Years Ago* and *Christ's Hospital Five-and-Thirty Years Ago*. Also L. I, p. 225, note 2.

32 1775–1812. The 'W' of Lamb's *Poor Relations*. Died of wounds at Salamanca as a young officer in 61st Foot. See Leigh Hunt's *Autobiography*, p. 72. Something of a poet. See L. I, pp. 111–112, note 1; I, p. 113. See also letter of Southey,

18

32 October 19, 1794, R.S. I, p. 224, in which a sonnet is quoted "on the subject of our emigration, by Favell." But it contains ll. 129–136 of the *Monody on the Death of Chatterton*. See J.D.C. note 14, pp. 562–563.

33 1775–1802. Followed his brother to Trinity College, Cambridge, 1794. Commissioned in 60th Foot. Died in Jamaica. See Leigh Hunt's *Autobiography*, p. 72, and *Lord Byron and his Contemporaries*, 1828; also C. V. Le Grice's letter in reply to the latter, E.S. XXII, pp. 58–59. See also *Christ's Hospital Five-and-Thirty Years Ago*; and C.L. I, p. 44.

34 See article, *Coleridge and Christ's Hospital*, by Edmund Blunden. C.M.V. p. 61 et seq.

19

35 William Evans. Became fellow clerk with Lamb in the India House. See Lamb's letter to Coleridge June 8–10, 1796. C.L. I, p. 19.

36 See Charles Lamb's *Recollections of Christ's Hospital*, 1813.

37 1736–1814. Scholar at Christ's Hospital, 1744–1752. Balliol College, Oxford. Upper Grammar Master, 1776. Vicar of Enford and Rector of Colne Engaine. See B.Lit.C. I, pp. 4–6; T.T. August 16, 1832, p. 180; *Christ's Hospital Five-and-Thirty Years Ago*: Leigh Hunt's *Autobiography*; *Elia and Christ's Hospital*, E.S. XXII, p. 36 et seq. also *Coleridge and Christ's Hospital*, C.M.V. p. 61 et seq. and *Charles Lamb and his Contemporaries*, 1934, by Edmund Blunden; L.L. I, p. 56 et seq.; *A History of the Royal Foundation of Christ's Hospital*, by A. W. Trollope, 1834; and *Recollections of a Blue-coat Boy*, by W. P. Scargill, 1829. "That sensible fool, Coleridge," was Boyer's description of his brilliant but erratic pupil.

38 *Christ's Hospital Five-and-Thirty Years Ago*. B.Lit.C. I, pp. 4–6. See also F.A. II, pp. 72–73 for eulogy of Wales, mathematics master.

39 See the sonnet entitled *Pain*, dated tentatively 1790, J.D.C. pp. 11–12; P. I, p. 17.

40 See *History of Christ's Hospital*; also article by J. Dykes Campbell, *Illustrated London News*, December 26, 1891.

41 J.G. pp. 21–22.

42 By Trenchard and Gordon, 1755. J.G. p. 23.

43 This translator and mathematician was born 1768, died 1835. In 1796 Coleridge described him to Thelwall as "the English pagan," L. I, p. 181.

44 Letter to Lady Beaumont, January 21, 1810, M.C. II, p. 107. Coleridge was referring in particular to Taylor's translation of Proclus's *Platonic Theology*.

45 *Christ's Hospital Five-and-Thirty Years Ago*.

46 B.Lit.B. I, p. 249. Note to Chapter XII. See also C.W. III, pp. 152–153.

47 B.Lit.C. I, p. 10.

21 48 J.G. p. 23.
22 49 J.G. pp. 23–24.   See also T.T. May 27, 1830, p. 84.   Cf. Coleridge's MS. Note, B.M. Add. MSS. 34225.
    50 *Recollections of Christ's Hospital* and *Christ's Hospital Five-and-Thirty Years Ago.*   See also J.G. pp. 17–18, 33.
    51 Thomas Hartwell Horne.   C.M.V. p. 62.
    52 C.M.V. p. 62.   A reminiscence of the Rev. Mr Smith.   Cf. J.G. pp. 18–19.
    53 J.G. p. 28.
    54 M. p. 11.
23 55 To Thomas Allsop, March 4, 1822.   A. II, p. 86.
    56 C.M.V. p. 58.   William Gill was at this time Treasurer of Christ's Hospital.
    57 See J.D.C. note, p. 562.
24 58 B.Lit.B. I, p. 13.   *Sonnets, written chiefly on picturesque spots during a tour,* 2nd edition, corrected, with additions.   Bath, 1789.   The volume contained twenty-one poems.   William Lisle Bowles, 1762–1850.   Rector of Cricklade, Wiltshire, 1792–97.   Later Rector of Shaftesbury.   For Coleridge's first sight of Bowles, see his letter to Thelwall, December 31, 1796.   L. I, p. 211.   This meeting probably took place in 1789, when Coleridge was on his way home for the summer holiday.   See also Clement Carlyon's *Early Years and Late Reflections* (4 vols., 1856–58) I, p. 8.
25 59 Two of these school themes are here printed together for the first time—the second essay was printed by E. H. C. in the *Illustrated London News,* April 1, 1893: *"NEC LUSISSE PUDET, SED NON INCIDERE LUDUM.*

"Our first deviations from the paths of rectitude the natural imbecillity of human nature may excuse.   In the beginning of Life Error and Folly wear their most alluring dress.   They have then all the charms of novelty to recommend them, and the inexperience, credulity, and rashness of the youthful mind to combat on their side.   That they too often obtain the conquest therefore produces rather Pity, than Wonder, in the candid mind.   Nor to any, but a malignant eye can the follies of Youth cast a shade over the virtues of a maturer age, nor will the retrospect excite a painful blush.   No—rather shall the remembrance of the praiseworthy exertion with which we extricated ourselves, afford the mind an honest exultation.

"To err then may be a debt to humanity, but to persevere in Error marks the weak and depraved mind.   For now more weighty claims should engage the attention.   Our Parents now expect the grateful Son, and Society demands the useful member.   Reason should now have dissipated the mists of passion, and Experience must have removed the specious veil, which once concealed the deformities and effects of Folly.   No plea now

remains to excuse our continuance in a state, from which
Experience, Reason and Shame conspire to rouse us.   To sacrifice all that is truly advantageous and honourable in life to
the pursuit of unselfish pleasures implies a disposition so congenial with Vice, that well may the conduct, which was pitied in
Youth, now be punished by the neglect and contempt of others,
and by the remorse of our own breasts.   For the very pleasures,
which influenced us, are fled!   If awoke from a pleasing dream
we will lay Reason and Shame asleep, that we may again enjoy
the delightful vision.   Alas! far different scenes must succeed—
darkness and haunts obscene and frightful, with all the gloomy
offspring of a diseased fancy.

"September 1790."

"QUID FAS,

ATQUE NEFAS, TANDEM INCIPIUNT SENTIRE
    PERACTIS
CRIMINIBUS.

"Before the perpetration of those actions, in which the Vice is
collected into one atrocious crime, the agitated mind anticipates
its future horrors.   But we exhibit the most striking picture of
our weakness in those distempered reasonings, with which we
deceive ourselves at the commencement of vicious *habits*.   The
superior enjoyments, which criminal pursuits promise, seem to
us then to form the only difference between Virtue and Vice.
We contemptuously compare the calm happiness of the one with
the keen delights of the other.   We call Temperance and
Sobriety joyless severity, and think, that we should have reason
to congratulate ourselves on exchanging Thorns for Flowers.

"But the value of a Blessing is never so fully known as by its
loss.   When we unfortunately come near enough to view the
background of the Picture, we shall find the loose hour punished
by still-attendant disgust and self-reproach.   We shall find, that
as high as the Spirits are artificially raised above their natural
standard, so far they must sink below it.   Will the pleasures of
riotous mirth compensate for the despondency, which follows it?
That despondency, which is able to create imaginary misfortunes, how will it aggravate great and real evils?   Then the
Debt and Embarrassments, which our irregularities have brought
upon us, will torture our minds with double suspense and dread.
Then shall the remembrance of our loss of Health be most painful.   Then shall we sigh more deeply for that perpetual sunshine of the breast, which Virtue and Temperance impart.   Then
shall we look back with keenest remorse to those happy times,
when we knew and feared no harm.

"What now remains but to return?   Alas! at the moment we
contract a habit we forego our free agency.   The remainder of

[425   ]

25 59 our life will be spent in making resolutions in the hour of dejection and breaking them in the hour of Passion. As if we were in some great sea-vortex, every moment we perceive our ruin more clearly, every moment we are impelled towards it with greater force. What is the event? Too trite to mention. We cut the knot, which we cannot untye.

"January 19, 1791."

60 B.Lit.C. I, p. 6. See also J.G. p. 27.

61 B.Lit.C. I, p. 11. See also ibid. II, p. 21.

62 Ibid. I, pp. 15–16.

63 In 1793 Wordsworth read the book through, seated in a recess on Westminster Bridge. Christopher Wordsworth, who was with William, had to wait until his enraptured brother had finished the quarto before he could persuade him to move. For Southey's acknowledgment of Bowles's influence see Preface R.S.W.

27 64 B.Lit.C. I, p. 14.

65 Ibid.

66 See J.D.C. notes 12 and 15, pp. 562–563. But it seems unlikely that Coleridge went home in 1789 *and* 1790. The first date is the more probable. See reference to his sister's pain in *Life*, dated 1789. Anne (Nancy) died in March 1791.

67 The sixth son. Born 1764. Pembroke College, Oxford. At this time assistant master at Newcome's Academy, Hackney. The headmaster was a Mr Sparrow.

68 The seventh son. Born 1765. Came from the west to walk the wards of London Hospital under Sir William Blizard. See J. G. pp. 22–23. Died 1790; but not before he had married and become the father of a son who (in 1824) was appointed first Bishop of Barbadoes. Luke left London in 1787 after passing his medical examinations. He died at Thorverton three years later.

69 Extract from the Minutes of the Committee of Almoners, January 12, 1791. Printed in *Christ's Hospital: List of Exhibitioners, from 1566–1885.*

28 70 The title of the MS. version in which these lines appear is *Upon the Author's leaving School and entering into Life.*

CHAPTER 2

29 1 To George Coleridge, October 1791. U.L. I, p. 1. For this and other particulars of Coleridge at Cambridge, see the *History of Jesus College*, by A. Gray, 1902.

2 In a letter to George Coleridge, November 28, 1791. U.L. I, p. 3.

30   3   1757–1841. Unitarian and mathematician. Fellow of Jesus. Had held and resigned (1787) the living of Madingley.

     4   Coleridge began writing sermons early. A MS. is in existence entitled *A Sermon written when the Author was but 17 years old.* The text was taken from Psa. xcv. 6–10. The MS. is dated September 1789, so that Coleridge was in fact not quite seventeen years of age.

     5   To George Coleridge, January 24, 1792. L. I, p. 23 et seq.

     6   Mainly on account of his 'republican' leanings. For comments upon Middleton cf. J.G. p. 43 et seq.

31   7   J.G. pp. 48, 54. See also F.A. I, pp. 246–247, where Coleridge writes: "My feelings, however, and imagination did not remain unkindled in this general conflagration [the French Revolution]; and I confess I should be more inclined to be ashamed than proud of myself if they had. I was a sharer in the general vortex, though my little world described the path of its revolution in an orbit of its own. What I dared not expect from constitutions of government and whole nations, I hoped from Religion." See also E. p. 117. Cf. note of June 23, 1834, T.T. pp. 289–290. Cf. R. p. 314 et seq. for Coleridge's later remarks on the subject.

     8   February 7, 1793. L. I, p. 50.

     9   1774–1839. Later Headmaster of Shrewsbury and Bishop of Lichfield and Coventry.

     10 February 5, 1793. L. I, pp. 45–46.

32   11 February, 1793. U.L. I, p. 10.

     12 Ibid. I, p. 11.

     13 See L. I, p. 57 note. Tuckett was at Cambridge with Coleridge.

33   14 *Gentleman's Magazine,* December 1834, May 1838. Reprinted as *College Reminiscences of Coleridge,* 1842. Cf. R. pp. 303–305.

     15 The *Gentleman's Magazine,* December 1834.

     16 The cause of the trial was Frend's publication in 1793 of a tract, *Peace and Union recommended to the Associated Bodies of Republicans and Anti-Republicans,* in which a good deal of the Church of England Liturgy was attacked. Frend was deprived of his Fellowship on April 17 and banished May 30, 1793. Cf. J.G. p. 55; *Reminiscences of Cambridge,* 1855, by Henry Gunning, I, p. 272 et seq; *Gentleman's Magazine,* August 1838, p. 124.

     17 1760–1843. The fourth son. Pembroke College, Oxford. Chiefly remarkable at this time for his marriage to a woman, in Coleridge's words, "twenty years older than his mother" (L. I, p. 7). He later married a first cousin, Anne Bowden.

     18 1759–1836. The third and oldest surviving son. Finally settled at Heath's Court, Ottery. Became Lieut.-Colonel of the local militia.

     19 A literary society of twelve members was founded at Exeter in 1786 by Hugh Downman and the Cathedral organist, William

33 19 Jackson, 1730–1803. (See Coleridge's later unfavourable remarks on this man and the musical profession in general, L. I, p. 309, in reply to Southey's letter of October 3, 1799. R.S. II, p. 26.) A volume of essays and verses read by members at the meetings was published in 1796. See Wordsworth's *Poems*, edited Thomas Hutchinson, who made this discovery. Presumably the poems heard by Coleridge were *An Evening Walk* and *Descriptive Sketches*, 1793, but see B.Lit.C. I, p. 56. Cf. B.Lit.B. I, p. 19. See also letter from Dorothy Wordsworth to Jane Pollard, February 16, 1793. W.L. I, pp. 85–86. Also comments in H. pp. 130–131. "During my first Cambridge vacation," wrote Coleridge, "I assisted a friend in a contribution for a literary society in Devonshire, and in that I remember to have compared Darwin's works to the Russian palace of ice, glittering, cold, and transitory." C.W. III, p. 155. With reference to the *Songs of the Pixies*, written at this time, it is interesting to note that the Pixies' Parlour which Coleridge visited at the time the poem was composed is still to be seen, a sandstone hollow in the midst of a hanger overlooking the Otter about half a mile from the town of Ottery. The initials S. T. C. carved there by Coleridge in his boyhood are still visible.

34 20 1774–1846. Later Fellow of Peterhouse. Afterwards Master of Trinity College, Cambridge.

21 *Social Life at the English Universities*, 1874. Entry date, November 5, 1793.

22 Ibid. Entry date, November 13, 1793.

35 23 February 23, 1794. U.L. I, p. 13.

24 There have been a number of speculations as to the origin of this name, but in the result none of them carries conviction. The only certainty is the initials. See Note in U.L. I, p. 18. But Coleridge's reference (A. I. p. 95) is surely only an instance of punning after the event. At the time the name was conceived Coleridge was in no punning mood See J.G. p. 57 et seq.; E.R. II, p. 54. Cf. *Gentleman's Magazine*, August 1838, p. 124.

37 25 To G. L. Tuckett, February 6, 1794. L. I, p. 59.

26 February 8, 1794. L. I, pp. 59–60. Cf. letters to the same, February 11 and March 21, 1794. L. I, pp. 60–61, 68–69; and the commencement of letter, February 23, 1794. U.L. I, pp. 12–13.

38 27 February 23, 1794. U.L. I, pp. 13–14. But see J.G. pp. 63–65.

28 February 20, 1794. L. I, pp. 61–62.

29 Miss Mitford and W. L. Bowles both stated later that Captain Ogle (a son of Dr Newton Ogle, Bowles' patron, and a schoolfellow of Bowles at Winchester) was solely responsible for procuring Coleridge's discharge. But the correspondence between Coleridge's brothers and the military authorities relative to the

38	29	discharge disproves this statement. Captain Ogle's name is not

38   29   discharge disproves this statement. Captain Ogle's name is not
even mentioned. See J.G. p. 61. See also *Reminiscences of Coleridge* in *Fra[er's Magazine*, October 1834; and *The late Mr Coleridge, a common Soldier*, in *The Times*, August 13, 1834; also *Memoir of Coleridge* in the *Gentleman's Magazine*, November 1834; R. pp. 277–287.

39   30   U.L. I, pp. 17–18.

      31   In *The Soother in Absence*, a projected work which did not materialize, Coleridge planned to include the '*Domus quadrata hortensis*, at Henley-on-Thames' and 'the beautiful girl.' MS. note, January 1805.

      32   Unpublished letter from Captain George Hopkinson, K.L.D., to George Coleridge.

      33   March 30, 1794. L. I, p. 68.

40   34   1740–*c.* 1820. Visited by Haydn, 1792. See *Grove's Dictionary of Music and Musicians*, 1927, I, p. 654. But the songs do not appear to have been published. See also Coleridge's reference to Charles Hague (1769–1821, Professor of Music at Cambridge, 1799–1821) in a letter to Mary Evans, February 7, 1793. L. I, pp. 50–51.

      35   April 7, 1794. L. I, p. 70.

      36   The College Register says "1794 Apl.: *Coleridge admonitus est per magistrum in praesentiâ sociorum.*"

      37   The Coleridge brothers were put to considerable financial inconvenience by this escapade as the unpublished correspondence between them and the authorities makes clear.

      38   From J Plampin, April 16, 1794. Cf. Coleridge to George, May 1, 1794. L. I, p. 70.

      39   May 1, 1794. L. I, pp. 71–72.

      40   May 4, 1794. U.L. I, p. 20.

      41   Advertisement in the *Cambridge Intelligencer*, June 14 and July 28, 1794: "Proposals for publishing by subscription *Imitations from the Modern Latin Poets, with a Critical and Biographical Essay on the Restoration of Literature*. By S. T. Coleridge, of Jesus College, Cambridge. The work will consist of two volumes, large octavo, elegantly printed on superfine paper: Price to Subscribers, 14s. in boards; to be paid on delivery." The 'Design' followed and the advertisement ended: "In the course of the Work will be introduced a copious Selection from the Lyrics of Casimir, and a new Translation of the Basia of Secundus. The Volumes will be ready for delivery shortly after next Christmas. Cambridge, June 10, 1794."

41   42   In the Fonthill Collection. There entitled *Song*. No date on MS. but dated June 1794 in the 1796 volume of Coleridge's *Poems*. See also letter of June 8–10, 1796. C.L. I, p. 17. E.H.C. suggests in a note to the poem, P. I, p. 62, that these verses were not written before August 1794. If this were so,

41   42   Coleridge must have sent a copy to Mary after seeing her at Wrexham—yet it is all but certain that he did not write to her between June and his 'proposal' at the end of the year. It would seem more reasonable to suppose that the sentiments expressed in the poem were the result of Coleridge's disastrous 'week' in London which ended in his enlistment—behaviour which he well knew to be repugnant to Mary. Indeed, Tuckett speaks of the fact that Coleridge was ashamed to meet the Evanses afterwards. And in fact most of what was to become the first stanza of *The Sigh* had been struck out by Coleridge in a letter to George Coleridge written as early as April 1792, under the heading:

First Love

When youth his fairy reign began,
Ere sorrow had proclaimed me man;
Then, Mary! mid my lightsome glee,
I heaved the painless sigh for thee—

S. T. C.

Printed in the *Illustrated London News*, April 8, 1893.

43   Later Fellow of Catherine Hall. Published an account of the tour: *A Pedestrian Tour through North Wales in a Series of Letters*, 1795.

44   1773–1856, Christ's Church, Oxford.

45   Born August 12, 1774.

46   R.S. I, p. 210.

47   See H.S. pp. 120–125.

42   48   1774–1811. Baptized Huntspill, October 25, 1774. Son of John and Ann Burnet (but spelt his name with the double t). At Balliol. See T.P. I, pp. 207–208. Edmund Seward, also of Balliol, was a member of the pantisocratic group, but soon withdrew. See R.S. I, pp. 211–212.

49   See E.S. XXII, p. 58. But Allen was never a pantisocrat. See L. I, p. 126.

50   O.E.D. pantisocracy (f. Greek παντ-, Panto—all + ἰσοκρατία Isocracy). A form of social organization in which all are equal in rank and social position; a Utopian community in which all are equal and all rule. See also *Coleridge's Critical Terminology*, by J. Isaacs, E.S. XXI, p. 86 et seq.

51   Letter from Robert Southey to his brother Tom, September 20, 1794. R.S. I, pp. 220–221.

43   52   T.P. I, pp. 96–99. In addition to Adam Smith, the writings of William Godwin must be given their due in forwarding the pantisocratic idea. Southey was a staunch admirer of *Political Justice*. Coleridge for a time worshipped before the same shrine. And Godwin had said "that all the conveniences of civilized life might be produced, if society would divide the

43 52 labour equally among its members, by each individual being employed in labour two hours during the day."

53 Southey's version of this time and the next few weeks was written to Cottle in a letter dated March 5, 1836, and published R. pp. 402–407, in a garbled form. For a quotation from the original in the Fonthill collection, see M. p. 31.

54 July 6, 1794. L. I, pp. 72–73.

55 O.E.D. aspheterism (f. Greek ἁ priv. + σφέτερ-ος one's own, after Greek σφετερισμός appropriation). The doctrine that there ought to be no private property; communism. Aspheterize (f. as prec. after Spheterize, Greek σφετερίζειν), to practise aspheterism. See letter to Southey, July 6, 1794. L. I, p. 73.

56 Letter to Tom Southey, September 20, 1794. R.S. I, pp. 220–221.

57 July 6, 1794. L. I, p. 72.

58 *Lines written at the King's Arms, Ross, formerly the House of the 'Man of Ross.'* J.D.C. p. 33; P. I, pp. 57–58. See note J.D.C. p. 571, for a description of the vicissitudes of these verses. Also for the fact that J.D.C. found an autograph copy of the verses (as also a copy of *Bala Hill*, see J.D.C. following note) in the Fonthill Collection, thus demonstrating that Coleridge, despite his avoidance of Mary, still maintained correspondence with the Evans family. The lines were sent by Coleridge to Southey in his letter of July 15–16, from Wrexham; and sent by Southey to Grosvenor Bedford from Bath on July 20, with the adjuration: "Admire the verses, Grosvenor, and pity the mind that wrote them from its genuine feelings." R.S. I, pp. 213–214.

44 59 To Robert Southey, July 15–16, 1794. L. I, p. 79.

60 So, at least, Coleridge has it in his letter to Southey of July 15–16, 1794. L. I, p. 80. But in his letter to Martin a week later, General Washington had become Dr Priestley. B.E. I, p. 36. Hucks, however, gives it as Washington. See *A Pedestrian Tour through North Wales*, p. 25 et seq.

61 July 22, 1794. *Gentleman's Magazine*, March 1836, pp. 242–244. Henry Martin was with Coleridge at Jesus. He took Orders and became incumbent of Cucklington. Coleridge later was to dedicate his and Southey's *The Fall of Robespierre* to this college friend. See also *Gentleman's Magazine*, June 1839, pp. 609–612.

45 62 July 14–15, 1794. L. I, p. 78.

63 Southey's uncle, the Rev. Herbert Hill, then at Lisbon, had helped his nephew to go to Oxford on the implied understanding that Southey would take Orders. See H.S. p. 52.

64 July 14–15, 1794. L. I, p. 75. But see note 49.

65 Ibid.

66 But see X. p. 503 and E.S. XIX, p. 103.

46 67 To Henry Martin, July 22, 1794. B.E. I, p. 39. See also B.Lit.B. II, p. 338.

46   68   B.E. I, p. 40.   See also T.T. May 31, 1830, p. 88.   According
to Coleridge the incident occurred on Plynlimmon, which they
also climbed.   But Hucks, who must be considered the more
reliable authority, gives it as Penmaenmawr.   Cf. *A Pedestrian
Tour through North Wales*, p. 62.   See also B.Lit.B. II, p. 338.

    69   1770–1845.   Coleridge later spelt the name Sara, but to avoid
confusion between Sarah and her daughter, the 'h' in the
name of the former is retained throughout except in Coleridge's
own letters.   For a time Coleridge became quite emphatic on
the subject.   ". . . why, dear Southey!" he wrote, "will you
write it always Sarah? Sara, methinks, is associated with times
that you and I cannot and do not wish ever to forget."   July
29, 1802, L. I, p. 387.

    70   1770–96.

47   71   R.S. I, pp. 220–221.

    72   1765–1837.   See De Quincey's description of Poole, Q. II, p.
141.   It appears true, except for the use of the word 'polished,'
which Poole certainly was not.   See also T.P. II, p. 308 et seq.
Cf. Coleridge's encomium in *On the Constitution of the Church
and State*, second edition, 1831, p. 115.   See also Wordsworth's
Prefatory Note to *The Farmer of Tilsbury Vale* and comments on
Michael (T.P. II, pp. 54–56).   Cf. T.P. II, p. 312; T.W. p. 106.

48   73   To a Mr Haskins.   T.P. I, pp. 96–97.

    74   See remarks in X. p. 604 S.

    75   John's *Journal* for August 18, records the meeting: "Horâ fere
7^{mâ} Thos. Poole, et frater Richardus, Henricus Poole, et duo
juvenes ei familiares huc veniunt.   Duo isti ignoti, intelligo, è
Cantabrigiâ exierant; et totam fere Walliam peragraverant. Unus
Oxoniensis Alumnus; alter Cantabrigiensis.   Uterque verò rabie
Democratica, quoad Politiam; et Infidelis quoad Religionem
spectat, turpiter fervet.   Ego maxime indignor.   Tandem verò,
horâ fere 8^{vâ}, omnes discedunt.   Post prandium ego me ad
Vitam Johnsonianam confero.   Horâ ferme 1^{mâ} D^{ns} Reekes
Stoweiâ venit; multum indignatur propter malitiam odiosam et
detestandam juvenum istorum, quibus, apud Avunculi mei
Thomae occurrerat.   Illi plus videntur cogitationes suas, quam
apud nos, illic indicâsse. . . ."   T.P. I, p. 103.

      Miss Helen Cam, of Girton College, Cambridge, has very
kindly drawn my attention to the strong possibility that Coleridge and Southey were introduced to Poole by Henry Poole
rather than by Burnett, and has put her notes at my disposal.   I
am very grateful for the opportunity to take advantage of the researches, extending over many years, which Miss Cam has undertaken on this question.   It may be mentioned that Miss Cam is
herself a descendant, both of the Poole family to which Henry
Poole belonged and of Thomas Ward, apprentice and partner
of Thomas Poole.

In 1793 the College Register of Jesus College, Cambridge, includes the name of Henry Poole, of Somerset, privately educated, aged twenty, son of William Poole, Esq., deceased. That this was both the Henry Poole mentioned in John Poole's *Journal* entry quoted above, and the Henry Poole who was baptized in Stogursey church on October 20, 1771, seems more than probable despite the difference of two years in the stated ages.   This Henry Poole was the grandson of William Poole of Shurton, Stogursey, and member of a large Poole clan living in Stogursey and in Cannington.   No connexion with the branch of the Poole family to which Thomas Poole belonged has been established, but would not be unreasonable to assume. The fact that Thomas Ward married Sarah Poole, a granddaughter of William Poole of Shurton, suggests that a connexion did exist.   Similarly, no contact between George Burnett and Henry Poole has been traced—but this, in view of Burnett's history, is not surprising.

The only existing authority for the suggestion that Burnett introduced Coleridge and Southey to Thomas Poole is contained in the letter written by Southey to Cottle on March 5, 1836 (corrected version of R. pp. 402–407, by the original in the Fonthill collection, M. p. 31).   Southey says: "In the summer of 1794 S. T. Coleridge and Hucks came to Oxford on their way into Wales for a pedestrian tour.   Then Allen introduced them to me, and the scheme [pantisocracy] was talked of, but not by any means determined on.   It was talked into shape by Burnett and myself, when, upon the commencement of the long vacation, we separated from them, they making for Gloucester, he and I proceeding on foot to Bath.   After some weeks, S. T. C., returning from his tour, came to Bristol on his way and slept there. Then it was that we resolved upon going to America, and S. T. C. and I walked into Somersetshire to see Burnett, and on that journey it was that he [Coleridge] first saw Poole.   He made his engagement with Miss Fricker on our return from this journey at my mother's house in Bath, not a little to my astonishment, because he had talked of being deeply in love with a certain Mary Evans."   This account in no way states that Burnett introduced Coleridge and Southey to Poole, although the inference until now, when the existence of Henry Poole at Jesus and in Somerset has been brought to light, was natural.

What actually occurred would seem to be this; that Coleridge and Southey duly visited Burnett at Huntspill; then alone, or with Burnett, looked up Henry Poole at Stogursey near by; and finally, that all four, or possibly the three, without Burnett, went on to Stowey to meet Poole.   It is perhaps significant that John Poole makes no mention of Burnett being present at Marsh Mills.

[433   ]

48	76	T.P. I, p. 101. See also ibid. I, pp. 104–105.
49	77	L.R. I, p. 3; R.S. I, p. 217.
50	78	The Barbou *Casimir*, Paris, 1759.
	79	No. 17. Burned down in 1884.
	80	1755–1841. Left Christ's Hospital while Coleridge was in the Lower School. His book had appeared in 1793. A Unitarian. See letter to Robert Southey, September 6, 1794. U.L. I, p. 22.
	81	U.L. I, p. 22.
	82	1733–1804. Scientist and theologian. A hero of Coleridge and Lamb. His position as one of the leaders of Unitarianism and his association with Frend in consequence would naturally endear him to an earnest disciple of the latter. Coleridge had already written a sonnet in praise of Priestley (J.D.C. p. 39; P. I, pp. 81–82) and paid him further tribute in *Religious Musings* (ll. 371–376, J.D.C. p. 60; P. I, p. 123). For Lamb's Priestley worship, see C.L. I, p. 11.
51	83	See letter to Robert Southey, September 6, 1794. U.L. I, p. 24.
52	84	B.E. I, pp. 44–45. See also R. p. 188; A. II, pp. 234–235.
	85	Dublin, 1794. See letter to Southey, October 21, 1794. L. I, pp. 91–92. Cowper should certainly be read Cooper. That Coleridge came to hear, if he had not already heard of "the colony established not far from the Susquehanna River" to be described in the *Gentleman's Magazine*, June 1795, may be assumed with some confidence. Note also his familiarity with the *New Travels in the United States of America*, by J. P. Brissot, quoted in *Conciones ad Populum*, p. 32.
	86	To Robert Southey, September 6, 1794. U.L. I, p. 23.
	87	Ibid.
53	88	George Caldwell. Friend of Coleridge at Jesus. Later took Orders and became Fellow and Tutor of Jesus. See Coleridge's letter to George Coleridge, January 24, 1792. L. I, p. 25. See also L.P. p. 452.
	89	September 18, 1794. L. I, pp. 81–82.
	90	September 19, 1794. L. I, pp. 84–85.
54	91	Ibid. I, p. 85.
	92	September 26, 1794. L. I, p. 86.
	93	E.R. I, p. 10. See also letter to Southey, October 21, 1794. L. I, p. 91.
	94	*The Fall of Robespierre.* An Historic Drama. By S. T. Coleridge, of Jesus College, Cambridge. Printed by Benjamin Flower, for W. H. Lunn, and J. and J. Merrill; and sold by J. March, Norwich, 1794. (Price one shilling.) Octavo, pp. 37. For Dedication to H. Martin and further details see J.D.C. note 228, p. 646.
	95	1755–1829. A Cambridge printer, editor of the *Cambridge Intelligencer*, to whom Coleridge later wrote some interesting letters. A Unitarian. First printed the *Monody on the Death of Chatterton* in his edition of Chatterton's *Rowley Poems*, 1794.

54   96   September 19, 1794.   L. I, p. 85.
     97   See L. I, p. 86 note.
     98   See L. I, pp. 82–83, 92–93, 107–112, 115–120.
55   99   L. I, pp. 87–89.
     100 In the letters to Wrangham and Southey the sonnet had no title, the first version commencing, "Thou Bleedest my poor Heart!" An autograph copy is dated October 21, 1794. When printed first in *Poems*, 1796, it was called *Effusion XIX*, but in the Contents it was given the title *To My Own Heart*.
56   101 1769–1842. Poet, translator, theologian. Fellow student of Coleridge. Formerly of Trinity Hall, where he was "done out of" a divinity fellowship. Took Orders. Private tutor to the Duke of Manchester's son. Curacy at Cobham with three West Indian pupils at £200 a year each. Rector of Hunmanby. Later Archdeacon of Cleveland and Prebendary of York and Chester. A lifelong friend of W. Wordsworth. See U.L. I, p. 45, for a description of him by Coleridge. See also *Archdeacon Francis Wrangham*, by Michael Sadleir. Supplement to the Bibliographical Society's Transactions No. 12.
     102 October 24, 1794.   U.L. I, p. 28.
     103 October 21, 1794.   L. I, p. 89.
     104 Ibid.
57   105 The suggestion that Shadrach Weeks and his wife Sally, with a Mr and Mrs Roberts, should join the pantisocrats appears to have come from Southey (see H.S. p. 146); but the conclusion that they would therefore be admitted on terms of equality was Coleridge's alone. Hence his enthusiastic "SHAD GOES WITH US. HE IS MY BROTHER," L. I, p. 82. And hence the misunderstanding.
     106 October 21, 1794.   L. I, p. 90.
58   107 To Robert Southey, Autumn, 1794.   L. I, p. 101. (This letter appears to be wrongly placed in L. It should come before XXXVIII. See Lushington reference.)
     108 To Robert Southey, November 1794.   L. I, pp. 95–96.
59   109 To Robert Southey, October 21, 1794.   L. I, pp. 90–91.
60   110 To Robert Southey, Autumn, 1794.   L. I, pp. 101–103.
     111 November, 1794.   L. I, p. 98.
     112 Ibid.   L. I, p. 97.
61   113 *Lines on a Friend who died of a Frenzy Fever induced by Calumnious Reports.* L. I, pp. 99–100. Also J.D.C. p. 35; P. I, pp. 76–78. The verses were also included in Coleridge's letter to his brother George, November 6, 1794. L. I, pp. 103–106. See A. II, pp. 135–137. The Rev. Fulwood Smerdon was buried in the Lady's Chapel, Ottery St. Mary, on August 7, 1794, aged forty.
     114 November, 1794.   L. I, p. 98.
     115 Ibid.
     116 November 6, 1794.   L. I, pp. 103–106.

61 117 See letter to Mary Evans, December 1794. L. I, p. 124. A probable reference to this "liberal proposal" made by Coleridge's family is to be found in the letter of November 13, 1795, to Southey, L. I, p. 138.

62 118 See letter of November 1794. L. I, p. 97. Evidently Coleridge stayed at the Salutation and Cat on this occasion—see M.W. II, p. 307.

119 The series began December 1, 1794, with a sonnet *To the Honourable Mr Erskine*. See J.D.C., p. 38, for letter accompanying the sonnet and for editorial note. Sonnets by Coleridge also appeared in the same paper at this time to *La Fayette*, December 15, 1794; *Pitt*, December 23, 1794; *Mrs Siddons*, December 29, 1794; and (although not one of the series) to *Lord Stanhope*, January 31, 1795 (see J.D.C. note, p. 43).

120 December 9, 1794. J.D.C. p. 38; P. I, pp. 80–81.

121 December 11, 1794. J.D.C. p. 39; P. I, pp. 81–82.

122 December 16, 1794. J.D.C. p. 39; P. I, pp. 82–83.

123 January 10, 1795. J.D.C. p. 41; P. I, p. 86. But Coleridge was dissatisfied with this sonnet and asked Southey to contribute the first eight lines. See L. I, p. 117. Cf. W.G. II, p. 224.

124 January 14, 1795. J.D.C. p. 42; P. I, p. 87.

125 January 29, 1795. J.D.C. p. 42; P. I, pp. 87–88.

126 *Address to a Young Jackass and its Tethered Mother*. See letter to Robert Southey, December 17, 1794. L. I, pp. 119–120. In the revised form with the title *To a Young Ass: Its Mother being tethered near it* (J.D.C. p. 35; P. I, pp. 74–76) the reference to pantisocracy is omitted. But there was an even earlier version entitled *Monologue to a Young Jackass in Jesus Piece. Its Mother near it, chained to a Log*. See J.D.C. Appendix C, p. 477 and note, p. 573

127 Thomas Holcroft (1749–1809), author, actor, playwright, translator. Wrote *The Road to Ruin*. His *Memoirs* were completed after his death by Hazlitt. Lovell, who had been in London on a visit, had endeavoured without success to convert Holcroft to pantisocracy. See note 109, Chapter IV. See also W.H. III, pp. 278–279 and XVII, p. 112; E.R. II, pp. 105, 107–110.

128 Richard Porson (1759–1808), Greek scholar. Edited the *Hecuba, Orestes, Phoenissae* and *Medea* of Euripides.

129 William Godwin (1756–1836), Dissenting minister. Later atheist and anarchical philosopher. In 1797 married Mary Woolstonecraft, who died at the birth of Mary, the future wife of Shelley.

63 130 W.G. I, p. 17. Cf. Ibid. pp. 119, 354–358.

131 Tried for sedition in March 1794 at Edinburgh. Placed in Newgate the following month where he stayed until May 1795, when he was transported to New South Wales and died soon after. See *Conciones ad Populum*, p. 22.

132 To Robert Southey, December 17, 1794. L. I, pp. 114–115.

63 133 J.D.C. p. 40; P. I, pp. 84–85. See also letter to Southey, December 11, 1794, L. I, p. 111.

134 David Hartley, the philosopher and physician, 1705–57.

135 December 11, 1794. L. I, p. 113.

65 136 The *Phaedrus, Phaedo, Timaeus, Cratylus* and *Parmenides*, 1792–93.

137 A reprint of the 1787 Ennead I, Book VI, *Concerning the Beautiful*, 1792. Also *Five Books of Plotinus*, 1794, containing *On Felicity, On the Nature and Origin of Evil, On Providence, On Nature, Contemplation, and the One*, and *On the Descent of the Soul*. Cf. *Coleridge's Idealism*, by C. Howard, 1925.

138 See B.Lit.C. I, p. 93. See also Introduction, p. xiv et seq. Also C.P. p. 38 et seq.

139 1749. Cf. Coleridge's letter to George of November 6, 1794: "And after a diligent, I may say an intense, study of Locke, Hartley, and others who have written most wisely on the nature of man, I appear to myself to see the point of possible perfection, at which the world may perhaps be destined to arrive." L. I, p. 105.

140 I, pp. 6–7.

141 Ibid. I, p. 6. In a pioneer attempt, insufficiently appreciated, to study psychology in the light of physical phenomena.

66 142 The following extract from *Observations of Man*, II, Introduction, pp. iii–iv explains Hartley's intentions: "... there are Difficulties both in the Word of God, and in His Works; and these Difficulties are sometimes so magnified, as to lead to Scepticism, Infidelity, or Atheism. Minute Contemplation of our own Frame and Constitution appears to me to have a peculiar Tendency to lessen these Difficulties attending Natural and Revealed Religion, and to improve their Evidences, as well as to concur with them in their Determination of Man's Duty and Expectations. With this View, I drew up the foregoing Observations on the Frame and Connexion of the Body and Mind; and, in Prosecution of the same Design, I now propose,

"First, To proceed upon this Foundation, and upon the other Phaenomena of Nature to deduce the Evidences for the Being and Attributes of God, and the general Truths of Natural Religion.

"Secondly, Laying down all these as a new Foundation, to deduce the Evidences for Revealed Religion.

"Thirdly, To inquire into the Rule of Life, and the particular Applications of it, which result from the Frame of our Natures, the Dictates of Natural Religion, and the Precepts of the Scriptures taken together, compared with, and casting Light upon, each other. And,

"Fourthly, To inquire into the genuine Doctrines of Natural and Revealed Religion thus illustrated, concerning the Expectations of Mankind, here and hereafter, in consequence of their Observance or Violation of the Rule of Life."

66 143 December 1794. L. I, p. 126. In the same letter, speaking of Mary Lamb's illness, Coleridge says that Charles Lamb "bore it with an apparent equanimity as beseemed him who, like me, is a Unitarian Christian, and an advocate for the automatism of man." L. I, p. 127.

144 In his letter of December 17, 1794, Coleridge told Southey that the authorities were "making a row" about his absence from Jesus. (Not printed with remainder of letter in L.)

67 145 December 1794. L. I, pp. 121–122.

69 146 The correct name is now inserted. Little is known of Mary Evans' husband. His wife was later to make another appearance in Coleridge's life. An undated letter from Coleridge exists which reads:

"DEAR MADAM,

"Undoubtedly the first moment of the meeting was an awful one to me. The *second* of time previous to my full recognition of you, the Mary Evans of 14 years ago, flashed across my eyes with a truth and vividness as great as its rapidity. But the confusion of mind occasioned by this sort of *double* presence was amply and more than balanced by the after-pleasure and satisfaction. Truly happy does it make me to have seen you once more, and seen you well, prosperous, and cheerful—all that your goodness gives you a title to.

"I shall, as soon as I am a little at liberty, call on you and Mr Todd, and believe me to be with most sincere regard and never extinguished esteem.

"Your friend,

"S. T. COLERIDGE."

The dating of the *Stanzas written after a long absence* which begin:
Mary! ten chequered years have passed
is not necessarily in conflict with the '14 years' of the letter. But U.L. I, p. 409, suggests that all was not well with Mary.

147 December 1794. L. I, pp. 122–124.

70 148 December 24, 1794. L. I, pp. 124–125.

149 See *Early Years and Late Recollections*, I, p. 27. See also the suggestion in *Samuel Taylor Coleridge and the English Romantic School*, by Alois Brandl, 1886 (Eng. trans. 1887), p. 80, that an inability to assent to the Thirty-nine Articles prevented Coleridge from taking his degree. This presumably follows the statement in J.G. p. 65. Cf. the remark of Mr Lloyd when writing to his son Robert, C.LL. p. 20. The final stages of Coleridge's connexion with Jesus College were these: A college resolution of April 6, 1795, orders that if Coleridge does not return before June 14 his name shall be removed from the boards. This information was passed on to the Treasurer of Christ's Hospital a few days later in reply to an enquiry as to the whereabouts of

70   149   Coleridge. This letter from Coleridge's tutor, dated April 14, 1795, and addressed to Thomas Smith (in error, for William Gill was the Treasurer at this time) reads as follows:

"Sir,

"Mr Coleridge left Cambridge a few days before he had kept the October term and has not since returned but on what account is unknown to any person here. The Master and fellows made an order a fortnight ago that his name shall be removed from the College boards provided he does not return before the 14th of June next and conform in other respects to the rules of the Society.

"I am Sir,
"Your obedient servant,
"J. Costobadie."

Thereupon the details were noted in the Minutes of the Committee of Almoners, April 22, 1795.

"The Committee were informed that in consequence of an enquiry relative to Samuel Coleridge, Scholar of Jesus College, Cambridge, his Tutor had written a Letter whereby it appeared the said Samuel Coleridge left Cambridge a few days before he had kept the last October Term, and had not since returned but on what account was unknown to any person there; and that the Master and Fellows had recently [April 6] made an Order that his Name should be removed from the College Boards unless he returned before 14 June next, and conformed in other respects to the rules of the Society. The Committee considering that the Exhibitions from this Hospital to their Scholars are voted by the General Court under a restriction that if they misbehave or absent themselves from College without permission, under the Order of 13 June 1744, their allowance is to cease; and having further considered that the general Example of a Scholar of such distinguished abilities may be highly detrimental to the welfare of the Youth of this House, it was unanimously agreed with submission to the Court that his Exhibitions which have been paid to the 5th inst. be from that time withheld until the Committee may see cause to make a further Report to the Court upon this subject."

The last half-yearly Exhibition payment to Coleridge was made by the school on April 4, 1795. It was, of course, the enquiries made by the Committee at the time of this payment that led to the official ending of Coleridge's connexion both with Jesus and Christ's Hospital.

150   December 1794. L. I, pp. 125–126.
151   Ibid. I, p. 126.
152   Ibid.
153   Ibid.

CHAPTER 3

PAGE NOTE

71   1   Charles Lamb to Coleridge, June 8–10, 1796. C.L. I, p. 16.

      2   Charles Lamb to Coleridge, December 2, 1796. C.L. I, p. 60.

      3   December 10, 1796. C.L. I, p. 73.

      4   January 28, 1798. (But see J.D.C. p. 600.) C.L. I, p. 118.

      5   R. p. 405.

72   6   A. I, p. 205.

      7   See letter to Robert Southey, November 13, 1795. L. I, p. 139. Also letter to Dyer (January) 1795. U.L. I, p. 29.

      8   Letter to Cottle, March 6, 1836. R. p. 405. Text corrected by the original letter. Cf. M. pp. 42–43.

73   9   n.d. U.L. I, pp. 29–30. This letter to Dyer is headed "25, College Street," yet it is difficult to see how Coleridge could be at this address and still talk of writing in conjunction with Southey. Save for the address, everything would point to the letter being written in January 1795 but Coleridge was at 48, not 25, College Street, at that time. E.H.C. in the *Illustrated London News*, April 22, 1893, states that Coleridge and Southey shared lodgings at 48 *and* 25. Presumably οὔτ' should be οὐκ.

    10   See letter from Southey to Sarah Fricker, October 18, 1794, quoted in L. I, pp. 107–108, note. See also letter to Thomas Southey, October 19, 1794. R.S. I, p. 222.

    11   See letter to Southey, December, 1794. L. I, p. 122. See also letter to Dyer (n.d.) U.L. I, p. 30.

    12   When the writer was last in Bristol (1938) some houses in this street, including No. 25, to which Coleridge subsequently moved, were being demolished, but No. 48 (now 54) was still standing.

    13   *Poems*, by Robert Lovell and Robert Southey, of Baliol College, Oxford: Printed by R. Cruttwell, 1795. The last two lines of the preface say: "The signature of *Bion* distinguishes the pieces of R. Southey;—*Moschus*, R. Lovell."

74   14   n.d. U.L. I, p. 30.

    15   n.d., but almost certainly January 1795. U.L. I, p. 32.

    16   1770–1853.

    17   It is necessary to mention here Cottle's habit in later years of garbling the text of letters written to him. This, due in part to vanity, in part to caution, when joined with a sense of humour that led frequently to exaggerated and misleading statements, render suspect a great deal of what would have been an important contemporary record of Coleridge and his friends at this time.

    18   E.R. I, p. 2 et seq.

75   19   H.S. p. 154. See also L. I, pp. 122, 146–147.

    20   *A Moral and Political Lecture, delivered at Bristol.* By S. T. Coleridge, of Jesus College, Cambridge, a pamphlet of 19 pages, was first printed February 1795. Reprinted in November with

75 20 *On the Present War* as *Conciones ad Populum*, 69 pages. *The Plot Discovered* was printed November 28, 52 pages.

21 The preface to the *Conciones*, written on Coleridge's honeymoon at Clevedon and dated November 16, 1795, claims that "Truth should be spoken at all times, but more especially at those times, when to speak Truth is dangerous." Unfortunately Coleridge was obliged, or saw fit, to alter his draft—"Fools! to commit ROBBERIES, and get hung, when they might MURDER with impunity," substituting for "MURDER" the safer but less impressive "fight for their King and Country."

22 Or ". . . in defence of natural and revealed Religion" to quote the printed version of the *Conciones*.

23 E.R. I, p. 27. In this and other quotations from Cottle it should be noted that variations often appear in the quoted texts of E.R. and R. respectively. The variations are not specified in these pages unless they reveal an important change or modification of attitude.

24 1747–1817. Minister of Lewin's Mead Chapel, Bristol.

76 25 The Rev. David Jardine, Minister of Trim Street Chapel, Bath.

26 H.S. p. 159; C.M.V. p. 12.

27 n.d. U.L. I, p. 31.

28 E.R. I, p. 15.

77 29 Letter dated Spring 1795. L. I, p. 133.

30 E.R. I, pp. 17–18.

31 February 8, 1795. R.S. I, p. 231.

32 n.d. U.L. I, p. 31.

78 33 E.R. I, p. 29.

34 R.S.L. I, p. 41. L. I, pp. 150–151.

35 R.S.L. II, pp. 188–189.

36 Letter to Miss Barker, January 29, 1810. R.S.L. II, p. 188. Southey was not the only person to notice this habit. Coleridge's clerk at Malta years later was to comment upon it. See Charles Wentworth Dilke's *The Papers of a Critic*, 1875, I, p. 32. Something of Coleridge's loquacity, if not his habit of repetition, is recalled in his letter to Southey of August 7, 1803. "I had a vivid recollection, indeed an ocular spectrum, of our room in College Street, a curious instance of association. You remember how incessantly in that room I used to be compounding those half-verbal, half-visual metaphors." L. I, p. 427.

79 37 L. I, pp. 149–150; H.S. p. 162.

38 U.L. I, p. 31.

39 L. I, p. 85.

80 40 See, for instance, L. I, p. 138.

41 L. I, p. 140.

42 L. I, p. 143.

81 43 See E.R. I, pp. 40–41.

81   44   See E.R. I, pp. 40–41. See also letter from Southey to Grosvenor Bedford, R.S. I, p. 239.

45   But "as early as the summer of 1795" Southey had lost confidence in Coleridge. See R.S.L. I, p. 41.

82   46   R.S.L. I, p. 41. See also H.S. pp. 164–165.

47   To Robert Southey, November 13, 1795. L. I, p. 141.

48   L. I, pp. 141–142.

49   For financial reasons, according to Southey. But he discovered, he says, that Coleridge "had been employing every calumny against me." See R.S.L. I, p. 41. Also R. p. 406.

50   See *The Eolian Harp*, J.D.C. p. 49; P. I, pp. 100–102. First entitled, when printed in 1796, *Effusion XXXV. Composed August 20th, 1795, at Clevedon, Somersetshire.*

83   51   U.L. I, p. 31.

84   52   T.P. I, pp. 125–126.

53   Ibid. I, p. 124.

54   J.G. p. 74. Gillman continues: "Mr Wordsworth then residing at Allfoxden." But this is clearly impossible (1) because of the terms Wordsworth uses and (2) because Southey and Coleridge were at that time no longer together in Bristol.

85   55   H. pp. 203–204.

56   Mary Wordsworth to Coleridge's daughter, Sara, November 7, 1845. K.W. I, p. 111. Sara's husband, H. N. Coleridge, said later: "Mr Coleridge and Mr Wordsworth first met in the house of Mr Pinney in the Spring or Summer of 1795"—but if this is correct the time must have been September, when Wordsworth is known to have been staying with the Pinneys, who lived at No. 7 Great George Street, Brandon Hill, Clifton.

57   Letter of Dorothy Wordsworth to Jane Marshall (*née* Pollard), September 2, 1795. W.L. I, p. 139.

58   Mr Pinney was under the impression that Wordsworth was renting the house. In fact, his son allowed the poet free use of it. This son, John Frederick, and his brother Azariah, were both pupils of Basil Montague and Wrangham in London— hence the acquaintance with Wordsworth. Racedown Lodge or Farm is roughly equidistant (about 7 miles) from Crewkerne, Chard, Axminster, Bridport, and Lyme Regis. See *Racedown and the Wordsworths*, by Bergen Evans and Hester Pinney, *Review of English Studies*, Vol. VIII, No. 29, January, 1932; also *A History of Broadwindsor, Dorset*, by Taylor Milne.

59   The full title of the poem is *Lines written at Shurton Bars, near Bridgewater, September 1795, in Answer to a Letter from Bristol*. J.D.C. p. 47; P. I, pp. 96–100. In the editions of 1796–97, a note was appended to the poem, referring to the quoted words 'green radiance' in line 5. The note said, "The expression 'green radiance' is borrowed from Mr Wordsworth, a Poet whose versification is occasionally harsh and his diction too frequently

85 59 obscure; but whom I deem unrivalled among the writers of the present day in manly sentiment, novel imagery, and vivid colouring." In a copy of the 1797 *Poems* Coleridge has written under this note—"This note was written before I had ever seen Mr Wordsworth, *atque utinam opera ejus tantum noveram.*" The expression 'green radiance' occurred in Wordsworth's *An Evening Walk*, 1793, in the line "Small circles of green radiance gleam around." Coleridge's other remarks on the subject are not very helpful. See letter to Estlin, L. I, p. 246, and B.Lit.C. I, p. 58, "I was in my twenty-fourth year, when I had the happiness of knowing Mr Wordsworth personally, and while memory lasts, I shall hardly forget the sudden effect produced on my mind, by his recitation of a manuscript poem. . . ." This was the *Female Vagrant* (see B.Lit.B. I, p. 86) but not the earlier version. Coleridge refers to the second meeting, of autumn 1796.

60 W.L. I, pp. 144–145. The satire came to nothing. It seems certain that the two men met (1) before the quarrel and separation of Coleridge and Southey, (2) before Coleridge's marriage (October 4) and (3) while Wordsworth was in Bristol (September 2 to 25). Indeed, Southey was "a coxcomb" by the following March 21. Letter to William Mathews. W.L. I, p. 155.

61 January 7, 1796. W.L. I, p. 149. . . . "he [Coleridge] has interleaved it [*Guilt and Sorrow*] with white paper to mark down whatever may strike him as worthy your notice," Azariah Pinney wrote Wordsworth on March 25, 1796. See *Review of English Studies*, January, 1932, pp. 12–13. Cf. Notes 114–117, Chapter IV.

62 E.R. I, pp. 57 58. Martha Fricker and Josiah Wade were the witnesses. See notices of the wedding in Bonner and Middleton's *Journal*, October 10; *Bristol Gazette and Public Advertiser*, October 15; and in Felix Farley's *Bristol Journal*, October 17.

86 63 October 7, 1795. L. I, p. 136.
64 Ibid.
65 Ibid. I, p. 137.
66 Ibid.
87 67 Ibid. I, pp. 136–137.
68 See R. p. 40.
69 Ibid.
70 G.M.B. *Memoir and Letters of Sara Coleridge*, 1873, I, pp. 10–11.
71 October 1795. L. I, p. 134.
72 L. I, p. 144.
88 73 H.S. p. 166
74 November 13, 1795. L. I, p. 137 et seq.
75 Ibid. I, p. 148.
76 In addition to the quotations which follow, there is proof of this statement in Coleridge's bitter reproach of later years. See U.L. I, p. 404. Cf. Coleridge's Note Book No. 21.
77 L. I, p. 138.

89   78   L. I, pp. 146–147.
     79   See letter from Lamb to Coleridge, May 24–31, 1796.   C.L. I,
          p. 7, and note p. 11.
     80   L. I, pp. 148–149.
     81   Cottle and his sister Sarah were the witnesses.   See R. p. 189;
          H.S. p. 168.   Despite the attempt at secrecy, news of the mar-
          riage was soon public property.   See R. p. 190.

CHAPTER 4

90   1   See *The Reading of Southey and Coleridge: The Record of their
         Borrowings from the Bristol Library, 1793–98*, by Paul Kaufman,
         Modern Philology, XXI, pp. 317–320; also *Books Read by
         Coleridge and Southey* in James Baker's *Literary and Biographical
         Studies*, 1908, pp. 211–218.
     2   ll. 43–48 *Reflections on Entering Into Active Life*; a title altered in
         1797 to *Reflections on having left a Place of Retirement.   Monthly
         Magazine*, October 1796.   J.D.C. p. 53; P. I, pp. 106–108.
     3   T.P. I, p. 130; E.R. I, p. 137.
91   4   See, for instance, U.L. I, p. 35.   Also R. p. 165; E.R. I, p. 146.
     5   See Cottle's story of the £50 gift of Dr Fox in 1796 "in admiration
         of Mr C's talents."   E.R. II, pp. 162–163.   Dr Fox it was with
         whom in later years Coleridge sought refuge.   See L. II, p. 619;
         U.L. II, p. 108.   See also U.L. I, p. 60, for an early mention
         of him.   Cf. the *Athenaeum*, May 2, 1908, p. 543.   Although
         it is not certain whether John Morgan also lent Coleridge money
         about the same time, this Bristol admirer was to become one of
         Coleridge's truest friends and helpers.   See R. pp. 237–247 for
         mention of Morgan's situation after Coleridge had left Bristol.
     6   But Cottle was not included—why, Coleridge explains in his
         letter B.E. I, p. 52.
     7   Letter to Thomas Poole, October 7, 1795.   L. I, p. 136.
     8   See Appendix to M.   First printed by J.D.C. in the *Athenaeum*,
         December 9, 1893.   The Motto is taken from the Gospel
         according to St. John ("And ye shall know the truth, and the
         truth shall make you free"), chapter viii. verse 32, not chapter
         xxxii. (which does not exist), as stated in U.L. I, p. 41.
92   9   Appendix to M.
93   10 B.Lit.C. I, pp. 114–115.
     11 To Josiah Wade, January 10, 1796.   U.L. I, p. 38.
     12 John Edwards of Gateacre Chapel, Liverpool, succeeded Priest-
         ley's colleague as minister (1791–1802) to the New Meeting.
         Coleridge preached from the New Meeting pulpit on January 17.
         He also met in Birmingham the ministers of the Old Meeting
         Congregation—Radcliffe Scholefield (1772–99), John Coates

93   12   (1785–1801), and Astley Meanley, of whom more is heard. Whether or not Coleridge preached from the Old Meeting Pulpit is uncertain.   A Birmingham newspaper report of the bicentenary of the Old Meeting, on May 18, 1887 (the chapel was actually built in 1689), says: "During the time of the occupation of the Livery Street Chapel by the burned-out congregations of the Old and New Meetings, the famous S. T. Coleridge preached, while on his tour 'in a blue coat and a white waistcoat,' to canvass for *The Watchman,* which was to regenerate the world.   He has left a curious sketch of his 'canvassing' but no report of his preaching has survived."   See also article *Samuel Taylor Coleridge and Unitarianism,* by H. W. Stevenson, and address *Our Indebtedness to Priestley,* by the Rev. H. J. Rossington, in the *Transactions of the Unitarian Historical Society,* vol. V, part 2, October 1932, p. 165 et seq., and vol. V, part 3, November 1933, p. 227 et seq. respectively.   See also E. H. Coleridge in C.M.V. p. 11 et seq.

13   To Josiah Wade, January 1796, from Nottingham.   B.E. I, pp. 55–56; R. p. 85.

94   14   To Josiah Wade, February 2, 1796, from Sheffield.   B.E. I, pp. 58–59.   See also Carpenter's *Presbyterianism in Nottingham,* 1862, pp. 172–173.

95   15   B.Lit.C. I, pp. 115–117.

96   16   Ibid. I, pp. 117–119.   Cf. W.H. XVII, pp. 114–115.

17   Written at Nottingham, January 27, 1796.   L. I, p. 152; B.E. I, p. 56.

97   18   1775–1839.

19   Letter to Josiah Wade, January 1796.   B.E. I, p. 56.

20   1736–97.

21   1731 1802.   See letter to Josiah Wade, January 27, 1796.   L. I, pp. 152–153; B.E. I, pp. 56–57.   Also letter to the Rev. John Edwards, January 1796.   U.L. I, pp. 39–40.   See also C.W. III, p. 155.

22   1726–97.

23   Letter to the Rev. John Edwards, January 1796.   U.L. I, p. 40. There is no record of Coleridge having preached at the Friargate Chapel in Derby on January 24.

24   To Josiah Wade, January 27, 1796.   L. I, pp. 153–154.

25   This charity sermon was given before the High Pavement Congregation on January 31.   George Walker, a man of parts, was one of the ministers of this chapel.   See *Trans. Unit. Hist. Soc.* V, 2.   Also *Presbyterianism in Nottingham.*

26   To Josiah Wade, February 2, 1796.   B E. I, p. 58.

27   To the Rev. John Edwards, January 1796.   U.L. I, p. 40.

28   To the same, February 4, 1796.   U.L. I, p. 42.

29   To the same, January 1796.   U.L. I, p. 40.

30   To the same, February 4, 1796.   U.L. I, pp. 42–43.   It was unfortunate that Coleridge had not been provided with an in-

97	30	troduction to the Rev. John Evans of the Upper Chapel at Sheffield, a man much his way of thinking. See *History of Upper Chapel*, by J. E. Manning, 1900, p. 82.
	31	Benjamin Naylor, assistant minister at the Upper Chapel, 1780–1798. Then minister, 1798–1805.
98	32	See note 12. Meanley (1758–94) was minister of a group of chapels in the Peak District with his centre at Platt Chapel, Rusholme. Then he settled at Stannington, outside Sheffield, to and from which place Coleridge walked with such discomfort. See U.L. I, pp. 42–43. See also *Trans. Unit. Hist. Soc.* V, 2.
	33	To the Rev. John Edwards, February 4, 1796. U.L. I, p. 42. Samuel Shore, to whom Naylor gave Coleridge a letter, was High Sheriff of the county of Derby in 1761. See *Trans. Unit. Hist. Soc.* vol. I, pp. 132, 139.
	34	1771–1854.
	35	To Josiah Wade, February 7, 1796, from Manchester. B.E. I, p. 59.
	36	Ibid. I, pp. 59–60. See also letter to the Rev. John Edwards, February 4, 1796. U.L. I, p. 43. See also B.Lit.C. I, p. 117.
	37	B.E. I, p. 60. With reference to Sarah's illness, see *On Observing a Blossom on the First of February, 1796*, as printed in *The Watchman*, VI, April 11, 1796, with the lines:

> From black anxiety that gnaws my heart
> For her who droops far off on a sick bed.

	38	February 1796. B.E. I, p. 60.
	39	E.R. I, p. 148.
	40	Ibid. I, pp. 156–157, note. This further example of Coleridge's habit of procrastination, to be many times multiplied in the future, displays a characteristic by no means overlooked by Coleridge himself. See, for instance, his remarks some years earlier to George Coleridge. "I intended to have written to my brother James, but Mr Pitt and I have the honour of resembling one another in one particular—he in his *bellatory*, and I in my epistolary department—we are both men of *Preparation*." May 17, 1891, *Illustrated London News*, April 1, 1893.
	41	C.M.V. pp. 17–18; B.Lit.C. I, pp. 119–120. But see E.R. I, p. 163.
99	42	February, 1796. *Illustrated London News*, April 15, 1893. L. I, p. 57, note.
	43	Letter to George Coleridge, April 1798. L. I, p. 240. Cf. B.Lit.C. I, p. 120
	44	B.Lit.C. I, p. 120.
	45	O.T. I, pp. 120–126.
	46	Isa. xv. 11: "Wherefore my bowels shall sound like an harp for Moab."
	47	The Rev. W. J. Hort was a master at Dr Estlin's School. See *To the Rev. W. J. Hort: While teaching a Young Lady some Song-tunes on his flute.* J.D.C. pp. 44–45; P. I, p. 92.

99	48	March 12, 1796. U.L. I, p. 47.
100	49	March 30, 1796. L. I, p. 157. See also letter to the Rev. John Edwards, March 20, 1796. U.L. I, p. 48.
	50	B.Lit.C. I, p. 120. Cf. C.M.V. pp. 18–20, for a description of *The Watchman.*
	51	May 3, 1796. T.P. I, pp. 137–139.
	52	Letter to Thomas Poole, March 30, 1796. L. I, p. 157; B.E. I, p. 69.
	53	Ibid.
101	54	L. I, pp. 154–155; B.E. I, pp. 63–64.
	55	U.L. I, pp. 45–46.
	56	Ibid. I, p. 47.
102	57	To the Rev. John Edwards. U.L. I, p. 48.
	58	Ibid. p. 49.
	59	Ibid.
	60	Ibid.
	61	To Thomas Poole, April 11, 1796. B.E. I, p. 73.
103	62	Ibid. See also C.M.V. p. 21.
	63	To Thomas Poole, March 30, 1796. L. I, p. 156.
	64	To Joseph Cottle, February 1796, from Stowey. " 'The Religious Musings,' " writes Coleridge, "I have altered monstrously." B.E. I, p. 63.
	65	*Poems on Various Subjects*, by S. T. Coleridge, late of Jesus College, Cambridge.

> Felix curarum, cui non Heliconia cordi
> Serta, nec imbelles Parnassi e vertice laurus!
> Sed viget ingenium, et magnos accinctus in usus
> Fert animus quascunque vices.—Nos tristia vitae
> Solamur cantu.—Stat. *Silv.* Lib. IV, 4.

Octavo, pp. xvi; 188 (plus one page of 'Errata').

	66	Cf. *Monthly Magazine*, II, 1796, p. 487.
	67	Cf. *Critical Review*, XVII, June 1796, p. 209.
	68	Cf. *Analytical Review*, XXVII, June 1796, p. 627.
	69	July 4. U.L. I, p. 54.
	70	April 1, 1796. B.E. I, pp. 68, 73. See also letter to Thelwall, May 1796. U.L. I, pp. 50–51. The poem, said Bowles mistakenly, was written "in a tap room at Reading" (see *A Wiltshire Parson and his Friends*, by Garland Greever, 1926). See E.R. II, p. 48 et seq.
104	71	ll. 343–357. J.D.C. p. 59; P. I, p. 122. The verses admired by Wordsworth were 364–375 and 403–428. See letter to Thelwall, May 13, 1796. L. I, pp. 163-164; C.L. I, pp. 9, 10, 16, 93; and *From Necessity to Transcendentalism in Coleridge*, by S. F. Gingerich, in P.M.L.A. vol. XXXV, No. 1, March 1920, for a discussion of the philosophical and religious views expressed in the poem. This was the passage declaimed, vainly, to the Brummagem tallow-chandler. B.Lit.C. I, p. 116.

104. 72 ll. 240–242. J.D.C. p. 57; P. I, p. 118.
73 ll. 317–322. J.D.C. p. 59; P. I, p. 121.
105 74 ll. 340–343. J.D.C. p. 59; P. I, p. 122.
75 ll. 371–375. J.D.C. p. 60; P. I, p. 123.
76 Note by Coleridge in the 1797 edition of his *Poems* to the lines following.
77 ll. 396–404. J.D.C. p. 60; P. I, p. 124. In 1797 Coleridge added a footnote to line 402. "This paragraph is intelligible to those, who, like the Author, believe and feel the sublime system of Berkley; and the doctrine of the final Happiness of all men."
78 ll. 368–370. J.D.C. p. 60; P. I, p. 123.
79 ll. 405–408. J.D.C. p. 60; P. I, p. 124.
106 80 To Josiah Wade, January 27, 1796. B.E. I, p. 57; L. I, p. 152.
81 See Coleridge's reply to 'Caius Graccus,' who had protested against the attack. *The Watchman*, April 2, 1796. B.E. I, pp. 69–71. See also letters to Thelwall, May 13, 1796, L. I, pp. 159–163; June 22, 1796, L. I, pp. 166–167. The original article, *Modern Patriotism*, appeared in the third number, on March 17.
82 See L. I, p. 91.
83 Cf. C.P. p. 42 et seq. Also *Gingerich*.
107 84 B.Lit.C. I, p. 98.
85 ll. 41–45. J.D.C. p. 54; P. I, pp. 110–111. In 1797 Coleridge added a footnote to line 44: "See this *demonstrated* by Hartley, vol. 1, p. 144, and vol. 2, p. 329. See it likewise proved, and freed from the charge of Mysticism, by Pistorius in his Notes and Additions to part second of Hartley on Man, Addition the 18th, the 653rd page of the third volume of Hartley, Octavo Edition." But no mention of Plotinus, from whom the thought would seem to have been derived.
86 ll. 413–415. J.D.C. p. 60; P. I, p. 124.
87 ll. 126–128. J.D.C. p. 55; P. I, pp. 113–114.
108 88 ll. 149–157. J.D.C. p. 56; P. I, pp. 114–115.
89 ll. 105–110. J.D.C. p. 55; P. I, p. 113.
90 B.E. I, p. 65; L. I, p. 156.
91 B.E. I, p. 66; L. I, p. 157. These were the Bristol lectures to be made into book form.
92 B.E. I, p. 72.
109 93 In *The Watchman*, No. V, April 2, 1796. J.D.C. p. 64. Count (Sir Benjamin Thompson) Rumford (1753–1814) later founded the Royal Institution, to which he invited Humphry Davy. See H.D.M. I, p. 132 et seq.
94 E.R. I, pp. 145–146. To Joseph Cottle, April 1796. B.E. I, pp. 74–75.
95 Ibid.
96 E.R. I, p. 146.
97 To Thomas Poole. May 5, 1796; B.E. I, p. 77.
98 C.M.V. p. 22. See also E.R. I, p. 30.

110	99	To Thomas Poole, May 5, 1796. B.E. I, pp. 77–78.
111	100	Ibid. pp. 78–79.
	101	E.R. I, p. 158.
	102	Ibid.
	103	T.P. I, p. 142. In addition to Thomas Poole, the contributors included Dr Beddoes, John Cruikshank, (Lord Egmont's agent), Josiah Wade, Dr Estlin, Dr Disney (colleague and successor of Theophilus Lindsey at the Unitarian Essex Street Chapel and of whom more will be heard), and Benjamin Hobhouse (later Sir Benjamin), a member of the Trim Street Chapel at Bath.
112	104	T.P. I, pp. 143–144. The letter was dated March 28, 1796.
113	105	May 12, 1796. L. I, p. 158; B.E. I, pp. 80–81.
	106	L. I, p. 159; B.E. I, p. 81.
	107	Ibid.
	108	T.P. I, p. 146.
114	109	1766–1834. Together with Horne Tooke, Thomas Holcroft, and Thomas Hardy, president of the London Corresponding Society, Thelwall was sent to the Tower in May 1794. The papers of the Society were seized and the men arraigned for treason. They were tried, found not guilty and discharged, in November of the same year. See Thelwall's *The Tribune*, vol. I, p. 90, 1795. Cf. W.P. 1805, X, ll. 646–657.
	110	May, 1796. U.L. I, p. 50.
115	111	May 13, 1796. L. I, pp. 159–160.
	112	Ibid. I, p. 163.
	113	Ibid.
116	114	For instance, see the Note to the 1797 *Poems* in which Coleridge states that he had not met Wordsworth as early as March 1796. See also letter to Estlin of May 1798 (dated mistakenly May 1797 in E.) in which Coleridge says, "I have now known him [Wordsworth] a year and some months": L. I, p. 246. See also L. I, p. 163, note. Cf. Notes 54–61, Chapter III.
	115	January 7, 1796. W.L. I, p. 149.
	116	See letter from Lamb to Coleridge, May 24–31, 1796. C.L. I, p. 9.
	117	B.Lit.C. I, p. 58.
117	118	To Joseph Cottle, February 22, 1796. L. I, p. 155; B.E. I, p. 64.
	119	B.Lit.C. I, p. 120. Some (J. Shawcross, for instance) have held that Poole is the friend mentioned but the wording does not bear this out. Sara Coleridge states (B.Lit.B. I, p. 188) that Wade was the man. Cf. Coleridge's letter to Wade, U.L. I, p. 74.
	120	May 24–31, 1796. C.L. I, p. 10.
	121	E.R. I, p. 176 et seq.
118	122	May 5, 1796. B.E. I, p. 79. Cf. E. pp. 48–50, 59.
	123	See letter from Lamb to Coleridge, June 10, 1796. C.L. I, p. 21. "mine will be the loss if your lot is to be cast at Bristol or Nottingham," writes Lamb. C.L. I, p. 22.

[449   ]

118   124   C.L. I, p. 21.

125   July 4, 1796. B.E. I, p. 83.

126   1760–1808. Founder of the Pneumatic Institute in Bristol. Father of T. L. Beddoes, the poet. See H.D.M. I, p. 65 et seq.; T.W. p. 33 et seq.

119   127   July 4, 1796. U.L. I, p. 52.

128   B.E. I, p. 84.

129   Ibid. pp. 83–84.

130   See letter from Lamb to Coleridge, July 6, 1796. C.L. I, pp. 35–36.

131   T.P. I, pp. 150–152.

120   132   Letter to John Fellowes of Nottingham, written at Tewkesbury, July 28, 1796 (on the way from Darley to Ottery). *Letters, hitherto uncollected, by Samuel Taylor Coleridge.* Edited with a prefatory note by Colonel W. F. Prideaux, 1913, pp. 2–4.

133   Letter to J. P. Estlin. E. p. 11.

134   C.M.V. p. 28.

135   Letter to J. P. Estlin. E. p. 11.

136   C.M.V. p. 28.

137   Saturday, August 1796. U.L. I, p. 56. See also letter to Thomas Poole, Monday morning, August 22, 1796. U.L. I, p. 56.

121   138   To Thomas Poole, August 22, 1796. U.L. I, p. 57.

139   T.P. I, p. 153.

140   See letter to Thomas Poole, August 22, 1796. U.L. I, p. 57. See also B.E. I, pp. 86, 88.

141   August, 1796. B.E. I, p. 88. See also U.L. I, p. 57.

142   To Thomas Poole, August 22, 1796. U.L. I, p. 58; T.P. I, pp. 152–154. Cf. E. pp. 12–13.

122   143   Ibid. Also B.E. I, pp. 86–87.

144   Just outside Birmingham.

145   Former Unitarian minister at Birmingham, at this time retired.

146   At Birmingham.

147   U.L. I, p. 57; B.E. I, p. 86.

148   E. p. 15. Cf. R. p. 93.

149   To Josiah Wade, August 1796. B.E. I, p. 88. Roscoe was one of the prominent Liverpool Unitarians, Abolitionists, and Liberals connected with Dr Crompton.

123   150   Letter to Thomas Poole, September 24, 1796. L. I, p. 168; B.E. I, p. 89.

151   Ibid.

152   September 1796. C.LL. p. 20.

153   To Thomas Poole, September 24, 1796. L. I, p. 169; B.E. I, p. 90.

124   154   *On receiving a letter informing me of the Birth of a Son: Composed on a Journey Homeward; the Author having received Intelligence of the Birth of a Son, Sept. 20, 1796: To a Friend who asked, how I felt when the Nurse first presented my Infant to Me.* J.D.C. p. 66; P. I, pp. 152–154.

124 155   To Thomas Poole, September 24, 1796.   L. I, p. 169; B.E. I, p. 90.

156   "I cannot as yet reconcile my intellect to the sacramental Rites," Coleridge told Estlin. "My conduct is this—I omit the rites, and wish to say nothing about it; everything that relates to Christianity is of importance, but yet all things are not of equal importance; and when the Incendaries have surrounded the building, it is idle to dispute among ourselves whether the staircase was placed in it by the original Architect or added afterwards by a meaner Hand." E. pp. 35–36; U.L. I, p. 79.

157   To Thomas Poole, September 24, 1796.   L. I, p. 169; B.E. I, p. 90.

158   To the same.   L. I, p. 168; B.E. I, p. 89.

159   To the same.   L. I, pp. 169–170; B.E. I, pp. 90–91.

160   To the same.   L. I, p. 170; B.E. I, p. 91.

161   Ibid.

125 162   Ibid.

163   To the same.   L. I, p. 169; B.E. I, p. 90.

126 164   November 19, 1796.   L. I, p. 178.

165   B.Lit.C. I, p. 121.

166   September 26, 1796.   T.P. I, p. 161.

167   Letter to Thomas Poole, November 1, 1796.   B.E. I, p. 97.

168   Ibid.

169   Act V, Sc. 16.   See B.E. I, p. 92.

170   December 31, 1796.   L. I, pp. 210–211.   Cf. Cottle's account in E.R. I, pp. 196–197.

127 171   See R.S.L. II, p. 188.   Cf. Wordsworth's opinion that Southey took "too rigid a view" of Coleridge.   Tom Moore's *Reminiscences*.   See also Southey's letters to Cottle, R. p. 406 et seq.

172   To Coleridge, June 8–10, 1796.   C.L. I, p. 19.

173   September 27, 1796.   C.L. I, p. 39.

128 174   September 29, 1796.   L. I, pp. 171–172; B.E. I, pp. 93–94.

129 175   The *Morning Chronicle* office.

176   Darley Hall.

177   Doctor Crompton.

178   Coleridge's latest plan—the settlement at Stowey.

179   October 17, 1796.   C.L. I, pp. 46–47.

180   Letter to Coleridge, October 3, 1796.   C.L. I, p. 42.

181   See, for instance, Lamb's letters of October 24 and 28, 1796. C.L. I, pp. 48–50.

130 182   October 15, 1796.   C.LL. pp. 20–23; B.E. I, pp. 106–107.

131 183   October 18, 1796.   B.E. I, pp. 95–96.

184   Lloyd's grandmother.   The first line of Coleridge's *Sonnet* prefacing the quarto was:

The piteous sobs that choke the virgin's breath.

131 185 Letter from Lamb to Coleridge, December 9, 1796. C.L. I, pp. 67–69. See article *A Letter of Charles Lamb*, by J. Dykes Campbell, in the *Athenaeum*, June 13, 1891. No copy of the Coleridge-Lloyd pamphlet is known to exist. A copy of the 16-page pamphlet containing twenty-eight sonnets by Coleridge, Bowles, and others is now in the South Kensington Museum. See L. I, pp. 177, 205–206 and note; J.D.C. pp. 542–544; and P.D.W. II, p. 375 et seq.

186 B.E. I, p. 96.

187 Ibid. I, p. 98.

188 L. I, p. 173; B.E. I, p. 99.

132 189 L. I, p. 176; B.E. I, p. 101.

190 L. I, pp. 173–175; B.E. I, pp. 100–101.

191 U.L. I, p. 59. "Oh! that S. T. C. had never taken more than 25 drops each dose" was Cottle's later comment, scribbled on the back of the letter.

133 192 Cf. *The Lancet*, April 11, 1936.

193 See W.L. I, p. 169, for instance, and L. I, pp. 238, 240. The suggestion has even been made (by J. D. Rea in *Modern Language Notes*, XLV, pp. 12, 18) that Coleridge's later troubles of mind can be traced to a physical cause—"osteomyelitis, or impacted teeth."

194 November 13, 1796. U.L. I, pp. 60–61.

195 John Horne Tooke, 1736–1812, philologist, Radical politician. Had taken Orders but afterwards left the Church. Author of *The Diversions of Purley*. See B.E. I, p. 88. Also T.T. May 1, 1832, p. 161. See also Coleridge's poem, first included in a letter to Estlin of July 4, 1796, to celebrate Horne Tooke's poll at the second Westminster election. E. pp. 24–25; U.L. I, pp. 54–55.

196 U.L. I, p. 61.

134 197 November 15, 1796. U.L. I, p. 61.

198 Ibid. I, p. 62.

199 Ibid.

200 To Charles Lloyd, senior, November 14, 1796. C.LL. pp. 27–28; B.E. I, p. 108.

201 To the same. C.LL. p. 28; B.E. I, p. 108.

135 202 To the same. C.LL. p. 29; B.E. I, p. 109.

203 December 4, 1796. C.LL. p. 33; B.E. I, pp. 110–111.

204 C.LL. pp. 31–32; B.E. I, p. 110.

136 205 To Thomas Poole, December 12, 1796. L. I, p. 186; B.E. I, p. 111, note.

137 206 November 19, 1796. L. I, pp. 180–181. See, in contrast, the description of Coleridge by the Rev. Leapidge Smith in his "Reminiscences of an Octogenarian" in *Leisure Hour*, 1870, p. 651. This is quoted in L. I. pp. 180–181, note.

207 L. I, p. 182. Presumably Coleridge really wanted Apollonius of Tyana rather than Apollinaris Sidonius.

137 208 December 17, 1796. L. I, p. 196.
    209 Ibid.
    210 Ibid. I, p. 197.
    211 Ibid. I, p. 204.
138 212 See, for instance, the commencement of the letter, December 31, 1796. L. I, p. 210.
    213 December, 1796. U.L. I, p. 65.
    214 The intention was to revise and enlarge his Bristol lectures for the press. G.M.B.
    215 ". . . the confidants who have *not* betrayed me, the friends whose silence was *not* detraction, and the inmates before whom I was not ashamed to complain, to yearn, to weep, or even to pray!" June 21, 1823; and again, earlier "my only full confidants," L. II, p. 597.   The name 'flycatchers' was given by Coleridge to his later notebooks—'Flycatcher No. 1' is dated July 5, 1827— which are filled chiefly with his theological notes and queries. But what might seem a misnomer if made by the ordinary man, is not only characteristic of Coleridge but, bearing the writer in mind, by no means an unsuitable title.
    216 These notebooks are now being edited—one of the two most important pieces of Coleridgean scholarship still to be completed.

    The following extracts are from one of the earliest and certainly the best known of the notebooks, dating from 1795 to 1798. The Gutch Memorandum Book (so called because the book came into the possession of Coleridge's old schoolfellow, John Matthew Gutch, before being purchased in 1868 for the British Museum) has been printed in German (*S. T. Coleridge's Notiz̧buch aus den Jahren 1795–1798* in *Herrigs Archiv für das Studium der neueren Sprachen und Litteraturen*, XCVII (1896), pp. 333–372), but in English has yet to be fully printed.   Apart from quotations in many books upon Coleridge, the most important printed sources in English are: A.P. (numerous entries in the first chapter); L.R. I; J.D.C. pp. 453–458; and P. II, pp. 988–995.

My Works.

———

Imitations of the Modern Latin Poets with an Essay Biog. and Crit. on the Rest. of Lit.—2 Vol., Octavo.
Answer to the System of Nature—
       ~~1 Vol.~~ Oct.

The Origin of Evil, an Epic Poem.
Essay on Bowles
Strictures on Godwin, Paley etc. etc.—
Pantisocracy, or a practical Essay on the abolition of Indiv[id]ual Property.
Carthon an Opera.

[453]

Poems

Edition of Collins and Gray with a preliminary Dissertation.

A Liturgy ⎰ On the different Sects of Religion and Infidelity—
A Tragedy ⎱ philosophical analyisis of their Effects on mind and manners—

Six Gallons of Water—
~~Eighteen~~ Twelve pounds of Sugar.
Half a pound of Ginger
Eighteen Lemons

Ginger to be sliced—Lemons to be peeled—The Sugar and Water to be boiled together, and the Scum—viz.—the Monarchica[l] part must go to Pot—and out of the Pot—*Then* put in the Ginger with the Peels of the Lemons, and let the whole be boiled together gently for half an hour—When cold, put in the Lemon juice strained etc—then let the Sum total be put in the Barrel with three Spoonfuls of Yeast—let it work three Days (Sundays excepted—) and then put in a gallon of Barrel—Close up the Barrel—Nota bene: you may do it legally the habeas corpus act being suspended,—let it remain a fortnight—then bottle it— The Wine not to be used even in warm weather till three Weeks after Bottling—in Winter not till after a month—

Very fond of Vegetables, particulary Bacon and Peas—Bacon and Broad Beans—

Receipt for brewing Wine—
Get two strong faithful men by proper Instruments—Vide Thieves' Calendar—break into a Wine merchant's Cellar—carry off a hogshead of best Claret or other ad arbitrium—given me by Mrs Danvers—expertae crede

Mem. To ~~write in~~ reduce to a regular form the Swedenborgian's Reveries—
Mem. To remember to examine into the Laws upon Wrecks as at present existing
Mem. I asserted that Cato was a drunkard—denied by S.—to examine it—
. . . Poem in ~~three~~ one Books in the manner of Dante on the excursion of Thor—
2 Satires in the manner of Donne.
1 Horace Walpole.
2 Monthly Reviewers (?) Bowles
Address to Poverty at thė end of the
In early youth— Ωσραλ! Console my SARA—
And grieve not, my son! that we &c: Tob.

Take a pound of Beef, Mutton, or Pork; cut it into small pieces; a pint of Peas; four Turnips sliced; six or seven Potatoes cut very small; four or five Onions; put to them three Quarts of

Water, and let it boil about two hours and a half—(thick)—then thicken it with a pound of Rice—and boil it a quarter of an (other) hour more—after which season it with salt & pepper—

N.B. better season it at first—peppering & salting the Meat, &c.—

1. An Essay on Tobit.

2. On the art of prolonging Life—by getting up in a morning.

3. On Marriage—in opposition to French Principles.

4. Jacob Behmen.

5. Life of John Henderson.

6. Ode to a Looking Glass.

7. Burnet de montibus: in English Blank Verse.

8. Escapes from Misery—a Poem—Halo round the Candle— Sigh visible.

9. Cavern—candle.

10. Life of David—a Sermon.

11. Wild Poem on Maniac—Eρα[τ]σου Γαληρος ἁτ

12. Ode on St. Withold.

13. Crotchets, by S. T. Coleridge.

14. Edition of Akenside.

15. Of Collins and Gray.

16. Hymns to the Sun, the Moon, and the Elements—six hymns.

In one of them to introduce a dissection of Atheism—particularly the Godwinian System of Pride—Proud of what? An outcast of blind Nature ruled by a fatal Necessity—Slave of an Ideot Nature! In the last Hymn a sublime enumeration of all the charms or Tremendities of Nature—then a bold avowal of Berkley's System!!!

17. Letter to Godwin.

18. Randolph consecrating D. of York's banners—

19. Ode to Southey
                Deproeliantium e carcere nubium.

20. Egomist, a metaphysical Rhapsody—

21. Berkley's Maxims—Vol. II, 345. Ode to a Moth— against accumulation.

22. Adventures of CHRISTIAN, the mutineer——

23. Military anecdotes—(N.B. promised to be sergeants)

24. History of Phrases—ex.gr. The King must have men.

25. Hymn to Dr Darwin—in the manner of the Orphics.

26. Address to the Clergy against the two Bills—

27. Satire addressed to a young Man who intended to study medicine at Edinburgh—

The Earth feared and was still, then God arose to Judgement to save the meek of the Earth. Surely, the Wrath of Man shall praise thee—: the remainder of Wrath shalt thou restrain.—

[455]

138   216   God shall cut off the spirit of Princes—he is terrible to the
Kings of the Earth.

Then shall the right-aiming Thunderbolt go abroad; & from
the Clouds, as from a strong Bow, shall they fly to the mark.

There be Spirits that are created for Vengeance—in the time of
Destruction they pour out their force and appease the Wrath
of him that made them.

Men that run mad unto prosperity compared to cats on beds of
Marum and Valerian—

There is not a new or strange opinion—Truth returned from
banishment—a river run under ground—fire beneath embers—

Men anxious for this world—Owls that watch all night to
catch mice—

Smooth, shining, & deceitful as thin Ice—

Wisdom, Mother of retired Thought,

Nature,

Wrote Rascal on his face by chiliographic art

Our quaint metaphysical opinions in an hour of anguish like
playthings by the bedside of a child deadly sick.

139   217   December 1796. U.L. I, p. 63.
     218   Ibid.
     219   Ibid.
     220   L. I, p. 183.
     221   The two, dated December 12 and 13, 1796, were sent together.
144   222   T.P. I, pp. 184–193; L. I, pp. 187–193.
     223   December 18, 1796. L. I, p. 209.
     224   Ibid.
     225   It appeared on December 31, 1796.
     226   The spare end-page was filled with his 'Indolence' sonnet to
Charles Lloyd.   The first title of the sonnet, as sent in a letter
to Thelwall of December 17, 1796 (L. I, pp. 207–208), was *To
a Young Man who abandoned himself to a causeless and indolent
melancholy*.   The later alteration to *Addressed to a Young Man
of Fortune*, etc., accounts presumably for E. H. C.'s suggestion
that the sonnet may have been intended in the first instance as
a rebuke to the author himself, being applied later to Charles
Lloyd instead.   The sonnet appeared first in the *Cambridge
Intelligencer* on December 17, 1796.

     227   See J.D.C. pp. 586–587.

CHAPTER 5

145   1   See letter to Thomas Poole, December 18, 1796.   L. I, p. 209.
Then on April 2, 1798, "Coleridge came to avoid the smoke;
stayed all night."   D.W.J. p. 15.

146   2   January 3, 1797. B.E. I, p. 123.

        3   n.d. L. I, pp. 213–214. But at a later date the cottage found little favour, either in Coleridge's or his wife's eyes. See T.P. I, p. 199; ibid. II, p. 8; and S.C. p. 75.

        4   The *Monthly Magazine.*

        5   December 17, 1796. L. I, p. 194.

        6   Ibid.

147   7   February 6, 1797. L. I, pp. 219–220.

        8   January 10, 1797. C.L. I, p. 85.

        9   Ibid. Also February 5, 1797. C.L. I, p. 95.

      10   Spring, 1797. U.L. I, pp. 71–72 See also T.T. April 28, 1832, p. 160. Cf. E.R. I, pp. 190–193, for an example of the manner in which Cottle garbled letters.

      11   Letter to Joseph Cottle, n.d. B.E. I, p. 125.

      12   Letter to Joseph Cottle. B.E. I, p. 124. Although dated January 10, 1797, in B.E., the actual date must have been February 10. Lamb's letter of criticism was not written until February 5. See C.L. I, p. 92 et seq. Other titles of the poem were: *Visions of the Maid of Orleans*; *Visions of the Maid of Arc*; *The Vision of the Patriot Maiden.* But when the verses eventually appeared in print, in *Sibylline Leaves*, 1817, they were called none of these things, but *The Destiny of Nations.*

148 13   February 13, 1797. C.L. I, p. 98 et seq.

      14   ll. 26–30; J.D.C. p. 70. ll. 27–31; P. I, p. 132.

      15   ll. 38–48; J.D.C. pp. 70–71. ll. 39–49; P. I, p. 133.

      16   ll. 49–51; J.D.C. p. 71. ll. 50–52; P. I, p. 133.

      17   ll. 55–58; J.D.C. p. 71. ll. 56–59; P. I, p. 133.

149 18   M. p. 65; R. p. 132; E.R. I, pp. 232–233.

      19   Letter to Coleridge, January 16, 1797. C.L. I, pp. 90–91.

      20   "My Mother has often told me how amiable Mr Lloyd was as a youth; how kind to her little Hartley; how well content with cottage accommodation; how painfully sensitive in all that related to the affections." Sara Coleridge in B.Lit.B.; B.E. I, p. 103.

      21   March 16, 1797. U.L. I, pp. 72–73. See also letter to Joseph Cottle (B.E. I, pp. 121–122) dated incorrectly January 1797. See also C.L. I, pp. 106–107.

150 22   See X. p. 454 for collected quotations.

      23   Poole's mother.

      24   February 6, 1797. L. I, pp. 219–220.

      25   J.G. pp. 94–95; M. pp. 65–66. A tradition of Coleridge's pulpit oratory at these towns still persists. See Note 86, Chapter VIII.

      26   Review of *The Monk* by M. G. Lewis, 1796, in the *Critical Review*, February 1797, Vol. XIX, pp. 194–200. One of four early reviews by Coleridge rediscovered and published in *A Wiltshire Parson and his Friends*, pp. 165–200. C.M.C. p. 370.

151 27   *Critical Review*, August 1794, Vol. II, pp. 361–372. C.M.C. p. 356.

151 28 *Critical Review*, February 1797. C.M.C. p. 373.
29 ll. 38–39. *To the Rev. George Coleridge of Ottery St. Mary, Devon, With some Poems.* J.D.C. p. 82; P. I, p. 174. Cf. letter to Cottle, Spring 1797. U.L. I, p. 72; B.E. I, p. 131. Letter to Thelwall, December 17, 1796, L. I, p. 194.
30 Letter to Joseph Cottle, 1797. B.E. I, p. 127. Cf. letter to Josiah Wade, March 16, 1797. U.L. I, p. 72.
31 Ibid.
152 32 U.L. I, p. 75.
33 Letter from Dorothy to Richard Wordsworth, March 19, 1797. W.L. I, p. 163. See also H. p. 220 et seq.
34 Coleridge's letter to Joseph Cottle, June 1797. L. I, p. 221. Cf. Richard Reynell on his visit to Stowey and Alfoxden in August. He describes Wordsworth as "of living men the greatest—at least, Coleridge, who has seen most of the great men of this country, says he is." *Illustrated London News*, April 22, 1893.
35 Letter to Joseph Cottle, June 1797, L. I, p. 221.
36 May 1797. U.L. I, p. 70; B.E. I, pp. 129–130. The date on this letter should probably be early April. The reference to Wordsworth is to his Bristol visit in March—not, as Cottle states, to the Alfoxden period. A part of this letter, badly garbled, is printed in E.R. I, pp. 190–193.
153 37 n.d. U.L. I, p. 74. See also E.R. I, p. 53 (a part only).
38 Letters of June 5, 1797, to Lloyd and Estlin. T.P. I, pp. 228–231.
39 Letter to Joseph Cottle, 1797. B.E. I, pp. 134–135. See also E.R. I, pp. 230–231.
40 To Josiah Wade, n.d. B.E. I, p. 132. See also letter to Joseph Cottle, n.d. B.E. I, p. 133. Coleridge here also tells of his reluctance to destroy the mice in the cottage: "The mice play the very devil with us. It irks me to set a trap. By all the whiskers of all the pussies that have mewed plaintively, or amorously, since the days of Whittington, it is not fair. 'Tis telling a lie. 'Tis as if you said 'Here is a bit of toasted cheese; come little mice! I invite you!' when, oh foul breach of the laws of hospitality! I mean to assassinate my too credulous guests."
154 41 See B.E. I, p. 65; U.L. I, p. 46; L. I, p. 155.
42 Coleridge's influence was to be demonstrated signally later in the year when the hapless Burnett, with what qualifications is not known, joined the Unitarian Chapel at Yarmouth, undertaking at the same time the tutoring of Southey's young brother, Henry. The records of the chapel show Burnett to have joined in 1797 and "declined the Ministry when he left Yarmouth," when the voluntary assistant minister, Henry Robert Bowles, continued the services. Cf. *Memoir of William Taylor of Norwich*, I. p. 212 et seq.
43 T.P. I, p. 231. But, as Coleridge told Estlin a few days later, it

154   43   is not always the most admired sermons that do the most good. E. p. 39.

44   Letter from Mrs Wordsworth to Sara Coleridge, November 7, 1845. K.W. I, p. 111.

155   45   It is not certain that Dorothy Wordsworth was addressing this letter ('written to a friend who had left Racedown early in 1797,' M.W. I, p. 98) to Mary Hutchinson. The question whether or not Mary had left Racedown, where she had been staying, before Coleridge arrived, has not finally been answered. Dr E. de Selincourt may be taken to represent the view that Mary was not at Racedown when Coleridge arrived. (See D.W.S. p. 73, and note to W.L. I, p. 167.) The opposite point of view has been well stated by Miss Catherine M. Maclean, D.W.M. p. 47; review of W.L. I, in *Modern Language Review*, January 1937, pp. 105–106; and in the following note kindly supplied by Miss Maclean: "The authority for Mary Hutchinson's meeting with Coleridge at Racedown is Mary's letter of November 7, 1845, to Sara Coleridge (Knight, *Life*, I, p. 111). Dr de Selincourt, in his *Life* of Dorothy Wordsworth, page 73, interprets this letter as excluding Mary Wordsworth's presence at the meeting with Coleridge. He suggests that as it stands it is wrongly punctuated, and that it should be punctuated as follows:

" 'Your father,' he says, 'came afterwards to see us at Racedown, where I was living with my sister' etc, so that the "we" which follows would refer only to Wordsworth and Dorothy. This re-arrangement of the punctuation is possible on formal grounds, although the change in construction it implies is exceedingly awkward. But there is one grave objection to it, arising out of the matter of the letter itself, which seems to me to put it out of court. It would be a very extraordinary thing for Wordsworth to inform Sara Coleridge, who would be acquainted with the main outlines of his life, and to whom the formative days at Racedown and Alfoxden would be 'matter of history,' that when he was at Racedown he was living with his sister, whereas it would be perfectly natural for Mrs Wordsworth, who had not been resident there but who had paid a visit, to tell Sara Coleridge, seeking specific information on a point of detail, that *she* had chanced to be there at the time Coleridge came.

"Dr de Selincourt's suggestion that this letter should be re-punctuated and re-interpreted, is based on the assumption that the letter Dorothy wrote to a friend describing Coleridge's visit, was written to Mary Hutchinson. Bishop Wordsworth, in the *Memoirs*, I, 98, says that this letter was written 'to a friend who had left Racedown early in 1797.' Knight gives it as 'to a correspondent unknown.' He more than once refers to this or that member of the Halifax circle, about which he knew little, as 'a

155   45   correspondent unknown.'   I do not think that, in the absence of
manuscript evidence, it can be assumed that this letter was to
Mary Hutchinson.   Dorothy had other correspondents at this
time, one of them being Elizabeth Threlkeld the younger, of
Halifax (Mr William Threlkeld's daughter).   She may have had
a visitor early in the year, of whom we know nothing.

"More than once, we know that in her letters, when they were
intermittent, she neglected to chronicle even visits of importance.
Thus, none of the letters of the autumn of 1803 give any indication that Hazlitt had been at Grasmere.

"Also, the words 'to a friend who had left Racedown early in
the year' do not apply very well to Mary Wordsworth, who told
Crabb Robinson in 1841 that she had been there 'a long winter
and spring.'

"Allowing for the fact that Mary, in a letter, was not endeavouring to be precise, this might include a visit that lasted till
the beginning of June; she was certainly at Racedown for some
time after May 28.

"But it is hardly applicable to the phrase 'early in the year.'

"It seems to me that if we reject the evidence of Mary Wordsworth's letter we reject what is substantial for what is shadowy
and insubstantial."

See also A.P. p. 8.

46   June 1797.   W.L. I, pp. 168–169.

47   June 7–8, 1797.   L. I, p. 221; B.E. I, p. 135.   Cf. K.W. I, p. 123.

48   "To a friend who had left Racedown early in 1797."   M.W. I,
p. 98; W.L. I, p. 169; K.W. I, pp. 111–112.   *The Borderers*
was to be read many times in like circumstances.   For instance,
there is Coleridge's note to Poole of July, from Alfoxden,
a few days after the Wordsworths had settled in: "I pray you,
come over if possible by eleven o'clock, that we may have
Wordsworth's Tragedy read under the Trees."   *Illustrated
London News*, April 22, 1893.

156   49   L. I, p. 221; B.E. I, p. 135.   "My Tragedy employed and
strained all my thoughts and faculties for six or seven months;
Wordsworth consumed far more time, and far more thought,
and far more genius."   R. p. 176.

50   To Jane Marshall, November 30, 1795.   W.L. I, p. 147.

51   Both letters in E. pp. 40–41; the second letter only, in U.L. I,
p. 76.

52   R. p. 142.   The letter has been garbled by Cottle.   A good
deal is omitted.

53   Letter to Joseph Cottle, June 29, 1797.   U.L. I, p. 78.

157   54   Probably to Mary Hutchinson, July 4, 1797.   W.L. I, p. 170.

55   Probably to Mary Hutchinson, August 14, 1797.   W.L. I, p. 170.
The name is commonly spelt Alfoxton and is shown thus on the
Ordnance Survey maps.

56 W.L. I, p. 170.

57 To Robert Southey, July 14–21, 1797. L. I, p. 224.

58 De Quincey was beset by as little scruple as Cottle in bending facts to suit his requirements. Indeed, of the main motives which moved them, many will prefer Cottle's vanity to the younger man's spite. Nevertheless, while De Quincey was by no means above embroidering a tale to satisfy at once a journalistic purpose and a pleasure in arousing or enhancing strife, there can be little doubt that he worked upon a substratum of fact. For that reason, what he wrote about his contemporaries cannot be ignored. Thus he writes of Sarah and Dorothy at Stowey:

". . . it is a bitter trial to a young married woman to sustain any sort of competition with a female of her own age for any part of her husband's regard, or any share of his company. Mrs Coleridge, not having the same relish for long walks or rural scenery, and their residence being, at this time, in a very sequestered village, was condemned to a daily renewal of this trial. Accidents of another kind embittered it still further: often it would happen that the walking party returned drenched with rain; in which case, the young lady, with a laughing gaiety, and evidently unconscious of any liberty that she was taking, or any wound that she was inflicting, would run up to Mrs Coleridge's wardrobe, array herself, without leave asked, in Mrs Coleridge's dresses, and make herself merry with her own unceremoniousness and Mrs Coleridge's gravity. In all this, she took no liberty that she would not most readily have granted in return; she confided too unthinkingly in what she regarded as the natural privileges of friendship; and as little thought that she had been receiving or exacting a favour, as, under an exchange of their relative positions, she would have claimed to confer one. But Mrs Coleridge viewed her freedoms with a far different eye: she felt herself no longer the entire mistress of her own house; she held a divided empire; and it barbed the arrow to her womanly feelings that Coleridge treated any sallies of resentment which might sometimes escape her as narrow-mindedness; whilst, on the other hand, her own female servant, and others in the same rank of life, began to drop expressions which alternately implied pity for her as an injured woman, or contempt for her as a very tame one . . . a situation which exposed Mrs Coleridge to an invidious comparison with a more intellectual person; as, on the other hand, it was most unfortunate for Coleridge himself to be continually compared with one so ideally correct and regular in his habits as Mr Southey."

The Lake Poets: Samuel Taylor Coleridge. Tait's Magazine, September 1834. Revised text in the Edinburgh Collective Edition, 1853–1860. Q. II, pp. 160–161. But see J.D.C. p. lxi, note 2; also Dorothy's reference to Mrs Coleridge, W.L. i. p. 190.

158   59   *The Destiny of Nations*, l. 168, J.D.C. p. 73; l. 175, P. I, p. 137: *Remorse*, Act 1, Sc. 1, l. 58. J.D.C. p. 361; P. II, p. 821.

        60   July 1797. B.E. I, pp. 136–137; R. p 144

        61   It was entitled *Poems, by S. T. Coleridge, Second Edition. To which are now added Poems by Charles Lamb, and Charles Lloyd.* Printed by N. Biggs, for J. Cottle, Bristol, and Messrs Robinsons, London, 1797, Octavo pp. xx; 278. The poems of Coleridge were followed by those of Lloyd; Lamb's 23 pages completing the volume.

        62   "Duplex nobis vinculum, et amicitiae et similium junctarumque Camoenarum; quod utinam neque mors solvat, neque temporis longinquitas!" *Groscoll. Epist. ad Car. Utenhov. et Ptol. Lux. Tast.*

        63   E.R. I, p. 147.

        64   In a copy of the 1797 edition of the *Poems*, Coleridge wrote under the Dedication: "N.B. If this volume should ever be delivered according to its direction, i.e. to Posterity, let it be known that the Reverend George Coleridge was displeased and thought his character endangered by this Dedication!"

        65   *Charles! my slow heart*, etc., and *Oft o'er my brain*, etc. J.D.C. p. 66; P. I, pp. 153–154.

159   66   J.D.C. p. 540. Cf. B.Lit.C. I, p. 3.

        67   J.D.C. p. 540.

        68   L. I, p. 196.

        69   See T.P. I, p. 202; E.R. I, pp. 275–277; W.H. XVII, p. 119.

160   70   ll. 47 and 53 in the version sent to Southey, July 1797. L. I, p. 227. The words 'My Sister and my Friends' were changed in both instances to 'My gentle-hearted Charles!' in the printed version.

        71   l. 6. J.D.C. p. 92; P. I, p. 179.

        72   ll. 28, 68, 75. J.D.C. pp. 93, 95; P. I, pp. 179, 181.

        73   Letters of August 6 and 14, 1800. C.L. I, pp. 198, 203.

        74   ll. 9–11. J.D.C. p. 92; P. I, p. 179.

        75   ll. 22–26. J.D.C. p. 93; P. I, p. 179.

        76   ll. 48–51. J.D.C. p. 93; P. I, p. 180.

        77   ll. 53–55. J.D.C. p. 93; P. I, pp. 180–181.

        78   ll. 58–59. J.D.C. p. 93; P. I, p. 181.

        79   ll. 68–69. J.D.C. p. 95; P. I, p. 181.

        80   ll. 73–74. J.D.C. p. 95; P. I, p. 181.

        81   l. 24. *Fears in Solitude.* J.D.C. p. 128; P. I, p. 257.

161   82   ll. 37–43. J.D.C. p. 93; P. I, p. 180. Cf. Dorothy's "We lay sidelong upon the turf, and gazed at the landscape till it melted into more than natural loveliness." February 26, 1798, D.W.J. p. 11.

162   83   T.P. I, pp. 225–226.

        84   Letter to Robert Southey, July 1797. L. I, p. 227.

PAGE NOTE
162 85 L. I, p. 224.
 86 August 14, 1797. W.L. I, p. 17c.

CHAPTER 6

FOR this and the following chapter, cf. *Wordsworth*, by Walter Raleigh, 1903; *Wordsworth, Lectures and Essays*, by H. W. Garrod, Second edn., 1927; *The Early Wordsworth*, by E. de Selincourt, 1936; *Wordsworth*, by C. H. Herford, 1930; *Wordsworth*, by F. W. H. Myers, 1880; *William Wordsworth: His Doctrine and Art in their Historical Relations*, by Arthur Beatty, 1922; *The French Revolution and English Literature*, by Edward Dowden, 1897; *La Révolution française et les poètes anglais, 1789–1809*, by C. Cestre, 1906.

PAGE NOTE
163 1 Born April 7, 1770.
 2 See W.H. XVII, p. 118.
164 3 W.P. 1805, I, l. 415 ff.; I, l. 611 ff.; II, l. 47 ff.
 4 Ibid. 1805, I, l. 311 ff.; I, l. 474 ff.; II, l. 321 ff.; II, l. 359 ff.
 5 *Lines written a few miles above Tintern Abbey*, July 13, 1798. ll. 76–83.
165 6 W.P. 1805, X, ll. 694–703, 729–736.
 7 From the expected payment by Lord Lonsdale. See letters of Dorothy Wordsworth to Jane Pollard, May 23 and December 7, 1791. W.L. I, pp. 45, 46, 63.
166 8 B.Lit.C. I, p. 56.
167 9 W.P. 1805, IX, ll. 36–37.
 10 See for example W.P. 1805, IX, ll. 192–196.
 11 W.P. 1805, IX, l. 293 ff. Beaupuy was Captain of the Garrison at Blois, where Wordsworth had gone early in 1792. See *Le Général Michel Beaupuy*, by Georges Bussière and Émile Legouis, 1891.
 12 W.P. 1805, VIII, ll. 485–486.
 13 W.P. 1805, IX, ll. 518–532.
168 14 See A.V. p. 13 et seq. Cf. Documents published by Professor Edith J. Morley from Crabb Robinson's Library in *T.L.S.*, August 3, 1922, March 8 and 15, 1923; also commentary on above by Émile Legouis in *La Revue Anglo-Américaine*, October 1923.
 15 See W.P. 1805, IX, ll. 190–192.
 16 W.P. 1805, IX, l. 361.
 17 A.V. pp. 28, 33. See also letter from Dorothy Wordsworth to Jane Pollard, June 16, 1793. W.L. I, p. 88 et seq. See also D.W.S. pp. 40–41.
169 18 See *The Story of the English Jacobins*, by Edward Smith, 1881.
 19 A.V. pp. 29–33, 124–133.
 20 H. pp. 150–151; A.V. pp. 34–36. See also W.P. 1805, IX, l. 178 and note p. 569.
 21 W.P. 1805, X, ll. 369–372, 374–376.
170 22 W.P. 1805, X, ll. 402–490.

[463]

170   23   On January 15, 1793, the Bishop published the sermon, with an appendix, entitled *Strictures on the French Revolution and the British Constitution.* Wordsworth's reply was signed "A Republican." See W.W. I, pp. 3–23.
The same Bishop of Llandaff, Richard Watson (1737–1816), Coleridge was to praise for his answer to Tom Paine. See letter to the Rev. John Edwards, March 20, 1796. U.L. I, p. 49. The book was *An Apology for the Bible; in a series of letters addressed to T. Paine* . . . 1796.

24   See letter from Lamb to Coleridge, May 24–31, 1796. C.L. I, p. 8.

25   B.Lit.C. I, p. 58.

26   *The Philanthropist* by name. See M.W. I, p. 83; K.W. I, p. 92; L.W. p. 250. Also letter to W. Mathews, May 23, 1794. W. I, pp. 115–116.

27   It was while engaged upon this work in 1795 that he used and praised some lines by Southey, "a friend of Coleridge." W.L. I, pp. 144–145. Cf. *Modern Language Notes,* XLV, pp. 209–215.

171   28   W.L. 1805, X, l. 465 ff.

29   Thomas Hardy, shoemaker and founder of the London Corresponding Society, 1792. The Society was formed to attempt the unification of the Liberals. The main plank in its platform was the demand for electoral reform, but its sympathies with the French Revolution were such that it was calling for English intervention on the side of the French and prophesying a republic in England.

172   30   But the French had become "oppressors in their turn" as early as 1794. See W.P. 1805, X, l. 781 ff.

31   I, p. 347, 2nd edn. See L.W. pp. 259–278; H. p. 181 et seq. Cf. *English Thought in the Eighteenth Century,* by Leslie Stephen, 1876; *Shelley, Godwin, and their Circle,* by H. N. Brailsford, 1913; and W.P., note pp. 584–587.

173   32   W.P. 1805, X, ll. 806–830.

33   Letter to Benjamin Flower, December 1796. U.L. I, p. 65.

174   34   W.P. 1805, X, ll. 873–879, 890–893.

35   Ibid. X, ll. 897-901.

36   At Windy Brow, near Keswick, a small farmhouse lent to them by Raisley Calvert in April 1794. See letters from Dorothy to Jane Pollard, April 1794, and to her aunt, Mrs Crackanthorpe, April 21, 1794. W.L. I, pp. 110–114.

175   37   Raisley Calvert was the brother of William Calvert, an old Hawkshead schoolfellow, to whom Wordsworth had acted as travelling companion in the Isle of Wight in 1793. Raisley died at Windy Brow. Wordsworth for some time looked after him. See L.W. pp. 282–284; H. pp. 176–178.

38   *The Borderers,* l. 1036.

[464]

PAGE NOTE

175 39 W.P. 1850, XI, ll. 321–333; L.W. p. 278. Mention may be made here of "A Glance at Wordsworth's Reading" by Lane Cooper, *Modern Language Notes*, XXII, pp. 87–89, 110–117.

176 40 W.P. 1805, XI, ll. 192–193, 195. Followed by the lines comparing this restlessness with Dorothy's satisfaction with common things. W.P. 1805, XI, ll. 207–221.

41 W.P. 1805, XI, ll. 157–158, 162–164.

177 42 A.V. pp. 28–29; D.W.S. pp. 38–39.

43 A.V. pp. 37–39, 47 et seq.

178 44 W.P. 1850, XIV, l. 241.

45 W.P. 1805, XIII, ll. 224–236.

46 ll. 17–18. *The Sparrow's Nest.*

47 ll. 26–28. *The Tables Turned.*

179 48 See L. I, pp. 164, 246.

49 1770–1850. Natural son of the fourth Earl of Sandwich and Martha Ray (murdered in 1779). Christ's College, Cambridge, 1786–95. Met Wordsworth in London, 1793, when widowed. Took pupils with Wrangham 1795. Called to Bar 1798. Edited *Works of Bacon* (1825–37) with Wrangham.

50 See, for instance, Wordsworth's *Anecdote for Fathers, Shewing how the practice of Lying may be taught. Lyrical Ballads*, 1798. See also Dorothy on their method of bringing up the boy. Letter to Jane Marshall, March 19, 1797. W.L. I, pp. 164–165.

51 W.P. 1805, XIII, ll. 236–246.

180 52 See, for instance, her remarks on *An Evening Walk* and *Descriptive Sketches* in the letter of February 16, 1793, to Jane Pollard. W.L. I, pp. 85–86.

CHAPTER 7

182 1 W.P. 1805, X, ll. 905–908. See also, for example, Wordsworth's reference to the influence of Coleridge in his Preface to the 1814 edition of *The Excursion*, where he speaks of ". . . a dear Friend, most distinguished for his knowledge and genius, and to whom the Author's Intellect is deeply indebted."

184 2 W.W. III, p. 441; K.W. I, p. 129.

3 M.W. II, p. 288, Cf. W.W. III, p. 492; R. p. 300.

4 M.W. II, pp. 288–289.

185 5 W.P. 1805, XIII, ll. 247–268. Also Wordsworth's later statement that "He [Coleridge] and my beloved sister are the two beings to whom my intellect is most indebted."

6 *Religious Musings*, l. 49. J.D.C. p. 54; P. I, p. 111.

186 7 Ibid. l. 408. J.D.C. p. 60; P. I, p. 124.

8 The passages admired by Wordsworth were ll. 364–375 and 403–428. See Coleridge's letter to John Thelwall, May 13, 1796. L. I, p. 164.

[465]

PAGE NOTE
188   9   From a fragment found in a MS. notebook containing *Peter Bell*. W.P., pp. lvii, 512.

189 10 ll. 41–45, 126–128, 130–131.

      11 ll. 79–87; J.D.C. p. 71. ll. 80–88; P. I, p. 134.

      12 ll. 17–22; J.D.C. p. 70. ll. 18–23; P. I, p. 132.

190 13 *The Borderers*, ll. 1490–1492, 1493–1496.

191 14 B.Lit.C. I, p. 58.

      15 Letter to Lady Beaumont, April 3, 1815. M.C. II, p. 175. Cf. letter to Cottle, March 8, 1798: "He [Wordsworth] has written more than 1200 lines of a blank verse, superior, I hesitate not to aver, to anything in our language which any way resembles it." L. I, p. 239; B.E. I, p. 152. Cf. T.T. July 21, 1832, p. 170.

192 16 W.P. 1850, XIII, ll. 352–365.

      17 W.W. III, p. 442.

193 18 B. Lit.C. I, p. 59.

194 19 Ibid. I, pp. 60–62.

195 20 Ibid. I, p. 64.

      21 Ibid. This mental restlessness in Coleridge, this unceasing search, it was that Keats deplored, fearing that so the heart of the mystery and its beauty, by analysis and attempted exposure, would be destroyed. See Keats's letter of December 21, 1817, to his brothers.

196 22 October 26, 1803. A.P. pp. 35–36.

197 23 Letter to Sarah, February 19, 1804. L. II, p. 460.

      24 Ibid.

      25 Ibid.

199 26 *Lines written a few miles above Tintern Abbey*, ll. 118–119. See also l. 148.

200 27 October 1807 was the date when De Quincey first saw Dorothy. The description first appeared in *Tait's Magazine*, January 1839, article *The Lake Poets: William Wordsworth*. Revised text as in the Edinburgh Collective Edition, 1853–1860. Q. II, pp. 238–239. Cf. Coleridge's "Dorothy, eager of soul." *Hexameters*, l. 16; J.D.C. p. 138; P. I, p. 304.

201 28 See, for instance, Coleridge's letter to Wordsworth in 1808. K.W. II, p. 104.

202 29 K.W. I, p. 129.

CHAPTER 8

204 1 Written probably to Mary Hutchinson, August 14, 1797. W.L. I, pp. 170–171.

     2 July 19–26, 1797. C.L. I, p. 112.

     3 Letter from Thelwall to his wife from Alfoxden, July 18, 1797. T.P. I, pp. 232–233. Cf. Thelwall's MS. Diary.

204   3 See M. p. 73, where part of the entry for July 21, 1797, is quoted—the discussion of "the moral character of Democrats, of Aristocrats," and of "pursuits proper for literary men—unfit for management of pecuniary affairs—Rousseau, Bacon, Arthur Young!"

       4 Thelwall to his wife, July 18, 1797. T.P. I, p. 233; M. p. 72.

       5 Thelwall to his wife, July 18, 1797. T.P. I, p. 233; K.W. I, p. 118.

       6 M.W. I, p. 105. Cf. T.T. July 26, 1830, p. 103.

205   7 T.T. July 26, 1830, p. 103.

       8 Doubtless fetching Basil, Peggy, and the Wordsworths' goods after the decision to rent Alfoxden had been made.

       9 Letter to Robert Southey, July 1797. L. I, p. 227.

     10 Letter to Joseph Cottle, June 29, 1797. B.E. I, p. 136. Also letter to the same. Ibid. I, p. 139. Cottle's description of his visit, when made eventually, is worth quoting:

". . . It was not convenient at this time to accept Mr C's invitation, but going to Stowey two or three weeks afterward, I learnt how pleasantly the interview had been between Charles Lamb and himself. It is delightful, even at the present moment, to recal the images connected with my then visit to Stowey, (which those can best understand, who, like myself, have escaped from severe duties to a brief season of happy recreation:) Mr Coleridge welcomed me with the warmest cordiality. He talked of his old school-fellow, Lamb, with affection, who had so recently left him; regretted he had not an opportunity of introducing me to one whom he so highly valued. Mr C. took peculiar delight in assuring me (at least, at that time) how happy he was; exhibiting, successively, his house, his garden, his orchard, laden with fruit; and also the contrivances he had made to unite his two neighbours' domains with his own.

"After the grand circuit had been accomplished, by hospitable contrivance, we approached the 'Jasmine harbour,' when, to our gratifying surprise, we found the tripod table laden with delicious bread and cheese, surmounted by a brown mug of the true Taunton ale. We instinctively took our seats; and there must have been some downright witchery in the provision which surpassed all of its kind; nothing like it on the wide terrene, and one glass of the Taunton, settled it to an axiom. While the dappled sun-beams played on our table, through the umbrageous canopy, the very birds seemed to participate in our felicities, and poured forth their selectest anthems. As we sat in our sylvan hall of splendour, a company of the happiest mortals, (T. Poole, C. Lloyd, S. T. Coleridge, and myself) the bright-blue heavens; the sporting insects; the balmy zephyrs; the feathered choristers; the sympathy of friends, all augmented the pleasurable to the highest point this side the celestial! Every interstice of our hearts being filled with happiness, as a consequence, there was no

205 10 room for sorrow, exorcised as it now was, and hovering around at unapproachable distance. With our spirits thus entranced, though we might weep at other moments, yet joyance so filled all within and without, that, if, at this juncture, tidings had been brought us, that an irruption of the ocean had swallowed up all our dear brethren of Pekin; from the pre-occupation of our minds, 'poor things,' would have been our only reply, with anguish put off till the morrow. While thus elevated in the universal current of our feelings, Mrs Coleridge approached, with her fine Hartley; we all smiled, but the father's eye beamed transcendental joy! 'But, all things have an end.' Yet, pleasant it is for memory to treasure up in her choicest depository, a few such scenes, (these 'sunny spots' in existence!) on which the spirit may repose, when the rough, adverse winds shake and disfigure all beside." E.R. I, pp. 274–277.

     11 U.L. I, p. 80.

     12 Ibid. I, pp. 80–81.

206 13 Ibid. I, p. 81.

     14 July 1797. L. I, pp. 222–223.

207 15 Ibid. I, p. 224.

     16 Ibid. I, p. 228.

     17 T.P. I, pp. 240, 248. Also R. pp. 181–182.

208 18 T.P. I, p. 235. The Mr Willmott who had taken Woodlands, a house just off the main road, between Alfoxden and Stowey, seems to have done nothing to deserve the implied censure. But the Wordsworths visited the house frequently (see D.W.J. pp. 8–12) and that fact would be sufficient to give the occupier a bad name in the district. On Poole's recommendation, Willmott later acted as confidential Steward to the Wedgwoods at Tarrant Gunville.

     19 The investigations carried out by A. J. Eagleston on this subject are recorded in *Wordsworth, Coleridge, and the Spy*, C.M.V. p. 73 et seq., which amplifies and confirms an article by the same writer in the *Nineteenth Century*, August 1908.

209 20 B.Lit.C. I, pp. 126–127.

     21 Ibid. I, p. 129.

     22 Ibid.

     23 See letter to John Thelwall, n.d. (probably autumn 1797). L. I, pp. 231–232.

     24 Ibid. See also letter to John Chubb, n.d. U.L. I, pp. 82–83.

210 25 n.d. L. I, pp. 233–234.

211 26 Anna Letitia Barbauld (1743–1825), wife of the Rev. R. Barbauld. A popular writer at this time. She wrote a poem to Coleridge after this visit, urging her impetuous visitor to "fair exertion for bright fame sustained."

     27 Letter to his brother, August 1797. See *Illustrated London News*, April 22, 1893. Reynell stayed at Nether Stowey for

211   27   a few days as a kind of trial before taking up a more permanent residence with the Coleridges. Reynell appeared to find everything and everybody much to his liking. In addition to his remarks on Wordsworth (see note 34, Chapter V) he found Burnett "agreeable and well-informed, and of a very benevolent turn of mind"; Sarah "sensible, affable, and good-natured, thrifty and industrious, and always neat and prettily dressed"; Hartley "noble, healthy-looking fellow, has strong eyebrows and beautiful eyes." He even found good words for the cottage: "It is very small and very simple. Three rooms below and three above—all small. The window to my room has no opening, but a pane of glass is made to slide in and out by a piece of wire." Nevertheless, as far as is known Reynell did not return to Stowey. See reference in L. II, p. 497. See also Coleridge's letter to Estlin from Racedown in June 1797, in which he says: "If this Mr Reynell settles with me, it will at least provide my immediate household expenses." E. p. 40.

    28   Letter to Coleridge, August 24, 1797. C.L. I, p. 114.

    29   Ibid.

    30   About September 20, 1797. C.L. I, p. 117. But Coleridge had sent Lloyd a version of *This Lime-Tree Bower my Prison* as late as July. See J.D.C. p. 591.

212   31   Letter from Wordsworth to Joseph Cottle, September 13, 1797. B.E. I, p. 140; W.L. I, p. 132.

    32   Some difference of opinion exists as to whether Coleridge did or did not take his Tragedy to Bowles at this time; and whether, having done so, he took or sent it to London. The letter of Wordsworth referred to in the previous note would seem conclusive. See also B.E. I, p. 140. Yet see M. p. 78; and *A Wiltshire Parson and his Friends*, p. 32, where the MS. is said to have been sent to Sheridan via Bowles on October 16. The most reasonable solution of the difficulty seems to be this: that Coleridge took his play, unfinished, to Bowles, early in September; and arranged to send it to Bowles when completed so that the latter might forward it to Sheridan, whom he knew. The facts that Coleridge visited Bowles; that he saw Linley at Donhead; and that he stayed in London shortly afterwards seem indisputable. But in no place does he say that he took the play to London with him. An undated letter to Thelwall, probably October 1797, saying, "Oh, my Tragedy! it is finished, transcribed, and to be sent off to-day; but I have no hope of its success, or even of its being acted," confirms the view that the play was sent eventually by post.

    33   Letter from Coleridge to Joseph Cottle, n.d. (probably September 1797). B.E. I, p. 140.

    34   E.R. I, p. 31; R. pp. 21, 133.

    35   *Lines to W. L. while he sang a Song to Purcell's music.* First

212   35   published in Southey's *Annual Anthology*, 1800.   Title of original MS. *To Mr William Linley*. J.D.C. p. 155; P. I, p. 236.

      36   n.d. (probably September 1797). B.E. I, pp. 140–141.

      37   1797 (probably October). L. I, p. 228.

213   38   Ibid.

      39   The lines quoted are:

> "Struck with the deepest calm of joy," I stand
> Silent, with swimming sense; and gazing round
> On the wide landscape, gaze till all doth seem
> Less gross than bodily, a living Thing
> Which acts upon the mind and with such hues
> As clothe th'Almighty Spirit, where He makes
> Spirits perceive His presence!

214   40   L. I, p. 229.

      41   Ibid. See also *Osorio*, Act V, Sc. 1, l. 39 ff. *Remorse*, Act IV, Sc. 3, l. 1 ff. J.D.C. pp. 507, 390-391; P. II, pp. 584, 868.

      42   The home of William Taylor, friend of Southey, who had published (1790) his much admired translation of Bürger's *Leonore*. Taylor was on very good terms with Dr Sayers and the Unitarians of Norwich.

      43   Letter to the Rev. J. P. Estlin, n.d. (possibly July 1797). E. pp. 34-37; U.L. I, p. 79. See also E. p. 50, where Coleridge speaks of the "motives which inclined me to reject Norwich." As pointed out in *Trans. Unit. Hist. Soc.* V, Part 2, October 1932, pp. 175–176, the Rev. William Enfield of the Octagon Chapel at Norwich died on November 3, 1797, and was presumably unable to perform his duties for some time before that date. Therefore it seems not unlikely that Estlin, who was keeping his eyes open on behalf of a Coleridge by this time all but resigned to a career in the Unitarian Ministry, may have suggested that Coleridge offer himself as a candidate. Whether Coleridge actually visited Norwich, made the acquaintance of the Rev. Pendlebury Houghton, the other minister, and perhaps preached there, is unknown. But Coleridge certainly writes as though he had seen Norwich; and it was about this time that Burnett proceeded to Yarmouth on a similar mission. It is not improbable that the two may have travelled together.

      44   Letter to John Thelwall, 1797 (probably October). L. I, p. 231.

      45   T.P. I, pp. 240–243.

      46   n.d. (probably Autumn 1797). L. I, p. 232.

      47   Letter to Cottle (probably November 1797). E.R. I, p. 251; R. p. 143. See E.S. XIX, pp. 86–87, for corrected text of the existing part of the letter, and comments.

      48   Letter from Dorothy, probably to Mary Hutchinson, November 20, 1797. W.L. I, p. 174.

215   49   J.D.C. pp. 110-111; P. I, pp. 209-211.

50   n.d. (probably November 1797). B.E. I, p. 142; E.R. I, p. 288; R. p. 159; corrected version from original, E.S. XIX, p. 86.

     51   Ibid.

     52   *Sonnets Attempted in the Manner of Contemporary Writers.* The first had no title, beginning:

> Pensive at eve on the *hard* world I mus'd.

     53   B.Lit.A. I, pp. 26–28.

     54   *To Simplicity.*

     55   *On a Ruined House in a Romantic Country.*

     56   B.Lit.A. I, pp. 26–28.

216

57   Probably early November. E.S. XIX, p. 86.

     58   Possibly the third and fourth parts of *The Three Graves.* (But see E.S. XIX, p. 86 et seq.) There seems little doubt that the idea for this poem came from Wordsworth in the first instance, who was working on the early part of it at Racedown. See *The Early Wordsworth* by E. de Selincourt, p. 23. See also the note to this passage, which quotes the following interesting extract from Barron Field's unpublished *Memoir of the Life and Poetry of William Wordsworth* (B.M. MS. Add. 4135–7): "Mr Wordsworth one day said to me: 'It is not enough for a poet to possess the power of mind; he must also have knowledge of the heart, and this can only be acquired by time and tranquil silence. No great poem has been written by a young man or by an unhappy one. It was poor dear Coleridge's constant infelicity that prevented him from being the poet that Nature had given him the power to be. He had always too much personal and domestic discontent to paint the sorrows of mankind. He could not

> afford to suffer
> With those whom he saw suffer.

I gave him the subject of his Three Graves; but he made it too shocking and painful, and not sufficiently sweetened by any healing views. Not being able to dwell on or sanctify natural woes, he took to the supernatural, and hence his Antient Mariner and Christabel, in which he shows great poetical power; but these things have not the hold on the heart which Nature gives, and will never be popular poems, like Goldsmith's or Burns's.' " In this patronising speech Wordsworth revealed, what he was to reveal too often in later years, that he rather than his old friend had departed from the spirit of poetry, and that he had forgotten more than he remembered of Coleridge and of their early days together. But of the many questionable statements pressed into this one quotation, the passage about the genesis of *The Three Graves* can at least be accepted without reserve.

     59   E.S. XIX, p. 86. See also E. pp. 47–48, where it is disclosed that this new plan, on which Coleridge said he had been working for the last three months of the year, had as its end the taking of

216 59 pupils in conjunction with Wordsworth's friend and debtor, Basil Montague. "Our scheme," wrote Coleridge, "was singular and extensive: extensive, for we proposed in three years to go systematically yet with constant reference to the nature of *man*, through the mathematical branches, chemistry, anatomy, the laws of life, the laws of intellect, and lastly, through universal history, arranging separately all the facts that elucidate the separate states of society—savage, civilized, and luxurious: singular, for we proposed ourselves not as Teachers, but only as Managing Students." Fortunately for both men, the plan shared the fate common to so many others.

      60 B.Lit.C. I, p. 129.

218 61 B.Lit.C. II, pp. 5–6. Cf. W.H. XVII, p. 120.

219 62 See letter from Dorothy Wordsworth, probably to Mary Hutchinson, November 1797. W.L. I, p. 174. The Valley of Rocks was called the Valley of Stones by Dorothy, Wordsworth, Coleridge, Cottle, and Hazlitt.

      63 Reminiscence of Wordsworth by the Rev. Alexander Dyce, communicated to H. N. Coleridge and printed as a Note in the *Poems of Samuel Taylor Coleridge*, edited by Derwent and Sara Coleridge, 1852, pp. 383–384. The question of the genesis of two of Coleridge's three great poems has been treated exhaustively in X. A later article, *Some Dates in Coleridge's Annus Mirabilis*, by E. K. Chambers (E.S. XIX, p. 85 et seq), discusses the time-relations of these poems, in particular those of *The Ancient Mariner* and *Christabel* Part One. After the subject has been treated at some length, the conclusions reached do not in essentials differ from the views expressed in the following pages.

      64 *The Poems of Samuel Taylor Coleridge*, 1852, pp. 383–384. See also J.D.C. p. 594; T.P. I, p. 249.

      65 Fenwick Note by Wordsworth, 1843. M.W. I, pp. 107–108. But in the original Fenwick Note, to *We Are Seven*, which appeared in the Moxon edition of Wordsworth's Poems, 1857, I, p. 181, the date of the excursion was given as Spring 1798. In the Preface to the 1816 *Poems* the poem is described as written "in the Summer of 1797." In a MS. copy of the poem in the possession of the Marquess of Crewe, Coleridge, in a note to Southey, seems to assign the writing of the poem to the "fall" of the same year. These dates, however, are almost certainly not correct. See Coleridge's note to *The Ancient Mariner* in *Sibylline Leaves*, 1817. "It was on a delightful walk from Nether Stowey to Dulverton, with him [Wordsworth] and his sister, in the Autumn of 1797, that this Poem was planned, and in part composed." Cf. Reminiscence of the Rev. Alex. Dyce. Note to the poem in C.W., reprinted J.D.C. p. 594.

      66 L. I, p. 181.

219 67 Letter from Dorothy Wordsworth, probably to Mary Hutchinson, November 20, 1797. W.L. I, p. 174. See also Coleridge's Note to ll. 226–227 in the *Sibylline Leaves*, 1817. "For the last two lines of this stanza, I am indebted to Mr Wordsworth. It was on a delightful walk from Nether Stowey to Dulverton ..." etc.

 68 November 20, 1797. W.L. I, p. 174.

220 69 M.W. I, pp. 107–108.

 70 n.d. (probably November 1797). Dated tentatively December 2 in B.E. I, p. 142; E.R. I, p. 288; R. p. 159. Corrected by original, E.S. XIX, p. 86.

 71 Ibid.

 72 Received December 2, 1797. U.L. I, p. 84. See also Coleridge's account to Greenough—*London Mercury*, April 1931, p. 561; and to Carlyon—*Early Years and Late Reflections*, I, pp. 179–180.

 73 See letters, from William Wordsworth to Joseph Cottle, December 13, and from Dorothy Wordsworth, December 21, 1797 (correspondent unknown). W.L. I, pp. 174–175. See also *London Mercury*, April 1931, p. 565.

221 74 1766–1846. Bought the *Morning Post* in 1795 and the *Courier* the following year.

 75 Letter from Daniel Stuart to Coleridge, January 20, 1798. Forwarded by Poole with accompanying letter, undated. See T.P. I, p. 261; M. p. 84. See also E. p. 52. Coleridge's first contribution to the *Morning Post* appeared December 7, 1797. Mackintosh apparently recommended Coleridge to Stuart from Cote House in December 1798. See the *Gentleman's Magazine*, May 1838, p. 485.

 76 Coleridge gave Montague a "last chance" of securing immediately eight pupils at £100 a year exclusive of board or lodging—the condition upon which Coleridge would join him. E. p. 49.

 77 Letter to J. P. Estlin. E. pp. 48–49.

 78 December 8, 1797. L. I, pp. 251–252 note.

 79 Letter to Charles Lamb, n.d. (spring 1798). L. I, p. 251.

222 80 Letter to J. P. Estlin. E. pp. 50–51.

 81 Ibid. pp. 51–52.

 82 1771–1805.

 83 1769–1843. Charles Darwin's uncle and a main factor in ensuring his nephew of an opportunity to become a scientist.

 84 E.R. I, p. 305. It is possible that Tom Wedgwood, whose sister Susannah married Erasmus Darwin's son, may have met Coleridge at Derby during the latter's *Watchman* tour. It is, in any event, probable that he had heard of Coleridge's visit.

 85 T.W. p. 51. Possibly in company with Wordsworth's friend Tobin. He also visited Stowey in March 1798. See D.W.J., p. 15. Coleridge's relations with Tom Wedgwood are also set

222   85   out in *A Group of Englishmen, 1795–1815*, by Eliza Meteyard, 1871—but the statements made therein are not always reliable.

86   E. p. 55.

223   87   December 27, 1797.   U.L. I, pp. 84–85.

227   88   January 5, 1798.   U.L. I, pp. 85–90.

89   Saturday (January 6, 1798).   U.L. I, p. 90.

228   90   Saturday morning (January 6, 1798).   U.L. I, p. 91.

229   91   Ibid.   There are several references to Coleridge taking the duty of Mr Howell at Bridgwater and Mr Toulmin at Taunton.   Cf. T.P. I, p. 231; *Christian Reformer*, 1834, pp. 838–840; U.L. pp. 101, 104–105; W.H. XVII, p. 122; R. p. 174.   There are also strong local traditions of this magnetic "hireless priest" and at least one record (*Christian Reformer*, 1853, p. 593) of a member of the congregation who had heard "the torrents of happily expressed language."   All of which goes far to support the statements in J.G., pp. 94–95, and M. pp. 65–66.

230   92   U.L. I, pp. 91–92.

93   This statement remains correct whether the ballad referred to is *The Ancient Mariner*, *Christabel*, or *The Three Graves*—one of which it must certainly have been.   In the writer's opinion, the ballad was *Christabel*.

94   1778–1830.

233   95   Sir James Mackintosh, 1765–1832, the philosopher.   Friend of the Wedgwoods, whose sister-in-law Catherine Allen he married the same year.   Wrote *Vindiciae Galliae*, 1791, in answer to Burke's *Reflections on the French Revolution* of the previous year.   See also W.H. XX, p. 217; and *Early Years and Late Reflections* I, pp. 68–69.   First met Coleridge, December 1798, at Cote House.

235   96   Cf. Carlyle's *Life of Sterling*, Centenary edn., 1897, XI, p. 54.   But see also suggestion in *Coleridge and S.T.C.*, by Stephen Potter, 1935, pp. 86–87.

237   97   *My First Acquaintance with Poets*, by W.H. in *The Liberal*, No. III, April 1823.   Based upon Hazlitt's letter to the editor of the *Examiner* (W.H. VII, pp. 128–129), January 12, 1817, headed *Mr Coleridge's Lay Sermon* and signed *Semper Ego Auditor*. W.H. XVII, pp. 106–115.   See also *Memoirs of William Hazlitt*, by W. Carew Hazlitt, 1867, and *Life of William Hazlitt*, by P. P. Howe, 1928.   The discrepancy between Hazlitt's description of Coleridge as "inclining to the corpulent," and Dorothy's "pale and thin" at Racedown a few months earlier, may reasonably be attributed to the fact that Hazlitt's account of his first meeting with Coleridge was not written in its completed form until 25 years after the event, when Coleridge, alas, fully merited the description.

238   98   T.P. I, pp. 257–259; T.W. pp. 55–56.

239   99   January 11–12, 1798.   T.P. I, pp. 259–261.

240   100   January 17, 1798. U.L. I, pp. 96–97.

241   101   U.L. I, pp. 92–96. In his letter to Mr Isaac Wood of Shrews-
              bury, withdrawing from the candidateship, Coleridge explains
              that: "I should have regarded the salary I received, not as pay-
              ment for my particular services to the congregation from whom
              I receive it, but only as the means of enabling myself to pursue a
              general scheme of Christian warfare, of which those particular
              services would have formed only a part." *Christian Reformer*,
              1834, pp. 838–840.

       102   January 24, 1798. B.E. I, p. 144.

       103   See T.P. I, p. 261.

       104   January 30, 1798. U.L. I, pp. 99–100.

       105   See letter from Lamb, C.L. I, p. 119. The date of this letter
              (January 28 in C.L., following Ainger) has been questioned.
              See J.D.C. p. 600.

       106   January 23, 1798. L. I, pp. 234–235.

       107   Ibid.

242   108   March 3, 1798, from Llyswen. L. I, p. 235, note.

       109   T.P. I, p. 261. Written on a letter of Stuart to Coleridge dated
              January 20, 1798.

       110   He wrote to Mr Wood: "Of course I retire from the candidate-
              ship for the ministerial office at Shrewsbury; and have deemed it
              proper to inform your Society of it, before I place myself within
              the contingency of their election, and antecedently to my being
              accepted or rejected." *Christian Reformer*, 1853, p. 593.

       111   Received January 27, 1798. U.L. I, p. 97.

       112   Ibid.

243   113   January 27, 1798. U.L. I, pp. 97–98, note. In his letter, Cole-
              ridge writes: "I have an humble trust, that many years will not
              pass over my head before I shall have given proof in some way
              or other that active zeal for Unitarian Christianity, not indolence
              or indifference, has been the motive of my declining a local and
              stated settlement as preacher of it. . . . My friends Mr Howell
              and Dr Toulmin are both in the descent of life, and both at a
              small distance from me; it is my purpose to relieve one or the
              other every Sunday." *Christian Reformer*, 1834, pp. 838–840.
              In this connexion a letter of Theophilus Lindsey (Unitarian
              Minister at the Essex Street Chapel with Dr Disney) to a
              Shrewsbury friend, in February 1798, goes far to confirm
              Coleridge's opinion of his success with the Unitarians of the
              town. "You cannot well conceive how much you have raised
              my opinion of Mr Coleridge by your account of him," he
              wrote. "Such shining lights, so virtuous and disinterested, will
              contribute to redeem the age we live in from being so destitute
              of apostolic zeal." *The Early History of Charles James Fox*,
              by G. O. Trevelyan, 1880. But see *Trans. Unit. Hist. Soc.* V. 2,
              p. 184.

PAGE NOTE
243   114   House of John Wedgwood, Tom Wedgwood's eldest brother.
      115   Letter to Thomas Poole, received January 27, 1798. U.L. I,
            p. 97.
      116   See letter to John Thelwall, January 30, 1798. U.L. I, p. 100.

CHAPTER 9

For this and the following chapter cf. *Lyrical Ballads Reprinted from the First Edition of 1798*, edited by Edward Dowden, 1890; *Lyrical Ballads by William Wordsworth and S. T. Coleridge, 1798*. Edited with certain poems of 1798 and an introduction and notes by Thomas Hutchinson, 1898; *The Lyrical Ballads, 1798–1805, Wordsworth and Coleridge*, with an introduction and notes by George Sampson, 1903; *Wordsworth and Coleridge, Lyrical Ballads, 1798*. Edited with Introduction, Notes and Appendix containing Wordsworth's Preface of 1800, by Harold Littledale, 1911; *Coleridge Biographia Literaria*, chapters I–IV, XIV–XXII, *Wordsworth Prefaces and Essays on Poetry, 1800–1815*. Edited by George Sampson with an Introductory Essay by Sir Arthur Quiller-Couch, 1920; *Coleridge as a Poet*, by Edward Dowden, *Fortnightly Review*, September 1889, later in *New Studies in Literature; The Golden Book of Coleridge*, with an Introduction by Stopford A. Brooke, 1906; *Poetical Works of William Wordsworth*, edited by Edward Dowden, 1892–93, and by Thomas Hutchinson, 1904; *Coleridge on Logic and Learning*, by Alice D. Snyder, 1929; *Coleridge on Imagination*, by I. A. Richards, 1934; *Coleridge and S. T. C.* by Stephen Potter; *La Vie d'un poète: Coleridge*, by J. Aynard, 1907.

PAGE NOTE
244   1   W.P. 1805, XIII, ll. 417–418.
      2   Ibid. XIII, ll. 390–409.
      3   Coleridge's letter to Wordsworth, January 23, 1798. L. I, p. 325.
245   4   January 31st.   Set forward to Stowey at half past five. D.W.J.
                          p. 5.
          February 3rd.   Walked with Coleridge over the hills. The sea
                          at first obscured by vapour; that vapour after-
                          wards slid in one mighty mass along the sea-
                          shore; the islands and one point of land clear
                          beyond it. D.W.J. p. 7.
             „   4th.   Walked a great part of the way to Stowey with
                          Coleridge. The morning warm and sunny.
                          The young lasses seen on the hill-tops, in the
                          villages and roads, in their summer holiday
                          clothes—pink petticoats and blue. Mothers with
                          their children in arms, and the little ones that
                          could just walk, tottering by their side. Midges
                          or small flies spinning in the sunshine; the songs
                          of the lark and redbreast; daisies upon the turf;
                          the hazels in blossom; honeysuckles budding.

245   4 February 4th.   I saw one solitary strawberry flower under a hedge. D.W.J. p. 7.

         ,,   5th.   Walked to Stowey with Coleridge, returned by Woodlands; a very warm day. D.W.J. pp. 7–8.

         ,,   6th.   Walked to Stowey over the hills, returned to tea, a cold and clear evening. D.W.J. p. 8.

         ,,   11th.   Walked with Coleridge near to Stowey. D.W.J. p. 8.

         ,,   12th.   Walked alone to Stowey. Returned in the evening with Coleridge. D.W.J. p. 8.

         ,,   13th.   Walked with Coleridge through the wood. A mild and pleasant morning, the near prospect clear. The ridges of the hills fringed with wood, showing the sea through them like the white sky, and still beyond the dim horizon of the distant hills, hanging as it were in one un-determined line between sea and sky. D.W.J. pp. 8–9.

         ,,   19th.   I walked to Stowey before dinner. D.W.J. p. 10.

         ,,   21st.   Coleridge came in the morning. D.W.J. p. 10.

         ,,   22nd. Coleridge came in the morning to dinner. D.W.J. p. 10.

         ,,   23rd.   William walked in the morning with Coleridge. D.W.J. p. 10.

         ,,   26th.   Coleridge came in the morning, and Mr and Mrs Cruikshank; walked with Coleridge nearly to Stowey after dinner. A very clear afternoon. We lay sidelong upon the turf, and gazed on the landscape till it melted into more than natural loveliness. The sea very uniform . . . only one distant bay bright and blue as a sky. D.W.J. p. 11. Cf. *This Lime-Tree Bower my Prison*, ll. 37–41.

         ,,   27th.   I walked to Stowey in the evening. Wm. and Basil went with me through the wood. The prospect bright, yet *mildly* beautiful. The sea big and white, swelled to the very shores, but round and high in the middle. Coleridge returned with me, as far as the wood. D.W.J. p. 11.

   March 2nd.   Went a part of the way home with Coleridge in the morning. D.W.J. p. 12.

         ,,   6th.   A pleasant morning, the sea white and bright, and full to the brim. I walked to see Coleridge in the evening. D.W.J. p. 12.

[477]

245   4 March 7th. William and I drank tea at Coleridge's.   D.W.J. p. 12.

„   8th.   Coleridge came after dinner.   D.W.J. p. 13.

„   9th.   A clear sunny morning, went to meet Mr and Mrs Coleridge.   D.W.J. p. 13.

„   10th.   Coleridge, Wm., and I walked in the evening to the top of the hill.   D.W.J. p. 13.

„   12th.   Tom Poole returned with Coleridge to dinner. D.W.J. p. 13.

„   13th.   Poole dined with us.   William and I strolled into the wood.   Coleridge called us into the house.   D.W.J. p. 13.

„   16th.   William, and Coleridge, and I walked in the Park a short time.   D.W.J. p. 13.

„   18th.   The Coleridges left us.   A cold, windy morning.   Walked with them half way.   D.W.J. pp. 13–14.

„   20th.   Coleridge dined with us.   We went more than half way home with him in the evening.   D.W.J. p. 14.

„   21st.   We drank tea at Coleridge's.   D.W.J. p. 14.

„   23rd.   Coleridge dined with us.   D.W.J. p. 14.

„   24th.   Coleridge, the Chesters, and Ellen Cruikshank called.   D.W.J. p. 14.

„   25th.   Walked to Coleridge's after tea.   Arrived at home at one o'clock.   D.W.J. p. 15.

„   26th.   Went to meet Wedgwood at Coleridge's after dinner.   D.W.J. p. 15.

„   29th.   Coleridge dined with us.   D.W.J. p. 15.

April 2nd.   A very high wind.   Coleridge came to avoid the smoke; stayed all night.   We walked in the wood, and sat under the trees.   The half of the wood perfectly still, while the wind was making a loud noise behind us.   The still trees only gently bowed their heads, as if listening to the wind.   D.W.J. p. 15.

„   3rd.   Walked to Crookham with Coleridge and Wm., to make the appeal.   Left Wm. there, and parted with Coleridge at the top of the hill. D.W.J. p. 15.   [Crookham is Crowcombe.]

„   5th.   Coleridge came to dinner.   D.W.J. p. 15.

„   6th.   Went a part of the way home with Coleridge. D.W.J. p. 16.

„   9th.   Walked to Stowey, a fine air in going, but very hot in returning.   The sloe in blossom, the hawthorns green, the larches in the park changed from black to green in two or three days.   Met Coleridge in returning.   D.W.J. p. 16.

245   4   April 13th.   I staid with Mr Coleridge. Wm. went to Poole's. Supped with Mr Coleridge. D.W.J. p. 16. [This should be Mrs Coleridge as Coleridge was at Ottery.]

     „   18th.   Walked in the wood, a fine sunny morning, met Coleridge returned from his brother's. He dined with us. We drank tea, and then walked with him nearly to Stowey. D.W.J. p. 17.

     „   24th.   Sat under the trees, in the evening walked on the top of the hill, found Coleridge on our return and walked with him towards Stowey. D.W.J. p. 17.

     „   25th.   Coleridge drank tea, walked with him to Stowey. D.W.J. p. 17.

     „   26th.   William went to have his picture taken. I walked with him. Dined at home. Coleridge and he drank tea. D.W.J. p. 17.

     „   27th.   Coleridge breakfasted and drank tea, strolled in the wood in the morning, went with him in the evening through the wood, afterwards walked on the hills: the moon, a many-coloured sea and sky. D.W.J. p. 18.

     May   6th.   Expected the painter, and Coleridge. A rainy morning—very pleasant in the evening. Met Coleridge as we were walking out. Went with him to Stowey; heard the nightingale; saw a glow-worm. D.W.J. p. 18.

     „   7th.   In the evening, to Stowey with Coleridge who called. D.W.J. p. 18.

     „   8th.   Coleridge dined, went in the afternoon to tea at Stowey. A pleasant walk home. D.W.J. p. 18.

     „   9th.   Wrote to Coleridge. D.W.J. p. 18.

     „   16th.   Coleridge, William, and myself, set forward to the Chedder rocks; slept at Bridgewater. D.W.J. p. 18.

     „   22nd.   Walked to Chedder. Slept at Cross. D.W.J. p. 18.

5   J.D.C. pp. 607–608, note 117.

6   But Wordsworth did not lose faith entirely in the French at this time, for the good reason that the invasion of Switzerland by no means expressed the wishes of the French nation as a whole. Indeed, even the French army was not unanimous in this action. See W.W. I, p. 164; see also K.W. I, p. 350; D.W.J. August 30, 1802, pp. 147–148; W.P. 1805, X, ll. 928–941; and L.W. p. 379. The coronation of Napoleon finally caused Wordsworth to lose sympathy for the French revolutionary

245   6   movement. There is his line "Creed which ten shameful years
            have not annulled"; W.P. 1805, X, l. 179. And there is his less
            specific statement in 1821 that "I abandoned France and her
            rulers where they abandoned liberty."
246   7   B.Lit.C. I, p. 132. See also U.L. I, p. 66.
       8   ll. 64–88. J.D.C. pp. 125–126; P. I, pp. 246–247.
247   9   Coleridge's expression of this gift is to be found frequently in his
            less successful poems. See, for instance, these stanzas in *The
            Three Graves:*

> 'The Sun peeps through the close thick leaves,
> See, dearest Ellen! see!
> 'Tis in the leaves, a little sun,
> No bigger than your ee;
>
> 'A tiny sun, and it has got
> A perfect glory too;
> Ten thousand threads and hairs of light
> Make up a glory gay and bright
> Round that small orb, so blue.'
>
> And then they argued of those rays,
> What colour they might be;
> Says this, 'They're mostly green'; says that,
> 'They're amber-like to me.'

            ll. 505–517. J.D.C. p. 92; P. I, p. 284. See also *Coleridge's
            Use of Light and Colour* in *A Miscellany*, by A. C. Bradley, 1931,
            p. 177 et seq.
      10   ll. 5–21. J.D.C. p. 124; P. I, p. 244.
248   11   ll. 4–23. J.D.C. p. 126; P. I, pp. 240–241.
      12   ll. 51–62. J.D.C. p. 127; P. I, p. 242.
      13   ll. 65–74. J.D.C. p. 127; P. I, p. 242. The poem ended in the
            Quarto at l. 80.
249   14   This threat of invasion lasted from October 1797, when the
            Treaty of Campo-Formio was signed, to May 19 in the year
            following, when the French army said to be massed ready for
            embarkation, was sent instead to Egypt. The scare may well
            have been begun by the 'invasion' under General Tate of
            February 22, 1797, at Careg Gwasted Point, Pembroke, tragi-
            comic though that episode now seems. See N. & Q. April 3, 1937.
      15   In a MS. copy of the poem the heading is *Written in April 1798
            during the Alarm of the Invasion—The Scene the Hill, near
            Stowey.* A note at the foot of the poem says: "N.B.—The
            above is perhaps not Poetry—but rather a sort of middle thing
            between Poetry and Oratory-sermoni propriora.—Some parts
            are, I am conscious, too tame even for animated prose." See
            J.D.C. p. 610.

249 16 ll. 1–11. J.D.C. p. 127; P. I, pp. 256–257.
17 ll. 17–28. J.D.C. pp. 127–128; P. I, p. 257.
250 18 ll. 104–124. J.D.C. p. 129 P. I, pp. 259–260. Cf. the

> specious names,
> Learned in soft childhood's unsuspecting hour,
> Serve as the sophisms with which mankind dims
> Bright Reason's ray, and sanctifies the sword
> Upraised to shed a brother's innocent blood.

of Shelley's *Queen Mab*.
19 ll. 182–197. J.D.C. p. 130; P. I, pp. 262–263.
251 20 ll. 203–220. J.D.C. pp. 130–131; P. I, p. 263. The words
suggest that Coleridge had been on the earthworks encircling the
top of Dowsborough Beacon—as indeed he might well have been,
to climb on the one side from the dell, and down on the other to
Stowey, which would then come into view.
21 ll. 12–23. J.D.C. pp. 131–132; P. I, pp. 264–265.
252 22 W.W. II, p. 211.
23 G.M.B. unaltered.
24 ll. 43–49. J.D.C. p. 132; P. I, p. 265.
25 ll. 69–86. J.D.C. pp. 132–133; P. I, p. 266. The 'gentle maid'
has commonly been taken to refer to Dorothy and the 'castle' to
the ruin and green fortification above Stowey, but E. H. C. in P.
names the 'castle' as Enmore, seat of the Earl of Egmont, and the
'maid' as Ellen Cruikshank, daughter of the Earl's Agent. The
possibility that Coleridge refers to Dorothy is further discounted
by the fact that he had earlier (l. 40) spoken of
> My Friend, and thou, our Sister!
this reference certainly being to Dorothy.
26 G.M.B.:
> "Hartley fell down and hurt himself. I caught him up angry
> and screaming—and ran out of doors with him. The moon
> caught his eye—he ceased crying immediately—and his eyes
> and the tears in them, how they glittered in the moonlight!"

Cf. and tears she sheds—
> Large tears that leave the lashes bright!
> And oft the while she seems to smile
> As infants at a sudden light!

Christabel, ll. 315–318. J.D.C. p. 120; P. I, p. 226.
253 27 ll. 91–105. J.D.C. p. 133; P. I, pp. 266–267.
28 At first sight it may appear invidious to mention a single work
dealing with this subject. Yet a list of works upon the three
great poems would be out of place here. Moreover, it may be
said with confidence that X. is unique in its method of treatment
and that a study of it is essential to a proper understanding of
The Ancient Mariner and *Kubla Khan*—claims that would be

253 28 difficult indeed to substantiate if made on behalf of any other work on the same subject.

29 A. I, p. 95.

30 l. 86, *Dejection: An Ode.* J.D.C. p. 161; P. I, p. 366; l. 242, *Coleridge's 'Dejection: An Ode,'* by E. de Selincourt. E.S. XXII, p. 23.

31 B.Lit.C. II, p. 6.

254 32 Fenwick Note. M.W. I, pp. 107–108.

33 B.Lit.C. I, p. 129.

255 34 November 19, 1796. L. I, p. 181.

35 Letter to Thomas Poole, October 3, 1803. U.L. I, p. 286.

36 See Note 30.

256 37 Preface to second edition (1797) of *Poems.* J.D.C. p. 540.

38 Letter to Thelwall, December 17, 1796. L. I, p. 196.

39 It might seem highly prejudicial to the magic of this poem that its tender flesh should be rent so as to expose its philosophical bones. Yet that *The Ancient Mariner* expresses a philosophy— and that of moment to a full understanding of Coleridge—few would deny. In any event, the attempt has been made more than once. See, for instance: C.P. p. 43; article, *Coleridge*, by Leslie Stephen, *D.N.B.*, and *Hours in a Library*, 1879, Vol. III; and *From Necessity to Transcendentalism in Coleridge*, by S. F. Gingerich.

40 Its chief fault, Coleridge told Mrs Barbauld, was "the obtrusion of the moral sentiment so openly on the reader as a principle or cause of action in a work of such pure imagination. It ought to have had no more moral than the 'Arabian Nights' tale of the merchant's sitting down to eat dates by the side of a well, and throwing the shells aside, and lo! a genie starts up, and says he *must* kill the aforesaid merchant, *because* one of the date shells had, it seems, put out the eye of the genie's son." T.T. May 31, 1830, p. 87.

41 On February 18, 1798. But see X. and E.S. XIX, p. 85 et seq.

257 42 B.Lit.A. I, p. 296. This postscript was withdrawn in B.Lit.B. See J.D.C. p. 595.

43 These comparisons appear, inevitably, in practically every book written upon Coleridge or the Wordsworths. A list, for instance, is given in X. pp. 511–512, 516, where two previous compilers are noted.

44 ll. 48–52. J.D.C. p. 116; P. I, p. 217.

45 D.W.J. pp. 12–13. The suggestion has been made, of course, that the priority of thought in this and other instances should be reversed.

46 l. 22. J.D.C. p. 116; P. I, p. 216.

47 D.W.J. p. 14.

48 Ibid. p. 5.

258 49 ll. 7 and 12. J.D.C. p. 116; P. I, p. 216.

258   50 D.W.J. p. 4.

        51 Ibid. p. 5.

        52 Ibid. pp. 5–6.

        53 G.M.B.

        54 ll. 16–19. J.D.C. p. 116; P. I, p. 216.

259   55 *Christabel, by Samuel Taylor Coleridge, illustrated by a Facsimile of the Manuscript*, edited by Ernest Hartley Coleridge. Published under the direction of the Royal Society of Literature, 1907, pp. 61–62. See A. I, p. 206. See also L.L. II, pp. 532–533.

        56 Ibid. See also P. I, p. 216.

        57 Ibid.

        58 Cf. X. and E.S. XIX, p. 85 et seq. But see Note 115.

260   59 Note to the published version, 1816. J.D.C. pp. 592–593. P. I, pp. 295–296. The precise words that Coleridge must have been reading just before he fell into his opiate-induced sleep were:

> "In Xamdu did Cublai Can build a stately Palace, encompassing sixteene miles of plaine ground with a wall, wherein are fertile Meddowes, pleasant springs, delightfull Streames, and all sorts of beasts of chase and game, and in the middest thereof a sumptuous house of pleasure which may be removed from place to place."—*Purchas his Pilgrimage*, 1617, p. 472.

        60 From a MS. Note Book dated 1810 in the possession of the Rev. G. H. B. Coleridge. This is the relevant passage:

> "If ever there was a time & circumstance in my life in which I behaved perfectly well, it was in that of C. Lloyd's mad & immoral & frantic ingratitude to me. He even wrote a letter to D.W., in which he not only called me a villain, but appealed to a conversation which had passed between him & *her*, as the grounds of it—& as proving that this was her opinion no less than his—She brought over the letter to me from Alfoxden with tears—I laughed at it—After this there succeeded on his side a series of wicked calumnies and irritations—infamous lies to Southey and to poor dear Lamb—in short, conduct which was not that of a fiend, only because it was that of a madman—on my side, patience, gentleness & good for evil— yet this supernatural effort injured me—what I did not suffer to act on my mind, preyed on my body—it prevented my finishing the Christabel—& at the retirement between Linton & Porlock was the first occasion of my having recourse to Opium; & all this was as well known to W. & D.W. as to myself—"

        61 Quoted from MS. in M. pp. 88–89, note.

        62 Ibid.

        63 M.W. II, p. 306.

261   64 It has been suggested, by the late Matthew Richardson, that the

261   64   effect of Coleridge's visit to the Cheddar Gorge with the Words-worths in the middle of May, 1798, is mirrored in the poem. But such an hypothesis is dependent upon the date the poem was written. See Note 115. Also *T.L.S.* August 21, 28, 1937.

65   April 12, 1798. W.L. I, p. 190; E.R. I, p. 310.

66   May (1798). L. I, p. 246.

67   W.H. XVII, p. 111.

68   T.T. July 21, 1832, pp. 170–171. See also A.P. p. 30.

69   James Tobin, brother of John Tobin, the dramatist. Later became assistant to Humphry Davy at the Pneumatic Institute. R. p. 269.

262   70   W.L. I, p. 188.

71   March 8, 1798. L. I, p. 239; B.E. I, p. 152. Coleridge had a big share in the inception of this poem; and perhaps a still greater share in the creation and sustainment of an enthusiasm for it in its author-to-be. See T.T. July 21, 1832, pp. 171–172.

72   Letter from Lamb to Coleridge, January 10, 1820. C.L. II, pp. 267–268. See also A. II, p. 30.

73   January 28 (but see J.D.C. p. 600), 1798. C.L. I, p. 118.

74   See T.P. I, p. 240 et seq. for Poole's letter of protest which he sent to Mrs St. Albyn, apparently without avail. Yet see Notes 52 and 58, Chapter XII, and Note 145, Chapter XIII. Also W.L. I. p. 201.

75   To Mary Hutchinson. W.L. I, p. 187.

76   To Mary Hutchinson, March 5, 1798. W.L. I, p. 176. Cf. Wordsworth's letter to James Tobin the following day. W.L. I, p. 188.

263   77   Of Woodside, near Carlisle. The translator. Later subscribed to *The Friend* and visited Coleridge at Greta Hall. See L. I, p. 219; L.P. p. 453.

78   W.L. I, pp. 189–190.

79   U.L. I, pp. 100–101; B.E. I, p. 150. Cf. E. p. 59.

80   1798 (March or April). B.E. I, p. 154.

264   81   Ibid. pp. 154–155.

82   R. p. 167.

83   May 14, 1798. U.L. I, p. 105.

265   84   To Joseph Cottle, n.d. (probably April 1798). B.E. I, p. 158.

85   April 12, 1798; May 9, 1798. W.L. I, pp. 190–192.

86   "A visit to Mr Coleridge, at Stowey, in the year 1797 [Note 10, Chapter VIII] had been the means of my introduction to Mr Wordsworth. [This is unlikely. See H. pp. 203–204.] Soon after… Mr W. happened to be in Bristol, and asked me to spend a day or two with him at Allfoxden. I consented, and drove him down in a gig. We called for Mr Coleridge, Miss Wordsworth, and the servant, at Stowey, and they walked, while we rode on to Mr W's. house at Allfoxden, distant two or three miles, where we purposed to dine. A London alderman would smile at our

preparation, or bill of fare.   It consisted of philosophers' viands;
namely, a bottle of brandy, a noble loaf, and a stout piece of
cheese; and as there were plenty of lettuces in the garden, with
all these comforts we calculated on doing very well.

"Our fond hopes, however, were somewhat damped, by finding, that our 'stout piece of cheese' had vanished!   A sturdy *rat*
of a beggar, whom we had relieved on the road, with his
olfactories all alive, no doubt, *smelt* our cheese, and while we
were gazing at the magnificent clouds, contrived to abstract our
treasure!   Cruel tramp!   An ill return for our pence!   We
both wished the rind might not choke him!   The mournful fact
was ascertained a little before we drove into the courtyard of the
house.   Mr Coleridge bore the loss with great fortitude, observing, that we should never starve with a loaf of bread and a bottle
of brandy.   He now, with the dexterity of an adept, admired by
his friends around, unbuckled the horse, and, putting down the
shafts with a jerk, as a triumphant conclusion of his work, lo!
the bottle of brandy that had been placed most carefully behind
us on the seat, from the force of gravity, suddenly rolled down,
and before we could arrest this spirituous avalanche, pitching
right on the stones, was dashed to pieces.   We all beheld the
spectacle, silent and petrified!   We might have collected the
broken fragments of glass, but the brandy! that was gone! clean
gone!

"One little untoward thing often follows another, and while
the rest stood musing, chained to the place, regaling themselves
with the Cogniac effluvium, and all miserably chagrined, I led
the horse to the stable, when a fresh perplexity arose.   I removed
the harness without difficulty, but after many strenuous attempts,
I could not get off the collar.   In despair, I called for assistance,
when aid soon drew near.   Mr Wordsworth first brought his
ingenuity into exercise, but after several unsuccessful efforts, he
relinquished the achievement, as a thing altogether impracticable.
Mr Coleridge now tried his hand, but showed no more grooming
skill than his predecessors; for after twisting the poor horse's
neck almost to strangulation, and to the great danger of his eyes,
he gave up the useless task, pronouncing that the horse's head
must have grown, (gout or dropsy!) since the collar was put on!
for, he said, It was a downright impossibility for such a large
Os Frontis to pass through so narrow a collar!   Just at this
instant the servant girl came near, and understanding the cause
of our consternation, 'La, Master,' said she, 'you do not go about
the work in the right way.   You should do like as this,' when
turning the collar completely upside down, she slipped it off
in a moment, to our great humiliation and wonderment; each
satisfied, afresh, that there were heights of knowledge in the
world, to which we had not yet attained.

[485]

265   86   "We were now summoned to dinner, and a dinner it was, such as every *blind* and starving man in the three kingdoms would have rejoiced to *behold*. At the top of the table stood a superb brown loaf. The centre dish presented a pile of the true cos lettuces, and at the bottom appeared an empty plate, where the 'stout piece of cheese' *ought* to have stood! (cruel mendicant!) and though the brandy was 'clean gone,' yet its place was well, if not *better* supplied by an abundance of fine sparkling Castilian champagne! A happy thought at this time started into one of our minds, that some condiment would render the lettuces a little more palatable, when an individual in the company, recollected a question, once propounded by the most patient of men, 'How can that which is unsavoury be eaten without *salt?*' and asked for a little of that valuable culinary article. 'Indeed, sir,' Betty replied, 'I quite forgot to buy salt.' . . ." R. pp. 182–184.

       87   E.R. I, p. 315.

       88   U.L. I, p. 104. Cf. *Modern Language Notes*, XLII, pp. 504–506.

269   89   Mr G. H. B. Coleridge recounts an incident which would seem to explain the source of the imagery. When E. H. Coleridge, in company with J. Dykes Campbell, paid his first visit to Kilve, where Wordsworth and Coleridge used often to sit on the bank above the sea (see B.Lit.C. I, p. 126), he looked at the ribs of shale which slant across the beach and exclaimed, "*Now* I understand why Wordsworth called them the 'ribbed sea-sands.'" See his article *The Genesis of the Ancient Mariner* (*Poetry Review*, January 1913).

271   90   *My First Acquaintance with Poets*, 1823. W.H. XVII, pp. 116–122.

       91   J.D.C. p. 112; P. I, pp. 286–287.

272   92   n.d. (probably May 1798). B.E. I, p. 160.

       93   Ibid.

       94   Ibid. p. 161.

273   95   L. I, pp. 239–240.

275   96   Ibid. pp. 240–244. The Cowper quotation is from *The Task*, Book V, "A Winter's Morning Walk."

276   97   Eventually printed in an altered form in *The Excursion*, IV, ll. 1198–1224. C.P.W. pp. 467–468.

       98   L. I, pp. 244–245.

       99   "met Coleridge returned from his brother's," April 18, 1798. D.W.J. p. 17.

     100   U.L. I, pp. 104–105.

277 101   1685–1753.

    102   Letter to Thomas Poole, May 14, 1798. L. I, p. 249.

    103   Letter to George Coleridge, May 14, 1798. U.L. I, pp. 104–105. See also E. p. 56. Coleridge had written to Estlin of Dr Toulmin nearly a year earlier: "The more I see of that man, the more I love him." E. pp. 39–40.

277 104 Written at Alfoxden in April 1798 (possibly the 14th), where Coleridge recuperated after his dental trouble. B.E. I, p. 155.

278 105 March 8, 1798. L. I, pp. 238–239; B.E. I, p. 152. *Blank Verse* was published in 1798.

    106 L. I, p. 239.

    107 April 1798.

    108 Such, it is to be supposed, as the details of his enlistment and trials in a regiment of light horse. The descriptions of the hero's slavery to laudanum: "if at any time thought-troubled, I have swallowed some spirits, or had recourse to my laudanum" (I, p. 245); "I have some laudanum in my pocket. I will quell these mortal upbraidings! I cannot endure them!" (I, p. 210); and "My brain phrensied with its own workings—I will again have recourse to my laudanum" (I, p. 218); together with the relation of his excesses in a 'pothouse in the Borough' prior to enlistment, painful though these obvious transcripts from life were, possibly hurt Coleridge less than the spirit in which they had been written. See his epigram, J.D.C. p. 448; P. II, p. 964.

    109 A. II, p. 30.

279 110 ll. 51–52, *The Pains of Sleep.* J.D.C. p. 171; P. I, p. 391; also in L. I, p. 437.

281 111 n.d. (probably April or May 1798). L. I, pp. 249–253.

    112 L. I, p. 246.

    113 Sunday evening (May 20, 1798). L. I, p. 249.

282 114 n.d. (probably May 20–22, 1798). L. I, p. 246. "Wordsworth is a great man, more inclined to Christianity than Theism, simply considered," Coleridge had told Estlin in June of the previous year. E. p. 41.

    115 Near Culbone Church. When did this 'retirement' occur? There are four possible periods: (1) Just before March 21, 1798, when Coleridge wrote Wade, "I have even now returned from a little excursion that I have taken for the confirmation of my health" (B.E. I, p. 153). (2) From May 9, 1798, when Dorothy "wrote to Coleridge" (D.W.J. p. 18), until not later than May 13 (Berkeley was born the following day). (3) After Cottle's visit to Alfoxden (after May 9, 1798), when Coleridge told him (n.d. but probably late May), "I walked to Linton the day after you left us, and returned on Saturday" (B.E. I, p. 161). (4) After Hazlitt's visit to Alfoxden and Stowey (probably late May) and before Coleridge's visit to the Wedgwoods at Stoke D'Abernon (early June). Of these, only the first date seems unlikely. Lloyd's novel had not then been published, and Coleridge gives a specific reason (his tooth) for his absence. Cf. E.S. XIX, p. 85 et seq., and M. p. 88 and note.

    116 L. I, p. 246.

    117 Ibid. The other man was, of course, Southey. Coleridge's

282 117 accusation, though dramatically worded seems not to have been without truth. Not only was Lloyd in general too weak-minded, too unstable, and too affectionate to have persisted without encouragement in an attitude of hostility towards anyone (a fact of which Coleridge was aware, hence his effort to 'capture' Lloyd when apart from Southey) but it is known, from a letter written to Grosvenor Bedford (R.S. I, p. 286) that Southey had projected a novel to be entitled "Edmund Oliver," as early as July 31, 1796. See also Southey's *Commonplace Book*, Series IV, 1850, pp. 9–10, in which there is a sketch for a novel much the same as Lloyd's, with a hero named Oliver Elton.

    118 June 7, 1798. E.R. I, p. 304.

    119 Letter of July 28, 1798. C.L. I, p. 126.

283 120 n.d. (probably May 1798). C.L. I, pp. 123–124.

    121 E.R. I, p. 301.

284 122 M. pp. 91–92.

    123 T.P. I, pp. 271–272.

    124 Letter from Dorothy to Richard Wordsworth, May 31, 1798. W.L. I, p. 192.

    125 July 3, 1798. W.L. I, pp. 195–196.

    126 Ibid. I, p. 196. Cf. p. 481.

285 127 U.L. I, p. 106. The ferry is at Combwich (pronounced Cummage).

    128 "Our going into Wales was quite an unpremeditated scheme," wrote Wordsworth to Henry Gardiner from Hamburg on October 3, 1798. "Mr Coleridge proposed it to us one evening and we departed the next morning at six o'clock. We had a very pleasant tour along the banks of the Usk and the Wye, into Brecknockshire." W.L. I, p. 201.

286 129 FEARS IN SOLITUDE, Written in 1798, during the alarm of an invasion. To which are added, FRANCE, an Ode; and FROST AT MIDNIGHT. By S. T. Coleridge. London: Printed for J. Johnson, in St. Paul's Church-yard, 1798. 4to, pp. 23.

    130 Correspondent unknown. W.L. I, p. 199.

    131 T.P. I, p. 273.

CHAPTER 10

287 1 On or about September 1, 1798. LYRICAL BALLADS, with a few other Poems. (1) Bristol: Printed by Biggs and Cottle, for T. N. Longman, Paternoster-Row, London, 1798. (2) London: Printed for J. & A. Arch, Grace-church Street, 1798. Small 8vo. Title, pp. viii + 210 + Errata, 1 p. Two unnumbered pages between pp. 69 and 70.

    2 See, for instance, *Coleridge–Echoes in Shelley's Poems* in *A Miscellany*, by A. C. Bradley, 1931, p. 171 et seq.

289   3   This first Preface was short and dealt with its subject in general terms (1) because the Poems were published anonymously and (2) because the reactions of the public to the poems were sought before the poets finally committed themselves (see Preface to second edition). But that what this Preface only implied vaguely was already clear in the poets' minds is undisputed. See following Note. The 'friend' was Hazlitt.

4   Letter to Robert Southey, July 29, 1802. L. I, p. 386. Indeed, it was at first intended that Coleridge should write the Preface. See letter to W. Southeby, July 13, 1802. L. I, pp. 373–375. This famous Preface to the second edition will be dealt with fully in its proper place. Nevertheless relevant extracts are given here (1) because it is not desirable to discuss the *Lyrical Ballads* without reference to it; and (2) because, although the Preface was not published until two years later, its inception and much of its content was thrashed out between Wordsworth and Coleridge at Alfoxden. Coleridge's words remain true of the Preface to the first edition. Indeed, they do not need the qualification that must be made in reference to the second edition. Already, in this letter to Southey, Coleridge displays uneasiness. He makes reservations. He goes on to say: "yet I am far from going all lengths with Wordsworth. He has written lately a number of Poems . . . some of them of considerable length . . . the greater number of these, to my feelings, very excellent compositions, but here and there a daring humbleness of language and versification, and a strict adherence to matter of fact, even to prolixity, that startled me. . . . I rather suspect that somewhere or other there is a radical difference in our theoretical opinions respecting poetry: this I shall endeavour to go to the bottom of, and, acting the arbitrator between the old school and the new school, hope to lay down some plain and perspicuous, though not superficial canons of criticism respecting poetry." L. I, pp. 386–387. See also letter to Southeby, L. I, pp. 373–375.

These are the most important parts of the Preface to the second edition of the *Lyrical Ballads*:

"The First Volume of these Poems has already been submitted to general perusal. It was published, as an experiment which, I hoped, might be of some use to ascertain, how far, by fitting to metrical arrangement a selection of the real language of men in a state of vivid sensation, that sort of pleasure and that quantity of pleasure may be imparted, which a Poet may rationally endeavour to impart. . . .

"The principal object, then, which I proposed to myself in these Poems was to make the incidents of common life interesting by tracing in them, truly though not ostentatiously, the primary laws of our nature: chiefly, as far as regards the manner in which we associate ideas in a state of excitement.

[489   ]

Low and rustic life was generally chosen, because, in that situation, the essential passions of the heart find a better soil in which they can attain their maturity, are less under restraint, and speak a plainer and more emphatic language; because in that situation our elementary feelings co-exist in a state of greater simplicity and consequently may be more accurately contemplated, and more forcibly communicated; because the manners of rural life germinate from those elementary feelings; and from the necessary character of rural occupations are more easily comprehended; and are more durable; and lastly, because in that situation the passions of men are incorporated with the beautiful and permanent forms of nature. The language too of these men is adopted (purified indeed from what appear to be its real defects, from all lasting and rational causes of dislike or disgust), because such men hourly communicate with the best objects from which the best part of language is originally derived; and because, from their rank in society and the sameness and narrow circle of their intercourse, being less under the action of social vanity they convey their feelings and notions in simple and unelaborated expressions. Accordingly such a language arising out of repeated experience and regular feelings is a more permanent and a far more philosophical language than that which is frequently substituted for it by Poets, who think that they are conferring honour upon themselves and their art in proportion as they separate themselves from the sympathies of men, and indulge in arbitrary and capricious habits of expression in order to furnish food for fickle tastes and fickle appetites of their own creation. . . .

"I have said that each of these poems has a purpose . . . to follow the fluxes and refluxes of the mind when agitated by the great and simple affections of our nature . . . but it is proper that I should mention one other circumstance which distinguishes these Poems from the popular Poetry of the day; it is this, that the feeling therein developed gives importance to the action and situation and not the action and situation to the feeling. . . .

". . . Except in a very few instances the Reader will find no personifications of abstract ideas in these volumes, not that I mean to censure such personifications: they may be well fitted for certain sorts of composition, but in these Poems I propose to myself to imitate, and, as far as possible, to adopt the very language of men; and I do not find that such personifications make any regular or natural part of that language. I wish to keep my Reader in the company of flesh and blood, persuaded that by so doing I shall interest him. Not but that I believe that others who pursue a different track may interest him likewise. I do not interfere with their claim, I only wish to prefer a different claim of my own.

There will also be found in these volumes little of what is

usually called poetic diction; I have taken as much pains to
avoid it as others ordinarily take to produce it; this I have
done for the reason already alleged, to bring my language near to
the language of men, and further, because the pleasure which I
have proposed to myself to impart is of a kind very different
from that which is supposed by many persons to be the proper
object of poetry.   I do not know how without being culpably
particular I can give my Reader a more exact notion of the style
in which I wished these poems to be written, than by informing
him that I have at all times endeavoured to look steadily at my
subject, consequently I hope it will be found that there is in these
Poems little falsehood of description, and that my ideas are expressed in language fitted to their respective importance.   Something I must have gained by the practice, as it is friendly to one
property of all good poetry, namely good sense: but it has
necessarily cut me off from a large portion of phrases and figures
of speech which from father to son have long been regarded as
the common inheritance of Poets.   I have also thought it expedient to restrict myself still further, having abstained from the
use of many expressions, in themselves proper and beautiful, but
which have been foolishly repeated by bad Poets till such feelings
of disgust are connected with them as it is scarcely possible by
any art of association to overpower. . . .

"Is there then, it will be asked, no essential difference
between the language of prose and metrical composition?   I
answer that there neither is, nor can be, any essential difference.
We are fond of tracing the resemblance between Poetry and
Painting and accordingly we call them Sisters: but where shall
we find bonds of connection sufficiently strict to typify the
affinity betwixt metrical and prose composition?   They both
speak by and to the same organs; the bodies in which both of
them are clothed may be said to be of the same substance, their
affections are kindred and almost identical, not necessarily
differing even in degree; Poetry sheds no tears 'such as Angels
weep,' but natural and human tears; she can boast of no celestial
ichor that distinguishes her vital juices from those of prose; the
same human blood circulates through the veins of them both.

"If it be affirmed that rhyme and metrical arrangement of themselves constitute a distinction which overturns what I have
been saying on the strict affinity of metrical language with that of
prose, and paves the way for other distinctions which the mind
voluntarily admits, I answer that the distinction of rhyme and
metre is regular and uniform, and not, like that which is produced
by what is usually called poetic diction, arbitrary and subject
to infinite caprices upon which no calculation whatever can be
made.   In the one case the Reader is utterly at the mercy of the
Poet respecting what imagery or diction he may choose to

connect with the passion, whereas in the other the metre obeys
certain laws to which the Poet and Reader both willingly submit
because they are certain, and because no interference is made by
them with the passion but such as the concurring testimony of
ages has shown to heighten and improve the pleasure which
co-exists with it.

"It will now be proper to answer an obvious question, namely,
why professing these opinions have I written in verse? To this
in the first place I reply, because, however I may have restricted
myself, there is still left open to me what confessedly constitutes
the most valuable object of all writing, whether in prose or verse,
the great and universal passions of men, the most general and
interesting of their occupations, and the entire world of nature,
from which I am at liberty to supply myself with endless combinations of forms and imagery. Now, granting for a moment
that whatever is interesting in these objects may be as vividly
described in prose, why am I to be condemned if to such
description I have endeavoured to superadd the charm which by
the consent of all nations is acknowledged to exist in metrical
language? . . .

" . . . The end of Poetry is to produce excitement in
coexistence with an overbalance of pleasure. Now, by the
supposition, excitement is an unusual and irregular state of the
mind; ideas and feelings do not in that state succeed each other
in accustomed order. But if the words by which this excitement is produced are in themselves powerful, or the images and
feelings have an undue proportion of pain connected with them,
there is some danger that the excitement may be carried beyond
its proper bounds. Now the co-presence of something regular,
something to which the mind has been accustomed when in an
unexcited or a less excited state, cannot but have great efficacy
in tempering and restraining the passion by an intertexture of
ordinary feeling. . . .

"I have said that Poetry is the spontaneous overflow of
powerful feelings: it takes its origin from emotion recollected in
tranquillity: the emotion is contemplated till by a species of
reaction the tranquillity gradually disappears, and an emotion
similar to that which was before the subject of contemplation, is
gradually produced, and does itself actually exist in the mind.
In this mood successful composition generally begins, and in a
mood similar to this it is carried on; but the emotion, of whatever
kind and in whatever degree, from various causes is qualified by
various pleasures, so that in describing any passions whatsoever,
which are voluntarily described, the mind will upon the whole
be in a state of enjoyment. Now if Nature be thus cautious in
preserving in a state of enjoyment a being thus employed, the
Poet ought to profit by the lesson thus held forth to him, and

289   4   ought especially to take care, that whatever passions he communicates to his Reader, those passions, if his Reader's mind be sound and vigorous, should always be accompanied with an overbalance of pleasure. Now the music of harmonious metrical language, the sense of difficulty overcome, and the blind association of pleasure which has been previously received from works of rhyme or metre of the same or similar construction, all these imperceptibly make up a complex feeling of delight, which is of the most important use in tempering the painful feeling which will always be found intermingled with powerful descriptions of the deeper passions. This effect is always produced in pathetic and impassioned poetry; while in lighter compositions the ease and gracefulness with which the Poet manages his numbers are themselves confessedly a principal source of the gratification of the Reader. I might perhaps include all which it is *necessary* to say upon this subject by affirming what few persons will deny, that of two descriptions either of passions, manners, or characters, each of them equally well executed, the one in prose and the other in verse, the verse will be read a hundred times where the prose is read once . . ."

     5   But as seen above, he was soon to have his doubts. He did, in fact, go on to "lay down . . . canons of criticism." His doubts culminated in the famous chapters in his *Biographia Literaria*. The best proof of Coleridge's adhesion at this time to Wordsworth's theory of poetic diction is provided, apart from the Preface, by his *The Three Graves* which, despite its author's later unconvincing denials (see his MS. Note in Mr. Stuart M. Samuel's copy of *Sibylline Leaves*, printed in *The Poetry of S. T. Coleridge*, edited by R. Garnett, p. 314), does illustrate Wordsworth's theory a great deal more successfully than Wordsworth himself was able to do. Moreover, this poem, written at the same time as *Peter Bell* (Wordsworth's declared effort to produce the effect of *The Ancient Mariner* without the aid of the supernatural) outdoes in no uncertain fashion this attempt in Wordsworth's own chosen field.

     6   B.Lit.C. II, pp. 5–6.

     7   Because the presence of *Lewti* in the volume would have threatened the anonymity the authors were so anxious to maintain for their *Lyrical Ballads* and thus, they hoped (vainly), giving their experiment a fair chance of judgment unprejudiced by any personal considerations. *Lewti* had appeared in the *Morning Post* on April 13, 1798 under the signature 'Nicias Erythraeus'—but Coleridge was known to have written it.

290   8   B.Lit.C. II, p. 6.

     9   Ibid. I, p. 60.

   10   Ibid. II, p. 6.

   11   Ibid.

   12   Ibid. II, p. 12.

291   13   See *History of English Prosody*, 1906–1910, by G. Saintsbury, III, pp. 55–67; *The Ancient Mariner and Christabel*, edited by A. Eichler, *Wiener Beiträge zur engl. Philologie*, 1907, XXVI, pp. 8–19; *Rhythm of Christabel*, by H. D. Bateson, *Manchester Quarterly*, 1894; *Milton's Prosody*, 1901, by R. Bridges, App. F. pp. 73–75; and *English Metrists*, by T. S. Omond, 1907, pp. 86–90. William Blake was working, independently, on similar lines— see *Jerusalem* and Preface. Cf. Coleridge's Note Book No. 3.

      14   W. P. 1850, XII, l. 279.

      15   B.Lit.C. II, p. 6.

      16   In the *Critical Review*, October, 1798. See W.L. I, pp. 229–230. Southey's review was signed 'Aristarchus.' For the reactions of Wordsworth and Coleridge when they discovered the identity of the reviewer see Note 63, Chapter XII.

      17   *Analytical Review*, December 1798.

292   18   William Wordsworth to James Losh, March 11, 1798. W.L. I, p. 189.

      19   Dorothy Wordsworth to Richard Wordsworth, April 30, 1798. W.L. I, p. 191.

      20   Letter to Joseph Cottle, May 1797. B.E. I, p. 130.

      21   B.E. I, p. 78.

      22   Ibid. pp. 130–131.

294   23   W.W. III, p. 469.

295   24   Letter to William Taylor, July 11, *Memoir of the Life and Writings of William Taylor of Norwich*, by J. W. Robberds, 1843, I, p. 215.

297   25   L. I, p. 113.

      26   Ibid. I, p. 126.

      27   Cf. C.P. p. 40 et seq.

      28   ll. 368–370. J.D.C. p. 60; P. I, p. 123.

298   29   ll. 28–31. J.D.C. p. 70; P. I, p. 132.

      30   This note was affixed to l. 34 in *Joan of Arc*, II, pp. 41–42, 1796. "Sir Isaac Newton at the end of the last edition of his Optics supposes that a very subtile and elastic fluid, which he calls aether, is diffused thro' the pores of gross bodies, as well as thro' the open spaces that are void of gross matter: he supposes it to pierce all bodies, and to touch their least particles, acting on them with a force proportional to their number or to the matter of the body on which it acts. . . . To the action of this aether he ascribes the attractions of gravitation and cohoesion, the attraction and repulsion of electrical bodies, the mutual influences of bodies and light upon each other, the effects and communication of heat, and the performance of animal sensation and motion. David Hartley, from whom this account of aether is chiefly borrowed, makes it the instrument of propagating those vibrations or configurative motions which are ideas. It appears to me, no hypothesis ever involved so many contradictions; for how can the

298   30   same fluid be both dense and rare in the same body at one time? . . . It has been asserted that Sir Isaac Newton's philosophy leads in its consequences to Atheism; perhaps not without reason. For if matter, by any powers or properties *given* to it, can produce the order of the visible world and even generate thought; why may it not have possessed such properties by *inherent* right? and where is the necessity of a God?" P. II, p. 1112; E.R. II, pp. 242–244.

31   Letter to Thomas Poole, September 24, 1796.   L. I, p. 169.

32   U.L. I, p. 94.

33   Ibid.

34   Cf. R. p. 21; E.R. I, p. 30.

35   ll. 396–401.   J.D.C. p. 60; P. I, p. 124.

299   36   December 17, 1796.   L. I, p. 195.

37   G.M.B.

38   C.L. I, p. 86.

39   L. I, p. 226 note.

40   W.H. XVII, p. 113.

300   41   Bentham's *Dictionary of Religion.*

301   42   B.Lit.C. I, p. 94.

43   December 1796.   U.L. I, p. 64.   See also G.M.B.

44   B.Lit.C. I, p. 132.   Cf. his words to George Coleridge in April, 1798: "I have for some time past withdrawn myself totally from the consideration of *immediate causes* . . . to muse on fundamental and general causes, the 'causæ causarum' . . . seeking with patience and a slow, very slow mind, 'Quid sumus, et quidnam victuri gignimus'—what our faculties are and what they are capable of becoming."   L. I, p. 243.

45   B.Lit.C. I, p. 98.   See entries in G.M.B. confirming Coleridge's knowledge of Boehme at least as early as 1796.

46   L. I, p. 211.   But cf. letter to J. Gooden, *Notes and Lectures upon Shakespeare* etc., edited Sara Coleridge, 1849, II, p. 273.

47   L. I, pp. 211–212.

302   48   ll. 28–31, 34–45.   J.D.C. p. 54; P. I, pp. 110–111.   But see Coleridge's note to the passage, Note 85, Chapter IV.

303   49   B.Lit.C. I, pp. lxii–lxiii, 107–109, 195.   See also notes, B.Lit.C. I., p. 249, on the derivation of esemplastic, sensuous and intuition —three of the words claimed by Coleridge.   See also A.P. p. 236; C.W. III, p. 272; cf. *Coleridge's Critical Terminology*, E.S. XXI.   And see N.&Q.   April 3, 1937, pp. 239–240 for remarks on yet another Coleridge word.

50   His note to *The Thorn*, for instance.   The relevant passage reads: "Superstitious men . . . have a reasonable share of imagination, by which word I mean the faculty which produces impressive effects out of simple elements; but they are utterly destitute of fancy, the power by which pleasure and surprise are excited by sudden varieties of situation and by accumulated imagery."

303   51   B.Lit.C. I, p. 64.

      52   *The Destiny of Nations.* ll. 17–19; J.D.C. p. 70. ll. 18–20; P. I, p. 132. (l. 6 added in 1834.)

      53   October 16, 1797. L. I, p. 16.

      54   Ibid.

304   55   B.Lit.C. I, p. 134.

      56   MS.H. p. 115.

      57   Ibid.

      58   A useful discussion of this point—though not specifically in connexion with Coleridge alone—appears in *Thought and Imagination in Art and Life,* by Katharine M. Wilson, 1937.

305   59   MS.C. Vol. II (numbering conjectural).

306   60   Letter to Josiah Wade, January 27, 1796. L. I, p. 152; B.E. I, p. 57. Cf. letter to Josiah Wedgwood, p. 225.

      61   B.Lit.C. I, pp. 95–96.

307   62   Coleridge's *Poetical Works,* 1828. Annotated copy. Cf. E.R. II, pp. 242–244; J.D.C. p. 586 and Note 28.

      63   L. I, pp. 203–204 note.

308   64   May 6, 1796. B.E. I, p. 78.

      65   April 1, 1796. B.E. I, p. 68.

      66   Letter to John Taylor Coleridge, April 8, 1825. L. II, p. 735. Cf. A.P. p. 106.

309   67   MS.C. Vol. II.

310   68   B.Lit.C. I, pp. 135–137.

311   69   Ibid. I, p. 134.

      70   C.R.D. May 29, 1812, I, p. 88. Yet see letter to Lady Beaumont, January 21, 1810, M.C. II, p. 105. Cf. letter to J. H. Green, December 13, 1817, L. II, p. 683; C.R.D. May 3, 1812, I, p. 70 et seq.; Aug. 13, 1812, I, p. 107; B.Lit.B. I, p. 303; B.Lit.C. I, pp. 102, 103; F.B. I, pp. 206, 211; C.W. II, pp. 91, 142; ibid. III, p. 691 et seq.; and MS.H.

      71   December 1796. L. I, p. 212.

      72   Letter to Thomas Poole, October 16, 1797. L. I, p. 16.

      73   Letter to John Thelwall, October 16, 1797. L. I, p. 228.

      74   F.A. Appendix A.

      75   B.Lit.C. I, p. 137.

CHAPTER 11

313   1   Letter to Henry Gardiner, October 3, 1798. W.L. I, p. 201. Indeed, Coleridge in his letter of September 19, 1798, to Sarah, marks Wordsworth down as one of the "horribly sick." L. I, p. 259.

      2   *Satyrane's Letters.* B.Lit.C. II, p. 135. Written originally to Poole and Sarah. Then published, with alterations, in *The*

313 2 *Friend*, Nos. 14, 16, 18. November-December 1809. Finally incorporated in *Biographia Literaria*. For the title see *Faery Queen*, Bk. I, Canto VI, and *A Tombless Epitaph*, J.D.C. p. 180. P. I, pp. 413–414. Cf. J.G. pp. 116–117; Note Book No. 3.

314 3 B.Lit.C. II, pp. 140–141. See also letter to Sarah, September 19, 1798. L. I, p. 260.

     4 B.Lit.C. II, p. 142.

     5 D.W.J. p. 21 et seq.; B.Lit.C. II, pp. 143–144.

     6 B.Lit.C. II, p. 151. Wordsworth had little good to say of it. See W.L. I, pp. 199, 201.

     7 B.Lit.C. II, p. 155.

315 8 Ibid. II, p. 156. But see letter to Benjamin Flower, April 1, 1796. B.E. I, p. 68.

     9 B.Lit.C. II, p. 165.

    10 January 4, 1799. L. I, p. 268.

    11 Ibid. I, p. 271.

316 12 *Samuel Taylor Coleridge*: By the English Opium Eater, *Tait's Magazine*, October 1834. Text as revised for Vol. II of the Edinburgh Collective Edition of 1853–60. Q. II, pp. 170–171.

    13 See B.Lit.C. II, p. 169 et seq.; H. pp. 280–281. See also E.R. II, p. 20; W.L. I, p. 482.

317 14 B.Lit.C. II, p. 171.

    15 October 8, 1798. T.P. I, p. 278.

    16 November 28, 1798. C.L. I, p. 141.

318 17 October 8, 1798. T.P. I, p. 278.

    18 Ibid. I, p. 279.

319 19 Ibid. I, pp. 279–280.

    20 Ibid. I, p. 280.

    21 T.P. I, p. 282.

    22 W.L. I, p. 200.

320 23 October 20, 1798. L. I, p. 262.

    24 B.Lit.C. I, pp. 137–138 note.

    25 Really Kielmansegge. L. I, p. 262.

    26 Letter dated December 13, 1798. L. I, p. 263 note.

321 27 November 26, 1798. L. I, p. 265.

    28 December 2, 1798. L. I, p. 266.

    29 Cf. L. I, pp. 259, 261, 265, 277, 281, for instance.

    30 See letter from Wordsworth to Coleridge, December 1798 or January 1799, W.L. I, pp. 203–204.

    31 Coleridge's Note to 1834 *Poems* when the heading was *Written during a temporary blindness in the year 1799*. "When I was ill and wakeful I composed some English hexameters." At the end he wrote: "There was a great deal more, which I have forgotten. . . . The last line which I wrote, I remember, and write it for the truth of the sentiment, scarcely less true in company than in pain and solitude." Then follows the quotation. J.D.C. p. 138; P. I, pp. 304–305. Cf. ll. 15–16.

322   32   December 1798. W.L. I, p. 208. Later, W.P. 1805 I, ll. 460–469. See also Coleridge's letter of December 10, 1798, in which he acknowledges Wordsworth's verses (later, W.P. 1805 V, ll. 389–422) sent to him probably early December 1798. "The blank lines gave me as much direct pleasure as was possible in the general bustle of pleasure with which I received and read your letter. I observed, I remember, that the 'fingers interwoven' etc. only puzzled me; and though I liked the twelve or fourteen first lines very well, yet I liked the remainder much better. Well, now I have read them again, they are very beautiful, and leave an affecting impression. That

> Uncertain heaven received
> Into the bosom of the steady lake

I should have recognised anywhere; and had I met these lines running wild in the deserts of Arabia, I should instantly have screamed out 'Wordsworth.'" See note, W.P. pp. 530–531.

      33   W.L. I, p. 208.
      34   Letter to Sarah, December 2, 1798. L. I, p. 266.
      35   W.L. I, p. 211.
      36   Ibid.

323   37   L. I, p. 267.
      38   Ibid. I, pp. 267–268.
      39   Ibid. I, pp. 268–269.

324   40   Ibid. I, pp. 269–270.
      41   Ibid. I, pp. 270–271.
      42   Thomas Ward was Poole's young apprentice. He transcribed Poole's letters and letters received into Poole's 'Copying Book.' Later he was taken into partnership with Poole. His was evidently a very happy disposition. Coleridge describes him as the "young man with the soul-beaming face." Letter to Poole, September 24, 1796. L. I, p. 170. See T.P. I, pp. 159–160; also X, p. 462.
      43   January 24, 1799. T.P. I, p. 284.

325   44   Ibid. I, pp. 285–286.
      45   January 14, 1799. L. I, pp. 271–272.

326   46   Ibid. I, pp. 272–273.
      47   Ibid. I, pp. 275–276.

327   48   Ibid. I, p. 277.
      49   W.L. I, pp. 212–213.

328   50   Ibid. I, p. 214.
      51   Ibid. I, p. 220.
      52   Ibid. I, p. 221.

329   53   Ibid.
      54   Ibid. I, p. 223.
      55   Ibid.

330   56   Cf. Coleridge's

> To be beloved is all I need,
> And whom I love, I love indeed.

ll. 51–52, *The Pains of Sleep*, J.D.C. p. 171; P. I, p. 391.   Also ll. 18–22, *Youth and Age*, J.D.C. p. 191; P. I, p. 440; and ll. 412–423, *Christabel* Part Two, J.D.C. p. 121; P. I, p. 229.   See also remarks on his rupture with Charles Lloyd and consequent retirement to the "lonely farm house between Porlock and Linton," Note 60, Chapter IX.   Cf. L. I, p. 296; A.P. p. 172; M.C. I, p. 15.   In the 1810 MS. Note Book, under *Ego-Ana*, Coleridge wrote: "One human Being, *entirely* loving me (this, of course, must have been a woman) would not only have satisfied all my Hopes, but would have rendered me happy and grateful, even tho' I had no Friend on earth, herself excepted." And again: "Unhappy I—I have loved many more than I ever loved myself and one beyond myself and beyond all things, and all persons, but never, never, have I met with any being who did not love many better than they loved me."

57   L. I, p. 278.

58   Ibid. I, p. 279.

59   Ibid.

60   Ibid.

61   Ibid.

62   Ibid. I, p. 280.

331   63   Ibid. I, pp. 280–281.

64   Brothers of the Arctic explorer.   Cottle (E.R. II, p. 74 note) mistakenly describes one of them as the explorer.   Charles (1779–1860) was later a doctor at Bath.

65   *Brandl*, p. 240.

66   1777–1864.   Later a doctor at Truro and author of *Early Years and Late Reflections*.

67   George Bellas Greenough, 1778–1855, later a well-known scientist and first president of the Geological Society.

68   Letter dated May 25, 1799, quoted in *Early Years and Late Reflections*, I, p. 101 note.   Coleridge, says Carlyon, dressed badly "but I have heard him say, fixing his prominent eyes upon himself (as he was wont to do whenever there was a mirror in the room), with a singularly coxcombical expression of countenance, that his dress was sure to be lost sight of the moment he began to talk, an assertion which, whatever may be thought of its modesty, was not without truth."   *Early Years and Late Reflections*, I, p. 29.

332   69   B.Lit.C. I, p. 138.   The following description of Coleridge at Göttingen, though not above suspicion, may be quoted here: "Benecke told me that Coleridge, when at Göttingen towards the close of the last century, was an idler, and did not learn the language thoroughly, and that he got a long ode of Klopstock by

332   69   heart and declaimed without understanding it, playfully mystify-
ing his countrymen with the apparent rapidity of his progress.
When the 'Opium Eater' appeared, Benecke at once attributed it
to Coleridge, from knowing, he said, that Coleridge took opium
when at Göttingen." *Göttingen in 1824,* author anonymous,
Putnam's Magazine, Vol. VIII, December 1856, p. 600. See X,
pp. 599–600.

      70   *Early Years and Late Reflections,* I, p. 100 note. But see L. I,
p. 298.

      71   B.Lit.C. I, pp. 138–141. For an impression of the extent of
Coleridge's reading at Göttingen see *Books Borrowed by Cole-
ridge from the Library of the University of Göttingen, 1799,* by
Alice D. Snyder, *Modern Philology,* XXV, pp. 377–380. See
also Coleridge's catalogue of work done in his letter to Josiah
Wedgwood of May 21, 1799. B.E. I, pp. 180–181.

333   72   *Brandl,* p. 242.

      73   That Coleridge read some Kant at Göttingen is known by
Carlyon's anecdote of the German girl who, discussing Kant with
Coleridge, was astonished to find that he could understand, in
her language, what she could not fathom. *Early Years and Late
Reflections,* I, p. 162. Cf. W.H. XII, p. 37; B.Lit.C. II, p. 179.

      74   *Brandl,* pp. 240–241.

      75   Ibid. p. 240.

      76   S.C. p. 1; T.P. I, pp. 289–290.

      77   T.P. I, p. 290.

      78   S.C. p. 1; T.P. I, p. 290.

335   79   T.P. I, pp. 290–293.

337   80   L. I, pp. 282–284. The last lines quoted are from one of
Wordsworth's "Lucy" poems-to-be. The previous four-line
quotation Coleridge took from his own *Osorio,* Act V, Sc. 1,
ll. 11–14, J. D. C. p. 506; P. II, p. 583.

      81   T.P. I, pp. 295–296.

338   82   L. I, pp. 284–285.

339   83   Ibid. I, pp. 285–287.

      84   Ibid. I, p. 287. Cf. *Early Years and Late Reflections,* I, p. 90.

340   85   L. I, p. 282 note.

      86   Ibid. I, pp. 288–289.

341   87   Ibid. I, p. 289 et seq.

      88   A blackbird. Not in this instance those who rip the bark from
oak logs for tanning, as stated in L. I, p. 296 note.

      89   T.P. I, pp. 297–298; L. I, pp. 295–296.

342   90   *Coleridge in Germany (1799) As portrayed in the Journal of George
Bellas Greenough and in some unpublished letters of the poet,* by
Edith J. Morley, *London Mercury,* April 1931, p. 555. Cole-
ridge described this expedition as "the Carlyon—Parry—
Greenation." *Early Years and Late Reflections,* I, p. 45; for
notes of the whole tour, see I, pp. 32–136. See also *Herrigs*

342   90   *Archiv für das Studium der neueren Sprachen und Litteraturen,* CXVIII, 1907, pp. 41–68; B.E. I, pp. 168–177; and U.L. I, pp. 107–115.

       91   *Early Years and Late Reflections,* I, p. 51.

       92   Ibid. I, p. 50.

       93   Greenough's *Diary,* p. 56; *London Mercury,* April 1931, p. 560.

       94   *Early Years and Late Reflections,* I, p. 114. Cf. Coleridge's jingle, "O'er damn'd bad roads, through damn'd delightful woods." Ibid. I, p. 33.

       95   *London Mercury,* April 1931, p. 559.

       96   B.E. I, p. 171.

       97   The first visit took place "soon after Coleridge's arrival at Göttingen" and before March 22, 1799. Carlyon suggests that the two men went for an excursion on this occasion, leaving Dorothy behind in Göttingen. *Early Years and Late Reflections,* I, pp. 196–197. The second visit occurred about April 20. See L. I, p. 288. Also K.W. I, pp. 183, 193.

344   98   T.P. I, pp. 298–299; L. I, pp. 296–297.

       99   L. I, pp. 298–299.

   100   Ibid. I, p. 299. See *Instructions for making Sugar, Molasses, and Vinous Spirit from Beet-root,* by F. C. Achard.

345 101   L. I, p. 300.

   102   U.L. I, p. 109.

   103   Ibid. I, p. 115; S.C. pp. 3–4.

   104   R. p. 425; B.E. I, p. 178.

   105   n.d. U.L. I, p. 116.

   106   Ibid.

   107   Ibid. I, p. 122.

346 108   Ibid. I, pp. 116–117.

   109   Many years later, after the death of Coleridge, Sarah wrote on the back of her letter to him of March 25, 1799, in which she spoke of Berkeley's death: "No secrets herein. I will not burn it for the sake of my sweet Berkeley." And see, for instance, her letter to Poole of September 20, 1819: "You will always live in my remembrance as connected with my early wedded-days, in the infancy of my beloved Hartley, and the *whole existence* of that other dear babe whose name you have *more than once unwittingly* given to my third son in your kind enquiries for him, thereby recalling many, many tender and *some* very bitter recollections connected with his birth and death, sweet child! But I do not wish him here." S.C. pp. 83–84. Cf. B.Lit.B. II, p. 411; *Memoir of Sara Coleridge,* I, pp. 2–3.

347 110   See letter of April 2, 1799. T.P. I, p. 300; S.C. pp. 2, 5.

   111   Written on the back of Coleridge's letter to Poole, May 6, 1799. T.P. I, p. 300.

   112   March 1799. T.P. I, p. 302; S.C. p. 4.

   113   April 2, 1799. T.P. I, p. 301; S.C. p. 5.

347 114 An opinion expressed in his review of October 1798, in the *Critical Review*. After pronouncing the venture as a whole a failure (see Chapter X) Southey described *The Ancient Mariner* in particular as "a Dutch attempt at German sublimity. Genius has been here employed in producing a poem of little merit." Cf. Lamb's comments, Chapter XIII, p. 379; C.L. I, pp. 240, 245–247.

348 115 April 2, 1799. T.P. I, p. 301; S.C. p. 5.

      116 See letter to Robert Southey, December 24, 1799. L. I, pp. 319–320. Letter from Poole to Coleridge, January 21, 1800. T.P. II, p. 3. Also Greenough's *Journal*, January 9, 1801; *London Mercury*, April 1931, p. 565. It would be as well in this place to refer to the statement in *A Group of Englishmen*, p. 99, that Wordsworth was lent money by the Wedgwoods for his German tour. This suggestion appears to have been disposed of adequately both in M. p. 91 note, and L. I, p. 269 note. Yet see T.W. p. 62 note.

      117 Letter to Sarah, April 23, 1799. L. I, p. 289.

349 118 B.Lit.C. I, p. 137.

      119 R. p. 427; B.E. I, p. 180.

      120 R. pp. 427–428; B.E. I, pp. 180–181.

350 121 R. p. 428; B.E. I, p. 181.

      122 An error for Sussmilch.

      123 R. p. 426; B.E. I, p. 179.

      124 B.E. I, p. 68.

      125 May 21, 1799. R. p. 428; B.E. I, pp. 180–181.

351 126 Letters from Sarah Coleridge to Thomas Poole, March and April 2, 1799. S.C. pp. 3–4; M. p. 100. Coleridge also considered writing a life of Giordano Bruno, whose doctrines he praised and expounded at Göttingen. *Early Years and Late Reflections*, I, pp. 95–97 note.

      127 L. I, pp. 269, 287, 288. But finally see p. 300.

      128 *Early Years and Late Reflections*, I, pp. 91, 95, 138.

      129 Ibid. I, pp. 35–37. See extract from Greenough's letter to his aunt, July 26, 1799; *London Mercury*, April 1931, pp. 556–557; R. p. 275.

      130 Greenough's *Diary*, p. 67; *London Mercury*, April 1931, p. 559.

352 131 Greenough's *Diary*, p. 112; *London Mercury*, April 1931, p. 563; *Early Years and Late Reflections*, I, pp. 178–179. When the party did visit Scandinavia—without Coleridge—the tour was a failure.

      132 At which function Coleridge appeared in high spirits—"the ladies delighted with him"—talking interminably "with the worst German accent imaginable," drawing a dictionary from his pocket whenever he paused at a loss for a word. *Early Years and Late Reflections*, I, pp. 161–162.

      133 Greenough's *Diary*, p. 184; *London Mercury*, April 1931, p. 562.

352 134 But for the second time the Brocken Spectre—a magnified reflection of the beholder's figure on a sheet of vaporous mist—
eluded them.   See, in this connexion, the G.M.B. entry

Vide Description of a Glory, by
John Haygarth, *Manchester Trans.* Vol. 3, p. 463.

For full note and comments, see X, pp. 470–471.

135 *Brandl*, pp. 250–251.   This was on June 30, 1799.   Attention
might well be drawn here to *German Influence in the English
Romantic Period 1788–1818*, by F. W. Stockoe, 1926, which
deals in part with Coleridge's months in Germany and their
after-effects.

136 Greenough's *Diary*, p. 212, and extracts from Coleridge's
letter to Greenough of July 6, 1799; *London Mercury*, pp.
563 564.

137 Apparently Coleridge and Chester were obliged to sail without
them.   See L. I, p. 321 and B.E. I, p. 187.

138 B.Lit.C. I, p. 99.

CHAPTER 12

353 1 *London Mercury*, April 1931, p. 564.
354 2 July 29, 1799.   L. I, pp. 303–304.
3 L. I, p. 304.
4 August 1799.   U.L. I, p. 123.
355 5 The full letter unpublished.   M. p. 103; L. I, p. 304; H.S. pp.
198–199.
6 *Memoir of William Taylor of Norwich*, I, pp. 232–233.
7 R.S.L. I, p. 78; H.S. p. 199.
8 H.S. p. 199.
9 R.S.W. p. 179.   See also Coleridge's letter to Southey, December 9, 1799.   L. I, p. 318.
10 Not until 1827.   See H.S. p. 200; J.D.C. pp. 621–623.
11 H.S. p. 201; A.P. pp. 290–291.   The result is to be seen in
J.D.C. pp. 139–140; P. I, pp. 329–330.   See also *Memoir of
William Taylor of Norwich*, I, pp. 294, 309, 325; and R.S. II,
p. 76.   For Southey early had his doubts as to the likelihood
of his partner's collaboration resulting in actual production of
verses: "From Coleridge I am promised the half," he told
William Taylor on February 3, 1800, "and we divided the
book according as the subject suited us, but I expect to have
nearly the whole work!   His ardour is not lasting . . ." R.S. II,
p. 48.
356 12 R.S.L. I, pp. 81–83.
13 September 16, 1799 (from Southey's lodgings, Fore Street Hill,
Exeter).   L. I, p. 306.

356 14 L. I, p. 306.
357 15 Ibid. I, pp. 306–307.
16 H.S. p. 199 et seq. Cf. R. p. 219.
17 September 16, 1799. L. I, p. 305.
18 1803 Notebook—portion printed L. I, p. 305, note 2.
19 U.L. I, p. 124.
358 20 Ibid. I, p. 125.
21 Ibid. Cf. *Memoir of William Taylor of Norwich*, I, p. 302.
22 U.L. I, p. 125.
23 Ibid.
24 Ibid.
359 25 September 30, 1799. U.L. I, pp. 126–127.
26 U.L. I, p. 128.
27 Ibid. I, pp. 128–129.
28 Ibid. I, p. 129. *Ideen zur Philosophie der Geschichte der Menschheit*, by J. G. von Herder, 1784–1791, translated by T. Churchill, 1800; *Geographische Geschichte des Menschen*, by E. A. W. von Zimmermann, 1778–83.
29 U.L. I, p. 129.
30 Ibid. I, pp. 129–130.
31 November 19, 1796. L. I, p. 183.
32 October 7, 1799. T.P. I, 304. But as Miss Helen Cam, owner of the original, points out, this "Letter the First" was in fact written on the same sheet and so sent at the same time as the "Letter the Second" quoted in the next Note.
360 33 T.P. I, p. 304. By the courtesy of Miss Helen Cam, the correct text of this "Letter the Second" can now be given. It is as follows:
"Most exquisite Benefactor!—I will speak dirt & daggers of the Wretch who shall deny thee to be the most heaven-inspired, munificent Penmaker that these latter Times, these superficial, weak, and evirtuate ages have produced—to redeem themselves from ignominy! And may he, great Calamist! who shall vilipend or derogate from thy penmaking merits, do *pen*ance & suffer *pen*itential *pen*alty, *pen*n'd up in some *pen*urious *pen*insular of *pen*al Fire & *pen*etrant Fire, *pen*sive and *pen*dulous, *pen*ding a huge slice of Eternity!—Were I to write till *Pen*tecost, filling whole *Pen*tateuchs, my grateful expressions would still remain merely a *Pen*umbra of my Debt of Gratitude.
"thine S. T. Coleridge"
34 T.P. I, p. 305. The text of T. P. has been corrected from the original in the possession of Miss Helen Cam. A Fable written by Coleridge on the paper in which the pens were wrapped, and returned to Ward, runs as follows:
"The Fox, the Goose and the Swan, a new Fable.
"The Fox observing a white Bird on the lake thought it a Goose—leapt in & meant to have payed his respects, but met

360   34   such a rebuff & had nearly made his fate similar to that of his namesake, the celebrated *Guy*. However he got off with a most profound respect for the supposed Goose & soon received a message from the Goose to this purport—Dear Friend! I have sent this hopping—hu'd has ow u dun mee the onnur of a vissat —sorry u dident hap to have meat with I—, That dowdy lanky neck'd Thing that u saw is a distant relashon of I's, and I suffers r to swum about the Pond when I is not at hum, but I is at hum now I hop for the onnur of ure company—

"your loving Friend   Guse.

"The Fox came—&—you guess the Rest—This Fable I address to the Writer of the above notable instance of Incapacity *self*-detected thro' vanity!"

35   1778–1829.

36   E.R. II, p. 31 et seq.; T.W. pp. 37–38; H.D.M. I, p. 58 et seq.; R. p. 261.

37   T.W. pp. 33–35; T.P. I, p. 254; H.D.F. p. 18 note 2.

361   38   T.W. pp. 33–35; T.P. I, p. 254.

39   T.P. I, p. 254. See H.D.M. I, p. 48 et seq.; H.D.F. pp. 1–19; R. p. 263.

40   H.D.M. I, p. 64; T.P. I, p. 276.

41   July 12, 1799, R.S. II, p. 21; H.S. p. 197.

42   Letter to Robert Southey, October 15, 1799. L. I, p. 308. Josiah Wedgwood was hoping to purchase the estate of Combe Florey near by, but the deal fell through, much to the disappointment of Poole, the negotiator and an admirer of the Wedgwoods, whom he wished to have as neighbours. See T.P. I, pp. 293–294; T.W. pp. 65–67. The suggestion in Meteyard's *Group of Englishmen*, p. 107 (repeated in L. I, p. 307) that the estate was actually purchased by Josiah Wedgwood, is incorrect.

43   E.R. II, p. 46; R. p. 274.

44   January 1800. B.E. I, p. 188. Cf. E.R. II, pp. 104–105; R. p. 431; L. I, p. 324; *The Life of Humphry Davy*, by John Ayrton, Paris, 1831, I, pp. 61, 74–75, 97.

362   45   L. I, pp. 307–308.

46   Ibid. I, p. 310.

47   Ibid.

48   Ibid.

49   Ibid. I, p. 311–312

50   Ibid. I, p. 312.

363   51   September 10, 1799, written at Exeter. MS. letter in B.M.

52   Ibid. Cf. Note 58; Note 74, Chapter IX; and Note 145, Chapter XIII.

53   Letter from Thomas Poole to Tom Wedgwood, November 27, 1799. R. pp. 475–476. Letter to Robert Southey, November 10, 1799. L. I, p. 313; D.W.M. p. 73. See also letter from Dorothy Wordsworth to Richard Wordsworth, September 3,

363   53   1799. W.L. I, p. 232. Cf. Coleridge's explanation to Southey: "I was called up to the North by alarming accounts of Wordsworth's health, which, thank God! are but little more than alarms." Letter of November 10, 1799, L. I, p. 313.

       54   MS. Diary of Tour in the Lake District. From Note Book No. 5½. Cf. Note Books Nos. 2 and 21.

       55   Ibid.

       56   Ibid. R. p. 259; K.W. I, pp. 198–200. Cf. E.R. II, pp. 82–83 note, on an incident at York.

       57   H. pp. 299–300; D.W.S. pp. 106–107; D.W.M. pp. 70–72.

       58   W.L. I, p. 228. Cf. Note 52; Note 74, Chapter IX; and Note 145, Chapter XIII.

364   59   May 13, 1799. W.L. I, p. 224.

365   60   July 27, 1799. W.L. I, p. 229. Cf. R. p. 260.

       61   June 24, 1799. W.L. I, pp. 226–227.

       62   Ibid. I, p. 227. Cf. Wordsworth's note on *The Ancient Mariner* in the second edition of the *Lyrical Ballads* with his Fenwick Note to *We are Seven* forty-three years later. Then see C.L. I, pp. 240, 245–247.

       63   1799. W.L. I, pp. 229–230. Coleridge, discovering the identity of 'Aristarchus,' wrote him an epigram as he had done to Lloyd:

To a Critic who extracted a passage from a poem without adding a word respecting the context, and then derided it as unintelligible

> Most candid critic, what if I,
> By way of joke, pull out your eye
> And holding up the fragment, cry
> 'Ha! ha! that men such fools should be!
> Behold this shapeless Dab!—and he
> Who own'd it, fancied it could *see!*'
> The joke were mighty analytic,
> But should you like it, candid critic?

Morning Post, December 16, 1801; J.D.C. p. 447; P. II, p. 962.

       64   July 27, 1799. W.L. I, p. 229.

       65   September 2, 1799. W.L. I, p. 231; R. pp. 258–259.

       66   Letters to Richard Wordsworth, May 13, 1799, W.L. I, p. 224; to Joseph Cottle, June 24, 1799, W.L. I, p. 227; and to Thomas Poole, July 4, 1799, W.L. I, p. 228.

366   67   Summer, 1799. M.W. I, p. 159; D.W.M. p. 72; A.P. p. 30; H. p. 300.

       68   Preface to the second edition of the *Lyrical Ballads*, 1800.

       69   W.P. 1805, XIII, ll. 270–271; D.W.M. pp. 72–73 and note.

       70   See Preface to *The Excursion*, 1814. *The Prelude* soon began to take shape in Wordsworth's mind as a self-examination in verse—a poem by which he might measure his fitness (with Coleridge as arbitrator or judge) for undertaking the greater task of writing the complete *The Recluse*.

PAGE NOTE

366 71 D.W.M. p. 73 and note.

367 72 October 12, 1799. M.W. I, p. 159; H. p. 301. Cf. Note 154, Chapter XIII.

73 "Few moments in Life are so interesting as those upon affectionate reception from those who have heard of you, yet are strangers to your person." Note Book No. 5½. See also D.W.M. pp. 73–74; D.W.S. p. 107.

74 D.W.S. p. 56. Sarah Hutchinson was born January 1 and baptized at Penrith January 20, 1775. Died 1835.

368 75 Letter to Daniel Stuart, 1808. L.P. p. 73; D.W.M. p. 74. Cf. Coleridge's letter to Southey, July 25, 1801, in which he describes Sarah Hutchinson as "so very good a woman that I have seldom indeed seen the like of her." L. I, p. 360.

76 Note Book No. 5½.

77 Ibid.

78 Ibid.

79 Ibid.

80 Ibid.

81 Ibid. Cf. The Visit of the Gods, Imitated from Schiller. J.D.C. pp. 142–143; P. I, pp. 310–311.

82 Note Book No. 5½. In this inn, Coleridge noted that "the handle of the bell rope in the parlour was made of a shell."

83 Note Book No 5½.

369 84 Ibid.

85 R. p. 259.

86 Note Book No. 5½. Cf. letter from Wordsworth to Dorothy, November 7, 1799, from Grasmere W.L. I, pp. 232–233

87 Note Book No. 5½.

88 W.L. I, p. 233.

89 Ibid.

90 Note Book No. 5½.

370 91 W.L. I, p. 233.

92 Letter of Coleridge to Dorothy Wordsworth, November 7, 1799, K.W. I, p. 198; D.W.M. p. 75.

93 Really Sour Milk Ghyll. Dorothy also writes Churn Milk on December 9, 1801. D.W.J. p. 69.

94 Willy good Wa-ers' Bridge.

95 Note Book No 5½.

96 Letter of Coleridge to Dorothy Wordsworth, November 7, 1799, K.W. I, p. 198. Cf. W.L. I, p. 233; D.W.M. p. 75.

97 K.W. I, p. 199. Cf. D.W.S. p. 107; H. p. 304.

98 W.L. I, p. 233. The cottage was known by the Wordsworths for some years by its local name, Town-end. H. pp. 306–307.

99 See letter to Dorothy Wordsworth, November 7, 1799, K.W. I, p. 199. ". . . there is no place in our island . . . which really equals the vale of Keswick" Coleridge tells Sarah on November 16, 1802. L. I, p. 411. Row Head, T. Tyson's house, still exists.

371 100 Note Book No. 5½. D.W.M. pp. 75–76; H. p. 304.
    101 November 10, 1799. L. I, p. 313. See Note 119.
    102 Ibid.
    103 Ibid. I, p. 314.
    104 Note Book No. 5½.
    105 "There is a Yew-tree, pride of Lorton Vale."
    106 Note Book No. 5½.
    107 Ibid.
372 108 Ibid.
    109 Ibid.
    110 Ibid. Part printed as Note to L. I, p. 312.
    111 Only two months before, Coleridge had walked in Devon with
        Southey.
    112 Note Book No. 5½.
373 113 Ibid.
    114 Ibid.
    115 Cf. ll. 509–517, *The Three Graves*. J.D.C. p. 92; P. I, p. 284.
    116 Note Book No. 5½.
    117 Ibid.
    118 Ibid.
374 119 See letter to Robert Southey, December 24, 1799. L. I, pp.
        319–320. Also letter to Tom Wedgwood, January 1800. T.W.
        pp. 74–76. Also C.M.V. pp. 42–43. Cf. The *Gentleman's
        Magazine*, May 1838, p. 487.
    120 A. I, p. 95.
375 121 December 21, 1799. B.E. I, p. 183. Coleridge is referring, of
        course, to William Camden, 1551–1623.
    122 See J.D.C. p. 613 note.
    123 ll. 1–4. J.D.C. p. 135; P. I, p. 330. ll. 20–24 in the *Morning
        Post* version. For the significance of this poem as an expression
        of his feelings for Sarah, see also the motto from Petrarch which
        Coleridge prefixed to the poem when reprinting it in *Sibylline
        Leaves*.
376 124 ll. 5–20. J.D.C. p. 135; P. I, pp. 331–332. ll. 25–40 in the
        Morning Post version. But the 1st and 4th stanzas differ from
        the later text.
    125 ll. 25–29, 77–80. J.D.C. pp. 135–136; P. I, p. 332. But in the
        Morning Post version these were ll. 41–44 and 97–100, a stanza
        being omitted later.
    126 ll. 101–104 in the *Morning Post*. The entire stanza omitted
        when reprinted in the *Lyrical Ballads*, second edition, 1800.
    127 ll. 105–108 in the *Morning Post*. ll. 81–84 in the *Lyrical
        Ballads*, the first line reading:
                Her bosom heav'd—she stepped aside
        J.D.C. p. 136; P. I, p. 334.
    128 ll. 109–116 in the *Morning Post*; ll. 85–92 in the *Lyrical Ballads*.
        J.D.C. p. 136; P. I, p. 334. This poem was first published with

376 128   seven additional stanzas (first four, last three) as the *Introduction to the Tale of the Dark Ladié* in the *Morning Post*, December 21, 1799. See L.R. I, pp. 50–52, for the seven stanzas. See pp. 34–35, *A Description of the Wordsworth and Coleridge MSS. in the possession of Mr. T. Norton Longman*, edited by W. Hale White, 1897, for facsimile of MS. as printed in *Lyrical Ballads*. Also *Coleridge's Poems*, A Facsimile Reproduction edited by J. Dykes Campbell, 1899, which collates the *Introduction to the Tale of the Dark Ladié* with MSS. copies (B.M. Add. MSS., No. 27902). Also see Appendices in P. II, p. 1052 et seq.

377 129   Which may be roughly translated: "And pressed Sara's hand a long time behind her back and then love first [pierced] me with a light arrow-tip, poisoned alas, and incurable." This extract from the Note Books, with a number of others relating to Sarah Hutchinson, has been printed in *Coleridge and "Asra,"* by T. M. Raysor, *Studies in Philology*, July 1929, Vol. XXVI, No. 3. Most, though not all, of the "Asra" references so far discovered have been included in the course of this article.

CHAPTER 13

378   1   T.P. I, p. 307.
      2   Ibid.
      3   Letter to Robert Southey, December 9, 1799. L. I, p. 318.
      4   Ibid. I, p. 318.
      5   Ibid. I, p. 318. The name was Hayes or Hays. Wrote *Memoirs of Emma Courtney* and *Female Biography or Memoirs of Illustrious and Celebrated Women*. See *Love Letters of Mary Hays*, by A. F. Wedd, 1925.
      6   L. I, p. 315.
      7   See *Metrical Letter written from London*, R.S.W. p. 149. See also H.S. p. 203; R. p. 213.
      8   L. I, p. 318.
379   9   *Lines written a few miles above Tintern Abbey*, which was placed last in the volume—*The Ancient Mariner* being placed first. The last place in every volume of his poems was always occupied by the poem considered by Wordsworth to be his best.
     10   November 8, 1798. C.L. I, pp. 136–137. Cf. Note 62, Chapter XII.
     11   See letter from Lamb to Coleridge, January 10, 1820. C.L. II, pp. 267–268. See also C.L. I, pp. 170–171. Also A. II, p. 30.
380 12   December 10–14, 1799. C.L. I, p. 163. Cf. R.S.L. I, p. 297.
     13   Letter to Robert Lloyd, December 17, 1799. C.L. I, p. 166; Cf. letter to Thomas Manning, December 28, 1799. C.L. I, p. 168.
     14   Coleridge headed his letter "12 o'clock."

PAGE NOTE
380 15 L. I, p. 319.
     16 See O.T. I, pp. 183–189.
     17 In the *Morning Post*, December 24, 1799.
     18 L. I, pp. 319–320.
381 19 The poem appeared in the issue of July 9, 1798—the last issue of the *Anti-Jacobin*. Lepaux, a member of the Directory, was the leading Theophilanthropist.

In the September 1798 number of the *Anti-Jacobin Review and Magazine*—successor to the *Anti-Jacobin*—a parody of the *Ode to the Passions* entitled *The Anarchists: an Ode*, attacked the four men again:

> See! faithful to their mighty dam,
> C——dge, S——th–y, L——d, and L—b,
> In splay-foot madrigals of love,
> Soft moaning like the widow'd dove,
> Pour, side by side, their sympathetic notes;
> Of equal rights, and civic feasts,
> And tyrant kings, and knavish priests,
> Swift through the land the tuneful mischief floats.
> And now to softer strains they struck the lyre,
> They sung the beetle or the mole,
> The dying kid, or ass's foal,
> By cruel man permitted to expire.

     20 See B.Lit.A. I, p. 70 note. Also H.S. pp. 49–50. The complete addition was:

"Some of these youths were sadly corrupted in the *metropolis*, and initiated into the mysteries of Theophilanthropism, when scholars at that excellent seminary, Christ's Hospital. C——dge was nominated to an Exhibition at Cambridge, and the Vice-Master (soon after his admission) sent to him, on account of his non-attendance at chapel. This illuminated gentleman affected astonishment that any criminality could attach to him for his non-performance of religious worship, the trickery of Priestcraft, but if his presence was required, *pro forma*, as at a muster roll, he had no great objection to attend. To the disgrace of discipline, and a Christian University, this avowed Deist was not expelled for such sin. His equalising spirit and eccentricities have reduced this poetaster occasionally to such difficulties, that almost in want of bread he once addressed a soldier in the Park—'*Are you one of the cut-throats of the despot?*'—The man was at first astonished, but he soon found that his distress had determined him to enlist. His friends have frequently extricated him from this and other embarrassments. He has since married. . . ." etc.

     21 L. I, p. 320. Lloyd printed a 'Letter to the *Anti-Jacobin* Reviewers' in Birmingham in 1799, defending Lamb from the attacks—although Lamb may well be imagined as remaining

[510]

381 21 unconcerned alike by attack and defence. Southey had previously commented calmly enough on the subject in his letters of August 15 and 29, 1798, to C. W. W. Wynn and to his brother Tom respectively. R.S. I, pp. 344–347.

     22 L. I, p. 321.

382 23 Ibid.

     24 Ibid. Moshes is, of course, little Hartley.

     25 U.L. I, p. 130.

383 26 Ibid. I, p. 131.

     27 Ibid. I, pp. 131–132.

     28 T.P. I, p. 2.

384 29 Ibid. II, p. 1.

     30 Ibid. II, p. 2.

386 31 Ibid. II, pp. 2–4.

     32 Sent to the *Morning Post*, January 10, 1800. B.E. I, pp. 184–185.

     33 T.P. II, p. 4.

     34 Ibid. pp. 4–5—except that 'button' is substituted for the original 'louse.'

     35 February 14, 1800. T.P. II, p. 5.

387 36 Thomas Norton Longman, the publisher, 1771–1842.

     37 1770–1844. M.P. for Boroughbridge, 1796; for Westminster, 1807–37. See also A.P. pp. 174, 255.

     38 1767–1840. Founder of the *Monthly Magazine*. He was later satirized in *Lavengro* as the publisher for whom Borrow wrote up his 'Newgate lives and trials.' See *Lavengro* (Norwich Edn.), I, p. 308 et seq. See also A. II, pp. 131–133. L. I, pp. 325, 327.

     39 Sarah Wesley (1760–1828) daughter of Charles and niece of John and Samuel Wesley.

     40 Elizabeth Ogilvy Benger (1778–1827) writer and prominent figure in literary circles.

     41 1758–1800. Mistress of the Prince of Wales (later George IV). By this time, however, she had won a considerable reputation as a writer. See article *Coleridge and Mrs Mary Robinson*, by E. L. Griggs, *Modern Language Notes*, February 1830.

     42 1749–1806. Novelist and poetess; author of *The Old Manor House*.

     43 A. II, pp. 73–74.

     44 R. p. 429; B.E. I, p. 186.

     45 Ibid. In fact, Southey left before *Thalaba* was finished.

388 46 R. p. 430; B.E. I, pp. 186–187.

389 47 R. pp. 430–431; B.E. I, pp. 187–188.

     48 The *Gentleman's Magazine*, May 1938, p. 487.

     49 See O.T. C.M.V. pp. 49–50; M. pp. 106–107. See also *Coleridge*, by H. D. Traill, 1909, p. 80 (but Coleridge was not contributing until 'about Midsummer').

     50 *Brandl*, p. 257; C.M.V. p. 43; *Traill*, p. 76. See articles in the

389   50   *Athenaeum* for June 15 and August 31, 1861, by Ferdinand
           Freiligrath, describing the MSS.   See also *Die Wallensteinüber-*
           setzung von Samuel T. Coleridge und ihr deutsches Original . . .
           vorgelegt von Hans Roscher.   Borna-Leipzig, 1905.
      51   See list in M. p. 106 note 2.
390   52   See *Traill*, p. 81 et seq.   Traill writes soundly on this part of
           Coleridge's career, although his conclusions may be questioned.
      53   See, for example, W.H. VII, pp. 115–116, 122, 152, 217–219,
           237–238, 386; XI, pp. 34, 37–38; XVI, pp. 102–103, 108.   See
           also *The Friend*, No. 23, February 8, 1810, and W.H. XIV, pp.
           159, 188 and note; XVI, p. 263.   Cf. *The Political Thought of*
           Coleridge, by Harold Beeley, C.M.V. p. 151 et seq.   Also *The*
           Political Thought of S. T. Coleridge, edited R. J. White, 1938.
391   54   The *Morning Post*, December 31, 1799; O.T. I, p. 184.
      55   B.Lit.C. I, pp. 141–142.
392   56   Ibid. I, pp. 142–145; T.T. (1835 edition only) I, p. 173.
      57   The *Gentleman's Magazine*, May and June 1838.
      58   T.P. II. 5–6.
393   59   February 1800.   L.P. pp. 4–6.
      60   T.P. II, p. 6.
      61   C.M.V. p. 50.
394   62   February 4, 1800.   R. pp. 433–434; B.E. I, pp. 189–190.
      63   R. pp. 434–435; B.E. I, pp. 190–191.
      64   B.E. I, p. 191.
395   65   n.d. (February 1800).   L. I, p. 324.
      66   February 18, 1800.   L. I, p. 327.
      67   In the *Morning Post*, February 18, 1800.   O.T. II, p. 293.   See
           also O.T. III, pp. 1009–1019.
      68   See O.T. III, p. 1009; J.G. pp. 207–208, 211; also the *Gentleman's*
           Magazine, May 1838, pp. 487–488; C.M.V. p. 40; and Coleridge's
           MS. Notes of 1810, intended for the collection of political
           essays he had planned. "I. The Morning Chronicle contains
           Mr Pitt's real speech—the Morning Post *my* Speech, & as far as
           it differs from the former.—Before two o'clock Mr Stuart had
           received from 35 to 40 letters from Persons of more or less
           eminence, asking who had reported it.   One from Sir James
           Mackintosh—beginning—Who reported Pitt's speech, I have
           not heard any thing so much the Talk of the Kerb and of the
           Town for the last 6 months.
           "II. This Character (which I still think my happiest produc-
           tion) gave the first decisive momentum to the sale of the Morning
           Post.
           "This is the improved Copy, or Rifacimento carried down to
           the present Day of the Character that was promised 3 weeks
           together every day in the Morning Post.   Otto twice called on
           the Editor at the express command of the First Consul—he had
           been so much interested by the Character of Mr Pitt, which he

395 68 had ordered to be translated. This was the main cause of my obstinate refusal to publish it—and on that occasion I wrote a prophetic Letter to Mr Stuart, who had considered this anxiety of the First Consul's as a proof of his regard for the Press—I deduced from it, that he would become its bitterest enemy.— Thus my refusal joined with my Essays in the M. Post during the Peace of Amiens, brought my Life into jeopardy when I was at Rome. An order for my arrest came from Paris to Rome at 12 at night—by the Pope's goodness I was off by one—and the arrest of all the English took place at six.—" Cf. *Journals of Caroline Fox*, 1882, I, pp. 122-123.

      69 A fairly full analysis of the business relations of Stuart and Coleridge will be found in C.M.V. p. 42 et seq.; and in M. p. 106 et seq. See also the *Gentleman's Magazine*, May and June 1838.

      70 February 22, 1800. T.P. II, p. 6.

396 71 Ibid.

      72 March 1800. O.T. I, p. xci (but £350 printed there in error). See also M, p. 107; B.E. I, pp. 191–192.

      73 See Note 69. Also *London Mercury*, April 1931, p. 564.

397 74 "In March," wrote Sarah to her sister Mary (Mrs Lovell), " I and the child left him [Coleridge] in London, and proceeded to Kempsford in Gloucestershire, the Rectory of Mr Roskilly; remained there a month. Papa was to have joined us there, but did not." See also Coleridge's letter of congratulation to Roskilly on his promotion. Both printed in L. I, p. 267.

      75 Letter of Coleridge to Robert Southey, February 1800. L. I, p. 326.

      76 Letter to Coleridge, January 21, 1800. T.P. II, p. 5. See also letter from Coleridge to Southey, February 1800. L. I, p. 326.

      77 L.P. p. 4.

      78 Ibid.

      79 C.L. I, p. 168.

      80 Thomas Manning (1772–1840). At this time private tutor in mathematics at Cambridge. Became a great friend of Lamb. See *The Letters of Thomas Manning to Charles Lamb*, edited by Mrs Anderson, 1925, and Lamb's *The Old and The New School-master*.

      81 C.L. I, pp. 168–169. "The philosopher" was the child Hartley.

      82 See letter from Sophia Lloyd (née Pemberton) to Manning, January 26, 1800. *The Letters of Thomas Manning to Charles Lamb*. "I was introduced to Coleridge," wrote Manning to Robert Lloyd soon after the event, "which was a great gratification to me. I think him a man of very splendid abilities and animated feelings." C. LL, p. 111.

      83 C.LL. p. 77 et seq.

398 84 January 25, 1800. L. I, p. 323.

      85 Ibid. I, p. 322.

398   86   Ibid. I, pp. 322–323.

       87   See *The Letters of Thomas Manning to Charles Lamb* and Lamb's letter to Manning, February 8, 1800, C.L. I, p. 171. The 'lye' was that Coleridge had told Caldwell, his old Cambridge friend, now Fellow and Tutor of Jesus, that he had no engagements with the newspapers.

399   88   February 8, 1800. C.L. I, pp. 170–171.

       89   A turkey Manning had sent Lamb. See C.L. I, p. 170.

       90   C.L. I, p. 172.

       91   March 9, 1800. *The Letters of Thomas Manning to Charles Lamb.*

400   92   C.L. I, p. 172.

       93   Ibid.

       94   March 1800. T.P. II, p. 7.

       95   W.G. II, p. 2.

401   96   C.L. I, p. 178.

       97   It is stated in H.S. p. 233 that Southey embarked on the Lisbon packet at Falmouth on April 2, 1800; but the letter to Coleridge from which a quotation is made on the same page and which is dated April 1, at Bristol, begins: "The day of our departure is now definitely fixed. We leave Bristol next week, on Thursday." R.S. II, p. 53. Cf. R.S.L. I, p. 108.

       98   L. I, pp. 321, 329; R.S. II. p. 35. H.S. p. 203.

       99   Letter of Coleridge to Robert Southey, n.d. (before January 25, 1800). L. I, p. 329; H.S. p. 203.

402   100   February 1800. L. I, p. 325. Coleridge hopes that Southey will "write a novel on that subject of yours! I mean the 'Rise and Progress of a *Laugher*'—Le Grice in your eye—the effect of Laughing on taste, manners, morals, and happiness!"

       101   Ibid. It is possible that Coleridge was speaking with experience, and that he had already "tossed up" a novel in his early Bristol days, if the MS. *The Son of Robespierre*, discovered by Mr Douglas Cleverdon of Bristol, assisted by Dr Walter Peck, proves to be the work of Coleridge.

       102   January 1800. L. I, pp. 329–330.

       103   December 9, 1799. L. I, p. 315.

       104   December 24, 1799. L. I, p. 319; H.S. p. 205.

       105   Ibid. See also E.R. II, pp. 26–27.

       106   L. I, p. 319.

       107   January 1800. L. I, p. 330. The proposed 'History of Levellers,' Coleridge refers to elsewhere as 'the Jacobin Book.' L. I, p. 325.

       108   Letter from Southey to Coleridge, February 15, 1800; and from Coleridge to Southey in reply, February 1800. L. I, p. 324; C.M.V. p. 47; H.S. p. 205.

       109   December 24, 1799. L. I, p. 319.

403   110   C.M.V. p. 47; H.S. p. 204. Profiting by Coleridge's admiration

403 110 of the poem, Southey made up his mind to ask at least £100 for the first edition only. H.S. p. 205.

111 February 1800. L. I, p. 325.

112 C.M.V. p. 47. (But it was Phillips, not Longman, who was willing to consider the idea.)

113 February 18, 1800. L. I, p. 327.

114 R.S.L. I, p. 98; H.S. p. 205.

115 February 28, 1800. L. I, p. 331.

116 H.S. p. 206.

117 February 28, 1800. L. I, p. 331.

118 Unpublished letter to Coleridge, February 15, 1800. L. I, p. 328 note; H.S. p. 206.

119 February 18, 1800. L. I, p. 328.

404 120 The donor was Peter Elmsley, an old school friend. R.S.L. I, p.102.

121 December 9, 1799. L. I, p. 315.

122 Ibid. I, pp. 315–316.

123 Ibid I, p. 316.

124 January 25, 1800. L. I, p. 323.

125 February 28, 1800. L. I, p. 332.

126 Letter from Coleridge to Robert Southey, January 25, 1800. L. I, p. 323.

405 127 Ibid. I, pp. 323–324.

128 L. I, p. 326.

129 *Traill*, p. 85; M. p. 108.

130 March 1, 1800. U.L. I, pp. 135–136.

131 Ibid. I, p. 136.

132 Ibid.

133 Ibid. I, p. 135.

406 134 Ibid. I, pp. 136–137.

135 Ibid. I, p. 137.

136 Letter to Robert Southey, February, 1800. L. I, p. 326.

137 Letter to Robert Southey. L. I, p. 321.

138 Letter to Robert Southey, January 25, 1800. L. I, p. 323.

139 Letter to Robert Southey, February 1800. L. I, p. 325.

140 Ibid. I, pp. 325–326.

141 Ibid. I, p. 326.

407 142 Ibid.

143 February 14, 1800. T.P. II, p. 5.

144 Ibid. II, p. 6.

145 March 1800. From a letter in the B.M. T.P. II, p. 7; H. p. 306 note; C.M.V. p. 48. Cf. Note 74, Chapter IX; Notes 52 and 58, Chapter XII.

146 T.P. II, p. 7. See also W.H. XVII, p. 117. Cf. *Early Years and Late Reflections*, I, p. 198: "When we have sometimes spoken complimentarily to Coleridge of himself, he has said that he was nothing in comparison with him [Wordsworth]."

408 147 T.P. II, p. 8.

408 148 T.P. II, p. 8.

149 Ibid. II, p. 9.

409 150 April 5, 1800.   C.L. I, p. 179.

151 Letter to Daniel Stuart, n.d.   L.P. p. 7.

152 March 1800.   From a letter in the B.M.   C.M.V. p. 49; H. p. 306 note.

153 Letter from Wordsworth to Coleridge, December 24, 1799. W.L. I, p. 234 et seq.

154 Ibid. I, p. 235.   Wordsworth refers to two letters from Coleridge already at Dove Cottage when he and Dorothy arrived. One of these read: "As to myself, I dedicate my nights and days to Stuart."   Then, anxious that Wordsworth's genius should neither rest nor run again into a multitude of small poems "By all means let me have the tragedy and 'Peter Bell' as soon as possible."   Two months later, his anxiety by no means allayed by what he has heard from Grasmere: "I grieve that 'The Recluse' sleeps."   M.W. II, p. 160.   But nothing short of a personal visit would set Wordsworth to full work again upon his masterpiece-to-be—so, at least, and with some reason, Coleride would argue; thus making possible the fulfilment of the desire that burned in him, under cover of the sense of necessity so dear to his heart and so essential to the preservation of his self-respect.

155 See the very favourable review in the *British Critic*, November 1799 (probably written by Wrangham).

410 156 W.L. I, p. 242.

157 Ibid. I, pp. 242–243.

158 M. p. 112.   "While I was translating the 'Wallenstein,'" Coleridge wrote W. Southeby, "I told Longman it would never answer; when I had finished it I wrote to him and foretold that it would be waste paper on his shelves."   September 10, 1802. L. I, p. 403.

159 M. p. 112.

160 Told to Mr Justice Coleridge in September 1836.   W.W. III, p. 428; J.D.C. p. 646.

161 Letter to Josiah Wedgwood, July 24, 1800.   R. p. 437; T.W. p. 104; B.E. I, p. 199.   Cf. Coleridge's MS. Notes, P. II, pp. 598–599.

162 A. I, p. 96.

163 *Brandl*, pp. 257–258.   See also *London Mercury*, April 1931, p. 564.   See the Preface affixed to *The Death of Wallenstein* for Coleridge's reasons for leaving *The Camp* untranslated. J.D.C. p. 305; P. II, p. 724.

164 See, for example, the Preface to the second edition of the *Lyrical Ballads*, of which Coleridge himself claimed part authorship (see Note 4, Chapter X), where "sickly and stupid German Tragedies" are condemned as panders to the modern craving for

410 164 "extraordinary incident." See also Coleridge's own recantation or apologia below.

411 165 In the October issue. *Brandl*, p. 263.

166 November 18, 1800. B.E. I, pp. 218–219; *Brandl*, pp. 263–264.

167 *Brandl*, p. 264; *Traill*, pp. 75–76.

168 F.A. I, pp. 203–204; III, p. 343; Lockhart's *Life of Scott*, IV, p. 193; Carlyle's *Life of Schiller*, Centenary Edition, 1899, XXV, pp. ix and 151 note; A. I, p. 96; *Brandl*, p. 264; *Traill*, pp. 76–77. See also Hazlitt's reference to it in *The Spirit of the Age*, 1825, as a "masterly production . . . faithful and spirited," W.H. XI, p. 35. *Coleridge's Wallensteinübersetzung*, by P. Machule, *Englische Studien*, 1902, XXXI, pp. 182–239, compares Coleridge's translation with the original in detail. Cf. *Leigh Hunt*, by Edmund Blunden, 1930, p. 134.

412 169 April 16–17, 1800. C.L. I, p. 184. Coleridge's 'shadows' had in one sense assumed a somewhat disconcerting reality; for, in his stead, Lamb was being shadowed by Coleridge's admirers, the Misses Benger and Wesley—"a tribe of authoresses"—in the hope of having their "nonsense put into a nonsensical Anthology." C.L. I, p. 184. But Miss Wesley, having wheedled Coleridge's address from Lamb, would not be satisfied with a substitute and continued her campaign upon the principal by post.

170 Some thirteen miles, in fact, by way of Dunmail Raise.

171 U.L. I, p. 138; B.E. I, pp. 193–194; W.G. II, p. 3.

172 U.L. I, p. 138; B.E. I, p. 194; W.G. II, p. 3.

413 173 On May 17 and 24, letters from Coleridge were received by Dorothy; on June 2 she started enquiring at Ambleside for lodgings for the Coleridges. Coleridge did at least look over the Porlock neighbourhood, according to his letter of June 12, 1800, to Josiah Wedgwood from Bristol, portions of which are quoted in T.W. p. 93.

174 April 16–17, 1800. C.L. I, p. 187.

175 W.G. I, pp. 357–358.

176 May 21, 1800. U.L. I, pp. 137–138; B.E. I, pp. 193–194; W.G. II, p. 3.

177 May 12, 1800. C.L. I, p. 188.

414 178 May 21, 1800. U.L. I, p. 138; B.E. I, p. 194; W.G. II, p. 3.

179 Ibid.

180 May 21, 1800. U.L. I, pp. 138–139; B.E. I, pp. 194–195; W.G. II, p. 4.

181 May 21, 1800. U.L. I, p. 139; B.E. I, p. 195; W.G. II, p. 4.

182 June 1800. U.L. I, p. 140. Nevertheless 'Perdita' died at the end of December of this year.

183 June 1800. U.L. I, p. 140; B.E. I, p. 196.

415 184 U.L. I, pp. 140–141; B.E. I, p. 197.

185 L.P. p. 7. Coleridge was still expecting to return to London

[517]

415 185 within the week when he wrote to Josiah Wedgwood on
April 21, 1800, from Grasmere.
186 July 11, 1800. L.P. pp. 7–8.
187 L.P. p. 8.
188 U.L. I, p. 140.
416 189 Letter to Josiah Wedgwood, July 24, 1800. R. p. 436; T.W.
p. 103; B.E., I, p. 198. Cf. Letter of Coleridge to Godwin,
October 16, 1800, printed in *Mary Shelley* by R. Glynn Grylls,
1937, p. 368.

INDEX

ACHARD, F. C., (501)

ACTON near Bristol, suggested by Poole as a more suitable place for Coleridge to live than Stowey, 139; Coleridge's loathing of the idea, 140

Ad Lyram, Casimir, translated by Coleridge, 32; and lost, 50

Addressed to a Young Jackass and its Tether'd Mother, Coleridge, published *Morning Chronicle*, 62 (436)

Addressed to a Young Man of Fortune who abandoned Himself to an Indolent and Causeless Melancholy, Coleridge, sonnet to Charles Lloyd, convalescent after epilepsy, 135, (456); gives offence, 215

ADELUNG, Johann Christoph, "The first of the Lexicographers," 332

ADSCOMBE near Stowey, Coleridge's wish to take a house there, 131, 139, 140

AISHOLT in the Quantocks, possible house for Coleridge found there by Poole, 384

AKENSIDE, Mark, signs of the new simplicity in his poems, 26; admired by Coleridge, 137; projected edition, (455)

ALFOXDEN, "A large mansion in a large park" (Dorothy Wordsworth) some three miles from Stowey, discovered by Wordsworths, 157, (460); Coleridge persuades Poole to arrange that it shall be let cheaply to the Wordsworths, 161-162; 198; the move in and D. W.'s description, 203-204, (467), 206; Thelwall's visit the final cause of Wordsworth's tenancy being ended, 207, 208,

211; trouble with landlord, 214; knowledge that the lease will not be renewed intensifies the pleasure of the last months, 241, 244-245; 262; Cottle visits it, 264-265, (484-486); Hazlitt visits it, 265, 267, 271; the Wordsworths leave it for ever, 284, 363; 387; Coleridge tries to lure them back, 406, 407, and fails, 409, 412

ALHADRA, character from Coleridge's tragedy, *Osorio*, 214

Allegro, L', Milton, 368

ALLEN, Catherine, sister-in-law of the Wedgwoods, m. Sir James Mackintosh, (474)

ALLEN, Robert, at Christ's Hospital with Coleridge, 18, (422), 22, 23, 24; at Oxford, 32; introduces Coleridge to Southey and Stoddart, 41; and pantisocracy, 42, from which he is a backslider, 45, (430), (433); reports to Coleridge Tuckett's prophecies of *The Watchman's* failure, 99

ALLSOP, Thomas, (417)

ANALYTICAL REVIEW, (447), (494). See REVIEWS

Ancient Mariner and Christabel, The, ed. A. Eichler, (494)

Ancient Mariner, The, opens Coleridge's great period, 219; evidence of exact date, (472); origins, 219-220, 253-255, (481-482); appreciation, 245, 255-257, 260, 261; 374, (474); Mrs Barbauld and the moral, 256, (482); given to Cottle for inclusion in the *Lyrical Ballads*, 265, 268; failure to collaborate with Wordsworth in the writing of it, 219-220, 271; published: its quality completely unappreciated by reviewers and public, 287, 291; mention in the preface to the first edition, 288-289; *Peter Bell's* relation to it, (493); its solitary place in the book, 289-290; the complete achievement of its declared purpose, 290; Wordsworth talks of omitting it from the second edition, 365; his criticism of and apology for it and Lamb's reproaches, (506); Lamb takes Southey to task for his adverse review of it, 378-379, (509)

ANDREWS, James Petit, his *History of England* (*History of Great Britain connected with the chronology of Europe*) to be used in the projected scissors-and-paste *History of Levellers*, 402

Anecdote for Fathers, Wordsworth, (465)

ANGEL, THE, inn in London, close to Christ's Hospital, Coleridge lodges there, 50, 72

Anima Poetae, ed. E. H. Coleridge, (418)

Annual Anthology, a miscellany of poems by Southey and his friends, Coleridge to contribute to the second number, 355; Humphry Davy a contributor, 361; *Lines to W. L. while he sang a Song to Purcell's music* first printed in this, (469-470); Coleridge decides *Christabel* is unsuitable for inclusion—and in fact has not finished it, 362, 371; 380; he contributes fourteen poems and several epigrams, 389

Anti-Jacobin, The, later the *Anti-Jacobin Review and Magazine*, contains *The New Morality*, a poem which attacks Coleridge, Southey, Lamb, and Lloyd, 380-381, (510); condemns *Wallenstein*, 411

Apology for the Bible, Watson, (464)

ARCHAIC FORMS IN FIRST VERSION OF *The Ancient Mariner*, 256

ARKWRIGHT, Sir Richard, predecessor of Jedediah Strutt of Derby, 97

ASHE, T., (418)

ASPHETERISM, word coined by Coleridge and defined by Southey as "the generalization of individual property," 43, (431); Coleridge aspheterizes, 43, 44, 50, 62; aspheterism in Coleridge's lectures, 76; difficulties in practical application: Southey rebels at supporting "indefinitely an eternally loquacious Coleridge," 78-80

ATHANASIOPHAGOUS, word coined by Coleridge to mean "devouring Immortality by anticipation," 383

Athenaeum, The, (444), (452), (512)

Autobiography, Leigh Hunt, (422), (423)

AYNARD, J. (476)

BACON, Lord, (467), 358

BAKER, James, (444)

BALA, Coleridge, on a walking tour with Hucks, writes *On Bala Hill* here, 44

BANFILL, Mr, "a pleasant man," 356

BARBAULD, Anna Letitia, (Mrs), visited by Coleridge at Bristol, 211, (468); complains that *The Ancient Mariner* has no moral, 256; Coleridge's answer, (482); in London, 387; praise from Coleridge, 406

BARR, Mr, advises against attempting to sell *The Watchman* at Worcester, 93

BATESON, H. D. (494)

BATH, Southey's mother at, 57, 67, 70; Coleridge preaches badly at, 117

BAXTER, Richard, "old Baxter," 298

BEATTY, Arthur, (463)

BEAUPUY, Michel, Wordsworth's friend, 167, (463), 182

[520]

Beauties of the 'Anti-Jacobin,' The. See *The New Morality*, 381

BEDDOES, Dr, of Bristol, contributes to Poole's annual subscription for Coleridge, (449); passes on suggestion that Coleridge might become assistant editor of the *Morning Chronicle*, 118-119, (450); called in for Lloyd's epilepsy, 134, and for Thomas Wedgwood, 222; establishes the Pneumatic Institute for relieving Diseases by Medicated Airs, 360-361; 383

BEDFORD, Grosvenor, friend of Southey, to whom Coleridge explains pantisocracy, 51; letter from Southey, 77, (488)

BEELEY, Harold, (512)

BEHMEN, see BOEHME, Jacob

BELL, John, an English publisher who owned the copyright of *Wallenstein* and sold it to Longman, 389, 410

Belle Dame sans Merci, La, John Keats. The greater successor to Coleridge's *Love*, 374

BENGER, Elizabeth Ogilvy, meets Coleridge in London, 387, (511); pursues him, (517)

BENTHAM, Jeremy, (495)

BERDMORE, a Jesus man, met (with Brookes) on the Welsh walking tour, 44; climbs Penmaenmawr with Coleridge: "You grinned like an idiot," 46; spreads Coleridge's opinions on pantisocracy "in mangled forms" at Cambridge, 53

BERKELEY, George, Bishop of Cloyne, influence of his thought on Coleridge at Cambridge, 65; his doctrines incorporated in Coleridge's lectures, 76; hailed in *Religious Musings*, 105, (448), and in conversation with Hazlitt and his father, 235-236, and (but that they were never written) in the last of the six *Hymns to the*

Elements, (455); Coleridge calls his second son after him, 276-277

Betty Foy (The Idiot Boy), Wordsworth. Coleridge reads it to Hazlitt, 265

BIBLIOGRAPHIES, (420)

BIGGS, Nathaniel, a partner of Cottle, and the printer of the privately printed pamphlets of 1796, which Coleridge finds difficulty in paying for, 152-153; £5 still owing, 229; Wordsworth supervises his printing of the *Lyrical Ballads*, 284, (488)

Biographia Epistolaris, ed. A. Turnbull, (417)

Biographia Literaria, Coleridge, (418), (476); commendation of Wordsworth's *Guilt and Sorrow*, 170; poetic diction, (493); (497)

BIRDLIPSCH, Count, expedition to his castle, 351

BIRMINGHAM, Coleridge there on *The Watchman* tour: the tallow chandler, 93-97; he preaches there, 122, (450); 129; a party, 236; Lloyd there, 282

BLACKWOOD, William, 268

BLAKE, William, and prosody, (494)

Blank Verse, projected volume of poems by Lamb and Lloyd, 277

BLIZARD, Sir William, of the London Hospital at which Luke Coleridge trained, 20

BLOIS, Annette Vallon's home, Wordsworth there, 168; she returns there as Mme Williams, with Caroline, 177

BLUMENBACH, Johann Friedrich, brother-in-law of Brandes, governor of Göttingen, 330; lectures on natural history, 332; his son goes to the Hartz Mountains with Coleridge and the Parrys, 341, 342; "flattering attentions" to Coleridge, 344; farewell party, 352, (502); Coleridge thinks of translating his *Manual of Natural History*, 414

BLUNDEN, Edmund,(418),(423),(517)

BOEHME, Jacob, influence of his Christian mysticism on Coleridge at Cambridge, 65; Coleridge acknowledges his debt to him, 106; (455), 295; he reverts to the writings of Boehme and the mystics, 301; "all Schelling had said he had thought out for himself, or found in Jacob Boehme," 311

Borderers, The, tragedy by Wordsworth, read to Coleridge on first visit to Racedown, 155, (460); his unmeasured praise of it, 156, (460), and the value of this praise to Wordsworth, 190-191; important as a key to Wordsworth's development—a Godwinian purging, 189-190; imitated by Coleridge in *Osorio*, 195; sent to Harris of Covent Garden, 214; rejected, 220; plan that Cottle should publish it abandoned, 263-264

BORROW, George, (511)

BOWDEN (or BOWDON), Anne, Coleridge's mother. See COLERIDGE, Anne

BOWDEN, Anne, 1st cousin of Coleridge, m. Edward, Coleridge's brother, (427)

BOWDEN, John, Coleridge's uncle who befriended him during his schooldays, 16, 17, 18, 27

BOWLES, The Rev. W. L., author of *Sonnets . . . on picturesque spots*; influence on Coleridge, 24-25, (424), 26; still admired by Coleridge in 1794, 63; Lamb's memories of his "repeating one of Bowles' sweetest sonnets," 71; some of his sonnets included in a privately printed collection, 1796, 131; attacked by Thelwall as Della Cruscan but admired by Coleridge, 137; Cole-

ridge's proposed essay on him, (453); (454); visit to Bowles at Shaftesbury prevented by Coleridge's unwillingness to leave Racedown, 156; influence on Wordsworth's early poetry, 166, (426); postponed visit (Sept. 1797) not very successful, 212, (did Coleridge take *Osorio* with him? 469); no more echoes of his poetry in Coleridge's by 1798, 256

Bowles, sonnet by Coleridge, 1794, published *Morning Chronicle*, 63, (437)

BOYER, The Rev. James, Upper grammar master of Christ's Hospital, influence on Coleridge: strict but sensible, 19, (423), 20; valuable training in the virtues of poetic simplicity, 24, 26; intervention on Coleridge's behalf after his enlistment, 38

BRADLEY, A. C., (420), (480), (488)

BRAHMIN CREED, "at other times I adopt the Brahmin creed," 214

BRAILSFORD, H. N., (464)

BRANDES, VON, Secretary of State and Governor of Göttingen University, 330

BRANDL, Alois, (438), (499), (500), (503), (511), (516), (517)

BRAY, Coleridge stays with Charles Clagget after his discharge from the army, 40

BRIDGES, R., (494)

BRIDGWATER, 145; Coleridge preaches there, 150, (457), (474), 154; suggestion that Thelwall should take lodgings there, 210; (479), 270, 336

BRISSOT, J. P., Coleridge quotes his *New Travels* in *Conciones ad Populum*, (434)

BRISTOL, Southey and Burnett walk there, elaborating pantisocracy, 43; arrival of Coleridge from walking tour, introduction to Frickers,

46, 49; 57; Coleridge's delays in returning there to see Sarah Fricker, 62, 66; return, 66-67; escape and further hesitations, 70; Southey fetches him back, 72-86; their joint lodgings, 73, (440), 78, abandoned, 82; marriages at St. Mary's, Redcliffe: Coleridge's, 85-86, Southey's, 89; the Coleridges return from Clevedon: advantage, nearness to library and friends, disadvantage, stepmother, 90; Coleridge reluctant to leave Bristol for London, 118-119; 120; he walks there from Stowey to see Mrs Barbauld, 211; the Wedgwoods there, seeking a cure for Thomas, 1797, 222; Coleridge walks there with Hazlitt, 270; Wordsworth looks for Lloyd there, 282; 284, 285, 308; "The Bristol library is a hum and will do us little good," 324; Sarah Coleridge there with Berkeley: he dies there, 324-325, 334; Coleridge there, 362-363; his dislike of it, 384

British Critic, The, condemns *Wallenstein,* 411; (516)

BROCKEN, sunrise from the, 352, (503)

Brook, The, projected poem by Coleridge, 209, 216, 217, 219

BROOKE, Stopford, (476)

BROOKES, a Jesus man met (with Berdmore) on the Welsh walking tour, 44, 46; spread Coleridge's opinions on pantisocracy "in mangled forms" at Cambridge, 53

BRONTË FAMILY, and local background, 13

BRÜCKER, Johann Jakob, his works to be used in the proposed scissors-and-paste History of the Levellers, 402

BRUNO, Giordano: Coleridge and Bruno, 301; projected life, (502)

BRUNTON, Miss, of Norwich, comes to Cambridge with a theatrical company: Coleridge dedicates *To a Young Lady* to her, and tries in her company to forget his Evans-Fricker troubles, 54, 56

BULLER, Francis, later Judge, old pupil of Coleridge's father, who helps Coleridge to a presentation to Christ's Hospital, 16, (422)

BURDETT, Sir Francis, meets Coleridge in London, 1799: they retreat to his house at Wimbledon from the gross conversation of Tooke and his friends, 387, (511)

BÜRGER, Gottfried August, 332

BURKE, Edmund, Coleridge "repeats whole pages verbatim" (Le Grice) from his pamphlets at Cambridge, 33; compares him favourably with Mackintosh, 233-234, and with Fox and Pitt, but unfavourably with Jeremy Taylor, 269

Burke, sonnet by Coleridge, 1794, published *Morning Chronicle,* 62, (436)

BURKE, Thomas, his *Reflections on the French Revolution,* (474)

BURNETT, George, friend of Southey: helps to hatch pantisocracy, 42, (430); walking tour, 43; 47; probably not the link between Coleridge and Thomas Poole, (432-433); lodges with Coleridge and Southey at Bristol, 73; bewildered by Southey's wholesale modifications of pantisocracy, 80, 82, 89; lives with the Coleridges at Clevedon, and tries to marry Martha Fricker, 87; dependent on Coleridge, 102; ill with jaundice at Huntspill, 153; his pathetic attachment to the corpse of pantisocracy, 153-154, (458); constant visitor at Stowey, 154; "agreeable, well-informed, and of a very benevolent turn of mind" (Reynell), (469); takes post as Unitarian minister at Yarmouth, (470); financial position, 406

BURNS, Robert, unknown to Coleridge in 1789, 25, 26

BURTON, Richard, Coleridge proposes Burton imitation to Lamb, 401

BUSSIÈRE, Georges, (463)

BUTLER, Samuel, father of the novelist, wins Craven Scholarship over Coleridge's head, 1793, 31, (427)

BUTLER, Joseph, Bishop of Durham, commended by Coleridge, 236; his theory of disinterestedness, 270

BYRON, Lord, 287

CALDWELL, George, of Jesus College, Cambridge, jeers at pantisocracy, 53, (434); with the Bruntons, 54; false rumour that Coleridge told him he had no newspaper engagements, 399, (514)

Caleb Williams, by William Godwin, not appreciated by Coleridge, 269

CALVERT, Raisley, whom Wordsworth nursed: died leaving Wordsworth £900, 175; lent Wordsworth Windy Brow near Keswick, (464)

CALVERT, William, brother of above, to whom Wordsworth acted as travelling companion, (464)

CAM, Miss Helen, research into the relationship of Coleridge, Southey, and the Poole family, (432)

CAMBRIDGE, Coleridge appointed to an exhibition at Jesus College, 27; in residence, 29-35, 40-41, 52-62, 69-70; Tuckett there, 36; Coleridge bemoans irregularities in his routine there, 37; his mental life there, (1) pantisocracy, (2) the struggle between Voltaire and Darwin, and Plato and the Neo-Platonists, 64-65; authorities restive at his absence, 66, (438); his name removed from the boards, (439); Wordsworth at, 164-165;

166; Coleridge plans to walk there every summer vacation so as to have access to libraries, 324

Cambridge Intelligencer, Flower's, advertisements of the projected Imitations in, (429) from 40; (434); suggested by Coleridge to readers as a substitute, after The Watchman's failure, 111; the Ode to the Departing Year sent for publication, 144, (456)

CAMDEN, William, 1551–1623, 375, (508)

Camp, The, Schiller, 410, (516)

CAMPBELL, J. Dykes, (417), (452), (486)

CANTHARADIZE, word coined by Coleridge, 46

CARLYLE, Thomas, (474), (517)

CARLYON, Clement, author of Early Years and Late Reflections, at Göttingen with a travelling scholarship from Pembroke College, Cambridge, 331, (499), (500); in Hartz mountains, 341-342, (501); lends Coleridge money, 348; ready to go to Scandinavia, 351-352, (502); (424)

CASIMIR, Coleridge translates his Ad Lyram, 32, and plans to translate "a copious selection" of his works, (429); loses it, 50, (434)

CASSEL, 351

CASTLE BARNARD, Lakes walking tour, 368

Castle Spectre, The, by Matthew Gregory Lewis, play seen at Bristol by Wordsworth, 267

CATO, essays on Liberty and Necessity in his Letters read by Coleridge at Christ's Hospital: these first arouse his interest in Neo-Platonism, 21, (423)

CESTRE, C., (463)

CHAMBERS, E. K., (472)

Character of Pitt, Coleridge's most successful contribution to the Morning Post, 1800, 405, (512)

Charles Lamb and his Contemporaries, Edmund Blunden, (423)
Charles Lamb and the Lloyds, ed. E. V. Lucas, (419)
Charles! My Slow Heart, Coleridge, sonnet to the child Hartley, (462)
CHEDDAR, visited by Coleridge and the Wordsworths, (479); the suggestion that this visit to the gorge is reflected in *Kubla Khan*, (483-484)
CHESTER, John, native of Nether Stowey, (478), friend of Coleridge, 267, 268, 270; goes to Germany with Coleridge, 285, 313, 314, 319, 320, 325, 328, 329, 341, 352, (503)
Christabel, evidence of exact date, (472); (474), (481), 245, 253; analysis and appreciation, 256-259, (483), 261; the Lloyd controversy blamed for its unfinished state, (483); intended for the first edition of the *Lyrical Ballads*, 290; (494), (499); not progressing: Coleridge decides that even if finished it would be unsuitable for Southey's *Annual Anthology*, 362, 371
CHRISTIANITY, a suggested cause of its easy propagation, 346
Christian Reformer, The, (474), (475)
CHRIST'S HOSPITAL, Coleridge admitted to, 16, 17; Coleridge at, 18-27; old Christ's Hospital friends at Cambridge, 32; some of the Grecians tell Tuckett of Coleridge's enlistment, 36; Coleridge enthuses the younger boys with the idea of pantisocracy, 50; news of Mary Evans through Christ's Hospital boys, 66; Favell at, 71; (421); Coleridge's exhibition suspended, (438-439)
Christ's Hospital Five-and-Thirty Years Ago, Lamb, (422), (423), (424)
CLAGGET, Charles, sets four of Coleridge's lyrics to music and suggests that he should write an opera, 40, (429)
CLARKSON, William, of Eusemere, friend of Wordsworth, 373
CLAUDE LORRAIN, landscape painter, 269
CLEVEDON, on the Bristol Channel, Aug. 1795, Coleridge rents a cottage there, 82; Oct. 1795, Coleridge and Sarah, newly married, live there for a few weeks only, 85-90; 209
CLEVERDON, Douglas, (514)
COATES, John, Unitarian minister in Birmingham, (444)
Coleridge and Christ's Hospital, Edmund Blunden, (423)
Coleridge and S.T.C., Stephen Potter, (474)
COLERIDGE, Anne, (born Bowden or Bowdon, 421), Coleridge's mother, 11, 14, 15, 16; he visits her at Ottery and is received "with transports," 120; a less successful visit, 356
COLERIDGE, Anne (Nancy), his sister, dies 1791, 27, (426)
Coleridge as a Poet, Dowden, (476)
Coleridge as Philosopher, John H. Muirhead, (418)
COLERIDGE, Berkeley, second son and child, born 1798, 276-277, 281, (487); called after George Berkeley, 300; illness, 321, 324, 325; death, 333-341; not forgotten by his mother, 346, (501)
COLERIDGE, David Hartley, first child, born 1796, 123; Coleridge writes three sonnets to mother and child, 124, (450); not baptized, 124, (451); as a baby, 136, 140, 146, 150, 152, (468), (469); in his father's poems, 248, 252, (481); named after the philosopher, 296; Coleridge homesick for him, 321; remains as a consolation after Berkeley's death, 335; 340; Coleridge fears for his safety, 341, 344-

345; Hartley has the itch, 357-359; laughs at Southey's letter, 359; to London, 378; his father talks of him in letters, 382, (511), 392, 404, 413; visit to Kempsford, 397, 400; to the Lakes, 416

COLERIDGE, Edward, second surviving brother, visited by Coleridge at Salisbury, 33, (427)

COLERIDGE, Ernest Hartley, (417), (483), (486)

COLERIDGE, Francis Snydercombe, the brother next older than Coleridge; trouble over cheese, 14

COLERIDGE, George, third surviving brother, 13; in London, 1785, 18, 27; as correspondent and mentor of Coleridge, 30, 31, 32, 34, 40, 61, 62; second edition of *Poems on Various Subjects* dedicated to him, but ill received, 158, (462); letter from Coleridge defending himself against the charge of harbouring republican sentiments, 272-276; visit from Coleridge at Ottery, 276; another visit: "Alas we have neither tastes nor feelings in common," 356

COLERIDGE, G. H. B., (483), (486)

COLERIDGE, Henry Nelson, (418)

COLERIDGE, James, oldest surviving brother, "the Colonel," visited by Coleridge at Tiverton, 1793, 33, (427); and at Ottery, 356

COLERIDGE, The Rev. John, Coleridge's father, vicar of Ottery and master of the grammar school, 11; author of *Critical Latin Grammar*, friendship with Coleridge, who was his Benjamin and resembled him, 15, 16; death, 1781, 16, (421)

COLERIDGE, John, Coleridge's grandfather, weaver and/or woollen draper of Crediton, 11

COLERIDGE, John Taylor, (496)

COLERIDGE, Lord, K.C., author of *The Story of a Devonshire House*, (421)

COLERIDGE, Luke, fourth surviving brother, trains at the London Hospital, 20; dies 1790, 27, (426)

Coleridge on Imagination, I. A. Richards, (476)

Coleridge on Logic and Learning, Alice D. Snyder, (476)

COLERIDGE, Samuel Taylor, his birth at Ottery, 1772, 11; his family, 11, (421); the childhood of a Benjamin, 11-16; early reading and education, 12-13; trouble over cheese: Coleridge's night by river bank a probable cause of later ill-health, 14-15; relationship with his father, and the latter's death, 15-16; his mother obtains presentation to Christ's Hospital, 1782, 16; introduction to London, 17; was Coleridge unhappy at school? 17-18; day-dreams in the Strand, 18; his school-friends— Lamb, etc., 18; his schoolmaster— Boyer: Coleridge profits by his strictness, 19, and by his drastic training in poetic simplicity, 24; becomes a Grecian, 19; first poems—*Genevieve* (? to daughter of his dormitory 'Nurse'), 19, *Monody on the Death of Chatterton* (in Boyer's album, 1787), 20; ill-health, 20; decision to be a cobbler, 20, a doctor, 20; interest in metaphysics—the Neo-Platonists—in theology and atheism— Voltaire and Darwin, 21; atheism cured by a flogging from Boyer, 22; his schooldays as pictured in Lamb's two essays, 22; introduction to the Evans family, and Coleridge's friendship with Mary Evans, 22-23; *The Nose, an Odaic Rhapsody*, 23; Bowles' *Sonnets* ... *on picturesque spots* and their electric effect on Coleridge: reasons for this, 24-27; school themes, (424-426); appointed to an Exhibition at Jesus College, Cambridge, 27;

Happiness written in the Long Vacation, 1792, at Ottery, 27-28; rapid progress at Cambridge and hopes of the Craven Scholarship in 1793, 29; interruptions: (1) letter writing, (2) ill-health (first references to opium), 29, (3) admiration for Frend: Coleridge becomes a Socinian, (427), (4) debts and wine parties, 30-31; the Craven Scholarship goes to Butler, with disintegrating effect on Coleridge, 31-32; his ostrich-like faculty for burying his head in new plans rather than contemplate unsuccessful or unfinished ones, 31-32; translation of Casimir's *Ad Lyram*, 32 (later lost, 50); he attends Frend's trial, 33; Long Vacation (1793) visits: attracted by Fanny Nesbitt to whom he writes *The Rose* and *Cupid Turn'd Chymist* or *Kisses*, 33; *Songs of the Pixies*, 33, (428); trouble with his brother George over debts: the money for settling them spent on other things, 34; *Lines: On an Autumnal Evening* and *To Fortune: On buying a Ticket in the Irish Lottery*, written during the next term, 34-35; his pathetic belief that he would win the lottery, and, this hope gone, his enlistment under the name of Silas Tomkyn Comberbacke, 35; life among horses, and nursing in Henley workhouse hospital, 36-38; efforts to secure his release, 36, 38, 39, (428); finally successful, 40, (429); plans, but never completes *Imitations from the Modern Latin Poets*, 40, (429); *The Sigh* written to Mary Evans, 41, (430); Long Vacation, 1794, to Oxford with Hucks: introduction to Southey: mutual liking and shared political views, 41; the hatching of pantisocracy by Coleridge, Southey,

Hucks, Burnett, and Allen, 42; immediate effect on Coleridge of this crystallization of his political sympathies and sociological views, 43; he coins the word "aspheterism," 43; the walking tour in Wales with Hucks, 43-46, (431-432); *On Bala Hill*, 44; embarrassing meeting with the Evans girls at Wrexham, 44; Coleridge's distress at Allen's desertion and Southey's first signs of back-sliding, 45; first draft of *Lewti*? 45; the thirsty climb of Penmaenmawr with Brookes and Berdmore: Berdmore, "You grinned like an idiot," cf. ". . . they for joy did grin" in *The Ancient Mariner*, 46, (432); arrival at Bristol and introduction by Southey to the Fricker household, now the headquarters of pantisocracy, 46; missionary work for pantisocracy, in Bristol, 46-47, and in Stowey where they visit Thomas Poole, 47-48, (432-433); Poole's impression of him, 47-48; Coleridge's admiration for the dead Robespierre, 48; *The Fall of Robespierre*, written by Coleridge, Southey, and Lovell, 49; Coleridge arranges to pair with Sarah, eldest and prettiest of the Fricker girls, 49; to London: evenings with Lamb, 50; failure to find a publisher for *The Fall of Robespierre* in spite of Dyer's help, 50; spreading the gospel of panti-socracy among Christ's Hospital boys, 50; Coleridge's account in a letter to Heath of the proposed pantisocratic settlement on the banks of the Susquehannah, 51-52; advice from an American land agent, 52; back to Cambridge: letter to Southey shows his lyrical worship of pantisocracy, 52-53; Southey's first protests against Coleridge's neglect of Sarah

[527]

Fricker: Coleridge's defence, 53, 54; *The Fall of Robespierre* published, 54; Coleridge dedicates *To a Young Lady* to Miss Brunton, and tries in her company to forget his Evans-Fricker troubles, 54, 56; disturbing letter from Mary Evans, 54-55; writes *To My Heart* (title later changed to *On a Discovery Made too Late*), 55; Coleridge gives up Mary for pantisocracy and Sarah, but continues to lament her loss, 56, 60, 70, 72, 88; distress at Southey's pantisocratic heresies; trouble over the status of servants, 57-58, (435), and over the inclusion of Mrs Southey and Mrs Fricker, 59-60; elegy on the vicar of Ottery—*Lines on a Friend*, 60-61; more trouble with his brothers, 61, and with Southey about Sarah Fricker, 61-62; Coleridge escapes to London, sees Lamb, Godwin and other friends, and has several poems accepted by the *Morning Chronicle*—sonnets on *Burke, Priestley, Kosciusko, Godwin, Southey* and *Sheridan*, also *Address to a Young Jackass and its Tethered Mother* (late 1794), 62, (436); Godwin's high opinion of his conversational powers, 62-63; discussion with Holcroft on the merits of Bowles whom Coleridge still admires fervently, 63; sonnet to *Bowles* in the *Morning Chronicle*, 63; the intense vitality of Coleridge's mental life contrasted with the indolence of his body, 63-64; his mental energy not wholly absorbed by pantisocracy: two divergent lines of thought— intellectual (Voltaire and Darwin), and mystical (Neo-Platonists and Christian Mystics), developing in the substratum of his mind, 64-65; his attempts to find in the teaching of one man a channel in which to combine these two streams: Hartley, 64-66; disappointment at Bristol: Sarah unable to supplant Mary Evans in his affections, 68, and Southey urging abandonment of Susquehannah scheme in favour of a farm in Wales, for men only, 66-67; return to London in despair which is deepened by news of Mary Evans' engagement, 68-70; letter to her fourteen years later, (438); final break with Cambridge, 70, (438) and resulting loss of Christ's Hospital Exhibition, (439); Coleridge and Lamb console each other, 71; Coleridge plans to tutor the Earl of Buchan's sons, 72; is carried off to Bristol by Southey, 72, (440); formal engagement to Sarah, and plans (unsuccessful) for getting a post on *The Telegraph*, 73; shares lodging aspheterically with Southey and Burnett, 73; more talk of the *Imitations*, 74; meeting with Joseph Cottle, 74-75; lectures (see LECTURES), 74-76; Cottle's offer to publish Coleridge and Southey's poems, 77; incompatibility of Coleridge's and Southey's working methods, 77-80, (441); the disastrous picnic to Tintern Abbey, 81; end of the joint menage: Coleridge robbed of Southey's friendship turns to Poole, 82; visit to Stowey, 83-84; meets Wordsworth, 85; marries Sarah and moves to a cottage at Clevedon which Cottle helps to furnish, 85, 86-87; further recriminations with Southey and a satisfyingly condemnatory letter to him, 87-89, (443); return to Bristol (Redcliffe Hill), 90; successful visit to Stowey, 90-91; Coleridge and the birth and death of *The Watchman*, 91-100, 106, 108-111 (see *The Watchman*), (444-

446); Cottle's difficulty in extracting copy for the *Poems*, 100-101; romantic bloom of the marriage worn off by financial worry, Mrs Fricker's nearness, and Sarah's illness, 101-103; the *Poems* including *Religious Musings*, q.v., finished, published as *Poems on Various Subjects*, 1796, and well reviewed (see REVIEWS), 103-109; enthusiasm for Count Rumford and project for Rumfordizing Bristol, Birmingham, and Manchester, 108-109; projects to found a school, and to become a Dissenting Minister, 110-111; annuity from Poole, and visit to Stowey, 111-113; correspondence with Thelwall: friendship grows out of a series of long happy epistolary wrangles, 114-115; further meetings with Wordsworth, 116-117; financial worry and many plans: the Dissenting Minister idea further considered, 117-118; suggestion that Coleridge should join the staff of the *Morning Chronicle*, 118-119; plan for tutorship of Mrs Evans' two boys at Darley Hall, 119-120, falls through, 120-121; visit to Ottery, 120; plan for founding a school at Derby, 121-122, 123, 125; plan for living near Liverpool, 122; plan for completing young Charles Lloyd's education, 123-125; birth of a son, (David Hartley), three sonnets to mother and child, 123-124, (450); growing wish to live near Poole at Stowey, 125, 126, 129, 131, amounts almost to hysteria, 133, 134, 139, 140-144; Derby scheme dropped, 126; partial reconciliation with Southey, 126; Coleridge's correspondence with Lamb before and after the disaster of Mrs Lamb's death, 127-129; Coleridge breaks to old Mr Lloyd the

abandonment of the Derby school in favour of a cottage at Stowey, 129-130; Cottle proposes a second edition of the poems, 130-131; two privately printed pamphlets, containing some of Coleridge's work, 131; bad attack of neuritis soothed by laudanum, 132-133, (452); Coleridge's prudent concern over Thelwall's lack of a plan in his life, 133; Charles Lloyd's epilepsy leads to a modification of the scheme for tutoring him, 134, 135, 149; Coleridge's "six companions" at Stowey, 136; self-portrait in a letter to Thelwall, 136-137; defence of his own and Bowles' poems against Thelwall's criticisms, and attempt to rescue the latter from the atheistical clutches of Godwin, 137; plan for an "answer to Godwin" (never written), 138; Coleridge's notebooks: their value in illustrating the range of his mind and his perception of nature, 138, 159: and their value to him: extracts, (453-456); passionate distress at Poole's counter-suggestion to the Stowey plan, 139-144; safe and triumphant establishment at Stowey, 144; the *Ode to the Departing Year* published in the *Cambridge Intelligencer*, and privately printed with a dedication to Poole, 144; Coleridge and Sarah happy at Stowey; neighbours, the garden, and an improbably industrious timetable, 145, 147, (but 457); more work on the second edition; *The Progress of Liberty* or *The Vision of the Maid of Orleans* shelved owing to Lamb's strictures (see *Destiny of Nations*), 147-148; Lloyd's health becoming worse, he and his £80 a year leave the Coleridge household, 149; Coleridge's happiness: better health, social success, frequent opportunities to preach and congenial reviewing, 150; affinity to the 'Gothic' school of novelists, 150-151; *Osorio* started at Sheridan's suggestion for production at Drury Lane, 151-152, 153; prediction that Southey "will be known to posterity as Shakespeare's great grandson," 151; a meeting with Wordsworth, and great admiration for him, 152, (458); financial crisis averted by Poole's organizing more help for Coleridge, 152-153; Coleridge tries Cottle's patience by repeated lateness with copy, but second edition finally in the printer's hands, 153; Coleridge visits Burnett at Huntspill, and hears from an old woman of "that vile Jacobin villain . . . Coleridge," 153; Burnett's pathetic attachment to Coleridge after Southey's defection, 153-154; Coleridge's dislike of mouse traps, (458); he preaches at Bridgwater, 154; walks to Racedown: leaps into the friendship of Wordsworth and Dorothy, 154-156; Dorothy's picture of him; his praise of Wordsworth, 155; and of *The Borderers*, 155-156; he reads them *Osorio*, 155-156; Wordsworth and Dorothy at Stowey, 156-161; Coleridge's first account of Dorothy, 158; detail of the second edition: the motto from Groscoll, the dedication to George Coleridge, new poems and the preface, 158-159, (462); he writes *This Lime-Tree Bower my Prison*, 159-161; his energy harnesses Poole's kindness and secures Alfoxden for the Wordsworths, 161-162; characters and capacities of Coleridge and Wordsworth compared, 163, 183-184; Wordsworth's reaction to Coleridge's impetuous leap into

friendship, and its value to him, 163; Coleridge's recognition of the advance which *Guilt and Sorrow* marks over Wordsworth's earlier poetry, 170; contrast of Wordsworth's brooding realism and Coleridge's explosively sanguine make-believe in the face of the French Revolution, the war with France, and the attack on the English Jacobins, 171, 173, 182, 183, 185; Coleridge's wide and varied interests act as shock-absorbers, 173, 183; his gifts to Wordsworth: relaxation, 163, a full mind, 175, 184, his version of Hartley's philosophy, 185-188, and, when Wordsworth outgrows this, of Berkeley's philosophy, 188-189, his generous admiration for *The Borderers* and *Guilt and Sorrow* which restores Wordsworth's self respect, 189-191; the Wordsworths' gifts to him: a development of his naturally fine perception of nature, 192; his pleasure in and inspiration from Wordsworths' growing power of creative imagination, 193-195; the interaction of the poets' work: Coleridge's imitations more obvious, Wordsworth's adoptions more fundamental, 195-196; Coleridge finds in Wordsworth a combination of Poole's steadfastness and his own mental liveliness, 196-197; his pleasure in Dorothy, 198, 200-201; Coleridge and Dorothy idolize different Wordsworths— she the actual and he the potential, 201-202; he settles the Wordsworths in, 203; Thelwall to stay, 204-206; Cottle to stay: the "Jasmine harbour," (467-468); Coleridge writes to Southey condemning the *Monody on the Death of Chatterton* and praising the Wordsworths, 206-207; suspicions roused among the patriotic by Thelwall's visit: Coleridge and the Government Spy, 207-209; he dissuades Thelwall from trying to settle in Stowey, 209-210; coldness with Lloyd, 211-212; visit to Bowles, 212, taking *Osorio*, (469); his natural religiousness leads him (in spite of the Wordsworths) to see nature as a symbol of God, 212-214, (470); Coleridge tries to place *The Borderers* in London, and writes parody sonnets for the *Monthly Magazine*, 214-215; begins to learn French and German: writes "a ballad of about 300 lines" (*The Three Graves*, parts 3 and 4?), 216, (471); plans a poem to be called *The Brook*, 216; the remarkable creative outburst of the next few months: the Wordsworths' part in releasing Coleridge's genius, 217-218; his own account of the origins of the *Lyrical Ballads*, 218; *The Ancient Mariner* launched, 219-220; distractions: poverty, rejection of *Osorio*, trouble over the parody sonnets, 220-222; the two cures for poverty: (1) the Wedgwood offer of £100, accepted, 222-223, then refused, 223-227, increased to £150 a year, 234, 237-239, accepted, 239-242, (2) the invitation to become Unitarian minister at Shrewsbury, 222, considered, 223-230, (Hazlitt's account of Coleridge on trial, 230-237), declined, 242; his popularity at Shrewsbury shown in a letter, 242-243 and (475); Coleridge's great period, November 1797–June 1798: Wordsworth on the delights of this time, 244; Dorothy on it, (476-479); *Lewti*, 245; *France: an Ode*, 245-247; *Frost at Midnight*, 247-249 (see COLERIDGE, S. T., and NATURE);

Fears in Solitude, 249-251; *The Nightingale*, 251-253, (481); *The Ancient Mariner*, 253-256, (482); *Christabel*, 256-259, (482-483); *Kubla Khan*, 259-261, (483-484); Coleridge helps to bring out Wordsworth's greatness: his pleasure at the start of *The Recluse*, 261-262; the German plan, 262-263; how to raise money for this? 263-264; Cottle's visit to Alfoxden, 265: his own account, (484-486); Hazlitt's visit and account of it, 265-271; failure of Coleridge and Wordsworth to write in collaboration (see also 219-220), *The Wanderings of Cain*, 271; Coleridge's lament on bad typography, 272; letter to George, foreshadowing *Kubla Khan* and renouncing political thought, 272-276; visit to George at Ottery and birth of second son, Berkeley, 276-277; trouble with Lloyd, Lamb, and Southey, 277-284, (487-488), drives him to the seclusion of the farm near Culbone Church, where he writes *Kubla Khan*, 282; visits to the Wedgwoods, Thelwall, etc., 284-285, (488); *Fears in Solitude, etc.*, published, 286, (488); sails for Germany with the Wordsworths, leaving his family in Poole's care at Stowey, 285-286; *Lyrical Ballads*, q.v., published, Sept. 1798, 287 (see REVIEWS); their reception, and their true value, 287-292; Coleridge's main motive in going to Germany: to resolve his philosophic questionings, 292-312; difference from Wordsworth's motive leads to their parting, 293, 317; résumé of Coleridge's philosophic pilgrimage to this point, 294-312; the voyage, 313-314; with the Wordsworths in Hamburg: visits to Ebeling and Klopstock, 314-317;

to Ratzeburg with Chester, 317-329; his neglect of the *Morning Post*, 319; enjoyments and homesickness, 320-321, (497); expenses to be repaid by a projected *Life of Lessing*, to collect material for which he plans a three months' stay in Göttingen, 323; discussion with Poole as to where to live in England, 324-325, 342-343; the pleasures of skating, 326, smoking, 327, and high society, 328; at Göttingen, 329-341; university life, 330-333, (499-500), 344; death of Berkeley, 333-341; fears for Hartley's safety, 341, 344-345; walking tour in the Hartz Mountains, 341-342; two Coleridgean inventions, 344; letters to Josiah Wedgwood: digression on National and World religions, 346; summary of his accomplishments in Germany, 349-350; expeditions with the Parrys, farewell party, (502), and return to England, 351-352; Coleridge patches up his friendship with Southey, 352-355; they collaborate in *The Devil's Walk*, 355; epic poem on Mohammed started, 355, (503); friendly (though trying) visit to Ottery, 356-357; return to Stowey: minor troubles but general cheerfulness, 357-360; punning letters, 360, (504); friendship with Davy, and taking of nitrous oxide, 360-361, (505); rheumatism and "Lloyd-and-Lambophobia," 361-362; to Sockburn with Cottle to see Wordsworth, 363, 367; Wordsworth's illness and his need of Coleridge, 363-365, (506); Coleridge urges the writing of a poem for those disillusioned by the French Revolution—"tailpiece of 'The Recluse,'" 365-367; first meeting with Sarah Hutchinson, 367-368,

(507-508); walking tour in the Lakes, 368-374, (507-508); Stuart offers a salaried post in London, 371, 374; Coleridge at Sockburn again: the writing of *Love* reflects his growing friendship with Sarah Hutchinson, 374-377, (509); the Coleridges in London: renewed friendship with Lamb, 378-380, 397, stands the test of the Hays controversy, 398-399; friendship with Godwin, 378, 382, 383, 387, 389; Coleridge works hard at journalism, 380, 388-389, 394, but is also exceedingly social, 382, 387, 397, 400; the *Anti-Jacobin* libel, 380-381, (510-511); letters to Southey, 381-382, and to poor Poole, who is house-hunting for the Coleridges near Stowey and realizing gradually that Coleridge has already decided to follow Wordsworth north, 383-386; and to Wedgwood, 387-389; translation of *Wallenstein* undertaken for Longman, 389, 392-393; 14 poems and several epigrams for Southey's second *Annual Anthology*, 389; the excellence of his journalism, 389-390, 392; his political attitude modified, 390-391; tries to withdraw from the *Morning Post*: refuses to tie himself down to journalism, 392-397; political reporting: Pitt's speech, 393-395, (512-513); meets Manning, 397; trouble over Lloyd and Miss Hays, 397-399, (514); visit to Lamb, and its value to the latter, 397, 400-401; money-making plans for Southey, 401-404, (514); plans for improving young George Fricker's prospects, 404; delight in Hartley, 404 (and see 468); *Character of Pitt*, 405, (512); pious letter to Estlin, 405-406; where to live: varying plans, 406-409; Poole accuses him of prostrating

[532]

himself before Wordsworth, (515); his defence, 407-408; visit to the Wordsworths at Dove Cottage, 409-412, (516); *Wallenstein* finished, published and unsuccessful —as he expected, 409-412, (516-517); finding of Greta Hall, 412; correspondence with Godwin and Lamb,413,with Southey and Davy, 414-415; final decision to go north, 415; the Coleridges depart, 416

As a Conversationalist, 33, 50, 62, 72; influence of his talk on Godwin, 63; habit of repetition, 78, (441); during his canvassing tour for *The Watchman*, 92-93; conversation 'flourished most when it assumed the character of a monologue,' hence his success as a preacher, 118; "In conversation I am impassioned," 137; Hazlitt's appreciation, 230-231, 232-237; Carlyon on, 342, (499)

Educational Projects:
To tutor the Earl of Buchan's sons, 72
To publish proposals for a school, 86
To study chemistry and anatomy at Jena and on returning start a school for eight young men at £105 each, for the study of Man, 110
To take another tutorship, 118, 119
To tutor Mrs Evans' sons, 119-121
To draw up a sketch of education, 121
To start a school at Derby, 121-123, 125-126, 129, 140
To train Charles Lloyd, 123, 130, 134, 135
To join with Basil Montague to take pupils for a three-year course of study which was to be "singular and extensive," 216, (471-472)
To write a schoolbook, 358, 359, "my money-book," 362

To get "a couple of Pupils," 359
To write "my Great Work," 359, and see 350

Health: origins of ill-health, 14-15, 20, 29; ill-health, 96, 132-133, (452), 144; better at Stowey, 145, 149-150; ill again, 272-273; "new and tender health," 277, (487); trouble with eyes, 322, (497)

Methods as a Workman: He "goes to work like a hound" (Southey), his apparent indolence incompatible with Southey's neat industry, 78-79. See (410), (460)

And Nature: "Nature looking at me with a thousand looks of beauty, and speaking to me in a thousand melodies of love," 136; first signs of his precise and passionate enjoyment shown in the notebooks, 138; first translation of this into poetry—*This Lime-Tree Bower my Prison,* 159-160; his discovery of "Religious meanings in the forms of Nature," 160-161; the relationship of his appreciation of nature to Wordsworth's and Dorothy's, 192, 193, 213; in *France: an Ode,* 246-247; in *Frost at Midnight,*247-248;in *Fears in Solitude,* 249-251; in *The Nightingale,* 251-253; in *Christabel,* 257-258; in *The Three Graves,* (480)

Personal Appearance: self-portrait,136-137; Dorothy Wordsworth on, 155; Hazlitt on, 230, 232-233, (474); Carlyon on, (499); Benecke on, (499-500)

Personal Qualities: Humility, "I feel myself *a little man by his side,*" (Wordsworth's), 155, 158; indolence, 61, bodily in origin, 63; sometimes apparent only, 79, "*indolence capable of energies,*" 136; need of affection, 329-330, (499); ostrich-like quality, 31; self-abasement, 36, 37, 98; self-analysis, 61; sense of humour, 342,

"I laugh more and talk more non-sense in a week than [most] other people do in a year," 342, 399; power of application, 103, 260, (460); rapidity of execution, 410; humanity, (458)

And Poetic Criticism: Coleridge, obliged to analyse the nature of poetry in order to prepare a defence of Bowles, lays a foundation for his powers of criticism while still at school, 26; admiration of Bowles, 24-25, 63, 71; criticism of Southey's poetry, 54, 62; his own account of the catholicity of his taste, 137; admiration of Wordsworth, 189-191, 407-408, etc.; the prefaces to the first and second editions of the *Lyrical Ballads*, 287-289, (489-493)

As a Preacher: Begins early to write sermons, 30, (427); preaches on *The Watchman* tour, 92, 93, (444-445), 97; 117-118; preaches at Birmingham and is pleased with his sermon, 122; preaches often at Taunton and Bridgwater, 150, 154, (457), 229, 270; Hazlitt's appreciation of the Shrewsbury sermon, 231-232; proposes to relieve Toulmin and Howell alternate Sundays, (475); success at Shrewsbury confirmed, (475)

Published Works:
The Fall of Robespierre, 1794, 54, (434)
A Moral and Political Lecture, 75, (440)
Conciones ad Populum, 75, (441)
The Plot Discovered, 75, (441)
The Watchman, 91, (444), 111
Poems on Various Subjects, 1796, 103, (447)
Two privately printed pamphlets, 1796, 131, (452)
Ode to the Departing Year, privately printed in an expanded form, 144

Second edition of *Poems on Various Subjects*, 1797, 158, (462)
Fears in Solitude, France: an Ode and *Frost at Midnight*, 1798, 286, (488)
Lyrical Ballads (with Wordsworth), 1798, 287, (488)
Translations:
Eight hymns of Synesius, 21
Ad Lyram, Casimir, 32
Demetrius Phalareus, 40
Plans to translate Casimir and Secundus, (429); plans to learn German and translate all Schiller's work, 110; learns some German and French: plans to translate Wieland's *Oberon*, 216; translates *Wallenstein*, q.v.

COLERIDGE, Sarah (see FRICKER), 1770–1845, m. Coleridge, 85-86; short stay at Clevedon, 86-90; successful visit to Stowey, 90; illness and miscarriage, 98, (446), 101-103; bewildered and unhappy, 117; birth of Hartley, 123; kept busy by Charles Lloyd's delicacy, 135; her part in the Stowey plan, 140, 141, 142; happy at Stowey, 145, 146, (but 457), 150; scalds Coleridge's foot, 157; possible resentment against Dorothy, 157, (461); helps with move to Alfoxden, 203; liking for Thelwall, 206; (467); (469), 212, (478), (479); left at Stowey with the children while Coleridge goes to Germany, 285; letters from Coleridge, 320-321; trouble over Berkeley's health, 321, 324, 325; letter from Coleridge, 329-330; Berkeley's death, 333-336, 337-340; implication that the love between her and Coleridge needs confirmation, 339; letter from Coleridge, 342; 343; stays with Southey and her sister, Edith, 346-348; suffers from delays in Coleridge's homecoming, 345, 351; from money worries, 346-348; from doubts as to her husband's greatness, 347-348; from not comprehending the growth of Coleridge's mind— "Pray furnish me," 348; from sorrow for Berkeley, 346, (501); Coleridge hesitates to move from Stowey because of her, 343; they return to Stowey, 357; Hartley ill, 358; they join Coleridge in London, 378; difficulty in finding a house to suit her and Coleridge, 384; 385; visit to Kempsford, 397, 400, (513); another child expected, 406, 415; plan to go to Ottery, 406-407; her sorrow at the decision to go north, 415-416; she leaves Stowey for the north, 416.

COLERIDGE, Sara, fourth child and only daughter, (457), (459)

Coleridge: Studies by Several Hands, ed. Edmund Blunden and Earl Leslie Griggs, (418)

COLERIDGE, Susannah, Coleridge's favourite aunt; kept a general shop at Crediton, 12

Coleridge's Critical Terminology, J. Isaacs, (430), (495)

Coleridge's Miscellaneous Criticism, ed. T. M. Raysor, (418)

Collected Writings of Thomas de Quincey, ed. David Masson, (420)

College Reminiscences of Coleridge, C. V. le Grice, (427)

COLLINS, William, projected edition of his poems,(454),(455); influence on Wordsworth's early poetry, 166; no echoes of Collins left in Coleridge's poetry by 1797, 256

Commonplace Book, Southey, (488)

COMBERBACKE, Silas Tomkyn, the name under which Coleridge enlisted, 1793, 35, (428)

Comparative View of the English Rebellion and the French Revolution, six lectures given by Coleridge in Bristol, 1795, 75

Complaint of a Poor Indian Woman,

Wordsworth: Hazlitt on, 266; ignored by reviewers of the *Lyrical Ballads*, 291

Complaints of the Poor People of England, George Dyer, 50

Complete Poetical Works of Robert Southey, (419)

Complete Poetical Works of Samuel Taylor Coleridge, ed. Ernest Hartley Coleridge, (417)

Complete Poetical Works of William Wordsworth, ed. John Morley, (419)

Complete Works of Samuel Taylor Coleridge, ed. Professor W. G. T. Shedd, (418)

Complete Works of William Hazlitt, ed. P. P. Howe, (420)

Conciones ad Populum or *Addresses to the People*, two political lectures given by Coleridge in Bristol, 1795: original titles, *A Moral and Political Lecture* and *On the Present War*, 75, (440-441); Thelwall takes exception to the reference to himself as an "unsupported Malcontent," 114; quotations from J. P. Brissot's *New Travels*, (434)

Conspiracy of Fiesco, Schiller, quoted by Southey, 126

CONSTITUTION OF SIEYES, 391

COOKE, friend of the Wordsworths and a visitor at Dove Cottage, 410

COOPER, Lane, (465)

COOPER, Thomas, Coleridge reads his *Some Information Respecting America*, 52, (434)

COOPER'S TOWN, nearest town to projected site of pantisocratic settlement, 51

CORN LAWS, Coleridge lectures on, at Bristol, 1795, 76; and (according to Cottle) recapitulates the lecture in an early sermon at Bath, 117

CORNISH, George, Cambridge friend of Coleridge who offered help during his time as a soldier, 39

COSTOBADIE, J., (439), Coleridge's tutor at Jesus

COTE HOUSE, John Wedgwood's home near Bristol: Coleridge meets Mackintosh there, 1798, (473); 242, 243

COTTLE, Joseph, a Bristol bookseller, friend, publisher, and financer of Southey and Coleridge, 74, 75, 77; his unreliability as a reporter, (440), (457), (460), (461); helps with Coleridge's lectures, 76; at Tintern Abbey, 81; meets Wordsworth: publication of *Guilt and Sorrow* discussed, 84; link between Wordsworth and Coleridge, 85; makes Coleridge's marriage possible, 86, and helps to furnish the cottage at Clevedon, 87; he and his sister witnesses at Southey's wedding, (444); difficulty of extracting work from Coleridge, 90-91, 100; help with *The Watchman*, 92; on "projecting," 98; publishes *Poems on Various Subjects*, 1796, 103; pays £3, 3s. to Coleridge for the plan of the Rumford pamphlets but "forbears publication," 109; 116; proposes second edition of the *Poems*, 130; (452); promises to correct proofs for Coleridge, 140; 142; owns copyright of the *Poems*, 130, 143; 147; 152; invited to Stowey, 205; his account of the delayed but happy visit, (467); he notes that Coleridge moderates his praise of Bowles after visiting him, 212; Coleridge asks him to buy a German grammar, 216; (472); told of the Wedgwood annuity, 241; Coleridge visits him, 243; 262; lends Coleridge £5 and discusses third edition of the *Poems*, 263; proposed publication of Coleridge's and Wordsworth's tragedies and of Wordsworth's poems, and final decision to publish the *Lyrical Ballads*, 264, 271; visits Stowey and Alfoxden and describes his stay, 265, (484-486); Coleridge's comments on typography, 272; Lloyd refuses to have his poems included in Coleridge's third edition, 277-278; publishes *Edmund Oliver* for Lloyd, 278; tries to patch up resultant quarrel, 282; houses the Wordsworths for a few days, 284-285; 286; (488); 298, 299; friendship with Davy, 361; goes north with Coleridge to see Wordsworth, who is ill, 363-367; discusses the failure of the *Lyrical Ballads*, 364-365; the Lakes tour, 368, abandoned by Cottle, 369; transactions with Longman, 402

Courier, The, a paper which Stuart controlled, 396

COWPER, William, undiscovered by Coleridge in 1789, 25; 26; Coleridge admires his "divine chitchat," 137; and plans a poem called *The Brook* on the lines of *The Task*, 209; Cowper "the best modern poet," 269; quoted by Coleridge, 274-275, (486)

CRAVEN SCHOLARSHIP, 1793, Coleridge is one of the four chosen to compete for it, 29, but fails, 31

Critical Latin Grammar, by the Rev. John Coleridge, 16

Critical Review, on *Poems on Various Subjects*, 103, (447); Coleridge reviews for it, 117, 135, the 'Gothic' school of novels, 150-151, (457), (458); Southey's unfavourable review of *The Ancient Mariner* displeases Wordsworth, 365, and Lamb, 378-379, (502), and Coleridge, (506)

CROMPTON, Dr., 97; suggests that Coleridge should start a school in Derby to which his own children should go, 121, (450)

CROMPTONS, The, of Eton House, near Liverpool, fêted Coleridge, 98

CROSS, the village of, where Coleridge parts from Wordsworth after their 'chase' of Lloyd, 282

CRUIKSHANK, Ellen, daughter of John (below), (478); in *The Nightingale*, (481)

CRUIKSHANK, John, agent of Lord Egmont, whose estate was near Stowey, employed by Thomas Poole in an attempt to give Coleridge an anonymous annuity, 111; contributes to this gift, (449); approached by Poole about a house at Adscombe for Coleridge, 131, 140

CRUIKSHANK, John, son of above, neighbour of Coleridge at Stowey, 145, 146, (477); his dream of a skeleton ship, 219

CRUTTWELL of Bath, publisher of Bowles, Southey, and Lovell, 73, (440)

Cupid Turn'd Chymist, or *Kisses*, Coleridge, 1793, dedicated to Fanny Nesbitt but later transferred to Sarah Fricker, 33

DANVERS, Charles, of Bristol, 119

Dark Ladié, The, Coleridge, not ready in time for inclusion in the first edition of the *Lyrical Ballads*, 290; (509)

DARLEY HALL near Matlock, home of Mrs Elizabeth Evans, 97; Coleridge and Sarah stay there, 120-121, (451); 214

DARWIN, Erasmus, his arguments against the existence of God, 21; his *Botanical Garden*, 25; satisfies the intellectual but not the mystical part of Coleridge, 64; meets Coleridge at Derby, 1796, 97; Coleridge unconvinced by his arguments for atheism, 105-106, 306; treats Charles Lloyd for epilepsy, 149; influence on Wordsworth's early poetry, 166; projected hymn to him, (455)

DAVY, John, (420)

DAVY, Humphry, (448), (484); experiments with medicated airs for the cure and relief of disease, 360-361; contributes to Southey's *Annual Anthology*, 361; friendship with Poole, Southey, Cottle, and Coleridge, 361; induces them to take his 'gaseous oxyde,' 361, (505); letter from Coleridge, 382-383; Godwin on Davy, his high opinion of him, 383, 389; Coleridge longs to include him in a settlement of men of rare minds, 382, 414; letters from Coleridge to Davy, 414-415

DE QUINCEY, Thomas, his picture of Dorothy Wordsworth, 199-200, (461); of Klopstock and Wordsworth, 315-316

DE SELINCOURT, Dr. E., (419), (459), (463), (471), (482)

DEATH, Coleridge on, 335-338

Death of Abel (*Tod Abels*), by Solomon Gessner, 1758, 269

Death of Wallenstein, Schiller, 410, and see under *Wallenstein*

Dejection: an Ode, Coleridge, (482) from 253

DERBY, Coleridge there on *The Watchman* tour, 97, (445); 119; the proposed school there, 121, 125, 129; 149

DESCARTES, René, Coleridge and, 301

Descriptive Sketches, Wordsworth, possibly heard by Coleridge at Exeter, (428); (465); helped to convince him that Wordsworth was the greatest poet of the day, 163, 166; 170

Destiny of Nations, The, Coleridge, later name for *The Progress of Liberty*, or *The Vision of the Maid of Orleans*, Coleridge's contribution to Southey's *Joan of Arc*: Lamb's strictures prevent its inclusion in the second edition, 147-148; shews that Coleridge had not allowed himself to perceive

the fundamental contradiction in Hartley's doctrines, 148, (457); effect of the poem on Wordsworth, 185, 189; effect — more superficial — of Wordsworth's *Guilt and Sorrow* upon it, 195; condemnation of Hartley as a materialist implicit in some passages, 297-298; note to a MS. copy, 307

Devil's Thoughts, The, later *The Devil's Walk,* a joint poem by Coleridge and Southey, published anonymously, *Morning Post,* Sept. 1799, 355

DISNEY, Dr., Unitarian Minister at the Essex Street Chapel, London, contributes to Poole's annual subscription for Coleridge, (449); (475); incurs Coleridge's censure by having frivolous Sunday parties, 405

Dictionary of Religion, Jeremy Bentham, (495)

DILKE, Charles Wentworth, (441)

DOMENICHINO, his landscapes contrasted by Hazlitt with a view of Dunster, 268

DONHEAD, Wiltshire, where Coleridge wrote a sonnet to Linley, 212

DONNE, John, (454)

DORING, Herr von, "a nobleman" of Ratzeburg, 330

Dorothy Wordsworth: A Biography, Ernest de Selincourt, (419)

Dorothy Wordsworth: The Early Years, Catherine Macdonald Maclean, (419)

DOVE COTTAGE, Grasmere: "The Dove and Olive Branch," 370; the Wordsworths move in, 409; visitors, 410

DOVEDALE, visited from Darley Hall, 121

DOWDEN, Edward, (463), (476)

DOWNMAN, Hugh, founded a literary society at Exeter, (427)

DRAMATIC CRITICISM, Coleridge's, 380, 388-389

DUNSTER, Hazlitt on, 268

DULVERTON, visited on the *Ancient Mariner* walk, 219, (472), (473)

Dungeon, The, a fragment of *Osorio,* published as one of Coleridge's four poems in the first edition of the *Lyrical Ballads,* 289

DYER, the bookseller, 358

DYER, George, author of *Complaints of the Poor People of England,* friend and admirer of Coleridge in London, 1794, 50, (434); helps to get "a few guineas worth of nonsense" sold to the booksellers, 53; tries to arrange for Coleridge to act as tutor to the Earl of Buchan's sons, 72; in London, 1799, 387

DYSON, George, influence on Godwin, 63

EAGLESTON, A. J., (468)

Early History of Charles James Fox, G. O. Trevelyan, (475)

Early Life of Robert Southey, William Haller, (419)

Early Life of William Wordsworth, Legouis, (419)

Early Recollections, Cottle, (417)

Early Wordsworth, The, Ernest de Selincourt, (463), (471)

Early Years and Late Reflections, Clement Carlyon, (424), (438), (473), (499), (500), (501), (502), (515)

EBELING, Professor, 314

EDINBURGH, Charles Lloyd at, 123

Edmund Oliver, a novel by Charles Lloyd, published 1798 by Cottle and dedicated to Lamb; contains obvious and malicious references to Coleridge, 278; quotations, (487); 280; Southey's projected novel of the same name, (488)

EDUCATION, difference of opinion between Thelwall and Coleridge

on the right to influence a child's mind, 205. And see under COLERIDGE, S. T., *Educational Projects*

EDWARDS, The Rev. John, Unitarian minister at Birmingham, met by Coleridge on his canvassing tour for *The Watchman*, 93, (444), 94; gives introduction to Coleridge to friends in Derby, 97; among Coleridge's correspondents, 114

EGMONT, Lord, owner of the house at Adscombe near Stowey which Coleridge wanted but failed to get, 1796, (449), 131

EICHLER, A., (494)

EICHORN, Johann Gottfried, lectures on the New Testament at Göttingen, 332; "most flattering attentions" to Coleridge, 344

ELLISTON, R. W., actor at Drury Lane in *Osorio* (*Remorse*), 270

ELMSLEY, the Rev. Peter, a schoolfriend of Southey's who gave him £100, (515) from 404

EMILIA GALOTTI, Lessing, 308, 350

ENFIELD, The Rev. William, Unitarian minister at Norwich, (470)

Englische Studien, P. Machule, (517)

English Metrists, T. S. Omond, (494)

English Thought in the Eighteenth Century, Leslie Stephen, (464)

Enquiry concerning Political Justice, An, William Godwin, 1793, 172

Eolian Harp, The, Coleridge, published 1796, (442), 103, 158; ideas tentatively suggested in this poem reappear in Wordsworth's *Lines written in Early Spring*, 195

EPIC POEM, Lamb goads Coleridge into considering the writing of one, 147; Coleridge lists the requirements of a poet's education before he is fit to produce this: one of his objects in going to Germany, 292; Mohammed chosen as the subject and Southey as collaborator, 355; "The Origin of Evil, an Epic Poem" in his list of projected works, (453)

EPITAPH, Wordsworth, "A slumber did my spirit seal," quoted by Coleridge with the suggestion that it was written for Dorothy, 336-337, (500)

Erskine, To the Hon. Mr, sonnet by Coleridge, published in the *Morning Chronicle*, December, 1794, (436)

"ESEMPLASTIC," word coined by Coleridge, 303, (495)

ESSAY ON EPIC POETRY, projected by Coleridge, 371

Essays of Elia, Charles Lamb, (422), (423), (424), (513)

Essays on His Own Times, Coleridge, (418)

ESTLIN, The Rev. John Prior, Unitarian minister and schoolmaster at Bristol: admires Coleridge's theological lectures, 75, (441); gives him money, 91, and an introduction to the minister in Birmingham, 93; "does not altogether relish" an indiscretion in *The Watchman*, 99; his sermons criticized by Coleridge, 102; contributes to Poole's annual subscription for Coleridge, (449); among Coleridge's correspondents, 114, 120, (451); gives him £15, 15s., 117; he and his wife favour the Stowey plan, 142; Coleridge applies to him for money, 156; he works to secure Coleridge for the ministry, 214, (470), and in particular for a position at Shrewsbury, 222, 223, 227, 229; pays £15 of Coleridge's debts, 230; 238; Coleridge explains why he has refused the Shrewsbury appointment, 240-241; and tells him of his admira-

tion of Wordsworth, 261; correspondence, 277, (486), 278, (487), 281, 298; opposes German trip, 284; pious letter from Coleridge, 405-406

EURIPIDES, ed. Porson, (436)

EVANS, Bergen, (442)

EVANS FAMILY, THE, Coleridge makes friends with, and becomes "Brother Coly," 22, and is very much at home in the Villiers St. house, 22-23; Mrs Evans among his correspondents, 29

EVANS, Anne, of Villiers St., 23

EVANS, Eliza, of Villiers St., 44

EVANS, Mrs Elizabeth (Strutt), widow, of Darley Hall near Matlock, meets Coleridge in Derby, 97; suggestion that Coleridge should be tutor to her boys falls through, 120; the Coleridges visit her at Darley Hall and are given money and baby clothes, 121; remarriage to Walter, her late husband's half brother, 214

EVANS, "the Grandfather," and Walter, relations of above, and successful in their opposition of her tutoring scheme, 120; Walter marries Mrs Evans, 214

EVANS, The Rev. John, Unitarian minister at Sheffield, (445-446)

EVANS, Mary, of Villiers St., first meetings with Coleridge, 23; his increasing devotion to her, 27, 28; correspondence, 29, 31; *The Sigh* enclosed in a letter to her, 41, (429-430); the struggle between pantisocracy and his love for Mary; an unlooked-for meeting at Wrexham, 44; (431); letter to Coleridge, 54; (433); Coleridge repines her loss, 56, 60, 70, 72, 88; engagement to Mr Todd, 68-69; a meeting with Coleridge fourteen years later, (438)

EVANS, William, of Villiers St., at Christ's Hospital with Coleridge,

19, (423); introduces Coleridge to his family, 1788, 22-23

Evening Walk, An, Wordsworth, possibly heard by Coleridge at Exeter, 1793, (428), (465)

Evidences of Natural and Revealed Religion, Coleridge's projected answer to Godwin, 137-138, 152, 173

Examiner, The, (474)

Excursion, The, Wordsworth, Preface to, (465), (506)

EXETER, (427), 356, 358

Expostulation and Reply, Wordsworth, 289

Faery Queen, Spenser, (497)

Fall of Robespierre, The, a play by Coleridge, Southey, and Lovell, 1794, (431), 49, 50, 54, (434); read by George Coleridge, 61

FANCY. See IMAGINATION AND FANCY

FANNY, the Coleridge's maid, suspected cause of Hartley's itch, 357

Farmer of Tilsbury Vale, The, Wordsworth, (432)

FAVELL, Samuel, at Christ's Hospital with Coleridge: a young disciple, 18, (422), 50; acts as intermediary between Coleridge and Southey on the subject of Sarah Fricker, 54, 71

FAWCET, Joseph, commended by Godwin as an "oral instructor," 63

Fears in Solitude, Coleridge, 1798, 249-251, (480-481); published, 286, (488)

FELLOWES, John, of Nottingham, Coleridge dines with him on *The Watchman* tour, 97

Female Biography, Mary Hays, (509)

Female Vagrant, The, Wordsworth, effect on Coleridge, (443), 116

FIELD, Barron, (471)

FIELDING, Henry, disliked by Coleridge, 269

Fire, Famine, and Slaughter, Coleridge, a denunciation of Pitt, 390

FLOWER, Benjamin, publisher of *The Fall of Robespierre*, 1794, 54, (434); of the *Cambridge Intelligencer*, q.v.; 103, 301, 308, (497), 350

Forsaken Indian Woman, The. See under *Complaint of a Poor Indian Woman*

Fortune, To: On buying a ticket in the Irish Lottery, Coleridge, 1793, 34

Foster Mother's Tale, The, fragment of *Osorio*, one of Coleridge's four poems in the first edition of the *Lyrical Ballads*, 289

Fox, Caroline, Journals of, (513)

Fox, Charles James, influence on Coleridge, 31, 41; compared unfavourably with Burke, 269; 390; reported by Coleridge in the House: "a great orator," 394

Fox, George, Coleridge acknowledges his debt to him, 106; and reverts to his writings, 301

Fox, Dr, gave Coleridge £50, (444)

Fragmentary Remains, Literary and Scientific, of Sir Humphry Davy, Bart., ed. John Davy, (420)

France: an Ode, Coleridge, first printed in the *Morning Post*, April 1798, under the title *The Recantation*, 245-247; published, 286, (488); 390

FRANKLIN, Frederick William, an ex-Grecian, at Cambridge with Coleridge: introduces him to Dyer in London, 50

FREILIGRATH, Ferdinand, (512)

FRENCH INVASION of England feared, 249, (480); of Switzerland, 245, (479)

FRENCH REVOLUTION, Coleridge and, (427); Coleridge and Southey enlarge on their reactions to it at Stowey, 48; Coleridge insists on taking over Southey's lecture on it, but forgets to attend it, 81; in *Religious Musings*, 104; effect on Wordsworth, 164-172, (464);

effect on Wordsworth and Coleridge contrasted, 182-183; Coleridge's later attitude to it, 273-274

French Revolution and English Literature, The, Edward Dowden, (463)

FREND, William, Coleridge's brothers worried about his growing friendship with Frend, 30, (427); Frend tried for sedition, 33, (427), 41; effect of his friendship on Coleridge's mental development, 64, 300; association with Priestley, (434)

FRICKER, Mrs, and her family, the backbone of the pantisocratic society, 46, 47; "If Mrs S. and Mrs F. go with us they can at least prepare the food of simplicity," Coleridge to Southey, 59; "I wish . . . that the two mothers were not to go," Coleridge to Southey, 60; an unwelcome mother-in-law, 90, 101; dependent on Coleridge, 102, 152; the Coleridges escape to Stowey, 145; Mrs Fricker's allowance advanced by Coleridge's friends, 156, 229

FRICKER, Edith, engaged to Southey, 46; "Make Edith my sister," Coleridge to Southey, 53, 59; the wish to support her in comfort and respectability leads Southey to give up pantisocracy, 80; at Tintern Abbey, 81; meeting with Wordsworth, 85; friction with Sarah, 85; secret marriage to Southey, 89. See SOUTHEY, Edith

FRICKER, Eliza, 46

FRICKER, George, 46; proposals to improve his prospects, 404

FRICKER, Martha, 46; witness at Coleridge's wedding with Sarah, (443); stays at Clevedon with Coleridge and Sarah and Burnett, 87

FRICKER, Mary. See LOVELL, Mary

FRICKER, Sarah, first meeting with Coleridge, 46; spelling of her

[541]

name, (432); 'Sarah was the prettiest': an understanding but no formal engagement, 49, (433); Southey scolds Coleridge for his neglect of her, 53, 66; Coleridge's unhappy hesitations, 55, 56, 57, 70, 71; 59; fails to supplant Mary Evans in Coleridge's affections, 68; Coleridge's capture and formal betrothal, 72-73; trouble at Tintern Abbey, 81; friction with Edith, 85; marriage, 85. See COLERIDGE, Sarah

Friend, The, 15, (418), (484), (496-497), (512)

Frost at Midnight, Coleridge, 247-249; published, 286, (422), (488)

GARDINER, Henry, correspondent of Wordsworth, (488), (496)

GARNETT, R., (493)

Général Michel Beaupuy, Le, Bussière and Legouis, (463)

Genevieve, Coleridge, possibly written to the daughter of the dormitory Nurse at Christ's Hospital, 1786, 19

Gentleman's Magazine, (422), (427), (428), (429), (431), (434), (473), (508), (511), (512), (513)

Geographie der Menschen, Von Zimmerman, 359

Georgics, Virgil, 269

GELLERT, Christian Furchtegott, 332

German Influence in the English Romantic Period, 1788–1818, F. W. Stockoe, (503)

GERMANY, Coleridge plans to go to Jena, 110; plans to go to Germany with the Wordsworths and Chester, 263, 270, 271, 282-283, 284, 285; they sail, 286; Coleridge's main motive in going, 292; different from Wordsworth's, 293-294; Coleridge in Germany, 286-352; summary of his accomplishments there, 349

GERRALD, Joseph, visited by Coleridge in Newgate, 1794, 63, (436); transported on a flimsy charge, 171

GILL, William, Lord Mayor of London in 1789 and Treasurer of Christ's Hospital, 23, (424), (439)

GILLMAN, James, (417)

GILLRAY, James, 'poor Gilly,' Thelwall on, 242

GINGERICH, S. F., (447), (448), (482)

GLOUCESTER, Coleridge and Hucks there on a walking tour, 1794; "the women have all sharp noses," 43

GLOVER, Richard, his blank verse preferred by Klopstock to Milton's, 317

GODWIN, Mary, Shelley's wife, (436)

GODWIN, William, the influence of his *Political Justice* on pantisocracy, (430); meets Coleridge, 62, (436); opinion of Coleridge as a talker, 63; influence on Coleridge's mind, 65; attacked in *The Watchman*, 99, 106; Thelwall takes Coleridge to task for this attack, 114; Coleridge tries to rescue Thelwall from Godwin's atheistical clutches, 137; Coleridge plans but never writes an *Answer to Godwin*, to be called *Evidences of Natural and Revealed Religion*, 137-138, 152, 173, 301, (453), (455); influence on Wordsworth, 172-174; decline of his influence on Wordsworth, 178, 182; and on Coleridge, 173, 234; Hazlitt meets Lamb at his house, 270; Godwin wishes to see Coleridge again, 284; they meet in London: Coleridge on Godwin, 378, 382, 383, 387; "I have seen a good deal of Godwin who has just published a novel," 389; financial success of this novel, *St. Neon*, 402; dines with Lamb, "I expect the roof to fall in and crush the atheist," 400; letter from Coleridge, 400; he values Wordsworth's work less

[542]

highly than Coleridge, 407; Coleridge invites him to his future house, 412; he misses Coleridge, and corresponds with him, 413; Coleridge longs to collect him, Wordsworth, and Davy under one roof, 414, 415

Godwin, sonnet by Coleridge, published *Morning Chronicle*, 1795, 62, (436)

GOETHE, Johann Wolfgang, Wordsworth on, 329; no reference to his works by Coleridge in Germany, 332

GOODEN, J., (495)

Goody Blake and Harry Gill, Wordsworth, founded on fact, 288; its value partially appreciated, 291

GOSLAR near the Brocken, the Wordsworths there, 317, 321; not a success, 322, 326, 327; they leave, 328; 329

'GOTHIC' SCHOOL OF NOVELS, reviewed and appreciated by Coleridge, 150

Gotten des Griechenland, Schiller, Coleridge plans to translate it, decides to write an antiphony to it, 368

GÖTTINGEN, 282, 283; Coleridge plans to go there for three months to collect materials for a life of Lessing, 323; Poole approves, 325; the Wordsworths are pleased, 328; Coleridge there, 329-341, (499-500), 342-345, (502), 351-352, 363

Grace before Meat, Lamb, (422)

GRAY, Thomas, projected edition, (454, 455); influence on Wordsworth's early poetry, 166; echoes of his work no longer to be heard in Coleridge's by the time of *The Ancient Mariner*, 256; Coleridge speaks with contempt of Gray to Hazlitt, 269

GRASMERE, Wordsworth takes Coleridge there on a walking tour, 369-370, and finds Dove Cottage,

370, 374; the Wordsworths move there, 409

GRECIANS of Christ's Hospital, The: Coleridge as a Grecian, 19, 22, 23; some of the Grecians pass on the news of Coleridge's enlistment to Tucket, 36; Coleridge meets them again in London, 50

GREENOUGH, G. B., at Göttingen, 331, (499); to Hartz Mountains, 341-342, (500), (501); ready to go to Scandinavia, 351-352, (502), (503)

GREEVER, Garland, (447)

GRENVILLE, William Wyndham, Baron Grenville, 397

GRETA BRIDGE, Lakes walking tour, 368

GRETA HALL, facing Derwent Water, house found by Coleridge, 412, (517)

GREY, the editor of the *Morning Chronicle*: Coleridge dines with him and Perry in London, 1794, 62; he dies, 118, 119

GRIGGS, E. L., (417), (418), (511)

GROSART, Alexander B., (419)

'GROSCOLL,' quotation from, as motto to second edition of *Poems on Various Subjects*, 158, (462), 277

Group of Englishmen, A, 1795–1815, Meteyard, (474), (502), (505)

GROVE'S *Dictionary of Music and Musicians*, (429)

Guilt and Sorrow, Wordsworth, publication discussed with Cottle, 84-85; sent to Coleridge to read, 85, (443); sent to Lamb, 116; helps to convince Coleridge that Wordsworth is the greatest poet of the day, 163; its purpose, 170; its poetic value and Coleridge's appreciation of it, 190-191; its value to Coleridge, 192, 302; imitated by Coleridge in *The Vision of the Maid of Orleans*, 195

GUTCH, John Matthew, schoolfellow of Coleridge, and possessor for a

[543]

time of one of the note-books, see below, (453)

Gutch Memorandum Book, The, (418)

HABEAS CORPUS ACT, suspended in 1794, to allow Pitt's attack on the English 'Jacobins,' 171

HAGUE, Charles, professor of music at Cambridge, (429)

HAIR POWDER TAX, Coleridge lectures on, 1795, 76, and (according to Cottle), recapitulates the lecture in an early sermon at Bath, 117

HALE, Sir Philip, of Cannington: not he, as Coleridge supposes, but Dr. Lysons of Bath, informs against the Wordsworths at Alfoxden, 208

HALLER, William, (419)

HAMBURG, disappoints Coleridge and the Wordsworths, 314-317, (497)

HAMILTON, a Cambridge man at Göttingen, 331

HANCOCK's house at Stowey, suggested by Poole as possible for the Coleridges: "I like it not," 325, 343

HANEY, John Louis, (420)

HANOVER, Coleridge there, 329

Happiness, Coleridge, 27, 28

HARDY, Thomas, tried for high treason, 1794, 171, (449), (464)

HARPER, George McLean, (419)

HARRIS, Thomas, of Covent Garden, interviews Coleridge, and considers but rejects *The Borderers* by Wordsworth, 214

HARTLEY, David, influence on Coleridge, 63, (437); temporarily satisfies the two divergent sides of Coleridge's mind, 65, 106; his thought as an ingredient in Coleridge's lectures, 76; hailed in *Religious Musings,* 105; (448); praised and interpreted in *The Vision of the Maid of Orleans,* 1797, 148; Wordsworth's reception of Coleridge's interpretation of Hartley's doctrines, 185-188; the two poets, Coleridge leading, pass on from Hartley to Berkeley, 188; reverence for Hartley still a power in Coleridge's mind, 240; analysis of Hartley's place in Coleridge's philosophical development, 295-300, (494), 304-305

HARTZ MOUNTAINS, expedition made by Coleridge, the Parrys, Carlyon, Chester, etc., Whitsun 1799, 341-342; 270

HARWOOD, "Harwood—pish! I say nothing of him," 53

HAWKES, Thomas, Unitarian minister, Coleridge stays with him at Moseley and preaches at Birmingham, 122, (450)

HAYDN, Joseph, (429)

HAYS, Mary, authoress, feminist, and friend of Mary Wollstonecraft, 378, (509); meets Coleridge in London, 387; trouble over her relationship with Lloyd, 397-399

HAZLITT, William, a discussion with Coleridge and Wordsworth, 196; (472); account of his first meeting with Coleridge, during the trial visit to Shrewsbury as Unitarian minister, 230-237, (474); his visit to Coleridge at Stowey and his first meeting with Wordsworth, 265-270, (487); meeting with Southey and Lamb, 270-271; his part in originating *Expostulation and Reply,* 289, (489); with Coleridge when he deprecates Johnson's view of Berkeley, 299; attacks Coleridge as inconsistent for the latter's dislike of Napoleon, 390; (460), (512)

HAZLITT, W. Carew, (474)

HENDERSON, John, projected life of, (455)

HENLEY, Coleridge at, 36, 39

Henry Crabb Robinson on Books and

their Writers, ed. Edith J. Morley, (420)

HERDER, Johann Gottfried, von, "*Ideas for the History of the Human Race*" (*Ideas on the Philosophy of the History of Mankind*), 359, (504)

Her Eyes are Wild, See *Mad Mother, The*

Herrigs Archiv für das Studium der Neueren Sprachen und Literaturen, (501)

HETTY, the Lambs' old servant: her death, 413

Hexameters. See *Written during a Temporary Blindness*

HEYNE, Professor Christian, "head librarian and in truth the real Governor of Göttingen," 330: no evidence that Coleridge attended his lectures, 333; his edition of Virgil at Stowey, 333

HIGGINBOTTOM, Nehemiah, Coleridge's pseudonym under which he published in the *Monthly Magazine* three sonnets, parodies of Lamb's, Lloyd's, and his own styles, 215, 221

HIGH WYCOMBE, Coleridge there, billeted at The Compasses (now The Chequers), 39

HILL, The Rev. Herbert, uncle of Southey, sends Southey to Oxford on the understanding that he will take Orders, (431); suggests that Southey shall go back to Oxford and carry out this programme, 1795, 81-82; Southey and his wife go to Lisbon at his invitation, 401

History of Broadwindsor, Dorset, A, Taylor Milne, (442)

History of English Prosody, George Saintsbury, (494)

History of Jesus College, A. Gray, (426)

HISTORY OF LEVELLERS, Coleridge suggests that Southey shall write scissors-and-paste book, 402, (514)

HISTORY OF POETRY, projected by Coleridge to be written by Southey, 403

History of the Royal Foundation of Christ's Hospital, A. W. Trollope, (423)

History of Upper Chapel, J. E. Manning, (446)

HOBHOUSE, Benjamin, of Bath, contributes to Poole's annuity scheme for Coleridge, (449), 229

HOLCROFT, Thomas, met by Coleridge, 1794, 62; commended by Godwin and described by Coleridge, 63; tried for treason, (436); 270

HOMER, recited by Coleridge in the cloister at school, 22

HOOKER, Richard; Coleridge's prose style at its best is like Hooker's, 389

HORNE, T. Hartwell, at Christ's Hospital with Coleridge, coached by Coleridge, 1790, 18-19, (424)

HORT, the Rev. W. J., a schoolmaster at Bristol: admiration of Coleridge's lectures, 75; "sighs more than he says" over the indiscretions of *The Watchman,* 99, (446)

HOUGHTON, The Rev. Pendlebury, of Norwich, (470)

HOUSE OF COMMONS, Coleridge reports there, 393-394

HOT WELLS, site of the Pneumatic Institute for research into Medicated Airs, 361

HOWE, P. P., (420), (474)

HOWELL, The Rev. John, Unitarian minister at Bridgwater, 229, (474); Coleridge proposes to relieve him of the duty alternate Sundays, (475)

HUCKS, Joseph, walking tour with Coleridge, 1794, 41, (430), 43, 44; references to his record of this—*Pedestrian Tour through North Wales,* (430-433); Hucks and

2 M

pantisocracy, 42; Coleridge meets him at Northmore's, 356

HUME, David, influence of his thought on Coleridge at Cambridge, 65; Coleridge speaks slightingly of him, 235; "the subtlety of Hume," 350; Coleridge on the danger of Hume for the young, 405; 412

HUNT, Leigh. See AUTOBIOGRAPHY

Hunt, Leigh, Edmund Blunden, (517)

HUNTSPILL, Somerset, village where Burnett lived, 47, (433), 153

HUTCHINSON, Jack, brother of Sarah and Mary, 377

HUTCHINSON, Mary, question of her presence at Racedown at the time of Coleridge's first visit, (459-460); Wordsworth's early love for her, 177; Wordsworth stays with her people, 363, 365, 367; Sarah more lively and intelligent than Mary, 368

HUTCHINSON, Sarah, first meeting with Coleridge, 367, (507); description and contrast with Dorothy Wordsworth and with her own sister Mary, 367-368; Sarah as the inspiration of *Love,* 375-377, (508-509); she was perhaps a reason for Coleridge's move to the North, 416

HUTCHINSON, Thomas, (476)

HUTCHINSON, Tom, brother of Sarah and Mary; Cottle rides on his mare, Lily, 368

Hymns to the Sun, the Moon, and the Elements, projected by Coleridge, (455)

IAMBLICHUS, expounded by Coleridge at school, 22; Thelwall buys his works for Coleridge, 137

Ideas for the History of the Human Race, Herder, 359, (504)

Idiot Boy, The, Wordsworth, fairly generally praised by the reviewers of the *Lyrical Ballads,* 291

ILAM, visited from Darley Hall, 121

Illustrated London News, (440), (446), (458), (460), (468)

IMAGINATION AND FANCY, 194, (495) from 303

Imitations from the Modern Latin Poets, planned, discussed, and subscribed for, but never finished, 40, (429), 74, 86, (453)

INOCULATION, Coleridge's dislike of it, 337

Instructions for Making Sugar Molasses and Vinous Spirit from Beetroot, F. C. Achard, (501)

Introduction to the Tale of the Dark Ladie, (509). See *Love*

INTRODUCTORY SONNET TO CHARLES LLOYD'S POEMS, Coleridge, 131

INTUITION, word claimed to have been coined by Coleridge, (495)

ISAACS, J., (430)

ISLE OF WIGHT, Wordsworth there, 169

I Stood on Brocken's Sovran Heights, Coleridge, 342

JACK, A. A., (420)

JACKSON, William, cathedral organist at Exeter, (427-428)

JACOBI, Heinrich Friedrich, The mysticism of, 301

JACOBINS, THE ENGLISH, "Jacobin and Democratic Patrons" of *The Watchman,* 100; "that vile Jacobin villain"—attack on Coleridge by the old woman of Huntspill, 153; the ardency of the English Jacobins difficult to recapture now, 168; 170; Habeas Corpus Act suspended by Pitt in order to suppress them, 171; effect of this on Coleridge and on Wordsworth, 183, 185; Coleridge convinces the Government spy that he is "no friend to Jacobinism," 208-209

JARDINE, Mr, Unitarian minister at Bath: his admiration of Coleridge as a lecturer, 76, (441)

JENA, Coleridge plans to go there and fit himself to instruct eight young men at £105 each per annum, 110
JESUS COLLEGE. See CAMBRIDGE, and PEARCE, Dr.
Joan of Arc, Southey, plans for, 74; accepted by Cottle, 77; Coleridge helps in revision, 79; he commends it, 151; 297-298
JOHN, Saint, 304
JOHNSON, Dr, Coleridge "exceedingly angry" with him over his opinion of Berkeley, 236, 299-300; Coleridge's dislike of him, 269
JOHNSON, J., of St. Paul's Churchyard, publishes *Fears in Solitude, France: an Ode*, and *Frost at Midnight*, 23 pages at 1s. 6d., 1798, 286, (488)
Journal of Dorothy Wordsworth, The, 245, (420), (462), (476-479), (482), (486); and *Christabel*, 257-259
JOURNALISM, Coleridge's success in, 389-390; standard of journalism raised by his contributions, 392; a spontaneous rather than a practised excellence, 392
JULIAN, The Emperor, Coleridge buys his works, through Thelwall, 137
"JUNIUS," Letters of, 1768-1771, Coleridge's low opinion of him as a writer, 269
JUVENAL, imitated by Wordsworth in a satire on leading English figures and habits, 170-171

KANT, Immanuel, 66; Coleridge plans to bring back all his works from Jena, and to instruct young men in "the new Kantean system", 110, 292, 308; his approach to the Kantean system, 300, 307; Baxter and Kant, 308-309; Coleridge anticipates Kant, 308-311; his name rarely mentioned by Coleridge in Germany, 332-333, but see (500); most of his work still unread by Coleridge on his return to England, 348, 352

KAUFMAN, Paul, (444)
KEATS, John, 287; his *La Belle Dame sans merci* a greater successor to Coleridge's *Love*, 374; he deplores Coleridge's mental restlessness, (466)
KEGAN, PAUL, C., (420)
KEMBLE, John Philip, made "some silly remarks" about *Osorio*, 220
KENDALL, William, "a poet who really looks like a man of genius," 356
KENNEDY, V. W., (420)
KESWICK, Windy Brow near Keswick lent to Wordsworth and Dorothy by Raisley Calvert, (464)
KEY, Dame, kept the "Reading" School at Ottery, 12, (421)
KIELMANSEGGE, Countess of, meets Coleridge at Ratzeburg, 320, (497)
KIRBY, Mr, of Sheffield, is out when Coleridge calls, 97
KLOPSTOCK, Friedrich Gottlieb, the poet: an unsatisfactory interview, 315-317; "a very *German* Milton," 316; 332
KLOPSTOCK, Victor, brother of the above, 314
KNIGHT, William, (417), (419), (420), (459)
Kosciusko, sonnet by Coleridge, published *Morning Chronicle*, 1794, 62, (436)
Kubla Khan, Coleridge, 245, 253, 259-261; where written, 259-260, 282; exact date discussed, 259-260, (487); *The Road to Xanadu* and *Kubla Khan*, (481-482)
KYRLE, Man of Ross, Coleridge writes a poem to him on his bedroom shutter, 43

La Fayette, sonnet by Coleridge published *Morning Chronicle*, 1794, (436)
La Révolution française et les poètes anglais, C. Cestre, (463)
La Vie d'un poète, J. Aynard, (476)
LAKE DISTRICT, much of Words-

worth's best work identified with it, 13; Wordsworth's childhood there, 163, 164; idea that the Wordsworths should move there, 324, 343; a Lakes walking tour suggested, 365, 367; Wordsworth, Coleridge, and Cottle set off, 368-374, (see under WALKING TOURS); Dove Cottage, 370, 409, 410; Coleridge in the Lakes again, 412; Greta Hall, 412; the Coleridges move to the Lakes, 416

LAMB, Charles, at Christ's Hospital with Coleridge, 18, (422); on Boyer, 19; on Coleridge as a schoolboy, 21, 22; in London with Coleridge, 50, 71; his Unitarian fortitude, (438); four of his sonnets published with Coleridge's *Poems on Various Subjects*, 103; among Coleridge's correspondents, 114, 116; advises Coleridge to revive *The Watchman* in a purely literary form, 117; reassures Coleridge about his scruples in becoming a Unitarian minister, 118, (449); holiday cancelled, 119; tragedy of his mother's death, 127; effect on Lamb's character, 128-129; expostulation on Coleridge's weathercock plans 129; his poem *The Grandame* printed with Lloyd's *Poems on the Death of Priscilla Farmer*, 1796, and some of his sonnets privately printed, 131, (452); tries to goad Coleridge into writing an epic poem instead of growing vegetables, 147; criticises *The Progress of Liberty* so severely that Coleridge abandons work on it, 147; more of Lamb's poems included in the second edition of the *Poems*, 148; liking for Lloyd, 149; visit to Stowey coincides with the Wordsworths', 157-162; *This Lime-Tree Bower my Prison* pictures Lamb on the Quantock heights, 159-

161; disappointment at missing Thelwall at Stowey, 204, 205, (467); friendship with Lloyd and Southey, 211; reproaches Coleridge with neglect of Lloyd, 211-212; parodied by Coleridge, 215; disbelieves Coleridge's explanations of this unlucky joke, 221; told news of Wedgwood annuity, 241; Coleridge on the Lloyd quarrel, (483); reconciliation, 262; Hazlitt on Lamb, 270-271; renewed friction, 277-284; dedication of Lloyd's *Edmund Oliver* to him, 278; letter from Coleridge, 279-281; satirical letter to Coleridge, 283; Lamb follows Coleridge's philosophic pilgrimage, 299; comments unkindly on the parting of Wordsworth and Coleridge in Germany, 317; he and Lloyd the cause of Coleridge's trouble with Southey, 354; "I have great affection for Lamb but I have likewise a perfect Lloyd-and-Lambophobia," 362; renewed friendship with Coleridge, 1799, 378-380, 397; reproaches Southey for his adverse criticism of the *Ancient Mariner*, 378-379, (502), also Wordsworth, (506); pilloried in the *Anti-Jacobin*, 380-381, but unruffled, (510); Coleridge recommends *My Great Aunt's Manuscript* to Stuart for the *Morning Post*, 397; the Mary Hays imbroglio, 397-399; Coleridge stays with Lamb, 397, 400, 407, to Lamb's enormous pleasure, "he tends me . . . as a gardener tends his young tulip," 401; false hopes of his engagement by the *Morning Post*, 401, 409; correspondence, 411-412; the death of Hetty, the old servant, overthrows Mary's reason again, 413-414, 415

LAMB, Mary, Charles' sister, her illness, (438); her insanity causes her mother's death, 127; recovers her reason, 129; Lamb's further fears for her, 401, justified after Hetty's death, 413

Lancet, The, (452)

LARDNER, Nathaniel, 241; "the profound erudition of our Lardner," 350; his *History of Heretics* to be used in the projected scissors-and-paste *History of Levellers*, 402

LAUDANUM, Coleridge's use of, 132-133, (452), 273. See OPIUM

Lavengro, George Borrow, (511)

LAW, William, Boehme's "pious and fervid" commentator, 106; Coleridge reverts to his writings, 301

LAWSON, Sir Gilford, Wordsworth hopes to have access to his library in the Lake District, 324

LE GRICE, Charles Valentine, at Christ's Hospital with Coleridge, 18, (422), 22, 24; at Cambridge with Coleridge, 32, (514)

LE GRICE, Samuel, at Christ's Hospital with Coleridge, 18, (423); 50

LECTURES given by Coleridge. (1) Three political lectures at The Plume of Feathers, Wine St., Bristol, 1795, *A Moral and Political Lecture. On the Present War. The Plot Discovered; or, An Address to the People against Ministerial Treason*, 75, (440-441); (2) Six political lectures at the Assembly Coffee House, Bristol, 1795, on *A Comparative View of the English Rebellion and the French Revolution*, 75; (3) Six theological lectures, Bristol, 1795, *On Revealed Religion, its Corruptions and its Political Views*, 75, 108, (448); (4) Single lectures, Bristol, 1795, on *The Slave Trade, The Corn Laws, The Hair Powder Tax*, etc., 76; he undertakes, but forgets to deliver Southey's lecture on the French Revolution, 81; help from Poole, 83

LEGOUIS, Émile, (419), (463)

LEIBNITZ, Gottfried Wilhelm, 308; quoted by Coleridge, 310; "the face of a god," 330

LEIPZIG, 282, 283

LÉPAUX, (Laréveillère-Lépaux), a member of the Directory, high priest of the Theophilanthropists, 381, (510)

LESSING, Gotthold Ephraim, Coleridge reads his *Emilia Galotti*, 308; "the most formidable infidel," 308, 350; Coleridge on his portrait, 315; the projected Life, 323, 349; 350, 352; Wordsworth does not feel competent to judge this work, 329; "Lessing, most acute of critics," 332; the Life not progressed with, 363; plans to start again as soon as he leaves London, 381, 389; 401

Letter from Talleyrand, Coleridge, 386, (511)

Letters, Conversations and Recollections of S. T. Coleridge, ed. Thomas Allsop, (417)

Letters Hitherto Uncollected, by S. T. Coleridge, (450)

Letters of Charles Lamb, ed. E. V. Lucas, (419)

Letters of S. T. Coleridge, ed. Ernest Hartley Coleridge, (417)

Letters of Thomas Manning to Charles Lamb, ed. Mrs Anderson, (513), (514)

Letters of William and Dorothy Wordsworth, ed. E. de Selincourt, (419)

Letters from the Lake Poets . . . to Daniel Stuart, (417)

LEWIS, Matthew Gregory, *The Monk* reviewed by Coleridge in the *Critical Review*, 1797, 151; Wordsworth's comments on *The Castle Spectre*, 267

Lewti, or The Circassian's Love Chant, Coleridge, 1794-1798. First draft probably begun at Wrexham on a walking tour: name of heroine successively Mary, Cora (Sara), and Lewti, 45; published in *Morning Post*, April 1798: hint of new metre, 245; 249; *The Nightingale* hurriedly substituted for *Lewti* in the first edition of the *Lyrical Ballads*, to preserve the author's anonymity, 289, (493)

Liberal, The, (474)

LICHFIELD, Charles Lloyd in a sanatorium there, 149; 98

Life, Coleridge, 1789, 27, (426)

Life and Correspondence of Robert Southey, ed. Charles Cuthbert Southey, (419)

Life of Charles Lamb, E. V. Lucas, (419)

Life of Humphry Davy, J. A. Paris, (505)

Life of Lorenzo the Magnificent, William Roscoe, 122

Life of Samuel Taylor Coleridge, James Gillman, (417)

Life of Schiller, Carlyle, (517)

Life of Scott, Lockhart, (517)

Life of Sterling, Carlyle, (474)

Life of William Hazlitt, P. P. Howe, (474)

Life of William Wordsworth, William Knight, (419), (459)

LIME STREET in Stowey, Coleridge's cottage here later rejected as unsuitable, 324, 325

Lime-Tree Bower my Prison, This, Coleridge, written during the Wordsworths' and Lamb's first visit to Stowey, 159-161, (462), (469); first draft sent to Southey, 207, 213, (470); compare D.W.J. (477); in a letter to Southey, "You know I am a *Berkeleian*," 299

LINDSEY, The Rev. Theophilus, Unitarian minister at Essex Street Chapel, London, (449), (475)

Lines Composed in a Concert Room, Coleridge, (422)

Lines on a Friend who Died of a

Frenzy Fever induced by Calumnious Reports, Elegy on the Vicar of Ottery, 60-61, (435)

Lines on a Yew Tree, Wordsworth, Southey the only reviewer to appreciate these when they appeared in the *Lyrical Ballads*, 291

Lines: On an Autumnal Evening, Coleridge, 1793, 34

Lines: To a Beautiful Spring in a Village, Coleridge, (422)

Lines written a few miles above Tintern Abbey, Wordsworth, quoted, 199, (466); 285; published in the *Lyrical Ballads*: their quality unappreciated by all the reviewers, 287, 291, except Southey, 291; Lamb's praise, (509) from 379. And see *Revisiting the Wye, On*

Lines written at Shurton Bars, a phrase in it borrowed from Wordsworth, 85; published 1796, 103, (442-443)

Lines written at the King's Arms, Ross, formerly the house of the Man of Ross, Coleridge, 43, (431)

Lines written in Early Spring, Wordsworth; Coleridge's *Eolian Harp* is one of the springs of this poem, 195

LINLEY, William, Sheridan's secretary and brother-in-law, 212; writes rejection of *Osorio*, 220

Linley, To Mr William, sonnet by Coleridge, 1797, written at Donhead, 212, (469-470)

LISBON, Southey goes there, 89; 401, 414; 81

LITCHFIELD, R. B., (420)

Literary and Biographical Studies: Books read by Coleridge and Southey, James Baker, (444)

Literary Remains of Samuel Taylor Coleridge, ed. H. N. Coleridge, (418)

LITTLEDALE, Harold, (476)

LLANDAFF, Bishop of, a one-time Jacobin: Wordsworth writes a letter of remonstrance on his recantation, 170, (464)

LLOYD, Charles, 1748-1828, a wealthy Quaker banker, father of Coleridge's friend; favourably impressed by Coleridge, 123; informed of change of plan: the cottage at Stowey instead of the school at Derby, 129; criticizes it, 134, 136; told of his son's illness and the abandonment of his tuition, 134, 135; sends £10 to Coleridge, 152

LLOYD, Charles, son of the above, meets Coleridge at Birmingham and idolises him, 97; meets him again at Moseley, 122; proposal that Lloyd should live with the Coleridges at Derby: Coleridge visits the Lloyds at Birmingham, 123; eulogized by Coleridge, 124, 131; 129; *Poems on the Death of Priscilla Farmer*, privately printed, 131; also some of his poems and sonnets, 131; epilepsy, 134-135; his part in the Stowey plan, 141, 142, 143, 144; his poems included in the second edition of the *Poems*, 148; visit to London: love for Sophia Pemberton: renewed attacks of epilepsy: to a sanatorium, 149, (457); 152; approached by Poole to join the Coleridge annuity scheme, 153; (467); plans runaway marriage, 211; friendship with Southey and Lamb and coolness with Coleridge, 211-212; (469); hurt by Coleridge's parody sonnet, and by *Addressed to a Young Man of Fortune*, 215; more trouble over the parodies, 221; Coleridge on these troubles, (483); Lloyd's "tattle," 262; collaborating in *Blank Verse*, 277; refusal to allow his poems to be republished with

Coleridge's, 277; publication of *Edmund Oliver* causes further friction with Coleridge, 278; quotations, (487); more tattle and friction, 278-281; attempts to clear matters up fail, 282, (487-488); Lloyd the chief cause of Southey's coolness to Coleridge, 354-355; Southey becomes aware of his shortcomings, 355, 362; Lamb also, 379-380, 397-399; his defence of Lamb against the *Anti-Jacobin*, (510); Lloyd and Mary Hays, 397-399

LLOYD, Priscilla, young Charles Lloyd's sister: Lamb hopes to match her with Christopher Wordsworth, 380

LLYSWEN near Swansea, where Thelwall eventually settles, 210; Coleridge and the Wordsworths visit him there, 285

LOCKE, John, influence of his thought on Coleridge at Cambridge, 65, (437); Berkeley his direct successor, 300

LOCKHART, J. G., (517)

LONDON, Coleridge in, at school, 16-27; from Cambridge, 34, 35, 50-52, 62-66, 68, 70-72; from Stowey, 214-216; on the way to Germany, 285-286; as a journalist, 308, 378-409

London Mercury, (473), (500), (502), (503), (513), (516)

LONGMAN, Thomas Norton, London publisher of the *Lyrical Ballads*, (488); (509); Coleridge meets him in London, 1799, 382, 387, (511); asks Coleridge to translate Schiller's drama *Wallenstein*, 389; "Mr Longman is kept in constant dread that some rival translation may pop out before mine," 392; buys Southey's *Joan of Arc* and the 1797 *Poems* for £370, 402; (515); (516); 414

LONSDALE, Lord, Wordsworth disappointed of a payment due from him, 165, (463)

Lord Byron and his Contemporaries, Leigh Hunt, (423)

Losh, James, Wordsworth's friend: a letter to him on the German plan, 263, (484)

Love, Coleridge, conceived and probably drafted at Sockburn: published in the *Morning Post,* December 1799, as *Introduction to the Tale of the Dark Ladié:* forerunner of Keats' *La Belle Dame sans merci,* 374; Sarah Hutchinson his model, 375-377, (508-509)

Love Letters of Mary Hays, ed. A. F. Wedd, (509)

Lovell, Mary, (Fricker), 46; Coleridge with her on the night of her husband's death, 109

Lovell, Robert, Quaker, poetaster and pantisocrat, married to Mary Fricker, 46; tries to convert Holcroft, (436); as a partner in Southey's Welsh scheme, 67; 71; lives near Coleridge in Bristol, 73; his poems and Southey's published by Cruttwell, 73, (440); the link between Cottle, Southey, and Coleridge, 74; doubts suitability of Coleridge's engagement to Sarah, 78; last illness and death, 109; in consequence "We are all become more religious than we were," 113

Lowes, John Livingston, (418)

Lucas, E. V., (419)

Lucy Poems, Wordsworth, quoted, 336-337, (500)

Luise, Voss, 308

Lushington, Prophesies to Coleridge the breakdown of pantisocracy through the women's shortcomings, 58

"Lutes, lobsters, seas of milk and ships of amber," misquotation of Otway by Coleridge: contrasted with Shakespeare's "What! have

his daughters brought him to this pass?" 194

Lynmouth, visited on the *Ancient Mariner* walk, 219

Lynton, the farm near Culbone Church, between Porlock and Lynton, 259, 282, (487). And see Valley of Rocks

Lyrical Ballads, 116, 117; origins of, 218; *The Nightingale,* 252; plans for publication, 264, 265, 271-272; Hazlitt reads them, 265, and hears Coleridge talk of them, 269; publication, 287, (488) (and see Reviews); the "advertisement" quoted, 287-289; relationship between this and the famous preface to the second edition, 289, (489); true authorship of this second preface, 289, (489); quotations from it, (489-493); effect on Sarah Coleridge of Southey's pronouncement of failure, 347; Wordsworth investigates the state of the market, 364, and considers omitting the *Ancient Mariner* from the second edition, 365; 369; *Love,* (508-509); Wordsworth tells Coleridge not to trouble to deny the rumour that all the poems were by Coleridge, 409-410, (516); various editions and reprints, (476)

Lysons, Dr., of Bath, informed against the Wordsworths as a "suspicious emigrant family," 208

Machule, P., (517)

Mackintosh, Sir James, recommended Coleridge to Stuart's attention from Cote House, (473); discussed by Coleridge and Hazlitt's father, 233-234, (474); 261; 387; Coleridge attends his lectures, 394; on Coleridge's report of Pitt's speech, (512)

Mad Mother, The, Wordsworth, later called *Her Eyes are Wild:*

[552]

Hazlitt on, 265; partially appreciated by reviewers of the *Lyrical Ballads*, 291
Madoc, Southey, Coleridge urges Southey to publish it "quam citissime," 371
Manchester Quarterly, (494)
MANNING, J. E., (446)
MANNING, Thomas, of Cambridge, Coleridge dines with Lamb to meet him, 397, (513); back chat and accusations, 398, discovered to have no foundation, 399; letter from Lamb, 400, 409
MARKES, Mr, a clergyman to whom Northmore presented Paine's books, 362
MARSH MILLS, John Poole's house, near Stowey: Poole introduces Coleridge and Southey there, 48, 84
MARTIN, Henry, a Cambridge friend, 44, (431)
MASSON, David, (420)
MATHEWS, William, friend to whom Wordsworth writes that he is going to Bristol "to see those two extraordinary young men, Southey and Coleridge," 84
MATLOCK, visited from Darley Hall, 121
MAY, John, friend of Southey's, 356
MEANLEY, The Rev. Astley, Unitarian minister in Birmingham, (445); 98, (446)
Memoir of the Life and Poetry of William Wordsworth, Barron Field, (471)
Memoir of the Life and Writings of William Taylor of Norwich, J. W. Robberds, (494), (503)
Memoirs of Emma Courtney, Mary Hays, (509)
Memoirs of the Life of Sir Humphry Davy, Bart., by John Davy, (420)
Memoirs of William Hazlitt, W. Carew Hazlitt, (474)
Memoirs of William Wordsworth, Christopher Wordsworth, (419)

Memorials of Coleorton, ed. William Knight, (417)
"METAPHYSICS . . . are my darling studies," 254-255
METEYARD, Eliza, (474), (502), (505)
METRE, the innovations of the *Lyrical Ballads*, 290; of *Christabel*, (494)
Metrical Letter written from London, Southey, (509)
MICHAELIS, Johann David, German theologian, 1717-1791: Coleridge plans to bring back his works from Jena, 110, 292
MIDDLETON, Thomas Fanshawe, at Christ's Hospital with Coleridge, 18, (422); draws Boyer's attention to Coleridge, 19; sends Bowles' *Sonets . . . on picturesque spots* to Coleridge from Cambridge, 24; his help in starting Coleridge at the university, 29, missed after he goes down, 30; 31, (427)
MILTON, John, read by Coleridge at Christ's Hospital, 24-25; "the solemn lordliness of Milton," 137; charged with obscurity by his contemporaries, 159; comments by Coleridge, 269; Klopstock— "a very *German* Milton," 316; Glover's blank verse preferred by Klopstock to his, 317; 358; 362; Coleridge plans two poems "in the manner of Penseroso and Allegro," 368; his *Accidence*, 403; Coleridge on Wordsworth as the greatest poet since Milton, 407-408
Milton's Prosody, R. Bridges, (494)
MINEHEAD, 209, 268, 354
MINNESINGER—and "the master singers, their degenerate successors," read by Coleridge at Göttingen, 332
Minnow among Tritons, (Sarah's letters to Poole), ed. Stephen Potter, (418)
MIRACLE PLAYS, 342
Miscellany, A, Bradley, (480)

[553]

Modern Language Notes, (452), (465), (511)
Modern Language Review, (459)
Modern Patriotism, Coleridge's article in The Watchman, attacking Godwin, (448)
Modern Philology, (444), (500)
MOHAMMED, subject of the projected epic poem by Southey and Coleridge, 355, 358, 362
MONADS, "Of the infinite mind," in Religious Musings, 105, 186; "All his involvéd Monads" and their various functions described in The Progress of Liberty, 148; Coleridge tells Wordsworth Hartley's theory that all visible things are symbols of reality, "Monads of the infinite mind," 185-186; Leibnitz, the adaptor or inventor of monadism, 330
"MONEY-BOOK, MY," the schoolbook which Coleridge planned to write for money, 358, 362
Monk, The, Lewis, reviewed by Coleridge in the Critical Review, 1797, 151
Monody on the Death of Chatterton, Coleridge, in Boyer's album, 20; (434); referred to in Poole's presentation letter, 111; Coleridge's later condemnation of it and refusal to allow a reprint, 206
MONTAGUE, Basil, friend of Wordsworth, (442); his child, 179; his history, (465); project for him and Coleridge to take pupils for a three-year course, (471-472), abandoned, 221, (473); and Wordsworth's money, 363; in London, 1797, 387
MONTAGUE, Basil, natural son of the above, lives with the Wordsworths at Racedown, 179, (465), and Alfoxden, 203, (467), 207, (477); 387
Monthly Magazine, The, or Monthly Review, (444), (447); "has catar-

acted panegyric" on Poems on Various Subjects, 103; suggested to the more literary of The Watchman's subscribers as a substitute after The Watchman stopped, 111; Coleridge contributes to it occasionally, 117, 135; publishes three parody sonnets by Coleridge, 215; 219; condemns Wallenstein, 411
MOORE, Thomas, (451)
Moral and Political Lecture, A, Coleridge, 75, (440-441); see Conciones ad Populum
MORE, Hannah, The Fall of Robespierre, first dedicated to her, 49
MORGAN, John, a Bristol friend of Coleridge, (444)
MORLEY, Professor Edith, (420), (500)
MORLEY, John, (419)
Morning Chronicle, The, publishes sonnets and some other poems of Coleridge's, 1794-1795, 62, (436); Coleridge dines with Perry and Grey, proprietor and editor, 62; suggestion that Coleridge, who had been contributing fairly regularly, should become assistant editor, 118; suggestion falls through, 119; (451); (512)
Morning Post, The, Coleridge contributes to it, 221, (473), 224; his discussion, in a letter to the Wedgwoods, of journalism as a livelihood, 224-225; Coleridge behind with his contributions, 242; excellence of his poems contributed in 1798, Lewti and France: an Ode (under the title The Recantation), 245; The Devil's Thoughts, written jointly with Southey, published anonymously, September 1799, 355; Stuart's offer of a salaried post to Coleridge in London, 374; publication of Love (as Introduction to the Tale of the Dark Ladié), December 1799, 374, (508-509); Coleridge's

[554]

work for the *Morning Post*, 380, (511), 389, becomes less radical, 390, and he finally conforms to the paper's general liberal policy, 391; 383; discussion of the merits of his contributions, 392-393; he reports a debate for it, 393-395, (512); Coleridge's picture of his financial prospects if he stays with the *Morning Post*, 396; he withdraws from it, 405; *Character of Pitt*, 405, (506), (510)

MOSELEY, Coleridge stays with Hawkes there, and meets Charles Lloyd, 122, (450)

MOUSETRAPS, Coleridge's dislike of, (458)

MUIRHEAD, John H., (418)

MURILLO, referred to by Hazlitt in his account of Coleridge, 233

MURRAY, Charles, "Secretary of the Bridge-street Junto," (Secretary to the Constitutional Association for opposing Disloyal and Seditious Principles), Hazlitt, 237

My First Acquaintance with Poets, Hazlitt, (474), (486)

My Heart, To, Coleridge, title later changed to *On a Discovery Made too Late*, 55, (435)

MYERS, F. W. H., (463)

MYERS, The Rev. Thomas, uncle by marriage of the Wordsworths, 369

Mysteries of Udolpho, Mrs Radcliffe, reviewed by Coleridge in the *Critical Review*, 151

MYSTICS, THE CHRISTIAN. See under FOX, George, BOEHME, Jacob, and LAW, William

NAPOLEON, tells his soldiers in Italy to pillage, 172; Wordsworth abandons his French sympathies on Napoleon's coronation, (479); 386; Coleridge and Hazlitt on, 390; and *Wallenstein*, 411

NAYLOR, Benjamin, of Sheffield, 97; part owner of the *Sheffield Iris*, and

so discouraging to Coleridge's *Watchman*, 98, (446)

NECESSITARIANISM, "I am a complete necessitarian," 63, 297; Wordsworth as a Godwinian necessitarian, 174

NEO-PLATONISTS, Coleridge's interest in them aroused at Christ's Hospital by the essays on Liberty and Necessity in Cato's *Letters*, 21; satisfy the mystical but not the intellectual side of Coleridge, 64; Coleridge still interested in them, 137; they teach him to regard beauty as the revelation of spirit through matter, 294, 295

NESBITT, Fanny, poems dedicated to her, 33

NETHER STOWEY, home of Thomas Poole, 47; Coleridge and Southey there, 47-48; Coleridge and Sarah visit Poole there, 1795, 90; Coleridge visits Poole after demise of *The Watchman*, 113, 120; his wish, growing almost to hysteria, to live near Poole at Stowey, 125, 126, 129, (451), 131, 133, 134, 139, 140-144; the move to Stowey, 144; life there, 145-162, 203-212, 216-285; discussion as to the possibility of leaving the Stowey district and of possible houses for the Coleridges, 324, 325, 337, 343; 336; Wordsworth deceived by Coleridge's firm announcement that he will not leave it, 363; 384, 406, 407, 408

New Morality, The, a poem published in the *Anti-Jacobin*, which attacked Coleridge and his friends. Reprinted in *The Beauties of the Anti-Jacobin*, 1799, with a footnote suggesting that Coleridge had deserted his wife and family, 381

New Studies in Literature, (476)

New Theory of Vision, The, Berkeley, 300

NEWTON, Sir Isaac, references in Hartley's writings, 65; Coleridge states that his philosophy expressed in his *Optics* leads to atheism, 298, (494-495)

NEWTON, Robert, an old soldier at whose cottage the Wordsworth brothers and Coleridge lodged at Grasmere, 369

Nightingale, The, Coleridge, 251-253; only one reviewer praises it after its appearance in the *Lyrical Ballads*, 291

Nineteenth Century, The, (468)

NORDHAUSEN, Wordsworth and Dorothy there, 328

NORTHCOTE, Sir Stafford, squire of Ottery district, former pupil of John Coleridge, 15, (421)

NORTHMORE, Thomas, "a pupil of Wakefield . . . edited a Tryphiodorus and part of Plutarch," 356; offensive to the aristocrats, 362

NORWICH, Coleridge refuses to become Unitarian minister there, 214, (470); 359

Nose, The: An Odaic Rhapsody, 23

NOTEBOOKS, COLERIDGE'S, their value in illustrating the range of his mind, and his perception of nature, 138, 159; Coleridge on their value to him: proposed edition of them: extracts, (453-456); 252, (481), (499)

Notes and Lectures upon Shakespeare, Coleridge, edited by his daughter, Sara, (495)

NOTTINGHAM. See under WATCHMAN. Coleridge hopes to be appointed Unitarian minister there, 118

OAKOVER, visited from Darley Hall, 121

Oberon, Wieland, Coleridge plans to translate it, 216, 292, 308

Observations on Man, by Hartley, 65-66, (437)

Ode to the Departing Year, Coleridge, 1796, prophesying the extinction of an England that took up arms against the friends of freedom: sent to Flower for the *Cambridge Intelligencer*, 144; included in the second edition of the *Poems*, 158

Oft o'er My Brain, Coleridge, sonnet to the child Hartley, (462)

OGLE, Captain, interested in the odd recruit who was Coleridge, 38, (428-429)

Old and the New Schoolmaster, The, Lamb, (513)

Old Manor House, The, Charlotte Smith, (511)

OMOND, T. S., (494)

On a Ruined House, Coleridge, parody sonnet, (471)

On Bala Hill, Coleridge, 1793. Written on walking tour, 44, (431)

On Observing a Blossom on the First of February, 1796, Coleridge, (446)

On Revealed Religion, its Corruptions and its Political Views, six lectures by Coleridge, 75, (441)

On the Constitution of Church and State, Coleridge, (432)

On the Present War, lecture by Coleridge, 75, (441). See *Conciones ad Populum*

OPITZ and the Silesian poets, "models of pure diction," 332

OPIUM, Coleridge's use of, 29; as a consolation for domestic miseries, 101; at Göttingen, (500). See LAUDANUM

Optics, Isaac Newton, 65, 298, (494)

Opus Maximum, Coleridge's projected, chapters from, (418), 350; "my Great Work," 359

Origin of Evil, The. See EPIC POEM

ORLEANS, Wordsworth at, 167

Osorio, Coleridge, 1797, begun at Sheridan's invitation for performance at Drury Lane, 151, 152; two and a half acts read to the Wordsworths at Racedown, 153-154,

189; imitative of Wordsworth's *Borderers*, 195; finished, 212; did Coleridge take it on his visit to Bowles? (469); thoughts from Brahmin philosophy put into Alhadra's mouth, 214; Coleridge depressed about its prospects, 214; its tardy rejection, 220; plan that Cottle should publish it abandoned, 263-264; quoted by Coleridge to Hazlitt, 270; two fragments published in the first edition of the *Lyrical Ballads*, 289; 308; quotation, 336, see (500)

OTTERY ST. MARY, Coleridge born there, 1772, 11; chief effect on Coleridge of a childhood spent there—ill-health, 13-15; 17, 27; death of Smerdon, vicar of Ottery, 1794, 60; Coleridge visits his family there, 1796, 120, (479); and in 1799, 356-357; 406

OTTFRIED, his metrical paraphrase of the gospel, 332

Pain, sonnet by Coleridge, (423)

PAINE, Thomas, his *Rights of Man* convinced Coleridge of man's inalienable right to self-government, 41, (464); "that rude blunderer," 313; Northmore offends public opinion by presenting Paine's books to a clergyman, 362

Pains of Sleep, The, Coleridge, (487), (499)

PALEY, William, projected strictures on him, (453); praised by Coleridge to Hazlitt, 236

PANTHEISM, in Coleridge and Wordsworth, 195; the logical conclusion of Spinoza's system, 305

PANTISOCRACY, derivation, (430); initiated by Coleridge, Hucks, Allen, Southey, and Burnett, 1794: Poole's account of the scheme, 42; effect on Coleridge, 43; Southey's first signs of backsliding, 45, 57; the Fricker nucleus, 46; missionary endeavour in Bristol and Stowey, 47-49; the understanding between Coleridge and Sarah a direct result of the scheme, 49; description by Coleridge, 51-52; advice on the site of the settlement by a young man from America, 52; jeers in Cambridge, 53; Coleridge's faith stands the shock of Mary Evans' disapproval, 54-57; position of servants, 57-58; Coleridge's fears for its corruption, 59-60; its long-term value in Coleridge's mental growth, 64; Southey's heretical amendment—the farm in Wales, 66, 67, 80; decay and death of pantisocracy, 73, 77; complete defection of Southey, 85, 87, 88, 89; echoes: in Coleridge's lectures, 76; in *Religious Musings*, 105; in Coleridge's hankering after a life of manual labour, 125; in Coleridge's wish to go abroad with Southey, 378; projected exposition, (453); the failure of pantisocracy mortal to Burnett, 153-154; 348

Papers of a Critic, The, Dilke, (441)

Paradise Lost, Milton, 408

PARODIES, three sonnets by Coleridge, parodying the styles of Lamb, Lloyd, and himself, published in the *Monthly Magazine* under the pseudonym Nehemiah Higginbottom, 215, 221

PARR, Samuel, "the learning of . . . Parr," 344

PARRY, Charles and Frederick, at Göttingen, and on expeditions from there, 331, (499), 332, 341-342, (500); the Scandinavian plan, 351-352, (502)

PARSONS, bookseller. Coleridge says Parsons owes him money, 229

PASCAL, Blaise, quoted by Coleridge, 335

PATRICK, David, the cousin who had brought up Sarah Hutchinson, 367

PAUL, SAINT, 304, 311
Peace and Union Recommended to the Associated Bodies of Republicans and Anti-Republicans, Frend: cause of his trial, (427)
PEARCE, Dr, Master of Jesus College, Cambridge, hints, according to Coleridge, at unfairness in the Craven Scholarship award, 32; remonstrates with Coleridge, 70
PECK, Dr Walter, (514)
Pedestrian Tour through North Wales in a Series of Letters, A, Hucks, (430), (431), (432)
PEGGY, the Wordsworths' maid at Alfoxden, 203, (467), (485)
PEMBERTON, Sophia, loved by Charles Lloyd, 149; elopement planned, 211; married, 397
PENMAENMAWR, Coleridge climbs it on a Welsh walking tour: a memorable phrase, 46, (432)
Penseroso, Il, Milton, 368
Pensive at Eve, Coleridge, parody sonnet, (471)
PERICLES, 313
PERRY, James, proprietor of the *Morning Chronicle*. Meets Coleridge in London, 1794, 62; considers Coleridge as assistant editor, 118-119
Peter Bell, Wordsworth, excelled in its own line by *The Three Graves*, (493); (516)
Philanthropist, The, monthly magazine projected by Wordsworth, (464), from 170
PHILLIPS, Sir Richard, Coleridge proposes to sell his Ballad to him for £5, 229; in London, 1799, 387, (511); Southey refuses to do business with him, 403
Philosophical Dictionary, Voltaire, Coleridge names this as the origin of his religious doubts, 21
PHLOGISTON, "There is *phlogiston* in your heart," 54, 79
Piccolomini, The, Schiller, 410

PIERCEBRIDGE, the George Inn, Lakes walking tour, 368, (507)
PINDAR, recited by Coleridge in the cloisters at Christ's Hospital, 22
PINNEY, family of, Bristol merchants, friends of Wordsworth, 85, (442); Azariah Pinney forwards *Guilt and Sorrow* to Coleridge via Cottle, 85, (443); John Pinney renews acquaintance with Coleridge in London, 1799, 387
PINNEY, Hester, (442)
PISTORIUS, The Rev. Herman Andrew, (448)
PITT, William, is held to be "one of the horns of the second beast in the Revelations" by the tallow chandler of Birmingham, 94, (446); attacks the English Jacobins, 171; compared unfavourably with Burke by Coleridge, 269; Coleridge, still opposed to him in 1799, attacks him in *Fire, Famine and Slaughter*, and in many leading articles, 390, 391; Coleridge reports Pitt in the House: "He argues but so-so and does not reason at all," 394, 395; 397; *Character of Pitt* by Coleridge published in the *Morning Post*, 1800, 405, (512)
Pitt, sonnet by Coleridge, printed in the *Morning Chronicle*, 1794, (436)
PLAMPIN, J., (429)
PLATO, *The Republic*, 41; translated by Thomas Taylor, 65, (437); and the Neo-Platonists, 64, 65, 294, 295; echoes from him in Berkeley's *Siris*, 300; "I love Plato, his dear, *gorgeous* nonsense," 301
Platonic Theology, Proclus, (423)
GEMISTUS or PLETHO (Gorgius), Coleridge studies his work, 301
Plot Discovered, The: or, An Address to the People against Ministerial Treason, the last of three lectures given by Coleridge in Bristol, in 1795, and later published, 75, (441)

PLOTINUS, expounded by Coleridge at school, 22; translated by Thomas Taylor, 65, (437), (448); Coleridge asks Thelwall to buy his works, 137; his influence in *Religious Musings*, 301-302

PLUME OF FEATHERS in Wine St., Bristol, Coleridge gives a series of lectures there, 75

PLUTARCH (*De Discernendo Adulatore ab Amico*), edited by Northmore, 356

Poem to Coleridge, The, Wordsworth and Dorothy's name for *The Prelude*, 366

Poems on the Death of Priscilla Farmer, Charles Lloyd, privately printed, 1796, with an introductory sonnet by Coleridge and *The Grandame* by Lamb, 131, (451)

Poems on Various Subjects, Coleridge, published April 1796: contents and reviews, 103-108, (447); second edition in preparation, 130, 140, 147; publication, 1797: the motto from 'Groscoll,' the dedication to George, new poems and the preface, 158-159, (462); third edition suggested: Lloyd asks for his poems to be omitted, 277

POETIC DICTION, Wordsworth's theory, and Coleridge's relation to it, 289, (489, 490-491, 493)

Poetical and Dramatic Works of Samuel Taylor Coleridge, The, (418)

Poetical Works of Samuel Taylor Coleridge, The, ed. James Dykes Campbell, (417)

Poetry Review, (486)

Political Justice, Godwin, influence on pantisocracy, (430); Coleridge attacks it, 114; effect on Wordsworth, 172-182

Political Thought of Coleridge, The, Harold Beeley, (512)

Political Thought of S. T. Coleridge, The, ed. R. J. White, (512)

POOLE, Charlotte, Thomas Poole's cousin, her first impressions of Coleridge, 84; further impressions —still unfavourable, 113; disapproves of Thelwall's visit to Stowey, and of the Wordsworths, 208

POOLE, Henry, at Cambridge with Coleridge: possible link between him and Thomas: at Marsh Mills, 47-48, 432-433

POOLE, John, of Marsh Mills, Coleridge and Southey meet him, 48; extract from his journal, (432)

POOLE, Richard, 48; congratulates Coleridge on *The Watchman*, but criticises it, 100; writes a "truly fraternal" letter to Coleridge, 109; his death, 281

POOLE, Thomas, on pantisocracy, 42; his character, and his picture of Coleridge, 47-48, (432); friendship with Coleridge resumed, 82; his value as a friend, 82-83; his poem to Coleridge, 83-84; visit of the Coleridges to Stowey, 90; probably gives money to Coleridge, 91; Coleridge apologizes for the Essay on Fasting, 100; Poole writes a letter to *The Watchman*, 100; generosity after the failure of *The Watchman*: raises an annual subscription for Coleridge, 111-113, (449), 117; among Coleridge's correspondents, 114; gives up sugar as a protest against slave labour, 115; told of Coleridge's plan to become a Dissenting Minister, 110-111, 118; on the inferiority of woman, 121; Coleridge sees in him the perfect workman, labouring with his hands by day, developing his mind by night, 125, 130; Coleridge's longing to live near him, 125; "my beloved friend," 136; he tries to dissuade Coleridge from the move to Nether Stowey, 139;

frenzied reply from Coleridge, 140-144; takes cottage for Coleridge at Stowey, 144; *Ode to the Departing Year* dedicated to him, 144; enthusiasm for *Osorio*, 152; organizes more financial help for Coleridge, 153; his garden, 159; his services in procuring Alfoxden, 161, (460); his relationship with Coleridge compared with Wordsworth's, 196; his single-mindedness and lack of jealousy, 197; visit from Thelwall, 204, (467); defended by Coleridge from probable results of Thelwall's settling in the neighbourhood, 209-210; Coleridge tells him of the rejection of *Osorio*, 220; advises Coleridge against rejecting the Wedgwoods' offer of £100, 223, 227; forwards the second Wedgwood offer, 238-239; 241; his joy at Coleridge's acceptance, 242; tries to get Alfoxden lease renewed, (484); tries to find another house for the Wordsworths, 262; Hazlitt meets him, 267; told of the arrival of Coleridge's second son, Berkeley, 277; letter from Coleridge on the death of his brother, Richard, 281; Mrs Coleridge and the children left in his care at Stowey, 285; Coleridge values his friendship, 286; his steadfastness, 311; his letters to Coleridge in Germany, and answers: advice, 318-319, 324-325; Coleridge homesick for his company, 321, 322-323; assurances of steadfastness, "*I will not part from you, if you will not part from me*," 325, 343; on Berkeley's death, 333-335, 335-337, 341, 346; correspondence with Sarah, 347-348, (501); called as a witness that Coleridge had "never discovered the least personal enmity" against Southey, 354-355; letter from

Coleridge, 356; friendship with Davy, 361, (505); disappointment about the Wedgwoods, (505); his value to Coleridge as a substitute for Wordsworth in the latter's absence, 364; Poole hurt by the gradual realization that Coleridge is not coming back to Stowey now that Wordsworth has settled in the Lakes, 383, 387; futile house-hunting, 384, 407, 408; praise of Coleridge's journalism, 386; warning against bad company, 386, 387; correspondence about the *Morning Post* job, 392, 393, 395-396, 397; reproaches Coleridge for prostrating himself before Wordsworth, and is answered, 407-409; visit from Coleridge, 412-413; the inevitable parting, "with pain and dejection," 415-416

Poor Relations, Lamb, (422)

POPE, Alexander, still revered prophet of an all-powerful creed in 1789, 25; influence on Wordsworth's early poetry, 166; Coleridge speaks "with intolerance" of him to Hazlitt, 269

POPE, The, (513)

PORLOCK, visited on the *Ancient Mariner* walk, 219; the intrusion of the "person . . . from Porlock" interrupts irretrievably the writing of *Kubla Khan*, 259-260, 282, (483); date of this, (487)

PORPHYRY, Coleridge asks Thelwall to buy his works, 137

PORSON, Richard, Greek scholar, meets Coleridge in London, 1794-1795, 62, (436); 344

POTTER, Stephen, (474)

POUSSIN, Gaspar, 268

Prelude, The, or *Growth of a Poet's Mind*, (419); Wordsworth, picture of Coleridge's schooldays, 17, (422); origins of, 216, 366-368, (506); the skating lines, 322, "had

I met these lines running wild ...",
(498)
Presbyterianism in Nottingham, Carpenter, (445)
PRIESTLEY, Joseph, scientist and theologian, (431); a hero of Coleridge and Lamb, 50, (434); 102; tribute in *Religious Musings*, 105; "I regard every experiment that Priestley made in Chemistry as giving *wings* to his more sublime theological works," 241; Coleridge discontented with Priestley's doubts as to the survival of infants, 338
PRIESTLEY, sonnet by Coleridge, published, *Morning Chronicle*, 1794, 62, (436)
Principles of Human Knowledge, Berkeley, 300
PROCLUS, Coleridge buys his works through Thelwall, 137; studies him, 301, (423)
Progress of Liberty, The. See *Destiny of Nations, The*
Prose Works of William Wordsworth, The, ed. Grosart, (419)
PROSODY, Coleridge and Wordsworth create a minor revolution in, 290-291, (494)
Provincial Magazine, The, projected by Coleridge and Southey, to be edited jointly, 1795, 74; plan abandoned owing to quarrel, 86, 91
PUNS, common with Coleridge when in high spirits, 342, (500), 359-360, (504)
Purchas his Pilgrimage, a source of *Kubla Khan*, 259, (483)
PURKIS of Brentford, a business friend of Poole's, 119, 284, 386, 397
Putnam's Magazine, (500)

Queen Mab, Shelley, (481)
QUILLER COUCH, Sir Arthur, (476)

RACEDOWN (Lodge or Farm), lent by John Pinney to Wordsworth, (442); the Wordsworths living there, 152, 154-156, 161, 175-181; Coleridge visits them there, 154, 156, 163, 182, 187-189, 193, 194, 196; Dorothy thinks of returning there after Alfoxden, 262
RALEIGH, Walter, (463)
RAMLER, Karl Wilhelm, 332
RAPHAEL, Coleridge indifferent to his work, 269
RATZEBURG, a small lakeside town near Hamburg: Coleridge and Chester there, 315, 317-329, 330, 332
RAWSON, Mrs, Dorothy Wordsworth's aunt, 284
RAYSOR, T. M., (418), (509)
REA, John D., (452)
READING, Coleridge billeted at the White Hart, 39
Reading of Southey and Coleridge, The, Paul Kauffman, in *Modern Philology*, (444)
Recantation, The, earlier name for *France: an Ode*, 245
Recluse, The, Wordsworth, projected, and 1,300 lines written, 261-262, (506); Coleridge's part in it, (484); Coleridge mainly responsible for its continuation, 364, 365-367, (516); plan to write a tail-piece to it, addressed to those who were disillusioned by the sequel to the French Revolution (see under *Prelude, The*), 366-368
Recollections of a Bluecoat Boy, W. P. Scargill, (423)
Recollections of Christ's Hospital, Lamb, (423), (424)
REED, Samuel, 406
Reflections on entering into Active Life (later, *Reflections on having left a Place of Retirement*), Coleridge, (444)
Reflections on Having Left a Place of Retirement, Coleridge, companion

piece to *The Eolian Harp*, included in the second edition of *Poems on Various Subjects*, 1797, 158, (444)

Religious Musings, Coleridge, (465); in progress, at Cambridge, 1794, 104; at Bristol, 1795,79; at Stowey, 90; quoted to the tallow-chandler of Birmingham, 95; completed and published in *Poems on Various Subjects*, 1796: "I rest all my credit on the *Religious Musings*," mistaken judgment, 103, (447); quotations and analysis, 104-105, 106, 107-108, (447-448); ecstatic praise in the *Monthly Review*, 103; criticized by Richard Poole as being "too metaphysical for common readers": Coleridge answers, "not written for common readers," 109; discussed with Thelwall, 137; 185; Wordsworth's admiration for it, 186; echoes of it in Wordsworth's poetry, 188-189; Coleridge hails Hartley in this, while condemning him implicitly in *The Destiny of Nations*, 297; Berkeleian tone of the poem, 298; lip service still paid to the principle of necessity, 301; influence of Plotinus, 301-302; tribute to Priestley, (434)

Reminiscences, Thomas Moore, (451)

Reminiscences of Cambridge, Henry Gunning, (427)

Reminiscences of Coleridge and Southey, Cottle, (417)

Review of English Studies, (442), (443)

REVIEWS, of *Poems on Various Subjects*: "The *Monthly* has *cataracted* panegyric on my poems, the *Critical* has *cascaded* it; and the *Analytical* has *dribbled* it with very tolerable civility. The *Monthly* has at least done justice to my *Religious Musings*; they place it 'on the very top of the scale of sublimity'!!!" 103; of the *Lyrical*

Ballads: importance entirely missed by the critics, 287, 291-292; Southey's unfavourable review, 291, (494), (502), displeases Wordsworth, 365, and Coleridge, (506), and Lamb, 378-379, (502); of 'Wallenstein': *The Anti-Jacobin Review*, the *Monthly Review*, and the *British Critic* all condemn it, 411

Revisiting the Wye, On (Lines written a few miles above Tintern Abbey), Wordsworth, 116

Revue Anglo-Americaine, La, (463)

REYNELL, Richard, visit to Stowey and comments on Coleridge's capacity as a walker, 211, (468-469)

REYNOLDS, Sir Joshua, quoted in the preface to the *Lyrical Ballads*, 288

"RIBBED SEA SANDS," 269, (486)

RICHARDS, I. A., (476)

RICHARDSON, Samuel, liked by Coleridge, 269

RIPPERS, 341, (500)

Road to Xanadu, John Livingston Lowes, (418), (481-482)

ROBBERDS, J. W., (494)

ROBERTS, Mr and Mrs, possible pantisocrats, 58

ROBESPIERRE, Maximilien Marie Isidore, extolled extravagantly after his death by Southey and Coleridge, 48; hated by Wordsworth, 171

ROBINSON, Henry Crabb, (420),(460)

ROBINSON, Mrs "Perdita," meets Coleridge in London, 1799, 387, (511); illness: Coleridge tries to get acid from Davy to cure her, 414; her death, (517)

ROMANTIC REVIVAL, Coleridge's contribution to it with his *Love*, 374; and the 'Gothic' School, 150

ROSCHER, Hans, (512)

ROSCOE, William, author of the *Life of Lorenzo the Magnificent*, suggests through Edwards that Coleridge should come and live at Liverpool where "a comfortable situation" could be found for him, 1796, 122, (450)

Rose, The, Coleridge, 1793, dedicated to Fanny Nesbitt, 33

ROSKILLY, Mrs, wife of the former curate at Stowey, now rector of Kempsford; Sarah and Hartley visit her, 397, (513)

Ross, Coleridge and Hucks visit it on a walking tour: Coleridge writes a poem to Kyrle, Man of Ross, on his bedroom shutter, 43

ROSSINGTON, The Rev. H. J., (445)

ROUSSEAU, Jean Jacques, (467)

ROWE, John, Unitarian minister at Shrewsbury, whom Coleridge considers succeeding, 221, 222, 230, 231, 238

Ruined Cottage, The, Wordsworth, read aloud to Coleridge on his first visit to Racedown, 1797, 155; Coleridge's admiration for it, 191, 193, 264

RUMFORD, Count, (Sir Benjamin Thompson), originator of garden cities in Bavaria; Coleridge reviews his essays favourably, writes a sonnet to him, and plans a pamphlet on the Rumfordizing of Bristol, Birmingham, and Manchester, 108-109, (448); the chimneys of the projected school at Derby to be Rumfordized, 122; Lamb teases Coleridge about his enthusiasm for Rumford, 127; chimneys of the cottage at Stowey not Rumfordized, 145

RUSSELL, William, his *History of Modern Europe,* 1799, to be used in the projected scissors-and-paste *History of Levellers,* 402

SACHS, Hans, enjoyed by Coleridge, 332; talk of him, 342

SACRAMENTAL RITES, Coleridge's dislike of them, 124, (451)

SADLEIR, Michael, (435)

SAINTSBURY, George, (494)

ST. ALBYN, Mrs, owner of Alfoxden; censures her tenant for sub-letting to the Wordsworths, 214; refuses to extend lease, 262, (484), 265

Salisbury Plain, Wordsworth, 264

SALLY. See WEEKS, Sally

SALUTATION AND CAT, The, London, Coleridge spends his evenings there with Lamb, 50, (434), 71; reminiscences of these times in Lamb's letters, 127

SAMPSON, George, (476)

SAMUEL, Stuart M., (493)

Samuel Taylor Coleridge, James Dykes Campbell, (417)

Samuel Taylor Coleridge and the English Romantic School, Alois Brandl, (438)

Samuel Taylor Coleridge and Unitarianism, H. W. Stevenson, (445)

SANDFORD, Mrs Henry, (419)

Satyrane's Letters, Coleridge, (496-497)

SAYERS, Dr, of Norwich, (470)

SCANDINAVIA, Coleridge plans a walking tour there, 351-352, (502)

SCHELLING, Friedrich Wilhelm Joseph von, Coleridge anticipates some of what he is later to find in him, 308-311; still unread, 348

SCHILLER, von J. C. F., Coleridge plans to learn German and translate all Schiller's works: also to go to Jena and meet him, 110, 292; his *Conspiracy of Fiesco* quoted by Southey, 126; his *Robbers* compared with Wordsworth's *Borderers* by Coleridge, 156, 283, 308; Coleridge plans to translate his *Gotten des Griechenland* and to write an antiphony to it, 368, (507); Coleridge translates his unpublished drama, *Wallenstein,* q.v., 389; correspondence with Coleridge about copyright, 410

The, pupils of Heyne,

Radcliffe, Unitarian
Birmingham, (444)
ter, 268, 287
mes Thomson, Cole-

..., an error for Suss-
MILCH, 350
Selections from the Letters of Robert Southey, ed. John Wood Warter, (419)
SEMLER, Johann Salomo, German theologian, 1725–1791. Coleridge wishes to go to Jena to study, and to bring back with him "all the works of Semler," 110, 292
SENSUOUS, word claimed to have been coined by Coleridge, (495)
SHADRACH (SHAD). See WEEKS, Shadrach
SHAKESPEARE, William, read by Coleridge at Christ's Hospital, 24-25; "profound touches of the human heart," 156; compared with Milton, "a mere stripling in the art," 269; talked of by Coleridge, 342
SHAWCROSS, J., (418)
SHEDD, Professor W. G. T., (418)
Shelley, Godwin and their Circle, H. N. Brailsford, (464)
SHELVOCKE, George, his *Voyage* the source of the albatross story which Wordsworth told Coleridge, 219
SHELLEY, Percy Bysshe, 287; Mary Wollstonecraft his mother-in-law, (436); his *Queen Mab* quoted, (481), (488)
SHERIDAN, Richard Brinsley, invites Coleridge to write a play for Drury Lane: hence *Osorio*, 151; 212, (469); delays in deciding for or against *Osorio*, 214, 220; rejects it, 220; 264; as a politician, 395
Sheridan, sonnet by Coleridge, published *Morning Chronicle*, 1795, 62, (436)

SHIREHAMPTON, the Wordsworths lodge there, 284
SHORE, Samuel, (446)
SHORT, Mrs, aunt of Coleridge, kind to him during his schooldays in London, 18, 27
SHREWSBURY, project that Coleridge should become Unitarian minister there, 221-227; Hazlitt's account of the trial visit, 230-237; 238, 240; Coleridge's popularity there, 242-243
SHUFFLEBOTTOM, Abel, Southey's parody pseudonym, 222
SHURTON BARS, 340; see also *Lines Written on Shurton Bars*
Sibylline Leaves, Coleridge, (457), (472), (473), (493), (508)
Siddons, Mrs, sonnet by Coleridge, published *Morning Chronicle*, 1794, (436)
SIDONIUS APOLLINARIS, Coleridge asks Thelwall to buy his works, 137, but perhaps meant Apollonius of Tyana, (452)
Sigh, The, Coleridge, 1794, to Mary Evans, 41, (429-430)
SYLVESTER, Matthew, edited *Reliquiae Baxterianae*, 1696, 308
Siris, by George Berkeley, echoes of Plato, 300
SKATING, de Quincey on Klopstock and Wordsworth, 316; Wordsworth's account in *The Prelude*, 322; Coleridge's in a letter to Sarah, 326
SLAVE TRADE, Coleridge lectures on, 1795, 76; Coleridge and Poole give up sugar as a protest, 115
SMERDON, The Rev. Fulwood, vicar of Ottery. Elegy on him by Coleridge, 1794, *Lines on a Friend who died in a Frenzy Fever induced by Calumnious Reports*, 60-61, (435)
SMITH, The Rev. Mr, Coleridge's fag at Christ's Hospital, (424)
SMITH, Adam, his *Wealth of Nations*, taken by Coleridge and his friends

as practically supporting the pantisocratic theory, 42

SMITH, Charlotte, meets Coleridge in London, 1799, 387, (511)

SMITH, Edward, (463)

SMITH, the Rev. Leapidge, description of Coleridge, (452)

SMOKING, Coleridge in Germany, 327

SNYDER, Alice D., (476), (500)

Social Life at the English Universities, (428)

SOCINIAN, Coleridge becomes a Socinian after contact with Frend, 31; 405

SOCKBURN-ON-TEES, the Wordsworths there, staying with the Hutchinsons, 363; 365; Coleridge and Cottle visit them there: Coleridge's first meeting with Sarah Hutchinson, 367-368; the stone figure of Sir Ralph Conyers in the church is the "arméd knight" of Love, 375; 384; the Wordsworths move from there to Dove Cottage, Grasmere, 409

Son of Robespierre, The, MS. anonymous novel, possibly the work of Coleridge, (514)

Songs of the Pixies, Coleridge, published 1796, 103, (428); 33

Sonnet: On Quitting School for College, Coleridge, 1791, (422)

Sonnet: To the River Otter, Coleridge, (422)

Sonnets attempted in the Manner of Contemporary Writers, by Nehemiah Higginbottom, Coleridge's three parody sonnets, 215, (471), 221

SONNETS on the birth of Hartley, Coleridge, 1796, 124, full titles, (450)

SONNETS to the child Hartley, Coleridge, 1797, 158, full titles, (462)

Soother in Absence, The, projected work by Coleridge, (429)

SOUTHEBY, W., letters to, (489), (516)

SOUTHEY, the Rev. Charles Cuthbert, (419)

SOUTHEY, Edith (see also FRICKER, Edith), secret marriage to Southey, 89; 205, 207; to Lisbon with Southey, 401

SOUTHEY, Robert, admiration for Bowles, 25; first meeting with Coleridge and mutual liking, 41, (430); the hatching of pantisocracy, 42; Southey and Burnett walk to Bristol, elaborating the scheme, 43; his definition of aspheterism, 43, (431); first signs of backsliding, 45; introduces Coleridge to the Frickers at Bristol, 46; his engagement to Edith Fricker, 46, 49; missionary work for pantisocracy, at Bristol, 46-47, 49, at Stowey, 47-48, (432); his extravagant praise of the dead Robespierre, 48; The Fall of Robespierre, 49; 51, 52; begins to harry Coleridge about his treatment of Sarah Fricker, 53, 54, 56-57; "There is phlogiston in your heart," Coleridge, 54; his accceptance of Coleridge's poetical criticisms, 54, 62; friction over the status of servants under pantisocracy, 57, 58; over the inclusion of Mrs Southey and Mrs Fricker, 59-60; Southey's intractability over Coleridge's waverings, 61, 62, 66; he proposes the Welsh farm scheme—a heretical amendment of pantisocracy, 66-67; 68, 70, 71; travels to London and fetches Coleridge back to Bristol and Sarah Fricker: reconciliation, 72; says (later) that he was surprised by Coleridge's engagement to Sarah, (433); money difficulties, 73; his poems published, 73, (440); he plans Joan of Arc, 74; joint plans with Coleridge: The Provincial Magazine, 74; Lectures, 74, 76; Joan of Arc accepted by Cottle, 77;

growing dislike of pantisocracy when it appears to mean supporting Coleridge in idleness, 80; friction, 81, (442); breach with Coleridge, 82; bitter quarrels, 85, (443); 87; abandons pantisocracy in favour of the Law, 88; marries Edith Fricker and goes to Lisbon, 89, (444); wish for a life of manual labour, 125; partial reconciliation with Coleridge, 126-127, (451); some of his sonnets privately printed, 1796, 131; friendship with Lloyd, 149; Coleridge prophesies "that he will be known to posterity as Shakespeare's great grandson," 151; effect of his defection from pantisocracy on Burnett, 153-154; (464); invitation to Stowey and Alfoxden, 205, 207, not accepted, 207; correspondence with Coleridge on the reprint of Chatterton's poems, 206; and on the Wordsworths, 207; attacks Coleridge about the parody sonnets, and copies the latter, 221-222; his *Vision of Judgment* referred to by Hazlitt, 237; further estranged from Coleridge, perhaps by Lloyd's mischief-making, 279; 280, 282, (487-488); described by Dorothy Wordsworth, 284; reviews the *Lyrical Ballads* unfavourably, 291, 365, 378-379, (506); jeers at what he takes to be Coleridge's philosophical instability, 295; 317, Sarah stays with him and his wife at Westbury after Berkeley's death, 346-348; effect on Sarah of his condemnation of the *Lyrical Ballads*, 347, (502); Coleridge effects a partial reconciliation, 352-355; they collaborate in *The Devil's Walk*, and project an epic on Mohammed, 355, (503); Southey on old Mrs Coleridge, 356; walking tour with Coleridge, 357, (508); letters from

Coleridge, 358-359, 371; friendship with Davy and enthusiasm over the new gas, 361; 362, (505); urged by Coleridge to finish and publish *Madoc*, 371; the news that he may go abroad to recuperate from illness revives in Coleridge pantisocratic longings, 378, 382; the *Anti-Jacobin* libels, 380, (510-511); correspondence with Coleridge, 380-382; 383; his ill-health, 387; second volume of his *Annual Anthology* q.v., 389, 394-395; the wrangle over Mary Hays, 398-399; departure to Lisbon with Edith, 401, (514); Coleridgean schemes for making the money for this trip, 402-404, (514); correspondence, 404-406; Southey not appreciative enough of Wordsworth's greatness to please Coleridge, 407; 415

Southey, sonnet by Coleridge, published *Morning Chronicle*, 1795, 62, (436)

Southey, projected ode by Coleridge, (455)

Southey, Thomas, Southey's brother. Letters to him about pantisocracy, 47; about the new gas, 361; about the *Anti-Jacobin* attack, (511)

Southey, Mrs, Southey's mother, 57; "If Mrs S. and Mrs F. come with us they can at least prepare the food of simplicity," 59; "I wish . . . that the two mothers were not to go," 60; Southey's wish to help her financially a reason for his defection from pantisocracy, 80; Southey joins her at Bath after split with Coleridge, 82

Sparrow's Nest, The, Wordsworth, (465)

Spinoza, Benedict, facetious story of the Government spy's mishearing, "Spy Nozy," 208; hold on Coleridge shewn by quotations from *This Lime-Tree Bower my Prison*, 213; analysis of his place in Coleridge's philosophical development, 295, 304, 305; rediscovered by Coleridge, "sunk in Spinoza," 358; 380, 415

Spirit of the Age, The, Hazlitt, (517)

SPY SCARE, investigations by a Government spy into the doings of Wordsworth and Coleridge after Thelwall's visit, 208-209

Stanhope, Lord, sonnet by Coleridge, published *Morning Chronicle*, 1795, (436)

Stanzas written after a Long Absence, Coleridge, (438)

STEINBURG, Baron, Minister of State at Hanover, 330

STEPHEN, Leslie, (464), (482)

STEVENSON, H. W., (445)

STOCKOE, F. W., (503)

STODDART, John, friend of Allen and Southey, 41, (430)

STOKE D'ABERNON, Coleridge stays with the Wedgwoods there, 284

Story of a Devonshire House, The, Lord Coleridge, K.C., (421)

Story of the English Jacobins, The, Edward Smith, (463)

STOWEY, See NETHER STOWEY

STOWEY BENEFIT CLUB, run by Poole; Thelwall endangers it, 210

STRUTT, Jedediah, cotton spinner of Derby: father of Mrs Elizabeth Evans of Darley Hall, and of William and Joseph, 97

STRUTT, Joseph, see above, 97

STRUTT, William, see above, 97; "dissuasive" of the plan whereby Coleridge was to tutor the Evans boys of Darley Hall, 120

STUART, Daniel, editor of the *Morning Post*, arranges for Coleridge to be paid a guinea a week for poems and articles, 221, (473); Coleridge fails to call on him about future contributions before leaving for Germany, 286; non-arrival of contributions from Germany, 318-319; offers to house Coleridge in London and pay him a handsome salary, 374; does so, 378, 380, 384, 387, 389; later controversy as to Coleridge's success in journalism, 392, 395; attempts to whip up Coleridge's flagging interest, 392-393, 394, 395; reception of the Pitt report, 395, (512-513); Coleridge states that Stuart offered him a half share in two papers, 396; Lamb's *My Great Aunt's Manuscript* introduced to Stuart by Coleridge, 397; Southey and Stuart, 402; Coleridge's work for him ceases temporarily, 405, 415

Studies in Philology, (509)

Strictures on the French Revolution and the British Constitution, Richard Watson, Bishop of Llandaff, (464)

SUGAR, given up by Coleridge and Poole as a protest against slave labour, 1796, 115; "Sugar from bete, oh! all Germany is mad about it," 344

SURVIVAL, Coleridge on, after Berkeley's death, 338

SUSQUEHANNAH RIVER, navigable, 47; projected site of the pantisocratic settlement, 49, 51-52, (434), 182

SWITZERLAND, invasion of by France, Coleridge's horror recorded in *France: an Ode*, 245-246, (479)

Table Talk and Omniana of Samuel Taylor Coleridge, ed. T. Ashe, (418)

Tables Turned, The, Wordsworth, (465)

Tait's Magazine, (461), (466), (497)

Tale of a Woman (*The Ruined Cottage*), Wordsworth, 264

Task, The, Cowper, the projected poem, *The Brook*, to be in the manner of *The Task*, 209; quoted, 275, (486)

TAUNTON, Coleridge breakfasts there, 154; preaches there, (474), 270, 277

TAYLOR, Samuel, godfather to Coleridge, (421)

TAYLOR, Jeremy, "Bishop Taylor, old Baxter, David Hartley and the Bishop of Cloyne are my men," 298; Coleridge on his richness of style and imagery, 269; talked of by Coleridge, 342; 358; Coleridge's own prose style at its best is like Taylor's, 389|

TAYLOR, Thomas, translator, 21, (423); his Plato and Plotinus, 65, (437); "the English pagan," 255

TAYLOR, William, of Norwich, (470), (503); books borrowed from him, 359

TENNYSON, Alfred Lord, 287

Thalaba, Coleridge urges Southey to finish it quickly, 402, (514-515); (511) from 387

THELWALL, John, revolutionary and poet: arrested and tried for high treason, 1794, 171; corresponds with Coleridge: objects to a passage in *Conciones ad Populum*, and later to *The Watchman* article on Godwin, 114, (449); friendship springs out of a series of long happy epistolary wrangles, 115; "Have you, my dear Thelwall!— no plan for your future Life?" 133; Coleridge describes himself to Thelwall, 136-137; and asks Thelwall to buy him books, 137; 138; Thelwall visits Stowey, 204, (466-467); his advocacy of free education countered by Coleridge's gardening analogy, 205; description by Coleridge, 205-206; his visit causes trouble to his friends, 207-211; his wish to settle near Stowey, 204, (467), and its abandonment, 209-210; 213; told

news of the Wedgwood annuity, 241; 298; Coleridge's wish to convert him from atheism, 301; 307, 359, (423)

Thomas Poole and his Friends, Mrs Henry Sandford, (419)

THOMPSON, Sir Benjamin. See RUMFORD, Count

THOMSON, James, influence on Wordsworth's early poetry, 166; Coleridge on *The Seasons*, 269

Thorn, The, Wordsworth, Hazlitt on, 265; mentioned in the preface to the first edition of the *Lyrical Ballads*, 288; its value, 291; partially appreciated by the critics, 291; his note to it quoted, (495)

"THOTH the Egyptian," 255

Thought and Imagination in Art and Life, Katharine Wilson, (496)

THRELKELD, Elizabeth, correspondent of Dorothy Wordsworth, (460)

Three Graves, The, Wordsworth the probable originator of the idea of it, (471); (474); and Wordsworth's theory of poetic diction: outdoes *Peter Bell* in Wordsworth's chosen field, (493), (508)

TIECK, Ludwig, pupil of Heyne, 333

TINTERN ABBEY, unsuccessful expedition to it, by Coleridge, Southey, Cottle, and the Fricker sisters, 81; the Wordsworths visit it and Wordsworth writes his *Lines written a few miles above Tintern Abbey*, q.v., 285

'Tis sweet to him who all the week, Coleridge, 342

TOBIN, James, Wordsworth's friend: letter to, 261-262, (473), 382, (484)

TOBIT, projected essay on, by Coleridge, (455)

TODD, Mr, engaged to Mary Evans, 68, and married to her, (438)

TOOKE, J. Horne, Coleridge criticises him in a letter to Thelwall, 133, (452); tried for high treason,

[568]

171, (449); "the learning of Tooke," 344; in London, 1799: "gross conversation," 387
To Simplicity, Coleridge, parody sonnet, (471)
Tom Wedgwood, The First Photographer, R. B. Litchfield, (420)
Tombless Epitaph, A, Coleridge, (497)
TOULMIN, Dr, minister at Taunton, 154; Coleridge preaches for him, (474), 270; his daughter drowns herself, 277; Coleridge proposes to relieve him of the duty alternate Sundays, (475); "the more I see of that man the more I love him," (486)
TRAILL, H. D., (511), (512), (515), (517)
Transactions of the Unitarian Historical Society, (445), (446), (470), (475)
TREVELYAN, G. O., (475)
Tribune, The, (449)
TRYPHIODORUS (Τρυφιοδώρου 'Ιλίου "Αλωσις), edited by Northmore, 356
TUCKETT, G. L., at Cambridge with Coleridge, 32, (427); informs Coleridge's family of his enlistment, 36, (430); gloomy prophecies of *The Watchman*'s history fulfilled, 99
TURNBULL, A., (417)
TYCHSEN, Professor, gives Coleridge lessons in "the Gothic of Ulphilas" at Göttingen, 332; 344
TYLER, Miss Elizabeth, Southey's aunt, upon whose favour he was mainly dependent, employer of Shadrach Weeks, 46
TYPOGRAPHY, Coleridge's plaint to Cottle, 272
TYSON, T., 372, (507)

UNITARIANISM, Frend's Unitarian teachings, 30; Coleridge a Unitarian (according to Poole), 48; Lamb a Unitarian, (438); in Coleridge's lectures: friendship with Estlin and others, 75; Coleridge's commercial-cum-evangelistic *Watchman* tour, 93-98; twitted by Darwin on his religion, 97; plans to become a minister, 110-111, 118; 122, 212, 214; proposal that he should become Unitarian minister at Shrewsbury, 221-243; his defence of this to the Wedgwoods, 223-227; his trial visit described by Hazlitt, 230-237; the plan abandoned owing to the Wedgwoods' annuity offer, 237-243, (475); "These principles I held *philosophically*, while in respect of revealed religion I remained a zealous Unitarian," 310
Unpublished Letters of S. T. Coleridge, ed. E. H. Coleridge, (422)
Unpublished Letters of S. T. Coleridge, ed. Earl Leslie Griggs, (417)
Unpublished Letters from S. T. Coleridge to the Rev. John Prior Estlin, (417)
UPCOTT, Coleridge stays with the Wedgwoods here, and perhaps meets Davy for the first time, 361
Upon the Author's leaving School and entering into Life (Happiness), Coleridge, cancelled lines, 28, (426)
URIAH, 226
URIEL, archangel, 283

"VACCIMULGENCE," word coined by Coleridge: "I am pleased with the word," 131-132
VALLEY OF ROCKS, Linton. Visited on the *Ancient Mariner* walk, 219; called The Valley of Stones by the two poets, (472); visited with Hazlitt, 268, 269; scene of *The Wanderings of Cain*, 269, 271
VALLON, Marie Anne, (Annette), Wordsworth's mistress, and mother of his daughter, Caroline, 167-169; Wordsworth's later reaction to their separation, 173, 175; plan that she and Caroline

[569]

should come to England, 174; her return to Blois with Caroline under the name Mme. Williams, 177

VALLON, Caroline, daughter of Annette: birth, 168; 174, 177

VALLON, Paul, Annette's brother, thrown into prison, 169, 177

VANE, Sir Frederick, Wordsworth plans to move to the north of England, "near Sir Frederick Vane's great library," 343

VELASQUEZ, referred to by Hazlitt in his account of Coleridge's appearance, 233

VIRGIL, Coleridge speaks on the *Georgics*, "but not well," Hazlitt, 269; Heyne's edition at Stowey, 333

Vision of the Maid of Orleans, The. See *Destiny of Nations, The*

Visit of the Gods, The, Coleridge, in imitation of Schiller, (507)

VOLTAIRE, F. M. A. de, his *Philosophical Dictionary*, 21; satisfies the intellectual but not the mystical part of Coleridge, 64, 294; "the wit of Voltaire," 350

VOSS, Johann Heinrich, Coleridge reads his *Luise*, 308; Wordsworth ignorant of him, 329

WADE, Josiah, of Bristol: an enthusiastic friend of Coleridge's, and witness at his wedding, (443); helps him start *The Watchman*, 92, and pays resulting debts, 117, 119; contributes to Poole's annual subscription for Coleridge, (449); letter from Sarah, 120; 142; invitation to Stowey, 205; letter from Coleridge about the Wedgwood offer, 227; application for money, 227, 229

WAKEFIELD, Gilbert, 356

WALES, William, mathematics master at Christ's Hospital, (423)

WALKER, George, Unitarian minister in Nottingham, (445)

WALKING TOURS:
To Wales with Hucks, 1794, 43-46; Gloucester: Ross: Hereford: Leominster: Bishop's Castle: Montgomery: Welshpool: Llanfyllin: Llangynog: Bala: Druid House: Llangollen: Wrexham: Ruthin: Denbigh: St. Asaph: Holywell: Rhuddlan: Abergele: Conway: Aber: Penmaenmawr: ferry to Beaumaris: Amlwch: Parys Copper Mines: Gwyndu: Moel-y-don: back to mainland, Caernarvon: Snowdon: Tan-y-Bwlch: Harlech: Barmouth: Dolgelly: Aberdovey: Aberystwyth: Llandovery: Brecon: Abergavenny: Tintern: Chepstow: Bristol.

In Devonshire with Southey, 1799, 357, (508), Exeter: Dartmouth: Totness: part of Dartmoor: Exeter.

To the Lakes with Wordsworth and Cottle, 1799, 368-374, (507-508). Neasham Bank: Hurworth: Croft: George Inn at Piercebridge: Gainford: Castle Barnard: Greta Bridge: Temple Sowerby: Mayburgh: Bampton: Long Sleddale: Kentmere: Troutbeck: Rayrigg: Bowness: Windermere: Hawkshead: Esthwaite: Blelham Tarn: Rydal: Grasmere: Grisedale Tarn: Easedale: Sour Milk Ghyll: Wastdale: Cockermouth: Bassenthwaite: Keswick: Derwentwater: Embleton: Low Lorton: Red How: Grasmoor: Scale Force: Gillerthwaite: Black Sail: Wastdale Head: Styhead Pass: Rosthwaite: Keswick: Grange: Lodore: Threlkeld: Matterdale: Ullswater: Patterdale: Lyulph's Tower: Eusemere, and back to Sockburn

Wallenstein, unpublished play by Schiller: copyright taken over by

[570]

Longman from Bell: Coleridge at work on the translation, 389, (511), 392, 393, 400, 409; translation finished, 410; misunderstanding with Schiller about copyright, 410; publication: its failure ensured by the likeness of its principal figure to the hated Napoleon, hostile reviews, 410-411, (516); its real merits: comparison of translation and original, 411, 412, (517)

Wallensteinübersetzung von Samuel T. Coleridge und ihr deutsches Original, Vorgelegt von Hans Roscher, (512)

WALPOLE, Horace, subject of a satire projected by Coleridge, (454)

Wanderings of Cain, The, planned as a prose tale, set in the Valley of Rocks, to be written jointly by Coleridge and Wordsworth, 269; collaboration fails, and only fragments are written by Coleridge, 271

WARD, Thomas, Poole's apprentice, (432), (433); his joy at the arrival of letters from Hamburg, 324, (498); punning letter from Coleridge to him, 359-360, (504); worships Coleridge and takes copies of his letters to Poole, 359

WARREN, Mr, the new schoolmaster at Ottery, 16, (421)

WARTER, J. W., (419)

WARTON, Thomas and Joseph, Bowles' debt to them, 26

WASHING, an invention for, and the Wordsworths, 329

WASHINGTON, General, Coleridge gives a toast to, at Bala, 44, (431)

WATCHET, visited on the *Ancient Mariner* walk, 220

Watchman, The, projected, 91; prospectus issued, 91, (444); Coleridge's canvassing tour to collect subscribers, 92-98, (445-446): *Worcester*, unsuccessful, 93:

Birmingham, very successful. Introduction to Edwards. Attempt at personal canvass, (447). Meeting with Charles Lloyd, 96-97: *Derby*, meets Wright, Darwin, and others, 97, (445): *Nottingham*, well entertained but homesick, 97, (445): *Sheffield*, abandoned, so as not to interfere with the sale of the *Sheffield Iris*, 97-98, (445-446): *Manchester: Liverpool*, fêted by the Cromptons of Eton House: *Lichfield: Bristol*; the result— nearly 1,000 subscribers, 98; the joys of projecting give way to the sorrows of work, 98; first number, March 1st, 1796, 99; reason for and disadvantages of the eight-day interval, 99; reasons for failure: radicals and conservatives alike offended: the *Essay on Fasting*, 99; typical criticisms of, 100; attacks Godwin, 106, (448); precarious situation of *The Watchman*: Coleridge loses interest, 108, 109, 110; last number, May 13, 1796, 111; Burnett's help in the compilation of *The Watchman*, 154

WATSON, Richard, Bishop of Llandaff. See LLANDAFF

WAY, John, from whom the presentation to Christ's Hospital for Coleridge was obtained, 16

We are Seven, Wordsworth, note to, (506)

Wealth of Nations. See SMITH, Adam

WEDD, A. F., (509)

WEDGWOOD, Thomas and Josiah, uncles of Charles Darwin, whom Josiah helped to become a scientist, (473); their offer of £100 to Coleridge to avert his entering the Unitarian ministry, 222, refused by Coleridge, 223-227; (474); offer of £150 a year, 234, 237-238, accepted, 239-240; Coleridge on their "magnificent liberality," 241;

[571]

"a very affectionate letter from Thomas Wedgwood," 243; Coleridge tells Thomas of his admiration for Wordsworth, 261; he stays with them, 243, 284; he anticipates his annuity, 323; "six huge letters" from Coleridge to Josiah, 345; they do not lend money to Wordsworth, (502); Tom a patient of Dr. Beddoes: gives £1,000 for research into "medicated airs," 360-361; plan to purchase Combe Florey falls through, (505); Coleridge visits them at Upcott, 361; (517); (518)

WEEKS, Sally, wife of Shadrach (below): discussion as to her status on the banks of the Susquehannah, 58

WEEKS, Shadrach, manservant of Southey's aunt, Miss Tyler: at Bristol during the early days of pantisocracy, 46; "SHAD GOES WITH US. HE IS MY BROTHER," 53; discussion of his position in the pantisocratic order, 57, 58, (435)

WEM, Shropshire, Hazlitt's father dissenting minister there, 230, 265

WESLEY, Sarah, meets Coleridge in London, 1799, 387, (511); pursues him, (517)

WESTBURY, Sarah Coleridge stays with the Southeys' there, 346

WHITE, R. J., (512)

WHITE, W. Hale, (509)

WICKSTEED, Mr, of Wem, a correspondent of Coleridge's, 265

WIELAND, Christoph Martin, Coleridge plans to translate his Oberon, 216, 292, 308; Wordsworth on, 329

Wiener Beiträge zur Engl. Philologie, (494)

William Godwin, Kegan Paul, (420)

William Wordsworth, George M'Lean Harper, (419)

William Wordsworth and Annette Vallon, Legouis, (419)

William Wordsworth: His Doctrine and Art in their Historical Relations, Arthur Beatty, (463)

WILLIAMS, Mme. See VALLON, Marie Anne

WILMOTT, Mr, rented Woodlands, a house near Alfoxden, (468), 325

WILSON, Katharine M., (496)

Wiltshire Parson and his Friends, A, Garland Greever, (447), (457), (469)

WISE, T. J., (420)

WOLF, Johann Christian von, 1679-1754, 308

WOLLSTONECRAFT, Mary, mother of Shelley's wife, (436); Coleridge talks of her, 233, 234; Godwin is "in heart and manner better for having been the husband of Mary Wollstonecraft": friend of Mary Hays, 378

WOOD, Mr, Unitarian Church official at Shrewsbury: letter to Coleridge, 242-243, (475)

WOODLANDS, house near Stowey wanted by Coleridge, 324; not available, 325, (468)

Wordsworth and Coleridge, with an Introduction and Notes by George Sampson, (476)

WORDSWORTH, Bishop, (459), (419)

Wordsworth, C. H. Herford, (463)

Wordsworth, F. W. H. Myers, (463)

Wordsworth, Walter Raleigh, (463)

Wordsworth, Lectures and Essays, H. W. Garrod, (463)

WORDSWORTH, Christopher, youngest brother of Wordsworth: with Coleridge at Cambridge, 1793, 34, (428); letter from Dorothy, 327-328; Lamb plans to match him with Priscilla Lloyd, 380

WORDSWORTH, Dorothy, first impressions of Coleridge, 154-155; information from her letters, (459-460), (474); visit to Stowey, and the move to Alfoxden planned, 157-162; her unceremoniousness, and Sarah's attitude to it, 157,

(461); Coleridge describes her to Cottle, 158; her gifts to Wordsworth, relaxation, 163, 174-5, a delicate perception of nature, 176, (465) 177-178, 245, belief in his high poetic destiny, 178, (465), faith in humanity, and a habit of friendliness with those they met, 179, help in throwing off Godwin's philosophy, 178-179, 181; her limitations, uncritical adoration which tended to make him complaisant and content with small endeavours, and complete lack of philosophic insight, 180-181, 200-201: she and Coleridge the two personal influences to which Wordsworth was amenable in 1797, 182; natural sympathy between her and Coleridge, 198; De Quincey's picture of her, 199-200; Coleridge's enjoyment of her qualities and perception of her limitations, 200-202; at Alfoxden, 203-220, 244, 262; drives with Coleridge, 205; "a most exquisite young woman in mind and heart," 207; the *Ancient Mariner* walk, 219, (472); to London and back, 220; in *The Nightingale*, (481); drawn into the Lloyd controversy, (483), 279; dinner at Alfoxden, (484); plans after Alfoxden, 262; sorrow at leaving: description of Southey, 284: to Wales, 285; on the German trip, 286, 292-294, 313-318, 321-322, 327-329; disadvantages of her having accompanied Wordsworth, 326, 342, (501); "A slumber did my spirit seal"—Coleridge thinks this may have been written in the event of her death, 336; letter to Christopher Wordsworth, 327-328; 329; compared with Sarah Hutchinson, 367-368; "Why were you not with us?" Coleridge in the Lakes, 370; Coleridge longs

for her company, 388; the move to Dove Cottage, 409; she wishes for Coleridge, 410; at Grasmere, 412; she looks for lodgings for the Coleridges' at Ambleside, (517). See also *Journal* of Dorothy Wordsworth.

WORDSWORTH, John, Wordsworth's sailor brother, joins him and Coleridge for part of a walking tour, 369-370; promises Wordsworth money to buy land for a house, 370; at Dove Cottage, 410

WORDSWORTH, Richard, Wordsworth's brother, 364, 410

WORDSWORTH, William, and the Lake Country, 13; on Coleridge's boyhood, 17; admiration for Bowles, 25; his *Descriptive Sketches* discussed by Coleridge's circle at Cambridge, 34; first meeting with Coleridge and Southey, 1795, 84; discussion with Cottle of the publication of *Guilt and Sorrow*, 84, (442); Coleridge ascribes to him a phrase in *Lines written at Shurton Bars*, 85, (442-443); he sends *Guilt and Sorrow* to Coleridge, 85; among Coleridge's correspondents, 114; "a very dear friend," 115-116; contradictory evidence of early meetings, 115-116, (449); thinks Southey takes "too rigid a view" of Coleridge, (451); Coleridge sends him *The Progress of Liberty*, 147; further meetings, 152; admired by Poole, 152, and by Coleridge, (458); Coleridge 'leaps into friendship' with the Wordsworths on his first visit to Racedown, 155, 156, 163; Coleridge on Wordsworth, "I feel myself a *little man by his side*," 155; visit to Stowey, and the move to Alfoxden planned, 157-162; résumé of his life up to 1797, 163-181; (463-465); character, 163; childhood, 164; the French Revolution and the war with France, 164, 168-172; relationship with Michel Beaupuy, 167, with Annette (Marie Anne Vallon), 167-169, 174, 177; *Guilt and Sorrow*, 170; acceptance of Godwin's theories, 172-174; the Calvert legacy makes life with Dorothy possible, 175; Dorothy's gifts to him and her value during his spiritual convalescence, 175-179; her limitations, 179-181; gradual rejection of Godwin's philosophy, 178-179; Coleridge's influence on Wordsworth, 182, (465); contrast of the effect of the French Revolution on the two poets, 182-183; their natures contrasted, 183-184; Wordsworth's reaction to Coleridge's Hartleian philosophy, 185-188, and later at Racedown to his Berkleian philosophy, 188-189; *The Borderers*: Wordsworth purges himself of the Godwinian doctrines, 190; his self-respect restored by Coleridge's generous admiration, (466), for *The Borderers* and *Guilt and Sorrow*, 189-191; self-respect merges into self-satisfaction: Wordsworth on his gifts to Coleridge, 191-192; Coleridge learns from the Wordsworths' perception of nature, 192, and discovers in Wordsworth a new demonstration of the creative imagination, 193-194, 302-303; the poets' discussion of imagination and fancy, 194-195, (495); interaction of their work on each other, 195-196; Wordsworth's great personal value to Coleridge compared with Poole's, 196-198, 199; Coleridge supplies Dorothy's shortcomings with regard to Wordsworth's poetry: Coleridge loves the potential, Dorothy the actual Wordsworth, 200-202; the

Wordsworths at Alfoxden: Thelwall's visit, 204-206, hastens their final departure, 210-211, 214, 244; the contrasted attitude to nature of Wordsworth and Coleridge, 213; patronizing criticism of Coleridge and *The Three Graves*, (471); the Wordsworths' part in releasing Coleridge's genius for its great creative outburst, 217-218; Wordsworth's rôle in the writing of the *Lyrical Ballads* as recorded later by Coleridge, 218; his share in the birth of *The Ancient Mariner*, 219-220, (472), and later questionable analysis of its weaknesses in second edition of *Lyrical Ballads*, (506); attempts at collaboration with Coleridge fail, 219-220, 269, 271; "ribbed sea sand," 269, (486); *The Borderers* rejected, 220; letter from Coleridge on the Wedgwood annuity, 241; Coleridge's great creative period as Wordsworth recorded it, 244; the invasion of Switzerland shakes his faith in France, 245, (479-480); in Dorothy's *Journal*, (476-479), (479-480); Wordsworth on the cheerful character of the nightingale, 251-252; his poetic growth during Coleridge's great period: *The Recluse* started, 261-262; plans for the time when the Alfoxden lease ended, 262-263: and particularly the German plan: money to be raised, 263-264; Cottle on dinner at Alfoxden, (484-486); Hazlitt's account of his visit to the poets, 265-267; plans for the *Lyrical Ballads*: anonymity and good typography, 271-272; quoted by Coleridge in a letter to his brother George, 275-276; Coleridge worried by Wordsworth's attitude to Christianity, 281-282, (487); the Wordsworths

[574]

leave Alfoxden: Stowey, Bristol, and a walking tour to Tintern Abbey, 284-285; *Lines written a few miles above Tintern Abbey*, 285; visit with Coleridge to Thelwall at Llyswen, to London, to Yarmouth, to Germany, 285-286, (488); the *Lyrical Ballads*, 287-292, (489-493); Wordsworth's and Coleridge's realization of the power of the imagination, 302-303, (495); Wordsworth in Germany, 292, 293, 294, 313-319, (496), 321-324, 326-329, 342-243; lines from *The Prelude* sent to Coleridge in Germany, 321-322; "had I met these lines running wild in the deserts of Arabia I should instantly have screamed out 'Wordsworth!'," (498); Coleridge quotes Wordsworth's "sublime epitaph," 336-337, (500); his wish to live in the Lake District, near a library and near Coleridge, 324, 343; Coleridge refers Southey to him on the question of the alleged slanders, 354; Wordsworth at Sockburn-on-Tees with Dorothy and Mary Hutchinson, 363; his illness, 363, (506); his need of Coleridge, 363-364, 365; his conclusions on the non-success of the *Lyrical Ballads*, 364-365, (506); Coleridge urges him to write a poem for those disillusioned by the turn of affairs in France: this "tail-piece of 'The Recluse'" undertaken, 365-367; it takes shape as *The Prelude*, (506); Coleridge's visit, and a walking tour to the Lakes, 367-374, (507); discovery of Dove Cottage, 370, 374; Coleridge's admiration—in their eyes excessive—for Wordsworth, a factor in the estrangement of Lamb, Lloyd, and Southey from Coleridge, 379, (509); Poole considers

Coleridge's attitude 'prostration,' 384-385, 407-408, (515); Coleridge's need of the Wordsworths, 388; Wordsworth, established firmly in the north, gradually draws Coleridge northwards, 407-410; Coleridge on a visit to Dove Cottage: discovery of Greta Hall, 412; the Coleridge family comes north, 416

WRANGHAM, Francis, friend of Wordsworth's, (422), (435), 56, 85, (443); helps Wordsworth with the Juvenal imitation, 170-171; (465), (516)

WREXHAM, Coleridge and Hucks meet the Evans girls unexpectedly there, 1794, 44, (430, 431); the first draft of *Lewti* possibly begun there, 45

WRIGHT, Joseph, meets Coleridge at Derby, 1796, 97

WRIGHT, Mr, of Nottingham, 97

Written during a Temporary Blindness in the Year 1799, Coleridge: hexameters to William and Dorothy Wordsworth, 321, (497)

WYNDHAM, William, Secretary for War in Pitt's administration, 397

WYNN, C. W. W., school friend of Southey's: offers Southey £160 a year provided he studies Law, 1795, 81, (511)

YARMOUTH, Wordsworths and Coleridge sail from here to Germany, 1798, 285-286

YOUNG, Arthur, (467)

YOUNG, Edward, influence on Wordsworth's early poetry, 166

Youth and Age, Coleridge, (499)

ZENO THE ELEATIC, 305

ZIMMERMAN, Professor von, meets Coleridge at Brunswick and catechises him about Kant, 352; his *Geographie der Menschen*, 359, (504)

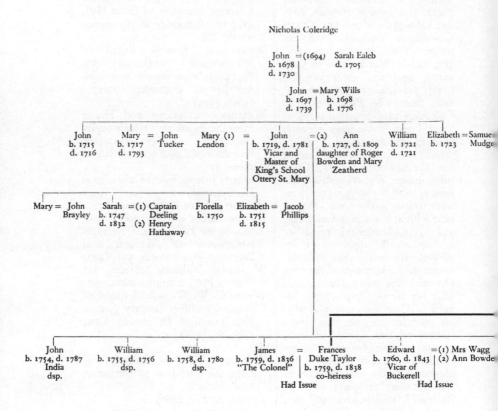

Nicholas Coleridge

John = (1694) Sarah Ealeb
b. 1678 | d. 1705
d. 1730

John = Mary Wills
b. 1697 | b. 1698
d. 1739 | d. 1776

John | Mary = John | Mary (1) = John = (2) Ann | William | Elizabeth = Samuel
b. 1715 | b. 1717 Tucker | Lendon | b. 1719, d. 1781 | b. 1727, d. 1809 | b. 1721 | b. 1723 Mudge
d. 1716 | d. 1793 | | Vicar and | daughter of Roger | d. 1721
| | | Master of | Bowden and Mary
| | | King's School | Zeatherd
| | | Ottery St. Mary

Mary = John | Sarah = (1) Captain | Florella | Elizabeth = Jacob
Brayley | b. 1747 Deeling | b. 1750 | b. 1751 Phillips
| d. 1832 (2) Henry | | d. 1815
| Hathaway

John | William | William | James = Frances | Edward = (1) Mrs Wagg
b. 1754, d. 1787 | b. 1755, d. 1756 | b. 1758, d. 1780 | b. 1759, d. 1836 Duke Taylor | b. 1760, d. 1843 | (2) Ann Bowde
India | dsp. | dsp. | "The Colonel" b. 1759, d. 1838 | Vicar of
dsp. | | | co-heiress | Buckerell

Had Issue | Had Issue

Richard Duke = Ciceley Power, of Powershayes, heiress
|
Richard Duke
|
Richard Duke
|
Henry Duke = Maud Whitte, of Ottery St. Mary
|
John Duke = Ellen Middleton
|
Richard Duke = (1) Martha Parker
of Otterton | (2) Katharine Prideaux, daughter of Serjeant Prideaux
|
Richard Duke = Margaret, daughter of Sir Arthur Bassett
of Otterton |
d. 1641 |
|
Robert Duke — Sarah Reynell, co-heiress of Creedywigier
of Otterton |
b. 1601, d. 1665 |
|
Thomas Duke = Anna Walrond of Bovey
of Colaton Ralegh |
b. 1629, d. 1710 |
|
George Duke = Dorothy Ayre,
of Colaton Ralegh | b. 1685, d. 1757,
b. 1679 | heiress
|
Frances Duke = Bernard Frederick Taylor
b. 1724, d. 1781 | b. 1724, d. 1783
co-heiress of Otterton |

George — Jane	Luke — Sarah	Anne (Nancy)	Francis	SAMUEL TAYLOR = (1795) SARAH FRICKER
764, d. 1828	Hart	Hermann	Hart	b. 1767, d. 1791	Snydercombe	b. 1772, d. 1834	b. 1770, d. 1845
Master of	b. 1765		b. 1770, d. 1792		
ng's School	d. 1790		India, dsp.		
Had Issue	Had Issue				

HARTLEY	BERKELEY	DERWENT = Mary	SARA = Henry Nelson
1796, d. 1849	b. 1798, d. 1799	b. 1800, d. 1883	Pridham	b. 1802	Coleridge
dsp.	dsp.	Rector of	d. 1852	b. 1798
		Hanwell		d. 1843
		Had Issue	Had Issue